WPA Outcomes for First-Year Composition	Where *The Allyn & Bacon Guide* Addresses These Outcomes
KNOWLEDGE OF CONVENTIONS By the end of first-year composition, students should • Learn common formats for different kinds of texts • Develop knowledge of genre conventions ranging from structure and paragraphing to tone and mechanics • Practice appropriate means of documenting their work • Control such surface features as syntax, grammar, punctuation, and spelling	Part 1, "A Rhetoric for Writers," Concepts 7, 11, and 12 Chapter 21, "Incorporating Sources into Your Own Writing" Chapter 22, "Citing and Documenting Sources" Handbook (Regular Edition) Additionally, all Writing Project chapters in Part 2 explain appropriate format, tone, and style.
COMPOSING IN ELECTRONIC ENVIRONMENTS By the end of first-year composition, students should • Use electronic environments for drafting, reviewing, revising, editing, and sharing texts • Locate, evaluate, organize, and use research material collected from electronic sources, including scholarly library databases; other official databases (e.g., federal government databases); and informal electronic networks and Internet sources • Understand and exploit the difference in the rhetorical strategies and in the affordances available for both print and electronic composing processes and texts	Chapter 24, "Portfolios and Reflective Essays" Chapter 19, "Asking Questions, Finding Sources" Chapter 20, "Evaluating Sources" Additionally, the Writing Project chapters in Part 2 make frequent reference to electronic formats and processes, including desktop-published material, posters, advocacy ads, and PowerPoint presentations.

THE ALLYN & BACON GUIDE TO WRITING

Why Do You Need This New Edition?

If you're wondering why you should buy this sixth edition of *The Allyn & Bacon Guide to Writing*, here are 8 great reasons!

1. Coverage of integrating researched sources effectively and ethically has been expanded with new instruction, visual presentations, and examples to help you improve skills fundamental to college readiness and success while avoiding plagiarism (Chapters 21 and 22).
2. MLA and APA coverage is thoroughly updated according to the most recent citation guidelines from each organization, ensuring that you are learning the most current national standards (Chapter 22).
3. A thoroughly revised chapter on image analysis helps you work effectively with the wide variety of visual texts you will encounter in other course areas and outside of college (Chapter 10).
4. Eight new readings offer engaging and contemporary topics for discussion, written response, and exploratory research—including banning laptops and cell phones from classes, sustainable environmental practices, and the growing gap between the rich and the poor.
5. New visual explanations present complex topics clearly so that information is displayed at-a-glance in charts or color-coded samples rather than in long passages of text (Chapters 21 and 22).
6. A new section on presenting data visually to reach different kinds of readers helps you create effective tables, graphs, and charts to support your arguments (Chapter 17).
7. New instruction on creating thesis statements and introductions helps you with parts of the writing process that are often tricky for writers, but have a great impact on the efficacy of your writing (Chapter 2).
8. The sixth edition is available as a CourseSmart eText, and you can subscribe to *The Allyn & Bacon Guide to Writing* at CourseSmart.com. The site includes all of the book's content in a format that enables you to search, bookmark, save notes, and print.

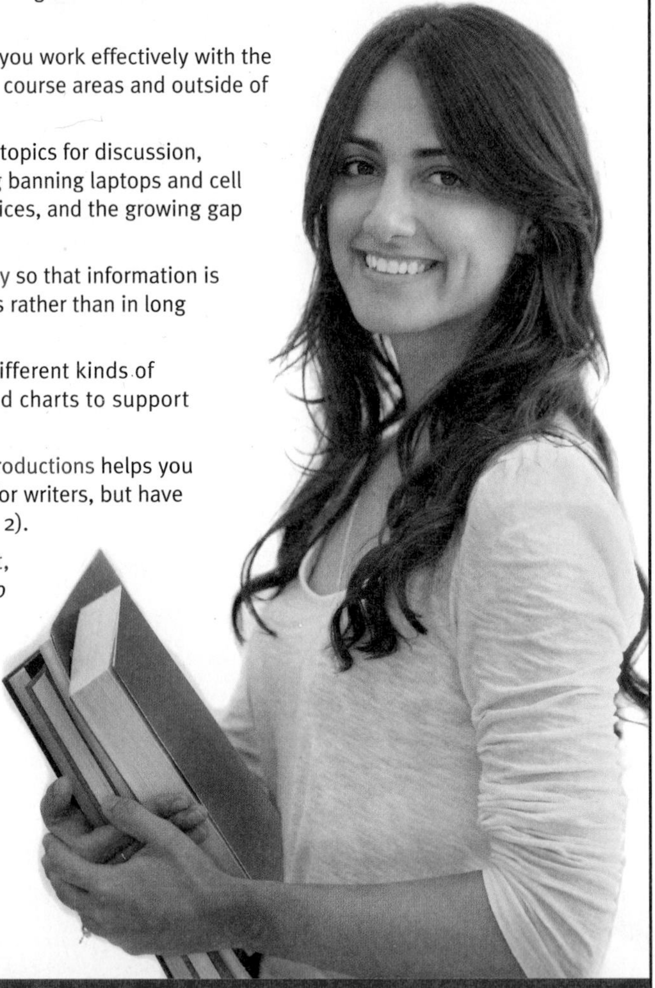

PEARSON

THE ALLYN & BACON GUIDE TO WRITING

SIXTH EDITION

John D. Ramage
Arizona State University

John C. Bean
Seattle University

June Johnson
Seattle University

Longman
Boston Columbus Indianapolis New York San Francisco Upper Saddle River
Amsterdam Cape Town Dubai London Madrid Milan Munich Paris Montréal Toronto
Delhi Mexico City São Paulo Sydney Hong Kong Seoul Singapore Taipei Tokyo

Senior Acquisitions Editor: Lauren A. Finn
Senior Development Editor: Marion B. Castellucci
Senior Marketing Manager: Sandra McGuire
Senior Supplements Editor: Donna Campion
Senior Media Producer: Stefanie Liebman
Production Manager: Savoula Amanatidis
Project Coordination, Interior Design, and Electronic Page Makeup: Integra Software Services, Inc.
Cover Designer/Manager: Wendy Ann Fredericks
Cover Art: Copyright © Fotalia.com
Photo Researcher: Rebecca Karamehmedovic
Senior Manufacturing Buyer: Roy L. Pickering, Jr.
Printer and Binder: R. R. Donnelley and Sons Company–Crawfordsville
Cover Printer: Lehigh-Phoenix Color Corporation–Hagerstown

For permission to use copyrighted material, grateful acknowledgment is made to the copyright holders on pp. 717–719, which are hereby made part of this copyright page.

Library of Congress Cataloging-in-Publication Data
Ramage, John D.
The Allyn & Bacon guide to writing/John D. Ramage, John C. Bean, June Johnson.— 6th ed.
p. cm.
Includes index.
ISBN-13: 978-0-205-72148-1 (Complete edition)
ISBN-10: 0-205-72148-6 (Complete edition)
ISBN-13: 978-0-205-82315-4 (Brief edition)
ISBN-10: 0-205-82315-7 (Brief edition)
1. English language—Rhetoric—Handbooks, manuals, etc. 2. English language—Grammar—Handbooks, manuals, etc. 3. Report writing—Handbooks, manuals, etc. 4. College readers. I. Bean, John C. II. Johnson, June, 1953- III. Title. IV. Title: Allyn and Bacon guide to writing.
PE1408.R18 2010
808'.042—dc22

2010033283

1 2 3 4 5 6 7 8 9 10—DOC—14 13 12 11

Longman
is an imprint of
PEARSON

Complete Edition
ISBN-13: 978-0-205-72148-1; ISBN-10: 0-205-72148-6
Brief Edition
ISBN-13: 978-0-205-82315-4; ISBN-10: 0-205-82315-7
Concise Edition
ISBN-13: 978-0-205-82314-7; ISBN-10: 0-205-82314-9

www.pearsonhighered.com

BRIEF CONTENTS

Detailed Contents vii
Writing Projects xxvi
Thematic Contents xxviii
Preface xxxv

PART 1 A RHETORIC FOR WRITERS

1 Thinking Rhetorically about Good Writing 5
2 Thinking Rhetorically about Your Subject Matter 25
3 Thinking Rhetorically about How Messages Persuade 51
4 Thinking Rhetorically about Style and Document Design 67

PART 2 WRITING PROJECTS

WRITING TO LEARN
5 Reading Rhetorically: The Writer as Strong Reader 87
WRITING TO EXPLORE
6 Writing an Autobiographical Narrative 132
7 Writing an Exploratory Essay or Annotated Bibliography 153
WRITING TO INFORM
8 Writing an Informative (and Surprising) Essay or Report 177
WRITING TO ANALYZE AND SYNTHESIZE
9 Analyzing Field Research Data 201
10 Analyzing Images 241
11 Analyzing a Short Story 280
12 Analyzing and Synthesizing Ideas 301
WRITING TO PERSUADE
13 Writing a Classical Argument 331
14 Making an Evaluation 378
15 Proposing a Solution 401

PART 3 A GUIDE TO COMPOSING AND REVISING

16 Writing as a Problem-Solving Process 437
17 Composing and Revising Closed-Form Prose 451
18 Composing and Revising Open-Form Prose 495

PART 4 A RHETORICAL GUIDE TO RESEARCH

19 Asking Questions, Finding Sources 517
20 Evaluating Sources 536
21 Incorporating Sources into Your Own Writing 553
22 Citing and Documenting Sources 574

PART 5 WRITING FOR ASSESSMENT

23 Essay Examinations 609
24 Portfolios and Reflective Essays 623

PART 6 A GUIDE TO EDITING

1 Improving Your Editing Skills 639
2 Understanding Sentence Structure 644
3 Punctuating Boundaries of Sentences, Clauses, and Phrases 657
4 Editing for Standard English Usage 666
5 Editing for Style 682
6 Editing for Punctuation and Mechanics 692

Acknowledgments 717
Index 720

DETAILED CONTENTS

Writing Projects xxvi

Thematic Contents xxviii

Preface xxxv

PART 1 A RHETORIC FOR WRITERS

1 THINKING RHETORICALLY ABOUT GOOD WRITING 5

CONCEPT 1 Good writing can vary from closed to open forms. 6

David Rockwood, *A Letter to the Editor* 6

Thomas Merton, *A Festival of Rain* 7

Distinctions between Closed and Open Forms of Writing 8

Where to Place Your Writing along the Continuum 10

CONCEPT 2 Good writers address problems rather than topics. 11

Shared Problems Unite Writers and Readers 12

Where Do Problems Come From? 12

CONCEPT 3 Good writers think rhetorically about purpose, audience, and genre. 15

What Is Rhetoric? 16

How Writers Think about Purpose 17

How Writers Think about Audience 19

How Writers Think about Genre 21

Chapter Summary 23

BRIEF WRITING PROJECT 1 TWO MESSAGES FOR DIFFERENT PURPOSES, AUDIENCES, AND GENRES 23

BRIEF WRITING PROJECT 2 A LETTER TO YOUR PROFESSOR ABOUT WHAT WAS NEW IN CHAPTER 1 24

2 THINKING RHETORICALLY ABOUT YOUR SUBJECT MATTER 25

CONCEPT 4 To determine their thesis, writers must often "wallow in complexity." 26

Learning to Wallow in Complexity 27

Seeing Each Academic Discipline as a Field of Inquiry and Argument 27

Using Exploratory Writing to Help You Wallow in Complexity 29

Believing and Doubting Paul Theroux's Negative View of Sports 33

CONCEPT 5 A strong thesis statement surprises readers with something new or challenging. 37

Trying to Change Your Reader's View of Your Subject 38

Giving Your Thesis Tension through "Surprising Reversal" 39

CONCEPT 6 In closed-form prose, a typical introduction starts with the problem, not the thesis. 42

A Protypical Introduction 43

Features of a Good Introduction 43

CONCEPT 7 Thesis statements in closed-form prose are supported hierarchically with points and particulars. 46

How Points Convert Information to Meaning 46

How Removing Particulars Creates a Summary 47

How to Use Points and Particulars When You Revise 48

Chapter Summary 49

BRIEF WRITING PROJECT PLAYING THE BELIEVING AND DOUBTING GAME 49

3 THINKING RHETORICALLY ABOUT HOW MESSAGES PERSUADE 51

CONCEPT 8 Messages persuade through their angle of vision. 52

Recognizing the Angle of Vision in a Text 52

Analyzing Angle of Vision 55

CONCEPT 9 Messages persuade through appeals to *logos*, *ethos*, and *pathos*. 58

CONCEPT 10 Nonverbal messages persuade through visual strategies that can be analyzed rhetorically. 58

Visual Rhetoric 59

The Rhetoric of Clothing and Other Consumer Items 62

Chapter Summary 64

BRIEF WRITING PROJECT ANALYZING ANGLE OF VISION IN TWO PASSAGES ABOUT NUCLEAR ENERGY 64

4 THINKING RHETORICALLY ABOUT STYLE AND DOCUMENT DESIGN 67

CONCEPT 11 Good writers make purposeful stylistic choices. 67

Factors That Affect Style 68

Four Powerful Strategies for Improving Your Style 69

CONCEPT 12 Good writers make purposeful document design choices. 75

Document Design for Manuscripts and Papers 75

Document Design for Published Works 76

Chapter Summary 81

BRIEF WRITING PROJECT TWO CONTRASTING DESCRIPTIONS OF THE SAME SCENE 82

PART 2 WRITING PROJECTS

WRITING TO LEARN

5 READING RHETORICALLY: THE WRITER AS STRONG READER 87

Exploring Rhetorical Reading 87

Michael Pollan, *Why Bother?* 88

Understanding Rhetorical Reading 95

What Makes College-Level Reading Difficult? 95

Using the Reading Strategies of Experts 97

Reading with the Grain and Against the Grain 98

Understanding Summary Writing 99

Usefulness of Summaries 99

The Demands that Summary Writing Makes on Writers 100

Summary of "Why Bother?" 100

Understanding Strong Response Writing 104

Strong Response as Rhetorical Critique 104

Strong Response as Ideas Critique 106

Strong Response as Reflection 108

Strong Response as a Blend 110

Kyle Madsen (student), *Can a Green Thumb Save the Planet? A Response to Michael Pollan* 111

WRITING PROJECT A SUMMARY 114
Generating Ideas: Reading for Structure and Content 114
Drafting and Revising 116
Questions for Peer Review 117
WRITING PROJECT A SUMMARY/STRONG RESPONSE ESSAY 118
Exploring Ideas for Your Strong Response 118
Writing a Thesis for a Strong Response Essay 121
Shaping and Drafting 122
Revising 123
Questions for Peer Review 123
READINGS
Thomas L. Friedman, ***30 Little Turtles*** 124
Stephanie Malinowski (student), ***Questioning Thomas L. Friedman's Optimism in "30 Little Turtles"*** 125
David Horsey, ***Today's Economic Indicator (editorial cartoon)*** 128
Mike Lane, ***Labor Day Blues (editorial cartoon)*** 129
Froma Harrop, ***New Threat to Skilled U.S. Workers*** 130

WRITING TO EXPLORE

6 WRITING AN AUTOBIOGRAPHICAL NARRATIVE 132

Exploring Autobiographical Narrative 133
Understanding Autobiographical Writing 133
Autobiographical Tension: The Opposition of Contraries 134
How Literary Elements Work in Autobiographical Narratives 134
WRITING PROJECT AUTOBIOGRAPHICAL NARRATIVE 138
Generating and Exploring Ideas 139
Shaping and Drafting Your Narrative 139
Revising 140
Questions for Peer Review 140
WRITING PROJECT LITERACY NARRATIVE 141
What Is a Literacy Narrative? 141
Typical Features of a Literacy Narrative 142
Generating and Exploring Ideas 144
Shaping and Drafting Your Literacy Narrative 144
Revising 145
Questions for Peer Review 145

READINGS
Kris Saknussemm, ***Phantom Limb Pain*** 146
Patrick José (student), ***No Cats in America?*** 148
Stephanie Whipple (student), ***One Great Book*** 150

7 WRITING AN EXPLORATORY ESSAY OR ANNOTATED BIBLIOGRAPHY 153

Exploring Exploratory Writing 154
Understanding Exploratory Writing 155
WRITING PROJECT AN EXPLORATORY ESSAY 157
Generating and Exploring Ideas 157
Taking "Double-Entry" Research Notes 159
Shaping and Drafting 161
Revising 163
Questions for Peer Review 163
WRITING PROJECT AN ANNOTATED BIBLIOGRAPHY 164
What Is an Annotated Bibliography? 164
Features of Annotated Bibliography Entries 165
Examples of Annotation Entries 165
Writing a Critical Preface for Your Annotated Bibliography 166
Shaping, Drafting, and Revising 167
Questions for Peer Review 167
READINGS
James Gardiner (student), ***How Do Online Social Networks Affect Communication?*** 169
James Gardiner (student), ***What Is the Effect of Online Social Networks on Communication Skills? An Annotated Bibliography*** 174

WRITING TO INFORM

8 WRITING AN INFORMATIVE (AND SURPRISING) ESSAY OR REPORT 177

Exploring Informative (and Surprising) Writing 178
EnchantedLearning.com, ***Tarantulas*** 178
Rod Crawford, ***Myths about "Dangerous" Spiders*** 179
Understanding Informative Writing 180
Informative Reports 181
Informative Essay Using the Surprising-Reversal Strategy 182

WRITING PROJECT INFORMATIVE REPORT 185

Generating and Exploring Ideas 185

Shaping and Drafting 186

Revising 186

Questions for Peer Review 187

WRITING PROJECT INFORMATIVE ESSAY USING THE SURPRISING-REVERSAL STRATEGY 187

Generating and Exploring Ideas 188

Shaping, Drafting, and Revising 189

Questions for Peer Review 191

READINGS

Pew Research Center, ***Muslim Americans: Middle Class and Mostly Mainstream*** 192

Kerri Ann Matsumoto (student), ***How Much Does It Cost to Go Organic?*** 195

Shannon King (student), ***How Clean and Green Are Hydrogen Fuel-Cell Cars?*** 196

Eugene Robinson, ***You Have the Right to Remain a Target of Racial Profiling*** 199

WRITING TO ANALYZE AND SYNTHESIZE

9 ANALYZING FIELD RESEARCH DATA 201

Exploring the Analysis of Field Research Data 201

Understanding the Analysis of Field Research Data 202

The Structure of an Empirical Research Report 202

How Readers Typically Read a Research Report 204

Posing Your Research Question 204

Collecting Data through Observation, Interviews, or Questionnaires 207

Reporting Your Results in Both Words and Graphics 213

Analyzing Your Results 214

Following Ethical Standards 217

WRITING PROJECT AN EMPIRICAL RESEARCH REPORT 218

Generating Ideas for Your Empirical Research Report 218

Designing Your Empirical Study and Drafting the Introduction and Method Sections 219

Doing the Research and Writing the Rest of the Report 219

Revising Your Report 220

Questions for Peer Review 220
Writing in Teams 221
WRITING PROJECT A SCIENTIFIC POSTER 222
What Is a Scientific Poster? 222
Content and Features of a Poster 222
Designing, Creating, and Revising Your Poster 223
Questions for Peer Review 224

READINGS

Gina Escamilla, Angie L. Cradock, and Ichiro Kawachi, ***Women and Smoking in Hollywood Movies: A Content Analysis*** 225

Lauren Campbell, Charlie Bourain, and Tyler Nishida (students), ***A Comparison of Gender Stereotypes in* SpongeBob SquarePants *and a 1930s Mickey Mouse Cartoon (APA-Style Research Paper)*** 231

Lauren Campbell, Charlie Bourain, and Tyler Nishida (students), **SpongeBob SquarePants *Has Fewer Gender Stereotypes than Mickey Mouse (scientific poster)*** 240

10 ANALYZING IMAGES 241

Exploring Image Analysis 241
Understanding Image Analysis: Documentary and News Photographs 243
Angle of Vision and Credibility of Photographs 245
How to Analyze a Documentary Photograph 245
Sample Analysis of a Documentary Photograph 249
Understanding Image Analysis: Paintings 252
How to Analyze a Painting 252
Sample Analysis of a Painting 253
Understanding Image Analysis: Advertisements 256
How Advertisers Think about Advertising 257
Mirrors and Windows: The Strategy of an Effective Advertisement 258
How to Analyze an Advertisement 261
Sample Analysis of an Advertisement 263
WRITING PROJECT ANALYSIS OF TWO VISUAL TEXTS 268
Exploring and Generating Ideas for Your Analysis 268
Shaping and Drafting Your Analysis 269
Revising 269
Questions for Peer Review 270

READINGS
Clark Hoyt, *Face to Face with Tragedy* 271
Manoucheka Celeste, *Disturbing Media Images of Haiti Earthquake Aftermath Tell Only Part of the Story* 273
Lydia Wheeler (student), *Two Photographs Capture Women's Economic Misery* 275

11 **ANALYZING A SHORT STORY 280**

Exploring Literary Analysis 280
Evelyn Dahl Reed, *The Medicine Man* 281
Understanding Literary Analysis 282
The Truth of Literary Events 282
Writing (about) Literature 282
WRITING PROJECT AN ANALYSIS OF A SHORT STORY 285
Reading the Story and Using Reading Logs 286
Generating and Exploring Ideas 288
Shaping, Drafting, and Revising 290
Questions for Peer Review 291
READINGS
Alice Walker, *Everyday Use (For Your Grandmama)* 292
Betsy Weiler (student), *Who Do You Want to Be?: Finding Heritage in Walker's "Everyday Use"* 298

12 **ANALYZING AND SYNTHESIZING IDEAS 301**

Exploring the Analysis and Synthesis of Ideas 302
Nikki Swartz, *Mobile Phone Tracking Scrutinized* 302
Terry J. Allen, *Reach Out and Track Someone* 303
Understanding Analysis and Synthesis 305
Posing a Synthesis Question 305
Synthesis Writing as an Extension of Summary/Strong Response Writing 306
Student Example of a Synthesis Essay 307
Kate MacAulay (student), *Technology's Peril and Potential* 308
WRITING PROJECT A SYNTHESIS ESSAY 310
Ideas for Synthesis Questions and Readings 310
Using Learning Logs 311
Exploring Your Texts through Summary Writing 312
Exploring Your Texts' Rhetorical Strategies 313

Exploring Main Themes and Similarities and Differences in Your Texts' Ideas 314
Generating Ideas of Your Own 316
Taking Your Position in the Conversation: Your Synthesis 317
Shaping and Drafting 318
Writing a Thesis for a Synthesis Essay 320
Organizing a Synthesis Essay 320
Revising 320
Questions for Peer Review 321

READINGS

Dee, ***Comprehensive Immigration Reform: PROs and ANTIs*** 324
Byron Williams, ***Immigration Frenzy Points Out Need for Policy Debate*** 325
Victor Davis Hanson, ***The Global Immigration Problem*** 326
Mike Crapo, ***Immigration Policy Must Help Economy While Preserving Ideals*** 328
Trapper John, ***The Progressive Case Against the Immigration Bill*** 328

WRITING TO PERSUADE

13 **WRITING A CLASSICAL ARGUMENT 331**

What Is Argument? 331
Exploring Classical Argument 332
Understanding Classical Argument 333
Stages of Development: Your Growth as an Arguer 333
Creating an Argument Frame: A Claim with Reasons 335
Articulating Reasons 336
Articulating Underlying Assumptions 337
Using Evidence Effectively 339
Evaluating Evidence: The STAR Criteria 342
Addressing Objections and Counterarguments 343
Responding to Objections, Counterarguments, and Alternative Views 346
Seeking Audience-Based Reasons 347
Appealing to *Ethos* and *Pathos* 348
A Brief Primer on Informal Fallacies 351

WRITING PROJECT A CLASSICAL ARGUMENT 353
Generating and Exploring Ideas 354
Shaping and Drafting 355
Revising 357
Questions for Peer Review 357

READINGS
Ross Taylor (student), ***Paintball: Promoter of Violence or Healthy Fun?*** 359
William Sweet, ***Why Uranium Is the New Green*** 362
Stan Eales, ***Welcome to Sellafield (editorial cartoon)*** 366
Los Angeles Times, ***No to Nukes*** 367
Leonard Pitts, Jr., ***Spare the Rod, Spoil the Parenting*** 370
A. J. Chavez (student), ***The Case for (Gay) Marriage*** 372

14 **MAKING AN EVALUATION 378**

Exploring Evaluative Writing 379
Understanding Evaluation Arguments 381
The Criteria-Match Process 382
The Role of Purpose and Context in Determining Criteria 384
Special Problems in Establishing Criteria 384
Distingushing Necessary, Sufficient, and Accidental Criteria 385
Using a Planning Schema to Develop Evaluation Arguments 386
Conducting an Evaluation Argument: An Extended Example 387
WRITING PROJECT AN EVALUATION ARGUMENT 390
Generating and Exploring Ideas 391
Shaping and Drafting 392
Revising 393
Questions for Peer Review 393

READINGS
Jackie Wyngaard (student), ***EMP: Music History or Music Trivia?*** 394
Diane Helman and Phyllis Bookspan, Sesame Street: ***Brought to You by the Letters M-A-L-E*** 396
Teresa Filice (student), ***Parents: The Anti-Drug: A Useful Site*** 398

15 **PROPOSING A SOLUTION 401**

Exploring Proposal Writing 401
Understanding Proposal Writing 402
Special Problems of Proposal Arguments 403
Developing an Effective Justification Section 404
Proposals as Visual Arguments and PowerPoint Presentations 406
WRITING PROJECT A PROPOSAL ARGUMENT 408
Generating and Exploring Ideas 409
Shaping and Drafting 410

Revising 411
Questions for Peer Review 411
WRITING PROJECT ADVOCACY AD OR POSTER 412
Using Document Design Features 412
Exploring and Generating Ideas 412
Shaping and Drafting 413
Revising 414
Questions for Peer Review 414
WRITING PROJECT PROPOSAL SPEECH WITH VISUAL AIDS 414
Developing, Shaping, and Outlining Your Proposal Speech 415
Designing Your Visual Aids 416
Slide Titles: Using Points, Not Topics 416
Student Example of a Speech Outline and Slides 418
Sam Rothchild (student), ***Reward Work Not Wealth (oral presentation with visual aids)* 418**
Delivering Your Speech 421
Revising 422
Questions for Peer Review 422
READINGS
Lucy Morsen (student), ***A Proposal to Improve the Campus Learning Environment by Banning Laptops and Cell Phones from Class*** 423
Jennifer Allen, ***The Athlete on the Sidelines*** 427
Dylan Fujitani (student), ***"The Hardest of the Hardcore": Let's Outlaw Hired Guns in Contemporary American Warfare*** 429

PART 3 A GUIDE TO COMPOSING AND REVISING

16 WRITING AS A PROBLEM-SOLVING PROCESS 437

SKILL 16.1 Follow the experts' practice of using multiple drafts. 438
Why Expert Writers Revise So Extensively 438
An Expert's Writing Processes Are Recursive 440
SKILL 16.2 Revise globally as well as locally. 440
SKILL 16.3 Develop ten expert habits to improve your writing processes. 442

SKILL 16.4 Use peer reviews to help you think like an expert. 445
Becoming a Helpful Reader of Classmates' Drafts 445
Using a Generic Peer Review Guide 446
Participating in Peer Review Workshops 449
Responding to Peer Reviews 450

17 COMPOSING AND REVISING CLOSED-FORM PROSE 451

SKILL 17.1 Understand reader expectations. 452
Unity and Coherence 452
Old before New 453
Forecasting and Fulfillment 454

SKILL 17.2 Convert loose structures into thesis/support structures. 455
Avoiding *And Then* Writing, or Chronological Structure 456
Avoiding *All About* Writing, or Encyclopedic Structure 457
Avoiding *Engfish* Writing, or Structure without Surprise 458

SKILL 17.3 Plan and visualize your structure. 459
Making Lists of "Chunks" and a Scratch Outline Early in the Writing Process 459
"Nutshelling" Your Argument as an Aid to Finding a Structure 460
Articulating a Working Thesis with Main Points 461
Using Complete Sentences in Outlines to Convey Meanings 461
Sketching Your Structure Using an Outline, Tree Diagram, or Flowchart 461
Letting the Structure Evolve 463

SKILL 17.4 Set up reader expectations through effective titles and introductions. 464
Avoiding the "Topic Title" and the "Funnel Introduction" 464
Hooking Your Reader with an Effective Title 465
From Old to New: The General Principle of Closed-Form Introductions 466
Typical Elements of a Closed-Form Introduction 468
Forecasting the Whole with a Thesis Statement, Purpose Statement, or Blueprint Statement 468

SKILL 17.5 Create effective topic sentences for paragraphs. 470
Placing Topic Sentences at the Beginning of Paragraphs 471
Revising Paragraphs for Unity 472
Adding Particulars to Support Points 473

SKILL 17.6 Guide your reader with transitions and other signposts. 474
Using Common Transition Words to Signal Relationships 474
Writing Major Transitions between Parts 476
Signaling Major Transitions with Headings 477

SKILL 17.7 Bind sentences together by placing old information before new information. 477

The Old/New Contract in Sentences 477

How to Make Links to the "Old" 479

Avoiding Ambiguous Use of "This" to Fulfill the Old/New Contract 481

SKILL 17.8 Learn four expert moves for organizing and developing ideas. 481

The *For Example* Move 482

The *Summary/However* Move 483

The *Division-into-Parallel Parts* Move 484

The *Comparison/Contrast* Move 485

SKILL 17.9 Use effective tables, graphs, and charts to present numeric data. 486

How Tables Tell Many Stories 487

Using a Graphic to Tell a Story 487

Incorporating a Graphic into Your Essay 490

SKILL 17.10 Write effective conclusions. 492

18 COMPOSING AND REVISING OPEN-FORM PROSE 495

Key Features of Open-Form Prose 496

SKILL 18.1 Make your narrative a story, not an *and then* chronology. 496

Depiction of Events through Time 498

Connectedness 499

Tension or Conflict 500

Resolution, Recognition, or Retrospective Interpretation 500

SKILL 18.2 Write low on the ladder of abstraction. 501

Concrete Words Evoke Images and Sensations 502

Use Revelatory Words and Memory-Soaked Words 503

SKILL 18.3 Disrupt your reader's desire for direction and clarity. 504

Disrupting Predictions and Making Odd Juxtapositions 505

Leaving Gaps 506

SKILL 18.4 Tap the power of figurative language. 506

SKILL 18.5 Expand your repertoire of styles. 508

SKILL 18.6 Use open-form elements to create "voice" in closed-form prose. 510

Introduce Some Humor 510

Use Techniques from Popular Magazines 511

PART 4 A RHETORICAL GUIDE TO RESEARCH

19 ASKING QUESTIONS, FINDING SOURCES 517

An Overview of Research Writing 517
- Characteristics of a Good Research Paper 517
- An Effective Approach to Research 518
- The Role of Documentation in College Research 518

SKILL 19.1 Argue your own thesis in response to a research question. 518
- Topic Focus Versus Question Focus 519
- Formulating a Research Question 519
- Establishing Your Role as a Researcher 520
- A Case Study: James Gardiner's Research on Online Social Networks 521

SKILL 19.2 Understand differences among kinds of sources. 523
- Primary and Secondary Sources 523
- Reading Secondary Sources Rhetorically 524

SKILL 19.3 Use purposeful strategies for searching libraries, databases, and web sites. 528
- Checking Your Library's Home Page 528
- Finding Print Articles: Searching a Licensed Database 529
- Illustration of a Database Search 531
- Finding Cyberspace Sources: Searching the World Wide Web 533

20 EVALUATING SOURCES 536

SKILL 20.1 Read sources rhetorically and take purposeful notes. 536
- Reading with Your Own Goals in Mind 536
- Reading Your Sources Rhetorically 537
- Taking Purposeful Notes 539

SKILL 20.2 Evaluate sources for reliability, credibility, angle of vision, and degree of advocacy. 541
- Reliability 541
- Credibility 514
- Angle of Vision and Political Stance 542
- Degree of Advocacy 544

SKILL 20.3 Use your rhetorical knowledge to evaluate web sources. 544
- The Web as a Unique Rhetorical Environment 544
- Criteria for Evaluating a Web Source 545
- Analyzing Your Own Purposes for Using a Web Source 546

21 **INCORPORATING SOURCES INTO YOUR OWN WRITING 553**

Roger D. McGrath, *The Myth of Violence in the Old West* 553

SKILL 21.1 Let your own argument determine your use of sources. 555

Writer 1: An Analytical Paper on Causes of Violence in Contemporary Society 555

Writer 2: A Persuasive Paper Supporting Gun Control 556

Writer 3: An Informative Paper Showing Shifting Definitions of Crime 557

SKILL 21.2 Know when and how to use summary, paraphrase, and quotation. 558

Summarizing 559

Paraphrasing 559

Quoting 561

SKILL 21.3 Use attributive tags to distinguish your ideas from a source's. 561

Attributive Tags Mark Where Source Material Starts and Ends 562

Attributive Tags Are Clearer than Parenthetical Citations 563

Attributive Tags Frame the Source Material Rhetorically 564

SKILL 21.4 Punctuate quotations correctly. 565

Quoting a Complete Sentence 566

Inserting Quoted Words and Phrases into Your Own Sentences 566

Modifying a Quotation 567

Omitting Something from a Quoted Passage 567

Quoting Something That Already Contains a Quotation 568

Using a Block Quotation for a Long Passage 568

SKILL 21.5 Avoid plagiarism by following academic conventions for ethical use of sources. 569

Why Some Kinds of Plagiarism May Occur Unwittingly 569

Strategies for Avoiding Plagiarism 571

22 **CITING AND DOCUMENTING SOURCES 574**

SKILL 22.1 Know what needs to be cited and what doesn't. 574

SKILL 22.2 Understand the connection between in-text citations and the end-of-paper list of cited works. 575

SKILL 22.3 Cite and document sources using MLA style. 576

In-Text Citations in MLA Style 576

Works Cited List in MLA Style 579

MLA Citation Models 579

James Gardiner (student), ***Why* Facebook *Might Not Be Good for You* *(MLA-Style Research Paper)*** 590

SKILL 22.4 Cite and document sources using APA style. 599
In-Text Citations in APA Style 599
References List in APA Style 600
APA Citation Models 600
Student Example of an APA-Style Research Paper 605

PART 5 WRITING FOR ASSESSMENT

23 ESSAY EXAMINATIONS 609

How Essay Exams Differ from Other Essays 610
Preparing for an Exam: Learning Subject Matter 610
Identifying and Learning Main Ideas 610
Applying Your Knowledge 611
Making a Study Plan 612
Analyzing Exam Questions 612
Understanding the Use of Outside Quotations 613
Recognizing Organizational Cues 613
Interpreting Key Terms 614
Dealing with the Limits of the Test Situation 618
Producing an "A" Response 620
Chapter Summary 622

24 PORTFOLIOS AND REFLECTIVE ESSAYS 623

Understanding Portfolios 624
Collecting Work for Paper and Electronic Portfolios 624
Selecting Work for Your Portfolio 625
Understanding Reflective Writing 625
Why Is Reflective Writing Important? 627
Reflective Writing Assignments 627
Single Reflection Assignments 627
Guidelines for Writing a Single Reflection 628
Comprehensive Reflection Assignments 629
Guidelines for Writing a Comprehensive Reflection 630
Guidelines for Writing a Comprehensive Reflective Letter 631

READINGS
Jaime Finger (student), *A Single Reflection on an Exploratory Essay* 633
Bruce Urbanik (student), *A Comprehensive Reflective Letter* 634

PART 6 A GUIDE TO EDITING

1 **IMPROVING YOUR EDITING SKILLS 639**

Why Editing Is Important 639

Improving Your Editing and Proofreading Processes 640

Keep a List of Your Own Characteristic Errors • Do a Self-Assessment of Your Editing Knowledge • Read Your Draft Aloud • Read Your Draft Backward • Use a Spell-Checker and (Perhaps) Other Editing Programs

Microtheme Projects on Editing 641

Microtheme 1: Apostrophe Madness • Microtheme 2: Stumped by *However* • Microtheme 3: The Comic Dangler • Microtheme 4: How's That Again? • Microtheme 5: The Intentional Fragment • Microtheme 6: Create Your Own

2 **UNDERSTANDING SENTENCE STRUCTURE 644**

The Concept of the Sentence 644

Basic Sentence Patterns 645

Pattern One: Subject + Verb (+ Optional Adverb Modifiers) • Pattern Two: Subject + Verb + Direct Object (DO) • Pattern Three: Subject + Verb + Subject Complement (SC) • Pattern Four: Subject + Verb + Direct Object + Object Complement (OC) • Pattern Five: Subject + Verb + Indirect Object (IDO) + Direct Object

Parts of Speech 647

Nouns • Pronouns • Verbs • Adjectives and Adverbs • Conjunctions • Prepositions • Interjections

Types of Phrases 652

Prepositional Phrases • Appositive Phrases • Verbal Phrases • Absolute Phrases

Types of Clauses 654

Noun Clauses • Adjective Clauses • Adverb Clauses

Types of Sentences 655

Simple Sentences • Compound Sentences • Complex Sentences • Compound-Complex Sentences

3 **PUNCTUATING BOUNDARIES OF SENTENCES, CLAUSES, AND PHRASES 657**

Why Readers Need Punctuation 658

Rules for Punctuating Clauses and Phrases within a Sentence 658

Identifying and Correcting Sentence Fragments 660

Types of Fragments • Methods for Correcting Sentence Fragments

Identifying and Correcting Run-Ons and Comma Splices 662

• Methods for Correcting Run-Ons and Comma Splices

Overview of Methods for Joining Clauses 664

4 EDITING FOR STANDARD ENGLISH USAGE 666

Fixing Grammatical Tangles 666

Mixed Constructions • Faulty Predication

Maintaining Consistency 667

Shifts in Tense • Shifts in the Person and Number of Pronouns

Maintaining Agreement 668

Subject-Verb Agreement • Pronoun-Antecedent Agreement

Maintaining Parallel Structure 672

Placement of Correlative Conjunctions • Use of *and which/that* or *and who/whom*

Avoiding Dangling or Misplaced Modifiers 674

Dangling Modifiers • Misplaced Modifiers

Choosing Correct Pronoun Cases 676

Cases of Relative Pronouns • Intervening Parenthetical Clauses • Pronouns as Parts of Compound Constructions • Pronouns in Appositive Constructions • Pronouns as Parts of Implied Clauses • Pronouns Preceding Gerunds or Participles

Choosing Correct Verb Forms 679

Choosing Correct Adjective and Adverb Forms 679

Confusion of Adjective and Adverb Forms • Problems with Comparative and Superlative Forms • Ambiguous Adverbs

5 EDITING FOR STYLE 682

Pruning Your Prose 682

Cutting Out Deadwood • Combining Sentences

Enlivening Your Prose 684

Avoiding Nominalizations • Avoiding Noun Pileups • Avoiding Pretentious Language • Avoiding Clichés, Jargon, and Slang • Creating Sentence Variety • Using Specific Details

Avoiding Broad or Unclear Pronoun Reference 686

Avoiding Broad Reference • Avoiding Unclear Antecedents

Putting Old Information before New Information 687

Deciding between Active and Passive Voice 687

Strength of the Active Voice • When to Use the Passive Voice

Using Inclusive Language 689

Avoiding Sexist Labels and Stereotypes • Avoiding Use of Masculine Pronouns to Refer to Both Sexes • Avoiding Inappropriate Use of the Suffix *-man* • Avoiding Language Biased Against Ethnic or Other Minorities

6 EDITING FOR PUNCTUATION AND MECHANICS 692

Periods, Question Marks, and Exclamation Points 692

Courtesy Questions • Indirect Questions • Placement of Question Marks with Quotations • Exclamation Points

Commas 693

Using Commas • Omitting Commas

Semicolons 700

Semicolon to Join Main Clauses • Semicolon in a Series Containing Commas

Colons, Dashes, and Parentheses 701

Colons • Dashes • Parentheses

Apostrophes 704

Apostrophe to Show Possession • Forming the Possessive • Apostrophes with Contractions • Apostrophes to Form Plurals

Quotation Marks 705

Punctuating the Start of a Quotation • Placement of Attributive Tags • Punctuating the End of a Quotation • Indirect Quotations • Indented Block Method for Long Quotations • Single Quotation Marks • Quotation Marks for Titles of Short Works • Quotation Marks for Words Used in a Special Sense

Italics (Underlining) 708

Italics for Titles of Long Complete Works • Italics for Foreign Words and Phrases • Italics for Letters, Numbers, and Words Used as Words

Brackets, Ellipses, and Slashes 709

Brackets • Ellipses • Slashes

Capital Letters 711

Capitals for First Letters of Sentences and Intentional Fragments • Capitals for Proper Nouns • Capitals for Important Words in Titles • Capitals in Quotations and Spoken Dialogue • Consistency in Use of Capitals

Numbers 712

Numbers in Scientific and Technical Writing • Numbers in Formal Writing for Nontechnical Fields • Numbers at the Beginning of a Sentence • Plurals of Numbers • Numbers in a Series for Comparison

Abbreviations 714

Abbreviations for Academic Degrees and Titles • Abbreviations for Agencies, Institutions, and Other Entities • Abbreviations for Terms Used with Numbers • Abbreviations for Common Latin Terms • Plurals of Abbreviations

Manuscript Form 715

Acknowledgments 717

Index 720

WRITING PROJECTS

BRIEF PROJECTS

CHAPTER 1 Write two messages with different audiences, purposes, and genres, and explain the differences in your rhetorical choices in each message. 23

Write a letter to your professor explaining how your thoughts about writing have changed. 24

CHAPTER 2 Use the "believing and doubting game" to explore a controversial assertion. 49

CHAPTER 3 Analyze the different angles of vision in two passages about nuclear energy. 64

CHAPTER 4 Write two contrasting descriptions of the same place, and then analyze them, indicating what you learned. 82

MAJOR PROJECTS

CHAPTER 5 Write a summary of a reading. 114

Write a summary and strong response essay. 118

CHAPTER 6 Write an autobiographical narrative shaped by contrary experiences or opposing tensions. 138

Write a literacy narrative. 141

CHAPTER 7 Write an exploratory narrative of your engagement with a problem and your attempts to resolve it. 157

Write an annotated bibliography for a research project. 164

CHAPTER 8 Write an informative report. 185

Write an informative article using the "surprising-reversal" strategy. 187

CHAPTER 9 Write an empirical research report based on a field research project using questionnaires, interviews, or observations. 218

Create a scientific poster to present the key elements of your field research project. 222

CHAPTER 10 Analyze two documentary or news photographs, two paintings, or two print advertisements. 268

CHAPTER 11 Pose an interpretive question about a short story and respond to it analytically. (Project uses reading log entries.) 285

CHAPTER 12 Analyze the ideas of other writers on a question and synthesize these ideas to arrive at your own point of view. (Project uses learning log entries.) 310

CHAPTER 13 Write a persuasive argument in the classical style. 353

CHAPTER 14 Develop criteria for an evaluation and test your chosen case against the criteria. 390

CHAPTER 15 Write a proposal to solve a local problem or address a public issue. 408

Create a public affairs advocacy advertisement or poster. 412

Prepare a proposal speech with visual aids. 414

THEMATIC CONTENTS

The Allyn & Bacon Guide to Writing contains 51 readings—28 by professional writers and 22 by students. In addition, the text has more than 70 visual texts (such as advertisements, news photographs, posters, and Web sites) that can lead to productive thematic discussions. These readings and visual texts can be clustered thematically in the following ways.

ENERGY SOURCES AND SUSTAINABILITY

Wind turbines photograph 3

David Rockwood, A Letter to the Editor 6

Two passages about nuclear power 64

Arctic National Wildlife Refuge photographs and texts 61

Food Is a Weapon poster 85

Michael Pollan, Why Bother? 88

Kyle Madsen (student), Can a Green Thumb Save the Planet? A Response to Michael Pollan 111

Shannon King (student), How Clean and Green Are Hydrogen Fuel-Cell Cars? 196

Greenpeace protest in Switzerland photograph 251

William Sweet, Why Uranium Is the New Green 362

Stan Eales, Welcome to Sellafield (editorial cartoon) 366

Los Angeles Times, No to Nukes 367

If You Are Not Using It . . . Turn It Off (poster) 637

THE INTERNET, SOCIAL NETWORKING, CELL PHONES, AND SURVEILLANCE

James Gardiner (student), How Do Online Social Networks Affect Communication? 169

James Gardiner (student), What Is the Effect of Online Social Networks on Communication Skills? An Annotated Bibliography 174

Nikki Swartz, Mobile Phone Tracking Scrutinized 302

Terry J. Allen, Reach Out and Track Someone 303

Kate MacAulay (student), Technology's Peril and Potential 308

Lucy Morsen (student), A Proposal to Improve the Campus Learning Environment by Banning Laptops and Cell Phones from Class 423

James Gardiner (student), Why *Facebook* Might Not Be Good for You 590

IMMIGRATION

Mike Lane, Labor Day Blues (editorial cartoon) 129

Froma Harrop, New Threat to Skilled U.S. Workers 130

Pew Research Center, Muslim Americans: Middle Class and Mostly Mainstream 192

Immigration photographs 242, 244

Dee, Comprehensive Immigration Reform: PROs and ANTIs (blog) 324

Byron Williams, Immigration Frenzy Points Out Need for Policy Debate (blog) 325

Victor Davis Hanson, The Global Immigration Problem (blog) 326

Mike Crapo, Immigration Policy Must Help Economy While Preserving Ideals (blog) 328

Trapper John, The Progressive Case Against the Immigration Bill (blog) 328

EMPLOYMENT AND OUTSOURCING

Angle of vision sweatshop cartoon 53

Thomas L. Friedman, 30 Little Turtles 124

Stephanie Malinowski (student), Questioning Thomas L. Friedman's Optimism in "30 Little Turtles" 125

David Horsey, Today's Economic Indicator (editorial cartoon) 128

Mike Lane, Labor Day Blues (editorial cartoon) 129

Froma Harrop, New Threat to Skilled U.S. Workers 130

Dee, Comprehensive Immigration Reform: PROs and ANTIs (blog) 324

Byron Williams, Immigration Frenzy Points Out Need for Policy Debate (blog) 325

Victor Davis Hanson, The Global Immigration Problem (blog) 326

Mike Crapo, Immigration Policy Must Help Economy While Preserving Ideals (blog) 328

Trapper John, The Progressive Case Against the Immigration Bill (blog) 328

Dylan Fujitani (student), "The Hardest of the Hardcore": Let's Outlaw Hired Guns in Contemporary American Warfare 429

American Indian College Fund public affairs advocacy advertisement 607

VIOLENCE, PUBLIC SAFETY, AND INDIVIDUAL RIGHTS

World Trade Center 9/11 attack photographs 244

Peter Turnley, Fall of the Berlin Wall (photograph) 250

Clark Hoyt, Face to Face with Tragedy 271

Ross Taylor (student), Paintball: Promoter of Violence or Healthy Fun? 359

Dylan Fujitani (student), "The Hardest of the Hardcore": Let's Outlaw Hired Guns in Contemporary American Warfare 429

Women Against Gun Control Web site 515

Million Mom March Web site factoids 548

Roger D. McGrath, The Myth of Violence in the Old West 553

OTHER PUBLIC POLICY ISSUES

Pew Research Center, Muslim Americans: Middle Class and Mostly Mainstream 192

Kerri Ann Matsumoto (student), How Much Does It Cost to Go Organic? 195

Eugene Robinson, You Have the Right to Remain a Target of Racial Profiling 199

World Trade Center 9/11 attack photographs 244

Peter Turnley, Fall of the Berlin Wall (photograph) 250

Clark Hoyt, Face to Face with Tragedy 271

Manoucheka Celeste, Disturbing Media Images of Haiti Earthquake Aftermath Tell Only Part of the Story 273

Leonard Pitts, Jr., Spare the Rod, Spoil the Parenting 370

A. J. Chavez (student), The Case for (Gay) Marriage 372

Images and graphs about binge drinking 379, 381

Teresa Filice (student), *Parents: The Anti-Drug*: A Useful Site 398

Common Sense for Drug Policy, White Kids Are Much More Likely to Be Using (and Selling) Drugs! (public affairs advocacy advertisement) 407

Sam Rothchild (student), Reward Work Not Wealth: A Proposal to Increase Income Tax Rates for the Richest 1 Percent of Americans (speech with visuals) 418–420

Jennifer Allen, The Athlete on the Sidelines 427

Dylan Fujitani (student), "The Hardest of the Hardcore": Let's Outlaw Hired Guns in Contemporary American Warfare 429

Army recruitment advertisement 435

James Gardiner (student), Why *Facebook* Might Not Be Good for You 590

American Indian College Fund public affairs advocacy advertisement 607

RACE AND CLASS

The visual rhetoric of workplace clothing photographs 63

Patrick José, No Cats in America? 148

Pew Research Center, Muslim Americans: Middle Class and Mostly Mainstream 192

Eugene Robinson, You Have the Right to Remain a Target of Racial Profiling 199

Immigration photographs 242

Clark Hoyt, Face to Face with Tragedy 271

Manoucheka Celeste, Disturbing Media Images of Haiti Earthquake Aftermath Tell Only Part of the Story 273

Lydia Wheeler (student), Two Photographs Capture Women's Economic Misery 275

Stephen Crowley, Isabel Bermudez, and Who Has Two Daughters and No Cash Income (photograph) 276

Dorothea Lange, Destitute Pea Pickers in California (*Migrant Mother*) photograph 277

Alice Walker, Everyday Use (For Your Grandmama) 292

Betsy Weiler (student), Who Do You Want to Be? Finding Heritage in Walker's "Everyday Use" 298

Dee, Comprehensive Immigration Reform: PROs and ANTIs (blog) 324

Byron Williams, Immigration Frenzy Points Out Need for Policy Debate (blog) 325

Victor Davis Hanson, The Global Immigration Problem (blog) 326

Mike Crapo, Immigration Policy Must Help Economy While Preserving Ideals (blog) 328

Trapper John, The Progressive Case Against the Immigration Bill (blog) 328

Common Sense for Drug Policy, White Kids Are Much More Likely to Be Using (and Selling) Drugs! (public affairs advocacy advertisement) 407

Evelyn Dahl Reed, The Medicine Man 281

Sam Rothchild (student), Reward Work Not Wealth: A Proposal to Increase Income Tax Rates for the Richest 1 Percent of Americans (speech with visuals) 418–420

American Indian College Fund public affairs advocacy advertisement 607

GENDER

Anonymous (student), Believing and Doubting Paul Theroux's Negative View of Sports 33

The visual rhetoric of workplace clothing photographs 63

Stephanie Whipple (student), One Great Book 150

Army recruitment advertisement 435

Gina Escamilla, Angie L. Cradock, and Ichiro Kawachi, Women and Smoking in Hollywood Movies: A Content Analysis 225

Lauren Campbell, Charlie Bourain, and Tyler Nishida (students), A Comparison of Gender Stereotypes in *SpongeBob SquarePants* and a 1930s Mickey Mouse Cartoon 231

Lauren Campbell, Charlie Bourain, and Tyler Nishida (students), *SpongeBob SquarePants* Has Fewer Gender Stereotypes than Mickey Mouse (scientific poster) 240

Pierre-Auguste Renoir, *La Loge* painting 254

Camille Pissarro, *Carousel* painting 255

Lydia Wheeler (student), Two Photographs Capture Women's Economic Misery 275

Stephen Crowley and Isabel Bermudez, Who Has Two Daughters and No Cash Income (photograph) 276

Dorothea Lange, Destitute Pea Pickers in California (*Migrant Mother*) photograph 277

A. J. Chavez (student), The Case for (Gay) Marriage 372

Diane Helman and Phyllis Bookspan, *Sesame Street*: Brought to You by the Letters M-A-L-E 396

Jennifer Allen, The Athlete on the Sidelines 427

Women Against Gun Control Web site 315

Million Mom March Web site 548

IDENTITY AND VALUES

Thomas Merton, A Festival of Rain 7

The visual rhetoric of workplace clothing photographs 63

Kris Saknussemm, Phantom Limb Pain 146

Patrick José (student), No Cats in America? 148

Stephanie Whipple (student), One Great Book 150

Kerri Ann Matsumoto (student), How Much Does It Cost to Go Organic? 195

Pierre-Auguste Renoir, *La Loge* painting 254

Camille Pissarro, *Carousel* painting 255

Evelyn Dahl Reed, The Medicine Man 281

Alice Walker, Everyday Use (For Your Grandmama) 292

Betsy Weiler (student), Who Do You Want to Be? Finding Heritage in Walker's "Everyday Use" 298

Kate MacAulay (student), Technology's Peril and Potential 308

Images and graphs about binge drinking 379, 381

Teresa Filice (student), *Parents: The Anti-Drug*: A Useful Site 398

Sam Rothchild (student), Reward Work Not Wealth: A Proposal to Increase Income Tax Rates for the Richest 1 Percent of Americans (speech with visuals) 418–420

Lucy Morsen (student), A Proposal to Improve the Campus Learning Environment by Banning Laptops and Cell Phones from Class 423

Army recruitment advertisement 435

James Gardiner (student), Why *Facebook* Might Not Be Good for You 590

American Indian College Fund public affairs advocacy advertisement 607

POPULAR CULTURE, MEDIA, AND ADVERTISING

Anonymous (student), Believing and Doubting Paul Theroux's Negative View of Sports 33

The visual rhetoric of workplace clothing photographs 63

James Gardiner (student), How Do Online Social Networks Affect Communication? 169

Gina Escamilla, Angie L. Cradock, and Ichiro Kawachi, Women and Smoking in Hollywood Movies: A Content Analysis 225

Lauren Campbell, Charlie Bourain, and Tyler Nishida (students), A Comparison of Gender Stereotypes in *SpongeBob SquarePants* and a 1930s Mickey Mouse Cartoon 231

Lauren Campbell, Charlie Bourain, and Tyler Nishida (students), *SpongeBob SquarePants* Has Fewer Gender Stereotypes than Mickey Mouse (scientific poster) 240

Geico billboard and Pemco Insurance bus panel advertisements 256, 259

Credit card advertisements 266–267

Clark Hoyt, Face to Face with Tragedy 271

Manoucheka Celeste, Disturbing Media Images of Haiti Earthquake Aftermath Tell Only Part of the Story 273

Kate MacAulay (student), Technology's Peril and Potential 308

Ross Taylor (student), Paintball: Promoter of Violence or Healthy Fun? 359

Images and graphs about binge drinking 379, 381

Experience Music Project photograph 387

Jackie Wyngaard (student), EMP: Music History or Music Trivia? 394

Diane Helman and Phyllis Bookspan, *Sesame Street*: Brought to You by the Letters M-A-L-E 396

Army recruitment advertisement 435

PARENTS, CHILDREN, AND FAMILY

Patrick José (student), No Cats in America? 148

Stephanie Whipple (student), One Great Book 150

Alice Walker, Everyday Use (For Your Grandmama) 292

Betsy Weiler (student), Who Do You Want to Be? Finding Heritage in Walker's "Everyday Use" 298

Lydia Wheeler (student), Two Photographs Capture Women's Economic Misery 275

Stephen Crowley and Isabel Bermudez, Who Has Two Daughters and No Cash Income (photograph) 276

Dorothea Lange, Destitute Pea Pickers in California (*Migrant Mother*) photograph 277

Leonard Pitts, Jr., Spare the Rod, Spoil the Parenting 370

Diane Helman and Phyllis Bookspan, *Sesame Street*: Brought to You by the Letters M-A-L-E 396

Teresa Filice (student), *Parents: The Anti-Drug*: A Useful Site 398

Army recruitment advertisement 435

NATURE AND ECOLOGY

Wind turbines photograph 3

David Rockwood, A Letter to the Editor 6

Thomas Merton, A Festival of Rain 7

Arctic National Wildlife Refuge photographs and texts 61

Michael Pollan, Why Bother? 88

Kyle Madsen (student), Can a Green Thumb Save the Planet? A Response to Michael Pollan 111

Shannon King (student), How Clean and Green Are Hydrogen Fuel-Cell Cars? 196

EnchantedLearning.com, Tarantulas 178

Rod Crawford, Myths about "Dangerous" Spiders 179

Kerri Ann Matsumoto (student), How Much Does It Cost to Go Organic? 195

Greenpeace protest in Switzerland photograph 251

PREFACE

Through five editions of *The Allyn & Bacon Guide to Writing*, users and reviewers have praised the book's ability to explain rhetorical concepts clearly, engage students in critical thinking, and teach reading and composing strategies that lead to thoughtful, interesting, and meaningful student work. In regular, brief, and concise editions, the text has been adopted at a wide range of two- and four-year institutions, where instructors admire its appeal to students, its focus on problem posing, its distinctive emphasis on writing and reading as rhetorical acts, its engaging classroom activities, and its effective writing assignments. Its flexibility enables composition teachers to capitalize on their own strengths and interests to create intellectually stimulating and pedagogically effective courses.

What's New in the Sixth Edition?

While retaining the signature strengths of earlier editions, the sixth edition features the following key changes and improvements:

- **Expanded coverage of integrating researched sources effectively and ethically** includes new instruction, visual presentations, and examples to help students improve skills fundamental to college readiness and success throughout their academic careers (Chapters 21 and 22).
- **A thoroughly revised chapter on image analysis** helps students work effectively with a wide variety of the visual texts they will encounter in other course areas and outside of college (Chapter 10).
- **Five new student models and three new professional texts** offer engaging and contemporary topics for discussion, written response, and exploratory research—including banning laptops and cell phones from classes, sustainable environmental practices, and the growing gap between the rich and the poor.
- **MLA and APA coverage is thoroughly updated** according to the most recent citation guidelines from each organization, ensuring that students are learning concepts formatted according to the most current guidelines (Chapter 22).
- **New visual pedagogy presents complex topics clearly** and at-a-glance to better suit today's learners and includes new Strategies Charts and new color-coded examples and explanations of incorporating sources using summary, paraphrase, and quotation (Chapters 21 and 22).
- **A new section on presenting data visually** to reach different kinds of readers helps students create effective tables, graphs, and charts to support their arguments (Chapter 17).

- **New instruction helps writers think rhetorically about introductions** (Chapter 2, Concept 6).
- **Chapters 3 and 4 have been extensively revised** to include the previous edition's Chapter 5 and to consolidate the presentation of angle of vision, the ladder of abstraction, and the value of sensory detail.
- **A revised Concept 2 helps writers develop meaningful thesis statements** by showing them how to start by investigating problems rather than topics (Chapter 1).

Distinctive Approach of *The Allyn & Bacon Guide to Writing*

The improvements in the sixth edition enhance the enduring strengths of *The Allyn & Bacon Guide to Writing* that have made this text pedagogically effective for students and intellectually satisfying for instructors. What follows are the distinctive elements of our approach to teaching composition:

- **Integration of rhetorical theory with composition research.** The authors of this text are scholars in rhetoric, composition studies, writing across the curriculum, critical thinking, global cultural studies, and active learning pedagogy. Together, they bring to *The Allyn & Bacon Guide to Writing* a distinctive pedagogical approach that integrates rhetorical theory with composition research by treating writing and reading as rhetorical acts and as processes of inquiry, problem posing, and critical thinking. The text helps students learn important skills that transfer across disciplines and professional fields.
- **Classroom-tested assignments that guide students through all phases of the reading and writing processes and make frequent use of collaboration and peer review.** The Writing Projects promote intellectual growth and stimulate the kind of critical thinking valued in college courses. Numerous "For Writing and Discussion" exercises make it easy to incorporate active learning into a course while deepening students' understanding of concepts. The text's focus on the subject-matter question that precedes the thesis helps students see academic disciplines as fields of inquiry rather than as data banks of right answers.
- **Coverage of a wide range of genres and aims including academic, civic, and professional genres as well as personal and narrative forms.** By placing nonfiction writing on a continuum from closed-form prose (thesis-based) to open-form prose (narrative-based), the text presents students with a wide range of genres and aims, and clearly explains the rhetorical function and stylistic features of different genres. The text focuses on closed-form writing for entering most academic, civic, and professional conversations, and on open-form writing for narrating ideas and experiences that resist closed-form structures and for creating stylistic surprise and pleasure.
- **Instructional emphases meet the Council of Writing Program Administrators (WPA) guidelines** for outcome goals in first-year

composition courses. The correlation of the WPA Outcomes Statement with the sixth edition of *The Allyn & Bacon Guide to Writing* appears on the front endpapers, part opening pages, and in the *Instructor's Resource Manual*. In addition to helping instructors plan their courses, these correlations help with program-wide internal and external assessments.

- **Great flexibility for instructors.** Because the chapters on rhetoric, on Writing Projects, and on composing and research strategies have been designed with self-contained modules, users praise the ease with which they can select chapters and sections and order them to fit the goals of their own courses.
- **Use of reader-expectation theory to explain how closed-form prose achieves maximum clarity and how open-form prose achieves its distinctive pleasures.** The skills explained in Chapter 17 on composing and revising closed-form prose (such as the reader's need for understanding the problem before encountering the thesis, for forecasting and signposts, for points before particulars, and for old information before new information) are taught as self-contained Skill Lessons that can be easily integrated into a variety of course structures. These explanations show students why certain principles of closed-form prose (such as unified and coherent paragraphs with topic sentences) derive from the psychology of cognition rather than from the rule-making penchant of English teachers. The skills explained in Chapter 18 on open-form prose show how writers create pleasurable surprise through purposeful disruptions and violations of the conventions of closed-form prose.
- **Emphasis on teaching students to read rhetorically.** An often-noted strength of *The Allyn & Bacon Guide to Writing* is its method for teaching students to read rhetorically so that they can summarize complex readings and speak back to them armed with their own powers of analysis and critical thinking. This skill is crucial for undergraduate research in any discipline. In its focus on rhetorical reading, the text teaches students to understand the differences between print and cyberspace sources; to analyze the rhetorical occasion, genre, context, intended audience, and angle of vision of sources; to evaluate sources according to appropriate criteria; and to negotiate the World Wide Web with confidence.
- **A sequenced skill-based approach to research** teaches students expert strategies for conducting academic research in a rhetorical environment.
- **Coverage of visual rhetoric and document design** focuses on Web sites, advertisements, posters, and other texts where words and images work together for rhetorical effect.
- **A friendly, encouraging tone** respects students and treats them as serious learners.

Key Features of *The Allyn & Bacon Guide to Writing*

- **An organization that emphasizes concepts and skills and promotes active learning.** The modular organization offers instructors great flexibility in designing courses and allows students to quickly navigate the text.

    - **Twelve rhetorical "Concepts" in Part 1** provide students with memorable takeaway ideas that enable them to situate verbal and visual texts in a rhetorical context and to think critically about how any text tries to persuade its audience.
    - **Writing Projects in Part 2,** arranged according to rhetorical aim, teach students the features of a genre while promoting new ways of seeing and thinking. The exploratory exercises for each Writing Project help students develop their skills at posing problems, generating ideas, delaying closure, valuing alternative points of view, and thinking dialectically.
    - **Numbered "Skills" in Parts 3 and 4,** designed as modular mini-lessons, teach the compositional and research skills that can be applied to any writing project.
- **Professional and student readings on current and enduring questions** that illustrate rhetorical principles, invite thematic grouping, and provide models for students' own writing.
- **"For Writing and Discussion" exercises,** which appear regularly throughout the text, provide class-tested critical thinking activities that promote conceptual learning or active exploration of ideas.
- **Strategies charts** present suggestions for approaching reading, writing, and research tasks in a handy format for student reference and use.
- **Framework charts for genres and writing assignments** help students understand the structural features of different genres, and serve as flowcharts that promote both idea generation and more purposeful structure.
- **Peer review guidelines for major assignments** help students conduct effective peer reviews of each other's drafts.

Strategies for Using *The Allyn & Bacon Guide to Writing*

The text's organization makes it easy to design a new syllabus or adapt the text to your current syllabus. Although there are many ways to use *The Allyn & Bacon Guide to Writing,* the most typical course design has students reading and discussing selected concepts from Chapters 1–4 (Part 1) during the opening weeks. The brief, informal write-to-learn projects in these chapters can be used either for homework assignments or for in-class discussion. In the rest of the course, instructors typically assign Writing Projects chapters from the array of options available in Part 2. While students are engaged with the Writing Projects in these chapters, instructors can work in mini-lessons on the writing and research "skills" in Parts 3 and 4. Typically during class sessions, instructors move back and forth between classroom exercises related directly to the current Writing Project (invention exercises, group brainstorming, peer review workshops) and discussions focused on instructional matter from the rest of the text. (For more specific suggestions on how to select and sequence materials, see the sample syllabi in the *Instructor's Resource Manual.*)

Supplements for *The Allyn & Bacon Guide to Writing*

***The Instructor's Resource Manual*, Sixth Edition,** has been revised by Susanmarie Harrington of the University of Vermont. The *Instructor's Resource Manual* integrates emphases for meeting the Council of Writing Program Administrators' guidelines for outcome goals in first-year composition courses. It continues to offer detailed teaching suggestions to help both experienced and new instructors; practical teaching strategies for composition instructors in a question-and-answer format; suggested syllabi for courses of various lengths and emphases; chapter-by-chapter teaching suggestions; answers to Handbook exercises; suggestions for using the text with nonnative speakers; suggestions for using the text in an electronic classroom; transparency masters for class use; and annotated bibliographies.

MyCompLab. The only online application that integrates a writing environment with proven resources for grammar, writing, and research, MyCompLab gives students help at their fingertips as they draft and revise. Instructors have access to a variety of assessment tools including commenting capabilities, diagnostics and study plans, and an e-portfolio. Created after years of extensive research and in partnership with faculty and students across the country, MyCompLab offers a seamless and flexible teaching and learning environment built specifically for writers.

Interactive Pearson eText. An e-book version of *The Allyn & Bacon Guide to Writing*, Sixth Edition, is also available in MyCompLab. This dynamic, online version of the text is integrated throughout MyCompLab to create an enriched, interactive learning experience for writing students.

CourseSmart. Students can subscribe to *The Allyn & Bacon Guide to Writing*, Sixth Edition, as a CourseSmart eText (at CourseSmart.com). The site includes all of the book's content in a format that enables students to search the text, bookmark passages, save their own notes, and print reading assignments that incorporate lecture notes.

Acknowledgments

We wish to give special thanks to the following composition scholars and teachers, who reviewed the fifth-edition text or the manuscript for the sixth edition, helping us understand how they use *The Allyn & Bacon Guide to Writing* in the classroom and offering valuable suggestions for improving the text: Ann Marie Ade, Embry-Riddle Aeronautical University; Terri A. Amlong, De Sales University; Larry Beason, University of Southern Alabama; Lisa Beckelhimer, University of Cincinnati; Linda Bingham, Hawkeye Community College; Rita M. Brown, Sanford-Brown College, Collinsville; Lizbeth A. Bryant, Purdue University Calumet; Allison Carr, University of Cincinnati; Laura Carroll, Abilene Christian University; Virginia Chappell, Marquette University; Jim Dervin, Winstson-Salem State University; Robert Grindy, Richland Community College; Kimberly Harrison, Florida International University; Jen Hazel, Owens Community College; Melissa Ianetta, University of Delaware; Gilda Kelsey,

University of Delaware; Lindsay Lewan, Arapahoe Community College; Theresa P. Maue, Embry-Riddle Aeronautical University; Amanda McGuire Rzicznek, Bowling Green State University; MaryGrace N. Paden, John Tyler Community College; Deirdre Pettipiece, University of the Sciences in Philadelphia; Jeanne Purtell, Harrisburg Area Community College, York; Jamey Trotter, Arapahoe Community College; Scott Warnock, Drexel University; and Derand Wright, Southern Illinois University Carbondale.

Thank you also to the students who reviewed *The Allyn & Bacon Guide to Writing,* telling us about their experiences using the fifth edition: Joseph Derosier, Embry-Riddle Aeronautical University; Roxanne Malick, Harrisburg Area Community College; Lindsey Shiflett, Richland Community College; Chelsea Stevenson, Richland Community College; and Heidi Thomas, Harrisburg Area Community College.

Thanks also to various scholars who have written commissioned sections of *The Allyn & Bacon Guide to Writing* for previous editions and whose work remains in the sixth edition. Thanks to Tim McGee of Philadelphia University, whose work still influences our material on oral presentation. Thanks also to Alice Gillam of the University of Wisconsin–Milwaukee, who authored the chapter on self-reflective writing (Chapter 24), and to Virginia Chappell of Marquette University, who contributed significantly to Chapter 11 on analyzing a short story. Finally, we wish to thank again Christy Friend of the University of South Carolina, Columbia, who wrote the chapter on essay examinations for the first edition.

Our deepest thanks and appreciation go to our editor, Lauren Finn, whose comprehensive view of the field, keen insights, and excellent people and communication skills make her a pleasure to work with. We are also particularly grateful to our development editor, Marion Castellucci, who has worked with us through multiple revisions and has become an invaluable part of our team. Her insight, sense of humor, professional experience, and extensive editorial knowledge have once again kept us on track and made the intense work of this revision possible.

We owe special thanks to three people whose expertise inform our new approaches to image analysis in Chapter 10: to Naomi Hume for her experience in teaching the analysis of paintings; to Claire Garoutte for her work on documentary photography; and to Kristopher Johnson for his insights from the fields of advertising and marketing.

We would also like to thank three Seattle University students who provided special research assistance for this edition as well as their perspective on important issues: Jon Carr, Kyle Madsen, and Lydia Wheeler. We'd also like to thank Stephen and Sarah Bean for their research help. Most of all, we are indebted to all our students, who have made the teaching of composition such a joy. We thank them for their insights and for their willingness to engage with problems, discuss ideas, and, as they compose and revise, share with us their frustrations and their triumphs. They have sustained our love of teaching and inspired us to write this book.

Finally, John Bean thanks his wife, Kit, also a professional composition teacher, whose dedication to her students as writers and individuals manifests the sustaining values of our unique profession. John also thanks his children, Matthew, Andrew, Stephen, and Sarah, who have grown to adulthood since he began writing textbooks. June Johnson thanks her husband, Kenneth Bube, for his loving support, his interest in teaching, and his expert understanding of the importance of writing in mathematics and the sciences. Finally, she thanks her daughter, Jane Ellen, who has offered encouragement and support in countless ways.

JOHN D. RAMAGE
JOHN C. BEAN
JUNE JOHNSON

PART 1

A RHETORIC FOR WRITERS

As the search for clean, renewable energy to relieve the pressure on oil gains momentum, photographs of wind turbines are appearing more frequently in magazines and newspapers. However, because this source of energy is controversial, *how* these massive technological windmills are depicted varies widely. Do they blend into the landscape or mar it with their industrial presence? Photographers and writers, conscious of the rhetorical effect of photos, carefully plan the impression they want photos of wind power to convey. This low-angle shot of wind turbines, emphasizing their size and power and hinting at barren hills in the background, participates in this public controversy.

This photograph is part of a discussion in Chapter 3, page 60, on the way that visuals make appeals to *logos*, *ethos*, and *pathos*.

PART 1 A RHETORIC FOR COLLEGE WRITERS

Part I addresses the following outcomes for first-year composition from the Council of Writing Program Administrators.

RHETORICAL KNOWLEDGE	• Focus on a purpose (Concepts 2 and 3) • Respond to the needs of different audiences (Concepts 1, 3, 8, 11, 12) • Respond appropriately to different kinds of rhetorical situations (Concepts 1, 3, 8, 9, 11, and 12; Brief Writing Projects) • Use conventions of format and structure appropriate to the rhetorical situation (Concepts 1, 3, 5-7, 11, 12; Brief Writing Projects) • Adopt appropriate voice, tone, and level of formality (Concepts 11 and 12; Brief Writing Projects) • Understand how genres shape reading and writing (Concepts 1 and 3, 11, 12; Brief Writing Projects) • Write in several genres (Brief Writing Projects)
CRITICAL THINKING, READING, AND WRITING	• Use writing and reading for inquiry, learning, thinking, and communicating (Concept 2, 4-6; Brief Writing Projects) • Understand a writing assignment as a series of tasks, including finding, evaluating, analyzing, and synthesizing appropriate primary and secondary sources (Concepts 4-7) • Integrate their own ideas with those of others (Concepts 2 and 4) • Understand the relationships among language, knowledge, and power (Concepts 8 and 9; Brief Writing Projects)
PROCESSES	• Understand writing as an open process that permits writers to use later invention and rethinking to revise their work (Concepts 2, 4, 5) • Use a variety of technologies to address a range of audiences (Concepts 10 and 12)
KNOWLEDGE OF CONVENTIONS	• Learn common formats for different kinds of texts (Concepts 1, 3, 12; Brief Writing Projects) • Develop knowledge of genre conventions ranging from structure and paragraphing to tone and mechanics (Concepts 1, 3, 11, 12; Brief Writing Projects)
COMPOSING IN ELECTRONIC ENVIRONMENTS	• Use electronic environments for drafting, reviewing, revising, editing, and sharing texts (Brief Writing Projects) • Understand and exploit the differences in the rhetorical strategies and in the affordances available for both print and electronic composing processes and texts (Concept 12)

THINKING RHETORICALLY ABOUT GOOD WRITING

1

It seems to me, then, that the way to help people become better writers is not to tell them that they must first learn the rules of grammar, that they must develop a four-part outline, that they must consult the experts and collect all the useful information. These things may have their place. But none of them is as crucial as having a good, interesting question.

—*Rodney Kilcup, Historian*

When new students ask us about the rules for good college writing, they are often surprised by history professor Rodney Kilkup's unexpected advice in the epigraph above. To become a better writer, says Kilcup, the most crucial thing is to have "a good, interesting question." We love Professor Kilcup's advice because we'd like you to think of good writers as critical thinkers who pose questions and problems.

As we show throughout this text, writing is closely allied to critical thinking and to the innate satisfaction you take in exercising your curiosity, creativity, and problem-solving ability. Writing helps you discover and express ideas that you would otherwise never think or say. Unlike speaking, writing gives you time to think deeply and long about an idea. Because you can revise writing, it lets you pursue a problem in stages, with each draft reflecting a deeper, clearer, or more complex level of thought. Moreover, the skills you learn in a writing course are transferable to all majors and to your professional careers. Research has shown that managers, accountants, lawyers, engineers, and other professionals spend, on average, forty-four percent of their professional time writing. In sum, writing has lifelong importance: It stimulates, challenges, and stretches your mental powers while giving you a voice in important academic, civic, and professional conversations.

In this chapter, you will learn three important concepts about writing:

- **CONCEPT 1** Good writing can vary from closed to open forms.
- **CONCEPT 2** Good writers address problems rather than topics.
- **CONCEPT 3** Good writers think rhetorically about purpose, audience, and genre.

CONCEPT 1 Good writing can vary from closed to open forms.

In our experience, beginning college writers are often discomforted by the ambiguity of the rules governing writing. They often wish for some consistent rules: "Never use 'I' in a formal paper" or "Start every paragraph with a topic sentence." The problem is that different kinds of writing have different criteria for effectiveness, leaving the writer with rhetorical choices rather than with hard-and-fast formulas for success. You'll be able to appreciate this insight for yourself through the following exercise.

Read the following short pieces of nonfiction prose. The first is a letter to the editor written by a professional civil engineer in response to a newspaper editorial arguing for the development of wind-generated electricity. The second short piece is entitled "A Festival of Rain." It was written by the American poet and religious writer Thomas Merton, a Trappist monk. After reading the two samples carefully, proceed to the discussion questions that follow.

David Rockwood
A Letter to the Editor

1 Your editorial on November 16, "Get Bullish on Wind Power," is based on fantasy rather than fact. There are several basic reasons why wind-generated power can in no way serve as a reasonable major alternative to other electrical energy supply alternatives for the Pacific Northwest power system.

2 First and foremost, wind power is unreliable. Electric power generation is evaluated not only on the amount of energy provided, but also on its ability to meet system peak load requirements on an hourly, daily, and weekly basis. In other words, an effective power system would have to provide enough electricity to meet peak demands in a situation when the wind energy would be unavailable—either in no wind situations or in severe blizzard conditions, which would shut down the wind generators. Because wind power cannot be relied on at times of peak needs, it would have to be backed up by other power generation resources at great expense and duplication of facilities.

3 Secondly, there are major unsolved problems involved in the design of wind generation facilities, particularly for those located in rugged mountain areas. Ice storms, in particular, can cause sudden dynamic problems for the rotating blades and mechanisms which could well result in breakdown or failure of the generators. Furthermore, the design of the facilities to meet the stresses imposed by high winds in these remote mountain regions, in the order of 125 miles per hour, would indeed escalate the costs.

4 Thirdly, the environmental impact of constructing wind generation facilities amounting to 28 percent of the region's electrical supply system (as proposed in your editorial) would be tremendous. The Northwest Electrical Power system presently has

a capacity of about 37,000 megawatts of hydro power and 10,300 megawatts of thermal, for a total of about 48,000 megawatts. Meeting 28 percent of this capacity by wind power generators would, most optimistically, require about 13,400 wind towers, each with about 1,000 kilowatt (one megawatt) generating capacity. These towers, some 100 to 200 feet high, would have to be located in the mountains of Oregon and Washington. These would encompass hundreds of square miles of pristine mountain area, which, together with interconnecting transmission facilities, control works, and roads, would indeed have major adverse environmental impacts on the region.

5 There are many other lesser problems of control and maintenance of such a system. Let it be said that, from my experience and knowledge as a professional engineer, the use of wind power as a major resource in the Pacific Northwest power system is strictly a pipe dream.

Thomas Merton
A Festival of Rain

1 Let me say this before rain becomes a utility that they can plan and distribute for money. By "they" I mean the people who cannot understand that rain is a festival, who do not appreciate its gratuity, who think that what has no price has no value, that what cannot be sold is not real, so that the only way to make something *actual* is to place it on the market. The time will come when they will sell you even your rain. At the moment it is still free, and I am in it. I celebrate its gratuity and its meaninglessness.

2 The rain I am in is not like the rain of cities. It fills the woods with an immense and confused sound. It covers the flat roof of the cabin and its porch with insistent and controlled rhythms. And I listen, because it reminds me again and again that the whole world runs by rhythms I have not yet learned to recognize, rhythms that are not those of the engineer.

3 I came up here from the monastery last night, sloshing through the corn fields, said Vespers, and put some oatmeal on the Coleman stove for supper. … The night became very dark. The rain surrounded the whole cabin with its enormous virginal myth, a whole world of meaning, of secrecy, of silence, of rumor. Think of it: all that speech pouring down, selling nothing, judging nobody, drenching the thick mulch of dead leaves, soaking the trees, filling the gullies and crannies of the wood with water, washing out the places where men have stripped the hillside! What a thing it is to sit absolutely alone, in a forest, at night, cherished by this wonderful, unintelligible, perfectly innocent speech, the most comforting speech in the world, the talk that rain makes by itself all over the ridges, and the talk of the watercourses everywhere in the hollows!

4 Nobody started it, nobody is going to stop it. It will talk as long as it wants, this rain. As long as it talks I am going to listen.

5 But I am also going to sleep, because here in this wilderness I have learned how to sleep again. Here I am not alien. The trees I know, the night I know, the rain I know. I close my eyes and instantly sink into the whole rainy world of which I am a part, and the world goes on with me in it, for I am not alien to it.

FOR WRITING AND DISCUSSION

Comparing Rockwood's and Merton's Writing

Working in small groups or as a whole class, try to reach consensus on the following specific tasks:

1. What are the main differences between the two types of writing? If you are working in groups, help your recorder prepare a presentation describing the differences between Rockwood's writing and Merton's writing.
2. Create a metaphor, simile, or analogy that best sums up your feelings about the most important differences between Rockwood's and Merton's writing: "Rockwood's writing is like . . ., but Merton's writing is like. . . ."
3. Explain why your metaphors are apt. How do your metaphors help clarify or illuminate the differences between the two pieces of writing?

Now that you have done some thinking on your own about the differences between these two examples, turn to our brief analysis.

Distinctions between Closed and Open Forms of Writing

David Rockwood's letter and Thomas Merton's mini-essay are both examples of nonfiction prose. But as these examples illustrate, nonfiction prose can vary enormously in form and style. From the perspective of structure, we can place nonfiction prose along a continuum that goes from closed to open forms of writing (see Figure 1.1).

Closed-Form Prose Of our two pieces of prose, Rockwood's letter illustrates tightly closed writing and falls at the far left end of the continuum because it has these elements:

- An explicit thesis in the introduction that informs readers of the point of the whole essay (i.e., wind-generated power isn't a reasonable alternative energy source in the Pacific Northwest)

FIGURE 1.1 A Continuum of Essay Types: Closed to Open Forms

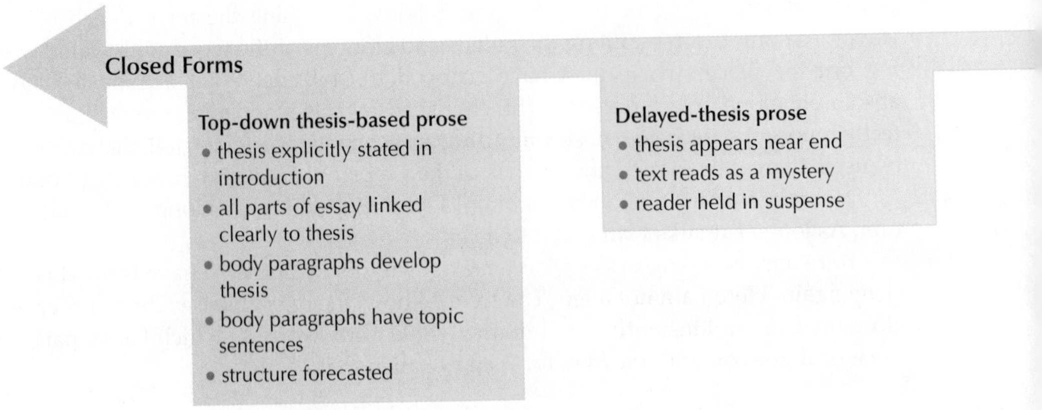

- Unified and coherent paragraphs (i.e., "First and foremost, wind power is unreliable. ... Secondly, there are major unsolved problems. ... Thirdly, ...")
- Sustained development of that thesis without digressions

Once the thesis is stated, readers know the point of the essay and can predict its structure. (You might note that the five-paragraph essay sometimes taught in high school is a by-the-numbers way to teach closed-form prose.) Because its structure is transparent and predictable, the success of closed-form prose rests entirely on its ideas, which must "surprise" readers by asserting something new, challenging, doubtful, or controversial. It aims to change readers' view of the subject through the power of reason, logic, and evidence. Closed-form prose is what most college professors write in their scholarly research, what they most often expect from their students, and what is most common in professional and business contexts.

Open-Form Prose In contrast, Merton's "A Festival of Rain" falls toward the right end of the closed-to-open continuum because it exhibits these features:

- No reduction to a single, summarizable thesis (Merton clearly opposes the consumer culture that will try to "sell" you the rain, but what exactly does Merton mean by "festival" or by rain's "gratuity and its meaninglessness"?)
- The use of story or narrative as an organizing principle (i.e., the story of Merton's leaving the monastery to sleep in the rain-drenched cabin) through which a point emerges suggestively

Although open-form prose does not announce its thesis and support it with reasons and evidence, it does have a focus. As Merton's piece illustrates, the focus is more like a theme in fiction that readers might discuss and even dispute than like a thesis in argument.

Consider also the extent to which Merton violates the rules for closed-form prose. Instead of using transitions between paragraphs, Merton juxtaposes passages that tell the story of his camping trip ("I came up here from the monastery last night ...") with passages that make cryptic, interpretive comments about his experience ("The rain I am in is not like the rain of cities"). Unlike paragraphs in

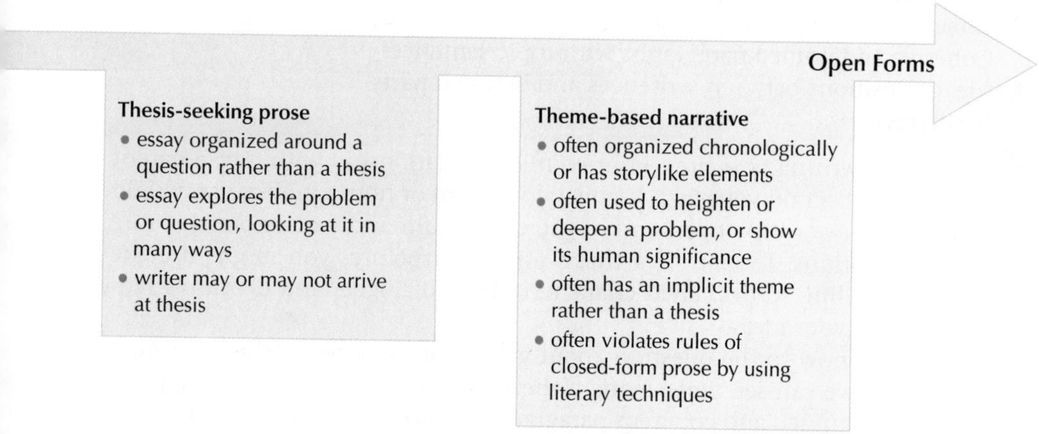

closed-form prose, which typically begin with topic sentences and are developed with supporting details, the paragraphs in Merton's piece have no clear hierarchical structure; paragraph 4, in fact, is only two lines long. These open-form elements often appear in personal essays, in blogs, in newspaper or magazine feature stories or character profiles, or in professional nonfiction.

Flexibility of "Rules" along the Continuum As you can see from the continuum in Figure 1.1, essays can fall anywhere along the scale. Not all thesis-with-support writing has to be top down, stating its thesis explicitly in the introduction. In some cases writers choose to delay the thesis, creating a more exploratory, open-ended, "let's think through this together" feeling before finally stating the main point late in the essay. In some cases writers explore a problem without *ever* finding a satisfactory thesis, creating an essay that is thesis seeking rather than thesis supporting, an essay aimed at deepening the question, refusing to accept an easy answer. Such essays may replicate their authors' process of exploring a problem and include digressions, speculations, conjectures, multiple perspectives, and occasional invitations to the reader to help solve the problem. When writers reach the far right-hand position on the continuum, they no longer state an explicit thesis. Instead, like novelists or short story writers, they embed their points in plot, imagery, dialogue, and so forth, leaving their readers to *infer* a theme from the text. This kind of writing is often called "literary nonfiction."

Where to Place Your Writing along the Continuum

Clearly, essays at opposite ends of this continuum operate in different ways and obey different rules. Because each position on the continuum has its appropriate uses, the writer's challenge is to determine which sort of writing is most appropriate in a given situation. Most college papers (but not all) and much professional writing are written in closed form. Thus if you were writing a business proposal, a legal brief, or an academic paper for a scholarly audience, you would typically choose a closed-form structure, and your finished product would include elements such as the following:

- An explicit thesis in the introduction
- Forecasting of structure
- Cohesive and unified paragraphs with topic sentences
- Clear transitions between sentences and between parts
- No digressions

But if you were writing to express your conflicted relationship with, say, a parent or friend or to reflect on your first discovery of racism or homophobia, you would probably move toward the open end of the continuum and violate one or more of these conventions. Instead of a thesis-support structure, you might use the power of compelling stories, vivid characterization, dialogue, and evocative language to convey your ideas.

If we return now to the question about good writing posed at the beginning of this chapter, we can see that having a thesis statement, topic sentences, good transitions, and unified and coherent paragraphs are not qualities of "good prose" but simply of "closed-form prose." What makes a piece of closed-form prose "good," as we will see in the next section, is the extent to which it addresses a problem or question that matters to the reader and brings to the reader something new, surprising, or provocative. In contrast, we have seen that open-form prose can be "good" without having a thesis-driven, hierarchical structure. Open-form prose conveys its pleasures and insights through narrative strategies rather than through thesis-with-support strategies.

FOR WRITING AND DISCUSSION

Thinking Personally about Closed and Open Forms

Do you and your classmates most enjoy writing prose at the closed or at the more open end of the continuum?

Individual task: Recall a favorite piece of writing that you have done in the past. Jot down a brief description of the kind of writing this was (a poem, a personal-experience essay, a piece of workplace writing, a research paper, a newspaper story, a persuasive argument). Where would you place this piece of writing on the closed-to-open continuum? Explore why you like this piece of writing. Are you at your best in closed-form writing that calls for an explicit thesis statement and logical support? Or are you at your best in more open and personal forms?

Small-group or whole-class task: Share the results of the individual tasks. Is there a wide range of preferences in your class? If so, how do you account for this variance? If not, how do you account for the narrow range?

CONCEPT 2 Good writers address problems rather than topics.

In the previous section, we explained how the rules for good writing vary along a continuum from closed to open forms. In this section, we return to the close connection between writing and critical thinking. From your previous schooling, you are probably familiar with the term **thesis statement**, which is the main point a writer wants to make in an essay. However, you may not have thought much about the *question* that lies behind the thesis, which is the problem or issue that the writer is wrestling with. Behind every thesis statement is an explicit or implied **thesis question**, which is the problem or issue to which the thesis responds. An essay's thesis statement is actually the writer's proposed answer to this question, and it is this question that has propelled the writer's thinking.

Thus, the problem that matters to engineer David Rockwood is whether wind power can be a viable alternative energy source. Rockwood writes to make his answer ("No!") persuasive to readers. Thomas Merton's question is more complex and subtle, one that leads him to use open-form narrative strategies. His question seems to be: What is the effect of a consumer economy on our understanding of meaning and value? He wants to raise readers' awareness of a problem with corporate capitalism (where corporations want to sell you even the rain), which alienates us from nature and from our deepest selves.

This focus on a writer's motivating problem or question differs somewhat from the common view that writers first choose a topic and then narrow it down. Of course, writers have broad areas of interest (which we might call topics), but what they are seeking isn't the topic itself but a cluster of problems or questions within the topic. Instead of "narrowing a topic," they seek a problem that grips their curiosity and gets them thinking.

Shared Problems Unite Writers and Readers

For college professors, "a good, interesting question" is at the heart of good writing. Professors want students to become gripped by problems because they themselves are gripped by problems. For example, at a workshop for new faculty members, we asked participants to write a brief description of the question or problem that motivated their Ph.D. dissertation or a recent conference paper or article. Here is how a biochemistry professor responded:

> During periods of starvation, the human body makes physiological adaptations to preserve essential protein mass. Unfortunately, these adaptations don't work well during long-term starvation. After the body depletes its carbohydrate storage, it must shift to depleting protein in order to produce glucose. Eventually, this loss of functional protein leads to metabolic dysfunction and death. Interestingly, several animal species are capable of surviving for extensive periods without food and water while conserving protein and maintaining glucose levels. How do the bodies of these animals accomplish this feat? I wanted to investigate the metabolic functioning of these animals, which might lead to insights into the human situation.

As you progress through your college career, you will find yourself increasingly engaged with the kinds of questions that motivate your professors. All around college campuses you'll find clusters of professors and students asking questions about all manner of problems ranging from puzzles in the reproductive cycles of worms and bugs to the use of nanotechnology to fight global warming, from the changing portrayal of race and gender in American films to the impact of digital technology on the dissemination of news. At the heart of all these communities of writers and readers is an interest in common questions and the hope for better or different answers. Writers write because they have something new or surprising or challenging to say in response to a question. Readers read because they share the writer's interest in the problem and want to deepen their understanding.

Where Do Problems Come From?

So where do these problems come from? How does a writer get hooked on a problem? Although this question is complex at a philosophical level, we can offer two relatively simple and helpful answers: Sometimes you encounter a problem that is already "out there" in a conversation already in progress in some human community. Some enduring problems have been sparking conversations that have lasted for thousands of years: Do humans have free will? What constitutes ethical action? What is the origin of the universe? Why do good people have to suffer? Thousands of less sweeping problems are being discussed by human communities all the time. In many of your college courses, you'll be introduced to long-standing problems that you hadn't encountered before and that may hook you and draw you into their spell. In these cases, a problem that is already "out there" initiates your search for a possible answer and invites you to join the conversation.

But sometimes you actually find, pose, or articulate a problem yourself, fresh from your own brain. In this case you start a conversation, rather than join an existing one. (It may turn out later that other people have asked the same question, but you didn't know that at the time.) For example, you find your own problem whenever you see something puzzling in the natural world, note curious or unexplained features in a cultural phenomenon or artifact, or discover conflicts or contradictions within your own way of looking at the world.

In the table below we describe some of the ways that writers can become gripped by a problem that may lead to engaged writing.

TABLE 1.1 How Writers Become Gripped by a Problem

Occasion That Leads to Problem	Your Interior Mental State	Example
	The problem is already "out there." *(You enter a conversation already in progress)*	
You encounter others arguing about a problem, and you don't know where you stand.	• You are equally persuaded by different views or dissatisfied with all the views • Part of you thinks X but another part thinks Y (you feel divided)	I don't know where I stand on the question of whether health care should be rationed. In *To Kill a Mockingbird,* I can't decide whether Atticus Finch is a good father.
You aren't satisfied with a common view of something or you disagree with someone on an issue.	• Your skepticism or intuition pushes against some popular view • You are committed to a view different from someone else's • *Note: You must go beyond simply having an opinion. You aren't gripped by a problem until you have seen the possible strengths of other views and the possible weaknesses of your own.*	My teacher's explanation of the causes for anorexia doesn't seem quite right to me. Shanita says that we should build more nuclear power plants to combat global warming, but I say nuclear power is too dangerous.
Someone gives you a question that you can't yet answer.	• You feel overwhelmed with unknowns • You feel that you can't begin to answer until you do more exploration and research • If you know enough to start proposing hypotheses, you aren't satisfied with any of your approaches	Your boss asks you whether the company should enact the proposed marketing plan. Your history professor asks you, "To what extent does Frederick Jackson Turner's frontier hypothesis reflect a Euro-centric world view?"

(*continued*)

TABLE 1.1 *continued*

Occasion That Leads to Problem	Your Interior Mental State	Example
	You pose the problem yourself. *(You initiate the conversation)*	
You see something puzzling in a natural or cultural phenomenon.	• Something deviates from what you would expect or is otherwise unexplainable • You begin testing possible solutions or answers. (Often you want to talk to someone—to start a conversation about the problem)	Why is this fungus appearing on some of these tomatoes but not on the others? Why is Twitter more popular among middle-aged adults than teenagers?
You see something unexpected, puzzling, or unexplained in a poem, painting, or other human artifact.	• You can't see why the artist/maker did something in such a way • You wonder why this particular artifact is different from other artifacts that you thought would be similar	Why does Merton call rain "meaningless"? If Hamlet really loves Ophelia, then why does he treat her like a whore in the nunnery scene?
You articulate something inconsistent or contradictory in your own view of the world.	• You feel unsettled by your own inconsistent views or values • You probe more deeply into your own identity and place in the world	I agree with Merton's argument against consumerism, but I really want a large plasma TV. Is consumerism really bad? Am I a materialist?

In each of these cases, the problem starts to spark critical thinking. As we'll explain in more detail in Chapter 2, you are starting to "wallow in complexity."

FOR WRITING AND DISCUSSION

Finding a Problem

This classroom exercise, based on the image in Figure 1.2, will give you the experience of posing a problem for yourself and then participating in a conversation initiated by shared questions from the class. It is designed to help you think about your own thinking as you ask questions and formulate problems that you might want to explore. Figure 1.2 is a photograph of a sculpture, called *The Foundling*, by Australian artist Patricia Piccinini. (The photograph is taken in an art museum; note the spectator walking by in the background.) The sculpture, which is made of silicone, fiberglass, human hair, leather, plywood, and clothing, is part of a larger Piccinini exhibit of similar life-size figures. Imagine that you came across this sculpture while visiting a museum. Consider the sculpture's title as well as its appearance and its effect on viewers.

Individual task: Working individually, spend several minutes writing down one or more thought-provoking questions that emerge from your looking

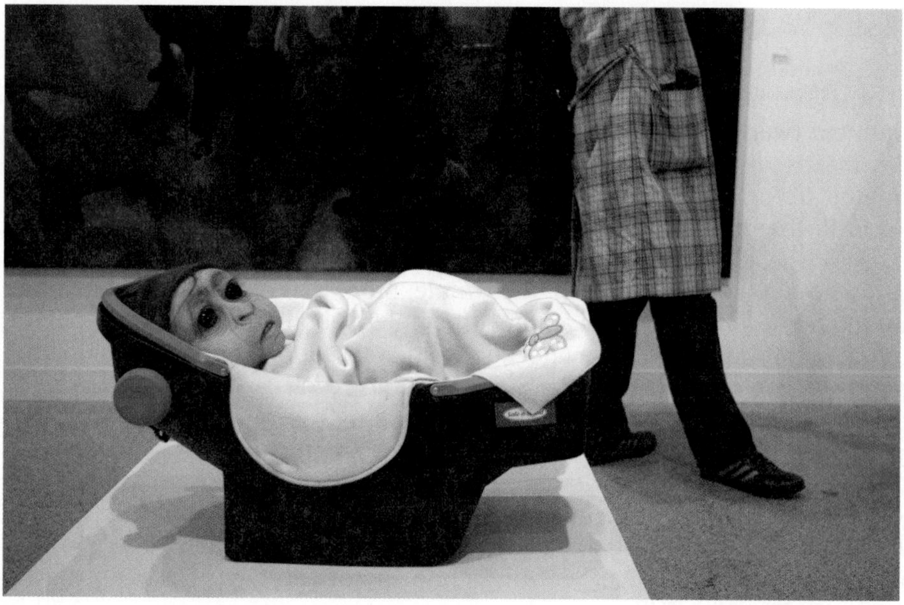

FIGURE 1.2 The Foundling

at the photo of the front view of this sculpture. By "thought-provoking," we mean questions that don't have simple "right answers" but that invite "possible answers" supported by different lines of reasoning, speculation, and argument.

Task for group or whole class discussion: Working in small groups or as a whole class, share your individual questions. Then speculate about possible answers to several of them. The best questions will lead to alternative responses—the feeling of a genuine conversation with different points of view. Each individual should now write down new questions that emerge from the conversation.

Individual reflection: To what extent did the activities provoked by this exercise help you think about where questions come from? How did the questions that you initially posed for yourself evolve as you participated in a conversation about the sculpture? Identify one question that now particularly intrigues you and explain why you find it a good question. (If you would like to find out more about Patricia Piccinini, a quick Web search will yield many results, including statements of her philosophy of art and photographs of her other works.)

CONCEPT 3 **Good writers think rhetorically about purpose, audience, and genre.**

So far, we have used the term "rhetoric"—as in "A Rhetoric for Writers" (the title of Part 1 of this text) or "thinking rhetorically"—without defining it. Now is the time for us to explain what we mean by *rhetoric*.

What Is Rhetoric?

At the broadest level, **rhetoric** is the study of how human beings use language and other symbols to influence the attitudes, beliefs, and actions of others. One prominent twentieth-century rhetorician, Kenneth Burke, calls rhetoric "a symbolic means of inducing cooperation in beings that by nature respond to symbols." To understand what Burke means by "symbols," consider the difference in flirting behavior between peacocks and humans. When male peacocks flirt, they spread their fantastic tail feathers, do mating dances, and screech weirdly to attract females, but the whole process is governed by instinct. Peacocks don't have to choose among different symbolic actions such as buying an Armani tail versus buying a knockoff from Wal-Mart or driving to the mating grounds in the right car. Unlike a peacock, however, a flirting human must make symbolic choices, all of which have meaning. Consider the different flirting messages humans send to each other by their choice of clothes, their method of transportation, their choice of major, their favorite music. Even word choices (for example, academic jargon words versus street slang) or texting behavior give further hints of a person's identity, values, and social groups. Rhetoricians study, among other things, how these symbols arise within a given culture and how they influence others.

In a narrower sense, rhetoric is the art of making messages persuasive. Perhaps the most famous definition of rhetoric comes from the Greek philosopher Aristotle, who defined rhetoric as "the ability to see, in any particular case, all the available means of persuasion." An effective speaker's task, in Aristotle's view, is to persuade listeners to accept the speaker's views on a question of action or belief. But to do so, the speaker must first understand all the arguments on all sides of the question ("all the available means of persuasion"). If we imagine the interaction of several speakers, each proposing different answers to a question, and if we imagine all the speakers listening to each other respectfully and open-mindedly, we can see how productive human conversation could emerge. The study of rhetoric can therefore help people write, speak, read, and listen more effectively.

At an operational level, writers can be said to "think rhetorically" whenever they are consciously aware of writing to an audience for a purpose within a genre. (A *genre*, to be explained in more detail shortly, is a recurring type of writing with distinguishing features and conventions such as a letter to the editor, a scholarly article, a business memo, or a blog.) To think rhetorically, writers consider questions like these:

- ***Purpose:*** What am I trying to accomplish in this paper? What do I want my readers to know, believe, see, or do?
- ***Audience:*** Who are my intended readers, and what are their values and assumptions? What do they already know or believe about my subject? How much do they care about it?
- ***Genre:*** What kind of document am I writing? What are its requirements for structure, style, and document design?

Let's look more closely at each of these components of a writer's rhetorical context.

How Writers Think about Purpose

In this section, we want to help you think more productively about your purpose for writing, which can be examined from several different perspectives: your rhetorical aim, the motivating occasion that gets you going, and your desire to change your reader's view. All three perspectives will help you make your awareness of purpose work for you and increase your savvy as a writer. Let's look at each in turn.

Purpose as Rhetorical Aim One powerful way to think about purpose is through the general concept of "rhetorical aim." In this text, we identify six different rhetorical aims of writing: to express, to explore, to inform, to analyze and synthesize, to persuade, and to reflect. Thinking of each piece of writing in terms of one or more of these rhetorical aims can help you understand typical ways that your essay can be structured and developed and can help you clarify your relationship with your audience. The writing projects in Part 2 of this text are based on these rhetorical aims. Table 1.2 gives you an overview of each of the six rhetorical

TABLE 1.2 Purpose as Rhetorical Aim

Rhetorical Aim	Focus of Writing	Relationship to Audience	Forms and Genres
Express or share (Chapter 6) May also include an artistic aim (Chapter 18)	Your own life, personal experiences, reflections	You share aspects of your life; you invite readers to walk in your shoes, to experience your insights	**Form:** Has many open-form features **Sample genres:** journal, blog, personal Web site, or online profile; personal essays or literacy narratives, often with artistic features
Explore or inquire (Chapter 7)	A significant subject-matter problem that puzzles you	You take readers on your own intellectual journey by showing your inquiry process (raising questions, seeking evidence, considering alternative views)	**Form:** Follows open form in being narrative based; is thesis seeking rather than thesis supporting **Sample genres:** freewriting; research logs; articles and books focused on process of discovery
Inform or explain (Chapter 8)	Factual knowledge addressing a reader's need or curiosity	You provide knowledge that your readers need or want, or you arouse curiosity and provide new, surprising information. You expect readers to trust your authority	**Form:** Usually has a closed-form structure **Sample genres:** encyclopedia articles; instruction booklets; sales reports; technical reports; informative magazine articles; informative Web sites

(continued)

TABLE 1.2 *continued*

Rhetorical Aim	Focus of Writing	Relationship to Audience	Forms and Genres
Analyze, synthesize, or interpret (Chapters 9–12)	Complex subject matter that you can break down into parts and put together in new ways for greater understanding	Using critical thinking and possibly research, you challenge readers with a new way of understanding your subject. Skeptical readers expect you to support your thesis with good particulars.	**Form:** Typically has a closed-form structure **Sample genres:** scholarly articles; experimental reports; many kinds of college research papers; public affairs magazine articles; many kinds of blogs
Persuade (Chapters 13–15)	Subject-matter questions that have multiple controversial answers	You try to convince readers, who may not share your values and beliefs, to accept your stance on an issue by providing good reasons and evidence and attending to alternative views.	**Form:** Usually closed form, but may employ many open-form features for persuasive effect **Sample genres:** letters to the editor; op-ed pieces; advocacy pieces in public affairs magazines; advocacy Web sites; researched academic arguments
Reflect (Chapter 24)	Subject matter closely connected to your interests and experience; often involves self-evaluation of an experience	Writing for yourself as well as for a reader, you seek to find personal meaning and value in an experience or course of study. You assume a sympathetic and interested reader.	**Form:** Anywhere on the closed-to-open-form continuum **Sample genres:** memoirs, workplace self-evaluations; introductory letter for a portfolio; personal essays looking back on an experience

aims and sketches out how the subject matter differs from aim to aim, how the writer's task and relationship to readers differ according to aim, and how a chosen aim affects the writing's genre and its position on the spectrum from open to closed forms.

Purpose as a Response to a Motivating Occasion Another important way to think about purpose is to think about each piece of writing as a response to a particular motivating occasion. Almost all writing is compelled by some sort of motivating occasion or exigency.* This exigency can be external (someone giving you a task and setting a deadline) or internal (your awareness of a problem stimulating your desire to bring about some change in people's views). Thus, when engineer David Rockwood read a newspaper editorial supporting wind-power projects, his own belief in the impracticality of wind power motivated him to write a letter to

*An *exigency* is an urgent or pressing situation requiring immediate attention. Rhetoricians use the term to describe the event or occasion that causes a writer to begin writing.

the editor in rebuttal (see pp. 6–7). But he also knew that he had to write the letter within one or two days or else it stood no chance of being published. His exigency thus included both internal and external factors.

College students' motivations for writing can be equally mixed: In part, you write to meet an assignment deadline; in part, you write to please the teacher and get a good grade. But ideally you also write because you have become engaged with an intellectual problem and want to say something significant about it. Our point here is that your purposes for writing are always more complex than the simple desire to meet an assignment deadline.

Purpose as a Desire to Change Your Reader's View Perhaps the most useful way to think about purpose is to focus on the change you want to bring about in your audience's view of the subject. When you are given a college writing assignment, this view of purpose engages you directly with the intellectual problem specified in the assignment. This view of purpose will be developed further in Concept 5 when we explain the importance of surprise as a measure of what is new or challenging in your essay. For most essays, you can write a one-sentence, nutshell statement about your purpose.

See Chapter 2, Concept 5, for an explanation of surprise in thesis statements.

> My purpose is to give my readers a vivid picture of my difficult struggle with Graves' disease.
>
> My purpose is to explain how Thoreau's view of nature differs in important ways from that of contemporary environmentalists.
>
> My purpose is to persuade the general public that wind-generated electricity is not a practical energy alternative in the Pacific Northwest.

In closed-form academic articles, technical reports, and other business and professional pieces, writers often place explicit purpose statements in their introductions along with the thesis. In most other forms of writing, the writer uses a behind-the-scenes purpose statement to achieve focus and direction but seldom states the purpose explicitly. Writing an explicit purpose statement for a paper is a powerful way to nutshell the kind of change you want to bring about in your reader's view of the subject.

Chapter 17, Skill 17.4, shows you how purpose statements can be included in closed-form introductions.

How Writers Think about Audience

In our discussion of purpose, we have already had a lot to say about audience. What you know about your readers—their familiarity with your subject matter, their reasons for reading, their closeness to you, their values and beliefs—affects most of the choices you make as a writer.

In assessing your audience, you must first determine who that audience is—a single reader (for example, your boss), a select group (a scholarship committee; attendees at an undergraduate research conference), or a general audience. If you imagine a general audience, you will need to make some initial assumptions about their views and values. Doing so creates an "implied audience," giving you a stable rather than a moving target so that you can make decisions about your own essay. Once you have identified your audience, you can use the following strategies for analysis.

Strategies for Analyzing Audience

Questions to Ask about Your Audience	Reasons for Asking the Question
How busy are my readers?	• Helps you decide on length, document design, and open versus closed features • In workplace writing, busy readers often require closed-form prose with headings that allow for skimming
What are my readers' motives for reading?	• If the reader has requested the document, you need only a short introduction • In most cases, your opening must hook your reader's interest
What is my relationship with my readers?	• Helps you decide on a formal or informal style • Helps you select tone—polite and serious or loose and slangy
What do my readers already know about my topic? Do my readers have more or less expertise than I have, or about the same expertise?	• Helps you determine what will be old/familiar information for your audience versus new/unfamiliar information • Helps you decide how much background and context to include • Helps you decide to use or avoid in-group jargon and specialized knowledge
How interested are my readers in my topic? Do my readers already care about it?	• Helps you decide how to write the introduction • Helps you determine how to make the problem you address interesting and significant to your reader
What are my readers' attitudes toward my thesis? Do my readers share my beliefs and values?	• Helps you make numerous decisions about tone, structure, reference to alternative views, and use of evidence • Helps you decide on the voice and persona you want to project

To appreciate the importance of audience, consider how a change in audience can affect the content of a piece. Suppose you want voters to approve a bond issue to build a new baseball stadium. If most voters are baseball fans, you can appeal to their love of the game, the pleasure of a new facility, and so forth. But non-baseball fans won't be moved by these arguments. To reach them, you must tie the new stadium to their values. You can argue that it will bring new tax revenues, clean up a run-down area, revitalize local businesses, or stimulate tourism.

Your purpose remains the same—to persuade taxpayers to fund the stadium—but the content of your argument changes if your audience changes.

In college, you often seem to be writing for an audience of one—your instructor. However, most instructors try to read as a representative of a broader audience. To help college writers imagine these readers, many instructors try to design writing assignments that provide a fuller sense of audience. They may ask you to write for the readers of a particular magazine or journal, or they may create case assignments with built-in audiences (for example, "You are an accountant in the firm of Numbers and Fudge; one day you receive a letter from ..."). If your instructor does not specify an audience, you can generally assume the audience to be what we like to call "the generic academic audience"—student peers who have approximately the same level of knowledge and expertise in the field as you do, who are engaged by the question you address, and who want to read your writing and be surprised in some way.

How Writers Think about Genre

The term *genre* refers to categories of writing that follow certain conventions of style, structure, approach to subject matter, and document design. Table 1.3 shows different kinds of genres.

The concept of genre creates strong reader expectations and places specific demands on writers. How you write any given letter, report, or article is influenced by the structure and style of hundreds of previous letters, reports, or articles written in the same genre. If you wanted to write for *Reader's Digest*, for example, you would have to use the conventions that appeal to its older, conservative readers: simple language, subjects with strong human interest, heavy reliance on anecdotal evidence in arguments, an upbeat and optimistic perspective, and an approach that reinforces the conservative *ethos* of individualism, self-discipline, and family.

TABLE 1.3 Examples of Genres

Personal Writing	Academic Writing	Popular Culture	Public Affairs, Civic Writing	Professional Writing	Literature
Letter	Scholarly article	Articles for magazines such as *Seventeen*, *Ebony*, or *Vibe*	Letter to the editor	Cover letter for a job application	Short story
Diary/journal	Research paper	Advertisements	Newspaper editorial	Résumé	Novel
Memoir	Scientific report	Hip-hop lyrics	Op-ed piece	Business memo	Graphic novel
Blog	Abstract or summary	Fan Web sites	Advocacy Web site	Legal brief	Play
Text message	Book review	Bumper stickers	Political blog	Brochure	Sonnet
E-mail	Essay exam	Reviews of books, films, plays, music	Magazine article on civic issue	Technical manual	Epic poem
Facebook profile	Annotated bibliography			Instruction booklet	Literary podcast
Personal essay	Textual analysis			Proposal	
Literacy narrative				Report	
				Press release	

If you wanted to write for *Seventeen* or *Rolling Stone*, however, you would need to use quite different conventions.

To illustrate the relationship of a writer to a genre, we sometimes draw an analogy with clothing. Although most people have a variety of different types of clothing in their wardrobes, the genre of activity for which they are dressing (Saturday night movie date, job interview, wedding) severely constrains their choice and expression of individuality. A man dressing for a job interview might express his personality through choice of tie or quality and style of business suit; he probably wouldn't express it by wearing a Hawaiian shirt and sandals. Even when people deviate from a convention, they tend to do so in a conventional way. For example, teenagers who do not want to follow the genre of "teenager admired by adults" form their own genre of purple hair and pierced body parts. The concept of genre raises intriguing and sometimes unsettling questions about the relationship of the unique self to a social convention or tradition.

These same kinds of questions and constraints perplex writers. For example, academic writers usually follow the genre of the closed-form scholarly article. This highly functional form achieves maximum clarity for readers by orienting them quickly to the article's purpose, content, and structure. Readers expect this format, and writers have the greatest chance of being published if they meet these expectations. In some disciplines, however, scholars are beginning to publish more experimental, open-form articles. They may slowly alter the conventions of the scholarly article, just as fashion designers alter styles of dress.

FOR WRITING AND DISCUSSION

Thinking about Purpose, Audience, and Genre

1. This exercise, which is based on Table 1.2 on page 17, will help you appreciate how rhetorical aim connects to choices about subject matter as well as to audience and genre. As a class, choose one of the following topic areas or another provided by your instructor. Then imagine six different writing situations in which a hypothetical writer would compose an essay about the selected topic. Let each situation call for a different aim. How might a person write about the selected topic with an expressive aim? An exploratory aim? An informative aim? An analytic aim? A persuasive aim? A reflective aim? How would each essay surprise its readers?

automobiles	animals	hospices or nursing homes
homelessness	music	dating or marriage
advertising	energy crisis	sports injuries

Working on your own or in small groups, create six realistic scenarios, each of which calls for prose in a different category of aim. Then share your results as a whole class. Here are two examples based on the topic "hospices."

Expressive Aim Working one summer as a volunteer in a hospice for dying cancer patients, you befriend a woman whose attitude toward death changes your life. You write an autobiographical essay about your experiences with this remarkable woman.

Analytic Aim	You are a hospice nurse working in a home care setting. You and your colleagues note that sometimes family members cannot adjust psychologically to the burden of living with a dying person. You decide to investigate this phenomenon. You interview "reluctant" family members in an attempt to understand the causes of their psychological discomfort so that you can provide better counseling services as a possible solution. You write a paper for a professional audience analyzing the results of your interviews.

2. Working in small groups or as a whole class, develop a list of the conventions for one or more of the following genres:
   - Cell phone text messages as typically created by teenagers
   - A Facebook profile
   - The home page for a college or university Web site

Chapter Summary

This chapter has introduced you to three transferable rhetorical concepts aimed at deepening your thinking about "good writing" in college.

- ***Concept 1: Good writing can vary from closed to open forms.*** Closed-form prose has an explicit thesis statement, topic sentences, unified and coherent paragraphs, and good transitions. At the other end of the continuum is open-form prose, which often uses narrative techniques such as storytelling, evocative language, surprising juxtapositions, and other features that violate the conventions of closed-form prose. Closed-form prose is "good" only if its ideas bring something new, provocative, or challenging to the reader.
- ***Concept 2: Good writers address problems rather than topics.*** Writers write because they have something surprising or challenging to say in response to a question that matters to the reader. Writers can pose their own problematic questions about a subject or become engaged in controversies or issues that are already "out there."
- ***Concept 3: Good writers think rhetorically about purpose, audience, and genre.*** In thinking about purpose, writers consider their rhetorical aim, their motivating occasion, or their desire to bring about change in their readers' view. They also think about their audience, analyzing how much their readers already know about (and care about) their subject and assessing their readers' values, beliefs, and assumptions. Writers attend to genre by thinking about the conventions of content, structure, and style associated with the kind of document they are writing.

Two Messages for Different Purposes, Audiences, and Genres

BRIEF WRITING PROJECT I

The purpose of this brief write-to-learn assignment is to let you experience firsthand how rhetorical context influences a writer's choices. The whole assignment, which has three parts, should not be more than two double-spaced pages long.

1. ***A Text Message to a Friend.*** Write a text message to a friend using the abbreviations, capitalization, and punctuation style typically used for text messages. Explain that you are going to miss an upcoming social event (movie, football game, dance, trip to the local diner or coffee house) because you are feeling sick. Then ask your friend to text you during the event to schedule another get-together. (Make up details as you need them.)
2. ***An E-Mail Message to a Professor.*** Compose an e-mail message to your professor explaining that you cannot meet an assignment deadline because you are sick and asking for an extension. (Use the same sickness details from Part 1.) Create a subject line appropriate for this new context.
3. ***Reflection on the Two Messages.*** Using items 1 and 2 as illustrative examples, explain to someone who has not read Chapter 1 of this text why a difference in your rhetorical context caused you to make different choices in these two messages. In your explanation, use the terms "purpose," "audience," and "genre." Your goal is to teach your audience the meanings of these terms.

BRIEF WRITING PROJECT 2

A Letter to Your Professor about What Was New in Chapter 1

Write a letter to your instructor in which you reflect on the extent to which the ideas in this opening chapter are new to you or have caused you to think about writing in new or different ways. Structure your letter in the following way:

- Describe for your instructor a piece of writing you did in high school or elsewhere that represents your most engaged work or about which you are most proud. Explain the context of this piece of writing (class or professional setting, nature of the assignment, length, and so forth) and provide a brief summary of your intentions and argument. Explain why this piece of writing particularly engaged you.
- Then analyze this piece of writing and your own thinking processes in producing it in light of the following three questions from this chapter:
  - Where would you place this piece of writing on the continuum from closed to open forms? Why?
  - To what extent was this piece of writing rooted in a "good, interesting question"? Explain.
  - To what extent did you think about purpose, audience, and genre as you wrote this piece?
- Finally, explain to your instructor the extent to which this chapter caused you to think about writing in any new or different ways.

THINKING RHETORICALLY ABOUT YOUR SUBJECT MATTER

2

"In management, people don't merely 'write papers,' they solve problems," said [business professor A. Kimbrough Sherman]. . . . He explained that he wanted to construct situations where students would have to "wallow in complexity" and work their way out, as managers must.

—*A. Kimbrough Sherman, Management Professor, Quoted by Barbara E. Walvoord and Lucille P. McCarthy*

In the previous chapter we explained how the rules for good writing vary along a continuum from closed to open forms, how writers become engaged with subject-matter questions, and how they think rhetorically about their purpose, audience, and genre. In this chapter we show how writers think rhetorically about their "subject matter"—that is, how they think about what is unknown, puzzling, or controversial in their subject matter and about how their view of the subject might be different from their audience's.

Because this chapter concerns academic writing, we focus on closed-form prose—the kind of thesis-governed writing most often required in college courses and often required in civic and professional life. As we will show, thesis-governed writing requires a behind-the-scenes ability to think rigorously about a problem and then to make a claim* based on your own solution to the problem. This claim should bring something new, interesting, useful, or challenging to readers.

In this chapter, you will learn four concepts of significant explanatory power:

- **CONCEPT 4** To determine their thesis, writers must often "wallow in complexity."
- **CONCEPT 5** A strong thesis surprises readers with something new or challenging.
- **CONCEPT 6** In closed-form prose, a typical introduction starts with the problem, not the thesis.
- **CONCEPT 7** Thesis statements in closed-form prose are supported hierarchically with points and particulars.

*In this text we use the words *claim* and *thesis statement* interchangeably. In courses across the curriculum, instructors typically use one or the other of these terms. Other synonyms for *thesis statement* include *proposition, main point,* or *thesis sentence.*

CONCEPT 4 **To determine their thesis, writers must often "wallow in complexity."**

As we explained in the previous chapter, the starting point of academic writing is a "good, interesting question." At the outset, we should say that these questions may lead you toward new and unfamiliar ways of thinking. Beginning college students typically value questions that have right answers. Students ask their professors questions because they are puzzled by confusing parts of a textbook, a lecture, or an assigned reading. They hope their professors will explain the confusing material clearly. Their purpose in asking these questions is to eliminate misunderstandings, not to open up controversy and debate. Although basic comprehension questions are important, they are not the kinds of inquiry questions that lead to strong college-level writing and thinking.

Instead, the kinds of questions that stimulate the writing most valued in college are open-ended questions that focus on unknowns or uncertainties (what educational researcher Ken Bain calls "beautiful problems") rather than factual questions that have single, correct answers.* Good open-ended questions invite multiple points of view or alternative hypotheses; they stimulate critical thinking and research. We don't mean to make this focus on problems sound scary. Indeed, humans pose and solve problems all the time and often take great pleasure in doing so. Psychologists who study critical and creative thinking see problem solving as a productive and positive activity. According to one psychologist, "Critical thinkers are actively engaged with life.... They appreciate creativity, they are innovators, and they exude a sense that life is full of possibilities."** Our way of thinking about problems has been motivated by the South American educator Paulo Freire, who wanted his students (often poor, illiterate villagers) to become *problematizers* instead of memorizers. Freire opposed what he called "the banking method" of education, in which students deposit knowledge in their memory banks and then make withdrawals during exams. The banking method, Freire believed, left third world villagers passive and helpless to improve their situations in life. Using the banking method, students being taught to read and write might learn the word *water* through drill-and-skill workbook sentences such as, "The water is in the well." With Freire's problematizing method, students might learn the word *water* by asking, "Why is the water dirty and who is responsible?" Freire believed that good questions have stakes and that answering them can make a difference in the world.

*Cognitive psychologists call these beautiful problems "ill-structured." An ill-structured problem has competing solutions, requiring the thinker to argue for the best solution in the absence of full and complete data or in the presence of stakeholders with different backgrounds, assumptions, beliefs, and values. In contrast, a "well-structured" problem eventually yields a correct answer. Math problems that can be solved by applying the right formulae and processes are well structured. That's why you can have the correct answers in the back of the book.

**Academic writers regularly document their sources. Two standard methods for documenting sources in student papers and in many professional scholarly articles are the MLA and APA citation systems explained in Chapter 22. In this text we have cited our sources in an "Acknowledgments" section. To find our source for this quotation (or the quotations from Kilcup or Kimbrough in the epigraphs or the "beautiful problem" quotation from Ken Bain), see the Acknowledgments at the end of the text.

Learning to Wallow in Complexity

This focus on important problems explains why college professors want students to go beyond simply understanding course concepts as taught in textbooks and lectures. Such comprehension is important, but it is only a starting point. As management professor A. Kimbrough Sherman explains in the epigraph to this chapter, college instructors expect students to wrestle with problems by applying the concepts, data, and thought processes they learn in a course to new situations. As Sherman puts it, students must learn to "wallow in complexity" and work their way out. To put it another way, college professors want students to "earn" their thesis. (Earning a thesis is very different from simply stating your opinion, which might not be deeply examined at all.) Because college professors value this kind of complex thinking, they often phrase essay exam questions or writing assignments as open-ended problems that can be answered in more than one way. They are looking not for the right answer, but for well-supported arguments that acknowledge alternative views. A C paper and an A paper may have the same "answer" (identical thesis statements), but the C writer may have waded only ankle deep into the mud of complexity, whereas the A writer wallowed in it and worked a way out.

What skills are required for successful wallowing? Specialists in critical thinking have identified the following:

CRITICAL THINKING SKILLS NEEDED FOR "WALLOWING IN COMPLEXITY"

- The ability to pose problematic questions
- The ability to analyze a problem in all its dimensions—to define its key terms, determine its causes, understand its history, appreciate its human dimension and its connection to one's own personal experience, and appreciate what makes it problematic or complex
- The ability (and determination) to find, gather, and interpret facts, data, and other information relevant to the problem (often involving library, Internet, or field research)
- The ability to imagine alternative solutions to the problem, to see different ways in which the question might be answered and different perspectives for viewing it
- The ability to analyze competing approaches and answers, to construct arguments for and against alternatives, and to choose the best solution in light of values, objectives, and other criteria that you determine and articulate
- The ability to write an effective argument justifying your choice while acknowledging counterarguments

We discuss and develop these skills throughout this text.

Seeing Each Academic Discipline as a Field of Inquiry and Argument

In addition to these general thinking abilities, critical thinking requires what psychologists call "domain-specific" skills. Each academic discipline has its own characteristic ways of approaching knowledge and its own specialized habits of mind. The questions asked by psychologists differ from those asked by historians or anthropologists; the evidence and assumptions used to support arguments in literary analysis differ from those in philosophy or sociology. As illustrations, here are some examples of how different disciplines might pose different questions about hip-hop:

- *Psychology:* To what extent do hip-hop lyrics increase misogynistic or homophobic attitudes in male listeners?
- *History:* What was the role of urban housing projects in the early development of hip-hop?
- *Sociology:* How does the level of an individual's appreciation for rap music vary by ethnicity, class, age, geographic region, and gender?
- *Rhetoric/Composition:* What images of urban life do the lyrics of rap songs portray?
- *Marketing and Management:* How did the white media turn a black, urban phenomenon into corporate profits?
- *Women's Studies:* What influence does hip-hop music have on the self-image of African-American women?
- *Global Studies:* How are other countries adapting hip-hop to their cultures?

As these questions suggest, when you study a new discipline, you must learn not only the knowledge that scholars in that discipline have acquired over the years, but also the processes they used to discover that knowledge. It is useful to think of each academic discipline as a network of conversations in which participants exchange information, respond to each other's questions, and express agreement and disagreement. As each discipline evolves and changes, its central questions evolve also, creating a fascinating, dynamic conversation that defines the discipline. Table 2.1 provides examples of questions that scholars have debated over the years as well as questions they are addressing today.

TABLE 2.1 Scholarly Questions in Different Disciplines

Field	Examples of Current Cutting-Edge Questions	Examples of Historical Controversies
Anatomy	What is the effect of a pregnant rat's alcohol ingestion on the development of fetal eye tissue?	In 1628, William Harvey produced a treatise arguing that the heart, through repeated contractions, causes blood to circulate through the body. His views were attacked by followers of the Greek physician Galen.
Literature	To what extent does the structure of a work of literature, for example, Conrad's *Heart of Darkness*, reflect the class and gender bias of the author?	In the 1920s, a group of New Critics argued that the interpretation of a work of literature should be based on close examination of the work's imagery and form and that the intentions of the writer and the biases of the reader were not important. These views held sway in U.S. universities until the late 1960s, when they came increasingly under attack by deconstructionists and other postmoderns, who claimed that author intentions and reader's bias were important parts of the work's meaning.

TABLE 2.1 *continued*

Field	Examples of Current Cutting-Edge Questions	Examples of Historical Controversies
Rhetoric/ Composition	How does hypertext structure and increased attention to visual images in Web-based writing affect the composing processes of writers?	Prior to the 1970s, college writing courses in the United States were typically organized around the rhetorical modes (description, narration, exemplification, comparison and contrast, and so forth). This approach was criticized by the expressivist school associated with the British composition researcher James Britton. Since the 1980s, composition scholars have proposed various alternative strategies for designing and sequencing assignments.
Psychology	What are the underlying causes of gender identification? To what extent are differences between male and female behavior explainable by nature (genetics, body chemistry) versus nurture (social learning)?	In the early 1900s under the influence of Sigmund Freud, psychoanalytic psychologists began explaining human behavior in terms of unconscious drives and mental processes that stemmed from repressed childhood experiences. Later, psychoanalysts were opposed by behaviorists, who rejected the notion of the unconscious and explained behavior as responses to environmental stimuli.

Using Exploratory Writing to Help You Wallow in Complexity

One of the important discoveries of research in rhetoric and composition is the extent to which experienced writers use writing to generate and discover ideas. Not all writing, in other words, is initially intended as a final product for readers. The very act of writing—often without concern for audience, structure, or correctness—can stimulate the mind to produce ideas. Moreover, when you write down your thoughts, you'll have a record of your thinking that you can draw on later. In Chapter 16 we explain this phenomenon more fully, showing you how to take full advantage of the writing process for invention of ideas and revision for readers. In this section we describe five strategies of exploratory writing and talking: freewriting; focused freewriting; idea mapping; dialectic talk in person, in class discussions, or in electronic discussion boards; and playing the believing and doubting game.

Freewriting *Freewriting*, also sometimes called *nonstop writing* or *silent, sustained writing*, asks you to record your thinking directly. To freewrite, put pen to paper (or sit at your computer screen, perhaps turning *off* the monitor so that you can't see what you are writing) and write rapidly, *nonstop*, for ten to fifteen minutes at a stretch. Don't worry about grammar, spelling, organization, transitions, or other features of edited writing. The object is to think of as many ideas as possible. Some freewriting looks like stream of consciousness. Some is more organized and focused, although it lacks the logical connections and development that would make it suitable for an audience of strangers.

Many freewriters find that their initial reservoir of ideas runs out in three to five minutes. If this happens, force yourself to keep your fingers moving. If you can't think of anything to say, write, "Relax" over and over (or "This is stupid" or "I'm stuck") until new ideas emerge.

What do you write about? The answer varies according to your situation. Often you will freewrite in response to a question or problem posed by your instructor. Sometimes you will pose your own questions and use freewriting to explore possible answers or simply generate ideas.

The following freewrite, by student writer James Gardiner, formed the starting point for his later exploration of issues connected to online social networks such as MySpace.com and Facebook.com. It was written in response to the prompt "What puzzles you about the new digital age?" We will return to James's story occasionally throughout this text. You can read his final paper in Chapter 22, pages 590–598, where he argues that online social networks can have unexpected detrimental effects on many users. You can also read his earlier exploratory paper (Chapter 7, pp. 169–173), which narrates the evolution of his thinking as he explored the popularity of MySpace and Facebook.

JAMES GARDINER'S INITIAL FREEWRITE

Hmm, what puzzles me about the new digital age? Let's see, let's see, OK I'm puzzled by what life used to be like before there was so much technology. I'm amazed by the growing role that technology has on the lives of people my age. It seems that my generation is spending an increasing amount of time surfing the net, talking on cell phones, listening to MP3 players, playing video games, and watching digital television. I wonder what type of effect these new technologies will have on our society as a whole and if the positive aspects that they bring into the lives of their users outweigh the negative aspects. Are kids happier now that they have all this technology? Hmm. What is the effect of text-messaging rather than talking directly to people? Also what about online social networks like Myspace and Facebook? A lot of my friends have a profile on these sites. I've never joined one of these networks or created a profile. What is my reason for avoiding them? Think. Think. OK, for one thing, I have seen how much time people can spend on these sites and I already feel that I spend enough time checking emails and voicemails. Here's another thing—I am a little hesitant to display personal information about myself on a website that can be viewed by anyone in the world. I feel I am a generally private person and there is something about posting personal details of my life in cyberspace that makes me a little uneasy. As these online social networks increase in popularity and membership, I am puzzled by how my generation will be affected by them. Although people use the sites to communicate with one another, they are usually (physically) alone at their computer. I wonder how this new type of online communication will affect other forms of interpersonal communication skills in the "real world." I also question whether young people should be encouraged to limit their time on these networks and what specifically they should use these sites for. [out of time]

Note how this freewrite rambles, moving associatively from one topic or question to the next. Freewrites often have this kind of loose, associative structure. The value of such freewrites is that they help writers discover areas of interest or rudimentary beginnings of ideas. When you read back over one of your freewrites, try to find places that seem worth pursuing. Freewriters call these places "hot spots," "centers of interest," "centers of gravity," or simply "nuggets" or "seeds." Because we believe this technique is of great value to writers, we suggest that you use it to generate ideas for class discussions and essays.

Focused Freewriting Freewriting, as we have just described it, can be quick and associational, like brainstorming aloud on paper. Focused freewriting, in contrast, is less associational and aimed more at developing a line of thought. You wrestle with a specific problem or question, trying to think and write your way into its complexity and multiple points of view. Because the writing is still informal, with the emphasis on your ideas and not on making your writing grammatically or stylistically polished, you don't have to worry about spelling, punctuation, grammar, or organizational structure. Your purpose is to deepen and extend your thinking on the problem. Some instructors will create prompts or give you specific questions to ponder, and they may call this kind of exploratory writing "focused freewriting," "learning log responses," "writer's notebook entries," or "thinking pieces."

Examples of focused freewriting can be found in the learning log entries on pp. 312–318 in Chapter 12.

Idea Mapping Another good technique for exploring ideas is *idea mapping*, a more visual method than freewriting. To make an idea map, draw a circle in the center of a page and write down your broad topic area (or a triggering question or your thesis) inside the circle. Then record your ideas on branches and subbranches that extend out from the center circle. As long as you pursue one train of thought, keep recording your ideas on subbranches off the main branch. But as soon as that chain of ideas runs dry, go back and start a new branch.

Often your thoughts will jump back and forth between one branch and another. This technique will help you see them as part of an emerging design rather than as strings of unrelated ideas. Additionally, idea mapping establishes at an early stage a sense of hierarchy in your ideas. If you enter an idea on a subbranch, you can see that you are more fully developing a previous idea. If you return to the hub and start a new branch, you can see that you are beginning a new train of thought.

An idea map usually records more ideas than a freewrite, but the ideas are not as fully developed. Writers who practice both techniques report that they can vary the kinds of ideas they generate depending on which technique they choose. Figure 2.1 shows a student's idea map made while he was exploring issues related to the grading system.

Dialectic Talk Another effective way to explore the complexity of a topic is through face-to-face discussions with others, whether in class, over coffee in the student union, or late at night in bull sessions. Not all discussions are productive; some are too superficial and scattered, others too heated. Good ones are *dialectic*—participants with differing views on a topic try to understand each other and resolve their differences by examining contradictions in each person's position. The key to dialectic conversation is careful listening, which is made possible by an openness to each other's views. A dialectic discussion differs from

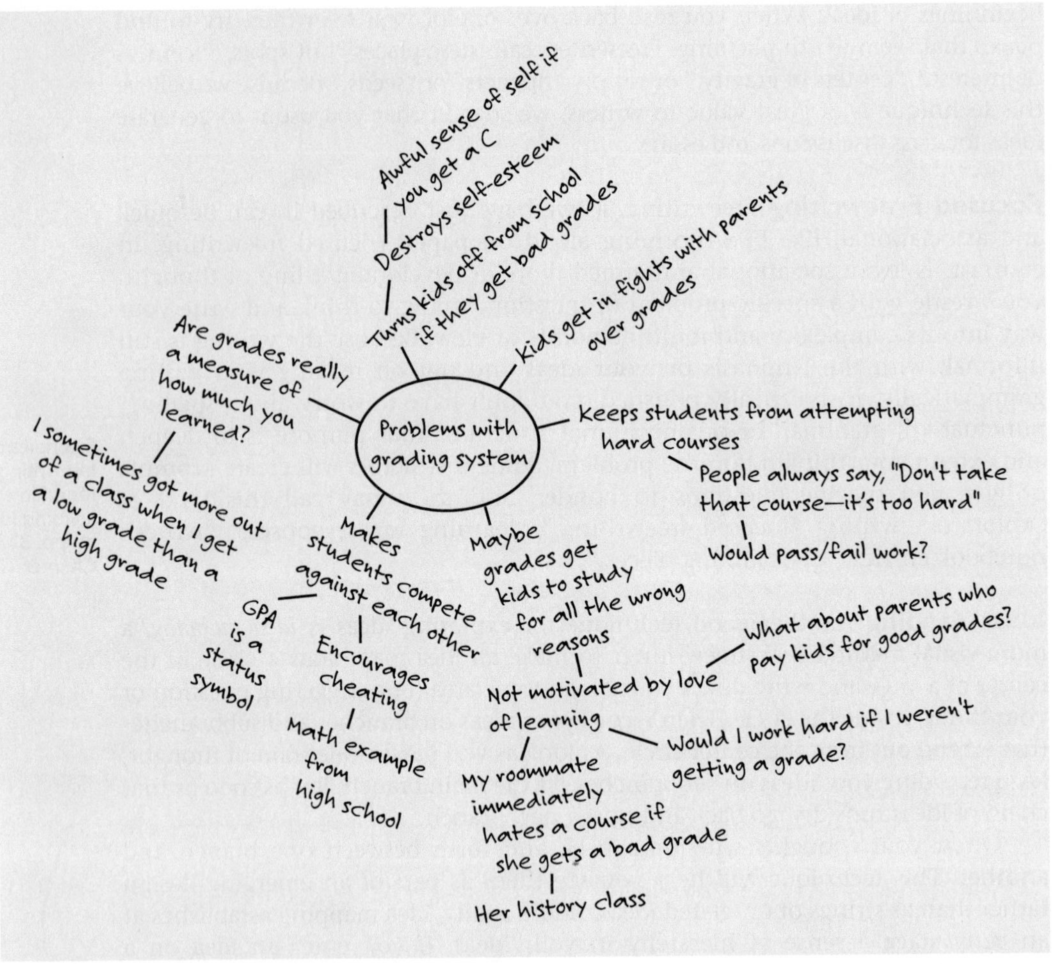

FIGURE 2.1 Idea Map on Problems with the Grading System

a talk show shouting match or a pro/con debate in which proponents of opposing positions, their views set in stone, attempt to win the argument. In a dialectic discussion, participants assume that each position has strengths and weaknesses and that even the strongest position contains inconsistencies, which should be exposed and examined. When dialectic conversation works well, participants scrutinize their own positions more critically and deeply, and often alter their views. True dialectic conversation implies growth and change, not a hardening of positions.

Dialectic discussion can also take place in electronic discussion boards, chat rooms, blogs, or other digital sites for informal exchange of ideas. If your goal is to generate ideas, your stance should be the exact opposite of the flamer's stance. A flamer's intention is to use brute rhetorical power (sometimes mindlessly obscene or mean, sometimes clever and humorous) to humiliate another writer and shut off further discussion. In contrast, the dialectician's goal is to listen respectfully to other ideas, to test new ways of thinking, to modify ideas in the face of other views, and to see an issue as fully and complexly as possible. If you go on to a discussion board to learn and change, rather than to defend your own position and shut off other views, you will be surprised at how powerful this medium can be.

Playing the Believing and Doubting Game One of the best ways to explore a question is to play what writing theorist Peter Elbow calls the "believing and doubting game." This game helps you appreciate the power of alternative arguments and points of view by urging you to formulate and explore alternative positions. To play the game, you imagine a possible answer to a problematic question and then systematically try first to believe that answer and then to doubt it. The game stimulates your critical thinking, helping you wallow in complexity and resist early closure.

When you play the believing side of this game, you try to become sympathetic to an idea or point of view. You listen carefully to it, opening yourself to the possibility that it is true. You try to appreciate why the idea has force for so many people; you try to accept it by discovering as many reasons as you can for believing it. It is easy to play the believing game with ideas you already believe in, but the game becomes more difficult, sometimes even frightening and dangerous, when you try believing ideas that seem untrue or disturbing.

The doubting game is the opposite of the believing game. It calls for you to be judgmental and critical, to find fault with an idea rather than to accept it. When you doubt a new idea, you try your best to falsify it, to find counterexamples that disprove it, to find flaws in its logic. Again, it is easy to play the doubting game with ideas you don't like, but it, too, can be threatening when you try to doubt ideas that are dear to your heart or central to your own worldview.

Here is how one student played the believing and doubting game with the following assertion from professional writer Paul Theroux that emphasizing sports is harmful to boys.

> Just as high school basketball teaches you how to be a poor loser, the manly attitude towards sports seems to be little more than a recipe for creating bad marriages, social misfits, moral degenerates, sadists, latent rapists and just plain louts. I regard high school sports as a drug far worse than marijuana.

Believing and Doubting Paul Theroux's Negative View of Sports

Believe

1 Although I am a woman I have a hard time believing this because I was a high school basketball player and believe high school sports are *very* important. But here goes. I will try to believe this statement even though I hate it. Let's see. It would seem that I wouldn't have much first-hand experience with how society turns boys

(*continued*)

into men. I do see though that Theroux is right about some major problems. Through my observations, I've seen many young boys go through humiliating experiences with sports that have left them scarred. For example, a 7-year-old boy, Matt, isn't very athletic and when kids in our neighborhood choose teams, they usually choose girls before they choose Matt. I wonder if he sees himself as a sissy and what this does to him? I have also experienced some first-hand adverse effects of society's methods of turning boys into men. In our family, my dad spent much of his time playing football, basketball, and baseball with my brother. I've loved sports since I was very young so I was eager to play. In order to play with them, I had to play like a boy. Being told you threw or played like a girl was the worst possible insult you could receive. The phrase, "be tough" was something I heard repeatedly while I was growing up. Whenever I got hurt, my dad would say, "Be tough." It didn't matter how badly I was hurt, I always heard the same message. Today, I think, I have a very, very difficult time opening up and letting people get to know me, because for so long I was taught to keep everything inside. Maybe sports does have some bad effects.

Doubt

2 I am glad I get to doubt this too because I have been really mad at all the sports bashing that has been going on in class. I think much of what Theroux says is just a crock. I know that the statement "sports builds character" is a cliché, but I really believe it. It seems to me that the people who lash out at sports clichés are those who never experienced these aspects of athletics and therefore don't understand them. No one can tell me that sports didn't contribute to some of my best and most meaningful friendships and growing experiences. I am convinced that I am a better person because through sports I have had to deal with failure, defeat, frustration, sacrificing individual desires for the benefit of the team, and so on. After my last high school basketball game when after many years of mind games, of hating my coach one minute and the next having deep respect for him, of big games lost on my mistakes, of hours spent alone in the gym, of wondering if the end justifies the means, my coach put his arm around me and told me he was proud. Everything, all the pain, frustration, anxiety, fear, and sacrifice of the past years seemed so worthwhile. You might try to tell me that this story is hackneyed and trite, but I won't listen because it is a part of me, and some thing you will never be able to damage or take away. I think athletes share a special bond. They know what it is like to go through the physical pain of practice time and again. They understand the wide variety of emotions felt (but rarely expressed). They also know what a big role the friendships of teammates and coaches play in an athlete's life.

We admire this writer a great deal—both for the passion with which she defends sports in her doubting section and for the courage of walking in a sports basher's shoes in the believing section. This exercise clearly engaged and stretched her thinking.

FOR WRITING AND DISCUSSION

Using Exploratory Writing and Talking to Generate Ideas

Background: In our discussion of problem posing in the last chapter (Concept 2: "Good writers address problems rather than topics," pp. 11–15), we explain two main ways that you can become gripped by a problem: (1) You can become engaged by a question or issue that is already "out there"—that is, already being examined or debated in some academic or civic community; or (2) you can pose your own question based on your observation of a puzzling phenomenon or artifact. You might have tried out these strategies in your thinking about the sculpture in Figure 1.2, page 15. Now in Concept 4, we have shown how exploratory writing and talking can help you learn to wallow in complexity. For this exercise we give you for analysis a poem by e. e. cummings and a pair of historical graphs on life expectancy and causes of death in the twentieth century.

next to of course god america i

"next to of course god america i
love you land of the pilgrims' and so forth oh
say can you see by the dawn's early my
country 'tis of centuries come and go

and are no more what of it we should worry
in every language even deafanddumb
thy sons acclaim your glorious name by gorry
by jingo by gee by gosh by gum
why talk of beauty what could be more beautiful than these heroic happy dead
who rushed like lions to the roaring slaughter
they did not stop to think they died instead
then shall the voice of liberty be mute?"

He spoke. And drank rapidly a glass of water

—*e. e. cummings*

1. ***Generating questions using freewriting and discussion***
   Individual task: Read e. e. cummings' poem three or four times, trying to make as much sense of it as you can. Then freewrite for five minutes in response to this prompt: *What do you find puzzling or thought provoking about this poem?* Let the ideas flow through your fingers. You are trying to identify aspects of the poem that you personally find puzzling or thought provoking while also trying to recall memories of conversations already "out there" about issues raised in the poem. While freewriting, you can also explore how you might try to "answer" some of these questions.
   Small-group or whole-class task: Share some of the questions or ideas raised in your freewrites and see how such "dialectic conversation" inspires more ideas.

(*continued*)

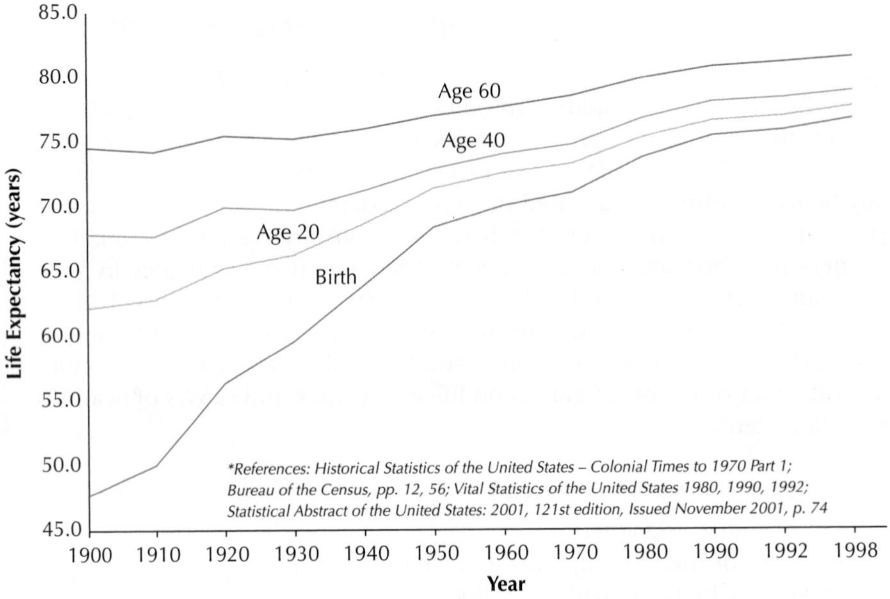

FIGURE 2.2 U.S. Life Expectancy at Birth, Age 20, Age 40, and Age 60, 1900–1998

2. ***Generating questions using idea mapping and discussion*** Repeat the same process, but this time look at the graphs in Figures 2.2 and 2.3, and use idea mapping rather than freewriting. Address the question, *What do you find puzzling or thought provoking in these graphs about changes in life expectancy and causes of death in the twentieth century?* On spokes coming out from the center of the idea map, write some questions or ideas raised by

FIGURE 2.3 U.S. Death Rates for Selected Causes, 1900–2000

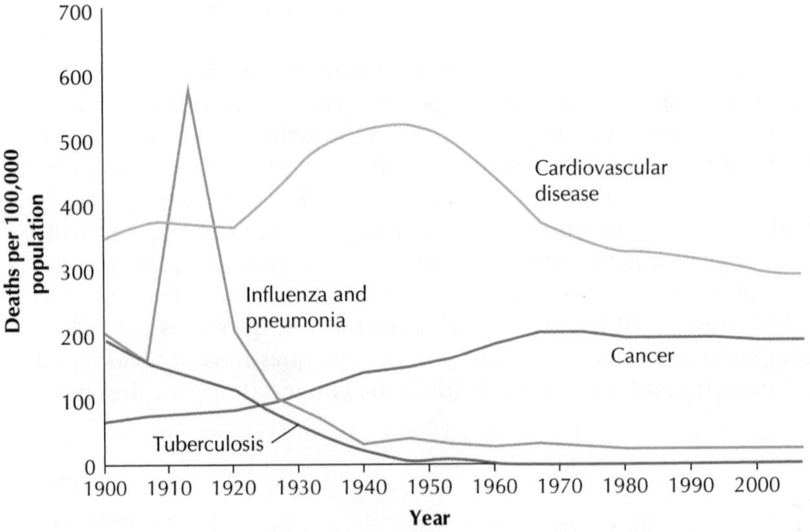

the graphs. Then pursue ideas from each of these spokes so that you begin making a branching map of thoughts. Then share your maps with classmates, using them to spark problem-centered conversations. Finally, discuss which technique works better for you, freewriting or idea mapping. How are they similar or different in the way they stimulate thinking?

3. ***Using freewriting or idea mapping to move from topics to problems*** Another valuable use of exploratory writing and talking is to turn broad topic areas such as "poverty," "music," "globalization," "climate change," "animal rights," or "food" into problematic questions that invite alternative points of view and opportunities for analysis or argument. Using freewriting or idea mapping, start with a broad topic area (either something that interests you or something that your instructor assigns) and explore it in search of questions or problems. Try to recall all the conversations about this topic that you have heard where people expressed confusion or disagreement. Also think of puzzling questions that might emerge from your own personal experiences with the topic area. Your goal is to find a question that interests you and eventually to discover a thesis that gives you an entry into the conversation.

CONCEPT 5 A strong thesis statement surprises readers with something new or challenging.

The strategies for exploring ideas that we offered in the previous section can prepare you to move from posing problems to proposing your own solutions. Your answer to your subject-matter question becomes your **thesis statement**. In this section we show that a good thesis surprises its readers either by bringing something new to the reader or by pushing against other possible ways to answer the writer's question.

Thus a strong thesis usually contains an element of uncertainty, risk, or challenge. A strong thesis implies a naysayer who could disagree with you. According to composition theorist Peter Elbow, a thesis has "got to stick its neck out, not just hedge or wander. [It is] something that can be quarreled with." Elbow's sticking-its-neck-out metaphor is a good one, but we prefer to say that a strong thesis *surprises* the reader with a new, unexpected, different, or challenging view of the writer's topic. By surprise, we intend to connote, first of all, freshness or newness for the reader. Many kinds of closed-form prose don't have a sharply contestable thesis of the sticking-its-neck-out kind highlighted by Elbow. A geology report, for example, may provide readers with desired information about rock strata in an exposed cliff, or a Web page for diabetics may explain how to coordinate meals and insulin injections during a plane trip across time zones. In these cases, the information is surprising because it brings something new and significant to intended readers.

In other kinds of closed-form prose, especially academic or civic prose addressing a problematic question or a disputed issue, surprise requires an argumentative, risky, or contestable thesis. In these cases also, surprise is not inherent in the material but in the intended readers' reception; it comes from the writer's providing an adequate or appropriate response to the readers' presumed question or problem.

In this section, we present two ways of creating a surprising thesis: (1) trying to change your reader's view of your subject; and (2) giving your thesis tension.

Trying to Change Your Reader's View of Your Subject

To change your reader's view of your subject, you must first imagine how the reader would view the subject *before* reading your essay. Then you can articulate how you aim to change that view. A useful exercise is to write out the "before" and "after" views of your imagined readers:

> Before reading my essay, my readers think this way about my topic: ________
> ____
>
> After reading my essay, my readers will think this different way about my topic:
> ____

You can change your reader's view of a subject in several ways.* First, you can enlarge it. Writing that enlarges a view is primarily informational; it provides new ideas and data to add to a reader's store of knowledge about the subject. For example, suppose you are interested in the problem of storing nuclear waste (a highly controversial issue in the United States) and decide to investigate how Japan stores radioactive waste from its nuclear power plants. You could report your findings on this problem in an informative research paper. (Before reading my paper, readers would be uncertain how Japan stores nuclear waste. After reading my paper, my readers would understand the Japanese methods, possibly helping us better understand our options in the United States.)

Second, you can clarify your reader's view of something that was previously fuzzy, tentative, or uncertain. Writing of this kind often explains, analyzes, or interprets. This is the kind of writing you do when analyzing a short story, a painting, an historical document, a set of economic data, or other puzzling phenomena or when speculating on the causes, consequences, purpose, or function of something. Suppose, for example, that you are analyzing the persuasive strategies used in various clothing ads. You are intrigued by a jeans ad that you "read" differently from your classmates. (Before reading my paper, my readers will think that this jeans ad reveals a liberated woman, but after reading my paper they will see that the ad fulfills traditional gender stereotypes.)

Another kind of change occurs when an essay actually restructures a reader's whole view of a subject. Such essays persuade readers to change their minds or make decisions. For example, engineer David Rockwood, in his letter to the editor that we reprinted in Chapter 1 (pp. 6–7), wants to change readers' views about

*Our discussion of how writing changes a reader's view of the world is indebted to Richard Young, Alton Becker, and Kenneth Pike, *Rhetoric: Discovery and Change* (New York: Harcourt Brace & Company, 1971).

wind power. (Before reading my letter, readers will believe that wind-generated electricity can solve our energy crisis, but after reading my letter they will see that the hope of wind power is a pipe dream.)

Surprise, then, is the measure of change an essay brings about in a reader. Of course, to bring about such change requires more than just a surprising thesis; the essay itself must persuade the reader that the thesis is sound as well as novel. Later in this chapter (Concept 7), we talk about how writers support a thesis through a network of points and particulars.

Giving Your Thesis Tension through "Surprising Reversal"

Another element of a surprising thesis is tension. By *tension* we mean the reader's sensation of being pulled away from familiar ideas toward new, unfamiliar ones. A strategy for creating this tension—a strategy we call "surprising reversal"—is to contrast your surprising answer to a question with your targeted audience's common answer, creating tension between your own thesis and one or more alternative views. Its basic template is as follows:

> *"Many people believe X (common view), but I am going to show Y (new, surprising view)."*

The concept of surprising reversal spurs the writer to go beyond the commonplace to change the reader's view of a topic.

One of the best ways to employ this strategy is to begin your thesis statement with an "although" clause that summarizes the reader's "before" view or the counterclaim that your essay opposes; the main clause states the surprising view or position that your essay will support. You may choose to omit the *although* clause from your actual essay, but formulating it first will help you achieve focus and surprise in your thesis. The examples that follow illustrate the kinds of tension we have been discussing and show why tension is a key requirement for a good thesis.

Question	What effect has the cell phone had on our culture?
Thesis without Tension	The invention of the cell phone has brought many advantages to our culture.
Thesis with Tension	Although the cell phone has brought many advantages to our culture, it may also have contributed to an increase in risky behavior among boaters and hikers.

Question	Do reservations serve a useful role in contemporary Native American culture?
Thesis without Tension	Reservations have good points and bad points.
Thesis with Tension	Although my friend Wilson Real Bird believes that reservations are necessary for Native Americans to preserve their heritage, the continuation of reservations actually degrades Native American culture.

In the first example, the thesis without tension (cell phones have brought advantages to our culture) is a truism with which everyone would agree and hence lacks surprise. The thesis with tension places this truism (the reader's "before" view) in an *although* clause and goes on to make a surprising or contestable assertion. The idea that the cell phone contributes to risky behavior among outdoor enthusiasts alters our initial, complacent view of the cell phone and gives us new ideas to think about.

In the second example, the thesis without tension may not at first seem tensionless because the writer sets up an opposition between good and bad points. But *almost anything* has good and bad points, so the opposition is not meaningful, and the thesis offers no element of surprise. Substitute virtually any other social institution (marriage, the postal service, the military, prisons), and the statement that it has good and bad points would be equally true. The thesis with tension, in contrast, is risky. It commits the writer to argue that reservations have degraded Native American culture and to oppose the counterthesis that reservations are needed to *preserve* Native American culture. The reader now feels genuine tension between two opposing views.

Tension, then, is a component of surprise. The writer's goal is to surprise the reader in some way, thereby bringing about some kind of change in the reader's view. As you are wallowing in complexity about your subject-matter problem, try the following strategies for bringing something new, surprising, or challenging to your targeted readers:

Strategies for Creating a Thesis with Tension or Surprise

How You Became Gripped with a Problem	Example of a Problem	Your Strategy While You "Wallow in Complexity"	Possible Thesis with Tension or Surprise
	The problem is already "out there." *(You enter a conversation already in progress)*		
You don't know where you stand on an issue.	Should health care be rationed?	Look at all sides of the issue, including all the available data, to determine where you stand based on your own examined values.	Although rationing health care at first seems inhumane, it may be the only ethical way to provide affordable health care to all citizens.
You do know where you stand on an issue. *[You need to move from an opinion to an earned thesis.]*	Shanita says that we should build more nuclear power plants to combat global warming, but I say nuclear power is too dangerous.	Research the strengths of the opposing views and the weaknesses of your own view. (*Note: You may change your mind.)*	Although nuclear power poses danger from storage of waste or possible meltdown, the benefits of reducing greenhouse gases and cutting coal pollution outweigh the dangers.

How You Became Gripped with a Problem	Example of a Problem	Your Strategy While You "Wallow in Complexity"	Possible Thesis with Tension or Surprise
Someone gives you a question that you can't yet answer.	Your boss asks you whether the company should enact the proposed marketing plan.	Do the research, critical thinking, and analysis needed to propose the "best solution" to the boss's question.	The marketing team's proposal, despite its creative use of advertising, is too risky to undertake at this time.
You pose the problem yourself. *(You initiate the conversation)*			
You see something puzzling in a natural phenomenon or a cultural activity or artifact.	Why does Merton call rain "meaningless"?	Through critical thinking and research, try to figure out a plausible "best solution" to your question.	Merton's puzzling use of "meaningless" in reference to the rain can perhaps be explained by his admiration for Buddhism.
You discover something inconsistent or contradictory in your own view of the world.	I agree with Merton's argument against consumerism, but I really want a large plasma TV. Is consumerism really bad? Am I a materialist?	Reflect on your own values and beliefs; try to achieve a consistent stand with regard to enduring social or ethical issues.	Although Merton makes me consider the potential shallowness of my desire for a huge plasma TV, I don't think I'm necessarily a materialist.

FOR WRITING AND DISCUSSION

Developing Thesis Statements Out of Questions

It is difficult to create thesis statements on the spot because a writer's thesis grows out of an exploratory struggle with a problem. However, in response to a question one can often propose a claim and treat it as a tentative thesis statement for testing. You may have already done some exploratory talking and writing in response to a problem provided by your instructor or about problems supplied so far in this text: the sculpture in Figure 1.2 (p. 15), the e. e. cummings poem (p. 35), or the graphs in Figures 2.2 and 2.3 (p. 36). Working individually, spend ten minutes considering possible thesis statements that you might make in response to one or more of the questions you have already been thinking about. (Remember that these are tentative thesis statements, done for practice, that you might abandon after doing research or more critical thinking.) Identify a possible audience for your thesis statement,

(continued)

and try to explain why this audience would find your thesis new, surprising, or challenging. Then, working in small groups or as a whole class, share your thesis statements. Select one or two thesis statements that your small group or class thinks are particularly effective and brainstorm the kinds of evidence that would be required to support the thesis.

Alternatively, your instructor might use the following exercises:

1. To what extent should the public support genetically modified foods? (possible audiences: readers of health food magazines; general public concerned about food choices; investors in companies that produce genetically modified seeds)
2. Should the government mandate more fuel-efficient cars? If so, how? (possible audiences: SUV owners; conservative legislators generally in favor of free markets; investors in the automobile industry)

Here is an example:

Problematic question: What can cities do to prevent traffic congestion?

One possible thesis: Although many people think that building light-rail systems won't get people out of their cars, new light-rail systems in many cities have attracted new riders and alleviated traffic problems.

Intended audience: Residents of cities concerned about traffic congestion but skeptical about light-rail

Kinds of evidence needed to support thesis: Examples of cities with successful light-rail systems; evidence that many riders switched from driving cars; evidence that light-rail alleviated traffic problems

CONCEPT 6 In closed-form prose, a typical introduction starts with the problem, not the thesis.

So far we've talked about the importance of finding a good problem and exploring its complexity. Eventually, however, your goal is to contribute to the conversation by stating and supporting your own thesis. First, however, readers need to know what problem your thesis addresses. One of the principles of closed-form prose—which we describe in detail later in this text—is that readers' need to attach new information to old information. In other words, before they can understand an answer, they must first understand the question. One function of the introduction in most closed-form prose is to show your readers what the problem is and to motivate their interest in it. This introduction can be long or short depending on whether your targeted audience is already familiar with the problem or already cares about it. Once readers know what problem you intend to address, they are prepared for your thesis statement.

For more on the old/new contract, see Chapter 17, Skill 17.7.

A Protypical Introduction

To show you how academic writers typically begin by asking a question, we will illustrate with several "prototype" examples.* In the following introduction by student writer Jackie Wyngaard, note how the author first presents a question and then moves, at the end of the introduction, to her thesis statement.

EMP: MUSIC HISTORY OR MUSIC TRIVIA?

Along with other college students new to Seattle, I wanted to see what cultural opportunities the area offers. I especially wanted to see billionaire Paul Allen's controversial Experience Music Project (known as EMP), a huge, bizarre, shiny, multicolored structure that is supposed to resemble a smashed guitar. Brochures say that EMP celebrates the creativity of American popular music, but it has prompted heated discussions among architects, Seattle residents, museum goers, and music lovers, who have questioned its commercialism and the real value of its exhibits. My sister recommended this museum to me because she knows I am a big music lover and a rock and roll fan. Also, as an active choir member since the sixth grade, I have always been intrigued by the history of music. I went to EMP expecting to learn more about music history from exhibits that showed a range of popular musical styles, that traced historical connections and influences, and that enjoyably conveyed useful information. However, as a museum of rock history, EMP is a disappointing failure.

Provides background on EMP

Begins to turn topic area (EMP) into a problem by showing that it has been controversial

Establishes her own purposes and expectations: She expects EMP to teach her about music history.

Implies her question: Is EMP a good place to learn about the history of rock music?

States her thesis

Features of a Good Introduction

Wyngaard's introduction, which shares the structure of many professionally written closed-form introductions, includes the following prototypical features:

- ***Background needed to identify the topic area and provide context.*** Readers need early on to know the specific topic area of the paper they are about to read—in this case a paper about the Experience Music Project in Seattle rather than, say, shower mold or medieval queenship. Sometimes writers also use a startling scene or statistic as an "attention grabber" as part of the opening background.
- ***A direct or implied question.*** As soon as possible, readers need to sense the problem, question, or issue that the writer will examine. In this case, Jackie Wyngaard implies her question: Will my expectations about EMP be fulfilled? Note that her question appears directly in her title: "EMP: Music History [her expectations] or Music Trivia [her claim]?"
- ***An indication of how the question invites tension or is otherwise problematic.*** An effective question or problem supposes the possibility of

*A *prototype* is the most typical or generic instance of a class and doesn't constitute a value judgment. For example, a prototype bird might be a robin or blackbird (rather than an ostrich, chicken, hummingbird, or pelican) because these birds seem to exhibit the most typical features of "birdiness." Likewise, a prototype dog would be a medium-sized mutt rather than a St. Bernard or toy poodle.

alternative points of view, different perspectives in tension with each other. In many cases, a writer summarizes alternative arguments sparked by the question or summarizes a particular point of view that the writer intends to oppose. Because Jackie initiates the conversation about EMP's status as a rock museum, she evokes this tension by contrasting her initial expectations with her later disappointment.

- ***An indication of how the question is significant or worth examining.*** In order to avoid a "so what?" response, writers must motivate readers' interest in the question. Somebody might say, "Who cares about EMP anyway?" Jackie's strategy is to imagine an audience who shares her interest in rock and roll music and her love of music history. These are the readers who will care whether it is worth big bucks to spend an afternoon in EMP. Readers who identify with Jackie's enthusiasm for rock history will share her engagement with the question. Other strategies for showing a question's significance include pointing to the good or bad consequences of a particular way of answering the question ("If we could understand why the crime rate in New York City dropped dramatically in the 1990s, we could apply these same principles to other cities today") or by showing how an answer to a smaller question might help readers begin to answer a larger question ("If we could better understand the role of the witches in *Macbeth*, we would better understand the ways gender was constructed in Shakespeare's time").

For more on thesis statements, purpose statements, and blueprint statements, see Skill 17.4. See also James Gardiner's full essay on pp. 169–173.

- ***The writer's thesis, which brings something new to the audience.*** Once readers are hooked on the writer's question, they are ready for the writer's answer. In this case, Jackie makes the claim that EMP fails as a rock history museum.
- ***[optional] A purpose statement ("The purpose of this paper is ... ") along with a mapping statement forecasting the content and shape of the rest of the article ("First I discuss X, then Y, and finally Z").*** Because her paper is short, Jackie ends the introduction with her thesis. An alternative strategy, common among longer closed-form essays, is to include a purpose statement along with a forecasting passage that maps what is coming. This strategy is used by student writer James Gardiner at the end of his introduction to a paper about the consequences of using online social networks like Facebook. Note how he poses his problematic question and then moves to a purpose statement and mapping statement.

States directly the question his paper will address

Purpose statement

Maps out the argument's structure while motivating readers' interest in question

> ... While "Facebook Trance" might describe only an occasional and therefore harmless phenomenon, it gives rise to an important question: What are the possible negative consequences of OSNs [online social networks]? What should youthful users be watchful for and guard against? The purpose of this paper is to identify the possible harms of OSNs. I will suggest that overuse of OSNs can be a contributing factor to a decline in grades as well as to other problems such as a superficial view of relationships, an increase in narcissism, and possible future embarrassment.

For a fuller look at the ways a writer can introduce readers to the problem he or she is addressing, consider the following strategies chart:

Strategies for Introducing Your Problem to Targeted Readers

Situation	Strategies
The problem is already "out there" *(You enter a conversation already in progress)*	*If readers are already familiar with the problem and care about it, use a mix of the following strategies:* • Provide background where needed • State the problem directly (often as a grammatical question ending with a question mark) or imply the question through context • Summarize the different points of view on the problem (or) • Summarize the particular point of view you intend to "push against" *If readers are less familiar with the problem:* • Summarize controversy in more depth • Explain why the problem is problematic (show why there are no easy answers to the problem; point out weaknesses in proposed answers; show the history of attempts to solve the problem) *If readers don't already care about the problem:* • Show why the problem is important (answer the "so what?" question) • Show how solving the problem will bring good consequences (or) • Show how answering the question will help us begin to answer a larger question

You pose the problem yourself *(You initiate the conversation)*	• Describe the artifact or phenomenon you are writing about and point to the specific features where you see an inconsistency, gap, or puzzle
	• State the problem directly (often as a grammatical question ending with a question mark)
	• Show how there isn't any immediate, easy answer to the question or problem or how the question can invite controversy/discussion; you can often employ a template such as the following:
	  • Some people might think…, but closer observation shows that….
	  • At first I thought…, but later I saw that….
	  • Part of me thinks…, but another part of me thinks that….
	  • I expected … ; but what I actually found was….
	• Show why the problem is important (answer the "so what?" question)
	• Show how solving the problem will bring good consequences (or)
	• Show how answering this question will help us begin to answer a larger question

FOR WRITING AND DISCUSSION

Examining Problem-Thesis Structure of Introductions

Background: As we explained in Concept 1, good writing can vary along a continuum from closed to open forms. Although academic essays are typically closed form, they can vary significantly along the continuum. Likewise, the introductions to closed-form essays don't always follow the prototypical structure we just described. But many do. In this exercise, we invite you to analyze additional introductions.

Task: Look at the following introductions. In each case, analyze the extent to which the introduction follows or varies from the prototypical introductions we have described in Concept 6.

1. Paragraphs 1–2 of Ross Taylor's "Paintball: Promoter of Violence or Healthy Fun?" (p. 359)
2. Paragraphs 1–4 of "No to Nukes," a *Los Angeles Times* editorial (p. 367)
3. Paragraphs 1–6 of Shannon King's "How Clean and Green Are Hydrogen Fuel-Cell Cars?" (pp. 196–197)

CONCEPT 7 **Thesis statements in closed-form prose are supported hierarchically with points and particulars.**

Of course, a surprising thesis is only one aspect of an effective essay. An essay must also persuade the reader that the thesis is believable as well as surprising. Although tabloid newspapers have shocking headlines ("Cloning Produces Three-Headed Sheep"), skepticism quickly replaces surprise when you look inside and find the article's claims unsupported. A strong thesis, then, must both surprise the reader and be supported with convincing particulars.

In fact, the particulars are the flesh and muscle of writing and comprise most of the sentences. In closed-form prose, these particulars are connected clearly to points, and the points precede the particulars. In this section, we explain this principle more fully.

How Points Convert Information to Meaning

When particulars are clearly related to a point, the point gives meaning to the particulars, and the particulars give force and validity to the point. Particulars constitute the evidence, data, details, examples, and subarguments that develop a point and make it convincing. By themselves, particulars are simply information—mere data without meaning.

In the following example, you can see for yourself the difference between information and meaning. Here is a list of information:*

- In almost all species on earth, males are more aggressive than females.
- Male chimpanzees win dominance by brawling.

*The data in this exercise are adapted from Deborah Blum, "The Gender Blur," *Utne Reader* Sept. 1998: 45–48.

- To terrorize rival troops, they kill females and infants.
- The level of aggression among monkeys can be manipulated by adjusting their testosterone levels.
- Among humans, preliminary research suggests that male fetuses are more active in the uterus than female fetuses.
- Little boys play more aggressively than little girls despite parental efforts to teach gentleness to boys and aggression to girls.

To make meaning out of this list of information, the writer needs to state a point—the idea, generalization, or claim—that this information supports. Once the point is stated, a meaningful unit (point with particulars) springs into being:

> Aggression in human males may be a function of biology rather than culture. (Point) In almost all species on earth, males are more aggressive than females. Male chimpanzees win dominance by brawling; to terrorize rival troops, they kill females and infants. Researchers have shown that the level of aggression among monkeys can be manipulated by adjusting their testosterone levels. Among humans, preliminary research suggests that male fetuses are more active in the uterus than female fetuses. Also, little boys play more aggressively than little girls despite parental efforts to teach gentleness to boys and aggression to girls. (Particulars)

Once the writer states this point, readers familiar with the biology/culture debate about gender differences immediately feel its surprise and tension. This writer believes that biology determines gender identity more than does culture. The writer now uses the details as evidence to support a point.

To appreciate the reader's need for a logical connection between points and particulars, note how readers would get lost if, in the preceding example, the writer included a particular that seemed unrelated to the point ("Males also tend to be taller and heavier than women"—a factual statement, but what does it have to do with aggression?) or if, without explanation, the writer added a particular that seemed to contradict the point ("Fathers play more roughly with baby boys than with baby girls"—another fact, but one that points to culture rather than biology as a determiner of aggression).

Obviously, reasonable people seek some kind of coordination between points and particulars, some sort of weaving back and forth between them. Writing teachers use a number of nearly synonymous terms for expressing this paired relationship: *points/particulars, generalizations/specifics, claims/evidence, ideas/details, interpretations/data, meaning/support.*

How Removing Particulars Creates a Summary

What we have shown, then, is that skilled writers weave back and forth between generalizations and specifics. The generalizations form a network of higher-level and lower-level points that develop the thesis; the particulars (specifics) support each of the points and subpoints in turn. In closed-form prose, the network of points is easily discernible because points are clearly highlighted with transitions, and main points are placed prominently at the heads of paragraphs. (In open-form prose, generalizations are often left unstated, creating gaps where the reader must actively fill in meaning.)

Being able to write summaries and abstracts of articles is an important academic skill. See Chapter 5 on strategies for writing summaries and strong responses, pp. 99–110.

If you remove most of the particulars from a closed-form essay, leaving only the network of points, you will have written a summary or abstract of the essay. As an example, reread the civil engineer's letter to the editor arguing against the feasibility of wind-generated power (pp. 6–7). The writer's argument can be summarized in a single sentence:

> Wind-generated power is not a reasonable alternative to other forms of power in the Pacific Northwest because wind power is unreliable, because there are major unsolved problems involved in the design of wind-generation facilities, and because the environmental impact of building thousands of wind towers would be enormous.

What we have done in this summary is remove the particulars, leaving only the high-level points that form the skeleton of the argument. The writer's thesis remains surprising and contains tension, but without the particulars the reader has no idea whether to believe the generalizations or not. The presence of the particulars is thus essential to the success of the argument.

FOR WRITING AND DISCUSSION

Analyzing Supporting Particulars

Compare the civil engineer's original letter with the one-sentence summary just given and then note how the engineer uses specific details to support each point. How do these particulars differ from paragraph to paragraph? How are they chosen to support each point?

How to Use Points and Particulars When You Revise

The lesson to learn here is that in closed-form prose, writers regularly place a point sentence in front of detail sentences. When a writer begins with a point, readers interpret the ensuing particulars not as random data but rather as *evidence* in support of that point. The writer depends on the particulars to make the point credible and persuasive.

This insight may help you understand two of the most common kinds of marginal comments that readers (or teachers) place on writers' early drafts. If your draft has a string of sentences giving data or information unconnected to any stated point, your reader is apt to write in the margin, "What's your point here?" or "Why are you telling me this information?" or "How does this information relate to your thesis?" Conversely, if your draft tries to make a point that isn't developed with particulars, your reader is apt to write marginal comments such as "Evidence?" or "Development?" or "Could you give an example?" or "More details needed."

Don't be put off by these requests; they are a gift. It is common in first drafts for main points to be unstated, buried, or otherwise disconnected from their details and for supporting information to be scattered confusingly throughout the draft or missing entirely. Having to write point sentences obliges you to wrestle with your intended meaning: Just what am I trying to say here? How can I nutshell that in a point? Likewise, having to support your points with particulars causes you to wrestle with the content and shape of your argument: What particulars will make this point convincing? What further research do I need to do to find these particulars? In Part 3 of this text, which is devoted to advice about composing and revising, we show how the construction and location of point sentences are essential for reader clarity. Part 3 also explains various composing and revising strategies that will help you create effective networks of points and particulars.

Chapter Summary

This chapter has introduced you to four concepts that will enable you to think about your subject matter from a rhetorical perspective.

- ***Concept 4: To determine their thesis, writers must often "wallow in complexity."*** What typically initiates the writing process is a problematic question that invites the writer to explore the problem's complexity. To do so, experienced writers often use exploratory techniques such as freewriting, idea mapping, dialectic talk, and the believing and doubting game to generate ideas.
- ***Concept 5: A strong thesis surprises readers with something new or challenging.*** A good thesis tries to change the reader's view of the subject and often creates tension by pushing against alternative views.
- ***Concept 6: In closed-form prose, a typical introduction starts with the problem, not the thesis.*** Readers need to be engaged with the writer's question before they can understand the thesis.
- ***Concept 7: Thesis statements in closed-form prose are supported hierarchically with points and particulars.*** Points give meaning to particulars; particulars make points persuasive. If you remove the particulars from a writer's argument and keep the points, you will have created a summary.

Playing the Believing and Doubting Game

BRIEF WRITING PROJECT

Part 1. The Game. Play the believing and doubting game with one of the assertions listed here (or with another assertion provided by your instructor) by freewriting your believing and doubting responses. Spend ten minutes believing and then ten minutes doubting the assertion, for a total of twenty minutes. When you believe an assertion, you agree, support, illustrate, extend, and apply the idea. When you doubt an assertion, you question, challenge, rebut, and offer counterreasons and counterexamples to the assertion. Note that when students first learn to do exploratory writing, they often run out of ideas quickly and want to stop. But the best ideas often happen when you push through that wall. If you run out of ideas, let your mind follow a tangent. Particularly explore your personal experiences with the subject. Eventually you will get back on track with new ideas.

1. Grades are an effective means of motivating students to do their best work.
2. Facebook is a good way to make new friends.
3. In recent years, advertising has made enormous gains in portraying women as strong, independent, and intelligent.
4. If there is only one kidney available for transplant and two sick persons need it, one in her thirties and one in her sixties, the kidney should go to the younger person.
5. The United States should reinstate the draft.
6. Humans have free will.
7. Fencing at the U.S.–Mexico border is not an effective immigration policy.
8. If students in a large lecture course can listen to a lecture and surf the Web or check e-mail at the same time, then they should be allowed to do so.

Part 2. Reflection. Write a reflective paragraph in which you assess the extent to which the believing and doubting game extended or stretched your thinking. Particularly, answer these questions:

- What was difficult about this writing activity?
- To what extent did it make you take an unfamiliar or uncomfortable stance?
- How can believing and doubting help you wallow in complexity?

THINKING RHETORICALLY ABOUT HOW MESSAGES PERSUADE

3

A way of seeing is also a way of not seeing.

—*Kenneth Burke, Rhetorician*

Every time an Indian villager watches the community TV and sees an ad for soap or shampoo, what they notice are not the soap and shampoo but the lifestyle of the people using them, the kind of motorbikes they ride, their dress and their homes.

—*Nayan Chanda, Indian-Born Editor of YaleGlobal Online Magazine*

In Chapters 1 and 2 we have focused on writing as a rhetorical act: When writers think rhetorically, they write to an audience for a purpose within a genre. We have also shown how academic writers pose subject-matter questions that engage their audience's interests, and then propose solutions to those problems that bring something new, surprising, or challenging to their audiences.

In this chapter we expand your understanding of a writer's choices by showing how messages persuade. We'll use the word *message* in its broadest sense to include verbal texts and nonverbal texts such as photographs and paintings or consumer artifacts such as clothing. When you understand how messages achieve their effects, you will be better prepared to analyze and evaluate those messages and to make your own choices about whether to resist them or accede to them.

In this chapter, you will learn three more important rhetorical concepts:

- **CONCEPT 8** Messages persuade through their angle of vision.
- **CONCEPT 9** Messages persuade through appeals to *logos, ethos,* and *pathos.*
- **CONCEPT 10** Nonverbal messages persuade through visual strategies that can be analyzed rhetorically.

CONCEPT 8 Messages persuade through their angle of vision.

One way that messages persuade is through their **angle of vision**, which causes a reader to see a subject from one perspective only—the writer's. Writers create an angle of vision through strategies such as the following:

- Stating point of view directly
- Selecting some details while omitting others
- Choosing words or figures of speech with intended connotations
- Creating emphasis or de-emphasis through sentence structure and organization

The writer's angle of vision—which might also be called a lens, a filter, a perspective, or a point of view—is persuasive because it controls what the reader "sees." Unless readers are rhetorically savvy, they can lose awareness that they are seeing the writer's subject matter through a lens that both reveals and conceals.

A classic illustration of angle of vision is the following thought exercise:

THOUGHT EXERCISE ON ANGLE OF VISION

Suppose you attended a fun party on Saturday night. (You get to choose what constitutes "fun" for you.) Now imagine that two people ask what you did on Saturday night. Person A is a close friend who missed the party. Person B is your parent. How would your descriptions of Saturday night differ?

Clearly there isn't just one way to describe this party. Your description will be influenced by your purpose and audience. You will have to decide:

- What image of myself should I project? (For your friend you might construct yourself as a party animal; for your parent, as a more detached observer.)
- How much emphasis do I give the party? (You might describe the party in detail for your friend while mentioning it only in passing to your parent, emphasizing instead all the homework you did over the weekend.)
- What details should I include or leave out? (Does my parent really need to know that the neighbors called the police?)
- What words should I choose? (The slang you use with your friend might not be appropriate for your parent.)

You'll note that our comments about your rhetorical choices reflect common assumptions about friends and parents. You might actually have a party-loving parent and a geeky friend, in which case your party descriptions would be altered accordingly. In any case, you are in rhetorical control; you choose what your audience "sees" and how they see it.

Recognizing the Angle of Vision in a Text

This thought exercise illustrates a key insight of rhetoric: There is always more than one way to tell a story, and no single way of telling it constitutes the whole truth. By saying that a writer writes from an "angle of vision," we mean that the writer cannot take a godlike stance that allows a universal, unfiltered, totally unbiased or objective way of knowing. Rather, the writer looks at the subject from a certain location, or, to use another metaphor, the writer wears a lens that colors or filters the topic in a certain way. The angle of vision, lens, or filter determines what part of a topic gets "seen" and what remains "unseen," what gets included or excluded, what gets emphasized or de-emphasized, and so forth. It even determines what words get chosen out of an array of options—for example, whether the writer says "panhandler" or "homeless person," "torture" or "enhanced interrogation," "universal health care" or "socialized medicine."

As an illustration of angle of vision, consider the cartoon in Figure 3.1, which shows different ways that stakeholders "see" sweatshops. For each stakeholder, some aspects of sweatshops surge into view, while other aspects remain unseen or invisible. An alert reader needs to be aware that none of these stakeholders can portray sweatshops in a completely "true" way. Stockholders and corporate leaders emphasize reduced labor costs and enhanced corporate profits and retirement portfolios while de-emphasizing (or omitting entirely) the working conditions in

FIGURE 3.1 Different Angles of Vision on "Sweatshops"

sweatshops or the plight of American workers whose jobs have been outsourced to developing countries. Consumers enjoy abundant low-cost goods made possible by sweatshops and may not even think about where or how the products are made. Opponents of sweatshops focus on the miserable conditions of sweatshop workers, their low wages, the use of child labor, and the "obscene" profits of corporations. Meanwhile, as the American union worker laments the loss of jobs in the United States, third world workers and their children may welcome sweatshops as a source of income superior to the other harsh alternatives such as scavenging in dumps or prostitution. The multiple angles of vision show how complex the issue of sweatshops is. In fact, most issues are equally complex, and any one view of the issue is controlled by the writer's angle of vision.

To get a hands-on feel for how a writer creates an angle of vision, try doing the following U. R. Riddle activity, which invites you to write a letter of recommendation for a student.

FOR WRITING AND DISCUSSION

U. R. Riddle Letter

Background: Suppose that you are a management professor who regularly writes letters of recommendation for former students. One day you receive a letter from a local bank requesting a confidential evaluation of a former student, Uriah Rudy Riddle (U. R. Riddle), who has applied for a job as a management trainee. The bank wants your assessment of Riddle's intelligence, aptitude, dependability, and ability to work with people. You haven't seen U. R. for several years, but you remember him well. Here are the facts and impressions you recall about Riddle:

- Very temperamental student, seemed moody, something of a loner
- Long hair and very sloppy dress—seemed like a misplaced street person; often twitchy and hyperactive
- Absolutely brilliant mind; took lots of liberal arts courses and applied them to business
- Wrote a term paper relating different management styles to modern theories of psychology—the best undergraduate paper you ever received. You gave it an A+ and remember learning a lot from it yourself.
- Had a strong command of language—the paper was very well written
- Good at mathematics; could easily handle all the statistical aspects of the course
- Frequently missed class and once told you that your class was boring
- Didn't show up for the midterm. When he returned to class later, he said only that he had been out of town. You let him make up the midterm, and he got an A.
- Didn't participate in a group project required for your course. He said the other students in his group were idiots.
- You thought at the time that Riddle didn't have a chance of making it in the business world because he had no talent for getting along with people.
- Other professors held similar views of Riddle—brilliant, but rather strange and hard to like; an odd duck.

You are in a dilemma because you want to give Riddle a chance (he's still young and may have had a personality transformation of some sort), but you also don't want to damage your own professional reputation by falsifying your true impressions.

Individual task: Working individually for ten minutes or so, compose a brief letter of recommendation assessing Riddle; use details from the list to support your assessment. Role-play that you have decided to take a gamble with Riddle and give him a chance at this career. Write as strong a recommendation as possible while remaining honest. (To make this exercise more complex, your instructor might ask half the class to role-play a negative angle of vision in which you want to warn the bank against hiring Riddle without hiding his strengths or good points.)

Task for group or whole-class discussion: Working in small groups or as a whole class, share your letters. Then pick representative examples ranging from the most positive to the least positive and discuss how the letters achieve their different rhetorical effects. If your intent is to support Riddle, to what extent does honesty compel you to mention some or all of your negative memories? Is it possible to mention negative items without emphasizing them? How?

Analyzing Angle of Vision

Just as there is more than one way to describe the party you went to on Saturday night or to write about sweatshops, there is more than one way to write a letter of recommendation for U. R. Riddle. The writer's angle of vision determines what is "seen" or "not seen" in a given piece of writing—what gets slanted in a positive or negative direction, what gets highlighted, what gets thrown into the shadows. As rhetorician Kenneth Burke claims in the first epigraph for the chapter, "A way of seeing is also a way of not seeing." Note how the writer controls what the reader "sees." As Riddle's former professor, you might in your mind's eye see Riddle as long-haired and sloppy, but if you don't mention these details in your letter, they remain unseen to the reader. Note too that your own terms "long-haired and sloppy" interpret Riddle's appearance through the lens of your own characteristic way of seeing—a way that perhaps values business attire and clean-cut tidiness. Another observer might describe Riddle's appearance quite differently, thus seeing what you don't see.

In an effective piece of writing, the author's angle of vision often works so subtly that unsuspecting readers—unless they learn to think rhetorically—will be drawn into the writer's spell and believe that the writer's prose conveys the "whole picture" of its subject rather than a limited picture filtered through the screen of the writer's perspective.

Contrasting Angles of Vision in Two Texts Consider the differences in what gets seen in the following two descriptions of the Arctic National Wildlife Refuge in Alaska (the ANWR), where proponents of oil exploration are locked in a fierce battle with anti-exploration conservationists. The first passage is from a pro-exploration advocacy group called Arctic Power; the second is from former President Jimmy Carter.

ARCTIC POWER'S DESCRIPTION OF THE ANWR

On the coastal plain [of the ANWR], the Arctic winter lasts for 9 months. It is dark continuously for 56 days in midwinter. Temperatures with the wind chill can reach –110 degrees F. It's not pristine. There are villages, roads, houses, schools, and military installations. It's not a unique Arctic ecosystem. The coastal plain is only a small fraction of the 88,000 square miles that make up the North Slope. The same tundra environment and wildlife can be found throughout the circumpolar Arctic regions. The 1002 Area [the legal term for the plot of coastal plain being contested] is flat. That's why they call it a plain. [. . .]

Some groups want to make the 1002 Area a wilderness. But a vote for wilderness is a vote against American jobs.

JIMMY CARTER'S DESCRIPTION OF THE ANWR

Rosalynn [Carter's wife] and I always look for opportunities to visit parks and wildlife areas in our travels. But nothing matches the spectacle of wildlife we found on the coastal plain of America's Arctic National Wildlife Refuge in Alaska. To the north lay the Arctic Ocean; to the south rolling foothills rose toward the glaciated peaks of the Brooks Range. At our feet was a mat of low tundra plant life, bursting with new growth, perched atop the permafrost.

As we watched, 80,000 caribou surged across the vast expanse around us. Called by instinct older than history, this Porcupine (River) caribou herd was in the midst of its annual migration. To witness this vast sea of caribou in an uncorrupted wilderness home, and the wolves, ptarmigan, grizzlies, polar bears, musk oxen and millions of migratory birds, was a profoundly humbling experience. We were reminded of our human dependence on the natural world.

Sadly, we were also forced to imagine what we might see if the caribou were replaced by smoke-belching oil rigs, highways and a pipeline that would destroy forever the plain's delicate and precious ecosystem.

How Angle of Vision Persuades To understand more clearly how angle of vision persuades, you can analyze the language strategies at work. Some of these strategies—which writers employ consciously or unconsciously to achieve their intended effects—are described in the following strategies chart.

Strategies for Constructing an Angle of Vision

Strategy	ANWR Example	U. R. Riddle Example
State your intention directly.	• Earlier passages directly state Arctic Powers' pro-drilling and Carter's anti-drilling stances.	• You might say "Riddle would make an excellent manager" or "Riddle doesn't have the personality to be a bank manager."
Select details that support your intentions; omit or de-emphasize others.	• Arctic Power writer (AP) "sees" the cold, barren darkness of the ANWR; Carter sees the beauty.	• A positive view of Riddle would select and emphasize Riddle's good traits and de-emphasize or omit his bad ones.

Strategy	ANWR Example	U. R. Riddle Example
	• AP spotlights the people who live on the coastal plain while making the animals invisible; Carter spotlights the caribou while omitting the people. • To AP, drilling means jobs; to Carter it means destructive oil rigs.	• A negative view would take opposite the tack.
Choose words that frame your subject in the desired way or have desired connotations.	• AP frames the ANWR as the dreary "1002 Area"; Carter frames it as a "spectacle of wildlife," a unique "delicate and precious ecosystem." • Arctic Power uses words with negative connotations ("wind chill"); Carter uses words connoting life and growth ("a mat of low tundra plant life").	• "Riddle is an independent thinker who doesn't follow the crowd" (frames him positively in value system that favors individualism). • "Riddle is a loner who thinks egocentrically" (frames him negatively in value system favoring consensus and social skills). • You could say, "Riddle is forthright" or "Riddle is rude"—positive versus negative connotations.
Use figurative language (metaphors, similes, and analogies) that conveys your intended effect.	• AP avoids figurative language, claiming objective presentation of facts. • Carter uses positive metaphors to convey ANWR's vitality (tundra "bursting with new growth") and negative metaphors for drilling ("smoke-belching oil rigs").	• To suggest that Riddle has outgrown his alienating behavior, you could say, "Riddle is a social late bloomer." • To recommend against hiring Riddle while still being positive, you could say, "Riddle's independent spirit would feel caged in by the routine of a bank."
Use sentence structure to emphasize and de-emphasize your ideas. *(Emphasize an idea by placing it at the end of a long sentence, in a short sentence, or in a main clause.)*	• AP uses short sentences to emphasize main points: "It's not pristine." It's not a unique ecosystem." "That's why they call it a plain." • Carter uses longer sentences for description, with an occasional short sentence to make a point: "We were reminded of our human dependence on the natural world."	Consider the difference between the following: • "Although Riddle had problems relating to other students, he is a brilliant thinker." • "Although Riddle is a brilliant thinker, he had problems relating to other students in the class."

CONCEPT 9 Messages persuade through appeals to *logos, ethos,* and *pathos.*

A fuller discussion of these classical appeals appears in Chapter 13, "Writing a Classical Argument."

Another way to think about the persuasive power of texts is to examine the strategies writers or speakers use to sway their audiences toward a certain position on an issue. To win people's consideration of their ideas, writers or speakers can appeal to what the classical philosopher Aristotle called *logos, ethos,* and *pathos*. Developing the habit of examining how these appeals are functioning in texts and being able to employ these appeals in your own writing will enhance your ability to read and write rhetorically. Let's look briefly at each:

- ***Logos* is the appeal to reason.** It refers to the quality of the message itself—to its internal consistency, to its clarity in asserting a thesis or point, and to the quality of reasons and evidence used to support the point.
- ***Ethos* is the appeal to the character of the speaker/writer.** It refers to the speaker/writer's trustworthiness and credibility. One can often increase one's *ethos* in a message by being knowledgeable about the issue, by appearing thoughtful and fair, by listening well, and by being respectful of alternative points of view. A writer's accuracy and thoroughness in crediting sources and professionalism in caring about the format, grammar, and neat appearance of a document are part of the appeal to *ethos.*
- ***Pathos* is the appeal to the sympathies, values, beliefs, and emotions of the audience.** Appeals to *pathos* can be made in many ways. *Pathos* can often be enhanced through evocative visual images, frequently used in Web sites, posters, and magazine or newspaper articles. In written texts, the same effects can be created through vivid examples and details, through connotative language, and through empathy with the audience's beliefs and values.

To see how these three appeals are interrelated, you can visualize a triangle with points labeled *Message, Audience,* and *Writer* or *Speaker.* Rhetoricians study how effective communicators consider all three points of this *rhetorical triangle.* (See Figure 3.2.)

We encourage you to ask questions about the appeals to *logos, ethos,* and *pathos* every time you examine a text. For example, is the appeal to *logos* weakened by the writer's use of scanty and questionable evidence? Has the writer made a powerful appeal to *ethos* by documenting her sources and showing that she is an authority on the issue? Has the writer relied too heavily on appeals to *pathos* by using numerous heart-wringing examples? Later chapters in this textbook will help you use these appeals competently in your own writing as well as analyze these appeals in others' messages.

CONCEPT 10 Nonverbal messages persuade through visual strategies that can be analyzed rhetorically.

Chapter 10 deals extensively with visual rhetoric, explaining how visual elements work together to create a persuasive effect.

Just as you can think rhetorically about texts, you can think rhetorically about photographs, drawings, and other images as well as artifacts such as clothing or cars.

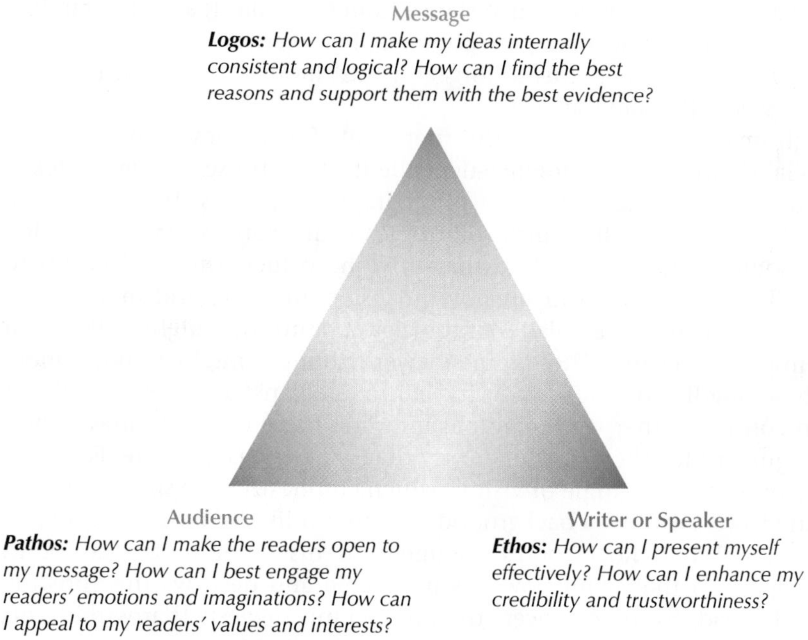

FIGURE 3.2 Rhetorical Triangle

Visual Rhetoric

Consider, for example, the persuasive power of famous photographs from the war in Iraq. Early in the war, several widely publicized images, particularly the film footage of the toppling of the statue of Saddam Hussein and the "Mission Accomplished" photograph of former President George W. Bush wearing a pilot's flight suit on the deck of the aircraft carrier *Abraham Lincoln*, served to consolidate public support of the war. Later, certain images began eating away at public support. For example, an unauthorized picture of flag-draped coffins filling the freight deck of a military transport plane focused attention on those killed in the war. Particularly devastating for supporters of the war were the images of American guards sexually humiliating Iraqi prisoners in the Abu Ghraib prison. Images like these stick in viewers' memories long after specific texts are forgotten.

What gives images this persuasive power? For one thing, they can be apprehended at a glance, condensing an argument into a memorable scene or symbol that taps deeply into our emotions and values. Images also persuade by appealing to *logos, ethos,* and *pathos*. They make implicit arguments (*logos*) while also appealing to our values and emotions (*pathos*) and causing us to respond favorably or unfavorably to the artist or photographer (*ethos*). Like verbal texts, images have an angle of vision, which can be crafted by selecting, manipulating, and often photoshopping images to control what viewers see and thus influence what they think. (Note that "angle of vision" is itself a visual metaphor.) Through the location and angle of the camera, the distance from the subject, and the framing, cropping, and filtering of the image, the photographer steers us toward a particular view of the subject, influencing us to forget, at least momentarily, that there are other ways of seeing the same subject.

Although images can have powerful rhetorical effects, these effects may be less controllable and more audience-dependent than those of verbal texts. Consider, for example, the wind farm photograph on page 3. In this striking image, the dominance of the whirling turbines could convey several implicit arguments. Some viewers might find that this photo fuels their objections to wind farms. They might zero in on how intrusive, massive, and unattractive wind turbines are. The blurred blades of the gigantic turbines might strike them as frightening or menacing. These same viewers, though, might respond more positively to a longdistance photo of wind turbines against a scarlet sunset over the hills. In contrast, other viewers might interpret these wind turbines in motion as an argument for the plentiful energy that wind farms generate. For these viewers, the photograph's angle of vision, which emphasizes the size and power of these wind towers against a background of barren hills and blue sky, could be used to counter David Rockwood's argument in his letter to the editor in Chapter 1 (pp. 6–7) that wind power is unreliable and destroys the "pristine wilderness." Instead, to these viewers the photograph suggests that wind farms make productive use of arid or barren land. Interpreted this way, this photo could be seen to use *pathos* to appeal to environmentalists' concerns (preserve beautiful landscape; don't harm wildlife) while evoking positive feelings about technology. In either case, viewers would agree that the photographer is obviously a professional, who uses an upward camera placement to emphasize the technological power of the wind turbines. One's feelings toward the photograph and the photographer may also depend on how much the photograph seems "natural" as opposed to being framed for artistic or political effect. Because images are somewhat open in the way they create visual arguments, writers of texts that include images should anticipate viewers' possible alternative interpretations.

FOR WRITING AND DISCUSSION

Analyzing Visual Messages

The following exercise asks you to think about how rhetorical effects of images can create implicit arguments. Figures 3.3–3.6 depict the controversial northernmost part of Alaska—the Arctic National Wildlife Refuge and the North Slope near the Brooks Range that Arctic Power and Jimmy Carter described on page 56. This region figures prominently in public debates about the United States' energy independence, climate change, environmental preservation, and unexplored sources of oil. Note that oil drilling has long been established in the North Slope but is currently forbidden in the adjacent ANWR. Working in small groups or as a whole class, explore the rhetorical effect of images by doing the following two tasks.

1. ***Analyzing the Photos.*** Explore the rhetorical effect of these images, noting how the effect may differ from person to person.
   a. In each photograph, on what details has the photographer chosen to focus? How do the details contribute to a dominant impression conveyed by the whole photograph? How does the photograph affect you emotionally? How does it make you feel about the ANWR/North Slope?
   b. Place your impression of the ANWR/North Slope, as conveyed by each of these images, on a continuum from ugly/forbidding to beautiful/fascinating or from barren/empty of animal life to biologically rich.
2. ***Using the Photos.*** Now imagine that you are creating a flyer for each of the following audiences and purposes. Which photo would you use to make the most compelling argument (consider *logos, ethos,* and *pathos*) for each audience? Explain your reasoning. Note that there is no "right answer" for these questions. If you think that none of the photographs would be

FIGURE 3.3 Caribou Crossing a River in the Arctic National Wildlife Refuge

FIGURE 3.4 Caribou Grazing Near Oil Pipeline in the Arctic North Slope

FIGURE 3.5 The ANWR Coastal Plain in Winter

FIGURE 3.6 Oil-Extraction Plant, North Slope

(*continued*)

appropriate for the designated audience and purpose, what kind of photograph would be more effective?

a. *Audience:* tourists
   Purpose: to invite people to buy tour packages to the Arctic National Wildlife Refuge and the North Slope
b. *Audience*: political leaders and voters
   Purpose: to persuade decision makers to take a pro-environment, anti-business stand on this region
c. *Audience*: political leaders and voters
   Purpose: to persuade decision makers to see this region as remote, empty, and therefore available for oil exploration and business development
d. *Audience*: undecided voters who want both more oil and a preserved environment
   Purpose: to persuade people to see that economic development in the ANWR can be compatible with preserving the region's unique natural beauty and wildlife

The Rhetoric of Clothing and Other Consumer Items

Not only do photographs, paintings, and drawings have rhetorical power, but so do the images projected by many of our consumer choices. Consider, for example, the rhetorical thinking that goes into our choice of clothes. We choose our clothes not only to keep ourselves covered and warm but also to project visually our identification with certain social groups and subcultures. For example, if you want to be identified as a skateboarder, a preppy socialite, a geek, a NASCAR fan, or a junior partner in a corporate law firm, you know how to select clothes and accessories that convey that identification. The way you dress is a code that communicates where you fit (or how you want to be perceived as fitting) within a class and social structure.

How do these symbolic codes get established? They can be set by fashion designers, by advertisers, or by trendy groups or individuals. The key to any new clothing code is to make it look different in some distinctive way from an earlier code or from a code of another group. Sometimes clothing codes develop to show rebellion against the values of parents or authority figures. At other times they develop to show new kinds of group identities.

Clothing codes are played on in conscious ways in fashion advertisements so that consumers become very aware of what identifications are signaled by different styles and brands. This aspect of consumer society is so ubiquitous that one of the marks of growing affluence in third world countries is people's attention to the rhetoric of consumer goods. Consider the second epigraph to this chapter, which indicates that villagers in India watching TV ads notice not only the soap or shampoo being advertised but also the brands of motorbikes and the lifestyles of the people in the ads. Buying a certain kind of consumer good projects a certain kind of status or group or class identity. Our point, from a rhetorical perspective, is that in making a consumer choice, many people are concerned not only with the quality of the item itself but also with its rhetorical symbolism. Note that the same item can send quite different messages to different groups: A Rolex watch might enhance one's credibility at a corporate board meeting while undercutting it at a barbecue for union workers.

FOR WRITING AND DISCUSSION

Clothing as Visual Arguments

The rhetorical power of clothing especially comes into play in the workplace. This exercise asks to you think about workplace dress codes, which are enforced by peer pressure and peer modeling as well as by company policies. Figures 3.7 to 3.10 show four different workplace environments. Working in small groups or as a whole class, consider the rhetoric of workplace clothing by sharing your responses to the following questions:

1. How would you describe the differences in dress codes in each of these environments?
2. If you were employed in one of these workplaces, how much do you think you could vary your style of dress without violating workplace codes?

FIGURE 3.7 Engineering firm

FIGURE 3.8 Warehouse

FIGURE 3.9 Associates, Law Firm

FIGURE 3.10 Espresso Bar

(continued)

3. Suppose that you are interviewing for a job in one of these workplaces. What clothing would be appropriate for your interview and why? (Note that how you dress for an interview might be different from how you dress once you have the job.) Share your rhetorical thinking about clothing choices aimed at making the best first impression on the people who interview you. Be as specific as possible for all items of clothing including shoes and accessories.
4. To what extent are dress codes for women more complex than those for men?

Chapter Summary

In this chapter we have looked briefly at rhetorical theory in order to explain the persuasive power of both verbal and visual texts.

- ***Concept 8: Messages persuade through their angle of vision.*** Any text necessarily looks at its subject from a perspective—an angle of vision—that selects and emphasizes some details while omitting or minimizing others. You can analyze writers' angle of vision by considering their direct statements of intention, their selection of details, their word choice, their figures of speech, and their manipulation of sentence structure to control emphasis.
- ***Concept 9: Messages persuade through appeals to* logos, ethos, *and* pathos.** *Logos* refers to the power of the writer's reasons and evidence; *pathos* to the way the writer connects to the reader's sympathies, emotions, values, and beliefs; and *ethos* to the way the writer portrays himself or herself as trustworthy and credible.
- ***Concept 10: Nonverbal messages persuade through visual strategies that can be analyzed rhetorically.*** Like verbal texts, visual texts have an angle of vision created by the way the image is framed and by the perspective from which it is viewed. Images also make implicit arguments (*logos*), appeal to the viewer's emotions and values (*pathos*), and suggest the creator's character and trustworthiness (*ethos*). One can also analyze consumer choices (clothing, jewelry, cars) rhetorically because such choices make implicit arguments about the consumer's desired identity.

BRIEF WRITING PROJECT

Analyzing Angle of Vision in Two Passages about Nuclear Energy

Background and Readings

This brief writing project will give you practice at analyzing the angle of vision in different texts. The assignment focuses on two passages about nuclear power plants.

The first passage is from the home page of NuclearPowerNow, a nuclear power advocacy site. It was posted in 2008.

PASSAGE 1

Nuclear Power Now

Nuclear power is the world's largest source of emission-free energy. Nuclear power plants produce no controlled air pollutants, such as sulfur and particulates, or greenhouse gases. The use of nuclear power in place of other energy sources helps to keep the air clean, preserve the Earth's climate, avoid ground-level ozone formation and prevent acid rain.

Nuclear power has important implications for our national security. Inexpensive nuclear power, in combination with fuel cell technology, could significantly reduce our dependency on foreign oil.

Nuclear power plants have experienced an admirable safety record. About 20% of electricity generated in the U.S. comes from nuclear power, and in the last forty years of this production, not one single fatality has occurred as a result of the operation of a civilian nuclear power plant in the United States. In comparison, many people die in coal mining accidents every year and approximately ten thousand Americans die every year from pollution related to coal burning.

The nuclear power industry generates approximately 2,000 tons of solid waste annually in the United States. In comparison, coal fueled power plants produce 100,000,000 tons of ash and sludge annually, and this ash is laced with poisons such as mercury and nitric oxide.

Even this 2,000 tons of nuclear waste is not a technical problem. Reprocessing of nuclear fuel, and the implementation of Integral Fast Reactor technology, will enable us to turn the vast majority of what is currently considered waste into energy.

Unfortunately, the voting public has been victimized by forty years of misinformation regarding the safety of nuclear power. The graphs on nuclear energy showing it to be safe, economical, and in our national interest are countered by anti-nuclear activists using fear tactics to frighten the electorate into inaction.

Until we can successfully educate the American electorate on the real pros and cons of nuclear power, we will not be able to engage in a healthy national discussion on the topic.

The second passage is by Carl Pope, the executive director of the Sierra Club. This brief article was posted in September 2009 on the "Great Debate" blog site hosted by Reuters, a news service focused on business and industry.

PASSAGE 2

Nuclear Power Is Not the Way Forward

Nuclear power is not a responsible choice and makes no sense as part of America's clean energy future. We can meet our energy needs through energy efficiency and renewable energy, and have a clean and healthy world without nuclear power.

There are four insurmountable problems with nuclear power.

First, nuclear power produces highly dangerous radioactive waste. Every nuclear reactor generates about 20 tons of highly radioactive spent nuclear fuel and additional low-level radioactive waste per year. The waste can kill at high doses and cause cancer and birth defects at low doses. Nuclear waste remains dangerous to humans for 200 thousand years.

Worse, we don't know what to do with this waste once it is generated. Some propose dumping nuclear waste in Yucca Mountain, NV; however, the mountain is seismically active. An earthquake in the 1990's caused over $1 million damage to a

Department of Energy (DOE) facility at the site. In addition, a Department of Energy panel of scientists has found that the nuclear material may leak from the containment vessels over time and will contaminate groundwater. On its way to Yucca Mountain, the waste would also pass through thousands of cities and towns and present multiple exposure risks.

Second, nuclear power is prohibitively expensive. The method is not anywhere near cost effective; nuclear plants in the states of Oregon, New York, Maine, Illinois, and Connecticut have been shut down because the owners found it was too expensive to keep them going.

American taxpayers are also subsidizing the nuclear industry. According to the Congressional Research Service, the industry has cost taxpayers tens of billions of dollars in research and development subsidies.

Third, an accident at a coal plant is a problem, but an accident at a nuclear plant can be a disaster. Because human beings operate plants and drive the trucks that transport nuclear waste, accidents can and will happen. The danger with nuclear power is that the stakes in accidents are extremely high. Anyone exposed to radiation leaks or accidents will likely sicken or die from that exposure.

And finally, there is a risk that nuclear material will fall into the wrong hands. Some have recommended that we consider "reprocessing" of spent nuclear fuel, a method that consolidates waste into weapons-usable plutonium. The government has elaborate plans to prevent rogue nations and terrorists from stealing the nuclear fuel or waste to make nuclear bombs. The more nuclear reactors, the more risk of radioactive material being stolen to make bombs.

Nuclear power is not the way forward. America deserves a safer, cleaner, and cheaper energy future.

Your task: Contrast the differences in angle of vision in these two passages by analyzing how they create their different rhetorical effects. Consider factors such as overt statements of meaning, selection/omission of details, connotations of words and figures of speech, and sentence emphasis. To help guide your analysis, review the strategies chart ("Strategies for Constructing an Angle of Vision") on pages 56–57. Your goal here is to explain to your readers how these two passages create different impressions of nuclear power.

THINKING RHETORICALLY ABOUT STYLE AND DOCUMENT DESIGN

4

Style is everything, and nothing. It is not that, as is commonly supposed, you get your content and soup it up with style; style is absolutely embedded in the way you perceive.

—*Martin Amis, Author*

. . . [C]larity and excellence in thinking is very much like clarity and excellence in the display of data. When principles of design replicate principles of thought, the act of arranging information becomes an act of thought.

—*Edward Tufte, Visual Design Researcher and Consultant*

In Chapters 1, 2, and 3, we explained the importance of rhetorical thinking for writers. In this chapter, we focus on the rhetorical effect of different writing styles and document designs and suggest ways to increase the power and effectiveness of your prose. As our two epigraphs suggest, style and document design are not decorative add-ons to jazz up dull content but rather means of guiding an audience to see what matters. Style and document design are thus "acts of thought."

To build on your understanding of rhetorical effectiveness, in this chapter you will learn two new concepts:

- CONCEPT 11 Good writers make purposeful stylistic choices.
- CONCEPT 12 Good writers make purposeful document design choices.

CONCEPT 11 Good writers make purposeful stylistic choices.

You can gain power as a writer by understanding the rhetorical effect of different writing styles.

Factors That Affect Style

Style refers to analyzable features of language that work together to create different effects. As shown in Figure 4.1, style can be thought of as a mixture of four factors:

- ***Ways of shaping sentences,*** such as length or complexity of sentence structure
- ***Word choice,*** such as abstract versus concrete or formal versus colloquial
- ***Voice, or persona,*** which refers to the reader's impression of the writer as projected from the page: expert versus layperson or scholarly voice versus popular voice
- ***Tone,*** which refers to the writer's attitude toward the subject matter or toward the reader, such as cold or warm, humorous or serious, detached or passionate

What style you adopt depends on your purpose, audience, and genre. Consider, for example, the differences in style in two articles about the animated sitcom *South Park*. The first passage comes from an academic journal in which the author analyzes how race is portrayed in *South Park*. The second passage is from a popular magazine, where the author argues that despite *South Park*'s vulgarity, the sitcom has a redeeming social value.

PASSAGE FROM SCHOLARLY JOURNAL

> In these cartoons, multiplicity encodes a set of nonwhite identities to be appropriated and commodified by whiteness. In the cartoon world, obscene humor and satire mediate this commodification. The whiteness that appropriates typically does so by virtue of its mobile positioning between and through imagined boundaries contrarily shown as impassible to black characters or agents marked as black. Let me briefly turn to an appropriately confusing example of such a character in *South Park*'s

FIGURE 4.1 Ingredients of Style

Ways of shaping sentences	Types of words	Voice or persona	Tone
Long/short Simple/complex Many modifiers/few modifiers Normal word order/frequent inversions or interruptions Mostly main clauses/many embedded phrases and subordinate clauses	Abstract/concrete Formal/colloquial Unusual/ordinary Specialized/general Metaphorical/literal Scientific/literary	Expert/layperson Scholar/student Outsider/insider Political liberal/ conservative Neutral observer/ active participant	Intimate/distant Personal/impersonal Angry/calm Browbeating/sharing Informative/ entertaining Humorous/serious Ironic/literal Passionately involved/aloof

scatological hero extraordinaire, Eric Cartman. . . . Eric Cartman's yen for breaking into Black English and interactions with black identities also fashion him an appropriator. However, Cartman's voice and persona may be seen as only an avatar, one layer of textual identity for creator Trey Parker, who may be regarded in one sense as a "blackvoice" performer.

—Michael A. Chaney, "Representations of Race and Place in *Static Shock, King of the Hill,* and *South Park*"

PASSAGE FROM POPULAR MAGAZINE

Despite the theme song's chamber of commerce puffery, *South Park* is the closest television has ever come to depicting hell on earth. Its inhabitants are, almost without exception, stupid, ignorant or venal—usually all three. Its central characters are four eight-year-olds: Stan, the high-achiever, Kyle, the sensitive Jew, Kenny, whose grisly death each week prompts the tortured cry, "Oh my God! They've killed Kenny! Those bastards!" and Eric Cartman, who has become the Archie Bunker of the '90s, beloved by millions. My 12-year-old son informs me that many of his schoolmates have taken to speaking permanently in Cartman's bigoted and usually furiously inarticulate manner. A (mild) sample: any display of human sensitivity is usually met by him with the rejoinder: "Tree-hugging hippie crap!" This has led to predictable calls for *South Park,* which is usually programmed late in the evening, to be banned altogether.

—Kevin Michael Grace, "*South Park* Is a Snort of Defiance Against a World Gone to Hell"

FOR WRITING AND DISCUSSION

Analyzing Differences in Style

Working in small groups or as a whole class, analyze the differences in the styles of these two samples.

1. How would you describe differences in the length and complexity of sentences, in the level of vocabulary, and in the degree of formality?
2. How do the differences in styles create different voices, personas, and tones?
3. Based on clues from style and genre, who is the intended audience of each piece? What is the writer's purpose? How does each writer hope to surprise the intended audience with something new, challenging, or valuable?
4. How are the differences in content and style influenced by differences in purpose, audience, and genre?

In the sections that follow, we highlight some ways of thinking about style that will be particularly relevant to you in your college writing.

Four Powerful Strategies for Improving Your Style

The preceding section has given you an overview of vocabulary and concepts for analyzing style. In this section we offer four powerful tips for making your own style forceful, clear, and effective. Of all the advice given about style in various handbooks, these four tips are usually regarded as essential—so much so that they rise to the level of rhetorical principles.

Streamline Your Prose by Cutting Deadwood In early drafts, writers often produce wordy, convoluted prose where unneeded words and roundabout expressions take up space without adding meaning. When they revise, experienced writers cut deadwood and use other strategies to make their prose as efficient and economical as possible. Their aim is to create streamlined sentences that keep the reader on track. In the following examples, consider how cutting words creates a leaner, more streamlined style:

Wordy/Verbose	Streamlined
As a result of the labor policies established by Bismarck, the working-class people in Germany were convinced that revolution was unnecessary for the attainment of their goals and purposes.	Bismarck's labor policies convinced the German working class that revolution was unnecessary.
In recent times a new interest has been apparent among many writers to make the language as it is used by specialists in the areas of government, law, and medicine more available to be understood and appreciated by readers who are not specialists in the aforementioned areas.	Recently writers have tried to make the language of government, law, and medicine more accessible to nonspecialist readers.

Control Emphasis with Sentence Structure Experienced writers vary the length and structure of their sentences to create a rhythm that emphasizes main ideas. For example, you can emphasize an idea by placing it in a main clause or by placing it in a short sentence surrounded by longer sentences. We illustrated this phenomenon in our discussion of the U. R. Riddle exercise (pp. 54–55), where variations in sentence structure created different emphases on Riddle's good or bad points:

> Although Riddle is a brilliant thinker, he had problems relating to other students in my class. (Emphasizes Riddle's personal shortcomings.)
>
> Although Riddle had problems relating to other students in my class, he is a brilliant thinker. (Emphasizes Riddle's intelligence.)

Neither of these effects would have been possible had the writer simply strung together two simple sentences:

> Riddle had problems relating to other students in my class. He is also a brilliant thinker.

In this version, both points about Riddle are equally emphasized, leaving the reader uncertain about the writer's intended meaning.

Our point is that subordinate structures help the reader distinguish between main and subordinate ideas. If you string together a long sequence of short sentences—or simply join them with words like *and, or, so,* or *but*—you create a choppy effect that fails to distinguish between more important and less important material. Consider the differences in the following examples.

Every Idea Equally Emphasized	Main Ideas Emphasized	Comment
Hisako usually attends each lab meeting. However, she missed the last one. She took the train to Boston to meet her sister. Her sister was arriving from Tokyo.	Although Hisako usually attends each lab meeting, she missed the last one because she took the train to Boston to meet her sister, who was arriving from Tokyo.	Sentence now focuses on main idea—why Hisako missed the lab.
I am a student at Sycamore College, and I live in Watkins Hall, and I am enclosing a proposal that concerns a problem with dorm life. There is too much drinking, so nondrinking students don't have an alcohol-free place to go, and so the university should create an alcohol-free dorm, and they should strictly enforce this no-alcohol policy.	As a Sycamore College student living in Watkins Hall, I am enclosing a proposal to improve dorm life. Because there is too much drinking on campus, there is no place for nondrinking students to go. I propose that the university create an alcohol-free dorm and strictly enforce the no-alcohol policy.	The fact that the writer is a Sycamore College student living in Watkins Hall is needed background information but not a main point. Focus of passage is now a crisp summary of the problem and her proposed solution.

In each of the above examples, the revised passage is easier to process because it subordinates less important material, focusing the reader's attention on main ideas.

Use Specific Details, Where Appropriate, to Stay Low on the Ladder of Abstraction In previous writing courses, you might have been offered advice such as "Show, don't tell" or "Use concrete, specific language." Our advice in this section follows the same spirit: to write as low on the ladder of abstraction as your context allows.

We use the metaphor of a ladder to show how words can vary along a continuum from the abstract ("crime") to the more specific and concrete ("aggravated assault with brass knuckles"). As a general rule, when you move from points to particulars in your prose, the more specific you can make these particulars, the more vivid the rhetorical effect on a reader. As an illustration, consider Figure 4.2, which depicts a "ladder of abstraction" descending from abstract terms at the top toward more specific ones at the bottom.

Choosing words low on the ladder of abstraction is particularly effective for descriptive writing, where your goal is to create a vivid mental image for readers. Writing teachers often express this advice through the maxim "Show, don't tell." *Tell* words interpret a scene or tell readers what to feel about a scene without describing it. ("The dog looked angry.") In contrast, *show* words describe a scene through sensory details. ("The neighbor's Doberman, growling and baring his

Level on Ladder	Clothing Example	Global Problem Example	Gendered Play Example
High level: Abstract or general ↕	• She chose new footwear.	• Should farmers in developing countries produce traditional crops or commercial crops?	• Sam exhibited traditionally gendered play behavior.
Middle level ↕	• She chose new flip-flops.	• In India, should farmers plant traditional crops or genetically engineered crops?	• Sam played with trucks and fire engines.
Low level: Specific or concrete	• She chose new purple platform flip-flops with rhinestones.	• For sale on the global market, should farmers of Northern India plant traditional mandua and jhangora or genetically modified soy beans?	• Sam gleefully smashed his toy Tonka fire engine into the coffee table.

FIGURE 4.2 The Ladder of Abstraction: From Abstract to Specific

teeth, lunged against his chain.") The description itself evokes the desired effect without requiring the writer to interpret it overtly. This difference in rhetorical effect can be seen in the following examples of descriptive writing:

Tell Words (mid-scale on the ladder) ⇩	• The awkward, badly dressed professor stood at the front of the room. ⇩	• The wonderful smell of food cooking on the barbecue fills my nose. ⇩
Show Words (low on the ladder)	• At the front of the room stood the professor, a tall, gawky man with inch-thick glasses, a wispy beard, an old brown-striped jacket, burgundy and gray plaid pants, and a green tie with blue koalas.	• The tantalizing smell of grilled hamburgers and buttered corn on the cob wafts from the barbecue area of the park, where men in their cookout aprons wield forks and spatulas and drink Budweisers.

Of course, not all writing needs to be this low on the ladder of abstraction. Our advice, rather, is to descend as low on the ladder as your context allows. Even the most abstract kind of prose will move up and down between several rungs on the ladder. In closed-form prose writers need to make choices about the level of specificity that will be most effective based on their purpose, audience, and genre. Note the differences in the levels of abstraction in the following passages:

PASSAGE 1: FAIRLY HIGH ON LADDER OF ABSTRACTION

Although lightning produces the most deaths and injuries of all weather-related accidents, the rate of danger varies considerably from state to state. Florida has twice as many deaths and injuries from lightning strikes as any other state. Hawaii and Alaska have the fewest.

Point sentence

Particulars high on ladder of abstraction

—Passage from a general interest informative article on weather-related accidents

PASSAGE 2: LOWER ON LADDER OF ABSTRACTION

Florida has twice as many deaths and injuries from lightning strikes as any other state, with many of these casualties occurring on the open spaces of golf courses. Florida golfers should carefully note the signals of dangerous weather conditions such as darkening skies, a sudden drop in temperature, an increase in wind, flashes of light and claps of thunder, and the sensation of an electric charge on one's hair or body. In the event of an electric storm, golfers should run into a forest, get under a shelter, get into a car, or assume the safest body position. To avoid being the tallest object in an area, if caught in open areas, golfers should find a low spot, spread out, and crouch into a curled position with feet together to create minimal body contact with the ground.

Point sentence

Particulars at midlevel on ladder

Particulars at lower level on ladder

—Passage from a safety article aimed at Florida golfers

Both of these passages are effective for their audience and purpose. The first passage might be compared to a distant shot with a camera, giving an overview of lightning deaths in the United States, while the second zooms in for a more detailed look at a specific case, Florida golf courses. Sometimes, low-on-the-ladder particulars consist of statistics or quotations rather than sensory details. For example, civil engineer David Rockwood uses low-on-the-ladder numerical data about the size and number of wind towers to convince readers that wind generation of electricity entails environmental damage. Your rhetorical decisions about level of abstraction are important because too much high-on-the-scale writing can become dull for readers, while too much low-on-the-scale writing can seem overwhelming or pointless.

See Rockwood's letter to the editor, pp. 6–7.

FOR WRITING AND DISCUSSION

Choosing Details for Different Levels on the Ladder of Abstraction

The following exercise will help you appreciate how details can be chosen at different levels of abstraction to serve different purposes and audiences. Working in small groups or as a whole class, invent details at appropriate positions on the ladder of abstraction for each of the following point sentences.

1. *Yesterday's game was a major disappointment.* You are writing an e-mail message to a friend who is a fan (of baseball, football, basketball, another sport) and missed the game; use midlevel details to explain what was disappointing.

(continued)

2. *Although the game stank, there were some great moments.* Switch to low-on-the-ladder specific details to describe one of these "great moments."
3. *Advertising in women's fashion magazines creates a distorted and unhealthy view of beauty.* You are writing an analysis for a college course on popular culture; use high-to-midlevel details to give a one-paragraph overview of several ways these ads create an unhealthy view of beauty.
4. *One recent ad, in particular, conveys an especially destructive message about beauty.* Choose a particular ad and describe it with low-on-the-ladder, very specific details.

Use a Voice Matched to Your Purpose, Audience, and Genre College students often wonder what style—and particularly, what voice—is appropriate for college papers. For most college assignments, we recommend that you approximate your natural speaking voice to give your writing a conversational academic style. By "natural," we mean a voice that strives to be plain and clear while retaining the engaging quality of a person who is enthusiastic about the subject.

Of course, as you become an expert in a discipline, you may need to move toward a more scholarly voice. For example, the prose in an academic journal article can be extremely dense with technical terms and complex sentence structure, but expert readers in that field understand and expect this voice. Students sometimes try to imitate a dense academic style before they have achieved the disciplinary expertise to make the style sound natural. The result can seem pretentiously stilted and phony—an "inflated" style. At the other extreme, students sometimes adopt an overly informal or street slang voice that doesn't fit an academic context. Writing with clarity and directness within your natural range will usually create the most effective and powerful voice. Consider the difference in the following examples:

Inflated Voice	Natural Speaking Voice	Overly Informal Voice
As people advance in age, they experience time-dependent alterations in their ability to adapt to environmental change. However, much prior research on the aging process has failed to differentiate between detrimental changes that result from an organism's aging process itself and detrimental changes resulting from a disease process that is often associated with aging.	As people get older, they are less able to adapt to changes in their environment. Research on aging, however, hasn't always distinguished between loss of function caused by aging itself and loss caused by diseases common among older people.	Old folks don't adapt well to changes in their environments. Some scientists who studied the cane and walker crowd found out that it was hard to tell the difference between bad stuff caused by age versus bad stuff caused by disease.

Although the "natural voice" style is appropriate for most college papers, especially those written for lower-division courses, many professors construct assignments asking you to adopt different voices and different styles. It is thus important to understand the professor's assignment and to adopt the style and voice appropriate for the assigned rhetorical situation.

FOR WRITING AND DISCUSSION

Revising Passages to Create a More Effective Style

Working individually or in small groups, try to improve the style of the following passages by cutting deadwood, by combining sentences to subordinate less important ideas and emphasize main points, or by achieving a more natural voice.

1. It is unfortunate that the mayor acted in this manner. The mayor settled the issue. But before he settled the issue he made a mistake. He fostered a public debate that was very bitter. The debate pitted some of his subordinates against each other. These subordinates were in fact key subordinates. It also caused many other people to feel inflamed passions and fears as a result of the way the mayor handled the issue.
2. Cheerleading should be seen as a sport. It should not be regarded as just sexy dancing. This issue is especially important to women. It is often the desire of junior high school girls to want to become cheerleaders, but their role models for achieving this desire are the Dallas Cowboys cheerleaders, but instead the vision they should strive to achieve is a vision of cheerleaders as athletes. Such athletes in order to become cheerleaders must be able to do very athletic moves and stunts such as handstands, cartwheels, handsprings, high jumps, and the splits. A great cheerleader is not a girl who makes suggestive moves like a pop star in an MTV video, but instead it is a girl who can participate in routines that are complex like lifts, tosses, flips, catches, and other gymnastic moves.

CONCEPT 12 Good writers make purposeful document design choices.

Document design refers to the format of a text including use of charts, illustrations, or visual images. The "look" of a document can signal to readers its purpose, its genre, its intended audience, and the writer's intended (or unintended!) *ethos*. Writers need to distinguish between document design appropriate for manuscripts—a category that includes most of the kinds of writing you will do in college—and document design for published works.

Document Design for Manuscripts and Papers

As a writer in an academic setting, you will usually be producing manuscript (keyboarded pages of typed text held together with a staple or folder, or submitted electronically) rather than a publication-ready document. Your document design choices mainly concern margins, font style and size, material in headers or footers (page number, document identification), and line spacing. Generally these choices are dictated by the style guidelines of an academic discipline such as the Modern

Language Association (MLA) or by the conventions established in a business or professional setting. If you deviate from the expected document design, readers will assume that you are doing so on purpose and will wonder what that purpose is. (If you use scripted font or design a personalized cover page for an academic paper, you'd make a "notice me" statement, analogous to wearing a green jump-suit to a business meeting—you might want to do so, but there's a risk.)

Attention to document design and the appearance of your manuscripts thus signals your membership in an academic or professional community. An inappropriately formatted or sloppy paper can hurt your *ethos* and may send a message that you are unprofessional. Figure 4.3 illustrates the first- and second-page manuscript formats for MLA and APA (American Psychological Association) style papers.

Document Design for Published Works

In contrast to manuscripts and college papers, published works require elaborate decisions about document design. The original manuscripts for a scholarly article, an article for a popular magazine, a newspaper op-ed piece, and a Web page may have all been double-spaced, typed documents with one-inch margins, but the published products look totally different, as you can see in Figure 4.4. Today's writers, especially in professional settings, often use desktop-publishing software to produce print-ready or Web-ready documents that have a professional visual appeal. For published documents, design is closely related to genre and involves decisions about type, use of space and layout, color, and graphics or images. Let's look at each in turn.

Type Type comes in different typeface styles, or **fonts**, that are commonly grouped in three font families:

1. **Serif fonts** have tiny extensions on the letters, which make them easier to read in long documents.
2. **Sans serif fonts** lack the extensions on the letters and are good for labels, headings, and short documents.
3. **Specialty fonts**, often used for decorative effect, include script fonts and special symbols.

Fonts also come in different sizes and can be formatted with **boldface**, *italics*, <u>underlining</u>, or shading.

In published documents, font use varies by genre. Scholarly print publications usually employ conservative typography: a consistently sized, plain, highly readable font like Times New Roman with variations mainly reserved for titles, headings, notes, and bibliography. Popular magazines, on the other hand, tend to use fonts playfully and artistically; they vary font styles and sizes to attract readers' attention and to make articles look pleasingly decorative on the page. Although the body text of articles is usually the same font throughout, the opening page often uses a variety of fonts and sizes. Font variations may highlight key ideas for readers who are reading casually or rapidly.

FIGURE 4.3 Manuscript Format for MLA and APA Papers

MLA Manuscript, page 1

Gardiner 1

James Gardiner

Professor Johnson

Writing Seminar: Inquiry and Argument

15 May 2007

Why *Facebook* Might Not Be Good For You:
Some Dangers of Online Social Networks

Walk into any computer lab located at any college campus across the country and you'll see dozens of students logged onto an online social network (OSN). In the last few years, the use of these networks has skyrocketed among Internet users, especially young adults. These new virtual communities are significantly influencing the way young people communicate and interact with one another. A report titled "E-Expectations: The Class of 2007" went so far as to label upcoming college freshmen "the Social-Networking Generation" (qtd. in Joly).

In late 2006, the Pew Internet Project, a nonpartisan, nonprofit research group that examines the social impact of the Internet, reported that 55 percent of online teens have created a personal profile on OSNs and that 48 percent of teens visit social networking Web sites daily, with 22 percent visiting several times a day (Lenhart and Madden 2). The two most popular OSNs are *MySpace* and *Facebook*. *MySpace* is a general networking site that allows anyone to join, develop a profile, and display personal information. In less than four years of existence, *MySpace* has exploded to become the third most visited Web site on the Internet behind only *Google* and *Yahoo* ("Top Sites") with more than 100 million members (Joly). *Facebook* is geared more toward college students (until recently it required that a person attend a university to join the network) and is the number one site accessed by 18- to 24-year-olds. According to research studies cited in an article in the *Toronto Star*, 90 percent of all undergraduates

APA Manuscript, page 1

Running head: GENDER STEREOTYPES 1

A Comparison of Gender Stereotypes in *SpongeBob SquarePants* and a 1930s Mickey Mouse Cartoon

Lauren Campbell, Charlie Bourain, and Tyler Nishida

November 10, 2006

MLA Manuscript, page 2

Gardiner 2

has also experienced unprecedented growth in its relatively short existence and now ranks as the seventh most visited site on the Internet ("Top Sites") and has a member base of more than 19 million (Joly).

With the use of OSNs increasing among young people, the term "Facebook trance" has emerged to describe a person who loses track of all time and stares at the screen for hours (Copeland). While "Facebook trance" might describe only an occasional and therefore harmless phenomenon, it gives rise to important questions: What are the possible negative consequences of OSNs? What should youthful users be watchful for and guard against? The purpose of this paper is to identify the possible harms of OSNs. I will suggest that overuse of OSNs can be a contributing factor to a decline in grades as well as to other problems such as a superficial view of relationships, an increase in narcissism, and possible future embarrassment.

I don't mean to deny that OSNs have positive consequences for young people. For one thing, they provide a "virtual hangout" that acts as a convenient and cost-effective way to stay in close contact with friends and family. According to the Pew survey, 91 percent of users use OSNs to keep in touch with their regularly seen friends, while 82 percent use the sites to stay in touch with distant friends (Lenhart and Madden). OSNs let young people regularly view their friends' profiles, leave short messages or comments, and share personal information. OSN researcher Danah Boyd also claims that these sites give young people a platform on which to experiment with identities, voice their opinions, and practice how they present themselves through personal data, pictures, and music placed in their profiles (Bowley). OSNs also assist them in learning more about people they've met offline. Used as an investigative tool, OSNs offer quick ways to get additional background information on someone. For example, a student could use an OSN to decide whom

APA Manuscript, page 2

GENDER STEREOTYPES 2

Abstract

Researchers in gender identity have continually argued whether gender differences are biological or social. Because television is a prime place for teaching children gender differences through socialization, we studied the extent of gender stereotyping in two1930s Mickey Mouse cartoons and two recent *SpongeBob SquarePants* cartoons. We analyzed the cartoons in one-minute increments and recorded the number of gender stereotypical and gender-non-stereotypical actions in each increment. Our results confirmed our hypothesis that *SpongeBob SquarePants* would have fewer gender stereotypes than Mickey Mouse. This study is significant because it shows that in at least one contemporary cartoon males and females have a range of acceptable behaviors that go beyond traditional gender stereotypes.

FIGURE 4.4 Examples of Published Documents

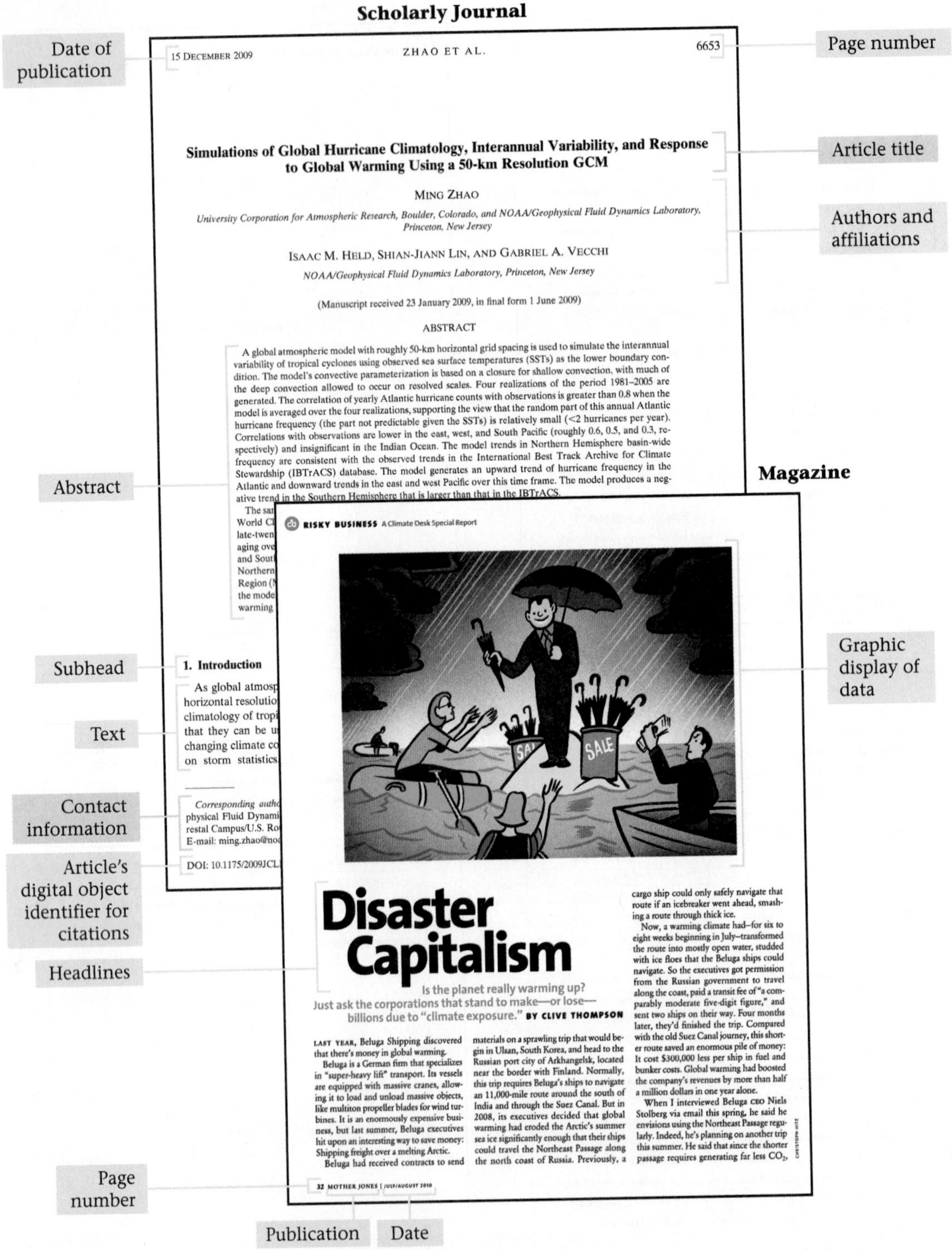

15 December 2009 ZHAO ET AL. 6653

Simulations of Global Hurricane Climatology, Interannual Variability, and Response to Global Warming Using a 50-km Resolution GCM

Ming Zhao

University Corporation for Atmospheric Research, Boulder, Colorado, and NOAA/Geophysical Fluid Dynamics Laboratory, Princeton, New Jersey

Isaac M. Held, Shian-Jiann Lin, and Gabriel A. Vecchi

NOAA/Geophysical Fluid Dynamics Laboratory, Princeton, New Jersey

(Manuscript received 23 January 2009, in final form 1 June 2009)

ABSTRACT

A global atmospheric model with roughly 50-km horizontal grid spacing is used to simulate the interannual variability of tropical cyclones using observed sea surface temperatures (SSTs) as the lower boundary condition. The model's convective parameterization is based on a closure for shallow convection, with much of the deep convection allowed to occur on resolved scales. Four realizations of the period 1981–2005 are generated. The correlation of yearly Atlantic hurricane counts with observations is greater than 0.8 when the model is averaged over the four realizations, supporting the view that the random part of this annual Atlantic hurricane frequency (the part not predictable given the SSTs) is relatively small (<2 hurricanes per year). Correlations with observations are lower in the east, west, and South Pacific (roughly 0.6, 0.5, and 0.3, respectively) and insignificant in the Indian Ocean. The model trends in Northern Hemisphere basin-wide frequency are consistent with the observed trends in the International Best Track Archive for Climate Stewardship (IBTrACS) database. The model generates an upward trend of hurricane frequency in the Atlantic and downward trends in the east and west Pacific over this time frame. The model produces a negative trend in the Southern Hemisphere that is larger than that in the IBTrACS.

The sa… World C… late-twen… aging ov… and Sout… Northern… Region (… the mode… warming…

1. Introduction

As global atmosp… horizontal resolutio… climatology of tropi… that they can be u… changing climate c… on storm statistics…

Corresponding auth… physical Fluid Dynami… restal Campus/U.S. Ro… E-mail: ming.zhao@no…

DOI: 10.1175/2009JCL…

RISKY BUSINESS A Climate Desk Special Report

Disaster Capitalism

Is the planet really warming up? Just ask the corporations that stand to make—or lose—billions due to "climate exposure." BY CLIVE THOMPSON

LAST YEAR, Beluga Shipping discovered that there's money in global warming.

Beluga is a German firm that specializes in "super-heavy lift" transport. Its vessels are equipped with massive cranes, allowing it to load and unload massive objects, like multiton propeller blades for wind turbines. It is an enormously expensive business, but last summer, Beluga executives hit upon an interesting way to save money: Shipping freight over a melting Arctic.

Beluga had received contracts to send materials on a sprawling trip that would begin in Ulsan, South Korea, and head to the Russian port city of Arkhangelsk, located near the border with Finland. Normally, this trip requires Beluga's ships to navigate an 11,000-mile route around the south of India and through the Suez Canal. But in 2008, its executives decided that global warming had eroded the Arctic's summer sea ice significantly enough that their ships could travel the Northeast Passage along the north coast of Russia. Previously, a cargo ship could only safely navigate that route if an icebreaker went ahead, smashing a route through thick ice.

Now, a warming climate had–for six to eight weeks beginning in July–transformed the route into mostly open water, studded with ice floes that the Beluga ships could navigate. So the executives got permission from the Russian government to travel along the coast, paid a transit fee of "a comparably moderate five-digit figure," and sent two ships on their way. Four months later, they'd finished the trip. Compared with the old Suez Canal journey, this shorter route saved an enormous pile of money: It cost $300,000 less per ship in fuel and bunker costs. Global warming had boosted the company's revenues by more than half a million dollars in one year alone.

When I interviewed Beluga CEO Niels Stolberg via email this spring, he said he envisions using the Northeast Passage regularly. Indeed, he's planning on another trip this summer. He said that since the shorter passage requires generating far less CO_2,

CHRISTOPH NIEMANN

32 MOTHER JONES | JULY/AUGUST 2010

Newspaper

Op Ed Page

Date and page number

Author biography

Headline

Author

Web Page

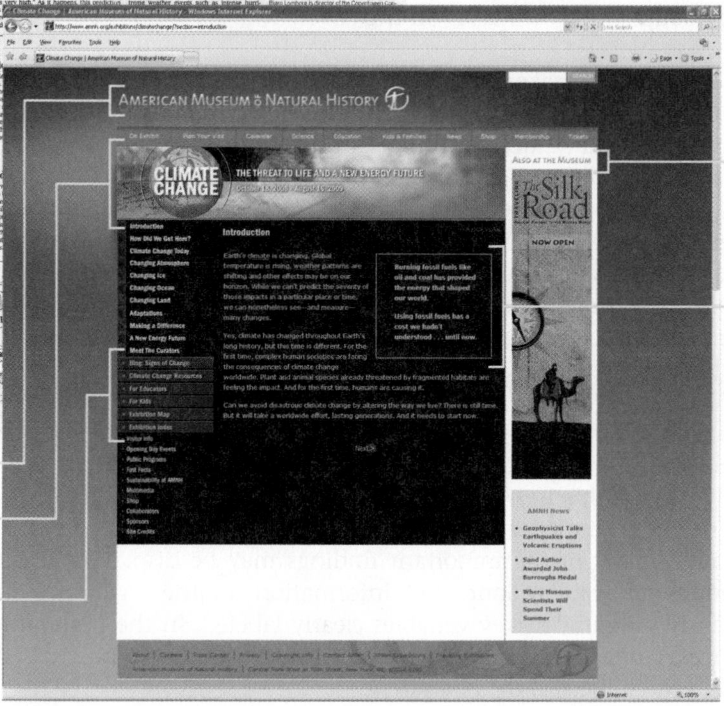

Links to main section of museum's site

Link to blog

Site sponsor

Site title

Links to sections of site

Space and Layout **Layout** refers to how the text is formatted on the page. Layout includes the following elements:

- Page size, margin size, proportion of text to white space
- Arrangement of text on the page (single or multiple columns, spaces between paragraphs)
- Use of justification (alignment of text with the left or right margins or both margins)
- Placement of titles, use of headings and subheadings, and spacing before and after headings
- Use of numbered or bulleted lists or of boxes and sidebars to highlight ideas or break text into visual units

Academic and scholarly publications, both in print and on the Web, use simple, highly functional document layouts. Most scholarly print journals use single or double columns of text that are justified at both margins to create a regular, even look. The layout of scholarly journals strikes a balance between maximizing the amount of text that fits on a page and ensuring readability.

In contrast, text layout in popular magazines and Web sites is more varied and playful, with text often wrapped around charts, sidebars, photographs, or drawings. While readability is important, so is visual appeal and entertainment: Readers must enjoy looking at the pages. For example, many popular print magazines try to blur the distinction between content and advertising so that ads become part of the visual appeal. This is why the table of contents is often buried a dozen or more pages into the magazine. The publisher wants to coax readers to think of the ads as part of the content. In contrast, the table of contents for most academic print journals is on the cover.

Color Colors make powerful appeals, even affecting moods. Whereas manuscripts are printed entirely in black ink, published documents often use color to identify and set off main ideas or important information. Color-tinted boxes can indicate special features or allow different but related articles to appear on the same page.

Academic and scholarly articles, books, and Web sites use color minimally, relying instead on different font styles and sizes to make distinctions in content. Popular magazines and Web sites, on the other hand, use colors playfully, artistically, decoratively, and strategically to enhance their appeal. They often vary colors of type or background for different kinds of content to give variety to the whole publication.

Graphics and Images **Graphics** include visual displays of information such as tables, line graphs, bar graphs, pie charts, maps, cartoons, illustrations, and photos.

As with the use of type, space, and color, the use of graphics indicates the focus, seriousness, function, and complexity of the writing. In scientific articles and books, many of the important findings may be displayed in complex, technical graphs and tables. Sources of information for these graphics are usually prominently stated, with key variables clearly labeled. In the humanities and social sciences, content-rich photos and drawings also tend to be vital parts of an article, even the subject of the analysis.

Popular publications typically use simple numeric visuals (for example, a colorful pie chart or a dramatic graph) combined with decorative use of **images**, especially photos. If photos appear, it is worthwhile to consider their rhetorical function. For example, some photos may be unscripted, realistic, and spontaneous, like news photos of a disaster scene or a sports highlight. Some may aim to look like news photos, but are in fact scripted and posed. Still others are concept (thematic) photos meant to illustrate an idea in an article. For example, an article on health care costs may include a photoshopped picture of a woman in a hospital gown surrounded by images of pills, doctors, expensive medical equipment, and wrangling employers and insurance agents.

FOR WRITING AND DISCUSSION

Analyzing Rhetorical Effect

Working individually or in small groups, analyze how genre and document design are interrelated in the examples shown in Figure 4.4.

1. How does the design of each document—its use of fonts, layout, color, and graphics—identify each piece as a scholarly article, an article in a popular magazine, a newspaper op-ed piece, or a Web page?
2. When you download an article from an electronic database (unless it is in pdf format), you often lose visual cues about the article's original genre. Even when an article is in pdf format, you lose cues about its original print context—the kind of magazine or journal the article appeared in, the magazine's layout and advertisements, and its targeted audience. Likewise, when you print a document from a Web site, you lose contextual cues about the original Web environment. How do document design and other visual features in the original print or Web source provide important contextual information for reading the article and using it in your own research?

Chapter Summary

In this chapter we have looked at how writers think rhetorically about style and document design.

- ***Concept 11: Good writers make purposeful stylistic choices.*** Style refers to analyzable language features—such as sentence structure, word choice, voice, and tone—that work together to create different rhetorical effects. You can improve your style by learning to cut deadwood, use sentence structure for emphasis, write low on the ladder of abstraction, and achieve a natural voice in your writing.
- ***Concept 12: Good writers make purposeful document design choices.*** Document design issues differ for manuscripts and published works. In producing manuscripts, expert writers follow the guidelines of their academic or professional communities, thereby signaling insider status. Design features for published documents concern type sizes and styles; layout and spacing; use of color; and use of graphics or images. Academic articles generally adopt a conservative design while more popular genres approach design playfully and artistically.

BRIEF WRITING PROJECT

Two Contrasting Descriptions of the Same Scene

This brief writing project is a write-to-learn task that will help you appreciate how writers construct an "angle of vision" (see Concept 8) and how aspects of style (particularly writing low on the ladder of abstraction) have strong rhetorical effects (Concept 11).

> Write two descriptions of the same scene, from contrasting angles of vision. Here is the catch: Your first description must convey a favorable impression of the scene, making it appear pleasing or attractive. The second description must convey a negative or unfavorable impression, making the scene appear unpleasant or unattractive. Both descriptions must contain only factual details and must describe exactly the same scene from the same location at the same time. It's not fair, in other words, to describe the scene in sunny weather and then in the rain or otherwise to alter factual details. Each description should be one paragraph long (approximately 125–175 words).
>
> Your instructor may ask you to discuss how you sought to create different rhetorical effects in these descriptions.

Establishing a Context

To get into the spirit of this unusual assignment, you need to create a personal rationale for why you are writing two opposing descriptions. Our students have been successful imagining any one of the following three rationales:

- ***Different moods.*** Pretend that you are observing this scene in different moods. How could you reflect a "happy" view of this scene and then a "sad" view? Let the mood determine your selection and framing of details, but don't put yourself into the scene. The reader should infer your mood from the description.
- ***Verbal game.*** Here you see yourself as a word wizard trying consciously to create two different rhetorical effects for readers. In this scenario, you don't worry how you feel about the scene but how you want your readers to feel. Your focus is on crafting the language to influence your audience in different ways.
- ***Different rhetorical purposes.*** In this scenario, you imagine your description in service of some desired action. You might dislike a certain space (for example, a poorly designed library reading room) and describe it in a way that highlights its bad features. This description is *the way you really feel.* Your next task is to see this same scene from an opposing perspective—perhaps that of the architect who designed the reading room.

Observing and Taking Notes

Once you have chosen your scene, you'll need to observe and take notes for fifteen or twenty minutes in preparation for writing the focused descriptions of the scene using specific, concrete, sensory details. You need to compose descriptions that are rich in sensory detail—sights, sounds, smells, textures, even on occasion tastes—all contributing to a dominant impression that gives the description focus.

You can train yourself to notice sensory details by creating a two-column sensory chart and noting details that appeal to each of the senses. Then try describing them, first positively (left column) and then negatively (right column). One student, observing a scene in a local tavern, made these notes in her sensory chart:

Positive Description	**Negative Description**
Taste	
salted and buttered popcorn	salty, greasy popcorn
frosty pitchers of beer	half-drunk pitchers of stale, warm beer
big bowls of salted-in-the-shell peanuts on the tables	mess of peanut shells and discarded pretzel wrappers on tables and floor
Sound	
hum of students laughing and chatting	din of high-pitched giggles and various obnoxious frat guys shouting at each other
the jukebox playing oldies but goodies from the early Beatles	jukebox blaring out-of-date music

Student Example

We conclude with a student example of this assignment.

DESCRIPTION 1—POSITIVE EFFECT

Light rain gently drops into the puddles that have formed along the curb as I look out my apartment window at the corner of 14th and East John. Pedestrians layered in sweaters, raincoats, and scarves and guarded with shiny rubber boots and colorful umbrellas sip their steaming hot triple-tall lattes. Some share smiles and pleasant exchanges as they hurry down the street, hastening to work where it is warm and dry. Others, smelling the aroma of French roast espresso coming from the coffee bar next to the bus stop, listen for the familiar rumbling sound that will mean the 56 bus has arrived. Radiant orange, yellow, and red leaves blanket the sidewalk in the areas next to the maple trees that line the road. Along the curb a mother holds the hand of her toddler, dressed like a miniature tugboat captain in yellow raincoat and pants, who splashes happily in a puddle.

DESCRIPTION 2—NEGATIVE EFFECT

A solemn grayness hangs in the air, as I peer out the window of my apartment at the corner of 14th and East John. A steady drizzle of rain leaves boot-drenching puddles for pedestrians to avoid. Bundled in rubber boots, sweaters, coats, and rain-soaked scarves, commuters clutch Styrofoam cups of coffee as a defense against the biting cold. They lift their heads every so often to take a small sip of caffeine, but look sleep-swollen nevertheless. Pedestrians hurry past each other, moving quickly to get away from the dismal weather, the dull grayness. Some nod a brief hello to a familiar face, but most clutch their overcoats and tread grimly on, looking to avoid puddles or spray from passing cars. Others stand at the bus stop, hunched over, waiting in the drab early morning for the smell of diesel that means the 56 bus has arrived. Along the curb an impatient mother jerks the hand of a toddler to keep him from stomping in an oil-streaked puddle.

PART 2

WRITING PROJECTS

This poster, one of hundreds created by the United States' Office of War Information during World War II, enlisted Americans' communal efforts, particularly women's help at home, in conserving resources to support the production for the war being fought on two fronts—the Pacific and Europe. This poster taps the urgency of that historical moment just as Michael Pollan's article, "Why Bother?", in Chapter 5 speaks to our current environmental problems. Think about how choice of words, images, color, and design in this poster work together to create an emotionally intense argument. Consider how you would design a poster to convey Pollan's argument or some other timely environmental message.

FOOD IS A WEAPON
DON'T WASTE IT!
BUY WISELY – COOK CAREFULLY – EAT IT ALL
FOLLOW THE NATIONAL WARTIME NUTRITION PROGRAM

PART 2 **WRITING PROJECTS**

Part 2 addresses the following outcomes for first-year composition from the Council of Writing Program Administrators.

RHETORICAL KNOWLEDGE	• Focus on a purpose: • To learn (Ch. 5) • To explore (Ch. 6,7) • To inform (Ch. 8) • To analyze/synthesize (Ch. 9–12) • To persuade (Ch. 13–15) • Respond to the needs of different audiences • Respond appropriately to different kinds of rhetorical situations • Use conventions of format and structure appropriate to the rhetorical situation • Adopt appropriate voice, tone, and level of formality • Understand how genres shape reading and writing (Readings and Thinking Critically activities) • Write in several genres: • Summary and Strong Response (Ch. 5) • Autobiographical Narrative, Literacy Narrative (Ch. 6) • Exploratory Essay, Annotated Bibliography (Ch. 7) • Informative Report, Informative and Surprising Article (Ch. 8) • Empirical Research Report, Scientific Poster (Ch. 9) • Analysis of Two Visual Texts (Ch. 10) • Analysis of a Short Story (Ch. 11) • Synthesis Essay (Ch. 12) • Classical Argument (Ch. 13) • Evaluation Argument (Ch. 14) • Proposal Argument, Advocacy Ad or Poster, Proposal Speech with Visual Aids (Ch. 15)
CRITICAL THINKING, READING, AND WRITING	• Use writing and reading for inquiry, learning, thinking, and communicating (Exploratory activities, For Writing and Discussion activities, Readings, and Thinking Critically activities) • Understand a writing assignment as a series of tasks, including finding, evaluating, analyzing, and synthesizing appropriate primary and secondary sources • Integrate their own ideas with those of others (Ch. 5, Summary/Strong Response; Ch. 7, Exploratory Essay; Ch. 12, Synthesis Essay; Ch. 13–15, Arguments)
PROCESSES	• Be aware that it usually takes multiple drafts to create a successful text • Develop flexible strategies for generating, revising, editing, and proofreading • Understand writing as an open process that permits writers to use later invention and re-thinking to revise their work • Understand the collaborative and social aspects of writing processes (Ch. 9, team-writing; For Writing and Discussion activities, Questions for Peer Review) • Learn to critique their own and others' work (Question for Peer Review) • Learn to balance the advantages of relying on others with the responsibility of doing their part (Ch. 9, team-writing) • Use a variety of technologies to address a range of audiences (Ch. 9, Scientific Poster; Ch. 15, Advocacy Ad, Proposal Speech with Visual Aids)
KNOWLEDGE OF CONVENTIONS	• Develop knowledge of genre conventions ranging from structure and paragraphing to tone and mechanics • Practice appropriate means of documenting their work (Ch. 5, Summary/Strong Response; Ch. 7, Exploratory Essay, Annotated Bibliography; Ch. 9, Empirical Research Report; Ch. 12, Synthesis Essay; Ch. 13–15, Arguments)
COMPOSING IN ELECTRONIC ENVIRONMENTS	• Understand and exploit the differences in the rhetorical strategies and in the affordances available for both print and electronic composing processes and texts (Ch. 8, Desktop-published Article; Ch. 9, Scientific Poster; Ch. 15, Advocacy Ad, Proposal Speech with Visual Aids)

READING RHETORICALLY

The Writer as Strong Reader

5

Many new college students are surprised by the amount, range, and difficulty of reading they have to do in college. Every day they are challenged by reading assignments ranging from scholarly articles and textbooks on complex subject matter to primary sources such as Plato's dialogues or Darwin's *Voyage of the Beagle.*

To interact strongly with challenging texts, you must learn how to read them both with and against the grain. When you read *with the grain* of a text, you see the world through its author's perspective, open yourself to the author's argument, apply the text's insights to new contexts, and connect its ideas to your own experiences and personal knowledge. When you read *against the grain* of a text, you resist it by questioning its points, raising doubts, analyzing the limits of its perspective, or even refuting its argument.

We say that readers read *rhetorically* when they are aware of the effect a text is intended to have on them. Strong rhetorical readers analyze how a text works persuasively and they think critically about whether to enter into or challenge the text's intentions. The two writing projects in this chapter, both of which demand rhetorical reading, introduce you to several of the most common genres of academic writing: the summary, and various kinds of strong response essays, which usually incorporate a summary of the text to which the writer is responding. Thus our goal is to help you become a more powerful reader of academic texts, prepared to take part in the conversations of the disciplines you study.

In this chapter, you will learn to:

- listen carefully to a text, recognize its parts and their functions, and summarize its ideas
- formulate strong responses to texts by interacting with them, either by agreeing with, interrogating, or actively opposing them

Exploring Rhetorical Reading

As an introduction to rhetorical reading, we ask you to imagine that you are investigating different strategies that individual Americans might take to protect the environment. You have come across the 2008 article "Why Bother?" by Michael Pollan in the *New York Times Magazine.* Pollan, a professor of journalism at the

University of California Berkeley's Graduate School of Journalism, is known for his popular books on reforming our food-production system for the benefit of humans, animals, and the environment: *The Omnivore's Dilemma: A Natural History of Four Meals* (2007), *In Defense of Food: An Eater's Manifesto* (2009), and *Food Rules* (2010). Before reading Pollan's article, respond to the following opinion survey, using a 1 to 5 scale, with 1 meaning "strongly agree" and 5 meaning "strongly disagree."

Item	Strongly agree	Agree	Neutral	Disagree	Strongly disagree
1. Global warming is a very serious problem.	1	2	3	4	5
2. Going green in my own lifestyle will have no effect on climate change—the magnitude of the problem is too great.	1	2	3	4	5
3. The only way to make a real difference in climate change is through hugely expensive actions taken by governments and businesses.	1	2	3	4	5
4. The best way to combat global warming is for individual Americans to go green in their own consumer choices.	1	2	3	4	5
5. Environmentally conscious people should change the way they eat.	1	2	3	4	5

When you have finished rating your degree of agreement with these statements, read Pollan's article, using whatever note-taking, underlining, or highlighting strategies you normally use when reading for a class. When you have finished reading, complete the exercises that follow.

Michael Pollan
Why Bother?

1 **Why bother?** That really is the big question facing us as individuals hoping to do something about climate change, and it's not an easy one to answer. I don't know about you, but for me the most upsetting moment in *An Inconvenient Truth* came long after Al Gore scared the hell out of me, constructing an utterly convincing case that the very survival of life on earth as we know it is threatened by climate change. No, the really dark moment came during the closing credits, when we are asked to ... change our light bulbs. That's when it got really depressing. The immense disproportion

between the magnitude of the problem Gore had described and the puniness of what he was asking us to do about it was enough to sink your heart.

2 But the drop-in-the-bucket issue is not the only problem lurking behind the "why bother" question. Let's say I do bother, big time. I turn my life upside-down, start biking to work, plant a big garden, turn down the thermostat so low I need the Jimmy Carter* signature cardigan, forsake the clothes dryer for a laundry line across the yard, trade in the station wagon for a hybrid, get off the beef, go completely local. I could theoretically do all that, but what would be the point when I know full well that halfway around the world there lives my evil twin, some carbon-footprint *doppelgänger* in Shanghai or Chongqing who has just bought his first car (Chinese car ownership is where ours was back in 1918), is eager to swallow every bite of meat I forswear and who's positively itching to replace every last pound of CO2 I'm struggling no longer to emit. So what exactly would I have to show for all my trouble?

3 A sense of personal virtue, you might suggest, somewhat sheepishly. But what good is that when virtue itself is quickly becoming a term of derision? And not just on the editorial pages of the *Wall Street Journal* or on the lips of the vice president,* who famously dismissed energy conservation as a "sign of personal virtue." No, even in the pages of the *New York Times* and the *New Yorker,* it seems the epithet "virtuous," when applied to an act of personal environmental responsibility, may be used only ironically. Tell me: How did it come to pass that virtue—a quality that for most of history has generally been deemed, well, a virtue—became a mark of liberal softheadedness? How peculiar, that doing the right thing by the environment—buying the hybrid, eating like a locavore—should now set you up for the Ed Begley Jr.* treatment.

4 And even if in the face of this derision I decide I am going to bother, there arises the whole vexed question of getting it right. Is eating local or walking to work really going to reduce my carbon footprint? According to one analysis, if walking to work increases your appetite and you consume more meat or milk as a result, walking might actually emit more carbon than driving. A handful of studies have recently suggested that in certain cases under certain conditions, produce from places as far away as New Zealand might account for less carbon than comparable domestic products. True, at least one of these studies was co-written by a representative of agribusiness interests in (surprise!) New Zealand, but even so, they make you wonder. If determining the carbon footprint of food is really this complicated, and I've got to consider not only "food miles" but also whether the food came by ship or truck and how lushly the grass grows in New Zealand, then maybe on second thought I'll just buy the imported chops at Costco, at least until the experts get their footprints sorted out.

5 There are so many stories we can tell ourselves to justify doing nothing, but perhaps the most insidious is that, whatever we do manage to do, it will be too little too late. Climate change is upon us, and it has arrived well ahead of schedule.

*Jimmy Carter was the Democratic president (1977–1981) who supported environmental policies, world peace, and human rights.
*Pollan is referring to Dick Cheney who served as George W. Bush's vice president from 2001–2009.
*Ed Begley, Jr., is a prominent television star who has his own green living reality TV show, *Living with Ed.* Begley has explored such topics as tapping the energy produced by people using exercise equipment.

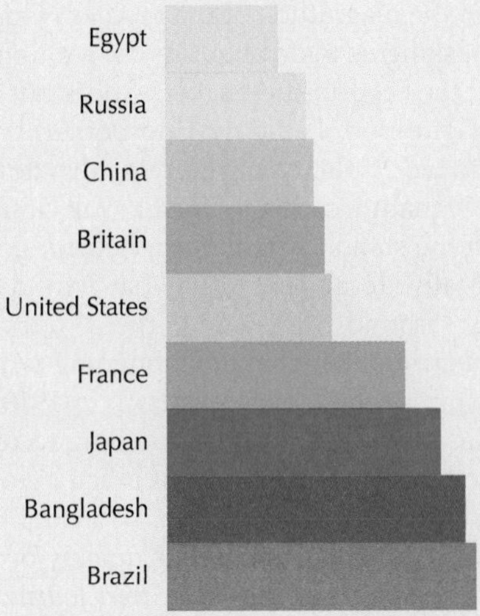

High Anxiety?
Percentage of people by country who view global warming as a "very serious" problem.

Scientists' projections that seemed dire a decade ago turn out to have been unduly optimistic: the warming and the melting is occurring much faster than the models predicted. Now truly terrifying feedback loops threaten to boost the rate of change exponentially, as the shift from white ice to blue water in the Arctic absorbs more sunlight and warming soils everywhere become more biologically active, causing them to release their vast stores of carbon into the air. Have you looked into the eyes
6 of a climate scientist recently? They look really scared.

7 So do you still want to talk about planting gardens?

8 I do.

Whatever we can do as individuals to change the way we live at this suddenly very late date does seem utterly inadequate to the challenge. It's hard to argue with Michael Specter*, in a recent *New Yorker* piece on carbon footprints, when he says: "Personal choices, no matter how virtuous [N.B.!], cannot do enough. It will also take laws and money." So it will. Yet it is no less accurate or hardheaded to say that laws and money cannot do enough, either; that it will also take profound changes in the way we live. Why? Because the climate-change crisis is at its very bottom a crisis of lifestyle—of character, even. The Big Problem is nothing more or less than the sum total of countless little everyday choices, most of them made by us (consumer spending represents 70 percent of our economy), and most of the rest of them made in the
9 name of our needs and desires and preferences.

For us to wait for legislation or technology to solve the problem of how we're living our lives suggests we're not really serious about changing—something our politicians cannot fail to notice. They will not move until we do. Indeed, to look to leaders and experts, to laws and money and grand schemes, to save us from our predicament represents precisely the sort of thinking—passive, delegated, dependent

*Michael Specter is a staff writer for the *New Yorker* and a national science reporter, who has most recently written a book, *Denialism*, about people's refusal to accept scientific evidence.

for solutions on specialists—that helped get us into this mess in the first place. It's hard to believe that the same sort of thinking could now get us out of it.

10 Thirty years ago, Wendell Berry, the Kentucky farmer and writer, put forward a blunt analysis of precisely this mentality. He argued that the environmental crisis of the 1970s—an era innocent of climate change; what we would give to have back *that* environmental crisis!—was at its heart a crisis of character and would have to be addressed first at that level: at home, as it were. He was impatient with people who wrote checks to environmental organizations while thoughtlessly squandering fossil fuel in their everyday lives—the 1970s equivalent of people buying carbon offsets to atone for their Tahoes and Durangos. Nothing was likely to change until we healed the "split between what we think and what we do." For Berry, the "why bother" question came down to a moral imperative: "Once our personal connection to what is wrong becomes clear, then we have to choose: we can go on as before, recognizing our dishonesty and living with it the best we can, or we can begin the effort to change the way we think and live."

11 For Berry, the deep problem standing behind all the other problems of industrial civilization is "specialization," which he regards as the "disease of the modern character." Our society assigns us a tiny number of roles: we're producers (of one thing) at work, consumers of a great many other things the rest of the time, and then once a year or so we vote as citizens. Virtually all of our needs and desires we delegate to specialists of one kind or another—our meals to agribusiness, health to the doctor, education to the teacher, entertainment to the media, care for the environment to the environmentalist, political action to the politician.

12 As Adam Smith and many others have pointed out, this division of labor has given us many of the blessings of civilization. Specialization is what allows me to sit at a computer thinking about climate change. Yet this same division of labor obscures the lines of connection—and responsibility—linking our everyday acts to their real-world consequences, making it easy for me to overlook the coal-fired power plant that is lighting my screen, or the mountaintop in Kentucky that had to be destroyed to provide the coal to that plant, or the streams running crimson with heavy metals as a result.

13 Of course, what made this sort of specialization possible in the first place was cheap energy. Cheap fossil fuel allows us to pay distant others to process our food for us, to entertain us and to (try to) solve our problems, with the result that there is very little we know how to accomplish for ourselves. Think for a moment of all the things you suddenly need to do for yourself when the power goes out—up to and including entertaining yourself. Think, too, about how a power failure causes your neighbors—your community—to suddenly loom so much larger in your life. Cheap energy allowed us to leapfrog community by making it possible to sell our specialty over great distances as well as summon into our lives the specialties of countless distant others.

14 Here's the point: Cheap energy, which gives us climate change, fosters precisely the mentality that makes dealing with climate change in our own lives seem impossibly difficult. Specialists ourselves, we can no longer imagine anyone but an expert, or anything but a new technology or law, solving our problems. Al Gore asks us to change the light bulbs because he probably can't imagine us doing anything much more challenging, like, say, growing some portion of our own food. We can't imagine it, either, which is probably why we prefer to cross our fingers and talk about the

promise of ethanol and nuclear power—new liquids and electrons to power the same old cars and houses and lives.

15 The "cheap-energy mind," as Wendell Berry called it, is the mind that asks, "Why bother?" because it is helpless to imagine—much less attempt—a different sort of life, one less divided, less reliant. Since the cheap-energy mind translates everything into money, its proxy, it prefers to put its faith in market-based solutions—carbon taxes and pollution-trading schemes. If we could just get the incentives right, it believes, the economy will properly value everything that matters and nudge our self-interest down the proper channels. The best we can hope for is a greener version of the old invisible hand. Visible hands it has no use for.

16 But while some such grand scheme may well be necessary, it's doubtful that it will be sufficient or that it will be politically sustainable before we've demonstrated to ourselves that change is possible. Merely to give, to spend, even to vote, is not to do, and there is so much that needs to be done—without further delay. In the judgment of James Hansen, the NASA climate scientist who began sounding the alarm on global warming 20 years ago, we have only 10 years left to start cutting—not just slowing—the amount of carbon we're emitting or face a "different planet." Hansen said this more than two years ago, however; two years have gone by, and nothing of consequence has been done. So: eight years left to go and a great deal left to do.

17 Which brings us back to the "why bother" question and how we might better answer it. The reasons not to bother are many and compelling, at least to the cheap-energy mind. But let me offer a few admittedly tentative reasons that we might put on the other side of the scale:

18 If you do bother, you will set an example for other people. If enough other people bother, each one influencing yet another in a chain reaction of behavioral change, markets for all manner of green products and alternative technologies will prosper and expand. (Just look at the market for hybrid cars.) Consciousness will be raised, perhaps even changed: new moral imperatives and new taboos might take root in the culture. Driving an S.U.V. or eating a 24-ounce steak or illuminating your McMansion like an airport runway at night might come to be regarded as outrages to human conscience. Not having things might become cooler than having them. And those who did change the way they live would acquire the moral standing to demand changes in behavior from others—from other people, other corporations, even other countries.

19 All of this could, theoretically, happen. What I'm describing (imagining would probably be more accurate) is a process of viral social change, and change of this kind, which is nonlinear, is never something anyone can plan or predict or count on. Who knows, maybe the virus will reach all the way to Chongqing and infect my Chinese evil twin. Or not. Maybe going green will prove a passing fad and will lose steam after a few years, just as it did in the 1980s, when Ronald Reagan took down Jimmy Carter's solar panels from the roof of the White House.

20 Going personally green is a bet, nothing more or less, though it's one we probably all should make, even if the odds of it paying off aren't great. Sometimes you have to act as if acting will make a difference, even when you can't prove that it will. That, after all, was precisely what happened in Communist Czechoslovakia and Poland, when a handful of individuals like Václav Havel and Adam Michnik resolved that they would

simply conduct their lives "as if" they lived in a free society. That improbable bet created a tiny space of liberty that, in time, expanded to take in, and then help take down, the whole of the Eastern bloc.

21 So what would be a comparable bet that the individual might make in the case of the environmental crisis? Havel himself has suggested that people begin to "conduct themselves as if they were to live on this earth forever and be answerable for its condition one day." Fair enough, but let me propose a slightly less abstract and daunting wager. The idea is to find one thing to do in your life that doesn't involve spending or voting, that may or may not virally rock the world but is real and particular (as well as symbolic) and that, come what may, will offer its own rewards. Maybe you decide to give up meat, an act that would reduce your carbon footprint by as much as a quarter. Or you could try this: determine to observe the Sabbath. For one day a week, abstain completely from economic activity: no shopping, no driving, no electronics.

22 But the act I want to talk about is growing some—even just a little—of your own food. Rip out your lawn, if you have one, and if you don't—if you live in a high-rise, or have a yard shrouded in shade—look into getting a plot in a community garden. Measured against the Problem We Face, planting a garden sounds pretty benign, I know, but in fact it's one of the most powerful things an individual can do—to reduce your carbon footprint, sure, but more important, to reduce your sense of dependence and dividedness: to change the cheap-energy mind.

23 A great many things happen when you plant a vegetable garden, some of them directly related to climate change, others indirect but related nevertheless. Growing food, we forget, comprises the original solar technology: calories produced by means of photosynthesis. Years ago the cheap-energy mind discovered that more food could be produced with less effort by replacing sunlight with fossil-fuel fertilizers and pesticides, with a result that the typical calorie of food energy in your diet now requires about 10 calories of fossil-fuel energy to produce. It's estimated that the way we feed ourselves (or rather, allow ourselves to be fed) accounts for about a fifth of the greenhouse gas for which each of us is responsible.

24 Yet the sun still shines down on your yard, and photosynthesis still works so abundantly that in a thoughtfully organized vegetable garden (one planted from seed,

nourished by compost from the kitchen and involving not too many drives to the garden center), you can grow the proverbial free lunch—CO2-free and dollar-free. This is the most-local food you can possibly eat (not to mention the freshest, tastiest and most nutritious), with a carbon footprint so faint that even the New Zealand lamb council dares not challenge it. And while we're counting carbon, consider too your compost pile, which shrinks the heap of garbage your household needs trucked away even as it feeds your vegetables and sequesters carbon in your soil. What else? Well, you will probably notice that you're getting a pretty good workout there in your garden, burning calories without having to get into the car to drive to the gym. (It is one of the absurdities of the modern division of labor that, having replaced physical labor with fossil fuel, we now have to burn even more fossil fuel to keep our unemployed bodies in shape.) Also, by engaging both body and mind, time spent in the garden is time (and energy) subtracted from electronic forms of entertainment.

25 You begin to see that growing even a little of your own food is, as Wendell Berry pointed out 30 years ago, one of those solutions that, instead of begetting a new set of problems—the way "solutions" like ethanol or nuclear power inevitably do—actually beget other solutions, and not only of the kind that save carbon. Still more valuable are the habits of mind that growing a little of your own food can yield. You quickly learn that you need not be dependent on specialists to provide for yourself—that your body is still good for something and may actually be enlisted in its own support. If the experts are right, if both oil and time are running out, these are skills and habits of mind we're all very soon going to need. We may also need the food. Could gardens provide it? Well, during World War II, victory gardens supplied as much as 40 percent of the produce Americans ate.

26 **But there are sweeter** reasons to plant that garden, to bother. At least in this one corner of your yard and life, you will have begun to heal the split between what you think and what you do, to commingle your identities as consumer and producer and citizen. Chances are, your garden will re-engage you with your neighbors, for you will have produce to give away and the need to borrow their tools. You will have reduced the power of the cheap-energy mind by personally overcoming its most debilitating weakness: its helplessness and the fact that it can't do much of anything that doesn't involve division or subtraction. The garden's season-long transit from seed to ripe fruit—*will you get a load of that zucchini?!*—suggests that the operations of addition and multiplication still obtain, that the abundance of nature is not exhausted. The single greatest lesson the garden teaches is that our relationship to the planet need not be zero-sum, and that as long as the sun still shines and people still can plan and plant, think and do, we can, if we bother to try, find ways to provide for ourselves without diminishing the world.

THINKING CRITICALLY
about "Why Bother?"

1. In three to four sentences, summarize Pollan's main points.
2. Freewrite a response to this question: In what way has Pollan's article caused me to reconsider one or more of my answers to the opinion survey on page 88?

3. Working in small groups or as a whole class, compare the note-taking strategies you used while reading this piece. (a) How many people wrote marginal notes? How many underlined or highlighted? (b) Compare the contents of these notes. Did people highlight the same passages or different ones? (c) Individually, look at your annotations and highlights and try to decide why you wrote or marked what you did. Share your reasons for making these annotations. The goal of this exercise is to make you more aware of your thinking processes as you read.
4. Working as a whole class or in small groups, share your responses to the questionnaire and to the postreading questions. What were the most insightful or provocative points in this article? To what extent did this article change people's thinking about the value of individual actions or about the impact of our individual lifestyles on climate change? As a result of Pollan's argument, are you more apt to try growing some of your own vegetables either now or in the future?

Understanding Rhetorical Reading

In this section, we explain why college-level reading is often difficult for new students and offer suggestions for improving your reading process based on the reading strategies of experts.

What Makes College-Level Reading Difficult?

The difficulty of college-level reading stems in part from the complexity of new subject matter. Whatever the subject—from international monetary policies to the intricacies of photosynthesis—you have to wrestle with new and complex materials that might perplex anyone. But in addition to the daunting subject matter, several other factors contribute to the difficulty of college-level reading:

- ***Vocabulary.*** Many college-level readings contain unfamiliar technical language such as the economic terms *assets, opportunity costs,* or *export subsidy* or the philosophic terms *hermeneutics* or *Neo-Platonism.* Even nontechnical readings and civic writing for the general public can contain unfamiliar terms. For example, in the Pollan article, the literary term *doppelgänger* or the ecological terms *feedback loops* or *pollution-trading systems* may have given you pause. In academia, words often carry specialized meanings that evoke a whole history of conversation and debate that may be inaccessible, even through a specialized dictionary. Good examples might be *postmodernism, string theory,* or *cultural materialism.* You will not fully understand these terms until you are initiated into the disciplinary conversations that gave rise to them.
- ***Unfamiliar rhetorical context.*** As we explained in Part 1, writers write to an audience for a purpose arising from some motivating occasion. Knowing an author's purpose, occasion, and audience will often clarify confusing parts

of a text. For example, Pollan's article was published in the *New York Times Magazine*, which attracts a liberal, well-educated audience. Pollan assumes that his audience already believes in global warming and takes climate change seriously. In fact, they may be so overwhelmed with the problem that they are ready to give up, shrug, and say, "Why bother?" His purpose is to motivate them to action. A text's internal clues can sometimes help you fill in the rhetorical context, but often you may need to do outside research.

- ***Unfamiliar genre.*** In your college reading, you will encounter a range of genres such as textbooks, trade books, scholarly articles, scientific reports, historical documents, newspaper articles, op-ed pieces, and so forth. Each of these makes different demands on readers and requires a different reading strategy.
- ***Lack of background knowledge.*** Writers necessarily make assumptions about what their readers already know. For example, Pollan makes numerous references to popular culture (Al Gore's *An Inconvenient Truth*; "the Ed Begley Jr. treatment"; "imported chops at Costco") or to general liberal arts knowledge (references to the economist Adam Smith or to the recent history of Communist Czechoslovakia and Poland). The more familiar you are with this cultural background, the more you will understand Pollan's argument on first reading.

FOR WRITING AND DISCUSSION

Appreciating the Importance of Background Knowledge

The importance of background knowledge is easily demonstrated any time you dip into past issues of a newsmagazine or try to read articles about an unfamiliar culture. Consider the following passage from a 1986 *Newsweek* article. How much background knowledge do you need before you can fully comprehend this passage? What cultural knowledge about the United States would a student from Ethiopia or Indonesia need?

> Throughout the NATO countries last week, there were second thoughts about the prospect of a nuclear-free world. For 40 years nuclear weapons have been the backbone of the West's defense. For almost as long American presidents have ritually affirmed their desire to see the world rid of them. Then, suddenly, Ronald Reagan and Mikhail Gorbachev came close to actually doing it. Let's abolish all nuclear ballistic missiles in the next 10 years, Reagan said. Why not all nuclear weapons, countered Gorbachev. OK, the president responded, like a man agreeing to throw in the washer-dryer along with the house.
>
> What if the deal had gone through? On the one hand, Gorbachev would have returned to Moscow a hero. There is a belief in the United States that the Soviets need nuclear arms because nuclear weapons are what make them a superpower. But according to Marxist-Leninist doctrine, capitalism's nuclear capability (unforeseen by Marx and Lenin) is the only thing that can prevent the inevitable triumph of communism. Therefore, an end to nuclear arms would put the engine of history back on its track.
>
> On the other hand, Europeans fear, a nonnuclear United States would be tempted to retreat into neo-isolationism.
>
> —Robert B. Cullen, "Dangers of Disarming," *Newsweek*

Working in small groups or as a class, identify words and passages in this text that depend on background information or knowledge of culture for complete comprehension.

Using the Reading Strategies of Experts

In Chapter 16, we describe the differences between the writing processes of experts and those of beginning college writers. There are parallel differences between the reading processes of experienced and inexperienced readers, especially when they encounter complex materials. In this strategies chart we describe some expert reading strategies that you can begin applying to your reading of any kind of college-level material.

Strategies for Reading Like an Expert

Strategies	What to Do	Comments
Reconstruct the rhetorical context.	Ask questions about purpose, audience, genre, and motivating occasion.	If you read an article that has been anthologized (as in the readings in this textbook), note any information you are given about the author, publication, and genre. Try to reconstruct the author's original motivation for writing.
Take notes.	Make extensive marginal notes as you read.	Expert readers seldom use highlighters, which encourage passive, inefficient reading.
Get in the dictionary habit.	Look up words whose meaning you can't get from context.	If you don't want to interrupt your reading, check off words to look up when you are done.
Match your reading speed to your goals.	Speed up when skimming or scanning for information. Slow down for complete comprehension or detailed analysis.	Robert Sternberg, a cognitive psychologist, discovered that novice readers tend to read everything at about the same pace, no matter what their purpose. Experienced readers know when to slow down or speed up.

(continued)

Strategies	What to Do	Comments
Read a complex text in a "multidraft" way.	Read a text two or three times. The first time, read quickly, skimming ahead rapidly, looking at the opening sentences of paragraphs and at any passages that sum up the writer's argument or clarify the argument's structure. Pay particular attention to the conclusion, which often ties the whole argument together.	Rapid "first-draft reading" helps you see the text's main points and structure, thus providing background for a second reading. Often, experienced readers reread a text two or three times. They hold confusing passages in mental suspension, hoping that later parts of the essay will clarify earlier parts.

Reading with the Grain and Against the Grain

For an explanation of the believing and doubting game, see Chapter 2, Concept 4.

The reading and thinking strategies that we have just described enable skilled readers to interact strongly with texts. Your purpose in using these strategies is to read texts both *with the grain* and *against the grain*, a way of reading that is analogous to the believing and doubting game we introduced in Chapter 2. This concept is so important that we have chosen to highlight it separately here.

When you read with the grain of a text, you practice what psychologist Carl Rogers calls "empathic listening," in which you try to see the world through the author's eyes, role-playing as much as possible the author's intended readers by adopting their beliefs and values and acquiring their background knowledge. Reading with the grain is the main strategy you use when you summarize a text, but it comes into play also when you develop a strong response. When making with-the-grain points, you support the author's thesis with your own arguments and examples, or apply or extend the author's argument in new ways.

When you read against the grain of a text, you question and perhaps even rebut the author's ideas. You are a resistant reader who asks unanticipated questions, pushes back, and reads the text in ways unforeseen by the author. Reading against the grain is a key part of creating a strong response. When you make against-the-grain points, you challenge the author's reasoning, sources, examples, or choices of language. You present alternative lines of reasoning, deny the writer's values, or raise points or specific data that the writer has omitted. Strategies for thinking with the grain and against the grain are shown in the following chart, along with particular occasions when each is helpful.

Strategies for Reading with and Against the Grain

Reading with the Grain	Reading Against the Grain
• Listen to the text, follow the author's reasoning, and withhold judgment.	• Challenge, question, and resist the author's ideas.

Reading with the Grain	Reading Against the Grain
• Try to see the subject and the world from the author's perspective. • Add further support to the author's thesis with your own points and examples. • Apply the author's argument in new ways.	• Point out what the author has left out or overlooked; note what the author has *not* said. • Identify what assumptions, ideas, or facts seem unsupported or inaccurate. • Rebut the author's ideas with counterreasoning and counterexamples.
Occasions When Most Useful	**Occasions When Most Useful**
• In writing summaries, you listen to a text without judgment to identify the main ideas. • In writing analyses, you seek to understand a text to determine points to elaborate on and discuss. • In synthesizing ideas from sources, you determine what ideas to adopt and build on. • In writing arguments, you inhabit an author's viewpoint to deepen your understanding of an issue and to understand alternative views so you can represent them fairly.	• In writing an initial strong response, you determine the ways in which your beliefs, values, and views might be different from the author's. • In writing analyses, you identify limitations in the author's view. • In synthesizing, you determine which ideas to reject, replace, or go beyond. • In writing arguments, you develop refutations and rebuttals to the author's views.

Strong readers develop their ability to read in both ways—with the grain and against the grain. Some readers prefer to separate these approaches by first reading a text with the grain and then rereading it with more against-the-grain resistance. Throughout the rest of this chapter, we show you different ways to apply these strategies in your reading and writing.

Understanding Summary Writing

A **summary** (often called an **abstract**) is a condensed version of a text that extracts and presents main ideas in a way that does justice to the author's intentions. As fairly and objectively as possible, a summary states the main ideas of a longer text, such as an article or even a book. Although the words "summary" and "abstract" are often used interchangeably, the term "abstract" is usually used for a stand-alone summary at the head of a published article. Scholars often present "abstracts" of their own work (that is, a summary of their argument) for publication in a conference program.

Usefulness of Summaries

Students often report later in their academic careers how valuable summary writing skills are. Summary writing fosters a close engagement between you and the text and demonstrates your understanding of it. By forcing you to distinguish between main and subordinate points, summary writing is a valuable tool for improving your reading comprehension. Summary writing is also useful in other ways. For example, summaries at the beginning of articles, in prefaces to books, and on book jackets help readers determine if they want to read the article or book. To participate in conferences, your professors—and perhaps you also—send abstracts of proposed papers to conference committees in hopes of getting the paper accepted for presentation. Engineers and business executives place "executive summaries" at the beginning of proposals of major reports. In the "literature review" section of scientific papers, summaries of previous research are used to demonstrate gaps in knowledge that the present researchers will try to fill. Finally, writing summaries is a particularly important part of research writing, where you often present condensed views of other writers' arguments, either in support of your own view or as alternative views that you are analyzing or responding to.

The Demands that Summary Writing Makes on Writers

Even though summaries are short, they are challenging to write. You must distinguish between the main and subordinate points in a text, and you must provide even coverage of the text. You must also convey clearly the main ideas—ideas that are often complex—in a limited number of words. Often, summaries are written to certain specifications, say, one-tenth of the original article, or 200 words, or 100 words.

One of the biggest challenges of summarizing is framing the summary so that readers can easily tell your own ideas from those of the author you are summarizing. Often, you are incorporating a summary into a piece of writing as a basis of your own analysis or argument, so this distinction is particularly important. You make this distinction by using frequent **attributive tags** (sometimes called "signal phrases") such as "Pollan claims," "according to Pollan," or "Pollan says"; by putting quotation marks around any passages that use the writer's original wording; and by citing the article using the appropriate documentation style. Typically, writers also introduce the summary with appropriate contextual information giving the author's name and perhaps also the title and genre (in research writing, this information is repeated in the "Works Cited" or "References" list). The first sentence of the summary typically presents the main idea or thesis of the entire article. Here is an example summary of the Pollan article using MLA citation and documentation style.

Chapter 21 provides additional instruction in summarizing, paraphrasing, and quoting sources. It also explains how to incorporate sources smoothly into your own writing and avoid plagiarism.

Identification of the article, journal, and author

Gives overview summary of whole article

Summary of "Why Bother?"

In "Why Bother?" published in the *New York Times Magazine*, environmental journalist Michael Pollan asks why, given the magnitude of the climate change problem, any individual should bother to go green, and argues that an individual's actions can bring multiple rewards for individuals, society, and the environment. Explaining that "the warming and the melting" (90) are occurring much faster than earlier models had predicted, Pollan acknowledges the apparent powerlessness of individuals to make a difference. Not only are we uncertain what actions to take to preserve the planet, but we realize that whatever we do will be offset by growing carbon emissions from emerging nations. Our actions will be "too little too late" (89). He asserts that our environmental problem is a "crisis of lifestyle"—"the sum total of countless little everyday choices" (90) made possible by cheap fossil fuel, which has led to our increasingly specialized jobs. Nevertheless, to counteract our practical and moral distance from the environment caused by this specialization, Pollan urges individuals to go green. Although he concedes that "'laws and money'" (90) are necessary, he still believes that individual actions may be influential by setting off a "process of viral social change" (92). A particularly powerful act, he claims, is to convert yards into vegetable gardens. Growing your own vegetables, he argues, will help us overcome "specialization," eat locally, reduce carbon emissions, get healthy exercise, reconnect with neighbors, and restore our relationship with the earth. (227 words)

Attributive tag

Short quotations from article, MLA documentation style; number in parentheses indicates page number of original article where quotation is found

Work Cited

Pollan, Michael. "Why Bother?" *New York Times Magazine* 20 Apr. 2008: 19+. Rpt. in *The Allyn and Bacon Guide to Writing.* John D. Ramage, John C. Bean, and June Johnson. 6th ed. New York: Pearson, 2012. 88–94. Print.

Bibliographic citation for Pollan's article using MLA style. In a formal paper, the "Works Cited" list begins on a new page at the end of the paper.

Note in this example how the use of attributive tags, quotation marks, and citations makes it easy to tell that the writer is summarizing Pollan's ideas rather than presenting his own. Note too the writer's attempt to remain neutral and objective and not to impose his own views. To avoid interjecting your own opinions, you need to choose your verbs in attributive tags carefully. Consider the difference between "Smith argues" and "Smith rants" or between "Brown asserts" and "Brown leaps to the conclusion that. . . . " In each pair, the second verb, by moving beyond neutrality, reveals the writer's judgment of the author's ideas.

In an academic setting, then, think of summaries as short, tightly written pieces that retain an author's main ideas while eliminating the supporting details. In the writing projects for this chapter, we'll explain the strategies you can use to write a good summary. The following chart lists the criteria for incorporating a summary effectively into your own prose.

CRITERIA FOR AN EFFECTIVE SUMMARY INCORPORATED INTO YOUR OWN PROSE

- Represents the original article accurately and fairly.
- Is direct and concise, using words economically.
- Remains objective and neutral, not revealing the writer's own ideas on the subject, but, rather, only the original author's points.
- Gives the original article balanced and proportional coverage.
- Uses the writer's own words to express the original author's ideas.
- Distinguishes the summary writer's ideas from the original author's ideas by using attributive tags (such as "according to Pollan" or "Pollan argues that").
- Uses quotations sparingly, if at all, to present the original author's key terms or to convey the flavor of the original.
- Is a unified, coherent piece of writing in its own right.
- Cites and documents the text the writer is summarizing and any quotations used according to an appropriate documentation system.

FOR WRITING AND DISCUSSION

Determining What Is a Good Summary

This exercise asks you to work with the "Criteria for an Effective Summary Incorporated into Your Own Prose" (above) as you analyze the strengths and weaknesses of three summaries of the same article: "Protect Workers' Rights" by Bruce Raynor, published in the *Washington Post* on September 1, 2003. Imagine three student writers assigned to summarize this editorial in approximately 200 words. The first of the summaries below we have rated as excellent. Read the excellent summary first and then determine how successful the other summaries are.

SUMMARY 1 (AN EXCELLENT SUMMARY OF THE RAYNOR ARTICLE)

In Bruce Raynor's op-ed article "Protect Workers' Rights," originally published in the *Washington Post* on September 1, 2003, union official Raynor argues that workers everywhere are threatened by the current rules of globalization that allow corporations and governments to seek out the cheapest and least regulated labor around the world. Using the example of the Pillowtex Corporation that recently shut down its plant in Kannapolis, North Carolina, he shows how ending manufacturing that has played a long and major role in the economies of towns leaves workers without severance pay, medical insurance, money to pay taxes and mortgages, and other options for employment. According to Raynor, in the last three years, millions of jobs have been lost in all branches of American manufacturing. While policymakers advise these workers to seek education to retool for white-collar jobs, Raynor points out that fields such as telemarketing and the computer industry are also losing millions of jobs. Furthermore, outsourcing has caused a drop in wages in the United States. The same dynamic of jobs moving to countries with cheaper and less stringent safety and health regulation has recently caused Mexican and Bangladeshi workers to lose their jobs to Chinese workers. Raynor concludes with a call to protect the rights of workers everywhere by rewriting the "rules for the global economy" (A25). (214 words)

Work Cited

Raynor, Bruce. "Protect Workers' Rights." *Washington Post* 1 Sept. 2003: A25. Print.

SUMMARY 2

The closing of the Pillowtex Corporation's factories in the United States represents a loss of sixteen textile plants and about 6,500 jobs, according to Bruce Raynor, president of UNITE, a union of textile workers.

The workers left in Kannapolis, North Carolina, former home of one of the largest Pillowtex plants, are experiencing financial problems as they are unable to buy medical insurance, pay their taxes or mortgages or find other jobs.

Raynor argues that the case of the Pillowtex workers is representative of workers in other industries such as metals, papers, and electronics and that "this is the longest decline since the Great Depression" with about three million jobs gone in the last three years.

He then explains that white-collar jobs are not safe either because millions of jobs in telemarketing, claims adjusting, and even government are predicted to go overseas in the next five years. Furthermore, Raynor states that the possibility of outsourcing jobs leads to lowering of wages within the United States, as "outsourcing has forced down hourly wage rates by 10 percent to 40 percent for many U.S. computer consultants" (A25).

However, according to Raynor, the developing countries like Mexico and Bangladesh that have acquired manufacturing jobs are also threatened by countries like China who can offer employees who are willing to work for even lower wages and under worse conditions.

Raynor concludes that "a prosperous economy requires that workers be able to buy the products that they produce" (A25) and that workers everywhere need to be protected. (251 words)

Work Cited

Raynor, Bruce. "Protect Workers' Rights." *Washington Post* 1 Sept. 2003: A25. Print.

SUMMARY 3

In his article "Protect Workers' Rights," Bruce Raynor, president of UNITE, a textile workers' union, criticizes free trade and globalization for taking away workers' jobs. Using the Pillowtex Corporation's closing of its plant in Kannapolis, North Carolina, as his prime example, Raynor claims that outsourcing has destroyed the economy of this town and harmed workers across the United States. Raynor threatens that millions of white-collar jobs are also being lost and going to be lost in the next five years. Raynor complains that the whole national and global economy is falling apart and is going to get worse. He implies that the only solution is to keep jobs here in the United States. He maintains that workers around the world are also suffering when factories are moved from one developing country to another that has even more favorable conditions for the corporations. Raynor naively fails to factor in the role of consumers and the pressures on corporations into his defense of workers' rights. Clearly, Raynor loves unions and hates corporations; he probably fears that he is going to lose his own job soon. (183 words)

Understanding Strong Response Writing

We have said that the summary or abstract is an important academic genre and that summary writing is an essential academic skill. Equally important is strong response writing in which you identify and probe points in a text, sometimes by examining how a piece is written and often by inserting your own ideas into the text's conversation. "Strong response" is an umbrella term that incorporates a wide variety of ways that you can speak back to a text. In all cases, you are called on to do your own critical thinking by generating and asserting your own responses to the text.

In this section we will explain four different genres of strong response writing:

- Rhetorical critique
- Ideas critique
- Reflection
- Blended version of all three of these

Strong Response as Rhetorical Critique

A strong response as **rhetorical critique** analyzes a text's rhetorical strategies and evaluates how effectively the author achieves his or her intended goals. When writing a rhetorical critique, you discuss how a text is constructed, what rhetorical strategies it employs, and how effectively it appeals to *logos*, *ethos*, and *pathos*. In other words, you closely analyze the text itself, giving it the same close attention that an art critic gives a painting, a football coach gives a game video, or a biologist gives a cell formation. The close attention can be with the grain, noting the effectiveness of the text's rhetorical strategies, or against the grain, discussing what is ineffective or problematic about these strategies. Or an analysis might point out both the strengths and weaknesses of the text's rhetorical strategies.

For example, suppose that you are writing a rhetorical critique of an article from a conservative business journal advocating oil exploration in the Arctic National Wildlife Refuge (ANWR). You might analyze the article's rhetorical strategies by asking questions like these:

- How is the argument shaped to appeal to a conservative, business-oriented audience?
- How has the writer's angle of vision influenced the selection of evidence for his or her argument?
- How does the writer make himself or herself seem credible to this audience?

You would also evaluate the *logos* of the argument:

- How sound is the logic of the argument?
- Is the evidence accurate and current?
- What are the underlying assumptions and beliefs on which the argument is based?

Rhetorical critiques are usually closed-form, thesis-driven essays. The essay has a thesis that captures the writer's overall assessment of the text and maps out the specific points that the writer will develop in the analysis. When you are writing a rhetorical critique, your goal is to find a few rhetorical points that you find particularly intriguing, important, or disturbing to discuss and probe. Typically, your analysis zeroes in on some key features that you, the writer, find noteworthy. In the following strategies chart, we suggest the kinds of questions you can ask about a text to construct a rhetorical critique.

Question-Asking Strategies for Writing a Rhetorical Critique

Ask Questions about Any of the Following:	Examples
Audience and purpose: • Who is the intended audience? • What is the writer's purpose? • How well does the text suit its particular audience and purpose?	Examine how Michael Pollan writes to the well-educated audience of the *New York Times Magazine*, who are aware of climate change debates and most likely concerned about the problems ahead. Consider how Pollan writes to move these readers beyond good intentions to action. Examine how the text's structure, language, and evidence support this purpose.
Influence of genre on the shape of the text: • How has the genre affected the author's style, structure, and use of evidence?	Examine how the genre of the feature editorial for a highbrow magazine accounts for the length, structure, and depth of Pollan's argument. Examine how his references to political and intellectual figures (Al Gore, then Vice President Cheney, Adam Smith, Wendell Berry, and so forth) carry weight in this magazine's investigation of contemporary issues.
Author's style: • How do the author's language choices and sentence length and complexity contribute to the impact of the text?	Examine how Pollan's casual and cordial connections with readers (use of "I," "you," and "we"), his urgency, and his use of questions contribute to the article's effect.
Appeal to *logos*, the logic of the argument: • How well has the author created a reasonable, logically structured argument?	Examine how well Pollan uses logical points to support his claim and make his claim persuasive.

(*continued*)

Ask Questions about Any of the Following:	Examples
Use of evidence: • How reputable, relevant, current, sufficient, and representative is the evidence?	Examine how Pollan uses references to scientific articles, newspaper accounts, and his own experiences to develop his points.
Appeal to *ethos* and the credibility of the author: • How well does the author persuade readers that he/she is knowledgeable, reliable, credible, and trustworthy?	Examine how Pollan conveys his knowledge of environmentalism, economics, and social trends. Examine the effects of genre and style in creating this *ethos*. Examine whether this *ethos* is effective for readers who are not familiar with Pollan's other writing, are skeptical of climate change, or are less in tune with environmental activism.
Appeal to *pathos*: • How well does the writer appeal to readers' emotions, sympathies, and values?	Examine how Pollan seeks to tap his audience's values and feelings. Consider how he conveys his familiarity with the everyday choices and decisions facing his readers.
Author's angle of vision: • How much does the author's angle of vision or interpretive filter dominate the text, influencing what is emphasized or omitted?	Examine how Pollan's angle of vision shapes his perspective on climate change, his choice of activist solutions, and his development of solutions. Consider how Pollan's reputation as the author of a number of books on food system reform influences his focus in this argument.

For a rhetorical critique, you would probably not choose all of these questions but would instead select three or four to highlight. Your goal is to make insightful observations about how a text works rhetorically and to support your points with examples and short quotations from the text.

Strong Response as Ideas Critique

A second kind of strong response, the **ideas critique,** focuses on the ideas at stake in the text. Rather than treat the text as an artifact to analyze rhetorically (as in a rhetorical critique), you treat it as a voice in a conversation—one perspective on an issue or one solution to a problem or question. Your strong response examines how the ideas of the original author mesh or conflict with your own. Based on your own critical thinking, personal experiences, and research, to what extent do you agree or disagree with the writer's thesis? A with-the-grain reading of a text would support all or some of the text's ideas, while also supplying additional evidence or extending the argument, perhaps applying it in a new context. An against-the-grain reading would challenge the writer's ideas, point out flaws and holes in the writer's thinking, and provide counterexamples and rebuttals. You might agree with some ideas and disagree with others in the text. In any case, in an ideas critique you speak back to the text from your own experience, background, reading, and thoughtful wrestling with the writer's ideas.

As an example, let's return to the article from the conservative business journal on drilling for oil in the ANWR. For an ideas critique, you would give your own views on oil exploration in the ANWR to support or challenge the writer's views, to raise new questions, and otherwise to add your voice to the ANWR conversation.

- You might supply additional reasons and evidence for drilling.
- You might oppose drilling in the ANWR by providing counterreasoning and counterexamples.
- You might propose some kind of synthesis or middle ground, where you would allow drilling in the ANWR but only under certain conditions.

When you write an ideas critique you are thus joining an important conversation about the actual subject matter of a text. Because much academic and professional writing focuses on finding the best solution to complex problems, this kind of strong response is very common. Usually this genre requires closed-form, thesis-governed prose. The following strategies chart suggests questions you can ask about a text to enter into its conversation of ideas.

Question-Asking Strategies for Writing an Ideas Critique

Questions to Ask	Examples
Where do I agree with this author? (with the grain)	Consider how you might amplify or extend Pollan's ideas. Build on his ideas by discussing examples where you or acquaintances have tried to change your lifestyle to lower carbon emissions. Show how these changes might have inspired others to do so.
What new insights has this text given me? (with the grain)	Explore Pollan's ideas that the environmental crisis is at heart a "crisis of lifestyle" or that specialization leads to a disjuncture between our everyday acts and their environmental consequences. Explore Pollan's argument that individual actions may lead to a social revolution. Think of how your eating habits or relationship to gardens has or could contribute to reform.

(*continued*)

Questions to Ask	Examples
Where do I disagree with this author? (against the grain)	Challenge Pollan's assumptions about the magnitude of the problem. Challenge Pollan's idea that individuals can make a difference. Challenge his assumptions that technological solutions won't work because we still will face a crisis of lifestyle. Challenge the practicality and value of his main solution—growing gardens.
What points has the author overlooked or omitted? (against the grain)	Recognize that Pollan overlooks the constraints that would keep people from gardening. Consider that Pollan chooses not to focus on problems of overpopulation, water shortage, or economic disruption caused by environmentalism.
What new questions or problems has the text raised? (with or against the grain)	Explain how Pollan minimizes the economic impact of environmental action and downplays the role of government and business. Consider how we might need to "change the system" rather than just change ourselves. Consider his apparent lack of interest in technological solutions to the energy crisis.
What are the limitations or consequences of this text? (with or against the grain)	Consider ways that Pollan excludes some of his readers even while reaching out to others. Consider how Pollan, given his books on food and his passion for replacing industrial food production with local food, has written a predictable argument. Consider what new ideas he brings to his readers.

Because critiques of ideas appear in many contexts where writers search for the best solutions to problems, this kind of thinking is essential for academic research. In writing research papers, writers typically follow the template "This other writer has argued A, but I am going to argue B." Often the writer's own view (labeled "B") results from the writer's having wrestled with the views of others. Because this kind of dialectic thinking is so important to academic and professional life, we treat it further in Chapter 7 on exploratory writing, in Chapter 12 on analysis and synthesis, and in Chapter 13 on classical argument. Each of these chapters encourages you to articulate alternative views and respond to them.

Strong Response as Reflection

A third kind of strong response is often called a "reflection" or a "reflection paper." (An instructor might say, for example, "Read Michael Pollan's article on climate change and write a reflection about it.") Generally, a **reflection** is an introspective genre; it invites you to connect the reading to your own personal experiences, beliefs, and values. In a reflection paper, the instructor is particularly interested in how the reading has affected you personally—what memories it has triggered, what personal experiences it relates to, what values and beliefs it has challenged, what dilemmas it poses, and so forth. A **reflection paper** is often more exploratory, open-ended, musing, and tentative than a rhetorical critique or an ideas critique, which is usually closed form and thesis governed.

To illustrate, let's consider how you might write a reflection in response to the article in the conservative business journal on drilling for oil in the ANWR. One approach might be to build a reflection around a personal conflict in values by exploring how the reading creates a personal dilemma:

- You might write about your own wilderness experiences, musing about the importance of nature in your own life.
- But at the same time, you might reflect on the extent to which your own life depends on cheap oil and acknowledge your own reluctance to give up owning a car.

In short, you want pristine nature and the benefits of cheap oil at the same time. Another quite different approach might be to reflect on how this article connects to discussions you are having in your other courses, say, the economic cost of individuals' and companies' going green.. Here are some strategies you can use to generate ideas for a reflective strong response:

Question-Asking Strategies for Writing a Reflective Strong Response

Questions to Ask	Examples
What personal memories or experiences does this text trigger?	Explore how Pollan's article evokes memories of your own frustrations about or successes with "green" living. Have you ever tried to change your habits for environmental reasons? If so, how did you go about doing it? Would your changes have met Berry's and Pollan's criteria for a change of "lifestyle"?
What personal values or beliefs does this text reinforce or challenge?	Explore the extent to which you can or can't identify with Pollan, Al Gore, and others who are proclaiming the seriousness of climate change and advocating changes in lifestyle. To what extent does Pollan as a person of conviction spark your admiration?

(*continued*)

Questions to Ask	Examples
What questions, dilemmas, or problems does this text raise for me?	Explore how Pollan has challenged readers to take actions that may be difficult for them. For instance, you may have arrived at other solutions or know groups or organizations that are contributing positively in other ways. Perhaps Pollan's level of commitment or his particular approach to living green disturbs you in some way.
What new insights, ideas, or thoughts of my own have been stimulated by this text?	Explore any moments of enlightenment you had while reading Pollan. For example, perhaps his focus on individual action rather than on "laws and money" seems problematic to you. Perhaps there are other causes besides the environment that spur you to concern or to action. Perhaps you are now interested in exploring what inspires people to make major changes in how they live.

As you can tell from these questions, a reflective strong response highlights your own personal experiences and beliefs in conversation with the text. Whereas the focus of a rhetorical critique is on analyzing the way the text works rhetorically and the focus of an ideas critique is on taking a stance on the ideas at stake in the text, a reflective response focuses on the personal dimension of reading the text. Reflections call for a degree of self-disclosure or self-exploration that would be largely absent from the other kinds of strong responses.

Strong Response as a Blend

It should be evident that the boundaries among the rhetorical critique, ideas critique, and reflection overlap and that a strong response could easily blend features of each. In trying to decide how to respond strongly to a text, you often don't have to confine yourself to a pure genre but can mix and match different kinds of responses. You can analyze and critique a text's rhetorical strategies, show how the text challenges your own personal values and beliefs, and also develop your own stance on the text's ideas. In writing a blended response, you can emphasize what is most important to you, while not limiting yourself to only one approach.

Before we turn to the writing project for this chapter, we show you an example of a student's summary/strong response that is a blend of rhetorical critique, ideas critique, and personal reflection. Note that the essay begins by conveying the writer's investment in environmental conservation. It then summarizes Pollan's article. Following the summary, the student writer states his thesis, followed by his strong response, which contains both rhetorical points and points engaging Pollan's ideas.

Kyle Madsen (student)

Can a Green Thumb Save the Planet?

A Response to Michael Pollan

When I was a child, our household had one garbage can, in which my family and I would deposit all of our cardboard, plastic, glass, and paper waste. No one on my block had ever heard of recycling or using energy saving bulbs, and we never considered turning down our thermostats during the frozen winters and ice storms that swept our region from November to March. It wasn't that we didn't care about what we were doing to our environment. We just didn't know any better. However, once I got to college all that changed. My university's policies requested that students separate glass bottles and pizza boxes from plastic candy wrappers and old food containers. Thanks in large part to the chilling success of Al Gore's documentary *An Inconvenient Truth,* many of my old neighbors were starting to catch on as well, and now my home town is as devoted to its recycling as any major metropolitan area. Still, even though we as a country have come a long way in just a few years, there is a long way to go. Environmental journalist Michael Pollan in his article "Why Bother?" for the *New York Times Magazine* examines why working to slow the threat of climate change is such a daunting task.

Introduces topic/problem and shows writer's investment in caring for the environment

Identifies Pollan's article and Pollan's purpose

In "Why Bother?" Michael Pollan explores how we have arrived at our current climate change crisis and argues why and how we should try to change our individual actions. Pollan sums up the recent scientific evidence for rapid climate change and then focuses on people's feeling overwhelmed in the face of this vast environmental problem. He presents his interpretation of how we have contributed to the problem and why we feel powerless. Pollan asserts that the climate-change crisis is "the sum total of countless everyday choices" made by consumers globally and that it is "at its very bottom a crisis of lifestyle—of character, even" (90). Our reliance on "cheap fossil fuel" has contributed to both the problem and to our sense of helplessness. In the final part of his article, Pollan concedes that "laws and money" (90) are necessary to create change, but he still advocates acting on our values and setting an example, which might launch a green social revolution. According to Pollan, "The idea is to find one thing to do in your life that does not involve spending or voting ... that will offer its own rewards" (93). He concludes by encouraging readers to plant gardens in order to reduce carbon emissions, to lessen our "sense of dependence and dividedness" (93)—to empower ourselves to contribute positively to our environment.

Summary of Pollan's article

Although Pollan has created an argument with strong logical, ethical, and emotional appeals, his very dominant angle of vision—seen in his assumptions, alarmist language, and exclusive focus on garden-growing—may fail to win neutral readers. I also think Pollan's argument loses impact by not discussing more realistic alternatives such as pursuing smart consumerism and better environmental education for children.

Thesis statement focused on rhetorical points

Second part of thesis focused on ideas critique

Pollan builds a forceful case in his well-argued and knowledgeable interpretation of our climate-change problem as a "crisis of lifestyle—of character, even" (90).

With-the-grain rhetorical point focused on the logos and ethos of Pollan's argument

His frank confrontation of the problem of how to motivate people is compelling, especially when he admits the contrast between "the magnitude of the problem" and the "puniness" of individual action (89). Pollan both deepens his argument and constructs a positive ethos by drawing on the ideas of environmental ethicist Wendell Berry and classical economist Adam Smith to explain how modern civilization has developed through the division of labor (specialization), which has brought us many advantages but also cut us off from community and environmental responsibility. In this part of his argument, Pollan helps readers understand how our dependence on cheap oil and our lifestyle choices have enhanced our roles as limited, specialized producers and major consumers. Pollan's development of his theory of the "cheap-energy mind" (92) and his reasonable support of this idea are the strongest part of his argument and the most relevant to readers like me. I have thought that we have become small cogs in an overbearing machine of consumption and only larger cogs such as the government can have enough influence on the overall system to make change happen. From time to time, I have wondered what I as one person could really do. This sense of insignificance, which Pollan theorizes, has made me wait until my regular light bulbs burned out before considering replacing them with energy-efficient ones.

Brief reflective comment

With-the-grain rhetorical point focused on the pathos of Pollan's argument

Another strength of Pollan's argument is the way he builds bridges to his audience through his appeals to *pathos*. He understands how overwhelmed the average person can feel when confronted with the climate-change problem. Pollan never criticizes his readers for not being as concerned as he is. Instead he engages them in learning with him. He explores with readers the suggestion of walking to work, a task on par with light bulb changing, when he writes, even if "I decide that I am going to bother, there arises the whole vexed question of getting it right. Is eating local or walking to work really going to reduce my carbon footprint?" (89). By asking questions like these, he speaks as a concerned citizen who tries to create a dialogue with his audience about the problem of climate change and what individuals can do.

Against-the-grain rhetorical point focused on angle of vision

However, despite his outreach to readers, Pollan's angle of vision may be too dominant and intense for some readers. He assumes that his *New York Times Magazine* readers already share his agreement with the most serious views of climate change held by many scientists and environmentalists, people who are focusing on the "truly terrifying feedback loops" (90) in weather and climate. He also assumes that his readers hold similar values about local food and gardening. This intense angle of vision may leave out some readers. For example, I am left wondering why gardening is more effective than, say, converting to solar power. He also tries to shock his readers into action with his occasional alarmist or overly dramatic use of language. For example, he tries to invoke fear: "Have you looked into the eyes of a climate scientist recently? They look really scared" (90). However, how many regular people have run-ins with climate scientists?

Transition to ideas critique, an against-the-grain point critiquing Pollan's ideas—Pollan

In addition, after appearing very in tune with readers in the first part of his argument, in the final part he does not address his readers' practical concerns. He describes in great detail the joys of gardening—specifically how it will connect readers not only to the earth, but to friends and neighbors as well—yet he glosses over the amount of work necessary to grow a garden. He writes, "Photosynthesis still works so abundantly that in a thoughtfully organized vegetable garden (one planted from seed, nourished by compost from the kitchen and involving not too many drives to the gardening center), you can grow the proverbial free lunch" (93–4). However, not everyone has a space for a garden or access to a public one to grow tomatoes themselves, and it takes hours of backbreaking labor to grow a productive vegetable garden—hardly a free lunch. Average Americans work upwards of sixty hours per week, so it is unrealistic to expect them to spend their free time working in a garden. In not addressing readers' objections to gardening or suggesting other ways to mend our cheap oil values, I think Pollan proposes simply another situation for semi-concerned individuals to again say, "Why bother?"

doesn't acknowledge the impracticality of expecting people to grow their own vegetables.

Also, besides gardens, I think Pollan could emphasize other avenues of change such as sustainable consumerism. In different places in the article, he mentions that individuals can use their consumer lifestyles to achieve a more sustainable way of life, but he chooses to insist that gardening be the main means. I would have liked him to discuss how we as consumers could buy more fuel-efficient cars, avoid plastic packaging, drink tap water, and buy products from green industries. This "going green" trend has already taken root in many of America's top industries—at least in their advertising and public relations campaigns. We can't leave a Starbucks without inadvertently learning about what they are doing to offset global warming. But we consumers need to know which industries really are going green in a significant way so that we can spend our shopping dollars there. If Pollan is correct, environmentally conscientious consumers can demand a change from the corporations they rely on, so why not use the same consumerism that got us into this mess to get us out?

Another point critiquing Pollan's ideas. Madsen proposes sustainable consumerism as an alternative to gardening.

Besides sustainable consumerism, I think we should emphasize the promotion of better environmental education for our children. Curriculum in K–12 classrooms presented by teachers rather than information from television or newspapers will shape children's commitment to the environment. A good example is the impact of Recycle Now, an organization aimed at implementing recycling and global awareness in schools. According to Dave Lawrie, a curriculum expert featured on their Web site, "Recycling at school is a hands-on way to show pupils that every single person can help to improve the environment. Everyone in our school has played a part in making a difference." With serious education, kids will learn the habits of respecting the earth, working in gardens, and using energy-saving halogen bulbs, making sustainability and environmental stewardship a way of life.

Another point addressing Pollan's ideas—environmental education in the schools as an alternative to gardening.

While Pollan is correct in pushing us into action now, asking Americans to grow a garden, when changing a light bulb seems daunting, is an unrealistic and limited approach. However, Pollan persuasively addresses the underlying issues in our attitudes toward the climate crisis and works to empower readers to become responsible and involved. Whether it be through gardening, supporting green businesses, or education, I agree with Pollan that the important thing is that you learn to bother for yourself.

Short conclusion bringing closure to the essay.

Works Cited

Lawrie, Dave. "Bringing the Curriculum to Life." School Success Stories. *RecycleNow* 11 Nov. 2009. Web. 28 Feb. 2010.

Pollan, Michael. "Why Bother?" *New York Times Magazine* 20 Apr. 2008: 19+. Rpt. in *The Allyn and Bacon Guide to Writing*. John D. Ramage, John C. Bean, and June Johnson. 6th ed. New York: Pearson, 2012. 88–94. Print.

Citation of works cited in the essay using MLA format

In the student example just shown, Kyle Madsen illustrates a blended strong response that includes both a rhetorical critique of the article and some of his own views. He analyzes Pollan's article rhetorically by pointing out both the persuasive features of the argument and the limiting angle of vision of a worried environmentalist and extremely committed gardening enthusiast. He seconds some of Pollan's points with his own examples, but he also reads Pollan against the grain by suggesting how Pollan's word choice and fixation on gardening as a solution prevent him from developing ideas that might seem more compelling to some readers.

WRITING PROJECT

A Summary

Write a summary of an article assigned by your instructor for an audience who has not read the article. Write the summary using attributive tags and providing an introductory context as if you were inserting it into your own longer paper (see the model on p. 100). The word count for your summary will be specified by your instructor. Try to follow all the criteria for a successful summary listed on page 100, and use MLA documentation style, including a Works Cited entry for the article that you are summarizing. (Note: Instead of an article, your instructor may ask you to summarize a longer text such as a book or a visual-verbal text such as a Web page or an advocacy brochure. We address these special cases at the end of this section.)

Generating Ideas: Reading for Structure and Content

Once you have been assigned an article to summarize, your first task is to read it carefully a number of times to get an accurate understanding of it. Remember that summarizing involves the essential act of reading with the grain as you figure out exactly what the article is saying. In writing a summary, you must focus on both a text's structure and its content. In the following steps, we recommend a process that will help you condense a text's ideas into an accurate summary. As you become a more experienced reader and writer, you'll follow these steps without thinking about them.

Step 1: The first time through, read the text fairly quickly for general meaning. If you get confused, keep going; later parts of the text might clarify earlier parts.

Step 2: Read the text carefully paragraph by paragraph. As you read, write gist statements in the margins for each paragraph. A *gist statement* is a brief indication of a paragraph's function in the text or a brief summary of a paragraph's content. Sometimes it is helpful to think of these two kinds of gist statements as "what it does" statements and "what it says" statements.* A "what

*For our treatment of "what it does" and "what it says" statements, we are indebted to Kenneth A. Bruffee, *A Short Course in Writing*, 2nd ed. (Cambridge, MA: Winthrop, 1980).

it does" statement specifies the paragraph's function—for example, "summarizes an opposing view," "introduces another reason," "presents a supporting example," "provides statistical data in support of a point," and so on. A "what it says" statement captures the main idea of a paragraph by summarizing the paragraph's content. The "what it says" statement is the paragraph's main point, in contrast to its supporting ideas and examples.

When you first practice detailed readings of a text, you might find it helpful to write complete *does* and *says* statements on a separate sheet of paper rather than in the margins until you develop the internal habit of appreciating both the function and content of parts of an essay. Here are *does* and *says* statements for selected paragraphs of Michael Pollan's article on climate change activism.

Paragraph 1: *Does*: Introduces the need for environmental action as a current problem that readers know and care about and sets up the argument. ***Says***: We as individuals often wonder if our small, minor actions are worth doing in light of the magnitude of the climate change problem.

Paragraph 2: *Does:* Explores another reason why individuals may doubt whether individual actions could make a difference. ***Says:*** People willing to change their lifestyles to combat climate change may be discouraged by the increase in a carbon-emissions lifestyle in other parts of the world such as China.

Paragraph 8: *Does:* Expresses an alternative view, partially concedes to it, and asserts a counterview. ***Says:*** Although big money and legislation will be important in reversing climate change, the problem at its heart is a "crisis of lifestyle—of character" (90), and therefore will require the effort of individuals.

Paragraph 18: *Does:* Presents and develops one of Pollan's main reasons that concerned individuals should take personal action to fight climate change. ***Says:*** Setting an example through our own good environmental choices could exert moral influence here and abroad, on individuals and big business.

Writing a *says* statement for a paragraph is sometimes difficult. You might have trouble, for example, deciding what the main idea of a paragraph is, especially if the paragraph doesn't begin with a closed-form topic sentence. One way to respond to this problem is to formulate the question that you think the paragraph answers. If you think of chunks of the text as answers to a logical progression of questions, you can often follow the main ideas more easily. Rather than writing *says* statements in the margins, therefore, some readers prefer writing *says* questions. *Says* questions for the Pollan text may include the following:

- What are some of the biggest obstacles that discourage people from undertaking individual actions to fight climate change?
- Despite our excuses not to act, why is individual action still necessary?
- How is the problem of climate a "crisis of lifestyle"?
- What are the reasons we should "bother"?
- Why is growing one's own vegetable garden a particularly powerful individual act?

No matter which method you use—*says* statements or *says* questions—writing gist statements in the margins is far more effective than underlining or highlighting in helping you recall the text's structure and argument.

Step 3: Locate the article's main divisions or parts. In longer closed-form articles, writers often forecast the shape of their essays in their introductions or use their conclusions to sum up main points. For example, Pollan's article uses some forecasting and transitional statements to direct readers through its parts and main points. The article is divided into several main chunks as follows:

- Introductory paragraphs, which establish the problem to be addressed and describe the reasons that people don't take action to help slow climate change (paragraphs 1–5)
- Two short transitional paragraphs (a one-sentence question and a two-word answer) stating the author's intention to call for individual action in spite of the obstacles. These two paragraphs prepare the move into the second part of the article (paragraphs 6 and 7).
- A paragraph conceding to the need for action beyond the individual (laws and money) followed by a counterclaim that the climate change problem is a "crisis of lifestyle" (paragraph 8)
- Eight paragraphs developing Pollan's "crisis of lifestyle" claim, drawing on Wendell Berry and explaining the concepts of specialization and the "cheap-energy mind" that have led us into both the climate change problem and our feelings of inadequacy to tackle it (paragraphs 9–16)
- A transitional paragraph conceding that reasons against individual action are "many and compelling," but proposing better ways to answer the "why bother" question. (paragraph 17)
- Two paragraphs developing Pollan's reasons for individual action—how individuals will influence each other and broader communities and lead to "viral social change" (paragraphs 18–19)
- Two paragraphs elaborating on the possibility of viral social change based on analogy to the end of Communism in Czechoslovakia and Poland and to various ways individuals might make significant changes in their lifestyles (paragraphs 20–21)
- Five paragraphs detailing Pollan's choice for the best solution for people to reduce their carbon emissions and make a significant environmental statement: grow gardens (paragraphs 22–26)

Instead of listing the sections of your article, you might prefer to make an outline or tree diagram of the article showing its main parts.

Drafting and Revising

Once you have determined the main points and grasped the structure of the article you are summarizing, combine and condense your *says* statements into clear sentences that capture the gist of the article. These shortened versions of your *says* statements will make up most of your summary, although you might mention the structure of the article to help organize the points. For example, you might say, "[Author's name] makes four main points in this article. ... The article concludes with a call to action. ... " Because representing an article in your own words in a greatly abbreviated form is a challenge, most writers revise their sentences to find the clearest, most concise way to express the article's ideas accurately. Choose and use your words carefully to stay within your word limit.

The procedures for summarizing articles can work for book-length texts and visual-verbal texts as well. For book-length texts, your *does* and *says* statements may cover chapters or parts of the book. Book introductions and conclusions as well as chapter titles and introductions may provide clues to the author's thesis and subthesis to help you identify the main ideas to include in a book summary. For verbal-visual texts such as a public affairs advocacy ad, product advertisement, Web page, or brochure, examine the parts to see what each contributes to the whole. In your summary, help your readers visualize the images, comprehend the parts, and understand the main points of the text's message.

Plan to create several drafts of all summaries to refine your presentation and wording of ideas. Group work may be helpful in these steps.

FOR WRITING AND DISCUSSION

Finding Key Points in an Article

If the whole class or a group of students is summarizing the same article, brainstorm together and then reach consensus on the main ideas that you think a summary of that article should include to be accurate and complete. Then reread your own summary and check off each idea.

When you revise your summary, consult the criteria on page 102 in this chapter as well as the Questions for Peer Review that follow.

Questions for Peer Review

In addition to the generic peer review questions explained in, Skill 16.4, ask your peer reviewers to address these questions:

1. In what way do the opening sentences provide needed contextual information and then express the overall thesis of the text? What information could be added or more clearly stated?
2. How would you evaluate the writer's representation and coverage of the text's main ideas in terms of accuracy, balance, and proportion? What ideas have been omitted or overemphasized?
3. Has the writer treated the article fairly and neutrally? If judgments have crept in, where could the writer revise?
4. How could the summary use attributive tags more effectively to keep the focus on the original author's ideas?
5. Has the writer used quotations sparingly and cited them accurately? Has the writer translated points into his or her own words? Has the writer included a Works Cited?
6. Where might the writer's choice of words and phrasing of sentences be revised to improve the clarity, conciseness, and coherence of the summary?

WRITING PROJECT

A Summary/Strong Response Essay

In response to a text assigned by your instructor, write a "summary/strong response" essay that incorporates a 150–250-word summary of the article. In your strong response to that reading, speak back to its author from your own critical thinking, personal experience, values, and, perhaps, further reading or research. Unless your instructor assigns a specific kind of strong response (rhetorical critique, ideas critique, or reflection), write a blended response in which you are free to consider the author's rhetorical strategies, your own agreement or disagreement with the author's ideas, and your personal response to the text. Think of your response as your analysis of how the text tries to influence its readers rhetorically and how your wrestling with the text has expanded and deepened your thinking about its ideas. As you work with ideas from the text, remember to use attributive tags, quotation marks for any quoted passages, and MLA documentation to distinguish your own points about the text from the author's ideas and language.

Exploring Ideas for Your Strong Response

Earlier in the chapter we presented the kinds of strong responses you may be asked to write in college. We also provided examples of the questions you can ask to generate ideas for different kinds of strong response. Your goal now is to figure out what you want to say. Your first step, of course, is to read your assigned text with the grain, listening to the text so well that you can write a summary of its argument. Use the strategies described in the previous writing project to compose your summary of the assigned text.

After you have written your summary, which demonstrates your full understanding of the text, you are ready to write a strong response. Because your essay cannot discuss every feature of the text or every idea the text has evoked, you will want to focus on a small group of points that enable you to bring readers a new, enlarged, or deepened understanding of the text. You may decide to write a primarily with-the-grain response, praising, building on, or applying the text to a new context, or a primarily against-the-grain response, challenging, questioning, and refuting the text. If your strong response primarily agrees with the text, you must be sure to extend it and apply the ideas rather than simply make your essay one long summary of the article. If your strong response primarily disagrees with the text and criticizes it, you must be sure to be fair and accurate in your criticisms. Here we give you some specific rereading strategies that will stimulate ideas for your strong response, as well as an example of Kyle Madsen's marginal response notes to Pollan's article (Figure 5.1).

See Chapter 1, Concept 3, for a discussion of audience analysis.

Strategies for Rereading to Stimulate Ideas for a Strong Response

Strategies	What to Do	Comments
Take notes.	Make copious marginal notes while rereading, recording both with-the-grain and against-the-grain responses.	Writing a strong response requires a deep engagement with texts. For example, in Figure 5.1, observe how Kyle Madsen's notes incorporate with-the-grain and against-the-grain responses and show him truly talking back to and interacting with Pollan's text.
Identify "hot spots" in the text.	Mark all hot spots with marginal notes. After you've finished reading, find these hot spots and freewrite your responses to them in a reading journal.	By "hot spot" we mean a quotation or passage that you notice because you agree or disagree with it or because it triggers memories or other associations. Perhaps the hot spot strikes you as thought provoking. Perhaps it raises a problem or is confusing yet suggestive.
Ask questions.	Write several questions that the text caused you to think about. Then explore your responses to those questions through freewriting, which may trigger more questions.	Almost any text triggers questions as you read. A good way to begin formulating a strong response is to note these questions.
Articulate your difference from the intended audience.	Decide who the writer's intended audience is. If you differ significantly from this audience, use this difference to question the author's underlying assumptions, values, and beliefs.	Your gender, age, class, ethnicity, sexual orientation, political and religious beliefs, interests, values, and so forth, may cause you to feel estranged from the author's imagined audience. If the text seems written for straight people and you are gay, or for Christians and you are a Muslim or an atheist, or for environmentalists and you grew up in a small logging community, you may well resist the text. Sometimes your sense of exclusion from the intended audience makes it difficult to read a text at all.

Michael Pollan

Why Bother?

Why bother? That really is the big question facing us as individuals hoping to do something about climate change, and it's not an easy one to answer. I don't know about you, but for me the most upsetting moment in *An Inconvenient Truth* came long after Al Gore scared the hell out of me, constructing an utterly convincing case that the very survival of life on earth as we know it is threatened by climate change. No, the really dark moment came during the closing credits, when we are asked to . . . change our light bulbs. That's when it got really depressing. The immense disproportion between the magnitude of the problem Gore had described and the puniness of what he was asking us to do about it was enough to sink your heart.

This idea is very direct and clear.

Short sentence sounds casual.

Informal speech.

Sounds like Pollan is talking to readers.

How I felt when I saw this film.

But the drop-in-the-bucket issue is not the only problem lurking behind the "why bother" question. Let's say I do bother, big time. I turn my life upside-down, start biking to work, plant a big garden, turn down the thermostat so low I need the Jimmy Carter signature cardigan, forsake the clothes dryer for a laundry line across the yard, trade in the station wagon for a hybrid, get off the beef, go completely local. I could theoretically do all that, but what would be the point when I know full well that halfway around the world there lives my evil twin, some carbon-footprint *doppelgänger* in Shanghai or Chongqing who has just bought his first car (Chinese car ownership is where ours was back in 1918), is eager to swallow every bite of meat I forswear and who's positively itching to replace every last pound of CO_2 I'm struggling no longer to emit. So what exactly would I have to show for all my trouble?

Another very informal statement.

Good word choice? Sounds prejudiced and alarmist.

Helpful examples.

Look up this word.

Exaggerated statement?

A sense of personal virtue, you might suggest, somewhat sheepishly. But what good is that when virtue itself is quickly becoming a term of derision? And not just on the editorial pages of the *Wall Street Journal* or on the lips of the vice president, who famously dismissed energy conservation as a "sign of personal virtue." No, even in the pages of the *New York Times* and the *New Yorker*, it seems the epithet "virtuous," when applied to an act of personal environmental responsibility, may be used only ironically. Tell me: How did it come to pass that virtue—a quality that for most of history has generally been deemed, well, a virtue—became a mark of liberal softheadedness? How peculiar, that doing the right thing by the environment—buying the hybrid, eating like a locavore—should now set you up for the Ed Begley Jr.* treatment.

This paragraph shows Pollan's liberal perspective.

Former Vice President Cheney?

What's the definition of this term?

FIGURE 5.1 Kyle Madsen's Marginal Response Notes

Practicing Strong Response Reading Strategies

FOR WRITING AND DISCUSSION

What follows is a short passage by writer Annie Dillard in response to a question about how she chooses to spend her time. This passage often evokes heated responses from our students.

> I don't do housework. Life is too short. ... I let almost all my indoor plants die from neglect while I was writing the book. There are all kinds of ways to live. You can take your choice. You can keep a tidy house, and when St. Peter asks you what you did with your life, you can say, "I kept a tidy house, I made my own cheese balls."

Individual task: Read the passage and then briefly freewrite your reaction to it.

Group task: Working in groups or as a whole class, develop answers to the following questions:

1. What values does Dillard assume her audience holds?
2. What kinds of readers are apt to feel excluded from that audience?
3. If you are not part of the intended audience for this passage, what in the text evokes resistance?

Articulate Your Own Purpose for Reading

Although you usually read a text because you are joining the author's conversation, you might occasionally read a text for an entirely different purpose from what the author intended. For example, you might read the writings of nineteenth-century scientists to figure out what they assumed about nature (or women, or God, or race, or capitalism). Or suppose that you examine a politician's metaphors to see what they reveal about her values, or analyze *National Geographic* for evidence of political bias. Understanding your own purpose will help you read deeply both with and against the grain.

Writing a Thesis for a Strong Response Essay

A thesis for a strong response essay should map out for readers the points that you want to develop and discuss. These points should be risky and contestable; your thesis should surprise your readers with something new or challenging. Your thesis might focus entirely on with-the-grain points or entirely on against-the-grain points, but most likely it will include some of both. Avoid tensionless thesis statements such as "This article has both good and bad points."

See Chapter 2, Concept 5, for a discussion of surprising thesis statements.

Here are some thesis statements that students have written for strong responses in our classes. Note that each thesis includes at least one point about the rhetorical strategies of the text.

EXAMPLES OF SUMMARY/STRONG RESPONSE THESIS STATEMENTS

- In "The Beauty Myth," Naomi Wolf makes a very good case for her idea that the beauty myth prevents women from ever feeling that they are good enough;

however, Wolf's argument is geared too much toward feminists to be persuasive for a general audience, and she neglects to acknowledge the strong social pressures that I and other men feel to live up to male standards of physical perfection.

- Although Naomi Wolf in "The Beauty Myth" uses rhetorical strategies persuasively to argue that the beauty industry oppresses women, I think that she overlooks women's individual resistance and responsibility.
- Although the images and figures of speech that Thoreau uses in his chapter "Where I Lived, and What I Lived For" from *Walden* wonderfully support his argument that nature is spiritually renewing, I disagree with his antitechnology stance and with his extreme emphasis on isolation as a means to self-discovery.
- In "Where I Lived, and What I Lived For" from *Walden*, Thoreau's argument that society is missing spiritual reality through its preoccupation with details and its frantic pace is convincing, especially to twenty-first century audiences; however, Thoreau weakens his message by criticizing his readers and by completely dismissing technological advances.
- Although the booklet *Compassionate Living* by People for the Ethical Treatment of Animals (PETA) uses the design features of layout, color, and image powerfully, its extreme examples, its quick dismissal of alternative views, and its failure to document the sources of its information weaken its appeal to *ethos* and its overall persuasiveness.

FOR WRITING AND DISCUSSION

Examining Thesis Statements for Strong Response Critiques

Working individually or in groups, identify the points in each of the thesis statements in the preceding section and briefly state them. Think in terms of the ideas you are expecting the writers to develop in the body of the essay. As a follow-up to this exercise, you might share in your groups your own thesis statements for your strong response essays. How clearly does each thesis statement lay out points that the writer will probe? As a group, discuss what new, important perspectives each thesis statement promises to bring to readers and how each thesis suits a rhetorical critique, ideas critique, or some combination of these.

Shaping and Drafting

Most strong response essays call for a short contextualizing introduction to set up your analysis. In the essay on pages 111–113, student writer Kyle Madsen begins by reflecting on personal and societal changes in environmental awareness and then raises the question that Pollan will address: What challenges confront us in changing how we live? Student writer Stephanie Malinowski (pp. 125–127) uses a similar strategy. She begins by tapping into her readers' experiences with outsourcing, and then poses the question that Thomas Friedman addresses in his op-ed piece: Should Americans support or question the practice of outsourcing?

Both student writers introduce the question addressed by the article they are critiquing, and both include a short summary of the article that gives readers a foundation for the critique before they present the points of the article they will address in their strong responses.

Each of the thesis statements in the preceding section as well as Kyle's and Stephanie's thesis statements identifies and maps out two or more points that readers will expect to see developed and explained in the body of the essay. In a closed-form, thesis-driven strong response, readers will also expect the points to follow the order in which they are presented in the thesis. If your strong response is primarily a rhetorical critique, your evidence will come mainly from the text you are analyzing. If your strong response is primarily an ideas critique, your evidence is apt to come from personal knowledge of the issue or from further reading or research. If your strong response is primarily reflective, much of your evidence will be based on your own personal experiences and inner thoughts. A blended response, of course, can combine points from any of these perspectives.

Each point in your thesis calls for a lively discussion, combining general statements and specifics that will encourage readers to see this text your way. Just as you do in your summary, you must use attributive tags to distinguish between the author's ideas and your own points and responses. In addition, you must document all ideas gotten from other sources as well as place all borrowed language in quotation marks or block indentations according to MLA format and include a Works Cited in MLA format. Most strong response essays have short conclusions, just enough commentary to bring closure to the essay.

Revising

In a summary/strong response essay, you may want to work on the summary separately before you incorporate it into your whole essay. Use the peer review questions for summaries (p. 117) for that part of your essay. You will definitely want to get feedback from readers to make your strong response as clear, thorough, and compelling as possible.

Questions for Peer Review

In addition to the generic peer review questions explained in Skill 16.4, ask your peer reviewers to address these questions:

1. How appealingly do the title and introduction of the essay set up the topic of critique, convey the writer's interest, and lay a foundation for the summary of the article and the writer's thesis?
2. How could the writer's thesis statement be clearer in presenting several focused points about the text's rhetorical strategies and ideas?
3. How could the body of the strong response follow the thesis more closely?
4. Where do you, the reader, need more clarification or support for the writer's points? How could the writer develop with-the-grain or against-the-grain points more appropriately?
5. Where could the writer work on the effectiveness of attributive tags, quotations, and documentation?

Readings

The readings for this chapter address the issue of outsourcing, the practice of moving jobs from developed countries like the United States to developing countries, which have a cheaper workforce. This practice affects available jobs for college graduates and American workers as well as the progress and vitality of the economies of many countries. Outsourcing continues to spark fiery debates about job creation and unemployment in the United States, about the distribution of benefits and harm, and about global economic competition. The readings that follow address these points from multiple perspectives. The questions for analysis have been omitted from all but the student essay by Stephanie Malinowski so that you can do your own independent thinking in preparation for writing your own summary/strong response essay.

Our first reading is an op-ed piece by prominent journalist Thomas L. Friedman, published in the *New York Times* on February 29, 2004. Friedman is known for his pro–free trade enthusiasm and his three books on globalization, *The Lexus and the Olive Tree* (1999), *The World Is Flat: A Brief History of the Twenty-First Century* (2005), and *Hot, Flat, and Crowded* (2008).

Thomas L. Friedman

30 Little Turtles

1 Indians are so hospitable. I got an ovation the other day from a roomful of Indian 20-year-olds just for reading perfectly the following paragraph: "A bottle of bottled water held 30 little turtles. It didn't matter that each turtle had to rattle a metal ladle in order to get a little bit of noodles, a total turtle delicacy. The problem was that there were many turtle battles for less than oodles of noodles."

2 I was sitting in on an "accent neutralization" class at the Indian call center 24/7 Customer. The instructor was teaching the would-be Indian call center operators to suppress their native Indian accents and speak with a Canadian one—she teaches British and U.S. accents as well, but these youths will be serving the Canadian market. Since I'm originally from Minnesota, near Canada, and still speak like someone out of the movie "Fargo," I gave these young Indians an authentic rendition of "30 Little Turtles," which is designed to teach them the proper Canadian pronunciations. Hence the rousing applause.

3 Watching these incredibly enthusiastic young Indians preparing for their call center jobs—earnestly trying to soften their t's and roll their r's—is an uplifting experience, especially when you hear from their friends already working these jobs how they have transformed their lives. Most of them still live at home and turn over part of their salaries to their parents, so the whole family benefits. Many have credit cards and have become real consumers, including of U.S. goods, for the first time. All of them seem to have gained self-confidence and self-worth.

4 A lot of these Indian young men and women have college degrees, but would never get a local job that starts at $200 to $300 a month were it not for the call centers. Some do "outbound" calls, selling things from credit cards to phone services to Americans and Europeans. Others deal with "inbound" calls—everything from tracing lost luggage for U.S. airline passengers to solving computer problems for U.S. customers. The calls are transferred here by satellite or fiber optic cable.

5 I was most taken by a young Indian engineer doing tech support for a U.S. software giant, who spoke with pride about how cool it is to tell his friends that he just spent the day helping Americans navigate their software. A majority of these call center workers are young women, who not only have been liberated by earning a decent local wage (and therefore have more choice in whom they marry), but are using the job to get M.B.A.'s and other degrees on the side.

6 I gathered a group together, and here's what they sound like: M. Dinesh, who does tech support, says his day is made when some American calls in with a problem and is actually happy to hear an Indian voice: "They say you people are really good at what you do. I am glad I reached an Indian." Kiran Menon, when asked who his role model was, shot back: "Bill Gates—[I dream of] starting my own company and making it that big." I asked C. M. Meghna what she got most out of the work: "Self-confidence," she said, "a lot of self-confidence, when people come to you with a problem and you can solve it—and having a lot of independence." Because the call center teams work through India's night—which corresponds to America's day—"your biological clock goes haywire," she added. "Besides that, it's great."

7 There is nothing more positive than the self-confidence, dignity and optimism that comes from a society knowing it is producing wealth by tapping its own brains—men's and women's—as opposed to one just tapping its own oil, let alone one that is so lost it can find dignity only through suicide and "martyrdom."

8 Indeed, listening to these Indian young people, I had a déjà vu. Five months ago, I was in Ramallah, on the West Bank, talking to three young Palestinian men, also in their 20's, one of whom was studying engineering. Their hero was Yasir Arafat. They talked about having no hope, no jobs and no dignity, and they each nodded when one of them said they were all "suicide bombers in waiting."

9 What am I saying here? That it's more important for young Indians to have jobs than Americans? Never. But I am saying that there is more to outsourcing than just economics. There's also geopolitics. It is inevitable in a networked world that our economy is going to shed certain low-wage, low-prestige jobs. To the extent that they go to places like India or Pakistan—where they are viewed as high-wage, high-prestige jobs—we make not only a more prosperous world, but a safer world for our own 20-year-olds.

Our second reading is a summary/strong response essay by student writer Stephanie Malinowski in response to the Friedman article. It follows primarily a "rhetorical critique" strategy for the strong response.

Stephanie Malinowski

Questioning Thomas L. Friedman's Optimism in "30 Little Turtles"

1 You are struggling to fix a problem that arises when you are downloading new computer software on to your computer. You're about to give up on the whole thing when an idea hits you: call the software company itself to ask for assistance. Should

you be surprised when the person who answers the phone to help you is based in India? Should Americans support or question outsourcing?

2 In "30 Little Turtles," an op-ed piece that appeared in the *New York Times* on February 29, 2004, journalist and foreign affairs columnist Thomas L. Friedman argues that outsourcing call center jobs from the Western world to India is transforming the lives of Indian workers and benefiting geopolitics. Friedman supports his argument by detailing his experience visiting a call center in India. He claims that the Indians working to serve Canadian and American markets are happy with how their work has improved their lives. Friedman points out that the working Indian women feel liberated now that they are making a decent wage and can afford such things as a college education. He describes Indian workers' view of their jobs, using words such as "self-confidence" and "independence." At the end of his article, Friedman states that he doesn't favor Indian employment over American employment but that outsourced jobs in countries like India or Pakistan create both prosperity and global security. Although Friedman's article clearly conveys to its audience how some Indian workers are benefiting from outsourcing, his argument relies heavily on personal experience and generalizations. I also think his condescending attitude hurts his argument, and he concludes his article too abruptly, leaving readers with questions.

3 Friedman succeeds in portraying the positive side of outsourcing to his *New York Times* readers who may be questioning the rationale for outsourcing. Friedman interviews the recipients of American jobs to see outsourcing from their perspective and enlightens Americans trying to understand how outsourcing is benefiting workers in other countries. Friedman's opening is vivid and captures the readers' interest by detailing his experience inside an Indian call center. He quotes the Indian workers expressing the joys of working for American and Canadian people. These workers testify to the financial and personal gains these jobs have brought. One woman says that she feels good about her job and herself "when people come to you with a problem and you can solve it" (125). The article is so full of optimism that the reader can't help but empathize with the Indians and feel happy that outsourcing has transformed their lives. Through these emotional appeals, Friedman succeeds in making readers who may have big reservations about outsourcing think about the human dimension of outsourcing.

4 However, Friedman also makes large generalizations based on his few personal experiences, lessening the credibility of his article. The first sentence of the article reads, "Indians are so hospitable." So are *all* Indians "so hospitable"? Friedman seems to make this generalization about national character based on the fact that he was applauded by a room full of Indians after reading a tongue twister paragraph in a perfect Canadian accent. I can see why Friedman appreciates his warm reception, but "feel good" moments can hardly provide evidence for the soundness of global economic policies. Friedman generalizes further about what he sees and hears in the call center room. He talks about the Indian employees in these terms: "All of them seem to have gained self-confidence and self-worth" (124). From this single observation, Friedman makes the assumption that almost every Indian working an outsourcing job must be gaining, and that the overall experience has done wonders for their lives. However, other articles that I have read have mentioned that call center work is basically a

deadend job and that $200 a month is not a big salary. Later in his conclusion, Friedman states that "we make not only a more prosperous world, but a safer world for our own 20-year-olds" (125). Can this conclusion be drawn from one visit to a call center where Indians expressed gratitude for their outsourcing work?

5 An even bigger problem with Friedman's article is the condescending way in which he describes the Indian workers. I think he portrays the culture as being incompetent before the American and Canadian outsourcing jobs came to improve their accents and their lives. One statement that conveys condescension is this remark: "Watching these incredibly enthusiastic young Indians preparing for their call center jobs—earnestly trying to soften their t's and roll their r's—is an uplifting experience ... " (124). This passage reminds me of the delight and pride of parents witnessing their children's growth milestones. Friedman is casting the accent neutralization of the Indian workers as overcoming a barrier in order to reach success. Friedman's condescending tone is apparent again when he restates the words of one American caller to an Indian worker, "They say you people are really good at what you do. I am glad I reached an Indian" (125). I see Friedman's reason for including this quote; he wants the reader to know that Indian workers are being valued for their work. However, the words that the American uses, which Friedman deliberately chooses to include in his article, "you people," suggest that Indians are a whole other kind of people different from American workers in their skills. Friedman's condescension also appears when he says that these are "low-wage, low-prestige jobs" (125). This remark is full of problems because it puts down the Indians taking the jobs and the Americans who have lost them, and it misrepresents the outsourcing scene that now includes many highly skilled prestigious jobs.

6 I also think that Friedman weakens his article by concluding abruptly and introducing new ideas to readers that leave them with unanswered questions. Friedman asks the reader, "What am I saying here? That it's more important for young Indians to have jobs than Americans?" (125). This point seems like a relevant question to investigate, but its weakness is that Friedman never even mentions any place in his article the loss that American workers are experiencing. At the end of the article, readers are left with questions. For example, the last sentence reads, "we make not only a more prosperous world, but a safer world for our own 20-year-olds" (125). Although Friedman is implying that outsourcing improves our relationships with other countries and enhances our national safety, nowhere in the article does he substantiate this claim. He seems to have thrown this statement into the conclusion just to end the article on a happy note.

7 Giving a human face to outsourcing is a good idea; however, Friedman does not support his main argument well, and this article comes across as a simplistic, unexplored view of outsourcing. I and other readers are left needing to look for answers to serious questions about outsourcing elsewhere.

Work Cited

Friedman, Thomas L. "30 Little Turtles." *New York Times* 29 Feb. 2004. Rpt. in *The Allyn & Bacon Guide to Writing.* John D. Ramage, John C. Bean, and June Johnson. 6th ed. New York: Pearson, 2012. 124–5. Print.

THINKING CRITICALLY

about "Questioning Thomas L. Friedman's Optimism in '30 Little Turtles'"

1. What rhetorical points has Stephanie Malinowski chosen to analyze in her strong response essay?
2. What examples and quotations from Friedman's article work particularly well as support for her points? Where might she have included more support?
3. Where does Stephanie use attributive tags effectively?
4. If you were to write a rhetorical critique of Friedman's article, what points would you select to analyze?
5. If you were to write an ideas critique, what would you choose to focus on? Where would you agree and disagree with Friedman?

Our third and fourth readings consist of two political cartoons that tell stories about employment and U.S. involvement in outsourcing. As you read these cartoons, identify the characters, the story line, the angle of vision, and the argument each presents.

David Horsey is a two-time Pulitzer Prize winner for editorial cartoons. This cartoon was originally published the *Seattle Post-Intelligencer* on June 4, 2003.

David Horsey

Today's Economic Indicator

The second cartoon, by Mike Lane, appeared in the *Baltimore Sun* in 2003 and was posted on Cagle Cartoons on August 27, 2003. Lane, a prize-winning and well-known liberal editorial cartoonist, left the Baltimore newspaper in 2004 after thirty-two years.

Mike Lane

Labor Day Blues

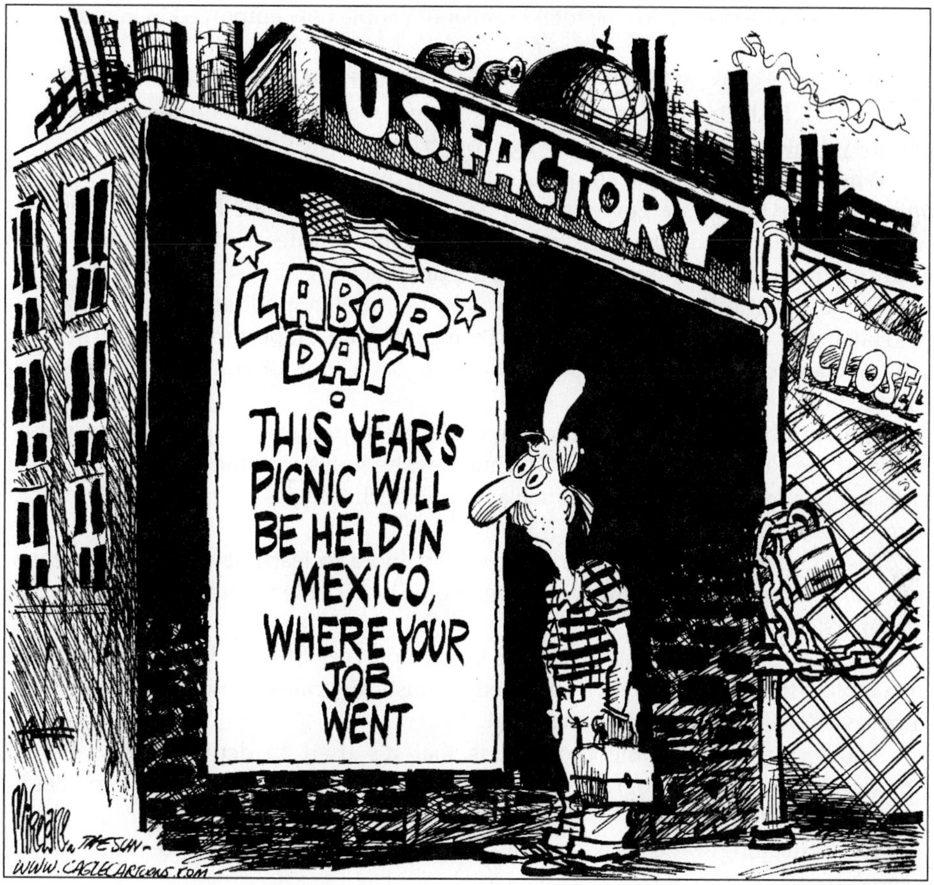

Our fifth reading is an op-ed piece by editorial writer and syndicated columnist Froma Harrop, who writes regularly for the *Providence Journal* and whose columns appear frequently in newspapers around the country. She is known for the articulate, forthright expression of her liberal views on current issues. This piece appeared in the *Seattle Times* on April 17, 2007.

Froma Harrop

New Threat to Skilled U.S. Workers

1 The master plan, it seems, is to move perhaps 40 million high-skill American jobs to other countries. U.S. workers have not been consulted.

2 Princeton economist Alan Blinder predicts that these choice jobs could be lost in a mere decade or two. We speak of computer programming, bookkeeping, graphic design and other careers once thought firmly planted in American soil. For perspective, 40 million is more than twice the total number of people now employed in manufacturing.

3 Blinder was taken aback when, sitting in at the business summit in Davos, Switzerland, he heard U.S. executives talk enthusiastically about all the professional jobs they could outsource to lower-wage countries. And he's a free trader.

4 What America can do to stop this is unclear, but it certainly doesn't have to *speed up* the process through a government program. We refer to the H-1B visa program, which allows educated foreigners to work in the United States, usually for three years. Many in Congress want to nearly double the number of H-1B visas, to 115,000 a year.

5 To the extent that the program helps talented foreign graduates of U.S. universities stay in this country while they await their green cards, it performs a useful service. But for many companies, the visa has become just a tool for transferring American jobs offshore.

6 Ron Hira has studied the dark side of the H-1B program. A professor of public policy at the Rochester Institute of Technology, he notes that the top applicants for visas are outsourcing companies, such as Wipro Technologies of India and Bermuda-based Accenture.

7 The companies bring recruits in from, say, India to learn about American business. After three years here, the workers go home better able to interact with their U.S. customers.

8 In other cases, companies ask their U.S. employees to train H-1B workers who then replace them at lower pay. "This is euphemistically called, 'knowledge transfer,'" Hira says. "I call it 'knowledge extraction.' "

9 Another rap against the program is that it's used to depress the wages of American workers. The program's defenders argue that the law requires companies to pay "the prevailing wage."

10 But "prevailing wage" is a legalism, Hira says. It does not translate into "market wage."

11 The median pay for H-1B computing professionals in fiscal 2005 was $50,000, which means half earn less than that. An American information-technology worker with a bachelor's degree makes more than $50,000 in an entry-level job.

12 Businesses bemoan the alleged shortage of Americans trained to do the work. But wait a second—the law of supply and demand states that a shortage of something causes its price to rise. Wages in information technology have been flat.

13 The companies fret that not enough young Americans are studying science and technology. Well, cutting the pay in those fields isn't much of an incentive, is it?

14 The threat that they will outsource if they can't bring in foreign temps is a hollow one. "There's nothing stopping those companies from working offshore anyway," Hira says. "They're not patriotic."

15 This vision for a competitive America seems to be a few rich U.S. executives commandeering armies of foreign workers. They don't have to train their domestic workforce. They don't have to raise pay to American standards.

16 A provision for revving up the H-1B program is contained in the immigration bill that last year passed the Senate. The co-sponsors, Democrat Ted Kennedy of Massachusetts and Republican John McCain of Arizona, have contended that their legislation requires employers to search for U.S. workers first. It does not.

17 Skilled U.S. workers had better start looking out for their interests. No one else is.

For additional help with writing, reading, and research, go to **www.mycomplab.com**

6 WRITING AN AUTOBIOGRAPHICAL NARRATIVE

This chapter focuses on the rhetorical aim "writing to express or share." Its writing projects ask you to write an autobiographical narrative about something significant in your own life. But rather than state the significance up front in a thesis, you let it unfold in storylike fashion. This narrative structure places autobiographical writing at the open end of the closed-to-open-form continuum, making it more like a nonfiction "short story" than a traditional academic essay. Consequently, many instructors pair this chapter with Chapter 18, which discusses in more detail the features of openform prose.

Autobiographical writing can help us explore, deepen, and complicate our perceptions of the world. In addition to telling stories to convey the complexity and significance of an event, we use stories to reveal something about ourselves. We also use others' stories, particularly during adolescence, to monitor our own growth. Many of us have read the stories of such people as Anne Frank, Maya Angelou, Helen Keller, Malcolm X, and Laura Ingalls Wilder in search of attitudes and behaviors to emulate. Reading their stories becomes a way of critiquing and understanding our own stories.

The writing projects for this chapter address two genres of narrative writing: (1) An **autobiographical narrative** on any significant event or moment in your life that uses the narrative strategies of plot, character, and setting to develop tension, move the story forward, and give it significance, and (2) a **literacy narrative** that uses the same narrative strategies but is centered on the writer's experience with language, reading, writing, school, teachers, or education. Both kinds of narratives draw on the sensibility that you bring to the ordinary as well as the unique events of your life. Good autobiographical narrative does not depend on having an exciting life with highly dramatic moments. On the contrary, some of the most memorable autobiographical and literacy narratives relate ordinary experiences in a vivid manner that shares the writer's humiliations, aspirations, self-discoveries, and revelations. All of us have experienced moments when our world became strange or new—perhaps a first day at a new school or job; a conflict with a parent, teacher, employer, lover, or friend; or an encounter in a lunchroom or on a street corner. Everyone enjoys hearing good writers describe how they coped with and understood these universal situations. It is precisely because readers have experienced these things that they can project themselves easily into the writer's world.

In this chapter, you will learn to:

- find and explore a significant moment in your life and
- write an autobiographical or literacy narrative using literary techniques

Exploring Autobiographical Narrative

One of the premises of this book is that good writing is rooted in the writer's perception of a problem. Problems are at the center not only of thesis-based writing but also of narrative writing. In effective narration, the problem usually takes the form of a *contrary*, two or more things in opposition—ideas, characters, expectations, forces, worldviews, or whatever. Three kinds of contraries that frequently form the plots of autobiographical narratives are the following:

1. ***Old self versus new self.*** The writer perceives changes in himself or herself as a result of some transforming or breakthrough moment or event.
2. ***Old view of person X versus new view of person X.*** The writer's perception of a person (favorite uncle, childhood hero, scary teacher) changes as a result of some revealing moment; the change in the narrator's perception of person X also indicates growth in the narrator's self-perception.
3. ***Old values versus new values that threaten, challenge, or otherwise disrupt the old values.*** The writer confronts an outsider (or a new, unfamiliar situation such as a class or a learning task) that challenges his or her worldview, or the writer undergoes a crisis that creates a conflict in values.

Prior to class discussion, freewrite for ten minutes about episodes in your own life that fit one or more of these typical plots. Then, working in small groups or as a whole class, share your discoveries. Your goal is to begin seeing that each person's life is a rich source of stories.

In considering experiences for a narrative, think of *significant* not as "unusual" or "exciting" but as "revealing" or "conveying an unexpected meaning or insight." Thought of in this way, a significant moment in a story might be a gesture, a remark, a smile, a way of walking or tying a shoe, the wearing of a certain piece of clothing, or the carrying of a certain object in a purse or pocket. Invent a short scene in which a gesture, smile, or brief action reverses one character's feelings about, or understanding of, another character.

1. You thought that Maria had led a sheltered life until ____________________.
2. You thought Mr. Watson was a racist until ____________________________.
3. Marco (Jillian) seemed the perfect date until ___________________________.

In each case, think of specific details about one revealing moment that reverse your understanding. Here is an example of a scene:

> My dad seemed unforgivingly angry at me until he suddenly smiled, turned my baseball cap backward on my head, and held up his open palm for a high five. "Girl, if you don't change your ways, you're going to be as big a high school screw-up as your old man was."

Understanding Autobiographical Writing

Autobiographical writing may include descriptions of places and people and depictions of events that are more entertaining than enlightening. However, the spine of most autobiographical writing is a key moment or event, or a series of key moments or events, that shapes or reveals the author's emerging character or growth in understanding.

Autobiographical Tension: The Opposition of Contraries

Key events in autobiography are characterized by a clash of opposing values or points of view. These oppositions are typically embodied in conflicts between characters or in divided feelings within the narrator. The contraries in a story can often be summed up in statements such as these:

> My best friend from the eighth grade was suddenly an embarrassment in high school.
>
> My parents thought I was too young to drive to the movies when in fact I was ready to ride off with Iggy's Motorcycle Maniacs.
>
> The school I had dreamed of attending turned into a nightmarish prison.
>
> The subject I had hated most in middle school—science—became my passion in high school.
>
> The job that bored me and made all my muscles ache rescued me from a hopeless summer.

Consider the differences between "No Cats in America?" (pp. 148–149) and "The Stolen Watch" (pp. 496–497).

An autobiographical piece without tension is like an academic piece without a problem or a surprising thesis. No writing is more tedious than a pointless "So what?" narrative that rambles on without tension. (You can read such a narrative in our discussion of the difference between a "story" and an "*and then* chronology" in Chapter 18. It is a good example of what *not* to do for this assignment.)

Like the risky thesis statement in closed-form writing, contrariety, or opposition, creates purpose and focus for open-form writing. It functions as an organizing principle, helping the writer determine what to include or omit. It also sets a direction for the writer. When a story is tightly wound and all the details contribute to the story line, the tension moves the plot forward as a mainspring moves the hands of a watch. The tension is typically resolved when the narrator experiences a moment of recognition or insight, vanquishes or is vanquished by a foe, or changes status.

How Literary Elements Work in Autobiographical Narratives

The basic elements of a literary narrative that work together to create a story are plot, character, setting, and theme.

The Importance of Plot By *plot* we mean the basic action of the story, including the selection and sequencing of scenes and events. Often stories don't open with the earliest chronological moment; they may start *in medias res* ("in the middle of things") at a moment of crisis and then flash backward to fill in earlier details that explain the origins of the crisis. What you choose to include in your story and where you place it are concerns of plot. The amount of detail you choose to devote to each scene is also a function of plot. How a writer varies the amount of detail in each scene is referred to as a plot's *pacing*.

Plots typically unfold in the following stages: (a) an arresting opening scene; (b) the introduction of characters and the filling in of background;

(c) the building of tension or conflict through oppositions embedded in a series of events or scenes; (d) the climax or pivotal moment when the tension or conflict comes to a head; and (e) reflection on the events of the plot and their meaning.

To help you recognize story-worthy events in your own life, consider the following list of pivotal moments that have figured in numerous autobiographical narratives:

- Moments of enlightenment or coming to knowledge
- Passages from one realm to the next: from innocence to experience, from outsider to insider or vice versa, from novice to expert, from what you once were to what you now are
- Confrontation with the unknown
- Moments of crisis or critical choice
- Problems maintaining relationships without compromising your own growth or denying your own needs
- Problems accepting limitations and necessities
- Contrasts between common wisdom and your own unique knowledge or experience:

The Importance of Character Which characters from your life will you choose to include in your autobiography? The answer to that question depends on the nature of the tension that moves your story forward. Characters who contribute significantly to that tension or who represent some aspect of that tension with special clarity belong in your story. Whatever the source of tension in a story, a writer typically chooses characters who exemplify the narrator's fears and desires or who forward or frustrate the narrator's growth in a significant way.

Sometimes writers develop characters not through description and sensory detail but through dialogue. Particularly if a story involves conflict between people, dialogue is a powerful means of letting the reader experience that conflict directly. The following piece of dialogue, taken from African-American writer Richard Wright's classic autobiography *Black Boy,* demonstrates how a skilled writer can let dialogue tell the story, without resorting to analysis and abstraction. In the following scene, young Wright approaches a librarian in an attempt to get a book by Baltimore author and journalist H. L. Mencken from a whites-only public library. He has forged a note and borrowed a library card from a sympathetic white coworker and is pretending to borrow the book in his coworker's name.

> "What do you want, boy?"
>
> As though I did not possess the power of speech, I stepped forward and simply handed her the forged note, not parting my lips.
>
> "What books by Mencken does he want?" she asked.
>
> "I don't know ma'am," I said avoiding her eyes.
>
> "Who gave you this card?"
>
> "Mr. Falk," I said.
>
> "Where is he?"

"He's at work, at the M— Optical Company," I said. "I've been in here for him before."

"I remember," the woman said. "But he never wrote notes like this."

Oh, God, she's suspicious. Perhaps she would not let me have the books? If she had turned her back at that moment, I would have ducked out the door and never gone back. Then I thought of a bold idea.

"You can call him up, ma'am," I said, my heart pounding.

"You're not using these books are you?" she asked pointedly.

"Oh no ma'am. I can't read."

"I don't know what he wants by Mencken," she said under her breath.

I knew I had won; she was thinking of other things and the race question had gone out of her mind.

—Richard Wright, *Black Boy*

It's one thing to hear *about* racial prejudice and discrimination; it's another thing to *hear* it directly through dialogue such as this. In just one hundred or so words of conversation, Wright communicates the anguish and humiliation of being a "black boy" in the United States in the 1920s.

Another way to develop a character is to present a sequence of moments or scenes that reveal a variety of behaviors and moods. Imagine taking ten photographs of your character to represent his or her complexity and variety and then arranging them in a collage.

The Importance of Setting Elements of setting are selected as characters are selected, according to how much they help readers understand the conflict or tension that drives the story. When you write about yourself, what you notice in the external world often reflects your inner world. In some moods you are apt to notice the expansive lawn, beautiful flowers, and swimming ducks in the city park; in other moods you might note the litter of paper cups, the blight on the roses, and the scum on the duck pond. The setting typically relates thematically to the other elements of a story. In "No Cats in America?" (pp. 148–149), for example, the author contrasts his parents' parties in the Philippines, replete with music and dancing, firecrackers, a mahjong gambling room, and exotic food and drink such as homemade mango juice and coconut milk, with the American school lunchroom where he opened his Tupperware lunchbox filled with fish and bagoong. The contrast of these settings, especially when the author's American classmates laugh at his lunch, embodies the story's tension.

FOR WRITING AND DISCUSSION

Capturing a Setting

In writing an autobiographical narrative, one of the challenges is to use words to capture scenes so vividly that readers can see in their own minds what you are describing and can share in your experience vicariously. The four photos in Figures 6.1 through 6.4 depict four common scenes: a wooded stream, a city street, an elementary school classroom, and an amusement ride at a fair. For this

FIGURE 6.1 A Wooded Stream

FIGURE 6.2 A City Street

FIGURE 6.3 An Elementary School Classroom

FIGURE 6.4 Amusement Ride at a Fair

exercise, choose one of these photos, and imagine a scene from your own life that might have taken place there.

Your goal in this exercise is to freewrite a vivid description of a setting, imagining that you are there. Describe the setting fully. What do you see? Hear? Smell? Once you have described the setting, imagine several characters entering this location and what conflict might play out. Try writing a short scene that portrays some tension. Then share your descriptions with your classmates, discussing how your settings might be used in an autobiographical narrative.

The Importance of Theme The word *theme* is difficult to define. Themes, like thesis statements, organize the other elements of the essay. But a theme is seldom stated explicitly and is never proved with reasons and factual evidence. Readers ponder—even argue about—themes, and often different readers are affected very differently by the same theme. Some literary critics view theme as simply a different way of thinking about plot. To use a phrase from critic Northrop Frye, a plot is "what happened" in a story, whereas the theme is "what happens" over and over again in this story and others like it. To illustrate this distinction, we summarize student writer Patrick José's autobiographical narrative "No Cats in America?", one of the essays in the Readings section of this chapter, from a plot perspective and from a theme perspective:

José's essay is on pp. 148–149.

> **Plot Perspective** It's the story of a Filipino boy who emigrates with his family from the Philippines to the United States when he is in the eighth grade. On the first day of school, he is humiliated when classmates snicker at the lunch his mother packed for him. Feeling more and more alienated each day, he eventually proclaims, "I hate being Filipino!"
>
> **Theme Perspective** It's the story of how personal identity is threatened when people are suddenly removed from their own cultures and immersed into new ones that don't understand or respect difference. The story reveals the psychic damage of cultural dislocation.

As you can see, the thematic summary goes beyond the events of the story to point toward the larger significance of those events. Although you may choose not to state your theme directly for your readers, you need to understand that theme to organize your story. This understanding usually precedes and guides your decisions about what events and characters to include, what details and dialogue to use, and what elements of setting to describe. But sometimes you need to reverse the process and start out with events and characters that, for whatever reason, force themselves on you, and then figure out your theme after you've written for a while. In other words, theme may be something you discover as you write.

WRITING PROJECT

Autobiographical Narrative

> Write a narrative essay about something significant in your life using the literary strategies of plot, character, and setting. Develop your story through the use of contraries, creating tension that moves the story forward and gives it significance. You can discuss the significance of your story explicitly, perhaps as a revelation, or you can imply it. (The readings at the end of this chapter illustrate different options.) Use specific details and develop contraries that create tension.

This assignment calls for a story. In Chapter 18, we argue that narrative qualifies as a story only when it depicts a series of connected events that create for the reader a sense of tension or conflict that is resolved through a new understanding or change in status. Your goal for this assignment is to write a story about your life that fulfills these criteria. The suggestions that follow will help you.

Generating and Exploring Ideas

Choosing a Plot

For some of you, identifying a plot—a significant moment or insight arising out of contrariety—will present little problem; perhaps you have already settled on an idea that you generated in one of the class discussion exercises earlier in this chapter. However, if you are still searching for a plot idea, you may find the following list helpful:

- A time when you took some sort of test that conferred new status on you (Red Cross lifesaving exam, driver's test, SAT, important school- or work-related test, entrance exam, team tryout). If you failed, what did you learn from it or how did it shape you? If you succeeded, did the new status turn out to be as important as you had expected it to be?
- A situation in which your normal assumptions about life were challenged (an encounter with a foreign culture, a time when a person you'd stereotyped surprised you).
- A situation in which you didn't fit or fulfill others' expectations of you, or a situation in which you were acknowledged as a leader or exceeded others' expectations of you (call to jury duty, assignment to a new committee, being placed in charge of an unfamiliar project).
- A time when a person who mattered to you (parent, spouse, romantic interest, authority figure) rejected you or let you down, or a time when you rejected or let down someone who cared for you.
- A time when you were irresponsible or violated a principle or law and thereby caused others pain (you shoplifted or drank when underage and were caught, you failed to look after someone entrusted to your care).
- A time when you were criticized unjustly or given a punishment you didn't deserve (you were accused of plagiarizing a paper that you'd written, you were blamed unjustly for a problem at work).

Shaping and Drafting Your Narrative

Once you've identified an event about which you'd like to write, you need to develop ways to show readers what makes that event particularly story-worthy. In thinking about the event, consider the following questions:

HOW TO START

- What are the major contraries or tensions in this story?
- What events and scenes portraying these contraries might you include in your narrative?

- What insights or meaning do you think your story suggests? How would you articulate for yourself the theme of your narrative?
- How might you begin your narrative?

HOW TO THINK ABOUT AND DEVELOP CHARACTERS AND SETTING

- What characters are important in this story?
- How will you portray them—through description, action, dialogue?
- What settings or scenes can you re-create for readers?
- What particulars or physical details will make the setting, characters, and conflicts vivid and memorable?

HOW TO THINK ABOUT AND DEVELOP THE PLOT OF YOUR NARRATIVE

- How might you arrange the scenes in your story?
- What would be the climax, the pivotal moment of decision or insight?

HOW TO CONCLUDE YOUR NARRATIVE

- What resolution can you bring to the tensions and conflicts in your story?
- How can you convey the significance of your story? What will make it something readers can relate to?
- How can the ending of your narrative leave readers thinking about larger human issues and concerns?

When stuck, writers often work their way into a narrative by describing in detail a vividly recalled scene, person, or object. You may not be able to include all the descriptive material, but in the act of writing exhaustively about this one element, the rest of the story may begin to unfold for you, and forgotten items and incidents may resurface. In the course of describing scenes and characters, you will probably also begin reflecting on the significance of what you are saying. Try freewriting answers to such questions as "Why is this important?" and "What am I trying to do here?" Then continue with your rough draft. Remember that it is the storyteller's job to put readers into the story by providing enough detail and context for the readers to see why the event is significant.

Revising

Testing your narrative out on other readers can give you valuable feedback about your effectiveness in grabbing and holding their interest and conveying an insight. Plan to write several drafts of your narrative.

Questions for Peer Review

In addition to the generic peer review questions explained in Skill 16.4, ask your peer reviewers to address these questions:

OPENING AND PLOT

1. How could the title and opening paragraphs more effectively hook readers' interest and prepare them for the story to follow?
2. How might the writer improve the tension, structure, or pacing of the scenes?
3. How could the writer improve the connections between scenes or use a different organization such as a collage of scenes or flashbacks to enhance the clarity or drama of the narrative?

CHARACTERIZATION

4. Where might the writer provide more information about characters or describe them more fully?
5. Where might the writer use dialogue more effectively to reveal character?

SETTING, THEME, AND LANGUAGE

6. How might the writer make the setting more vivid and connected to the action and significance of the story?
7. What insight or revelation do you get from this story? How could the narrative's thematic significance be made more memorable or powerful?
8. Where do you find examples of specific language? Where could the writer use more concrete language?

Literacy Narrative

WRITING PROJECT

Write an autobiographical narrative that focuses on your experiences with language, reading, writing, or education. You could explore positive or negative experiences in learning to read or write, breakthrough moments in your development as a literate person, or some educational experiences that have shaped your identity as a person or student. Incorporate the literary elements of plot, character, setting, theme, and descriptive language in the telling of your story. Think of your task as finding new significance for yourself in these experiences and sharing your discoveries with your readers in ways that hold their interest and bring them new understanding.

What Is a Literacy Narrative?

A literacy narrative uses the elements of a story to recount a writer's personal experience with language in all its forms—reading and writing, acquiring a second language, being an insider or outsider based on literacy level and cultural context—or with learning how to learn in general through experiences inside and outside of school. The academic and public fascination with literacy narratives has grown out of—and contributed to—contemporary discussions about cultural diversity in the United States and the connections between literacy and cultural power.

Literacy narratives are a frequently encountered and important genre. For example, one of the most famous literacy narratives is by Frederick Douglass, the ex-slave and abolitionist leader who describes learning to read and write as the key to his liberation from slavery. Another well-known literacy narrative is by Zitkala-Ša (Gertrude Bonnin), a Native American woman who exposes the forceful assimilation tactics employed by missionary schools to separate Native American children from their tribes in the late nineteenth and early twentieth centuries. Perhaps the most famous literacy narrative is by Helen Keller, who recounts the moments when an understanding of language broke through the isolation created by her blindness and deafness. More recently, literacy narratives by immigrants from many cultures have explored the role of education in thwarting or encouraging their integration into American society.

Writing a literacy narrative in college classes can help students explore their adjustment to college, link their earlier learning experiences to the literacy demands of college courses, and take ownership of their own education. Thinking about your own literacy experiences compels you to ponder your educational path and your own ideas of the purpose of education. In contemplating the way that ethnic, economic, gender, class, and regional considerations have shaped your own learning to read and write, you will experience the pleasure of self-discovery and cultural insight.

Typical Features of a Literacy Narrative

Literacy narratives resemble other autobiographical narratives in their open-form structure and their inclusion of some or all of these literary features: a plot built on some tensions and presented as well-sequenced scenes, vivid descriptions of settings, well-drawn characters, dialogue, and theme. Like other autobiographical narratives, literacy narratives rely on vivid, concrete language to make settings and dramatic moments come alive for readers. While literacy narratives share many elements with other autobiographical narratives, they differ in their attention to the following features:

DISTINCTIVE FEATURES OF LITERACY NARRATIVES

- A focus on a writer's experience with language, reading, writing, schooling, teachers, or some other important aspect of education.
- A focus on bringing an insight about the significance of learning, language, reading, or writing to readers through an implied theme (although this theme might be explicitly stated, most likely at the end of the narrative).
- A focus on engaging readers and connecting them to an understanding of the writer's educational/learning experience, prompting them to think about their own educational experiences and larger questions about the purpose and value of education.

FOR WRITING AND DISCUSSION

Analyzing Features of Literacy Narratives

Read the following passages that depict key moments in two students' literacy experiences, and answer the questions about them that direct your attention to specific features.

EXCERPT FROM MEGAN LACY'S LITERACY NARRATIVE

... I was placed in the remedial reading group. Our books had red plastic covers while the other kids had books with yellow covers that looked gold to me. When it was reading time, the rest of the red group and I congregated around a rectangular wood table where Mrs. Hinckley would direct each of us to read a passage from the story aloud. The first time this happened, my stomach dropped. Even the remedial kids were sounding out the words, but I had no idea what those symbols on the page meant.

When my turn came, I muttered meekly, "I can't. ... "

"Don't say 'can't' in my classroom!" Mrs. Hinckley snapped. Then, more gently, she said, "Just sound it out. ... "

I did as she recommended and could hardly believe what was happening. I was reading. I felt superhuman with such a power. After that moment, I read to my mom every night. ...

EXCERPT FROM JEFFREY CAIN'S LITERACY NARRATIVE

In the Walla Walla Public Library, I remember the tomato soup colored carpet, the bad oil paintings of pioneers fording the Columbia River, the musty smell, the oak card catalog with brass knobs, the position of the clock when I first read Jerzi Kosinski's *The Painted Bird.*

"Just read it," my sister-in-law said. "I know you don't read much fiction, but just read this one," she pleaded

Reluctantly, at first, I turned the pages. But each word covertly seduced me; slowly the odyssey of the dark-skinned gypsy affected my spirit like an exotic opiate, until Lehki's painted bird lay pecked to death on the ground. The image haunted my conscience for days. During some of my more restless nights, I was chased like the characters by Nazis through the Black Forest.

Who was this Kosinski? Why did his book affect me this way? How and why did he write like this? Did all writers write like Kosinski?

The novel incited a series of questions that forced me to begin writing notes and summarizing my thoughts. I began a reading journal and my development as a writer shadowed my habits as a reader. ...

1. What literacy experiences have Megan and Jeffrey chosen to focus on?
2. How do Megan and Jeffrey use the narrative elements of plot, setting, and concrete, specific language to involve their readers in their experiences?
3. Based on these excerpts, how would you articulate the theme of each piece?
4. What educational memories of your own are triggered by these excerpts?

Generating and Exploring Ideas

Many of the questions for generating and exploring ideas for the autobiographical narrative (pp. 139–140) apply equally to literacy narratives. To discover ideas that you could fruitfully explore in your literacy narrative, try asking yourself the following questions:

- ***Questions about your experiences with reading and writing*** (obstacles you encountered and perhaps overcame; particularly vivid memories; role of literacy in your self-identity; ways you have changed or grown)
- ***Questions about adjusting to college or educational challenges*** (unexpected problems with reading and writing encountered in college, or earlier in middle school or high school; discovery of holes or weaknesses in your education; educational issues related to your "difference"—ethnic, class, physical/mental, sexual orientation—from the norm)
- ***Questions about your experiences with language*** (issues arising from learning a second language; from being bilingual; from speaking a nonstandard dialect; from having a speech or hearing impairment or a learning disability; from preferring math or art or athletics or video games rather than reading and writing)
- ***Questions about influential (or inhibiting) teachers or mentors*** (influence of people who have helped or hindered your literacy development; people who have changed your view of yourself as a reader or writer)
- ***Questions about literacy and social status or citizenship*** (issues connected to literacy and cultural power or economic success; role of education in preparing you for local, national, or global citizenship).

FOR WRITING AND DISCUSSION

Discovering Experiences with Literacy

Using one or more of the preceding question areas to trigger ideas, freewrite about some of your literacy experiences. Try to identify moments in your life—in the form of scenes that you could describe using the story elements of plot, dialogue, and setting—that might engage readers. What themes about literacy might these scenes uncover? What is at stake?

Shaping and Drafting Your Literacy Narrative

The following questions, which apply the contraries listed on page 133 (old self versus new self, old view of a person versus new view of person, and old values versus new, threatening, or challenging values), can help you shape your narrative in terms of tensions, scenes, and unfolding story.

- Can you portray your literacy experience in terms of a breakthrough or transforming moment that created a new sense of yourself as a reader, writer, or learner?
- Can you depict your literacy experience in terms of your relationship to a teacher or mentor who helped you or hindered you and led to a new view of this person?

- Can you depict your literacy experience as a conflict of values or as a process of change from one way of regarding literacy to another way? What will your readers understand, in terms of what you most value, by reading your literacy narrative?

While some literacy narratives will follow a clear chronological pattern or a tightly connected scene sequence, others may assume the pattern of a collage or a series of snapshots of key moments in your development. Your challenge is to find what pattern best fits the story you want to tell. Note how in her literacy narrative on pages 150–152, student writer Stephanie Whipple builds her literacy narrative around two contrasting scenes.

Revising

In writing about experiences that are very close to you, it is particularly important to get responses from readers. Your readers can help you determine how effectively you are capturing and holding their attention and conveying the significance behind your experiences.

Questions for Peer Review

The peer review questions for the autobiographical narrative (pp. 140–141) apply equally well to the literacy narrative. In addition, you can ask your peer reviewers the following questions, which focus specifically on the literacy narrative:

- What insight, revelation, or new understanding about the importance of reading, writing, or education does this narrative offer you?
- How can the narrative's thematic point about literacy be made more memorable or powerful?

Readings

Our first reading is by Kris Saknussemm, a poet and fiction writer. He is the author of the dystopian, futuristic novel Zanesville (2005), and his poems and short stories have appeared in literary magazines around the country, including *The Boston Review, New Letters, The Antioch Review,* and *ZYZZYVA*. This selection is taken from his autobiographical work in progress.

Kris Saknussemm

Phantom Limb Pain

1 When I was thirteen my sole purpose was to shed my baby fat and become the star halfback on our football team. That meant beating out Miller King, the best athlete at my school. He was my neighbor and that mythic kid we all know—the one who's forever better than we are—the person we want to be.

2 Football practice started in September and all summer long I worked out. I ordered a set of barbells that came with complimentary brochures with titles like "How to Develop a He-Man Voice." Every morning before sunrise I lumbered around our neighborhood wearing ankle weights loaded with sand. I taught myself how to do Marine push-ups and carried my football everywhere so I'd learn not to fumble. But that wasn't enough. I performed a ceremony. During a full moon, I burned my favorite NFL trading cards and an Aurora model of the great quarterback Johnny Unitas in the walnut orchard behind our house, where Miller and I'd gotten into a fight when we were seven and I'd burst into tears before he even hit me.

3 Two days after my ceremony, Miller snuck out on his older brother's Suzuki and was struck by a car. He lost his right arm, just below the elbow. I went to see him the day after football practice started—after he'd come back from the hospital. He looked pale and surprised, but he didn't cry. It was hard to look at the stump of limb where his arm had been, so I kept glancing around his room. We only lived about 200 feet away, and yet I'd never been inside his house before. It had never occurred to me that he would also have on his wall a poster of Raquel Welch from *One Million Years* B.C.

4 I went on to break all his records that year. Miller watched the home games from the bench, wearing his jersey with the sleeve pinned shut. We went 10–1 and I was named MVP, but I was haunted by crazy dreams in which I was somehow responsible for the accident—that I'd found the mangled limb when it could've been sewn back on—and kept it in an aquarium full of vodka under my bed.

5 One afternoon several months later, toward the end of basketball season, I was crossing the field to go home and I saw Miller stuck going over the Cyclone fence—which wasn't hard to climb if you had both arms. I guess he'd gotten tired of walking around and hoped no one was looking. Or maybe it was a matter of pride. I'm sure I was the last person in the world he wanted to see—to have to accept assistance from. But even that challenge he accepted. I helped ease him down the fence, one diamond-shaped hole at a time. When we were finally safe on the other side, he said to me, "You know, I didn't tell you this during the season, but you did all right. Thanks for filling in for me."

6 We walked home together, not saying much. But together. Back to our houses 200 feet apart. His words freed me from my bad dreams. I thought to myself, how many things I hadn't told him. How even without an arm he was more of a leader. Damaged but not diminished, he was still ahead of me. I was right to have admired him. I grew bigger and a little more real from that day on.

THINKING CRITICALLY
about "Phantom Limb Pain"

Perhaps the first thing the reader realizes about Saknussemm's narrative is that the climactic event—one boy helping another climb down a Cyclone fence—is a small action; however, it has a big psychological and emotional meaning for the narrator. The events leading to this moment have prepared us to understand the writer's revelation of his new relationship to his rival. Saknussemm's last paragraph comments on the preceding narrative, making connections and pulling out threads of meaning.

1. Saknussemm chooses to leave a lot unsaid, depending on his readers to fill in the gaps. Why do you suppose that he had never been inside Miller King's house before? Why does he feel "somehow responsible for the accident"? What details does Saknussemm use to sketch in Miller's admirable traits?

2. What examples can you find in this narrative of revelatory words, memory-soaked words, and other concrete words low on the ladder of abstraction? Where does Saknussemm use words that *show* what is happening in the narrative instead of simply telling readers?

See Skill 18.2 for a discussion of concrete language including revelatory words and memory-soaked words. See Chapter 4, Concept 11, for a discussion of *show* words and *tell* words.

3. In closed-form prose, writers seldom use sentence fragments. In open-form prose, however, writers frequently use fragments for special effects. Note the two fragments in Saknussemm's final paragraph: "But together. Back to our houses 200 feet apart." Why does Saknussemm use these fragments? What is their rhetorical effect?

4. Part of Saknussemm's style in this narrative is to use understatement and minimalistic language while also using words that resonate with multiple meanings. For example, he lets readers imagine what Miller would look like trying to climb the Cyclone fence with one arm. However, some phrases and words are figurative and symbolic. What does Saknussemm mean by the phrases "grew bigger" and "a little more real" in his final sentence? How do the ideas of size and of reality versus illusion play a role in this narrative and relate to the theme?

For a different approach to narrative, consider student writer Patrick José's "No Cats in America?" Unlike Saknussemm's narrative, José's includes plentiful description. Note also how José creates tension through contrasts in his narrative: between an ideal image of America and a factual image, between life in the Philippines and life in California.

Patrick José (student)

No Cats in America?

1 "There are no cats in America." I remember growing up watching *An American Tail* with my sisters and cousins. Ever since I first saw that movie, I had always wanted to move to America. That one song, "There Are No Cats in America," in which the Mousekewitz family is singing with other immigrating mice, had the most profound effect on me. These were Russian mice going to America to find a better life—a life without cats. At first, I thought America really had no cats. Later, I learned that they meant that America was without any problems at all. I was taught about the American Dream with its promise of happiness and equality. If you wanted a better life, then you better pack up all your belongings and move to America.

2 However, I loved living in the Philippines. My family used to throw the best parties in Angeles City. For a great party, you need some delicious food. Of course there would be lechon, adobo, pancit, sinigang, lumpia, and rice. We eat rice for breakfast, lunch, and dinner, and rice even makes some of the best desserts. (My mom's bibingka and puto are perfect!) And you mustn't forget the drinks. San Miguel and Coke are usually sufficient. But we also had homemade mango juice and coconut milk. And a party wouldn't be a party without entertainment, right? So in one room, we had the gambling room. It's usually outside the house. Everybody would be smoking and drinking while playing mahjong. And sometimes, others would play pepito or pusoy dos. Music and dancing is always a must. And when there are firecrackers, better watch out because the children would go crazy with them.

3 Then one day, a mixed feeling came over me. My dad told us that he had gotten a job … in California. In the span of two months, we had moved to America, found a small apartment, and located a small private Catholic school for the kids. We did not know many people in California that first summer. We only had ourselves to depend on. We would go on car trips, go to the beach, cook, play games. In August, I thought we were living the American Dream.

4 But at the end of summer, school began. I was in the eighth grade. I had my book bag on one shoulder, stuffed with notebooks, folder paper, calculators, a ruler, a pencil box, and my lunch. I still can remember what I had for lunch on the first day of school—rice and tilapia and, in a small container, a mixture of vinegar, tomatoes, and bagoong. My mom placed everything in a big Tupperware box, knowing I eat a lot.

5 When I walked into the classroom, everyone became quiet and looked at me. I was the only Filipino in that room. Everyone was white. We began the day by introducing ourselves. When it got to my turn, I was really nervous. English was one of the courses that I took in the Philippines, and I thought I was pretty proficient at it. But when I first opened my mouth, everyone began to laugh. The teacher told everyone to hush. I sat down, smiling faintly not understanding what was so funny. I knew English, and yet I was laughed at. But it had nothing to do with the language. It was my accent.

6 Some students tried to be nice, especially during lunch. But it didn't last long. I was so hungry for my lunch. I followed a group of students to the cafeteria and sat down at an empty table. Some girls joined me. I didn't really talk to them, but they asked if they could join me. As I opened my Tupperware, I saw their heads turn away. They didn't like the smell of fish and bagoong. The girls left and moved to another table of girls. From the corner of my eye I saw them looking and laughing at me. I tried to ignore it, concentrating on eating my lunch as I heard them laugh. In the Philippines, the only way to eat fish and rice is with your hands. But that was in the Philippines. My manners were primitive here in America. I was embarrassed at the smell, was embarrassed at the way I ate, was embarrassed to be me.

7 When I got home, I lied to my parents. I told them school was great and that I was excited to go back. But deep down, I wanted to go back to the Philippines. When lunch came the next day, I was hungry. In my hand was my lunch. Five feet away was the trash. I stood up, taking my lunch in my hands. Slowly, I walked my way towards the trashcan, opened the lid, and watched as my lunch filled the trashcan. Again, I told my parents I enjoyed school.

8 When my grades began to suffer, the teacher called my parents and scheduled an appointment. The next day, my parents came to the classroom, and when they started talking to the teacher I heard laughter in the background. It humiliated me to have my classmates hear my parents talk.

9 That night, my parents and I had a private discussion. They asked why I lied to them. I told them everything, including my humiliation. They told me not to worry about it, but I pleaded for us to return to the Philippines. My parents said no. "Living here will provide a better future for you and your sisters," they said. Then the unexpected came. I didn't know what I was thinking. I yelled to them with so much anger, "I hate being Filipino!" Silence filled the room. Teardrops rolled down my cheeks. My parents were shocked, and so was I.

10 I went to my room and cried. I didn't mean what I said. But I was tired of the humiliation. Lying on my bed, with my eyes closed, my mind began to wander. I found myself in the boat with the Mousekewitz family singing, "There are no cats in America." If only they knew how wrong they were.

THINKING CRITICALLY
about "No Cats in America?"

Patrick José lets the reader infer his essay's significance from the details of the narrative and from their connection to the framing story of the fictional mice and cats.

1. How do the settings help you understand José's theme at different points in the narrative?
2. What would you say is the narrative's climax or pivotal moment?
3. José's title, first paragraph, and last paragraph are about a children's movie that features the Mousekewitz's song proclaiming that there are no cats in America. How does the "no cats" image function both as part of the underlying tension

of this narrative and as a symbolic vehicle for conveying the theme of José's essay? What is the insight that José has achieved at the end?

4. During a rough draft workshop, José asked his peer reviewers whether he should retain his description of parties in the Philippines, which he thought was perhaps unconnected to the rest of the narrative. His classmates urged him to keep those details. Do you agree with their advice? Why?

See Skill 18.2 for a discussion of the power of memory-soaked words.

5. For Filipinos and Filipinas, the specific names of foods and party games would be rich examples of memory-soaked words. For other readers, however, these names are foreign and strange. Do you agree with José's decision to use these specific ethnic names? Why?

Our final reading, a literacy narrative, is by student writer Stephanie Whipple.

Stephanie Whipple (student)

One Great Book

1 When first asked to remember my earliest experiences with reading, I thought of my favorite books as a young teen, and I was excited to explore how they shaped the person that I am today. However, upon trying to remember the very first books that I ever read as a child, some quite negative and frankly painful memories were brought to the surface.

2 When I was a little girl living in Memphis, Tennessee, I was a well-behaved bright child who never had trouble learning at a good pace or working with other children. In what I am guessing was my first grade class I remember being so excited when I found out that that year I was going to learn to read. My entire life, my mother and both of my older sisters have all loved reading. I was so excited to be able to read with them and join the big girls' conversations about the books that they were reading.

3 My very first vivid memory of reading was in the playroom of our house in Memphis. I was sitting with my father reading *The Poky Little Puppy* with him, and my younger brother, who had just started kindergarten, was playing with his Nerf gun.

4 "Okay, Steph. Start with this word." My dad points to the first word on the page.

5 "Ff ... i ... fi—"

6 "Five!" My little brother pops his little freckled face over my shoulder.

7 "Stevie, Steph and I are reading this first. You can read it after her" says my father turning to me. "Go ahead Steph."

8 "Five ... li ... lit—"

9 "Little puppies!" yells Stevie from right behind me.

10 I turn away from the book, discouraged.

11 "Stephen!" says our father sternly. "Let Stephanie read. She knows the words; she just has to think about it for a little while. Go play over there and we will read a book when she is done." My Dad turns to me and smiles.

12 "Five little puppies ... d ... dug ... a ... h ... h—"

13 "A hole under the fence!" My brother is behind me again, and I cannot believe that he is smatter than I am. He is only in kindergarten. You're not even supposed to start learning words until the first grade! I drop *The Poky Little Puppy* and run to my mommy, telling myself that reading is stupid, and I don't want to learn how anymore. Drawing and doing other arts and crafts are much more fun anyway, and Stevie can't even draw a bunny!

14 I was by no means a slow learner; Steve was just an exceptionally fast learner when it came to reading. He knew how to read whole chapter books before any of his peers could even read *The Poky Little Puppy.* However, the fact that my little brother could read better than I could made me feel stupid and I lost all of my previous enthusiasm about books.

15 Both of my parents desperately tried to get me to like reading. They were always sure to separate my brother and me when they were helping me with my reading, but I had shut down. My rnom always tried to read to me before bed, but I told her that I hated books. Instead I wanted her to make up stories and tell them to me, or tell me stories about when she was a little girl. I had made up my mind that I hated reading. If I didn't like it, I wouldn't have to be good at it. So, I did just as much reading as my teacher and my parents forced me to do, but that was it. When my brother was reading every word of *Calvin and Hobbes* comics and needing no help from my father, I was coloring Calvin's hair pink and turning Hobbes into a purple tiger with big black sunglasses on.

16 I continued to dislike reading for years. As I got older, I never finished any of the chapter books that I was required to read for school, and I certainly never read the other books that my mother was constantly trying to get me to read. I remember her telling me, "If you just find one book that you really love, you will love reading forever. I promise." My response was always, "Mom, reading is boring. I'm not a nerd." I wanted to spend my spare time playing with my friends and making friendship bracelets, not reading *A Wrinkle in Time* like my dorky little brother.

17 My parents have since told me that my not liking to read broke their hearts. My dad felt like it was his fault for reading with me around my brother. They did not know what to do, and they were convinced that I would go through my entire life without ever enjoying a good book.

18 One rainy summer day when I was about fourteen years old, however, all of this changed. My family and I were at our mountain house in the Poconos and the weather was too bad to go out on the boat or play outside, so I was bored. I approached my mom to ask her to play a game with me while she was sitting on our screened-in porch reading. She told me that she bought me a book that she loved when she was my age, and suggested that she read some of it to me just to see if I might like it. I don't know if it was out of utter boredom, being worn down by my mom constantly nagging me to read, or just out of really wanting to spend time with my mother, but I agreed. The book was about a little girl named Francie who was extremely poor and lived in a city that I was completely unfamiliar with, but I still related to her. I loved Francie, and after my mom finished reading the first chapter to me and left to go to the store, I continued reading the book and didn't put it down

until it was time for dinner. I loved reading! When I was not reading, I was thinking about Francie and hoping that everything would turn out all right for her. The book had opened up a whole new world for me in which a family could be so poor and have almost none of the things that I was accustomed to, but still be happy and full of love and warmth and hope. I spent the whole week reading my book and discussing it with my mom and sisters.

19 I do not remember the next good book or even the next five good books that my mother gave me and I enthusiastically poured myself into. However, to this day whenever anyone mentions *A Tree Grows in Brooklyn*, or I see the movie on TV, or I read about another character named Frances or Francie, I get a warm feeling in my heart, and I thank God for my mother and her persistence. Without my mom, and without that one great book, I might not be the person and the reader that I am today. If anyone ever tells me that they do not like reading, I smile and tell them, "If you just find one book that you really love, you will love reading forever. I promise."

THINKING CRITICALLY
about "One Great Book"

1. In this literacy narrative, how does Stephanie Whipple create tension and establish the main conflicts?
2. In her desire to engage readers with her characters and setting, Stephanie chooses to use the present tense rather than the past tense for her early scene about reading. Do you find this choice effective? (It violates the normal rules about needless shifting of tense.) How else does she try to engage readers in her characters and setting?
3. This piece leads up to a moment of breakthrough and new insight about the significance of reading. How does Stephanie use story elements rather than straight exposition to convey her transformation in her attitude toward literature?
4. In much of this narrative, Stephanie includes words that are specific and descriptive—that is, low on the ladder of abstraction. What passages are vivid and memorable?
5. This piece is fairly straightforward, yet it points to some deeper themes about learning. What new understanding about children and reading does Stephanie want readers to grasp?

WRITING AN EXPLORATORY ESSAY OR ANNOTATED BIBLIOGRAPHY

7

In Part 1, we explained how writers wrestle with subject-matter problems. During exploration, experienced writers often redefine their problem, discover new ideas, and alter or even reverse their initial thesis. In contrast, inexperienced writers often truncate this process, closing off the period of exploratory thinking. Asserting a thesis too soon can prevent writers from acknowledging an issue's complexity, whereas dwelling with a question invites writers to contemplate multiple perspectives, entertain new ideas, and let their thinking evolve. In this chapter, we introduce two genres of writing built on exploratory thinking:

- An **exploratory essay** narrates a writer's thinking process while doing research. The essay recounts your attempt to examine your question's complexity, explore alternatives, and arrive at a solution or answer. Because an exploration often requires research, many instructors pair this project with Part 4, "A Rhetorical Guide to Research."
- An **annotated bibliography** summarizes and briefly critiques the research sources a writer used while exploring a problem. It encourages exploration and inquiry, provides a "tracing" of your work, and creates a guide for others interested in your research problem.

Even though academic readers usually expect and need thesis-driven arguments, exploratory essays are becoming more common in scholarly journals, and annotated bibliographies are a frequently encountered academic genre. Exploratory essays exist in embryo in the research or lab notebooks of scholars. For students, both the exploratory essay and the annotated bibliography serve as an intermediate stage in the research process. Student James Gardiner's exploratory paper and annotated bibliography in this chapter are products of the exploratory phase of his research about online social networking, which later resulted in a researched argument. You can compare his exploratory essay with the final thesis-driven argument in Chapter 22.

In this chapter, you will learn to:

- explore an issue and narrate your thinking process in an exploratory essay
- summarize and critique your research sources in an annotated bibliography

Exploring Exploratory Writing

Through our work in writing centers, we often encounter students disappointed with their grades on essay exams or papers. "I worked hard on this paper," they tell us, "but I still got a lousy grade. What am I doing wrong? What do college professors want?"

To help you answer this question, consider the following two essays written for a freshman placement examination in composition at the University of Pittsburgh, in response to the following assignment:

> Describe a time when you did something you felt to be creative. Then, on the basis of the incident you have described, go on to draw some general conclusions about "creativity."

How would you describe the differences in thinking exhibited by the two writers? Which essay do you think professors rated higher?

ESSAY A

I am very interested in music, and I try to be creative in my interpretation of music. While in high school, I was a member of a jazz ensemble. The members of the ensemble were given chances to improvise and be creative in various songs. I feel that this was a great experience for me, as well as the other members. I was proud to know that I could use my imagination and feelings to create music other than what was written.

Creativity to me means being free to express yourself in a way that is unique to you, not having to conform to certain rules and guidelines. Music is only one of the many areas in which people are given opportunities to show their creativity. Sculpting, carving, building, art, and acting are just a few more areas where people can show their creativity.

Through my music I conveyed feelings and thoughts which were important to me. Music was my means of showing creativity. In whatever form creativity takes, whether it be music, art, or science, it is an important aspect of our lives because it enables us to be individuals.

ESSAY B

Throughout my life, I have been interested and intrigued by music. My mother has often told me of the times, before I went to school, when I would "conduct" the orchestra on her records. I continued to listen to music and eventually started to play the guitar and the clarinet. Finally, at about the age of twelve, I started to sit down and to try to write songs. Even though my instrumental skills were far from my own high standards, I would spend much of my spare time during the day with a guitar around my neck, trying to produce a piece of music.

Each of these sessions, as I remember them, had a rather set format. I would sit in my bedroom, strumming different combinations of the five or six chords I could play, until I heard a series which sounded particularly good to me. After this, I set the music to a suitable rhythm (usually dependent on my mood at the time), and ran through the tune until I could play it fairly easily. Only after this section was complete did I go on to writing lyrics, which generally followed along the lines of the current popular songs on the radio.

At the time of the writing, I felt that my songs were, in themselves, an original creation of my own; that is, I, alone, made them. However, I now see that, in this

> sense of the word, I was not creative. The songs themselves seem to be an oversimplified form of the music I listened to at the time.
>
> In a more fitting sense, however, I *was* being creative. Since I did not purposely copy my favorite songs, I was, effectively, originating my songs from my own "process of creativity." To achieve my goal, I needed what a composer would call "inspiration" for my piece. In this case the inspiration was the current hit on the radio. Perhaps, with my present point of view, I feel that I used too much "inspiration" in my songs, but, at the time, I did not.
>
> Creativity, therefore, is a process which, in my case, involved a certain series of "small creations" if you like. As well, it is something the appreciation of which varies with one's point of view, that point of view being set by the person's experience, tastes, and his own personal view of creativity. The less experienced tend to allow for less originality, while the more experienced demand real originality to classify something a "creation." Either way, a term as abstract as this is perfectly correct, and open to interpretation.

Working as a whole class or in small groups, analyze the differences between Essay A and Essay B. What might cause college professors to rate one essay higher than the other? What would the writer of the weaker essay have to do to produce an essay more like the stronger?

Understanding Exploratory Writing

The essential move for exploratory thinking and writing is to keep a problem alive through consideration of multiple solutions or points of view. The thinker identifies a problem, considers a possible solution or point of view, explores its strengths and weaknesses, and then moves on to consider another possible solution or viewpoint. The thinker resists closure—that is, resists settling too soon on a thesis.

To show a mind at work examining multiple solutions, let's return to the two student essays you examined in the previous exploratory activity (pp. 154–155). The fundamental difference between Essay A and Essay B is that the writer of Essay B treats the concept of "creativity" as a true problem. Note that the writer of Essay A is satisfied with his or her initial definition:

> Creativity to me means being free to express yourself in a way that is unique to you, not having to conform to certain rules and guidelines.

The writer of Essay B, however, is *not* satisfied with his or her first answer and uses the essay to think through the problem. This writer remembers an early creative experience—composing songs as a twelve-year-old:

> At the time of the writing, I felt that my songs were, in themselves, an original creation of my own; that is, I, alone, made them. However, I now see that, in this sense of the word, I was not creative. The songs themselves seem to be an oversimplified form of the music I listened to at the time.

This writer distinguishes between two points of view: "On the one hand, I used to think *x*, but now, in retrospect, I think *y*." This move forces the writer to go beyond the initial answer to think of alternatives.

The key to effective exploratory writing is to create a tension between alternative views. When you start out, you might not know where your thinking process will end up; at the outset you might not have formulated an opposing, countering, or alternative view. Using a statement such as "I used to think . . . , but now I think" or "Part of me thinks this . . . , but another part thinks that . . . " forces you to find something additional to say; writing then becomes a process of inquiry and discovery.

The second writer's dissatisfaction with the initial answer initiates a dialectic process that plays one idea against another, creating a generative tension. In contrast, the writer of Essay A offers no alternative to his or her definition of creativity. This writer presents no specific illustrations of creative activity (such as the specific details in Essay B about strumming the guitar) but presents merely space-filling abstractions ("Sculpting, carving, building, art, and acting are just a few more areas where people can show their creativity"). The writer of Essay B scores a higher grade, not because the essay creates a brilliant (or even particularly clear) explanation of creativity; rather, the writer is rewarded for thinking about the problem dialectically.

We use the term *dialectic* to mean a thinking process often associated with the German philosopher Hegel, who said that each thesis ("My act was creative") gives rise to an antithesis ("My act was not creative") and that the clash of these opposing perspectives leads thinkers to develop a synthesis that incorporates some features of both theses ("My act was a series of 'small creations'"). You initiate dialectic thinking any time you play Elbow's believing and doubting game or use other strategies to place alternative possibilities side by side.

See Chapter 2, Concept 4, for an explanation of the believing and doubting game.

Essay B's writer uses a dialectic thinking strategy that we might characterize as follows:

1. Sees the assigned question as a genuine problem worth puzzling over.
2. Considers alternative views and plays them off against each other.
3. Looks at specific examples and illustrations.
4. Continues the thinking process in search of some sort of resolution or synthesis of the alternative views.
5. Incorporates the stages of this dialectic process into the essay.

These same dialectic thinking habits can be extended to research writing where the researcher's goals are to find alternative points of view on the research question, to read sources rhetorically, to consider all the relevant evidence, to search for a resolution or synthesis of alternative views, and to use one's own critical thinking to arrive at a thesis.

FOR WRITING AND DISCUSSION

Keeping a Problem Open

1. Working individually, read each of the following questions and write out the first plausible answer that comes to your mind.
   - Why on average are males more attracted to video games than females? Are these games harmful to males?

- Have online social networks such as Facebook improved or harmed the lives of participants? Why?
- The most popular magazines sold on college campuses are women's fashion and lifestyle magazines such as *Glamour, Elle*, and *Cosmopolitan*. Why do women buy these magazines? Are these magazines harmful?

2. As a whole class, take a poll to determine the most common first-response answers for each of the questions. Then explore other possible answers and points of view. The goal of your class discussion is to postulate and explore answers that go against the grain of or beyond the common answers. Try to push deeply into each question so that it becomes more complex and interesting than it may at first seem.
3. How would you use library and Internet research to deepen your exploration of these questions? Specifically, what keywords might you use in a database search? What databases would you use?

See Chapters 19–22 for instruction on doing college-level academic research.

WRITING PROJECT

An Exploratory Essay

Choose a question, problem, or issue that genuinely perplexes you. At the beginning of your essay, explain why you are interested in this problem, why you think it is significant, and why you have been unable to reach a satisfactory answer. Then write a first-person, chronologically organized narrative account of your thinking process as you investigate your question through research, talking with others, and doing your own reflective thinking. Your goal is to examine your question, problem, or issue from a variety of perspectives, assessing the strengths and weaknesses of different positions and points of view. Your goal is not to answer your question but to report on the process of wrestling with it.

This assignment asks you to dwell on a problem—and not necessarily to solve that problem. Your problem may shift and evolve as your thinking progresses. What matters is that you are actively engaged with your problem and demonstrate why it is problematic.

Generating and Exploring Ideas

Your process of generating and exploring ideas is, in essence, the *subject matter* of your exploratory essay. This section will help you get started and keep going.

Posing Your Initial Problem

If your instructor hasn't assigned a specific problem to be investigated, then your first step is to choose one that currently perplexes you. Perhaps a question is problematic for you because you haven't yet had a chance to study it (Should the United States turn to nuclear power for generating electricity?). Maybe the available data seem conflicting or inconclusive (Should women younger than fifty get annual mammograms?). Or, possibly, the problem or issue draws you into an uncomfortable conflict of values (Should we legalize the sale of organs for transplant?).

The key to this assignment is to choose a question, problem, or issue *that truly perplexes you.* (Your instructor may limit the range of topics you can choose.) Here are several exercises to help you think of ideas for this essay:

- Make a list of issues or problems that both interest and perplex you within the range of subjects specified by your instructor. Then choose two or three and freewrite about them for five minutes or so. Use as your model James Gardiner's freewrite on page 30, which marked the origin of his exploratory paper for this chapter. Share your questions and your freewrites with friends and classmates because doing so often stimulates further thinking and discovery.
- A particularly valuable kind of problem to explore for this assignment is a current public controversy. Often such issues involve disagreements about facts and values that merit open-ended exploration. This assignment invites you to explore and clarify where you stand on such public issues as gay marriage, immigration, health care reform, energy policies, and so forth. Make a list of currently debated public controversies that you would like to explore. Share your list with classmates and friends.

Formulating a Starting Point

After you've chosen a problem, you are ready to write a first draft of your introduction in which you identify your chosen problem and show why you are interested in it, why you find it perplexing, and why it is significant. You might start out with a sharp, clearly focused question (Should the United States build a fence between the United States and Mexico?). Often, however, formulating a focused question will turn out to be part of the *process* of writing the paper. Instead of a single, focused question, you might start with a whole cluster of related questions swimming in your head. That's fine too because you can still explain why you are interested in this cluster of questions.

The goal of your introduction is to hook your reader's interest in your chosen problem. Often the best way to do so is to show why you yourself became interested in it. For example, James Gardiner opens his exploratory essay by noting the popularity of online social networks such as MySpace and Facebook and mentioning the shocked look of his friends when he tells them he doesn't have a Facebook profile (see p. 169). He then introduces the questions he wants to investigate—why students are attracted to Facebook or MySpace, how students use the sites, and how their communication skills are being affected. Another student, Dylan Fujitani, opened his exploratory essay by explaining his shock when seeing a newspaper photograph of mutilated corpses hanging from a bridge in Falluja, Iraq. Later, he discovered that the bodies were not American soldiers but hired contractors. This experience gave rise to a number of issues he wanted to explore about mercenary soldiers under the general question, "Is the use of private contractors in military roles a good idea?"

Dylan Fujitani's final argument essay appears on pp. 429–433.

Taking "Double-Entry" Research Notes

After you have formulated your initial problem, you are ready to start your research. As you read, take purposeful notes, as explained in Skill 20.1 in Part 4, "A Rhetorical Guide to Research." Whereas novice researchers often avoid taking notes and instead create a pile of photocopied or downloaded-and-printed articles, experienced researchers use note taking as a discipline to promote strong rhetorical reading. We recommend "double-entry" notes in which you use one column for taking notes on a source and another column for recording your own thinking about the source. When you have finished taking notes in the first column, write a "strong response" to the source in the second column, explaining how the source advanced your thinking, raised questions, or pulled you in one direction or another.

What follows is James Gardiner's double-entry research notes for one of the articles he used in his exploratory essay. When you read both his exploratory essay in this chapter and his final researched argument in Chapter 22, you'll be able to see how he used this article at a crucial place in his research.

James's Double-Entry Research Log Entry for *Financial Times* Article

February 24

Date of entry so you can reconstruct chronological order

Bowley, Graham. "The High Priestess of Internet Friendship." *Financial Times Weekend Magazine* 27 Oct. 2006. *LexisNexis Academic*. Web. 22 Feb. 2007.

Bibliographic citation following assigned format, in this case MLA

Newspaper feature article in journalistic style

Rhetorical notation about genre, purpose, audience

Reading Notes	Strong Response Notes
—Begins with Danah Boyd, an expert on OSNs. Talks about how she enjoyed Internet connections when she was growing up. Says the Internet "could change the way all of us order our world, interact with each other, get information and do business." (p. 1 of printout)	*—I want to find out more about Danah Boyd.* *—good quote*
—Two-page section on history of OSNs beginning with Friendster.	
—Returns to profile of Boyd. Boyd compares MySpace to an "electronic version of the local mall" (p. 2). She claims that these public spaces are no longer available so kids have gone virtual.	*—I don't think I agree with this; kids still hang out at malls.*

Reading notes in column 1 on content of the source

Include full quotations if you won't keep a copy of the full source

Strong response notes in column 2 show reactions to the source

(*continued*)

James's Double-Entry Research Log Entry for *Financial Times* Article

—Quote from blogger Cory Doctorow on OSN messages as "simple grooming exercises" (p. 3)—not serious talk—just saying "hi" online.	*—good quote; I should use it.*
—Paragraph on the "explosion of self-expression" on the sites—poems, songs, pictures, etc.—everyone trying to self-express creatively.	*—very interesting passage; I should try to use it.*
—Generational shift in attitudes toward privacy. Compares kids on OSNs trying to become celebrities like Paris Hilton (p. 3)—mentions Christine Dolce (AKA ForBiddeN) as example of someone who achieved celebrity status.	*—very important for my research question*
—Quotes Boyd: OSNs are about "identity production"—kids are trying to "write themselves into being." Quotes researcher Fred Stutzman about kids using OSN profiles like their bedroom walls—their private place where they can invite friends. They are "testing out identities." (p. 4)	*—I have another article by Stutzman; should read it soon.* *—great analogy*
—Has a section on online games; also has a section on how sociologists are doing interesting experiments seeing how news travels on OSNs.	*—I don't quite understand the experiments.*
—Raises some questions about dangers—stalkers—especially dangers to minors. How legislators are trying to come up with laws to make it harder for stalkers to find victims.	*—good for challenging OSNs and constructing alternative views*
—Returns to Boyd, who says these dangers are "painfully overblown." Boyd really supports OSNs as places where kids can "negotiate this new world."	*—important points; good longer quote on p. 5*
— Last part focuses on commercial aspects of OSNs; they apparently aren't yet big moneymakers. Also if there is too much advertising, kids might not like the OSN as well.	*—points make sense; might use them*

Strong response summary:
Very useful article, not scholarly but fairly deep and well-researched. I can use it to give arguments in favor of Facebook, MySpace, or other OSNs. However, Danah Boyd doesn't support OSNs in the same way that many other supporters do. Most supporters talk about how OSNs help young people enlarge their list of friends and have a feeling of connection, etc. Boyd is much more edgy and sees the dangers out there and all the role playing and phoniness. Boyd seems to like that unstable atmosphere where the rules and norms aren't really clear. She thinks that the online world is really helping students learn to find their identities and discover who they are. I still have reservations, though. I like the parts of the article where Bowley talks about students wanting to become celebrities and competing with each other for the most friends because that seems like self-enhancement rather than making connections. Also Boyd doesn't seem worried about all the time young people spend at these sites. I need to do more research into the downside of OSNs.

Shaping and Drafting

Your exploratory essay records the history of your researching and thinking process (what you read or whom you talked to, how you responded, how your thinking evolved). Along the way you can make your narrative more colorful and grounded by including your strategies for tracking down sources, your conversations with friends, your late-night trips to a coffee shop, and so forth. What you will quickly discover about this exploratory assignment is that it forces you actually to do the research. Unless you conduct your research in a timely fashion, you won't have any research process to write about.

Exploratory essays can be composed in two ways—what we might call the "real-time strategy" and the "retrospective strategy."

Strategies for Composing an Exploratory Essay

Strategies	Advantages
Real-time strategy. Compose the body of the essay during the actual process of researching and thinking.	Yields genuine immediacy—like a sequence of letters or e-mails sent home during a journey.
Retrospective strategy. Look back over your completed research notes and then compose the body of the essay.	Allows for more selection and shaping of details and yields a more artistically designed essay.

In either case, the goal when writing with an exploratory aim is to reproduce the research and thinking process, taking the readers on the same intellectual and emotional journey you have just traveled. The exploratory essay has the general organizational framework shown in Figure 7.1.

There are a number of keys to writing successful exploratory papers. As you draft, pay particular attention to the following:

- *Show how you chose sources purposively and reflectively rather than randomly.* As you make a transition from one source to the next, help your reader see your thought processes. Note the following examples of bridging passages that reveal the writer's purposeful selection of sources:

  For the next stage of my research, I wanted to explore in more detail what students actually did while online in an OSN. I located my next source by searching through the Academic Search Complete database (from James Gardiner's essay, para. 6, p. 170).

  After reading Friedman's views of how globalization was changing lives in India and China, I realized that I needed to talk to some students from these countries, so I grabbed my backpack and headed to the International Student Center.

- *Give your draft both open-form and closed-form features.* Because your exploratory paper is a narrative, it follows an unfolding, open-form structure. Many of your paragraphs should open with chronological transitions such as "I *started*

FIGURE 7.1 Framework for an Exploratory Essay

Introduction (one or more paragraphs)	• Establishes that your question is complex, problematic, and significant • Shows why you are interested in it • Presents relevant background You can begin with your question or build up to it, using it to end your introductory section.
Body section 1 on first source	• Introduces your first source and shows why you started with it • Provides rhetorical context and information about the source • Summarizes the source's content and argument • Offers your strong response to this source, frequently including both with-the-grain and against-the-grain points • Talks about what this source contributes to your understanding of your question: What did you learn? What value does this source have for you? What is missing from this source that you want to consider? Where do you want to go from here?
Body section 2 on second source	• Repeats the process with a new source selected to advance the inquiry • Explains why you selected this source (to find an alternative view, pursue subquestions, find more data, and so forth) • Summarizes the source's argument • Provides a strong response • Shows how your cumulative reading of sources is shaping your thinking or leading to more questions
Body sections 3, 4, 5, etc., on additional sources	• Continues the process
Conclusion	• Wraps up your intellectual journey and explains where you are now in your thinking and how your understanding of your problem has changed • Presents your current answer to your question based on all that you have read and learned so far, or explains why you still can't answer your question, or explains what further research you might do
Works Cited or References list	• Includes a complete list of citations in MLA or APA format, depending on your assignment

by reading," "*Early the next morning,* I headed for the library to . . . ," "On the *next* day, I decided," or "*After* finishing . . . I *next* looked at. . . . " At the same time, your summaries of your sources and your strong responses to them should be framed within closed-form structures with topic sentences and logical transitions: "This article, in raising objections to genetic screening of embryos, began changing my views about new advances in reproductive technology. Whereas before I felt . . . , now I feel. . . . "

- *Show yourself wrestling with ideas.* Readers want to see how your research stimulates your own thinking. Throughout, your paper should show you responding strongly to your sources. Here is a good example from James's paper on online social networks.

> After considering the views of Boyd and Stutzman, I felt I understood why they think that OSNs give young people the opportunity for self-definition and self-expression. However, I still had doubts about the beneficial effects of OSNs. They still seem to me to send superficial messages about a person's identity. I found myself wondering if it is detrimental to spend all that time in virtual space rather than actually being with one's friends. I felt I needed to start looking for articles that examine the dangers of OSNs.

Although you might feel that sentences that show your mind talking its way through your research will sound too informal, they actually work well in exploratory essays to create interest and capture your critical thinking.

Revising

Because an exploratory essay describes the writer's research and thinking in chronological order, most writers have little trouble with organization. When they revise, their major concern is to improve their essay's interest level by keeping it focused and lively. Often drafts need to be pruned to remove extraneous details and keep the pace moving. Frequently, introductions can be made sharper, clearer, and more engaging. Peer reviewers can give you valuable feedback about the pace and interest level of an exploratory piece. They can also help you achieve the right balance between summarizing sources and showing the evolution of your own thinking. As you revise, make sure you use attributive tags and follow proper stylistic conventions for quotations and citations.

Questions for Peer Review

In addition to the generic peer review questions explained in skill 16.4 ask your peer reviewers to address these questions:

POSING THE PROBLEM:

1. In the introduction, how has the writer tried to show that the problem is interesting, significant, and problematic? How could the writer engage you more fully with the initial problem?
2. How does the writer provide cues that his/her purpose is to explore a question rather than argue a thesis? How might the opening section of the draft be improved?

NARRATING THE EXPLORATION:

3. Is the body of the paper organized chronologically so that you can see the development of the writer's thinking? Where does the writer provide chronological transitions?
4. Part of an exploratory essay involves summarizing the argument of each new research source. Where in this draft is a summary of a source particularly clear

and well developed? Where are summary passages either undeveloped or unclear or too long? How could these passages be improved?

5. Another part of an exploratory paper involves the writer's strong response to each source. Where in this draft is there evidence of the writer's own critical thinking and questioning? Where are the writer's ideas particularly strong and effective? Where are the writer's own ideas undeveloped, unclear, or weak?
6. Has the writer done enough research to explore the problem? How would you describe the range and variety of sources that the writer has consulted? Where does the writer acknowledge how the kinds of sources shape his or her perspective on the subject? What additional ideas or perspectives do you think the writer should consider?

WRITING PROJECT

An Annotated Bibliography

Create an annotated bibliography that lists the research sources you have used for your exploratory project. Because annotated bibliographies can vary in the number, length, and kinds of entries, follow guidelines provided by your instructor. Some instructors may also require a critical preface that explains your research question and provides details about how you selected the bibliographic sources.

What Is an Annotated Bibliography?

Bibliographies are alphabetized lists of sources on a given topic, providing readers with the names of authors, titles, and publication details for each source. Unlike a plain list of sources, an **annotated bibliography** also includes the writer's "annotation" or commentary on each source. These annotations can be either *summary-only* or *evaluative.*

- A **summary-only annotation** provides a capsule of the source's contents without any additional comments from the bibliography's author.
- An **evaluative annotation** adds the author's critique or assessment of the work, including comments about the source's rhetorical context, its particular strengths or weaknesses, and its usefulness or value.

Whichever type is used, the length of the annotation is a function of its audience and purpose. Brief annotations comprise only a few sentences (one standard approach—to be described later—uses three sentences) while longer annotations can be up to 150 words. Brief annotations are most common when the annotated bibliography has numerous entries; longer annotations, which allow for fuller summaries and more detailed analyses, are often more helpful for readers but can make an annotated bibliography too long if there are many sources.

Annotated bibliographies serve several important functions. First, writing an annotated bibliography engages researchers in exploratory thinking by requiring that they read sources rhetorically like experts, entering critically into scholarly conversations. Annotated bibliographies can also be valuable time-saving tools for new researchers in a field. By providing overview information about potential sources, they help new researchers determine whether a particular source might be useful for their own purposes. Think of source annotations as analogous to short movie reviews that help you select your next film. (What's this movie about? How good is it?) Additionally, annotated bibliographies can establish the writer's *ethos* by showing the depth, breadth, and competence of the writer's research. (A good annotated bibliography proves that you have read and thought about your sources.)

Features of Annotated Bibliography Entries

Each entry has two main parts, the bibliographic citation and the annotation. The **bibliographic citation** should follow the conventions of your assigned documentation style such as the Modern Language Association (MLA) or the American Psychological Association (APA).

See Skills 22.3 and 22.4.

An **evaluative annotation** (the most common kind) typically includes three elements. In a three-sentence evaluative annotation, each element is covered in one sentence.

- ***Rhetorical information,*** including the source's rhetorical context, particularly its genre and (if not implied by the genre) its purpose and audience. Is this source a scholarly article? An op-ed piece? A blog? What is the author's purpose and who is the intended audience? Are there any political biases that need to be noted?
- ***A summary of the source's content.*** In some cases, a writer simply lists what is covered in the source. Whenever possible, however, summarize the source's actual argument. (Note: In a *summary-only* annotation, this summary is the only element included.)
- ***The writer's evaluation of the source.*** What are the source's particular strengths or weaknesses? How useful is the source for specific purposes? How might the writer use the source for his or her research project? (Or, if the annotated bibliography comes at the end of the project, how did the writer use the source?)

Examples of Annotation Entries

Here are examples of different kinds of annotations based on James Gardiner's research notes for one of his sources (see pp. 159–160):

SUMMARY-ONLY ANNOTATION

Bowley, Graham. "The High Priestess of Internet Friendship." *Financial Times Weekend Magazine* 27 Oct. 2006. *LexisNexis Academic*. Web. 22 Feb. 2007.

In this feature story, Bowley explains the development of OSNs from their origins in *Friendster* to their current popularity in *MySpace* and *Facebook*. He also traces further developments of OSNs and explains their difficulties in making profits through commercial advertising. Finally, Bowley uses interviews with researchers to show how young people use OSNs to maintain social relationships and to play with different identities through self-expression.

EVALUATIVE ANNOTATION

Bowley, Graham. "The High Priestess of Internet Friendship." *Financial Times Weekend Magazine* 27 Oct. 2006. *LexisNexis Academic.* Web. 22 Feb. 2007.

This article is a feature story in the "Arts and Weekend" section of the *Financial Times Weekend Magazine.* Bowley's information comes from interviews with researchers who study online social networks (OSNs). Bowley explains the development of OSNs from their origins in *Friendster* to their current popularity in *MySpace* and *Facebook,* traces further developments of OSNs, and explains their difficulties in making profits through commercial advertising. Bowley also shows how young people use OSNs to maintain social relationships and to play with different identities through self-expression. A particularly valuable section mentions the dangers of OSNs, such as sexual predators. However, Danah Boyd, a researcher whom Bowley quotes extensively, defends OSNs as a place where young people can explore their identities and "negotiate this new world." This article gives a mostly positive view of OSNs and goes beyond other articles by showing how OSNs provide a new space for "identity production."

THREE-SENTENCE EVALUATIVE ANNOTATION

Bowley, Graham. "The High Priestess of Internet Friendship." *Financial Times Weekend Magazine* 27 Oct. 2006. *LexisNexis Academic.* Web. 22 Feb. 2007.

This article is a journalistic feature story written for readers of a major business and finance newspaper. It gives the history of online social networks (OSN) including *Friendster, MySpace,* and *Facebook,* explains their difficulties in making money through commercial advertising, and shows how young people use OSNs to maintain social relationships and to play with different identities through self-expression. This is a valuable article that gives a mostly positive view of OSNs by showing how they provide a new space for "identity production" and self-expression.

Writing a Critical Preface for Your Annotated Bibliography

Scholars who publish annotated bibliographies typically introduce them with a critical preface that explains the scope and purpose of the bibliography. When you write a critical preface for your own annotated bibliography, you have a chance to highlight your critical thinking and show the purposeful way that you conducted your research. Typically the critical preface includes the following information:

- A contextual overview that shows the purpose of the annotated bibliography and suggests its value and significance for the reader
- The research question posed by the author
- The dates during which the bibliography was compiled
- An overview of the number of items in the bibliography and the kinds of material included

A student example of an annotated bibliography with a critical preface is found in the Readings section of this chapter (pp. 174–176).

Shaping, Drafting, and Revising

The key to producing a good annotated bibliography is to take good research notes as you read. Compare the various versions of the above annotations with James Gardiner's research notes (pp. 159–160). Before composing your annotated bibliography, make sure that you understand your instructor's preferences for the number of entries required and for the length and kinds of annotations. Arrange the bibliography in alphabetical order as you would in a "Works Cited" (MLA format) or "References" (APA format) list.

The specific skills needed for an annotated bibliography are taught in various places in this text. If you are having problems with aspects of an annotated bibliography, you can find further instruction as follows.

Problems with:	Where to Find Help
Formatting the citations.	Refer to Skill 22.3 for MLA style, and Skill 22.4 for APA style.
Describing the rhetorical context and genre.	Review Skill 20.1, and reread Chapter 1, Concept 3.
Writing a summary.	Read Chapter 5, pages 99–102, on summary writing; read also Skill 21.2.
Writing an evaluation.	Use the strategies for strong response in Chapter 5, pages 104–110, and also Skills 20.1–20.3.
Wordiness—the annotation is more than 150 words.	See Chapter 4, Concept 11, on wordy versus streamlined sentences.

Questions for Peer Review

The following questions are based on the assumption that your instructor requires evaluative annotations and a critical preface. Adjust the questions to fit a different assignment.

CRITICAL PREFACE

1. Where does the writer explain the following: The purpose and significance of the bibliography? The research question that motivated the research? The dates of the research? The kinds of sources included?
2. How could the critical preface be improved?

BIBLIOGRAPHIC CITATIONS

3. Does each citation follow MLA or APA conventions? Pay particular attention to the formatting of sources downloaded from a licensed database or from the Web.
4. Are the sources arranged alphabetically?

ANNOTATIONS

5. Where does each annotation include the following: Information about genre or rhetorical context? A capsule summary of the source's contents? An evaluative comment?
6. Identify any places where the annotations are confusing or unclear or where the writer could include more information.
7. How could one or more of the annotations be improved?

Our first reading is an exploratory essay by student writer James Gardiner on online social networks. After completing the exploratory essay, James continued his research, writing an argument on potential negative consequences of OSNs. James's final argument is our sample MLA student research paper in Chapter 22 (pp. 590–598).

James Gardiner (student)

How Do Online Social Networks Affect Communication?

1 Walk into any computer lab located at any college campus across the country and you'll see dozens of students logged onto an online social network (OSN). In the last few years, the use of these networks has sky-rocketed among Internet users, especially young adults. As a college student, I am one of the few people I know who does not have a profile on either *MySpace* or *Facebook*, and I'm constantly met with shocked looks when I inform my fellow students of this. Today, OSNs have become a staple in the life of most American young people. Although I was conscious that OSNs were impacting the way young people communicate with each other, I was largely unaware of the specific ways that people used these OSNs or how their communication skills were being affected by this new technology. For this research project, I decided to pursue the question, How are online social networks influencing the way young people communicate with each other? This question deserves to be examined because the more people move toward these new modes of communication, the more influence these networks will have on society as a whole. I suspect that these new virtual communities are changing the way people communicate with one another to an incredible degree.

2 Before I could focus on the impact of OSNs on people's communication skills, I first needed to learn more about who used these networks and for what specific purposes they joined them. I started by reading a short news article, "The Web of Social Networking," from *U.S. News & World Report* (Green), to give me a basic understanding of this phenomenon. I learned that by far the two most popular OSNs are *MySpace* and *Facebook*. *MySpace* is a general networking site that allows anybody to access it. *Facebook* is geared more toward college students, and until recently a user needed a university - e-mail address to join. According to Green, in 2005, *MySpace* was one of the 20 most popular sites on the Internet while *Facebook* was the top site for 18- to 24-year-olds. Moreover, Green points out that 60% of *Facebook* members logged in daily. This high number surprised me.

3 Needing more in-depth information about how young people use OSNs, I next turned to the *Pew Internet Project* website, based on a recommendation from my composition instructor. Pew is a non-partisan, non-profit research center that examines the social impact of the Internet. On the website, I found the results of the Parents and Teens 2006 survey in which researchers conducted telephone interviews of 935 teenagers and their parents living in the United States. The key findings include the following, which I quote from this report:

- 55% of online teens have created a personal profile on OSNs.
- 66% of teens who have created a profile say that their profile is not visible to all Internet users. They limit access to their profiles.
- 48% of teens visit social networking websites daily or more often; 26% visit once a day, 22% visit several times a day.
- Older girls ages 15–17 are more likely to have used social networking sites and created online profiles; 70% of older girls have used an online social network compared with 54% of older boys, and 70% of older girls have created an online profile, while only 57% of older boys have done so. (Lenhart and Madden 2)

The survey reveals how young people were using OSNs as tools to communicate with each other. It states that 91% of users logged on to keep in touch with their regularly seen friends, while 82% used the sites to stay in touch with distant friends. The survey also indicates that 49% use the sites to make new friends (Lenhart and Madden 2).

4 The Pew survey gave me a clearer picture of how and why young people are using OSNs. Although I wasn't surprised to learn that over half of all online teens were members of OSNs, I was caught off guard by the frequency that these teens logged on to these sites. I was also unaware that almost half of all social networking teens used these sites to meet new people. These discoveries helped me to better form my understanding of OSNs as I proceeded with my investigation focusing on their effects on communication skills.

5 I was now several days into my project. Because I am kind of a private person, I would be hesitant to put much personal information on a profile. Since all online social networks are comprised of profiles created by their members, I thought it would be a good idea to next examine how extensively these people disclosed personal information. By plugging "personal information" and "Online Social Networks" into *Google*, I located a study titled, "An Evaluation of Identity-Sharing Behavior in Social Network Communities" by Frederic Stutzman, a graduate student at the School of Information and Library Science at the University of North Carolina in Chapel Hill. In this scholarly piece from a conference, Stutzman recounts how his research attempted to uncover how much and what kind of identity information young people are disclosing in OSNs. Stutzman identified a random sample of UNC students and asked them to complete a survey about their use of these social networks and their feelings about disclosure of identity information. The results showed that 90% of UNC undergraduates have a *Facebook* profile. At the heart of Stutzman's article is a graph that shows the percentage of polled students who disclose certain personal information on their *Facebook* page. For example, 75% of users post a photograph, 65% post relationship information, 55% disclose political views, and 35% disclose sexual orientation (sec. 4.3). Stutzman concludes that as the Internet grew in popularity and the tools and places for self-expression became more widely available and easier to use, many people went from wanting to be anonymous online to revealing a lot of personal information.

6 I was taken aback by the percentage of students willing to put their photographs and other personal information online. What kinds of photographs did they actually put online? How did the whole profile contribute to the way they communicated? For the next stage of my research, I wanted to explore in more detail what students actually

did while online in an OSN. I located my next source by searching through the *Academic Search Complete* database. I was fortunate to come upon a very helpful article. It was a feature article in the international business newspaper *Financial Times.* Its author, Graham Bowley, bases much of his information on an interview with OSN researcher Danah Boyd. Through a *Google* search, I found Boyd's personal website, where I learned that she is a PhD candidate at the University of California-Berkeley and a Fellow at the University of Southern California Annenberg Center for Communications. Her research focuses on "how people negotiate a presentation of self to unknown audiences in mediated contexts" (Boyd). According to Bowley, Boyd is widely known online as "the high priestess of Internet friendship" for her writings and research on the subject. His interview with Boyd confirms findings that I found in the Pew survey that while some OSN users try to find new friends on the Internet, the majority were not using OSNs for that purpose. Instead, according to Bowley, "they were using it to reinforce existing relations with the group of friends they already had from their offline lives. For them, *MySpace* had become an electronic version of the local mall or park, the place they went to with their friends when they just wanted to hang out." Besides a "virtual hang out," OSNs offer young people a way to stay in touch with friends by allowing them to view their friends' profiles and leave short messages or comments. According to Cory Doctorow, another person interviewed by Bowley, this practice can be likened to "simple grooming exercises—in the same way that other primates groom each other to reinforce their relationships" (qtd. in Bowley).

7 Throughout the article, Bowley shows why Boyd supports OSNs. Boyd believes that "online social networks have become a vital space for young people to express themselves and build their personal identities" (Bowley). What I find interesting is that she particularly seems to like some of the edgy, unstable, dangerous aspects of OSNs that cause parents to be nervous about having their children online.

> Is there porn on MySpace? Of course. And bullying, sexual teasing and harassment are rampant among teenagers. It is how you learn to make meaning, cultural roles, norms. These kids need to explore their life among strangers. Teach them how to negotiate this new world. They need these public spaces now that other public spaces are closed to them. They need a place that is theirs. We should not always be chasing them and stopping them from growing up. (qtd. in Bowley)

Danah Boyd's observations have helped me understand how OSNs provide a place for self-expression as well as for communication with friends. She says that online sites give students practice at "identity production," where they can construct an identity through the kinds of items they post in their profile while also getting feedback and recognition from their friends. I got further understanding of this aspect of OSNs from another researcher interviewed by Bowley, Fred Stutzman (a person whose article on Internet identity-sharing I had already read). Stutzman calls students' OSN profiles an online version of their bedroom wall. Just as young people place posters on bedroom walls to express their special interests, they place items (pictures, music, and so forth) in their profiles to express themselves while also searching for an identity. "They are tuning into an audience," explains Stutzman. "One of the things students do at college is they test out identities. Maybe that is one new thing we are seeing now—more rapid changes of identity. Online you get feedback and you can change at a moment's notice" (qtd. in Bowley).

8 After considering the views of Boyd and Stutzman, I felt I understood why they think that OSNs give young people the opportunity for self-definition and self-expression. However, I still had doubts about the beneficial effects of OSNs. They still seem to me to send superficial messages about a person's identity. I found myself wondering if it is detrimental to spend all that time in virtual space rather than actually being with one's friends. I felt I needed to start looking for articles that examine the dangers of OSNs.

9 Although the next two sources I found didn't focus on the dangers of OSNs, they did provide interesting information on how students use *Facebook* to gain information about people they have met offline. The first article, another proceeding from an academic conference, reports data from two surveys of 1,440 first-year students at Michigan State University who had profiles on *Facebook.* Results show that "users are largely employing *Facebook* to learn more about people they meet offline, and are less likely to use the site to initiate new connections" (Lampe, Ellison, and Steinfield 167). The study reveals that *Facebook* users primarily use *Facebook* as a tool to investigate people they've already met offline. My second article, "Click Clique: *Facebook*'s Online College Community," written by Libby Copeland and published in the reputable newspaper the *Washington Post* in December of 2004, gives specific examples of this new social practice. One student explains how she would meet someone new at a friend's party that interested her and minutes later would be in her friend's room looking at his *Facebook* profile. Another student used the site to learn about the people in his classes: "If you meet someone in class and can't remember his name, you can look him up on the class lists kept on the *Facebook.* You can also research his interests, gathering information that you keep to yourself when you talk to him so he won't ever know you looked him up." Copeland also cites another student, who went as far as to call *Facebook* a "Stalker book."

10 After learning more about how users of OSNs practice self-disclosure, how they interact with friends online, and how they used the networks to find out information about people, I wanted to address something that had caught me off guard earlier in my research: the frequency with which OSN members are logged on to the community. Copeland mentions how much time students spent logged onto *Facebook.* She uses the term "Facebook Trance," which describes a person who loses track of all time and stares at the screen for hours. Copeland quotes one student who says "You stare into it [*Facebook* profiles] FOR-EV-ER." For the next stage of my research, I wanted to learn more about this "Facebook trance" and about the concept of Internet addiction.

11 I discovered that there is a lot of material on Internet addiction, so I started with an article appearing in the *Educational Psychology Review* in 2005 (Chou, Condron, and Belland). This is a long, scholarly article, most of which doesn't talk directly about OSNs. Nevertheless, parts of the article are valuable. In contrast to most of my research so far, this article sheds light on the potential problems of OSNs—the other side of this double-edged communication sword. One section states that 13% of respondents (in one of the studies the authors reviewed) reported that Internet use

had interfered with "their academic work, professional performance, or social lives." Among them, about 2% perceived the Internet as having an "overall negative effect on their daily lives" (369). Although OSNs can help to maintain and create new relationships, the authors claim that "over-dependence on online relationships may result in significant problems with real-life interpersonal and occupational functioning" (381). Students may believe that they are "in touch" with people, when in actuality they are physically alone with their computers. Although online communication can be used to enhance relationships, this article warns that it can become a problem when it begins to replace offline interaction.

12 After learning some of the ways that online social networks affect their users' communication skills, I have concluded that these networks can improve the ability to communicate, but if overused can negatively affect these skills. Although OSNs are offering their users new tools to express themselves, stay in touch with friends, and meet new people, these networks can turn counterproductive when a person becomes addicted and thus isolated from offline interpersonal interactions.

13 As I continue with my research, I am not sure what thesis I will assert for my final project. I still want to do more research on the negative effects of OSNs. For example, I haven't found studies that explore the possible phoniness of *Facebook* relationships. I remember a passage from Copeland where one user labels *Facebook* interaction as "communication lean." According to this student, "It's all a little fake—the 'friends'; the profiles that can be tailored to what others find appealing; the 'groups' that exist only in cyberspace." I'm still thinking about that quotation. Do OSNs contribute to deeper, more meaningful relationships or do they promote a superficial phoniness? I hope to explore this issue further before writing my major paper.

Works Cited

Bowley, Graham. "The High Priestess of Internet Friendship." *Financial Times Weekend Magazine* 27 Oct. 2006. *LexisNexis Academic.* Web. 22 Feb. 2007.

Boyd, Danah. Home page. Web. 21 Feb. 2007.

Chou, Chien, Linda Condron, and John C. Belland. "A Review of the Research on Internet Addiction." *Educational Psychology Review* 17.4 (2005): 363–89. *Academic Search Complete.* Web. 22 Feb. 2007.

Copeland, Libby. "Click Clique: *Facebook*'s Online College Community." *Washingtonpost.com.* Washington Post, 28 Dec. 2004. Web. 24 Feb. 2007.

Green, Elizabeth Weiss. "The Web of Social Networking." *U.S. News & World Report* 14 Nov. 2005: 58. *Academic Search Complete.* Web. 15 Feb. 2007.

Lampe, Cliff, Nicole Ellison, and Charles Steinfield. "A Face(book) in the Crowd: Social Searching Versus Social Browsing." *Proceedings of the 2006 20th Anniversary Conference on Computer Supported Cooperative Work.* 2006: 167–70. *The ACM Digital Library.* Web. 24 Feb. 2007.

Lenhart, Amanda, and Mary Madden. "Social Networking Websites and Teens: An Overview." *Pew Internet & American Life Project.* Pew Research Center, 3 Jan. 2007. Web. 19 Feb. 2007.

Stutzman, Frederic. "An Evaluation of Identity-Sharing Behavior in Social Network Communities." *Proceedings of the 2006 iDMAa and IMS Code Conference.* Oxford, OH, 2006. Web. 20 Feb. 2007.

THINKING CRITICALLY

about "How Do Online Social Networks Affect Communication?"

1. Earlier in this chapter, we suggested ways to organize and strengthen an exploratory essay. Where do you see James including the following features: (a) A blend of open-form narrative moves with closed-form focusing sentences? (b) A purposeful selection of sources? (c) A consideration of the rhetorical context of his sources—that is, an awareness of the kinds of sources he is using and how the genre of the source influences its content? (d) Reflective/critical thinking that shows his strong response to his sources? Where might he develop these features further?
2. Trace the evolution of James's ideas in this paper. How does his thinking evolve? What subquestions does he pose? What issues connected to his main question does he pursue?
3. Read James's argument for limiting use of OSNs on pages 172–173. What new research did he do for his final argument? How do you see the exploratory paper contributing to James's argument in the final paper? How do differences in purpose (exploration versus persuasion) lead to different structures for the two papers?
4. What are the strengths and weaknesses of James's exploration of OSNs?

Our next reading is an excerpt from James's annotated bibliography based on the same research he did for his exploratory paper. We have used James's research for both examples so that you can compare an exploratory paper with an annotated bibliography. His original annotated bibliography contained six entries. We have printed three of these, along with his critical preface. Additionally, the evaluative annotated bibliography entry for Graham Bowley is shown on page 166.

James Gardiner (student)

What Is the Effect of Online Social Networks on Communication Skills?

An Annotated Bibliography

Critical Preface

1 Today, online social networks (OSNs) such as *MySpace* and *Facebook* have become staples in the lives of most American young people. Although I was conscious that OSNs were impacting the way young people communicate with each other, I was largely unaware of the specific ways that the people used these OSNs or how their communication skills were being affected by this new technology. For this research project, I set out to discover how online social networks influence the way young

people communicate with each other. I posed several specific questions that I hoped my research could help me answer: (1) Why are OSNs so popular? (2) How do young people use OSNs? (3) How do OSNs affect communication skills? And (4) To what extent might OSNs be harmful or detrimental? These questions deserve to be examined because as more people move toward these new modes of communication, these networks will increasingly influence society as a whole.

2 I conducted this research during a one-week period in late February 2007. The bibliography contains different kinds of sources: two articles from popular magazines or newspapers; three articles from scholarly journals; and one survey report from a major Internet site devoted to research on people's use of the Internet. These sources gave me preliminary answers to all my initial research questions. They show why young people are attracted to OSNs and why and how they use them. Particularly valuable for my research are the articles by Bowley and by Lampe, Ellison, and Steinfield showing the positive potential of OSNs and the article by Chou, Condron, and Belland showing the possible negative potential if persons become addicted to OSNs.

Annotated Bibliography

Chou, Chien, Linda Condron, and John C. Belland. "A Review of the Research on Internet Addiction." *Educational Psychology Review* 17.4 (2005): 363–89. *Academic Search Complete.* Web. 22 Feb. 2007.

This lengthy academic article written for scholars reviews research on Internet addiction. It has four sections: (1) explanations of how Internet addiction is defined and assessed; (2) problems created by Internet addiction and variables such as gender or psychosocial traits associated with addiction; (3) explanations for why the Internet creates addictions; and (4) ways to treat Internet addiction. For my project, section 2 on problems was most valuable. In one study 13% of respondents reported that Internet use interfered with their personal lives or academic performance. Although Internet addiction didn't seem as harmful as other addictions, the authors observed that too much dependence on online relationships can interfere with real relationships. The tables in this article show the key findings from dozens of research studies.

Lampe, Cliff, Nicole Ellison, and Charles Steinfield. "A Face(book) in the Crowd: Social Searching Versus Social Browsing." *Proceedings of the 2006 20th Anniversary Conference on Computer Supported Cooperative Work.* 2006: 167–70. *The ACM Digital Library.* Web. 24 Feb. 2007.

This scholarly research report is based on questionnaires about *Facebook* usage received from 1,440 first-year students at Michigan State University in fall 2006. The researchers investigated whether students used *Facebook* primarily to meet new people ("social browsers") or to maintain or develop friendships with persons whom they had already met ("social searchers.") The findings contradicted the popular view that *Facebook* users are social browsers. Rather, the majority of respondents used the network to keep in touch with existing friends or to find out additional information about classmates or other recent acquaintances. This article has useful data about perceived audiences for profiles (peers rather than professors or administrators) and about primary reasons for using *Facebook.* The article provided insights into why *Facebook* is popular.

Lenhart, Amanda, and Mary Madden. "Social Networking Websites and Teens: An Overview." *Pew Internet & American Life Project.* Pew Research Center, 3 Jan. 2007. Web. 19 Feb. 2007.

This source is an online memo from researchers working for the Pew Internet and American Life Project, a non-profit research organization. It reports the results of a telephone survey of a random national sample of 935 youths aged 12 to 17 in fall 2006. The document has numerous tables showing demographic data about teens' use of OSNs, the most popular sites, the frequency of use, and the reasons teens give for using the sites. Because of the scientific method of polling, this article provides reliable data for understanding how teens currently use OSNs.

THINKING CRITICALLY

about "What Is the Effect of Online Social Networks on Communication Skills? An Annotated Bibliography"

1. Explain how James includes the three common elements of an evaluative annotation (genre/rhetorical context, summary of content, evaluation) in each of his annotations.
2. Compare James's annotated bibliography with his exploratory essay (pp. 169–173), noting differences between the way each source is described in the bibliography versus the essay. What insights do you get from the exploratory essay that are missing from the bibliography? What information about the sources comes through more clearly in the bibliography than in the essay?
3. How might James use information and points in this annotated bibliography in his researched argument?

WRITING AN INFORMATIVE (AND SURPRISING) ESSAY OR REPORT

8

As a reader, you regularly encounter writing with an informative aim, ranging from the instruction booklet for a smart phone to a newspaper feature story on the South African AIDS crisis. Informative documents include encyclopedias, cookbooks, voters' pamphlets, and various kinds of reports, as well as informative Web sites and magazine articles. In some informative prose, visual representations of information such as diagrams, photographs, maps, tables, and graphs can be as important as the prose itself.

A useful way to begin thinking about informative writing is to classify it according to the reader's motivation for reading. From this perspective, we can place informative prose in two categories.

In the first category, readers are motivated by an immediate need for information (setting the clock on a new microwave) or by curiosity about a subject (the impressionist movement in painting or new developments in rooftop solar panels). Informative writing in this category does not necessarily contain a contestable thesis. Documents are organized effectively, of course, but they often follow a chronological, step-by-step organization (as in a set of instructions) or an "all-about" topic-by-topic organization (as in an encyclopedia article on, say, Pakistan, divided into "Geography," "Climate," "Population," "History," and so forth). The writer provides factual information about a subject without necessarily shaping the information specifically to support a thesis.

In contrast, the second category of informative writing *is* thesis-based and is therefore aligned with other kinds of thesis-based prose. The thesis brings new or surprising information to readers who may not be initially motivated by a need-to-know occasion or by their own curiosity. In fact, readers might not be initially interested in the writer's topic at all, so the writer's first task is to hook readers' interest and motivate their desire to learn something new or surprising about a topic. An excellent strategy for creating this motivation is the technique of "surprising reversal," which we explain later.

In this chapter, you will learn to:

- write an informative report for a targeted audience
- write an informative essay using the surprising-reversal strategy

Exploring Informative (and Surprising) Writing

Let's say that you have just watched an old James Bond movie featuring a tarantula in Bond's bathroom. Curious about tarantulas, you do a quick Web search and retrieve the following short informative pieces. Read each one, and then proceed to the questions that follow.

Our first mini-article comes from the Web site EnchantedLearning.com, a commercial site aimed at providing interesting, fact-filled learning lessons for children.

EnchantedLearning.com

Tarantulas

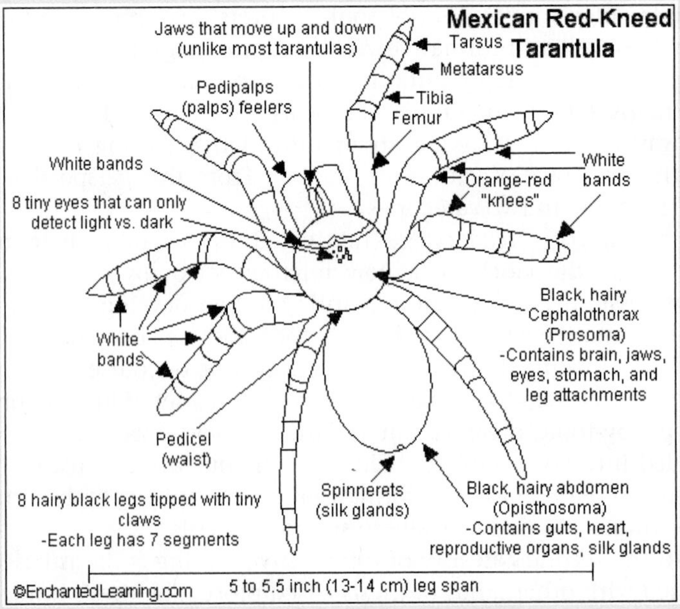

1 Tarantulas are large hairy spiders that live in warm areas around the world, including South America, southern North America, southern Europe, Africa, southern Asia, and Australia. The greatest concentration of tarantulas is in South America. There are about 300 species of tarantulas. The biggest tarantula is *Pseudotherathosa apophysis,* which has a leg span of about 13 inches (33 cm). These arachnids have a very long life span; some species can live over 30 years.

2 **Habitat:** Some tarantulas live in underground burrows; some live on the ground, and others live in trees. They live in rain forests, deserts, and other habitats.

3 **Diet:** Tarantulas are carnivores (meat-eaters). They eat insects (like grasshoppers and beetles), other arachnids, small reptiles (like lizards and snakes), amphibians (like frogs), and some even eat small birds. Tarantulas kill their prey using venomous fangs; they also inject a chemical into the prey that dissolves the flesh. Tarantulas can crush their prey using powerful mouthparts. No person has ever died of a tarantula bite.

4 **Anatomy:** Tarantulas have a hairy two-part body and very strong jaws (with venomous fangs). They have eight hairy legs; each leg has 2 tiny claws at the end and a cushioning pad behind the claws. The hairs on the body and legs are sensitive to touch, temperature, and smell. Tarantulas have a hard exoskeleton and not an internal skeleton.

The second mini-article comes from the Web site of the University of Washington's Burke Museum. The author of this piece is the curator of arachnids at the Burke Museum.

Rod Crawford

Myths about "Dangerous" Spiders

1 **Myth:** Tarantulas are dangerous or deadly to humans.

2 **Fact:** Outside of southern Europe (where the name is used for a wolf spider, famous in medieval superstition as the alleged cause of "tarantella" dancing), the word tarantula is most often used for the very large, furry spiders of the family Theraphosidae.

3 Hollywood is squarely to blame for these spiders' toxic-to-humans reputation. Tarantulas are large, photogenic and easily handled, and therefore have been very widely used in horror and action-adventure movies. When some "venomous" creature is needed to menace James Bond or Indiana Jones, to invade a small town in enormous numbers, or to grow to gigantic size and prowl the Arizona desert for human prey, the special-effects team calls out the tarantulas!

4 In reality, the venom of these largest-of-all-spiders generally has **very low toxicity to humans**. I myself was once bitten by a Texan species and hardly even felt it. None of the North American species or those commonly kept as pets are considered to pose even a mild bite hazard. There are some reports that a few tropical species may have venom more toxic to vertebrates, but human bite cases haven't been reported, so we can't know for sure.

5 The only health hazard posed by keeping pet tarantulas comes from the irritating chemicals on the hairs of the abdomen, which can cause skin rashes or inflammation of eyes and nasal passages. To prevent such problems, simply keep tarantulas away from your face and wash your hands after handling one.

6 Compared to common pets such as dogs, tarantulas are not dangerous at all. (For more information see the American Tarantula Society.)

European tarantula
Lycosa Tarentula
Southern Europe; body length 2–3 cm
(photo courtesy of Manuel J. Cabrero)
Click image to enlarge

Pink toe tarantula
Avicularia avicularia
Brazil to Trinidad; body length 6–7 cm
(photo courtesy of Ron Taylor)
Click image to enlarge

Both the *European wolf spiders* (**left**) originally called tarantulas, and the *theraphosid spiders* (**right**), often kept as pets and called tarantulas now, have been reputed dangerous to humans. They aren't.

THINKING CRITICALLY
about "Tarantulas" and "Myths about 'Dangerous' Spiders"

1. Why do you think the reading from EnchantedLearning.com uses a diagram of a tarantula while the Burke Museum Web site uses photographs? How is each choice connected to the piece's targeted audience and purpose?
2. How would you describe the difference in organizational strategies for each of the readings?
3. One might suppose that informational writing would be unaffected by the writer's angle of vision—that facts would simply be facts and that informational pieces on the same topic would contain the same basic information. Yet these two short pieces give somewhat different impressions of the tarantula. For example, how do these readings differ in the way they portray the bite of the tarantula? How else do they differ in overall effect?

Understanding Informative Writing

In informative writing, the writer is assumed to have more expertise than the reader on a given subject. The writer's aim is to enlarge the reader's view of the subject by bringing the reader new information. The writer's information can come from a variety of sources:

- From the writer's preexisting expertise in a subject
- From the writer's own personal experiences
- From field research such as observations, interviews, questionnaires, and so forth
- From library or Internet research

We turn now to a closer look at two commonly assigned genres with an informative aim.

Informative Reports

Although the term *report* can have numerous meanings, we will define a **report** as any document that presents the results of a fact-finding or data-gathering investigation. Sometimes report writers limit themselves to presenting newly discovered information, while at other times they go further by analyzing or interpreting the information to explain its implications and significance or to uncover patterns of cause and effect.

Reports of various kinds are among the most common genres that you will read and write as a workplace professional. Often managers have to prepare periodic reports to supervisors on sales, operations, expenses, or team productivity. Equally important are solicited reports, usually assigned by supervisors to individuals or task forces, requesting individuals to investigate a problem, gather crucial information, and report the results.

Characteristics of a Report The text of a report should be concise, with a tightly closed-form structure often broken into sections marked by headings. Individual points might be bulleted. Numeric data are usually displayed in graphs or tables. Long reports usually include a cover page and a table of contents and often begin with an "executive summary" that condenses the main findings into a paragraph.

The Introduction to a Report How you write the introduction to a report depends on the audience you are addressing. In some cases a report is aimed at general readers and published in, say, a popular magazine. In such cases, you must arouse your readers' interest and provide necessary background, just as you would do in most closed-form introductions. Kerri Ann Matsumoto's "How Much Does It Cost to Go Organic?" (p. 195) is a student example of an informative report written for a magazine audience. (Note how Matsumoto "desktop-published" her essay in two-column format to look like a magazine article.)

In other cases, the report is solicited (say, by a supervisor); it is aimed at a specific reader who is already interested in the information and is waiting for you to provide it. In this case, the report is often written as a memorandum. Instead of a title, short reports usually have an informative "subject line" that identifies the report's topic and purpose. The introduction typically creates a brief context for the report, states its purpose, and maps its structure. Here is an example of an introduction:

PROTOTYPE INTRODUCTION FOR A SOLICITED REPORT

To: Ms. Polly Carpenter, Business Manager
From: Ralph Hiner
Subject: Projected costs for the new seed catalog

As you requested, I have researched the projected costs for the new seed catalog. This memo provides background on the marketing plan, itemizes projected expenses, and presents an overall figure for budget planning.

For an example of a short informative report written for a general audience, see "Muslim Americans: Middle Class and Mostly Mainstream" on pages 192–193.

The following exercise will give you a taste of workplace report writing. Suppose that you are a marketing researcher for a company that designs and produces new video games. One day you receive the following memo from your manager:

To: You
From: Big Boss
Subject: Information about gender differences in video game playing

The marketing team wants to investigate differences in the amount of time male and female college students spend playing video games and in the kinds of video games that each gender enjoys. I want you to conduct appropriate research at local colleges using questionnaires, interviews, and focus groups. Specifically, the marketing team wants to know approximately how many minutes per week an average college male versus a college female spends playing video games. Also investigate whether there is any difference in the kinds of games they enjoy. We need your report by the end of the month.

FOR WRITING AND DISCUSSION

Producing a Solicited Report

1. Assume that your classroom is a "focus group" for your investigation. As a class, create an informal questionnaire to gather the information that you will need for your report.
2. Give the questionnaire to the class and tabulate results.
3. Working individually or in small groups, prepare a memo to Big Boss reporting your results.

For guidance on developing a questionnaire, see Chapter 9, pp. 210–213.

Informative Essay Using the Surprising-Reversal Strategy

Another commonly encountered genre is an informative article with surprising information, often found in magazines or newspapers. In this section, we focus on a specific version of this kind of essay—a thesis-based informative article aimed at general audiences. Because readers are assumed to be browsing through the pages of a magazine, the writer's rhetorical challenge is to arouse the reader's curiosity and then to keep the reader reading by providing interesting new information. The writer's first task is to hook the reader on a question and then to provide a surprising thesis that gives shape and purpose to the information. A good way to focus and sharpen the thesis, as we will show, is to use the "surprising-reversal" strategy.

"All-About" Versus "Thesis-Governed" Informative Prose Let's begin by revisiting the difference between an encyclopedic (or "all-about") informative piece and a thesis-based piece. To appreciate this distinction, consider again the difference between the EnchantedLearning.com Web site on tarantulas (pp. 178–179) and the Burke Museum piece "Myths about 'Dangerous' Spiders" (pp. 179–180). The EnchantedLearning.com piece is a short "all-about" report organized under the topic headings "Habitat," "Diet," and "Anatomy." The Web writer may simply have adapted an encyclopedia article on tarantulas into a format for children. In contrast, the Burke Museum piece by Rod Crawford is thesis-based. Crawford wishes to refute the myth that "[t]arantulas are dangerous or deadly to humans." He does so by providing information on the low toxicity of tarantula venom to humans and the relative painlessness of tarantula bites. All of Crawford's data focus on the danger potential of tarantulas. There are no data about habitat, diet, or other aspects of tarantula life—material that would be included if this were an all-about report. Because the piece also includes data about misconceptions of tarantulas, it follows the basic pattern of surprising reversal: "Many people believe that tarantulas are toxic to humans, but I will show that tarantulas are not dangerous at all."

Surprising-Reversal Pattern **Surprising reversal**, as we explained in Chapter 2, Concept 5, is our term for a strategy in which the writer's thesis pushes sharply against a counterthesis. This structure automatically creates a thesis with tension focused on a question or problem. Because of its power to hook and sustain readers, surprising-reversal essays can be found in many publications, ranging from easy-reading magazines to scholarly journals. Here, for example, is an abstract of an article from *Atlantic Monthly*.

"REEFER MADNESS" BY ERIC SCHLOSSER

> Marijuana has been pushed so far out of the public imagination by other drugs, and its use is so casually taken for granted in some quarters of society, that one might assume it had been effectively decriminalized. In truth, the government has never been tougher on marijuana offenders than it is today. In an era when violent criminals frequently walk free or receive modest jail terms, tens of thousands of people are serving long sentences for breaking marijuana laws.

This article asserts a surprising, new position ("the government has never been tougher on marijuana offenders than it is today") that counters a commonly held view (marijuana laws are no longer enforced). Here are additional examples of the surprising-reversal pattern:

Commonly Held, Narrow, or Inaccurate View	New, Surprising Information
Native Americans used to live in simple harmony with the earth.	Many American Indians used to "control" nature by setting fire to forests to make farming easier or to improve hunting.
Having fathers present in the delivery room helps the mother relax and have an easier birth.	Having fathers present in delivery rooms may reduce the amount of oxytocin produced by the mother and lead to more caesarian sections.

A similar pattern is often found in scholarly academic writing, which typically has the following underlying shape:

> Whereas some scholars say X, I am going to argue Y.

Because the purpose of academic research is to advance knowledge, an academic article almost always shows the writer's new view against a background of prevailing views (what other scholars have said). This kind of tension is what often makes thesis-based writing memorable and provocative.

The writer's surprising information can come from personal experience, field research, or library/Internet research. If a college writer bases an informative piece on research sources and documents them according to academic conventions, the magazine genre doubles as an effective college research paper by combining academic citations with a tone and style suitable for general readers. Shannon King's article on hydrogen cars (p. 196) is an example of a student research paper written in magazine article style.

"Surprise" as a Relative Term When using the surprising-reversal strategy, keep in mind that *surprise* is a relative term based on the relationship between you and your intended audience. You don't have to surprise everyone in the world, just those who hold a mistaken or narrow view of your topic. The key is to imagine an audience less informed about your topic than you are. Suppose, as an illustration, that you have just completed an introductory economics course. You are less informed about economics than your professor, but more informed about economics than persons who have never had an econ class. You might therefore bring surprising information to the less informed audience:

> The average airplane traveler thinks that the widely varying ticket pricing for the same flight is chaotic and silly, but I can show how this pricing scheme makes perfect sense economically. [written to the "average airplane traveler," who hasn't taken an economics course]

This paper would be surprising to your intended audience, but not to the economics professor. From a different perspective, however, you could also write about economics to your professor because you might know more than your professor about, say, how students struggle with some concepts:

> Many economics professors assume that students can easily learn the concept of "elasticity of demand," but I can show why this concept was particularly confusing

for me and my classmates. [written to economics professors who aren't aware of student difficulties with particular concepts]

Additionally, your surprising view doesn't necessarily have to be diametrically opposed to the common view. Perhaps you think the common view is *incomplete* or *insufficient* rather than *dead wrong*. Instead of saying, "View X is wrong, whereas my view, Y, is correct," you can say, "View X is correct and good as far as it goes, but my view, Y, adds a new perspective." In other words, you can also create surprise by going a step beyond the common view to show readers something new.

Informative Report

WRITING PROJECT

Write a short informative report based on data you have gathered from observations, interviews, questionnaires, or library/Internet research. Your report should respond to one of the following scenarios or to a scenario provided by your instructor:

- Your boss runs a chain of health food stores that sell high-nutrition smoothies. Because sales have been flat, she wants to create an advertising campaign to attract more customers to her smoothie bars. She has heard that the boutique coffee drinks sold at coffee shops such as Starbucks are actually high in calories and fat. She has asked you to research the nutritional information on coffee drinks. She would also like you to compare the fat/calorie content of various coffee drinks to that of cheeseburgers, fries, and milkshakes sold at fast-food restaurants. She's hoping that the information you provide will help her launch a campaign to lure customers from coffee shops to her smoothie bars. Write your report in the form of a memorandum to your boss, providing the requested information in a closed-form, crisply presented style.
- You are doing a service-learning project for a health maintenance organization. Your manager is worried about hearing loss in young people, possibly caused by listening to loud music through earbuds plugged into iPods or MP3 players. Your manager asks you to write a short informative article, suitable for publication in the HMO's newsletter, that reports on research on hearing loss due to earbuds. Write your report for a general audience who read the HMO newsletter for helpful health information.

Generating and Exploring Ideas

Your initial goal is to use effective research strategies to find the requested information. If your report draws on library/Internet research, consult Part 4 of this textbook. If your report draws on field research, consult Chapter 9 on gathering and

FIGURE 8.1 Framework for an Informative Report

Title	• For a report addressed to a general audience, an interest-grabbing title • For a solicited report, an informative subject line
Introduction (one to several paragraphs)	• For general audiences, provides background and context and arouses interest • For a solicited report, refers to the request, explains the purpose of the report, and maps its structure
Body section 1 (brief)	• Explains your research process and the sources of your data
Body section 2 (major)	• Provides the information in a logical sequence • Uses closed-form organizational strategies • Displays numeric data in graphs or tables referenced in the text
Conclusion	• Suggests the significance of the information provided

analyzing data. Particularly helpful will be pages 208–213, on using questionnaires and interviews. For displaying numerical information in graphs or tables, consult Skill 17.9.

Shaping and Drafting

Although there is no one correct way to organize an informative report, such reports typically have the structure shown in Figure 8.1. Kerri Ann Matsumoto's essay on the cost of organic food (p. 195), aimed at general audiences, exhibits this typical structure. Her title and introduction announce her research question and engage her readers' interest (how much does it cost to buy organic food versus non-organic food?). The body of the paper then explains her process (she did comparison pricing for a chicken stir-fry for a family of four at an organic and a non-organic store); presents her findings in both words and graphics (organic foods cost more); and suggests the significance of her research (helps readers sort out the advantages of organic foods versus the advantages of spending the extra money in other ways).

Revising

As you revise, make sure that your graphics (if you used them) and your words tell the same story and reinforce each other. As you edit, try to achieve a clear, concise style that allows your intended audience to read quickly. For workplace reports, show your respect for the busy business environment that places many simultaneous demands on managers. When you have a near-final draft, exchange it with a classmate for a peer review.

Questions for Peer Review

In addition to the generic peer review questions explained in Skill 16.4, ask your peer reviewers to address these questions:

1. If the report is solicited, does the document have a professional appearance (memo format, pleasing use of white space, appropriate use of headings)? Do the subject line and opening overview passage effectively explain the report's occasion, purpose, and structure?
2. If the report is aimed at a general audience, does it follow the manuscript style and document design specified by the instructor? Do the title and introduction provide context and motivate reader interest?
3. Does the writer explain how the research was conducted?
4. Is the report clear, concise, and well organized? How might the presentation of the information be improved?
5. If the report uses graphics, are the graphics referenced in the text? Are they clear, with appropriate titles and labels? How might they be improved?

Informative Essay Using the Surprising-Reversal Strategy

WRITING PROJECT

> Using personal experience, field research, or library/Internet research, write an informative magazine article using a surprising-reversal strategy in a tone and style suitable for general readers. Your task is to arouse your readers' curiosity by posing an interesting question, summarizing a common or expected answer to the question, and then providing new, surprising information that counters or "reverses" the common view. You imagine readers who hold a mistaken or overly narrow view of your topic; your purpose is to give them a new, surprising view.

Depending on the wishes of your instructor, this assignment can draw either on personal experience or on research. Shannon King's "How Clean and Green Are Hydrogen Fuel-Cell Cars?" (pp. 196–198) is an example of a researched essay that enlarges the targeted audience's view of a subject in a surprising way. Although it is an example of a short academic research article, it is written in a relaxed style suitable for magazine publication.

For this assignment, try to avoid issues calling for persuasive rather than informative writing. With persuasive prose, you imagine a resistant reader who may argue back. With informative prose, you imagine a more trusting reader, one willing to learn from your experience or research. Although you hope to enlarge your reader's view of a topic, you aren't necessarily saying that your audience's original view is wrong, nor are you initiating a debate. For example, suppose a writer wanted to develop the following claim: "Many of my friends think that having an alcoholic mother would be the worst thing that could happen to you, but I will show that my mother's disease forced our family closer together." In this case the writer isn't arguing that alcoholic mothers are good or that everyone should have an alcoholic mother. Rather, the writer is simply offering readers a new, unexpected, and expanded view of what it might be like to have an alcoholic mother.

Generating and Exploring Ideas

If you do field research or library/Internet research for your article, start by posing a research question. As you begin doing initial research on your topic area, you will soon know more about your topic than most members of the general public. Ask yourself, "What has surprised me about my research so far? What have I learned that I didn't know before?" Your answers to these questions can suggest possible approaches to your paper. For example, Shannon King began her research believing that fuel-cell technology produced totally pollution-free energy. She didn't realize that one needs to burn fossil fuels in order to produce the hydrogen. This initial surprise shaped her paper. She decided that if this information surprised her, it should surprise others also.

What follows are two exercises you can try to generate ideas for your paper.

Individual Task to Generate Ideas

Here is a template that can help you generate ideas by asking you to think specifically about differences in knowledge levels between you and various audiences.

> I know more about X [topic area] than [specific person or persons].

For example, you might say, "I know more about [computer games/gospel music/the energy crisis] than [my roommate/my high school friends/my parents]." This exercise helps you discover subjects about which you already have expertise compared to other audiences. Likewise, you can identify a subject that interests you, do a couple of hours of research on it, and then say: "Based on just this little amount of research, I know more about X than my roommate." Thinking in this way, you might be able to create an intriguing question that you could answer through your research.

Small-Group Task to Generate Ideas

Form small groups. Assign a group recorder to make a two-column list, with the left column titled "Mistaken or Narrow View of X" and the right column titled "Groupmate's Surprising View." Using the surprising-reversal strategy, brainstorm ideas for article topics until every group member has generated at least one entry for the right-hand column. Here are several examples:

Mistaken or Narrow View of X	Groupmate's Surprising View
Being an offensive lineman in football is a no-brain, repetitive job requiring size and strength, but only enough intelligence and athletic ability to push people out of the way.	Jeff can show that being an offensive lineman is a complex job that requires mental smarts as well as size, strength, and athletic ability.
Pawnshops are disreputable places.	Samantha's uncle owns a pawnshop that is a wholesome family business that serves an important social function.
To most straight people, *Frankenstein* is a monster movie about science gone amuck.	Cody can show how to the gay community, *Frankenstein* holds a special and quite different meaning.

To help stimulate ideas, you might consider topic areas such as the following:

- ***People:*** computer programmers, homeless people, cheerleaders, skateboarders, gang members, priests or rabbis, reality show stars, feminists, mentally ill or developmentally disabled persons.
- ***Activities:*** washing dishes, climbing mountains, wrestling, modeling, gardening, living with a chronic disease or disability, owning a certain breed of dog, riding a subway at night, posting status updates on Facebook, entering a dangerous part of a city.
- ***Places:*** particular neighborhoods, specific buildings or parts of buildings, local attractions, junkyards, college campuses, places of entertainment, summer camps.
- ***Other similar categories:*** groups, events, animals and plants, gadgets, and so forth; the list is endless.

Next, go around the room, sharing with the entire class the topics you have generated. Remember that you are not yet committed to writing about any of these topics.

Shaping, Drafting, and Revising

A surprising-reversal informative essay has the features and organization shown in Figure 8.2.

To create the "surprising-reversal" feel, it's important to delay your thesis until after you have explained your audience's common, expected answer to your opening question. This delay in presenting the thesis creates an open-form feel that readers often find engaging. Shannon King's research paper on hydrogen cars (pp. 196–198) has this surprising-reversal shape.

As a way of helping you generate ideas, we offer the following five questions. Following each question, we speculate about what King might have written if she had used the same questions to help her get started on her essay.

FIGURE 8.2 Framework for an Informative Essay Using the Surprising-Reversal Strategy

Introduction (one to several paragraphs)	• Engages readers' interest in the writer's question • Provides background and context
Body section 1 (brief)	• Explains the common or popular answer to the writer's question
Body section 2 (major)	• Provides a delayed thesis—the writer's surprising answer to the question • Supports the thesis with information from personal experience or research • Displays numeric data in graphs or tables referenced in the text
Conclusion	• Suggests the significance of the writer's new perspective on the question

1. ***What question does your essay address?*** (King might have asked, "Will hydrogen fuel-cell automobiles solve our nation's energy and pollution crises?")
2. ***What is the common, expected, or popular answer to this question held by your imagined audience?*** (King might have said, "Most people believe that hydrogen fuel-cell cars will solve our country's pollution and energy crises.")
3. ***What examples and details support your audience's view?*** Expand on these views by developing them with supporting examples and details. (King might have noted her research examples praising fuel-cell technology such as the Bush/Cheney National Energy Report or California Governor Arnold Schwarzenegger's desire to build hydrogen fuel stations across the state.)
4. ***What is your own surprising view?*** (King might have said, "Although hydrogen fuel-cell cars are pollution free, getting the hydrogen in the first place requires burning fossil fuels.")
5. ***What examples and details support this view? Why do you hold this view? Why should a reader believe you?*** Writing rapidly, spell out the evidence that supports your point. (King would have done a freewrite about her research discoveries that hydrogen has to be recovered from carbon-based fossils or from electrolysis of water—all of which means continued use of pollution-causing fossil fuels.)

After you finish exploring your responses to these five trigger questions, you will be well on your way to composing a first draft of your article. Now finish writing your draft fairly rapidly without worrying about perfection.

Once you have your first draft on paper, the goal is to make it work better, first for yourself and then for your readers. If you discovered ideas as you wrote, you may need to do some major restructuring. Check to see that the question you are addressing is clear. If you are using the surprising-reversal strategy, make sure that you distinguish between your audience's common view and your own surprising view. Apply the strategies for global revision explained in Chapter 16.

Questions for Peer Review

In addition to the generic peer review questions explained in Skill 16.4, ask your peer reviewers to address these questions:

1. What is the question the paper addresses? How effective is the paper at hooking the reader's interest in the question?
2. Where does the writer explain the common or popular view of the topic? Do you agree that this is the common view? How does the writer develop or support this view? What additional supporting examples, illustrations, or details might make the common view more vivid or compelling?
3. What is the writer's surprising view? Were you surprised? What details does the writer use to develop the surprising view? What additional supporting examples, illustrations, or details might help make the surprising view more vivid and compelling?
4. Is the draft clear and easy to follow? Is the draft interesting? How might the writer improve the style, clarity, or interest level of the draft?
5. If the draft includes graphics, are they effective? Do the words and the visuals tell the same story? Are the visuals properly titled and labeled? How might the use of visuals be improved?

Readings

Our first reading, "Muslim Americans: Middle Class and Mostly Mainstream," published in May 2007, illustrates an informative report. Based on field and research data compiled by the Pew Research Center for the People and the Press, this reading is the widely disseminated summary of the Center's longer, more detailed report. The complete report can be read on the Pew Research Center's Web site. This report summary has many features of a workplace document except that it is addressed to a general audience rather than a specific workplace audience.

The Pew Research Center for the People and the Press

Muslim Americans: Middle Class and Mostly Mainstream

1 The first-ever, nationwide, random sample survey of Muslim Americans finds them to be largely assimilated, happy with their lives, and moderate with respect to many of the issues that have divided Muslims and Westerners around the world.

2 The Pew Research Center conducted more than 55,000 interviews to obtain a national sample of 1,050 Muslims living in the United States. Interviews were conducted in English, Arabic, Farsi and Urdu. The resulting study, which draws on Pew's survey research among Muslims around the world, finds that Muslim Americans are a highly diverse population, one largely composed of immigrants. Nonetheless, they are decidedly American in their outlook, values and attitudes. This belief is reflected in Muslim American income and education levels, which generally mirror those of the public.

3 Key findings include:

- Overall, Muslim Americans have a generally positive view of the larger society. Most say their communities are excellent or good places to live.
- A large majority of Muslim Americans believe that hard work pays off in this society. Fully 71% agree that most people who want to get ahead in the U.S. can make it if they are willing to work hard.
- The survey shows that although many Muslims are relative newcomers to the U.S., they are highly assimilated into American society. On balance, they believe that Muslims coming to the U.S. should try and adopt American customs, rather than trying to remain distinct from the larger society. And by nearly two-to-one (63%–32%) Muslim Americans do not see a conflict between being a devout Muslim and living in a modern society.

Muslim Americans: Who Are They?

	Total
Proportion who are . . .	%
Foreign-born Muslims	**65**
Arab region	24
Pakistan	8
Other South Asia	10
Iran	8
Europe	5
Other Africa	4
Other	6
Native-born Muslims	**35**
African American	20
Other	15
	100
Foreign-born Muslims	**65**
Year immigrated:	
2000–2007	18
1990–1999	21
1980–1989	15
Before 1980	11
Native-born Muslims	**35**
Percent who are . . .	
Converts to Islam	21
Born Muslim	14

- Roughly two-thirds (65%) of adult Muslims in the U.S. were born elsewhere. A relatively large proportion of Muslim immigrants are from Arab countries, but many also come from Pakistan and other South Asian countries. Among native-born Muslims, roughly half are African American (20% of U.S. Muslims overall), many of whom are converts to Islam.
- Based on data from this survey, along with available Census Bureau data on immigrants' nativity and nationality, the Pew Research Center estimates the total population of Muslims in the United States at 2.35 million.
- Muslim Americans reject Islamic extremism by larger margins than do Muslim minorities in Western European countries. However, there is somewhat more acceptance of Islamic extremism in some segments of the U.S. Muslim public than others. Fewer native-born African American Muslims than others completely condemn al Qaeda. In addition, younger Muslims in the U.S. are much more likely than older Muslim Americans to say that suicide bombing in the defense of Islam can be at least sometimes justified. Nonetheless, absolute levels of support for Islamic extremism among Muslim Americans are quite low, especially when compared with Muslims around the world.
- A majority of Muslim Americans (53%) say it has become more difficult to be a Muslim in the U.S. since the Sept. 11 terrorist attacks. Most also believe that the government "singles out" Muslims for increased surveillance and monitoring.
- Relatively few Muslim Americans believe the U.S.-led war on terror is a sincere effort to reduce terrorism, and many doubt that Arabs were responsible for the 9/11 attacks. Just 40% of Muslim Americans say groups of Arabs carried out those attacks.

U.S. Muslims More Mainstream

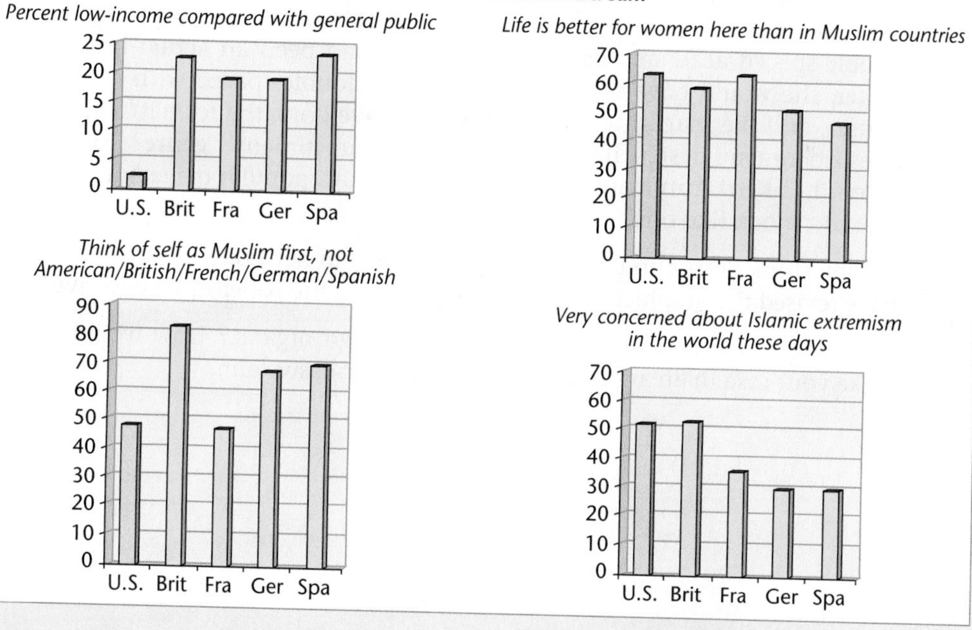

THINKING CRITICALLY

about "Muslim Americans: Middle Class and Mostly Mainstream"

1. Note how this document includes the typical features, with some modifications, of a typical informative report (see Figure 8.1). Where does the document include the following:
   a. An overview sentence that orients readers to the purpose and content of the document?
   b. An explanation of the writer's research process?
   c. Presentation of the writer's findings using both verbal text and graphics?
2. Typically, informative writing is valuable to the extent that it brings something needed, new, or surprising to the audience and therefore enlarges their view of the topic. What did you find new, surprising, or otherwise worthwhile in this informative report?

Our second reading, by student writer Kerri Ann Matsumoto (p. 195), is formatted to look like a popular magazine article.

THINKING CRITICALLY

about "How Much Does It Cost to Go Organic?"

1. In our teaching, we have discovered that students appreciate the concept of genre more fully if they occasionally "desktop-publish" a manuscript to look like a magazine article, a poster, or a brochure rather than a standard double-spaced academic paper. If Kerri Ann had been an actual freelance writer, she would have submitted this article double-spaced with attached figures, and the magazine publisher would have done the formatting. How does document design itself help signal the document's genre? To what extent has Kerri Ann made this article *sound* like a popular magazine article as well as look like one?
2. Do you think Kerri Ann used graphics effectively in her essay? How might she have revised the graphics or the wording to make the paper more effective?
3. Do you think it is worth the extra money to go organic? How would you make your case in an argument paper with a persuasive aim?

HOW MUCH DOES IT COST TO GO ORGANIC?

Kerri Ann Matsumoto

Organic foods, grown without pesticides, weed killers, or hormone additives, are gaining popularity from small privately owned organic food stores to large corporate markets. With the cost of living rising, how much can a family of four afford to pay for organically grown food before it becomes too expensive?

To find out more information about the cost of organic foods, I went to the Rainbow Market, which is a privately owned organic food store, and to a nearby Safeway. I decided to see what it would cost to create a stir-fry for a family of four. I estimated that the cost of organic vegetables for the stir-fry would cost $3.97. Non-organic vegetables for the same stir-fry, purchased at Safeway, would cost $2.37. If we imagined our family eating the same stir fry every night for a year, it would cost $1,499 for organic and $865 for non-organic for a difference of $584.

After pricing vegetables, I wanted to find out how much it would cost to add to the stir-fry free-range chicken fed only organic feeds, as opposed to non-organic factory farmed chicken. For good quality chicken breasts, the organic chicken was $6.99 per pound and the non-organic was $3.58 per pound. Projected out over a year, the organic chicken would cost $5,103 compared to $2,613 for non-organic chicken.

Comparative Cost of Ingredients in an Organic Versus Non-Organic Stir-Fry

	Vegetables per day	Chicken per day	Total per day	Total per year
Organic	$3.97	$13.98	$17.95	$6552
Non-Organic	$2.37	$7.16	$9.53	$3478

If we add the cost of chicken and vegetables together (see the table and the graph), we can compute how much more it would cost to feed our family of four organic versus non-organic chicken stir-fry for a year.

My research shows that over the course of one year it will cost $6,552 per year to feed our family organic stir-fry and $3,478 for non-organic for a difference of $3,074. If a family chose to eat not only organic dinner, but also all organic meals, the cost of food would sharply increase.

Before going to the Rainbow Market I knew that the price of organic foods was slightly higher than non-organic. However, I did not expect the difference to be so great. Of course, if you did comparison shopping at other stores, you might be able to find cheaper organic chicken and vegetables. But my introductory research suggests that going organic isn't cheap.

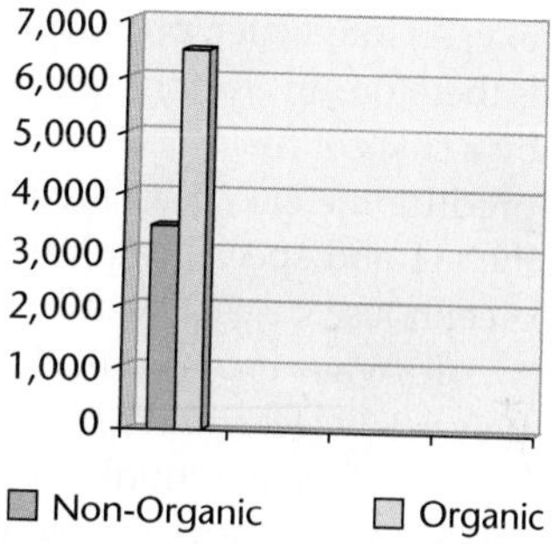

Cost of Feeding a Family of Four for One Year: Organic Versus Non-Organic Stir-Fry

Is it worth it? Many people today have strong concerns for the safety of the foods that they feed to their family. If you consider that organic vegetables have no pesticides and that the organic chicken has no growth hormone additives, the extra cost may be worth it. Also if you are concerned about cruelty to animals, free-range chickens have a better life than caged chickens. But many families might want to spend the $3,074 difference in other ways. If you put that money toward a college fund, within ten years you could save over $30,000. So how much are you willing to pay for organic foods?

The next reading, by student writer Shannon King, is a short academic research paper using the surprising-reversal strategy. Shannon's paper uses research information to enlarge her readers' understanding of hydrogen fuel-cell vehicles by showing that hydrogen fuel is not as pollution-free as the general public believes.

Shannon King (student)

How Clean and Green Are Hydrogen Fuel-Cell Cars?

1 The United States is embroiled in a controversy over energy and pollution. We are rapidly using up the earth's total supply of fossil fuels, and many experts think that children being born today will experience the end of affordable oil. One energy expert, Paul Roberts, believes that serious oil shortages will start ccurring by 2015 when the world's demand for oil will outstrip the world's capacity for further oil production. An equally serious problem is that the burning of fossil fuels spews carbon dioxide into the atmosphere, which increases the rate of global warming.

2 One hopeful way of addressing these problems is to develop hydrogen fuel cell cars. According to Karim Nice, the author of the fuel cell pages on the *HowStuffWorks* Web site, a fuel cell is "an electrochemical energy conversion device that converts hydrogen and oxygen into water, producing electricity and heat in the process." A hydrogen-fueled car is therefore an electric car, powered by an electric motor. The car's electricity is generated by a stack of fuel cells that act like a battery. In the hydrogen fuel cell, the chemicals that produce the electricity are hydrogen from the car's pressurized fuel tank, oxygen from the air, and special catalysts inside the fuel cell. The fuel cell releases no pollutants or greenhouse gases. The only waste product is pure water.

3 To what extent will these pollution-free fuel cells be our energy salvation? Are they really clean and green?

4 Many people think so. The development of hydrogen fuel cells has caused much excitement. I know people who say we don't need to worry about running out of oil because cars of the future will run on water. One recent *New York Times* advertisement produced by General Motors has as its headline, "Who's driving the hydrogen economy?" The text of the ad begins by saying "The hydrogen economy isn't a pipe dream.... The hydrogen economy is the endgame of a multifaceted strategy General Motors set in motion years ago, with steps that are real, progressive, and well-underway" (General Motors). The Web site for the Hydrogen Fuel Cell Institute includes a picture of a crystal clear blue sky landscape with a large letter headline proclaiming "At long last, a technology too long overlooked promises to transform society." At the bottom of the picture are the words, "Offering clean & abundant power, hydrogen-based fuel cells could soon end our reliance on oil and minimize emissions of pollution and global-warming gases." According to CNN News, the Bush administration proposed devoting 1.7 billion dollars of federal funds to developing hydrogen fuel cells (CNN). The biggest nationally known proponent of hydrogen fuel cells is California Governor Arnold Schwarzenegger, who signed an Executive Order that California's "21 interstate freeways shall be designated as the 'California Hydrogen Highway Network.'" (California). In this executive order, Schwarzenegger envisioned

> a network of hydrogen fueling stations along these roadways and in the urban centers that they connect, so that by 2010, every Californian will have access to hydrogen fuel, with a significant and increasing percentage produced from clean, renewable sources. (2)

Schwarzenegger's optimism about the hydrogen highway sums up the common view that hydrogen is a clean alternative energy source that is abundant throughout nature. All we have to do is bottle it up, compress it, and transport it to a network of new "gas stations" where the gas being pumped is hydrogen.

5 But what I discovered in my research is that hydrogen is not as green as most people think. Although hydrogen fuel cells appear to be an environmentally friendly alternative to fossil fuels, the processes for producing hydrogen actually require the use of fossil fuels. The problem is that pure hydrogen doesn't occur naturally on earth. It has to be separated out from chemical compounds containing hydrogen, and that process requires other forms of energy. What I discovered is that there are only two major ways to produce hydrogen. The first is to produce it from fossil fuels by unlocking the hydrogen that is bonded to the carbon in coal, oil, or natural gas. The second is to produce it from water through electrolysis, but the power required for electrolysis would also come mainly from burning fossil fuels. These problems make hydrogen fuel cell cars look less clean and green than they first appear.

6 One approach to creating hydrogen from fossil fuels is to use natural gas. According to Matthew L. Wald, writing in a *New York Times* article, natural gas is converted to hydrogen in a process called "steam reforming." Natural gas (made of hydrogen and carbon atoms) is mixed with steam (which contains hydrogen and oxygen atoms) to cause a chemical reaction that produces pure hydrogen. But it also produces carbon dioxide, which contributes to global warming. According to Wald, if fuel cell cars used hydrogen from steam reforming, they would emit 145 grams of global warming gases per mile compared to 374 grams an ordinary gas-powered car would emit. The good news is that using hydrogen power would cut carbon emissions by more than half. The bad news is that these cars would still contribute to global warming and consume natural gas. Moreover, Wald suggests that the natural gas supply is limited and that natural gas has many better, more efficient uses than converting it to hydrogen.

7 Another method for producing hydrogen would come from coal, which is the cheapest and most abundant source of energy. However, the current method of generating electricity by burning coal is the leading source of carbon dioxide emission. At Ohio University, engineers state we still have enough coal to last us two hundred and fifty years and that we should find some better uses for coal. The engineers have received a 4 million dollar federal grant to investigate the production of hydrogen from coal. They plan on mixing coal with steam, air, and oxygen under high temperatures and pressure to produce hydrogen and carbon monoxide ("Ohio University"). But this too would generate greenhouse gases and is a long way off from producing results.

8 The next likely source of hydrogen is to produce it directly from water using an electrolyzer. Wald explains that the electrolyzer uses an electrical current to break down water molecules into hydrogen and oxygen atoms. Creating hydrogen through electrolysis sounds like a good idea because its only waste product is oxygen. But the

hazardous environmental impact is not in the electrolysis reaction, but in the need to generate electricity to run the electrolyzer. Wald claims that if the electricity to run the electrolyzer came from a typical coal-fired electrical plant, the carbon dioxide emissions for a fuel cell car would be 17 percent worse than for today's gasoline powered cars. One solution would be to run the electrolyzer with wind-generated or nuclear-powered electricity. But wind power would be able to produce only a small fraction of what would be needed, and nuclear power brings with it a whole new set of problems including disposal of nuclear waste.

9 Although there seem to be various methods of producing hydrogen, the current sources being considered do not fulfill the claim that hydrogen fuel cell technology will end the use of fossil fuels or eliminate greenhouse gases. The problem is not with the fuel cells themselves but with the processes needed to produce hydrogen fuel. I am not arguing that research and development should be abandoned, and I hope some day that the hydrogen economy will take off. But what I have discovered in my research is that hydrogen power is not as clean and green as I thought.

Works Cited

California. Executive Dept. "Executive Order S-7-04." 20 Apr. 2004. Web. 24 May 2004.
CNN. "The Issues/George Bush." *CNN.com*. Cable News Network, 2004. Web. 23 May 2004.
General Motors. Advertisement. *New York Times* 28 July 2004: A19. Print.
Hydrogen Fuel Cell Institute. Wilder Foundation, 2001. Web. 27 May 2004.
Nice, Karim, and Jonathan Strickland. "How Fuel Cells Work." *HowStuffWorks.com*. HowStuffWorks, 18 Sept. 2000. Web. 27 May 2004.
"Ohio University Aims to Use Coal to Power Fuel Cells." *Fuel Cell Today*. N.p., 24 Nov. 2003. Web. 3 June 2004.
Roberts, Paul. "Running Out of Oil—and Time." *Los Angeles Times*. Common Dreams News Center, 6 Mar. 2004. Web. 23 Mar. 2004.
Wald, Matthew L. "Will Hydrogen Clear the Air? Maybe Not, Some Say." *New York Times* 12 Nov. 2003: C1. Print.

THINKING CRITICALLY

about "How Clean and Green Are Hydrogen Fuel-Cell Cars?"

1. Explain Shannon King's use of the surprising-reversal strategy. What question does she pose? What is the common answer? What is her surprising answer? How effectively does she use research data to support her surprising answer?

2. The line between information and persuasion is often blurred. Some might argue that Shannon's essay has a persuasive aim that argues against hydrogen fuel-cell cars rather than an informative aim that simply presents surprising information about hydrogen production. To what extent do you agree with our classification of Shannon's aim as primarily informative rather than persuasive? Can it be both?

Our final essay, by syndicated columnist Eugene Robinson, illustrates how an informative article for the general public can be based on data from a major research study—in this case a statistical report by the federal Bureau of Justice. At first glance, the study seems to indicate that no racial profiling occurs at the rate at which white, African-American, and Hispanic drivers are pulled over by police. But in this op-ed piece Robinson pushes deeper into the statistics and presents information showing that "driving while black" is "unsafe at any speed."

Eugene Robinson

You Have the Right to Remain a Target of Racial Profiling

1 Washington—This just in: Driving while black is still unsafe at any speed, even zero miles per hour. The same goes for driving while brown.

2 The federal Bureau of Justice Statistics released a report Sunday showing that white, African-American and Hispanic drivers are equally likely to be pulled over by police for an alleged traffic offense. In 2005, the year covered by the study, black drivers were actually less likely—by a tiny margin—to be stopped by police than drivers belonging to the other groups. You might be tempted to conclude that the constitutional imperative of equal protection had finally been extended to America's streets and highways.

3 But you would be wrong. The study reports that African-American and Hispanic drivers who are stopped by police are more than twice as likely as whites to be subjected to a search. Specifically, police searched only 3.6 percent of white drivers pulled over in a traffic stop, while they searched 9.5 percent of African-Americans who obeyed the flashing lights and 8.8 percent of Hispanics.

4 The report says the "apparent disparities" between racial groups "do not constitute proof that police treat people differently along demographic lines," since there could be "countless other factors and circumstances" that go into the decision of whom to spread-eagle on the hood.

5 All right, those figures alone might not constitute "proof" of bias that would convince a jury beyond a reasonable doubt. They are pretty compelling, though, especially when you also consider that black and Hispanic drivers are much more likely to experience "police use of force" than whites.

6 And besides, the following paragraph in the report pretty effectively demolishes that "move along, folks, nothing to see here" disclaimer about bias:

7 "Police actions taken during a traffic stop were not uniform across racial and ethnic categories. Black drivers (4.5 percent) were twice as likely as white drivers (2.1 percent) to be arrested during a traffic stop, while Hispanic drivers (65 percent) were more likely than white (56.2 percent) or black (55.8 percent) drivers to receive a ticket.

8 "In addition, whites (9.7 percent) were more likely than Hispanics (5.9 percent) to receive a written warning, while whites (18.6 percent) were more likely than blacks (13.7 percent) to be verbally warned by police."

9 African Americans have been putting up with the "driving while black" thing for so long that we've become somewhat cynical. For example, nearly three-quarters of whites and Hispanics who were pulled over for allegedly running a red light or a stop sign were willing to concede that they had been caught dead to rights, while nearly half of African Americans in that situation believed they had committed no infraction. About 90 percent of white drivers detained for some sort of vehicle defect, such as a busted taillight, thought the stop was legitimate, as opposed to 67 percent of black drivers.

10 Think that's just paranoia? Then try to reconcile the counterintuitive fact that while blacks are much more likely than whites to be arrested in a traffic stop, they are also more likely to be released with no enforcement action, not even a warning. This looks to me like powerful evidence that racial profiling is alive and well. It suggests there was no good reason to stop those people.

11 "About one in 10 searches during a traffic stop uncovered evidence of a possible crime," the report says. What could be wrong with that? Isn't that what police should be doing—enforcing the nation's laws, capturing criminals, making law-abiding Americans that much safer?

12 Of course that's what we pay our police officers to do, but not selectively. Whites, too, drive around with drugs, illegal weapons, open containers of alcohol or other contraband in their cars. The numbers in the report suggest that if white drivers stopped by police were searched at the same rate as blacks or Hispanics, police would uncover evidence of tens of thousands of additional crimes each year, doubtless putting thousands of dangerous people behind bars.

13 But, of course, we don't want a society in which everybody is being patted down by police officers all the time. We don't want a society in which people have to stand by the side of the road, fuming, while police arbitrarily rummage through the stuff in their cars—shopping bags, children's toys, McDonald's wrappers—on the off chance of finding something illegal.

14 If you're black or brown, though, may I see your license and registration, please?

THINKING CRITICALLY

about "You Have the Right to Remain a Target of Racial Profiling"

1. Nationally syndicated African-American columnist Eugene Robinson highlights statistical data to support his thesis about subtle but pervasive racial discrimination. In doing so, he gives his report a "surprising-reversal structure." What is the common view, seemingly supported by the report, that Robinson believes is mistaken? What is his surprising view? How does he use report data to support his surprising view?
2. What pieces of information from the report do you find most compelling in supporting Robinson's thesis?
3. Analyze this piece from the perspectives of *logos*, *ethos*, and *pathos*.

For support in learning this chapter's content, follow this path in **MyCompLab**: Resources ⇒ Writing ⇒ Writing Purposes ⇒ Writing to Inform.

ANALYZING FIELD RESEARCH DATA

9

Field research—which uses strategies such as questionnaires, interviews, or direct observation—is one of the most powerful methods that scholars use to investigate our world. If you plan to major in the social or physical sciences or in professional fields such as business, nursing, or education, this chapter will introduce you to two common genres of scientific writing that are based on field research: the empirical research report and the scientific poster.

If your major is in the humanities, this chapter will familiarize you with ways that scientists and other professionals gather and interpret research data as they investigate empirical questions.

In this chapter, you will learn to:

- pose an empirical question about a phenomenon that interests you
- collect relevant data through observation, interviews, or a questionnaire
- present your findings in a scientific style—either in a research report or a poster

Exploring the Analysis of Field Research Data

The following task, which anticipates some of the research issues discussed later in this chapter, will help you begin thinking about the analysis of field research data.

Suppose you want to find out whether there is any difference in the exercise habits of male versus female college students. You might hypothesize that there are no differences in the percentage of male versus female students who exercise regularly or in the amount of time spent exercising by men versus women. However, you might speculate that the kinds of exercise vary by gender. For example, you might hypothesize that male students spend more time than females on muscle-building activities such as weight training or on pickup team sports such as basketball or touch football. Conversely, you might hypothesize that female students select exercises aimed at weight loss, muscle toning, and psychological well-being. Your study will help you confirm or disconfirm your initial hypothesis.

1. Working in small groups, create your own hypothesis in answer to the research question, "Are there gender differences in the exercise habits of male versus female college students?" Then create a short questionnaire (or set of interview questions) that will give you the data needed to confirm or disconfirm your hypothesis. At a minimum, your group's questionnaire will have to provide data on two variables: the respondent's gender and the amount of

time each week the respondent typically spends on physical exercise. You might also wish to determine the kinds of exercise preferred by the respondents and their motivations for exercising, but try to develop an uncluttered questionnaire that yields answers that you can count and tabulate.

2. Choose one or more of the questionnaires you created in small groups and field-test them on the class. Ask class members—on a volunteer basis—to try responding to the questions. Your goal here is to discover whether the questions might be unclear or ambiguous.
3. As a class, discuss problems that arose in creating the questionnaire and then in responding to the questions. Were any questions unclear? Did they yield answers that could be counted and tabulated? How would you revise your questionnaire based on difficulties you encountered?
4. Suppose on two successive days you gave one of your class's questionnaires to all students entering your college library and tabulated the results. To what extent would the results be generalizable to the whole student body? Generalizable to college students overall? Generalizable to the public at large?
5. Discuss the ethics of this study. Might some students feel embarrassed or even harmed by this study if their answers were made public? Is it anyone's business how much a person exercises? How might safeguards be built into the study to minimize the chances of any person's being made to feel uncomfortable?

Understanding the Analysis of Field Research Data

The Structure of an Empirical Research Report

A framework chart for a typical research report is shown in Figure 9.1. Formatting conventions call for section headings so that readers can quickly find the sections labeled "Introduction," "Method," "Results," and "Discussion." What is noteworthy about this structure is that the main sections of a research report follow the logic of the scientific method, as the following explanation suggests.

Introduction (Stage 1: Posing the question) Scientists begin by posing a research question and formulating their own hypothetical answer based on their initial theories, assumptions, hunches, and reasoning. The "Introduction" section of the research report corresponds to this stage: It describes the research question, explains its significance, and reviews previous scientific research addressing the same or a similar question. (Note: The writing projects for this chapter do not ask you to do a literature review.) Typically, the introduction ends with the scientist's hypothesis predicting what the observed data will show.

Method (Stage 2: Collecting data) Scientists develop a method for collecting the data needed to confirm or disconfirm the hypothesis. The materials and methods used to conduct the research, along with operational definitions of any key terms, are described in detail in the "Method" section of the report. The Method section is like a recipe that allows future researchers to replicate the research process exactly. It also allows peer reviewers to look for possible flaws or holes in the research design.

FIGURE 9.1 Framework for an Empirical Research Report*

(Title Page)	• For format of an APA title page and body of research report, see pages 231–238 • Gives title of paper and author's name; short version of title appears flush left, the page number in the upper right-hand corner with, on this and all subsequent pages
ABSTRACT	• Provides a 120-word or less summary of paper (research question, methods, major findings, significance of study)
INTRODUCTION	• Explains the problem to be investigated • Shows importance and significance of the problem • *Reviews previous studies examining the same problem (called a "literature review") and points to conflicts in these studies or to unknowns meriting further investigation*† • Poses the determinate research question(s) to be investigated • Presents the researcher's hypothesis
METHOD	• Describes how the study was done (enables future researchers to replicate the study exactly) • Often has subheadings such as "Participants," "Materials," and "Procedure" • Often provides operative definitions of key concepts in the problem/hypothesis
RESULTS	• Presents the researcher's findings or results • Often displays findings in figures, charts, or graphs as well as describes them in words • Usually does not present raw data or behind-the-scenes mathematics; data focus on composite results • *Presents statistical analysis of data to show confidence levels and other advanced statistical implications or meanings*†
DISCUSSION	• Presents the researcher's analysis of the results • Interprets and evaluates the collected data in terms of the original research question and hypothesis • Speculates on causes and consequences of the findings • Shows applications and practical or theoretical significance of the study • Usually includes a section pointing out limitations and possible flaws in the study and suggests directions for future research
REFERENCES	• Bibliographic listing of cited sources • For format of APA references, see Skill 22.4, and page 238.
APPENDICES	• Provides place to include questionnaires or other materials used in study

*Based on guidelines in *Publication Manual of the American Psychological Association,* 6th ed., Washington, DC: APA, 2010, pp. 21–59.

Italicized sections are not required for the writing project in this chapter

Results (Stage 3: Determining results) Scientists examine the collected data carefully. The findings are reported in the "Results" section, usually displayed in tables or graphs as well as described verbally. To help determine the extent to which researchers can have confidence in the gathered data, expert researchers perform a variety of statistical tests that show, among other things, whether the results might be attributable simply to chance. (The writing projects for this chapter do not require statistical tests.)

Discussion (Stage 4: Analyzing results) Finally, scientists interpret and analyze their findings, drawing conclusions about what the findings mean and how the research advances knowledge. This stage of the scientific process corresponds to the "Discussion" section of the research report. Typically, the Discussion section also points to limitations and flaws in the research design and suggests directions for future research.

Other Sections In addition to the four main sections, research reports often include an abstract of 120 words or less that summarizes the research problem, research design, results, and major implications of the study. The abstract allows readers at a glance to get a basic understanding of the research. At the end of the report, a "References" section lists bibliographic details about any cited sources. Finally, scientists can add, in the "Appendices" section, copies of questionnaires used, interview questions asked, or special calculations that might interest readers.

How Readers Typically Read a Research Report

What is unusual about research reports is that readers typically don't read them in a linear fashion. The advantage of a well-marked structure is that readers can skim a report first and then, if they're interested, read it carefully in an order that meets their needs. Readers will typically skim the Introduction to understand the problem under investigation and then skip directly to the Discussion section, where the researcher's findings are analyzed in depth. Readers with special interest in the question being investigated may then go back to read the Introduction, Method section, and Results section in detail to evaluate the soundness of the research design and the accuracy and reliability of the data. Some readers may follow a different order. For example, researchers primarily interested in developing new research designs might read the Method section first to learn how the research was conducted. Our point is that the conventional format of a research report allows readers to tailor their reading practices to their own interests.

We will now go back through the sections of a research report, offering you suggestions for doing the kinds of thinking needed at each stage of the research process.

Posing Your Research Question

When you pose your research question for this writing project, you need to appreciate the difference between the broad, open-ended questions we have emphasized throughout this text and the very narrow questions that scientists use when doing empirical studies. Scientists, of course, pose big, open-ended questions all the time: What is the origin of the universe? What is the role of nature versus nurture in human gender behavior? But when they conduct actual research, scientists transform these big, speculative, indeterminate questions into narrow determinate questions. By "determinate," we mean questions that can be answered either with yes or no or with a single fact, number, or range of numbers. The kinds of determinate questions that scientists typically ask can be placed in five categories in ascending order of complexity (see Table 9.1).*

FOR WRITING AND DISCUSSION

Generating Research Questions

This exercise encourages you to brainstorm ideas for your own research question. The goal here is not to settle on a research question but to get a feeling for the range of options you might choose for your own investigation.

Background: The following list shows how students might use the five categories in Table 9.1 to frame questions about the exercise habits of college students.

CATEGORIES OF RESEARCH QUESTIONS APPLIED TO STUDY OF EXERCISE HABITS

1. ***Existence Questions ("Does X exist in domain Y?"):*** Does "yoga" appear as an exercise choice among the respondents to this questionnaire?
2. ***Measurement Questions ("How large/small/fast/much/many/bright is X?"):*** On average, how many hours per week do female (and male) college students devote to physical exercise? Or, what percentage of females (and males) report five or more hours per week of physical exercise?
3. ***Comparison Questions ("Is X greater/less than Y or different from Y?"):*** Do a higher percentage of male college students than female college students report five or more hours per week of physical exercise?
4. ***Correlation Questions ("If X varies, does Y vary?"):*** Do students who report studying more than thirty hours per week exercise more than students who report studying fewer than thirty hours per week?
5. ***Experimental Questions ("Does a variation in X cause a variation in Y?"):*** Will an experimental group of students asked to keep an exercise log exercise more regularly than a control group of students who do not keep such a log?

Individual task: Spend ten minutes thinking of possible ideas for your own research project. Try using the five categories of questions to stimulate your thinking, but don't worry whether a question exactly fits one category or another. Remember to ask determinate questions that can be answered by yes/no or by a single number, percentage, or range of numbers.

Group task: Working in small groups or as a whole class, share your initial ideas, using your classmates' proposed research questions to stimulate more of your own thinking. Your goal is to generate a wide range of possible research questions you might like to investigate.

*Table 9.1 is based on an unpublished paper by psychologist Robert Morasky, "Model of Empirical Research Question." Morasky's model was used for the section on "Asking Empirical Research Questions for Science" in John C. Bean and John D. Ramage, *Form and Surprise in Composition: Writing and Thinking Across the Curriculum* (New York: Macmillan, 1986), pp. 183–189.

TABLE 9.1 Asking Determinate Research Questions

Question Type	Explanation	Natural Science Example	Social Science Example	Question That You Might Ask for This Chapter's Writing Project
1. *Existence Questions:* "Does X exist in domain Y?"	Researchers simply want to determine if a given phenomenon occurs or exists in a given domain	Do fragments of fungi exist in Precambrian sediments?	Do racial stereotypes exist in current world history textbooks?	Do advertisements for computers appear in women's fashion magazines?
2. *Measurement Questions:* "How large/small/fast/much/many/bright is X?"	Researchers want to measure the extent to which something occurs (percentages) or the degree or size of a phenomenon	How hot is the surface of Venus?	What percentage of homeless persons suffer from mental illness?	What percentage of children's birthday cards currently displayed at local stores contain gender stereotyping?
3. *Comparison Questions:* "Is X greater/less than Y or different from Y?"	Researchers want to study how two events, groups, or phenomena differ according to some measure	Is radiation from Io greater in volcanic areas than in nonvolcanic areas?	Is the incidence of anorexia greater among middle-class women than among working-class women?	Do humanities majors report fewer study hours per week than nonhumanities majors?
4. *Correlation Questions:* "If X varies, does Y vary?"	Researchers determine whether differences in X are accompanied by corresponding differences in Y	Does the aggression level of male rats vary with testosterone levels in their blood?	Do students' evaluations of their teachers vary with the grades they expect to receive for the course?	Does students' satisfaction with university food services vary with their family size?
5. *Experimental Questions:* "Does a variation in X cause a variation in Y?"	Researchers move beyond correlations to try to determine the direct causes of a certain phenomenon	If male rats are forced into stress situations to compete for food, will the level of testosterone in their blood increase?	Will preschool children taken shopping after watching TV commercials for high-sugar cereals ask for such cereals at a higher rate than children in a control group who did not see the commercials?	Will persons shown a Monsanto ad promoting biotech corn reveal a more favorable attitude toward genetically modified foods than a control group not shown the ad?

**Direct experiments can be difficult to design and conduct in some of the social sciences. Also, experimental questions often raise ethical issues whenever experiments place human subjects in psychological stress, cause physical pain and suffering to laboratory animals, or otherwise bring harm to individuals. See pages 217–218 for further discussion of ethical issues in research.*

Collecting Data through Observation, Interviews, or Questionnaires

Once you have formulated your research question, you need to develop a plan for collecting the needed data. In this section, we give you suggestions for conducting your research through direct observation, interviews, or questionnaires.

Using Observation to Gather Information The key to successful observation of human behavior or other natural phenomena is having a clear sense of your purpose combined with advance preparation. We offer the following practical strategies for carrying out observational research:

Strategies for Using Observation to Collect Data

Strategies	What to Do	Comments
Determine the purpose and scope of your observation.	Think ahead about the subject of your observation and the details, behaviors, or processes involved. Make a list.	Some phenomena can be observed only once; others can be observed regularly. If you plan on a series of observations, the first one can provide an overview or baseline, while subsequent observations can enable you to explore your subject in more detail or note changes over time.
Make arrangements ahead of time.	In making requests, state clearly who you are and what the purpose of your observation is. Be cordial in your requests and in your thanks after your observations.	If you need to ask permission or get clearance for your observation, be sure to do so long before you plan to start the observation.
Take clear, usable notes while observing.	Bring note-taking materials—either a laptop or plenty of paper, a clipboard or binder with a hard surface for writing, and good writing utensils. Document your notes with exact indications of location, time, and names and titles of people (if relevant).	Make sure that your notes are easy to read and well labeled with helpful headings.
Go through your notes soon afterward.	Fill in gaps and elaborate where necessary. You might then write a first draft while your observations are still fresh in your mind.	Don't let too much time go by, or you will not be able to reconstruct details or recapture thoughts you had while observing.

Here are two examples of how students have used direct observation to conduct research:

- A student wanting to know how often people violated a "Do Not Walk on the Grass" sign on her campus observed a lawn for one week during mornings between classes and counted persons who took a shortcut across the grass rather than followed the sidewalks. She also recorded the gender of shortcut-takers to see if there were any gender differences in this behavior.
- A student research team hypothesized that episodes of the cartoon *SpongeBob SquarePants* would contain fewer gender stereotypes than episodes of a 1930s Mickey Mouse cartoon. The researchers watched the cartoons in one-minute segments and for each segment recorded the presence of behaviors that they categorized as stereotypical or nonstereotypical male behavior and stereotypical or nonstereotypical female behavior. (You can read their research report and their poster in the Readings section of this chapter.)

Conducting Interviews Interviews can be an effective way to gather field research information. They can range from formal interviews lasting thirty or more minutes to quick, informal interviews. As an example of informal interviews, consider the hypothetical case of a researcher investigating why customers at a local grocery store choose to buy or not buy organic vegetables. This researcher might ask persons buying vegetables if they would be willing to be briefly interviewed. (The researcher would need to be very polite, keep the interviews brief, and get the store manager's permission in advance.)

In other kinds of field research studies, you might rely on longer, formal interviews with persons whose background or knowledge is relevant to your research question. Although asking a busy professional for an interview can be intimidating, many experts are generous with their time when they encounter a student who is interested in their field. To make interviews as useful as possible, we suggest several strategies.

Strategies for Conducting an Interview

Strategies	What to Do	Comments
	Before the Interview	
Consider your purpose.	Determine what you hope to learn from the interview. Think about your research question and the aim of the paper you are planning to write.	This thinking will help you focus the interview.

Strategies	What to Do	Comments
Learn about your subject.	Research important subjects related to your research question and the person you will be interviewing. Although you needn't become an expert, you should be conversant about your subject.	Ideally, interviews should give you knowledge or perspectives unavailable in books or articles.
Formulate your questions.	Develop a range of questions, including short-answer questions like the following: How long have you been working in this field? What are the typical qualifications for this job?	Be as thorough with your questions as possible. Most likely you will have only one chance to interview this person. Avoid yes-or-no questions that can stall conversation with a one-word answer.
	Create open-ended questions, which should be the heart of your interview. For example: What changes have you seen in this field? What solutions have you found to be the most successful in dealing with . . . ? What do you see as the causes of . . . ? Questions framed in this way will elicit the information you need but still allow the interviewee to answer freely.	Avoid leading questions. The more you lead the interviewee to the answers you want, the less valid your research becomes.
Gather your supplies.	If you plan to record the interview, be sure to get your interviewee's permission, and spend time familiarizing yourself with recording equipment. Bring a laptop or pad of paper to take notes.	Using a recorder allows you to focus your attention on the substance of the interview. Most likely, you will want to take notes even if you are recording.
	During the Interview	
Manage your time.	Arrive on time. Also agree to a time limit for the interview and stick to it. (If necessary, you can request a second interview, or your interviewee may be willing to stay longer.)	You will show a lack of professionalism if you are not particularly careful to respect the interviewee's time.

(continued)

Strategies	What to Do	Comments
Be courteous.	Thank the interviewee for his or her time. During the interview, listen attentively. Don't interrupt.	Your attitude during the interview can help set up a cordial and comfortable relationship between you and the person you are interviewing.
Take notes.	Take down all the main ideas and be accurate with quoted material. Don't hesitate to ask if you are unsure about a fact or statement or if you need to double-check what the person intended to say.	If you are recording the interview, you can double-check quotations later.
Be flexible.	Ask your questions in a logical order, but also be sensitive to the flow of the conversation. If the interviewee rambles away from the question, don't jump in too fast.	You may learn something valuable from the seeming digression. You may even want to ask unanticipated questions if you have delved into new ideas.
	After the Interview	
Go through your notes soon afterward.	No matter how vivid the words are in your mind, take time *very* soon after the interview to go over your notes, filling in any gaps, or to transcribe your tape.	What may seem unforgettable at the moment is all too easy to forget later. Do not trust your memory alone.

Using Questionnaires In constructing a questionnaire, your goal is to elicit responses that are directly related to your research question and that will give you the data you need to answer the question. The construction of a questionnaire—both its wording and its arrangement on the page—is crucial to its success. As you design your questionnaire, imagine respondents with only limited patience and time. Keep your questionnaire clear, easy to complete, and as short as possible, taking care to avoid ambiguous sentences. Proofread it carefully, and pilot it on a few volunteer respondents so that you can eliminate confusing spots. Some specific examples of types of questions often found on questionnaires are shown in Figure 9.2.

When you have designed the questions you will ask, write an introductory comment that explains the questionnaire's purpose. If possible, encourage responses by explaining why the knowledge gained from the questionnaire will be beneficial to others. Make your completed questionnaire as professionally attractive and easy to read and fill out as possible. As an example, Figure 9.3 shows a questionnaire, introduced with an explanatory comment, prepared by a student investigating the parking problems of commuter students on her campus.

FIGURE 9.2 Types of Questions Used in Questionnaires

1. Fixed-choice question

Compared to other campuses with which you are familiar, this campus's use of alcohol is (mark one):

—— greater than other campuses'
—— less than other campuses'
—— about the same as other campuses'

2. Open-ended question

How would you say alcohol use on this campus compares to other campuses?

Comment: Fixed-choice questions are easier to tabulate and report statistically; open-ended questions can yield a wider variety of insights but are impractical for large numbers of respondents.

3. Question with operationally defined rather than undefined term

Undefined term: Think back over the last two weeks. How many times did you engage in binge drinking?

Operationally defined term: Think back over the last two weeks. How many times have you had four or more drinks in a row?

Comment: An "operational definition" states empirically measurable criteria for a term. In the first version of the question, the term "binge drinking" might mean different things to different persons. Moreover, respondents are apt to deny being binge drinkers given that it is an unflattering categorization. In the revised question, the term "binge drinking" is replaced with an observable and measurable behavior; respondents are more apt to give an honest response.

4. Category question

What is your current class standing?

—— freshman
—— sophomore
—— junior
—— senior
—— other (please specify)

Comment: In category questions, it is often helpful to have an "Other" category for respondents who do not fit neatly into any of the other categories.

5. Scaled-answer question

This campus has a serious drinking problem (circle one):

strongly agree	agree	neither agree nor disagree	disagree	strongly disagree
5	4	3	2	1

How much drinking goes on in your dormitory on Friday or Saturday nights?

a lot	some	not much	none

Comment: Although scaled-answer questions are easy to tabulate and are widely used, the data can be skewed by the subjective definitions of each respondent (one person's "a lot" may be another person's "not much").

FIGURE 9.3 Example of a Questionnaire

Dear Commuter Student:
I am conducting a study aimed at improving the parking situation for commuter students. Please take a few moments to complete the following questionnaire, which will provide valuable information that may lead to specific proposals for easing the parking problems of commuters. If we commuter students work together with the university administration, we may be able to find equitable solutions to the serious parking issues we face. Please return the questionnaires to the box I have placed at the south entrance to the Student Union Building.

1. When do you typically arrive on campus?

   Before 8 A.M. ______
   Between 8 A.M. and 9 A.M. ______
   Between 9 A.M. and noon ______
   During noon hour ______
   Between 1 P.M. and 5 P.M. ______
   Between 5 P.M. and 7 P.M. ______
   After 7 P.M. ______

2. How frequently do you have problems finding a place to park?

   Nearly every day ____
   About half the time ____
   Occasionally ____
   Almost never ____

3. When the first lot you try is full, how long does it typically take you to find a place to park (for those who buy a commuter parking permit)?

   Less than 10 minutes ___
   10–15 minutes ___
   More than 15 minutes ___

4. For those who use street parking only, how long does it take you to find a place to park?

   Less than 10 minutes ___
   10–15 minutes ___
   More than 15 minutes ___

5. Do you currently carpool?

   Yes ____
   No ____

6. The university is considering a proposal to raise parking fees for single-driver cars and lower them for car pools. If you don't currently carpool, how difficult would it be to find a car-pool partner?

   Impossible ___
   Very difficult ___
   Somewhat difficult ___
   Fairly easy ___

7. If finding a car-pool partner would be difficult, why?

   Few fellow students live in my neighborhood ___
   Few fellow students match my commuting hours ___
   Other ___

8. What suggestions do you have for improving the parking situation for commuter students?

When you distribute your questionnaire, try to obtain a random sample. For example, if you assessed student satisfaction with a campus cafeteria by passing out questionnaires to those eating in the cafeteria at noon on a particular day, you might not achieve a random sampling of potential cafeteria users. You would miss those who avoid the cafeteria because they hate it; also, the distribution of noon users of the cafeteria might be different from the distribution of breakfast or dinner users. Another problem with sampling is that people who feel strongly about an issue are more likely to complete a questionnaire than those who don't feel strongly. The student who prepared the parking questionnaire, for example, is likely to get a particularly high rate of response from those most angry about parking issues, and thus her sample might not be representative of all commuter students.

In some situations, random sampling may be unfeasible. For the assignment for this chapter, check with your instructor whether a "convenience sample" would be acceptable (for example, you would pass out questionnaires to persons in your dorm or in your class as a matter of convenience, even though these persons would not represent a random sample of the larger population).

FOR WRITING AND DISCUSSION

Developing a Research Plan

Write a possible research question that you might investigate for your project. Working individually, consider ways that you might use one of the research methods just discussed—observation, interviews, or questionnaires—to answer your question. Begin designing your research plan, including procedures for observations or formulation of questions for your questionnaire or interviews. Then, working in small groups or as a whole class, share your brainstorming. Your goal is to develop the beginnings of a research plan. Help each other talk through the stages of a possible investigation.

Reporting Your Results in Both Words and Graphics

Once you have completed your research and tabulated your findings, you are ready to write the "Results" section of your paper, which reports your findings in words often supplemented with tables and graphs. In reporting results, your aim is to create a scientific *ethos* that is objective and unbiased. Your purpose is to help readers understand your findings concisely and clearly. Do not report raw data. Rather, create composite results by tabulating totals or calculating averages and report these results in words and in appropriate graphics. Try to report your data in such a way that readers can quickly see whether the data support or do not support your hypothesis. For help on creating appropriate graphics for displaying your data, see Skill 17.9, which explains how to create reader-effective tables, pie charts, line graphs, and bar graphs.

Once you have created effective graphics, you then need to integrate them into your own text, making sure that your words and graphics tell the same story in a clear, easy-to-follow manner. Skill 17.9 also provides guidance on integrating graphics into a paper.

FOR WRITING AND DISCUSSION

Revising a Poor Graph

Background: A frequent problem with graphics designed by inexperienced writers is unclear purpose (What is this graphic supposed to show? What is its story?). Often this confusion comes from a missing or incomplete title, from missing or misleading labels for the *x*- and *y*-axes, or from inclusion of extraneous information.

Your task: Working in small groups or as a whole class, explain what is confusing about the graphic in Figure 9.4. The writer's purpose is to explain respondents' answers to the question, "Which fast-food restaurant produces the best chicken nuggets?" How might you redesign the graphic to tell the story more clearly?

Analyzing Your Results

The "Discussion" section of a research report is devoted to the writer's analysis of the results. This section most resembles a thesis-governed essay addressing an open-ended problem. Think of your Discussion section as answering the following questions: What do my results mean? What do we learn from them? How are these results important or significant?

The Discussion section should open with a thesis statement that indicates whether your findings support or do not support your original hypothesis and that summarizes or forecasts the other main points of your analysis. Here is an example of how a thesis statement from a professional research report entitled

FIGURE 9.4 Example of an Unclear Student Graphic

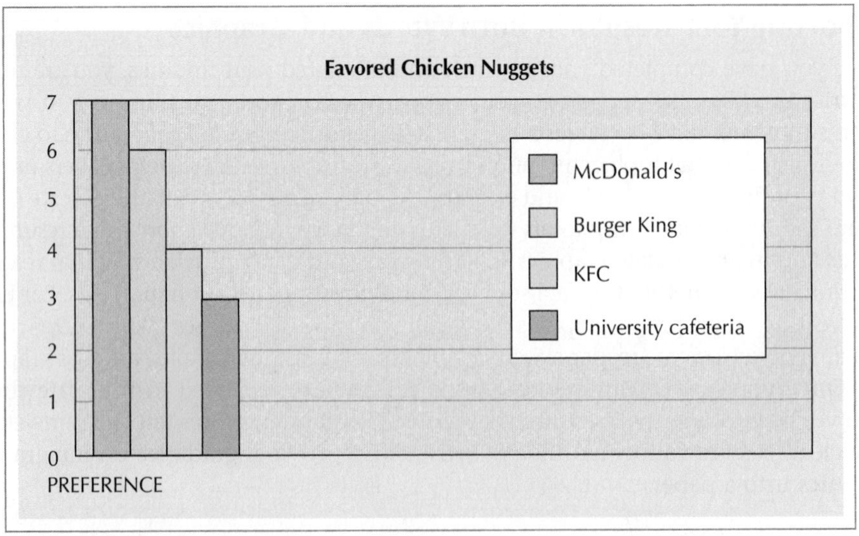

"Marital Disruption and Depression in a Community Sample" is connected to the research problem in the Introduction:

RESEARCH QUESTION AND HYPOTHESIS FROM INTRODUCTION

Research question: Researchers have long known that recently divorced persons tend to show high degrees of depression, but the direction of causation is unknown: Does divorce cause depression or does depression cause divorce?

Hypothesis: Marital disruption contributes to higher levels of depression in recently divorced persons.

Early in the Discussion section, the authors create an explicit thesis statement that directly responds to the hypothesis:

THESIS STATEMENT FROM THE "DISCUSSION" SECTION

According to the results, marital disruption does in fact cause a significant increase in depression compared to pre-divorce levels within a period of three years after the divorce.

Although there are no formulas for the Discussion section of a research report, most reports contain the following four conventional features:

1. Identification of significant patterns and speculation about causes
2. Implications and significance of the results
3. Limitations of the study
4. Suggestions for further research

Let's look at each in turn.

Identification of Significant Patterns and Speculation about Causes

The first part of a Discussion section often points out patterns within the results that bear directly on the researcher's hypothesis. For example, in studying exercise habits of college students, you might find that, contrary to your hypothesis, women exercise more than men. Depending on other findings derived from your questionnaire, you might note additional patterns—for example, that persons claiming to be on a diet exercise more than those who don't or that persons who are regular runners tend to spend more time studying than do persons who play lots of pickup team sports.

The discovery of significant patterns leads naturally to speculation about causes. Understanding how a certain event or condition leads to other events or conditions contributes to our knowledge of the world and often may have practical consequences for improving the world or our situation in it. As you contemplate questions raised by your research, consider the following ways that data may suggest causality:

- ***Causality induced from a recurring pattern:*** If numerous observations reveal a recurring pattern, you may be justified in inducing causality. For example, psychologists attempting to understand the causes of anorexia have discovered that many (but not all) anorexics come from perfectionist, highly work-oriented homes that emphasize duty and responsibility. This frequently recurring element is thus a suspected causal factor leading to anorexia.

- ***Causality hypothesized from correlations:*** **Correlation** is a statistical term indicating the probability that two events or phenomena will occur together. For example, various studies have shown a correlation between creativity and left-handedness. (The percentage of left-handed people within a sample of highly creative people is considerably higher than the percentage of left-handed people in the general population.) But does being left-handed cause a person to be more creative? Or does some other factor cause both left-handedness and creativity? The presence of this puzzling correlation leads scientists to speculate about its causes and to design further research that might pin down an answer.
- ***Causality demonstrated through experimental control of variables:*** In some cases, scientists try to resolve causal questions through direct experiment. By controlling variables and testing them one at a time, scientists can sometimes isolate causal factors quite precisely. For example, through experimentation, scientists now know that a particular bacterium causes typhoid fever and that particular antibiotics will kill that bacterium.

FOR WRITING AND DISCUSSION

Analyzing Results

Working in small groups or as a whole class, speculate on possible explanations for each of the following phenomena:

1. White female teenagers are seven times more likely to smoke than African-American female teenagers (a finding based on several professional studies).
2. When asked about the "car of their dreams," ninety-one percent of students polled listed an SUV, luxury car, or high-performance sports car. Only three percent specifically mentioned a fuel-conserving vehicle such as a hybrid.

Implications and Significance of the Results Another typical portion in the Discussion section focuses on the implications and significance of your research—the "So what?" question. What is important about this research? How does it advance our knowledge? What, if any, are its practical applications? For example, the discovery that white female teenagers smoke at a higher rate than African-American female teenagers could lead to speculation on ways to reduce teenage smoking among white females or offer clues into the psyches of white versus African-American women. (One theory proposed in the scientific literature is that white women are more obsessed with weight and body image than African-American women and see smoking as a way to suppress appetite.) Or, to take our other example, the study showing that only three percent of students mentioned a fuel-conserving car as their "dream car" could lead to speculation on how consumer preferences might be changed to promote the goal of environmental preservation.

Limitations of the Study Another common feature of the Discussion section is the researcher's skeptical analysis of his or her own research methods and data.

It may seem counterintuitive that authors would explicitly point out problems with their own research, but this honesty is part of the scientific *ethos* aimed at advancing knowledge. By nature, scientists are skeptical and cautious. Typically, authors go out of their way to mention possible flaws and other limitations of their studies and to caution other scholars against overgeneralizing from their research. They might refer to problems in sample size or duration of the study, flaws in the research design that might contaminate results, possible differences between an experimental group and a control group, or lack of statistical confidence in the data.

Your own research for this assignment will probably exhibit a number of problems that would limit other researchers' confidence in your findings. To increase your own *ethos* as a scientific writer, you should make these objections yourself as part of the Discussion section.

Suggestions for Further Research At the conclusion of their Discussion sections, researchers often suggest avenues for future research. Typically they show how their own research raises new questions that could be profitably explored. You might try this approach at the conclusion of your own Discussion section by mentioning one or more questions that you think would be the logical next steps for researchers interested in your area of study.

Following Ethical Standards

When research involves human subjects, researchers must scrupulously adhere to ethical standards. In the past, there have been horrible cases of unethical research using human subjects. Among the most notorious are Nazi medical experiments on Jews in concentration camps and the Tuskegee syphilis study in which four hundred low-income African-American males with syphilis were denied treatment—even though a cure for syphilis had been discovered—because the researchers wanted to continue studying the progress of the untreated disease.

As a response to problems like these, scientific bodies have established strict ethical guidelines for research using human subjects. Today, almost all colleges and universities have Institutional Review Boards that provide oversight for such research. In the case of your own research, for example, consider how certain items on a questionnaire might cause stress to a potential respondent or be considered an invasion of his or her privacy. It's one thing to ask persons if they prefer a Mac to a PC; it is quite another to ask them if they have ever cheated on an exam or gotten drunk at a party. As a general rule, the kind of first-time research that you do for this writing project will not require oversight from your university's Institutional Review Board, but you should nevertheless adhere to the following guidelines:

- ***Obtain informed consent***. Explain to potential respondents the purpose of your research, your methods for collecting data, and the way your data will be used. In the case of interviews, reach agreement on whether the respondent will be named or anonymous. Obtain direct permission for recording the session.

- ***Explain that participation in your study is voluntary.*** Do not apply any kind of personal or social pressure that would make it difficult for a respondent to say no.
- ***In the case of questionnaires, explain that no respondent will be individually identified and that results will be reported as statistical aggregates.*** If possible, ensure that all responses are anonymous to you (don't try to identify handwriting or otherwise match responses to an identified individual). If such anonymity is impossible (for example, you might be conducting an oral survey), then assure the respondent that you will keep all answers confidential.
- ***If any of your respondents are minors, check with your instructor because human-subject regulations are particularly strict in such instances.*** Parents or guardians generally have to give consent for interviews with their children.

WRITING PROJECT

An Empirical Research Report

The assignment for this project is a modified version of a standard empirical research report. We have omitted advanced features that would be required of upper-division science majors, such as a statistical analysis of the data or a review of previous research.

> Write a scientific report in APA style that presents and analyzes your research findings in response to an empirical question about a phenomenon, behavior, or event. Your research can be based on direct observations, interviews, or questionnaires. Your report should have a title page and abstract, followed by the four main sections of a research report: Introduction, Method, Results, and Discussion. Also include a "References" page if you cite any sources.

An example of a student empirical research report written for this writing project is found on pages 231–238. In the Introduction section of this report, the student researchers present a brief review of the literature based on readings in gender identity that the instructor had used in class for this unit. In most cases, you will not be expected to have a similar section in your report.

Generating Ideas for Your Empirical Research Report

In addition to the ideas presented earlier in this chapter, here are some suggestions for possible research projects:

- Using a questionnaire to gather evidence, investigate students' usage patterns or levels of satisfaction with some aspect of student services on your campus (for example, computer labs, security escorting service, student newspaper, recreational facilities in the student union, study skills workshops).

- Using direct observation, investigate the degree of gender stereotyping in randomly selected children's birthday cards from a local card store or supermarket. Or investigate adherence to road rules at a chosen intersection, testing variables such as car type, weather conditions, time of day, amount of traffic, and so forth.
- Using interviews or a questionnaire, investigate the way students spend their time during a typical week (for example, studying, watching television, playing video games, logging onto Facebook or MySpace, playing recreational sports, working, and so forth). You might also try to determine whether there are differences in these patterns depending upon factors such as gender, major, GPA, ethnicity, career aspirations, job status, part time/full time, or commuter/residential.

Designing Your Empirical Study and Drafting the Introduction and Method Sections

To design your study, you'll need to begin with a determinate research question that can be answered with yes/no or with a number, range of numbers, or percentage. Review pages 205–206 on asking a determinate research question.

We recommend that you write a draft of your Introduction and your Method section *before* you do the actual research. Drafting these sections first not only gets them out of the way but helps you think through your whole research process. Drafting your Introduction helps you understand your purpose more clearly and serves to clarify your research question and hypothesis. Drafting the Method section helps you plan exactly the steps you will take to do the research. If your research uses a questionnaire, make sure that it is carefully designed, tested on a few volunteers, and revised before you start distributing it. Many research projects are ruined when the researcher discovers that the questionnaire had ambiguous questions or didn't ask the right questions.

Doing the Research and Writing the Rest of the Report

Your next step is to do the research, record your raw numbers, and do the calculations needed for creating composite numbers that answer your research question. What follows is brief advice on drafting the rest of the report.

- ***Writing the Results section:*** This section simply presents your results both in words and in graphics. Refer to Skill 17.9 for advice on how to reference graphs and tables.
- ***Writing the Discussion section:*** Novice science writers often have trouble determining what goes in the Results section versus the Discussion section. The Results section answers the question, "What are my findings?" In contrast, the Discussion section addresses the question, "What do my findings mean?" It is the place where you bring your own critical thinking to bear on your results, creating your own thesis and argument. Reread page 215 to understand the typical features of a Discussion section.

- ***Writing the Abstract:*** When you have finished your draft, write a summary (no more than 120 words) of your report. In a few sentences indicate the broad problem you were investigating and the narrower purpose of your research; state your research question and your hypothesis. Then briefly describe your methods. In the last half of the abstract, describe your results and the extent to which they support your hypothesis. Conclude by suggesting the significance and implications of your research.

Revising Your Report

Because a scientific report follows a conventional structure, you should check your draft against the framework chart on page 203 (Figure 9.1). Make sure you have placed the right type of material in the appropriate section. Inside each section, revise for effective transitions, conciseness, and clarity. Getting feedback from peers can be very helpful.

Questions for Peer Review

In addition to the generic peer review questions explained in Skill 16.4, ask your peer reviewers to address these questions:

TITLE AND ABSTRACT

1. Can the title be improved to better focus the paper and pique reader interest?
2. Can the abstract be improved for accuracy, coverage, or clarity? Where does it state the research question and hypothesis? Briefly summarize the methods? Briefly state the results? Discuss the significance of the results?

INTRODUCTION

1. Where does the writer present the research question(s) and hypothesis(es)? Are these clear and focused?
2. Where does the writer suggest the importance or significance of the research question? What overall suggestions might you make to improve the introduction?

METHOD

1. Will the writer's method provide the data necessary to answer the research question?
2. If you had to replicate the writer's research, where might you have problems? How could the Methods section be improved?

RESULTS

1. Are the writer's results clearly stated in both words and graphics? Are there any graphics that need more explanation?
2. Are the graphics well designed? What suggestions might you have for improving the titles, labels, legends, and overall design of graphics?

DISCUSSION

1. Where is the thesis statement that shows whether the research supports the hypothesis? Can you suggest ways to improve the thesis?
2. Where does the writer: (a) Identify significant patterns in the data and speculate about possible causes? (b) Show the significance and importance of the study? (c) Describe the limitations of the study? (d) Suggest ideas for future research or next steps? How might the Discussion section be improved?

Writing in Teams

Because professional field research is often done in teams, resulting in jointly authored articles, your instructor may ask you to work in teams to plan and carry out your research projects. In such cases, instructors sometimes ask team members to write their own individual reports and sometimes require jointly authored reports. If you are assigned to write in teams, consider our advice for team-writing as shown in the following strategies chart.

Strategies for Team-Writing of Documents

Strategies	What the Team Does	What an Individual Does
Do as a team what teams do best. Do as individuals what individuals do best.	• Brainstorm ideas. • Set goals; plan and organize. • Develop research questions and methods. • Divide up the work. • Tabulate and analyze results. • Give feedback on ideas.	• Write drafts of each section. • Revise drafts of each section. • Edit for uniform voice and style. • Format the paper in APA style.
Talk through your document before you write it. Draft individually; revise as a team.	• Plan what will go into each section by taking notes on a large sheet of paper. • Assign the drafting of each section. • Review drafts for accuracy, completeness, clarity, development, and style. • Assign the revision of each section. • Repeat the team-review process for the revised draft.	• Understand the contents of each section and feel qualified to write any section as assigned. • Volunteer to draft the section with which you are most comfortable. • Make copies of your drafted section for team members to review. • Revise the section you are assigned.

(continued)

Strategies	What the Team Does	What an Individual Does
Prepare the final document.	• Assign one person to do the final editing so that it seems written in one voice. • Assign one person to edit for APA formatting and style.	• Edit and prepare the final draft. • Check APA formatting and style.

WRITING PROJECT

A Scientific Poster

Publish the results of your empirical research project as a scientific poster suitable for display at an undergraduate research conference. Your poster should combine visual and verbal elements to hook participants' interest in your project, show your research question and results, and provide a frame for further personal discussion of your research.

An example of a student-produced poster is found in the Readings section, page 240.

What Is a Scientific Poster?

A poster is a common means of disseminating research at a scientific conference.* Unlike a fifteen-minute talk to a sitting audience (which is the other means of presentation at a conference), a poster presentation occurs in a large room where dozens of researchers display their work on posters taped to walls or placed upright on tables. As researchers stand next to their displays, conference participants wander around the room, perusing posters and stopping to talk to researchers whose work particularly interests them.

Content and Features of a Poster

The content of a scientific poster, like an abstract, follows the same structure as the research report. In fact, a poster is sometimes called an "illustrated abstract" that presents at a glance the research question, hypothesis, methods, key results, and significance.

The function of a poster is to engage viewers' interest in your research project and invite discussion. Professional scientists make posters using special software

*Our discussion of posters is indebted to two excellent Web sites: Hess, G. R., K. Tosney, and L. Liegel. 2006. *Creating Effective Poster Presentations*. http://www.ncsu.edu/project/posters, accessed July 25, 2007, and Purrington, C. B. 2006. *Advice on Designing Scientific Posters*. http://www.swarthmore.edu/NatSci/cpurrin1/posteradvice.htm, accessed July 25, 2007.

and plotting printers. A typical poster is thirty-six by fifty-four inches, the largest sheet that most plotting printers can handle. If you don't have access to these professional tools, you can print sections of your poster using regular paper, arrange the sheets on poster board, and tape them in place.

An effective poster has the following features:

- Is readable from four feet away (text fonts should be at least 24 points; heading fonts should be 36 points)
- Uses phrases rather than sentences with text elements limited to fifty words or fewer
- Uses lots of white space with content arranged in columns
- Where appropriate, uses headings to tell your story
- Uses effective visual elements to supplement text, to create a balanced appearance, and to tell your story visually
- Has an easy-to-follow structure; readers know where to start and what sequence to follow

The most common poster mistake is using small fonts to cram in more text. An effective poster takes a "sound-bite" approach; it entices viewers into discussion with the research team rather than tries to substitute for the whole paper.

Designing, Creating, and Revising Your Poster

Begin by blocking sections of your poster for your Title, Introduction, Method, Results, and Discussion. Determine what graphics or drawings will make your poster visually attractive and meaningful. Then create sound-bite headings and text, limiting text blocks to fifty words or fewer. Researchers often reword the title and figure captions of the original research report by turning them from phrases into sentences that highlight key meanings (again following the sound-bite principle):

Also, a poster sometimes recasts the writer's research question and hypothesis as an "objective":

OBJECTIVE

To determine whether *SpongeBob SquarePants* has fewer gender stereotypes than a 1930s Mickey Mouse cartoon.

	Original Research Report (uses phrases)	**Poster (converts phrases to sentences)**
Title	A Comparison of Gender Stereotypes in *SpongeBob SquarePants* and a 1930s Mickey Mouse Cartoon	*SpongeBob SquarePants* Has Fewer Gender Stereotypes than Mickey Mouse
Figure caption	Figure 1: Stereotypical Behaviors by Gender in *SpongeBob SquarePants* and Mickey Mouse	More Non-Stereotypical Behavior for Males and Females in *SpongeBob SquarePants*

Questions for Peer Review

Ask your peer reviewers to address these questions:

1. Is the poster visually attractive? Can you tell where to start reading and where to go next from beginning to end? Where are possible problem areas that make the poster cluttered, unattractive, confusing, or too text-oriented?
2. Are all elements of the poster, including the legends and axis labels on graphics, readable from four feet away? If not, how can the problem be resolved?
3. To highlight meanings, are the title and figure captions stated as sentences rather than phrases? Where might readers need more highlighting of the results and significance of the research?

The following readings show a professional and a student example of a research report followed by a student example of a poster. The first reading, by authors from the Department of Health and Social Behavior in the Harvard School of Public Health, was published in the peer-reviewed scholarly journal *The American Journal of Public Health* in March 2000. You should find this article generally accessible even though the specific meaning of terms such as "odds ratios" or "confidence levels" may be unclear. As with most scientific articles, you can skim those portions of "Results" that focus on statistical analyses, moving on to those parts of the article that you can understand.

Gina Escamilla, B.A., Angie L. Cradock, M.S.,
and Ichiro Kawachi, M.D., Ph.D.

Women and Smoking in Hollywood Movies:

A Content Analysis

1 According to the Centers for Disease Control and Prevention, over one third (34.7%) of female high school students in a national survey reported smoking at least 1 cigarette in the previous month, up 10% since 1993 and 32% since 1991.[1] Cigarette smoking is initiated primarily in adolescence. Among adult regular smokers, 71% reported having formed the habit before the age of 18 years.[2]

2 Television and popular films have contributed to the allure of smoking. A recent study found that young adults smoked in about 75% of music videos.[3] Although tobacco industry documents suggest that manufacturers have not engaged in deliberate product placement in Hollywood movies since the late 1980s,[4] recent evidence indicates that smoking continues to be depicted at very high levels. Moreover, the gap between the prevalence of tobacco use in movies and in actual life has steadily widened through the 1990s.[5] A recent analysis of G-rated children's animated films found that more than two thirds featured tobacco or alcohol use in story plots, with no clear reference made to the adverse health consequences associated with these substances.[6]

3 Popular film actresses are likely to be role models for young women and adolescent girls. The way that movie stars portray cigarette smoking on the screen may influence young girls' attitudes toward the habit. In this study, we analyzed the portrayal of smoking by 10 leading Hollywood actresses.

Methods

Selection of Actresses

4 We selected 10 leading Hollywood actresses by surveying the 1997 issues of 5 popular magazines that had the highest readership among women aged 18 to 24 years, according to *Simmons Study of Media and Markets*.[7] Magazine titles from the "Special Interest" and "Women's Magazines" categories were selected if the editorial descriptions taken from *Bacon's Magazine Directory*[8] included 1 or more of the following key words or phrases: entertainment, contemporary or current, Hollywood, celebrity, film or movie, personality profiles, women in their 20s, or young women. All issues for the period January 1997 through December 1997 were obtained for the

magazines *Cosmopolitan, Glamour, Vogue, Vanity Fair*, and *Rolling Stone*. Each issue was analyzed for the appearance of female film stars. Advertisements were excluded, and the search was limited to women whose careers are primarily in film. The number of magazine appearances was tallied for each actress, and the 10 actresses with the greatest number of appearances were selected.

Selection of Films

5 A list of films starring each selected actress was generated from the Web site www.tvguide.com. This Web site, maintained by TV Guide Entertainment Network, provides information on the cast, credits, and reviews for some 35,000 movies. Five titles released between 1993 and 1997 were randomly selected for each of the 10 actresses. We excluded period dramas as well as movies in which the actresses did not play a lead or major supporting role. The title, year of release, rating (R, NC-17, PG, PG-13, G), and genre of each film were recorded.

Content Analysis

6 We followed the analytic approach described by Hazan et al.[9] Each film was divided into 5-minute intervals. The occurrence of smoking episodes in each interval was recorded on a coding sheet. We recorded both actual and implied smoking behavior (e.g., holding or smoking a lit or unlit tobacco product); the presence of cigarettes or other smoking paraphernalia (e.g., cigars, matches, and ashtrays); and environmental messages, including "no smoking" signs, tobacco advertising, and tobacco merchandise. Additionally, we recorded smoker characteristics (e.g., gender; whether lead, supporting, or other character); location (i.e., outdoors or in a bar, restaurant, home, or car); the social context of the event (i.e., smoking alone or with others and whether consideration was shown to nonsmokers). We also noted verbal and nonverbal tobacco messages (i.e., positive or negative consequences of smoking behavior and discussion about tobacco products, including positive, negative, or mixed reference to tobacco use). To establish interrater reliability, 5 films (10% of total sample) were randomly selected and independently rated by graduate student coders (G. Escamilla and A. L. Cradock). The coders had 99% agreement on all of the parameters examined regarding the depiction of smoking.

7 After viewing each film, the coders also completed a qualitative assessment of smoking themes and behaviors, addressing contextual issues such as the emotional valence attached to the smoking behavior and the significance of smoking for the character portrayed. All statistical analyses were performed with Stata.[10]

Results

8 The 50 films, representing approximately 96 hours of footage, were broken down into 1116 5-minute intervals (excluding introductions and credits). Of these, 317 (28.4%) of the intervals depicted smoking behavior (Table 1). Cigarettes were the most common tobacco product shown (23.9%). Over half of the smoking episodes (58.7%) occurred in the presence of others who were not smoking.

9 As Table 2 indicates, smoking was significantly more likely to be depicted in R-rated or unrated films than in PG/PG-13-rated films ($P < .001$). Although the percentage of lead actors or supporting actors shown smoking was similar for men and women (38% and 42%, respectively), sex differences were apparent according to the

TABLE 1 Depiction of Smoking Behavior and Paraphernalia, Smoking Context, and Location of Smoking Behaviors in 50 Hollywood Movies

	No. of 5-Min Intervals	Total 5-Min Movie Intervals, % (n = 1116)	Intervals Containing Smoking Behavior, % (n = 317)
Smoking behavior and paraphernalia			
Smoking (actual or implied) behavior	317	28.4	—
Cigarettes	267	23.9	—
Cigarette packs	64	5.7	—
Matches/lighter	108	9.7	—
Cigars, pipes, or smokeless tobacco	71	6.4	—
Ashtray	105	9.4	—
Social context of smoking behavior[a]			
Alone	46	—	14.5
With others (nonsmokers)	186	—	58.7
With others, including smokers and nonsmokers	71	—	22.4
Consideration shown to nonsmokers	5	—	1.6
Location of smoking behavior[b]			
Bar/lounge	25	—	7.9
Home/apartment	84	—	26.5
Restaurant	28	—	8.8
Car	40	—	12.6
Outside	103	—	32.5
Other location	69	—	21.8

[a] *A total of 4.4% of intervals depicted incidental smoking of characters other than the lead/supporting actors.*
[b] *Percentages total more than 100 as smoking may have occurred in more than one context in the same interval.*

TABLE 2 Odds Ratios (ORs) and 95% Confidence Intervals (95% CIs) for the Occurrence of Smoking Behavior in R-Rated/Unrated Movies

	OR[a]	95% CI
Overall smoking behavior	1.62	1.20–2.14
Smoking by male lead or supporting actor	2.48	1.55–3.97
Smoking by female lead or supporting actor	1.23	0.88–1.86

[a] *Referent is PG/PG-13 movies.*

film's rating. Males in lead or supporting roles were 2.5 times more likely to be shown smoking in R-rated/unrated movies than in PG/PG-13-rated films (P <.001). By contrast, the portrayal of smoking by a female lead or supporting character was not significantly different according to the movie's rating; that is, female actresses were *equally likely* to light up in movies aimed at juvenile audiences as in those aimed at mature audiences.

10 Smoking was also more likely to be depicted in the movies starring younger actresses. The mean age of the 10 actresses was 29.3 years (range = 21–40 years). When we categorized actresses according to quartiles by age, movies starring actresses in the youngest quartile featured 3.6 times as many intervals depicting smoking as did movies starring actresses in the oldest age group (95% confidence interval [95% CI] = 2.4, 5.4).

11 Negative messages regarding tobacco product use (e.g., depictions of the consequences of the use of tobacco products, such as coughing or grimacing at the smell of smoke) were more common than positive messages (30 vs 23) among the 50 films viewed. However, only 9 of 22 messages in PG/PG-13 films depicted smoking in a negative light, compared with 21 of 31 messages in R-rated/unrated films; that is, movies aimed at young audiences were *less* likely (odds ratio = 0.33; 95% CI = 0.11, 1.01) to carry negative messages associated with tobacco use than were movies made for mature audiences.

12 In a qualitative analysis of the social context of smoking, sex differences were detected in the themes associated with tobacco use. Women were likely to be portrayed using tobacco products to control their emotions, to manifest power and sex appeal, to enhance their body image or self-image, to control weight, or to give themselves a sense of comfort and companionship. Men were more likely to be depicted using tobacco products to reinforce their masculine identity; to portray a character with power, prestige, or significant authority; to show male bonding; or to signify their status as a "protector" (the last 3 themes were associated with cigar smoking).

13 ***Discussion***

The results of this study raise concerns about exposure to smoking in popular movies. According to social learning theory, by paying attention to the behaviors of a person who possesses the qualities, skills, and capacities one hopes to achieve, a young observer learns to model these behaviors.[11] Among third- through sixth-grade students who had smoked, having role models who smoked was more common, and having beliefs about the adverse consequences of smoking was less common than among their peers who never smoked.[12]

14 The prevalence of smoking by both female (42%) and male (38%) lead or supporting actors was substantially higher than the national smoking prevalence for females (24.3%) and males (29.2%) aged 18 to 44.[13] This discrepancy is significant, given that adolescents who overestimate smoking prevalence among young people and adults are more likely to become smokers themselves.[2] In the films viewed, over half of the smoking episodes occurred in the presence of others who were not smoking, and in fewer than 2% of the intervals was consideration shown to nonsmokers (e.g., smoker leaves the room or asks permission to smoke). The depiction of smoking in Hollywood would thus appear to reinforce smoking as an acceptable

and normative behavior in society. While most young people older than 18 years are able to acknowledge that on-screen smoking is part of a movie role, this may be more difficult for younger females aged 12 to 17 years, among whom smoking initiation is taking place.

15 Our qualitative analysis of smoking identified several themes related to smoking. One of the most prominent themes was using smoking to control emotion, which was specific to female characters and occurred during times of stress or difficulty, when the character was trying to regain or establish control, to repress or deny emotion, or to exit a negative or threatening situation.

16 Important limitations of this study should be noted. First, the sampling of magazine titles was limited to those with the highest readership among women aged 18 to 24 years. On the other hand, given the content and focus of the magazines, it is highly likely that they are widely read by adolescent girls. Surveying the issues of only 5 magazines may have biased our sample of actresses. However, a recent study on the influence of movie stars on adolescent smoking identified 6 of the 10 actresses in our sample as being the "most favorite" among girls.[14] Given that African American and Latina women have become targets for tobacco advertisements, it would also be informative to survey movies starring actresses of different racial/ethnic backgrounds. Future studies need to be extended to popular male actors as well. Finally, replication of our findings through the use of raters who are unaware of the hypotheses would be desirable, since the smoking-related themes emerging from our qualitative analyses may have been biased.

17 Our findings, in conjunction with those of others,[14] suggest the need for the development of policies—such as the adoption of a voluntary code of ethics by the entertainment industry—to eliminate the depiction of smoking in ways that appeal to adolescent audiences.

References

Centers for Disease Control and Prevention. Tobacco use among high school students—United States, 1997. *MMWR Morb Mortal Wkly Rep*. 1998; 47:229–233.

Preventing Tobacco Use Among Young People: A Report of the Surgeon General. Atlanta, Ga: National Center for Chronic Disease Prevention and Health Promotion, Office on Smoking and Health; 1994.

DuRant, RH, Rome ES, Rich M, Allred E, Emans SJ, Woods ER. Tobacco and alcohol use behaviors portrayed in music videos: a content analysis. *Am J Public Health*, 1997;87:1131–1135.

http://www.philipmorries.com/getallimg.asp.DOC_ID=2025863645/3659. Accessed July 1998.

Stockwell TF, Glantz SA. Tobacco use is increasing in popular films. *Tob Control*. 1997; 6:282–284.

Goldstein AO, Sobel RA, Newman GR. Tobacco and alcohol use in G-rated children's animated films. *JAMA*, 1999; 281:1131–1136.

Simmons Market Research Bureau. *Simmons Study of Media and Markets, M1*. New York, NY: Simmons Market Research Bureau; 1994; 0162–0163.

Bacon's Magazine Directory: Directory of Magazines and Newsletters. Chicago, III: Bacon's Information Inc; 1988.

Hazan AR, Lipton HL, Glantz S. Popular films do not reflect current tobacco use. *Am J Public Health*. 1994; 84:998–1000.

Stata Statistical Software: Release 5.0. College Station, Tex: Stata Corporation; 1997.

Greaves L. *Mixed Messages: Women, Tobacco and the Media*. Ottawa, Ontario: Health Canada; 1996.

Greenlund KJ, Johnson CC, Webber LS, Berenson GS. Cigarette smoking attitudes and first use among third- through sixth-grade students: the Bogalusa Heart Study. *Am J Public Health*. 1997; 87: 1345–1348.

Centers for Disease Control and Prevention. Cigarette smoking among adults—United States, 1995. *MMWR Morb Mortal Wkly Rep*. 1997; 46: 1217–1220.

Distefan JM, Gilpin EA, Sargent JD, Pierce JP. Do movie stars encourage adolescents to start smoking? Evidence from California. *Prev Med*. 1999; 28: 1–11.

THINKING CRITICALLY

about "Women and Smoking in Hollywood Movies: A Content Analysis"

1. The introduction to this article doesn't state its research question directly, even though a question is clearly implied. In your own words, what is the question these researchers are asking? Why is this question significant?

2. How did the researchers determine which actresses they were going to study? How did they select the films for each actress? How did they analyze smoking behavior within the films selected for study?

3. What were their findings?

4. In the Discussion section, where do the researchers (a) analyze causes and effects connected to their findings, (b) suggest the significance of their study, (c) point out limitations of their study, and (d) suggest areas for further research?

Our second reading, which was written for this chapter's writing project, was jointly authored by a team of three students. We have reproduced it in manuscript format to illustrate the form and documentation style of the APA (American Psychological Association) system for research papers. For further explanation of APA style, see Skill 22.4.

Include shortened title and page number on each page. On p. 1, include "Running head"

A Comparison of Gender Stereotypes in *SpongeBob SquarePants* and a 1930s Mickey Mouse Cartoon

Lauren Campbell, Charlie Bourain, and Tyler Nishida

November 10, 2006

Center title and authors.

Brief abstract summarizes paper and appears on a separate page.

Abstract

Researchers in gender identity have continually argued whether gender differences are biological or social. Because television is a prime place for teaching children gender differences through socialization, we studied the extent of gender stereotyping in two 1930s Mickey Mouse cartoons and two recent *SpongeBob SquarePants* cartoons. We analyzed the cartoons in one-minute increments and recorded the number of gender stereotypical and gender-non-stereotypical actions in each increment. Our results confirmed our hypothesis that *SpongeBob SquarePants* would have fewer gender stereotypes than Mickey Mouse. This study is significant because it shows that in at least one contemporary cartoon males and females have a range of acceptable behaviors that go beyond traditional gender stereotypes.

A Comparison of Gender Stereotypes in *SpongeBob SquarePants* and a 1930s Mickey Mouse Cartoon

Repeat title before body of paper.

Researchers in gender identity have long argued over the role of biology versus culture in causing gendered behavior. Pinker (2005) has argued that biology plays a more significant role in gender identity. In contrast, Barres (2006) has argued that culture plays the more significant role in gender identity. Proponents of socialization over biology have shown that cultural influences begin at a very young age. For example, Clearfield and Nelson (2006) show that mothers are more verbal and nurturing towards girls but are more focused on promoting independence and use more commands with boys.

Double-space all text.

Also of interest are the effects of media and popular culture on children and adults. A large part of a child's life is spent watching cartoons; therefore we believe it is important to find how much of a role gender stereotypes play in the media. In response to this question, we have examined data about gender stereotypes from two different kinds of children's cartoons. The first is a recent, somewhat controversial cartoon called *SpongeBob SquarePants*. The other is a popular 1930s Mickey Mouse cartoon.

Use italics for titles.

The purpose of our study is to see if there is a difference in the extent of gender stereotypes between *SpongeBob SquarePants* and the earlier Mickey Mouse cartoon. We asked the following research question: To what extent has *SpongeBob SquarePants* rejected or reinforced gender stereotypes compared to the Mickey Mouse cartoon? Our hypothesis is that *SpongeBob SquarePants* will show fewer gender stereotypes than the older Mickey Mouse cartoon. We believe this because SpongeBob SquarePants has been attacked by some conservative religious groups as a gay character (Kirkpatrick, 2005). We hypothesize that this characterization comes from the cartoon's male characters' not exhibiting stereotypical male behaviors. In contrast, we believe that the older Mickey

APA Style

GENDER STEREOTYPES 4

Mouse cartoon will show Mickey exhibiting stereotypical male behavior and Minnie stereotypical female behavior.

Center section headings in bold.

Methods

To analyze the cartoons, we developed four specific categories for coding the data: Stereotypical Female Action, Stereotypical Male Action, Non-Stereotypical Female Action, and Non-Stereotypical Male Action. For each category we developed certain criteria that can be viewed in Table 1

Reference tables in text.

We watched two episodes of each cartoon (obtained from the Internet) in one-minute intervals. After each minute, we stopped the cartoon and waited for each team member to record his or her analysis. We all watched the same episodes at the same time, but recorded our data separately and later compiled the data after the last episode had been watched.

Table 1

Coding Criteria for Gender Stereotypes

Category	Criteria for Making Category Decision
Stereotypical Female Action	Female character behaves in a timid, submissive, or passive way; breaks into tears; shows caring, nurturing, empathic, or motherly behavior; dresses in stereotypical way (frilly clothes, dresses, feminine accessories)
Stereotypical Male Action	Male character behaves in an aggressive, fearless, or competitive way; is cocky or taunting; shows physical strength; dresses in stereotypical male way
Non-Stereotypical Female Action	Female character exhibits stereotypical male behavior
Non-Stereotypical Male Action	Male character exhibits stereotypical female behavior

Here is a representative example of how we applied our coding scheme: In one one-minute segment from *SpongeBob SquarePants*, SpongeBob and his friend Patrick decide to lift weights. While lifting weights, SpongeBob infuriates a body building fish who is much bigger and stronger than SpongeBob. SpongeBob runs away in fear while his friend Sandy (the female squirrel) stands up to the mean body building fish. She then makes sure SpongeBob is okay before she returns to lifting weights. We coded this example as containing a stereotypical male action (body building fish), a non-stereotypical male action (SpongeBob showing fear), a stereotypical female action (Sandy expressing concern for others), and non-stereotypical female actions (Sandy challenging the fish and also lifting weights).

Results

Our results (see Figure 1) show that the Mickey Mouse cartoon had a higher percentage of stereotypical male and female actions than did *SpongeBob SquarePants*, which had an almost equal amount of non-stereotypical and stereotypical gendered actions.

Reference figures in text.

As shown in Figure 1, female actions in *SpongeBob SquarePants* were 59% gender stereotypical and 40% gender non-stereotypical while in Mickey Mouse female actions were 84% gender stereotypical and only 16% gender non-stereotypical. Similarly, male actions in *SpongeBob SquarePants* were 48% gender stereotypical and 52% gender non-stereotypical, while in Mickey Mouse male actions were 87% gender stereotypical and 12% gender non-stereotypical.

Discussion

Our hypothesis that *SpongeBob SquarePants* will have fewer gender stereotypes than the Mickey Mouse cartoon was confirmed. The data show that overall *SpongeBob SquarePants* is the more gender-neutral cartoon, showing balance between non-stereotypical and stereotypical actions, while Mickey Mouse showed strong gender stereotypes.

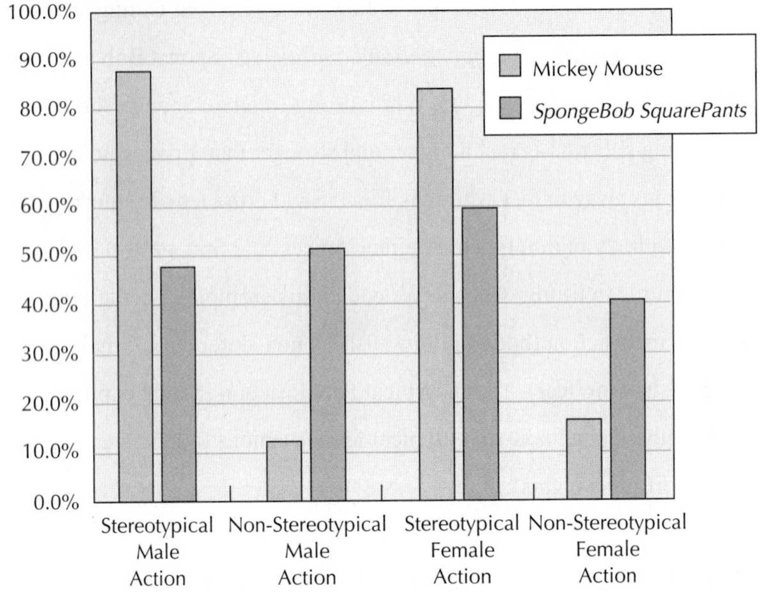

Figure 1 Stereotypical Behaviors by Gender in *SpongeBob SquarePants* and Mickey Mouse.

The study we have done is important because it shows that *SpongeBob SquarePants* does not reveal gender stereotyping in the stereotypical ways exhibited in the Mickey Mouse cartoon. In *SpongeBob SquarePants*, almost every gender stereotypical action (like SpongeBob acting tough or macho) was followed by a gender non-stereotypical action (like SpongeBob crying). This was not the case for Mickey Mouse, where there were many more gender stereotypical actions (for instance, Mickey Mouse rescuing Minnie Mouse) than gender non-stereotypical actions (for instance, Mickey Mouse quivering in fear).

The trends found in the *SpongeBob SquarePants* and Mickey Mouse cartoons suggest to us that these cartoons reveal ways that society's view of gender is evolving. In *SpongeBob SquarePants*, the greater variation and complexity of behavior may reflect such cultural and social changes as women and mothers in the workforce, stay-at-home dads raising the kids, shared household responsibilities, women in the military, and nontraditional families. These recent social and cultural changes have complicated our culture's views of gender, and we speculate that it is these less rigid gender restrictions that we glimpse in *SpongeBob SquarePants*. However, there is still a cultural war going on over gender roles in the media. Our class's discussion of advertising showed that the media in the 21st century still promote gender stereotypes, and the continuation of these stereotypes could explain why *SpongeBob SquarePants* has been controversial and has come under attack from cultural conservatives.

A potential limitation of our study could be that we didn't observe enough episodes of the two cartoons to get a representative sample. Another limitation was our difficulty in deciding how to code continuous actions that lasted more than one minute. For example, in a one-minute segment, *SpongeBob SquarePants* characters would exhibit many different actions, while actions in Mickey Mouse would last longer. For example, there might be a chase scene in which Mickey exhibited the same male action for several minutes or a scene where Minnie cried for several minutes. Should we count the chase scene or the crying scene as one action or as several because it continued across one-minute increments? We decided to count the same continuous action as several actions. Making another choice might have changed our data.

For future studies, researchers could ask questions like the following: Do other modern cartoons follow the trend of *SpongeBob SquarePants*? New research could compare *SpongeBob SquarePants* with other recent cartoons like *The Justice League* or *Jimmy Neutron* to see if they follow *SpongeBob SquarePants*' gender-neutral tendencies. If we believe that gender stereotyping is harmful, furthering the research on gender stereotypes in the media could help identify how to promote a more gender-neutral society in the future.

APA Style

Center page heading.

Use initials for first names.

Place date after author's name.

Italicize publication names.

Use initial cap for article titles.

Check that everything cited in report is in References list (except personal communications).

References

Barres, B. A. (2006, July 13). Does gender matter? *Nature, 442*, 133–136.

Clearfield, M., & Nelson, N. (2006, January). Sex differences in mothers' speech and play behavior with 6-, 9-, and 14-month-old infants. *Sex Roles, 54*(1/2), 127–137.

Kirkpatrick, D. (2005, January 20). Conservatives pick soft target: A cartoon sponge. *The New York Times*. Retrieved from http://www.nytimes.com

Pinker, S. (2005, February 7). The science of difference. Sex ed. *The New Republic Online*. Retrieved from http://www.tnr.com

THINKING CRITICALLY

about "A Comparison of Gender Stereotypes in *SpongeBob SquarePants* and a 1930s Mickey Mouse Cartoon"

1. Explain how this paper follows the genre conventions for a scientific report.
2. To what extent do you think the authors' research design was effective? Are you persuaded that *SpongeBob SquarePants* has moved away from gender stereotypes?
3. This research project was part of a class unit on issues in gender identity that included the readings by Pinker, Barres, and Clearfield and Nelson referred to in the introduction. What does this brief "review of the literature" add to the paper? How much more extensive is the review of the literature in the previous reading by Escamilla, Cradock, and Kawachi?
4. The authors located the reference to Kirkpatrick on their own. How does the use of this source contribute to the paper?
5. How might the authors expand their speculations about causes of new approaches to gender in cartoons and their ideas about the significance of the study? How has this study inspired you to think about gender and cartoons?

Our final reading is the poster created by the authors of the *SpongeBob SquarePants* paper for presentation at a poster session (see p. 240).

THINKING CRITICALLY

about "*SpongeBob SquarePants* Has Fewer Gender Stereotypes than Mickey Mouse"

1. To what extent does this poster present the same scientific content as the complete research report? If you attended a conference, would you rather listen to a fifteen-minute talk by the authors or view their poster and ask them questions? Why?
2. How does this poster employ the "sound-bite" principle by using minimal text connected to visual elements?
3. In what ways do you think this poster is effective? What questions would you want to ask the creators of this poster?

PEARSON mycomplab

For support in learning this chapter's content, follow this path in **MyCompLab**: Resources ⇒ Writing ⇒ Writing Purposes ⇒ Writing to Analyze. Review the Instruction and Multimedia resources, then complete the Exercises and click on Gradebook to measure your progress.

SpongeBob SquarePants Has Fewer Gender Stereotypes than Mickey Mouse

Lauren Campbell, Charlie Bourain, and Tyler Nishida

Introduction

Television cartoons may influence children's learning of gender stereotypes. Knowing how a contemporary cartoon portrays gender stereotypes would help us understand messages children receive.

Objective

We wanted to see if there is a difference in gender stereotypes between *SpongeBob SquarePants* and a 1930s Mickey Mouse cartoon.

Method

We analyzed cartoons in one-minute increments.

We coded behavior in four categories:
- *Stereotypical female* [timid, passive, tearful; caring, motherly; wearing frilly clothes, accessories]
- *Stereotypical male* [aggressive, fearless, competitive; cocky; showing physical strength; wearing typical male clothing]
- *Non-stereotypical female* [female exhibiting stereotypical male action]
- *Non-stereotypical male* [male exhibiting stereotypical female action]

Results

More Non-Stereotypical Behavior for Males and Females in SpongeBob

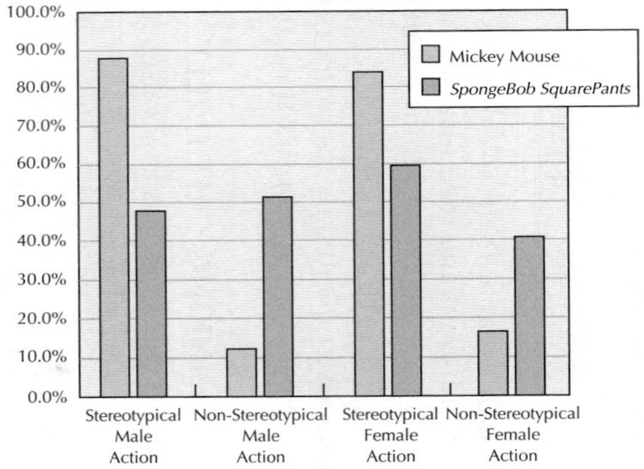

- *SpongeBob SquarePants* has almost equal ratio of stereotypical and non-stereotypical behaviors for both males and females (49%/51% for males; 59%/41% females)
- Mickey Mouse has mostly stereotypical behaviors (88%/12% for males; 84%/16% for females)

Discussion

SpongeBob SquarePants showed males and females engaged in wider range of behavior with fewer gender stereotypes than Mickey Mouse.

- *SpongeBob SquarePants* intermixed gender stereotypical action (SpongeBob acting tough, Sandy being nurturing) and non-stereotypical behavior (SpongeBob crying, Sandy rescuing SpongeBob)
- Mickey Mouse had mostly gender stereotypical actions (Mickey rescuing Minnie, who is in tears).

These differences may match changes in culture since 1930s (women's movement, working women, stay-at-home dads) and may explain why *SpongeBob SquarePants* has been attacked by cultural conservatives.

ANALYZING IMAGES

10

This chapter asks you to think about three major kinds of communication through images—documentary or news photos, paintings, and advertisements—to increase your visual literacy skills. By **visual literacy**, we mean your awareness of the importance of visual communication and your ability to interpret or make meaning out of images by examining their context and visual features. We focus on the ways that images influence our conceptual and emotional understanding of a phenomenon and the ways that they validate, reveal, and construct the world.

This chapter invites you to analyze images in order to understand their rhetorical and experiential effects. To **analyze** means to divide or dissolve the whole into its parts, examine these parts carefully, look at the relationships among them, and then use this understanding of the parts to better understand the whole—how it functions, what it means. As Chapter 1, Concept 2, explains, when you analyze, your goal is to raise interesting questions about the image or object being analyzed—questions that perhaps your reader hasn't thought to ask—and then to provide tentative answers, supported by points and particulars derived from your own close examination.

The ability to analyze visual texts is particularly important because we are surrounded by images from photojournalism, the Internet, billboards, newspapers, television, and magazines. These images, as one critic has stated, "have designs on us." Although glamorous and disturbing images saturate our environment, we do not necessarily have a deep understanding of how they affect us.

By writing in a common academic genre—a comparative analysis of two visual texts—in this chapter you will learn to:

- analyze the persuasive effects of images and how these effects are created
- respond to visual images as a more informed citizen and perceptive cultural critic

Exploring Image Analysis

To introduce you to image analysis, we provide an exercise that asks you to interact with several news photographs on the issue of immigration reform.

Immigration reform is one of the most complex issues facing the United States today; the problem is particularly acute with respect to immigrants from Mexico and Central America. Immigrants are drawn to the United States by employment opportunities not found in their own countries. U.S. citizens benefit from immigrants' inexpensive labor, which helps keep the prices of services and goods low. In addition to a sizable Mexican-American citizenry, more than ten million illegal immigrants currently live in the United States. All these factors give rise to a number of controversial questions: Should the United States increase border security and focus on building impassable barriers? Should it deport illegal immigrants or explore easier routes to making them citizens? Should it crack down on employers of illegal immigrants or should it implement a guest worker program to legitimize immigrant labor?

Public debate about these issues is particularly susceptible to manipulation by the rhetorical appeal of images. The following exercise asks you to examine the news photos in Figures 10.1 through 10.4. Working individually or in groups, consider the rhetorical effect of these photos, first by recording your responses to

FIGURE 10.1 Wall between Tijuana, Mexico, and the United States

FIGURE 10.2 Immigrants Crossing the Border Illegally

FIGURE 10.3 Protestors Marching for Compassionate Treatment of Immigrants

FIGURE 10.4 Immigrants Saying Their Citizenship Pledge

them and then by speculating how you might use these images to increase the persuasiveness of different positions on immigration reform.

1. What objects, people, or places stand out in each photo? Does the photo look candid or staged, taken close-up or from a distance? How do the angle of the photo (taken from below or above the subject) and the use of color contribute to the effect?
2. What is the dominant impression conveyed by each photo?
3. Examine how the similarities and differences among the four photos convey different rhetorical impressions of immigrants, Latino culture, or the role of immigrants and ethnic diversity in U.S. culture.
4. Now imagine how you might use these photos to enhance the persuasiveness of particular claims. Choose one or two photos to support or attack each claim below and explain what the photo could contribute to the argument.
   - The United States should seal its border with Mexico by building a wall and increasing border patrols.
   - The United States should offer amnesty and citizenship to immigrants who are currently in the United States illegally.

Understanding Image Analysis: Documentary and News Photographs

Documentary and news photos are aimed at shaping the way we think and feel about an event or cultural/historical phenomenon. For example, consider the newspaper photos, TV news footage, or Internet videos of the billowing clouds of smoke and ash from the collapsing World Trade Center towers on September 11, 2001. Figures 10.5, 10.6, and 10.7 present three well-known documentary images of this event, taken from three different positions and at three slightly different moments as the event unfolded.

Although all three photos convey the severity of the terrorist attack, each has a different impact. Figure 10.5 records the event shortly before the north tower collapsed and just after the south tower was struck by the second plane, marked in the photo by the red flames. The sheer magnitude and horror of the moment-by-moment action unfolding before our eyes evoked shock, anger, and feelings of helplessness in Americans.

In contrast to the first image, which was taken from a distance below the towers, Figure 10.6 was taken by a police detective in a helicopter searching for survivors on the roof of the north tower before it collapsed. This photo suggests the apocalyptic explosion and implosion of a contemporary city. The destruction pictured here is too massive to be an ordinary event such as a fire in a major building, and yet the streams of ash and smoke don't reveal exactly what is happening.

Another well-publicized view of this event is that of the firefighters on the ground, seen in Figure 10.7. Here the firefighters, risking their lives while trying to rescue the people in the towers, have come to symbolize the self-sacrifice, courage, and also vulnerability of the human effort in the face of such colossal

FIGURE 10.5 Terrorist Attack on the World Trade Center

FIGURE 10.6 World Trade Center Attack Seen from the Air

FIGURE 10.7 Firefighters in the World Trade Center Wreckage

destruction. This image also suggests the terror and suspense of a science-fiction-like conflict. All three photos, while memorializing the same event, have different specific subjects, angles of vision, and emotional and mental effects.

The rest of this section introduces you to the ways that photographers think about their use of the camera and the effects they are trying to achieve.

Angle of Vision and Credibility of Photographs

Although the word "documentary" is associated with an objective, transparent, unmediated glimpse of reality, the relationship of documentary photography to its subject matter has always been complex. Historians are now reassessing early documentary photographs, exploring the class and race agendas of the photographers in the kinds of scenes chosen, the photographers' stance toward them, and the wording of the narratives accompanying the photographs. In other words, despite a photograph's appearance of capturing a moment of reality (whose reality?), its effect is always influenced by the photographer's rhetorical angle of vision conveyed through the framing and focusing power of the camera. Perhaps now more than ever, we are aware that the photographer's purpose and techniques actually shape the reality that viewers see. (Think of the multiple cameras tracking a football game and replaying a touchdown from different angles, often creating very different impressions of a particular play.)

The photographer's power to shape reality is enhanced by various strategies for making "unnatural" photographs seem "natural" or "real." For example, photographs can be manipulated or falsified in the following ways:

- staging images (scenes that appear spontaneous but are really posed)
- altering images (airbrushing, reshaping body parts)
- selecting images or parts of images (cropping photographs so that only certain parts are shown)
- mislabeling images (putting a caption on a photograph that misrepresents the image)
- constructing images (putting the head of one person on the body of another)

Research has revealed that many famous photographs were tampered with. As early as the Civil War, composite photos of generals were created by combining heads, bodies, and scenery and inserting figures into scenes. Today this manipulation is also conducted by amateur photographers using photo-editing software. The potential for altering images gives us additional reasons for considering the active role of the photographer and for investigating the credibility and purpose behind images.

How to Analyze a Documentary Photograph

Photographs are always created and interpreted within a social, political, and historical context—the original context in which the photograph was made and viewed and your own context as a current viewer and interpreter. At play are the assumptions, values, and cultural knowledge of the photographer, the original viewers, and the later viewers. Also at play are the sites in which the photograph is viewed—whether in an original news story, a museum, an upscale art exhibit, an expensive coffee-table book, a documentary film, an Internet site, or a textbook. These sites invite us to respond in different ways. For example, one site may call us to social action or deepen our understanding of an event, while another aims to elicit artistic appreciation or to underscore cultural differences.

Examining the Rhetorical Contexts of a Photo A first step in analyzing a documentary photograph is to consider its various rhetorical contexts. The following chart will help you ask illuminating questions.

Strategies for Analyzing the Rhetorical Contexts of Documentary Photographs

Context	Questions to Ask
Photographer's purpose and context in making the photograph	• What was the photographer's original intention/purpose in making the image (to report an event, convey information, persuade viewers to think about the event or people a certain way)? • What was the original historical, cultural, social, and political context in which the photograph was taken?
Original context for displaying the photograph	• Where was the photograph originally viewed (news story, photo essay, scientific report, public exhibit, advocacy Web site)? • How does the original title or caption, if any, reflect the context and shape impressions of the image?
Cultural contexts for interpreting the photograph	• How does the photograph's appearance in a particular place influence your impression of it? • How does your own cultural context differ from that of original viewers? • What assumptions and values do you bring to the context?

Examining the Effects of a Photo on a Viewer In addition to considering the contexts of photographs, we can explore how photographs achieve their effects—that is, how they move us emotionally or intellectually, how they imply arguments and cause us to see the subject in a certain way. An image might soothe us or repel us; it might evoke our sympathies, trigger our fears, or call forth a web of interconnected ideas, memories, and associations.

Before you begin a detailed analysis of a photograph, you will find it helpful to explore the photograph's immediate impact.

- What words come to mind when you view this photograph?
- What is the mood or overall feeling conveyed by the photo?
- Assuming that photographs "have designs on us," what is this photograph trying to get you to feel, think, do, or "see"?

The following chart will help you examine a photograph in detail in order to analyze how it achieves its persuasive effects.*

Strategies for Analyzing the Persuasive Effects of Photographs and Other Images

What to Examine	Some Questions to Ask about Rhetorical Effect
Subject matter: People in portraits Portraits can be formal or informal and can emphasize character or social role. The gaze of the human subjects can imply power through direct eye contact and deference or shyness through lack of eye contact.	Is the emphasis on identity, character, and personality, or representative status (wife of wealthy merchant, king, soldier, etc.), or symbolic (an image of wisdom, daring, etc.)? What do details of clothing and setting (a room's furnishings, for example) reveal about historical period, economic status, national or ethnic identity?
Subject matter: People in scenes Scenes can make a statement about everyday life or capture some aspect of a news event or crisis.	What is the relationship of the people to each other and the scene? Can you re-create the story behind the scene? Does the scene look natural/realistic or staged/aesthetically attractive?
Subject matter: Landscape or nature Scenes can focus on nature or the environment as the dominant subject.	If the setting is outdoors, what are the features of the landscape: urban or rural, mountain or desert? What aspects of nature are shown? If people are in the image, what is the relationship between nature and the human figures? What vision of nature is the artist constructing—majestic, threatening, hospitable, tamed, orderly, wild?

(continued)

*We are indebted to Terry Barrett, Professor Emeritus of Art Education at Ohio State University, for his formulation of questions, "Looking at Photographs, Description and Interpretation," and to Claire Garoutte, Assistant Professor of Photography at Seattle University, for informing our discussion of context in analyzing documentary photographs.

What to Examine	Some Questions to Ask about Rhetorical Effect
Distance from subject: Close-ups tend to increase the intensity of the image and suggest the importance of the subject. Long shots tend to blend the subject into the environment.	Are viewers brought close to the subject or distanced from it? How does the distance from the subject contribute to the effect of the photo or painting?
Angle and orientation: The vantage point from which the photograph was taken and the positioning of the photographer to the subject determine the effect of images. Low angle makes the subject look larger. High angle makes the subject look smaller. A level angle implies equality. Front views tend to emphasize the persons in the image. Rear views often emphasize the scene or setting.	How does the angle influence what you see? Why do you think this angle was chosen? How would the photograph have changed if it had been taken from another angle?
Framing: Framing determines what is inside the image and what is closed off to viewers; it's a device to draw the attention of viewers.	How does the framing of the image direct your attention? What is included and what is excluded from the image? How does what the photo or painting allows you to see and know contribute to its effect? Why do you think this particular frame was chosen?
Light: The direction of the light determines the shadows and affects the contrasts, which can be subtle or strong. Lighting has different effects if it is natural or artificial, bright, soft, or harsh.	How does the light reveal details? What does the direction of the light contribute to the presence of shadows? How do these shadows affect the mood or feeling of the photo?
Focus: Focus refers to what is clearly in focus or in the foreground of the photo versus what is blurry. The range between the nearest and farthest thing in focus in the photo is referred to as the depth of field.	What parts of the image are clearly in focus? Are any parts out of focus? What effect do these choices have on viewers' impression of the image? How great is the depth of field and what effect does that have?
Scale, space, and shape: Size/scale and shape affect prominence and emphasis. Size and scale can be natural, minimized, or exaggerated. Use of space can be shallow, deep, or both.	How do the scale, space, and shape of objects direct viewers' attention and affect a feeling or mood? Are shapes geometric and angular or flowing and organic?

What to Examine	Some Questions to Ask about Rhetorical Effect
Both positive shapes and voids can draw viewers' attention.	Are shapes positive such as objects, or negative such as voids?
Use of repetition, variety, and balance: Repetition of elements can create order, wholeness, and unity. Variety can create interest. Balance can create unity and harmony.	What elements are repeated in this image? What variety is present, say, in shapes? Does the visual weight of the photo seem to be distributed evenly on the sides, top, and bottom? What roles do repetition, variety, and balance play in the impression created by the photo?
Line: Lines can be curved and flowing, straight, or disjointed and angular. Lines can be balanced/symmetrical, stable, and harmonious, or disjointed and agitated.	Does the use of line create structure and convey movement/action or calm/stasis? How does the use of line control how viewers look at the photo or painting?
Color: Choice of black and white can reflect the site of publication, the date of the photo, or an artistic choice. Colors can contribute to the realism and appeal; harmonious colors can be pleasing; clashing or harsh colors can be disturbing.	How many colors are used? What is the relationship of the colors? Which colors dominate? Are the colors warm and vibrant or cool, bright, or dull? How are light and dark used? How does the use of color direct viewers' attention and affect the impression of the image? What emotional response do these colors evoke?

Sample Analysis of a Documentary Photograph

To illustrate how a documentary photograph can work on the viewer's mind and heart, we show you our own analysis of a photo titled *The Fall of the Berlin Wall* (Figure 10.8), taken by photojournalist Peter Turnley in 1989. At the time, the Berlin Wall, which separated communist East Berlin from democratic West Berlin, symbolized the oppression of communism. In 1987 President Ronald Reagan appealed to Mikhail Gorbachev, president of the Union of Soviet Socialist Republics, saying in a famous speech, "Mr. Gorbachev, tear down this wall." When the border opened in November 1989, marking the end of communist rule in Eastern Europe, East Berliners flooded into West Berlin, sparking weeks of celebration. Peter Turnley is a world-famous American photojournalist whose photos of major world events have appeared on the covers of *Newsweek* as well as international magazines. This photograph appeared in a 1996 exhibit (and later a book) entitled *In Time of War and Peace* at the International Center of Photography in New York.

This documentary photograph of a celebratory scene following the opening of the Berlin Wall in 1989 uses elements of framing, orientation, focus, balance, and color to convey the dominant impression of a life-changing explosion of energy and emotion triggered by this significant event. This distance photo is divided

FIGURE 10.8 Fall of the Berlin Wall, 1989, by Peter Turnley

into three horizontal bands—the sky, the wall, and the celebratory crowd—but the focal point is the yelling, triumphant German youth sitting astride the wall, wearing jeans, a studded belt, and a black jacket. The graffiti indicate that the photo was taken from the West Berlin side (East Berliners were not permitted to get close to the wall), and the light post between the two cranes was probably used to illuminate the no-man zone on the communist side.

Every aspect of the photograph suggests energy. In contrast with the mostly homogeneous sky, the wall and the crowd contain many diverse elements. The wall is heavily graffitied in many colors, and the crowd is composed of many people. The wall looks crowded, tattered, and dirty, something to be torn down rather than cleaned up. Most of the graffiti consist of tags, people's response to the ugly obstruction of the wall; West Berliners had no power to destroy the wall, but they could mark it up. The slightly blurred crowd of heads suggests that the people are in motion. At first it is hard to tell if they are angry protesters storming the wall or celebrators cheering on the German youth. The photograph captures this dual emotion—anger and joy—all at once.

At the center of the photograph is the German youth, whose dark jacket makes him stand out against the light blue sky. A few days earlier the wall had fenced him in (at that time, it would have been unthinkable even to approach the wall lest he be shot by border guards). Now he rides the wall like an American cowboy at a rodeo. He has conquered the wall. He has become transformed from prisoner to liberator. His cowboy gesture, reflecting European fascination with American cowboy movies, becomes the symbol of the ideological West, the land of freedom, now the wave of the future for these reunited countries. He holds in his hand a tool (a hammer or chisel?) used to chip away the wall symbolically, but the position of his arm and hand suggests a cowboy with a pistol.

What makes this photograph so powerful is the distance. Had Turnley used a telescopic lens to focus on the German youth up close, the photograph would have been about the youth himself, a personal story. But by placing the youth into a larger frame that includes the crowd, the long expanse of ugly wall, and the cranes and lamppost behind the wall, Turnley suggests both the enormous public and political nature of this event and the implications for individual lives. The youth appears to be the first of the energized crowd to demonstrate the conquering of the powerful barrier that had shaped so many German lives for almost three decades. Thus the composition of this photo packs many layers of meaning and symbolism into its depiction of this historical event.

FOR WRITING AND DISCUSSION

Exploring a Photograph's Compositional Elements and Rhetorical Effect

In the last five years, documentary photographs have played a key role in persuading audiences that climate change is a serious threat. One recurring image shows mountains with receding or disappearing glaciers. An example is Figure 10.9, a photo of the Gormer glacier near Zermatt, Switzerland, that was taken by photojournalist Jean-Christophe Bott on August 25, 2009, during the Switzerland Greenpeace Protest. The staging and showing of the photograph were intended to put pressure on national legislation to enact stricter carbon dioxide emission limits and to influence negotiators at the Copenhagen Summit on climate change in September 2009.

1. Working in groups or individually, use the strategies for analyzing the context, composition, and rhetorical effects of photos presented in the strategies charts on pages 246–249 to describe and interpret this photo. What is the dominant impression conveyed by this photograph?

FIGURE 10.9 Greenpeace Climate Change Protest in Zermatt, Switzerland

2. Then using the Internet, search for another photograph that is currently being used in the public discussion of climate change and analyze its context, composition, rhetorical effect, and possible additional uses. What does your photograph contribute to its context?
3. If you were writing to underscore to young voters the importance of climate change, would you use the Greenpeace protest photograph or the one you located? Why?

Understanding Image Analysis: Paintings

When you analyze a painting, many of the strategies used for analyzing documentary photographs still apply. You still look carefully at the subject matter of the painting (the setting, the people or objects in the setting, the arrangement in space, the clothing, the gaze of persons, the implied narrative story, and so forth). Likewise, you consider the painter's distance from the subject, the angle of orientation, the framing, and other features that paintings share with photographs. Additionally, your analysis of paintings will be enriched if you consider, as you did with documentary photographs, the context in which the painting was originally created and originally viewed as well as your own cultural context and place of viewing.

But painters—by means of their choice of paints, their brushstrokes, their artistic vision, and their methods of representation—often do something quite different from photographers. For example, they can paint mythological or imaginary subjects and can achieve nonrepresentational effects not associated with a camera such as a medieval allegorical style or the striking distortions of Cubism. Also, the long history of painting and the ways that historical periods influence painters' choices of subject matter, medium, and style affect what viewers see and feel about paintings. Background on the artist, historical period, and style of paintings (for example, Baroque, Impressionism, Expressionism, and Cubism) can be found in sources such as the Oxford Art Online database. In analyzing paintings, art critics and historians often contrast paintings that have similar subject matter (for example, two portraits of a hero, two paintings of a biblical scene, two landscapes) but that create very different dominant impressions and effects on viewers.

How to Analyze a Painting

Just as with photographs, you should ground your interpretation of a painting in close observation. Many of the elements introduced in the strategies chart on pages 247–249 for analyzing photographs can apply or be adapted to the analysis of paintings. In addition, you will want to examine the following elements of the paintings you are analyzing.

Strategies for Analyzing the Particular Elements of Paintings	
Elements to Analyze	**Questions to Ask about Rhetorical Effect**
Design and shape of the painting: The width to height, division into parts, and proportional relationship of parts influence the impression of the painting.	What is viewer's impression of the shape of the painting and the relationship of its parts? How does line organize the painting? Is the painting organized along diagonal, horizontal, or vertical lines?
Medium, technique, and brushstrokes: The material with which the painting is made (for example, pen and ink, tempura/water colors, charcoal, oil paints on paper or canvas), and the thickness and style of brushstrokes determine the artistic effect.	In what medium is the artist working? How does the medium contribute to the impression of the painting? Are brushstrokes sharp and distinct or thick, layered, fused? Are they delicate and precise or vigorous? What effect does the awareness or lack of awareness of brushstrokes have on the appearance of the painting?

Sample Analysis of a Painting

As an example of a visual analysis of a painting, we offer an interpretation of a famous painting by Pierre-Auguste Renoir (1841–1919), a French Impressionist painter of the late nineteenth century. The French Impressionists were recognized for their refusal to paint old themes; their embrace of scenes of modern society, especially the city and suburbs; and their experimentation with light and brushstrokes as a way to capture fleeting impressions. Figure 10.10 shows Renoir's oil painting *La Loge* (The Theater Box), which he painted as his main contribution to the first exhibit of Impressionist paintings in 1874. Impressionist paintings were considered too *avant garde* to be displayed at the conservative state-controlled Salon, which was the official arbiter and channel of the work of established French artists.

Renoir's *La Loge* depicts social life in nineteenth-century urban society as an occasion to act out social roles. This painting of a man and a woman elegantly dressed in a theater box at the opera, a popular social spot of the period, suggests that attending the theater/opera entailed displaying one's wealth, being seen, and inspecting others as much as it did watching a performance. This painting focuses intensely on two members of the audience and specifically on the woman, who catches and holds our gaze. While the man in the background is looking at someone in the audience through his opera glasses, the woman looks directly at viewers and invites their attention.

Renoir has compelled viewers to dwell on this woman by a number of his choices in this painting. He has chosen to paint her in a tightly framed close-up image, which the slightly off-center woman dominates. Her face and eyes convey

FIGURE 10.10 Renoir's *La Loge* (1874)

the impression that she and the viewer are staring at each other, while in the shadows the man's eyes are blocked by his opera glasses. Thus this painting combines the woman's portrait with a scene at the opera, even though most of the setting, the theater box, is excluded from the painting. (We know we are at the opera because of the painting's title and the man's and woman's accessories.) There seems to be a story behind the scene: what is the man looking at and why is he not noticing the woman as we, the viewers, are compelled to do? This depiction of a moment seems to be less a shared experience of relationship and more a site for performance: men engaged in looking, women inviting the gaze of others.

Another choice Renoir has made to focus viewers' attention on the woman is his striking use of color. In this painting, the color palette is not large—white, black, brown/gold/sepia, with her red lips and red flowers on her bodice. The white of her face and her upper body is the brightest, suggesting light shining on her. Renoir also highlights the woman with short, thick brushstrokes, which give her shimmering, elegant dress texture and the impression of silk, velvet, and lace. As additional signs of wealth, she wears earrings, a gold bracelet, a flower in her hair, and a flower at her bosom. The stark contrast of the black and white in her dress, the white of her face, and the red of her lips—and the agitated diagonal but converging lines of the stripes of her dress that, along with her arms angled out from her body, shape her into a diamond—all work to direct viewers' eyes to her bosom and most of all to her face. Although the expression of the woman is calm, smiling in mild amusement or subtle emotion, the painting captures intensity, perhaps excitement or anticipation, through the sharp contrast of the red, white, and black. The piece is fairly still and yet we are transfixed by this woman's eyes and lips. With the complex interaction of artistic elements in this painting, Renoir has invited viewers to experience an exciting scene of privileged nineteenth-century urban life.

FOR WRITING AND DISCUSSION

Contrasting the Compositional Features of Two Paintings

This exercise asks you to apply the analysis strategies presented on pages 253 and 261–263 to examine the pastel painting *Carousel* by Camille Pissarro shown in Figure 10.11 and to contrast it with Renoir's painting in Figure 10.10. Camille Pissarro (1830–1903) was also a French Impressionist who regularly exhibited his works in Impressionist exhibitions. He painted *Carousel* in 1885; the medium is pastel on paper mounted on board.

Your task: Working individually or in groups, analyze Pissarro's painting and then find some striking points of commonality or difference with the Renoir painting that you think merit discussion.

- Begin by applying the strategies for analyzing photographic images and paintings on pages 247–249 and 253.
- After you have analyzed the visual features of the paintings, consider why Pissarro titled his painting *Carousel*.

FIGURE 10.11 *Carousel* by Camille Pissarro (1885)

- Finally, what are the thematic differences between these two paintings? How do these paintings, both Impressionistic images of well-dressed women at leisure, create similar or different effects on viewers? What view or feeling about life or about the artists' worlds is conveyed in each painting? What way of seeing or thinking are these paintings persuading you to adopt?

Understanding Image Analysis: Advertisements

The images in advertisements are fascinating to analyze. Like other images, they employ the rhetorical strategies we described in the section on documentary photographs. Often, the ad's words (called the "copy") also contribute to its rhetorical effect. Moreover, ads make a more direct and constant demand on us than do documentary photographs and paintings. Advertising, a multibillion-dollar global industry whose business is communicating across a wide range of media to stimulate the purchase of products or services, comes to us in multiple forms: not just as slick, glamorous magazine ads, but also as direct mail, billboards, radio and television commercials, e-advertisements, banners, pop-ups, and spam. Figures 10.12 and 10.13, a billboard and a bus ad, illustrate

FIGURE 10.12 A Billboard Ad

FIGURE 10.13 Ad on a City Bus

the ordinary ubiquity of ads. Because of advertising's powerful role in shaping our culture and influencing our self-images, we have good reason to analyze the rhetorical strategies of advertisers.

FOR WRITING AND DISCUSSION

Examining the Appeal of Ads

Think about the images and words in the two car insurance ads in Figures 10.12 and 10.13.

1. What do you notice most about the images and copy in these ads?
2. What is the appeal of these ads?
3. How are these ads designed to suit their contexts, a billboard and a bus panel? Why would they be less suitable for a magazine?

How Advertisers Think about Advertising

Although cultural critics frequently focus on ads as manipulative messages that need to be decoded to protect unwary consumers, we confess that we actually enjoy ads, appreciate how they hold down the consumer cost of media, and admire their often-ingenious creativity. (We suspect that others secretly enjoy ads also: Think of how the Super Bowl is popular both for its football and for its ads.) In this section, we take a look at advertising from a marketer's point of view in order to deepen your awareness of an ad's context and the many behind-the-scenes decisions and negotiations that produced it. Whether marketing professionals design an individual ad or a huge marketing campaign, they typically begin by asking questions.

Who Is Our Target Audience? At the outset, marketers identify one or more target audiences for their product or service. They often use sophisticated psychological research to identify segments of the population who share similar values, beliefs, and aspirations and then subdivide these categories according to age, gender, region, income level, ethnicity, and so forth. Think of the different way you'd pitch a product or service to, say, Wal-Mart shoppers versus Neiman Marcus shoppers, steak eaters versus vegans, or skateboarders versus geeks.

How Much Media Landscape Can We Afford? While identifying their target audience, marketers also consider how much terrain they can afford to occupy on the enormous media landscape of billboards, newspapers, magazines, mailing lists, Internet pop-ups, TV and radio commercials, posters, naming rights for sports stadiums, T-shirts, coffee mugs, product placements in films, sandwich boards, or banners carried across the sky by propeller airplanes. Each of these sites has to be rented or purchased, with the price depending on the perceived quality of the location and the timing. For example, a thirty-second TV commercial during the 2010 Super Bowl cost $2.6 million, and a one-time full-page ad in a nationally circulated popular magazine can cost up to $500,000 or more. Overall, advertisers hope to attain the best possible positioning and timing within the media landscape at a price they can afford.

What Are the Best Media for Reaching Our Target Audience? A marketer's goal is to reach the target audience efficiently and with a minimum of overflow—that is, messages sent to people who are not likely buyers. Marketers are keenly aware of both media and timing: Note, for example, how daytime TV is dominated by ads for payday loans, exercise equipment, or technical colleges, while billboards around airports advertise rental cars. Women's fashion magazines advertise lingerie and perfume but not computers or life insurance, while dating services advertise primarily through Internet ads.

Is Our Goal to Stimulate Direct Sales or to Develop Long-Term Branding and Image? Some ads are intended to stimulate retail sales directly: "Buy two, get one free." In some cases, advertisements use information and argument to show how their product or service is superior to that of their competitors. Most advertisements, however, involve parity products such as soft drinks, deodorants, breakfast cereals, or toothpaste. (*Parity products* are roughly equal in quality among competitors and so can't be promoted through any rational or scientific proof of superiority.) In such cases, advertisers' goal is to build brand loyalty based on a long-lasting relationship with consumers. Advertisers, best thought of as creative teams of writers and artists, try to convert a brand name appearing on a cereal box or a pair of jeans to a field of qualities, values, and imagery that lives inside the heads of its targeted consumers. Advertisers don't just want you to buy Nikes rather than Reeboks but also to see yourself as a Nike kind of person, who identifies with the lifestyle or values conveyed in Nike ads.

Mirrors and Windows: The Strategy of an Effective Advertisement

A final behind-the-scenes concept that will help you analyze ads is the marketers' principle of *"mirrors and windows,"* a psychological and motivational strategy to associate a product with a target audience's dreams, hopes, fears, desires, and wishes (often subconscious).

- ***The mirror effect*** refers to the way in which the ad mirrors the target audience's self-image, promoting identification with the ad's message. The target audience has to say, "I am part of the world that this ad speaks to. I have this problem (pimples, boring hair, dandelions, cell phone service without enough bars)."
- ***The window effect*** provides visions of the future, promises of who we will become or what will happen if we align ourselves with this brand. The ad implies a brief narrative, taking you from your ordinary self (mirror) to your new, aspirational self (window).

For example, the acne product Proactiv Solutions uses a very common mirrors/windows strategy. Proactiv infomercials create the mirror effect by featuring regular-looking teenagers with pimples and the window effect by using a gorgeous actress as endorsing spokesperson: If I use Proactiv Solutions, ordinary "me" will look beautiful like Jessica Simpson.

FIGURE 10.14 Geico Gecko Billboard Ad

But the mirrors and windows principle can be used in much more subtle and creative ways. Consider the brilliance of the Geico insurance gecko ads promoting what advertisers call a "a resentful purchase"—that is, something you need to have but that doesn't give you material pleasure like a new pair of shoes or money in a savings account. Insurance, a hassle to buy, is also associated with fear—fear of needing it, fear of not having it, fear of not being able to get it again if you ever use it. In this light, think of the Geico campaign featuring the humorous, big-eyed gecko (friendly, cute) with the distinctive cockney voice (working-class swagger). When this chapter was being written, Geico billboards were sprouting up all over the country (see Figure 10.14), while large-print ads were appearing in popular magazines along with numerous TV and radio commercials. Here are some of the particular advantages of the gecko for Geico's layered advertising campaign across many media:

- ***"Gecko" sounds like "Geico."*** In fact, this sound-alike feature was the inspiration for the campaign.
- ***The gecko is identifiable by both sight and sound.*** If you see a print ad or a billboard, you remember what the voice sounds like; if you hear a radio ad, you remember what the gecko looks like; on TV or YouTube, you get both sight and sound.
- ***The gecko is cheap.*** The cost of the computer simulations that produce the gecko is minimal in comparison to the royalties paid to celebrities for an advertising endorsement.

- ***The gecko is ethnically/racially neutral.*** Marketers didn't have to decide whether to choose a white versus black versus Asian spokesperson, yet a person of any race or nationality can identify with the little lizard. (Think Kermit the Frog on *Sesame Street.*) Feminist critics, however, might rightly ask why the gecko has to be male.
- ***The gecko is scandal-proof.*** When in 2010 the Tiger Woods imbroglio ruined the golfer's public image, the huge insurance company Accenture, along with TagHauer watches and other companies, had to drop his endorsement ads, forcing them at great expense to create new advertising campaigns and to lose media visibility in the interim.

Yet we must still ask why the gecko is a good advertising device for an insurance company. How does the gecko campaign incorporate mirrors and windows? Let's start with the mirror effect. It is easy to identify with the Geico ads because everyone has to buy insurance and because everyone wants to save money. (The gecko's main sales pitch is that Geico will save you 15 percent.) Moreover, our long cultural history of identifying with animated characters (*Sesame Street, ET*) makes it easy to project our own identities onto the gecko. Additionally, the cockney voice makes the gecko a bit of an outsider, someone breaking into corporate culture through sheer bravado. (Many people think of the gecko's accent as Australian more than cockney, giving the lizard a bit of sexy, macho Crocodile Dundee appeal.)

The ads also create a window effect, which comes from the way the gecko humanizes the insurance company, removing some of the fear and anxiety of buying insurance. You don't think of the gecko as *selling* you the insurance so much as *buying* it for you as your agent, hopping right up on the corporate desk and demanding your rights. Geico becomes a fun company, and you as consumer picture yourself going away with a pile of saved money. Recent ads have added another symbolic feature to the gecko—a pair of glasses—which makes him seem intellectual and responsible, more serious and grown-up. Meanwhile, another Geico campaign, the talking-money ad (see the billboard ad in Figure 10.12), extends the concept of a humorous, friendly creature, like the gecko, that turns Geico insurance into a savings, not an expense.

FOR WRITING AND DISCUSSION

Designing Ads

This exercise asks you to apply these marketing concepts to designing your own ad. Imagine you are an advertising professional assigned to the Gloopers account. Gloopers is a seaweed (kelp)-based snack treat (a fiction, but pretend it is real) that is very popular under another name in Japan. It was introduced earlier in the American market and failed miserably—what sort of a treat is seaweed? But now, you have laboratory evidence that Gloopers provides crucial nutritional benefits for growing bodies and that it is a healthy alternative to junk food. Many food companies would kill for the endorsement of nutritious content that you now have to work with, but the product is still made out of gunky seaweed. Working in groups or individually, develop a campaign for this product by working out your answers to the following questions:

- Who is your target audience? (Will you seek to appeal to parents as well as children?)
- What is your core message or campaign concept? (Think of a visual approach, including a mirror and window appeal, and perhaps a tagline slogan.)
- What is the best positioning in the media landscape for this campaign?
- How will you build a brand image and brand loyalty?

How to Analyze an Advertisement

In addition to thinking about the decision making behind an ad, when you analyze a print ad you need to ask three overarching questions:

1. How does the ad draw in the target audience by helping them identify with the ad's problematic situation or story (mirror effect)?
2. How does the ad create a field of values, beliefs, and aspirations that serve as windows into a more fulfilled life?
3. How do the ad's images and words work together to create the desired persuasive effects?

For the images in an ad, all the strategies we have already described for documentary photographs and for paintings continue to apply—for example, angle of vision, framing, and so forth. (Review the strategies chart on pp. 247–249.) With many ads you also have to factor in the creative use of words—puns, connotations, and intertextual references to other ads or cultural artifacts. Note that in professionally created ads, every word, every punctuation mark, and every visual detail down to the props in the photograph or the placement of a model's hands are consciously chosen.

The following strategies chart focuses on questions particularly relevant to print ads.

Strategies for Analyzing the Compositional Features of Print Ads

What to Do	Some Questions to Ask
Examine the settings, furnishings, and all other details.	• Is the room formal or informal; neat, lived-in, or messy? • How is the room furnished and decorated? • If the setting is outdoors, what are the features of the landscape: urban or rural, mountain or meadow? • Why are particular animals or birds included? (Think of the differences between using a crow, a hummingbird, or a parrot.)

(continued)

What to Do	Some Questions to Ask
Consider the social meaning of objects.	• What is the emotional effect of the objects in a den: for example, duck decoys and fishing rods versus computers and high-tech printers? • What is the social significance (class, economic status, lifestyle, values) of the objects in the ad? (Think of the meaning of a groomed poodle versus a mutt or a single rose versus a fuchsia in a pot.)
Consider the characters, roles, and actions.	• Who are these people and what are they doing? What story line could you construct behind the image? • Are the models regular-looking people, "beautiful people," or celebrities? • In product advertisements, are female models used instrumentally (depicted as mechanics working on cars or as a consumers buying cars) or are they used decoratively (bikini-clad and lounging on the hood of the latest truck)?
Observe how models are dressed, posed, and accessorized.	• What are the models' facial expressions? • What are their hairstyles and what cultural and social significance do they have? • How well are they dressed and posed?
Observe the relationships among actors and among actors and objects.	• How does the position of the models signal importance and dominance? • Who is looking at whom? • Who is above or below, in the foreground or background?
Consider what social roles are being played out and what values appealed to.	• Are the gender roles traditional or nontraditional? • Are the relationships romantic, erotic, friendly, formal, uncertain? • What are the power relationships among characters?
Consider how document design functions and how the words and images work together.	• What features of document design (variations of font style and size, placement on the page, formal or playful lettering) stand out?

What to Do	Some Questions to Ask
	• How much of the copy is devoted to product information or argument about superiority of the product or service? • How much of the copy helps create a field of values, beliefs, aspirations? • How do the words contribute to the "story" implied in the visual images? • What is the style of the language (for example, connotations, double entendres, puns)?

Sample Analysis of an Advertisement

With an understanding of possible photographic effects and the compositional features of ads, you now have all the background knowledge needed to begin doing your own analysis of ads. To illustrate how an analysis of an ad can reveal the ad's persuasive strategies, we show you our analysis of an ad for Coors Light (Figure 10.15) that ran in a variety of women's magazines in the mid-1990s. The marketers aimed to attract a new target audience—twenty-something or thirty-something middle-class women—and decided that print ads in magazines constituted the best medium.

This Coors Light ad uses an unusual strategy to target young adult women. Unlike typical beer ads aimed at men, which feature beach girls in bikinis or men bonding together on fishing trips or in sports bars, this Coors Light ad with its "Sam and Me" theme associates beer drinking with the warm friendship of a man and a woman.

Part of the ad's emotional appeal is the totally relaxed "story" shown in the image. The ad reveals a man and a woman, probably in their early- to mid-twenties, in relaxed conversation; they are sitting casually on a tabletop, with their legs resting on chair seats. The woman is wearing casual pants, a summery cotton top, and informal shoes. Her shoulder-length hair has a healthy, mussed appearance, and a braid comes across the front of her shoulder. She is turned away from the man, leans on her knees, and holds a bottle of Coors Light. Her sparkling eyes are looking up, and she smiles happily, as if reliving a pleasant memory. The man is wearing slacks, a cotton shirt with the sleeves rolled up, and scuffed tennis shoes with white socks. He also has a reminiscing smile on his face, and he leans on the woman's shoulder. The words "Coors Light. Just between friends." appear immediately below the picture next to a Coors Light can.

This ad creates its mirror effect by making it easy for women to identify with its story, which includes a good-looking but nonglamorous model and which is told from a woman's point of view (the "me" is the woman in the photograph). The ad's window effect is its opening onto a happy future. It appeals to women's

FIGURE 10.15 Beer Ad Aimed at Women

desire for close friendships and relationships. Everything about the picture signifies long-established closeness and intimacy—old friends rather than lovers. The way the man leans on the woman shows her strength and independence. Additionally, the way they pose, with the woman slightly forward and sitting up more than the man, results in their taking up equal space in the picture. In many ads featuring male-female couples, the man appears larger and taller than the woman; this picture signifies mutuality and equality.

The words of the ad help interpret the relationship. Sam and the woman have been friends since the first grade, and they are reminiscing about old times. The relationship is thoroughly mutual. Sometimes he brings the Coors Light and sometimes she brings it; sometimes she does the listening and sometimes he does; sometimes she leans on his shoulder and sometimes he leans on hers. Sometimes the ad says, "Sam and me"; sometimes it says, "me and Sam." Even the "bad grammar" of "Sam and me" (rather than "Sam and I") suggests the lazy, relaxed absence of pretense or formality. "Sam" is a "buddy" kind of name rather than a romantic-hero name. But the last three lines of the copy give just a hint of potential romance: "Me and Sam? Together? I've never even thought about it. Okay, so I've thought about it."

Whereas beer ads targeting men portray women as sex objects, this ad appeals to many women's desire for relationships and for romance based on friendship. Its window function is mutuality and love rather than sexual acquisition.

The Coors Light ad was designed to appeal to young adult women. But cultural critics might also point out that the ad reproduces a worldview in which heterosexuality is the norm and in which women find their identities in romance and marriage. From the perspective of cultural criticism, then, advertisements are powerful cultural forces that both reflect cultural values and help construct and reproduce those values, including our sense of what is normal and not normal and our ideas about gender, race, and class. Identifying these cultural values in ads is an important part of ad analysis.

FOR WRITING AND DISCUSSION

Analyzing Ads from Different Perspectives

1. ***Credit card campaigns:*** Credit card companies have always faced a challenge: persuading consumers to buy with credit cards rather than cash and checks (with the expectation that many customers will not pay off the balance each month and thus pay substantial interest charges). Currently, banks and credit card companies must also overcome consumers' anger and distrust in this age of the banking crisis, overextended consumer debt, and high credit card interest.

   Choose one or more of the magazine ads for credit cards on pages 266–267, and analyze them using the strategies suggested in the charts on pages 261–263 as well as the ideas presented throughout this section (target audience, choice of medium, brand building, mirror and window strategy, and compositional features).
2. ***Cultural Criticism***
   a. Reexamine the same credit card ads from the perspectives of gender, class, and ethnicity. To what extent do these ads break or reinforce traditional notions of gender, race, and class?
   b. Look at the U.S. Army recruiting ad on page 435. Analyze this ad from the perspectives of gender, race, and class. Why does it pair a father and daughter rather than a mother and son?

FIGURE 10.16 MasterCharge Ad from the 1970s

c. Locate a gallery of older ads on the Web, and choose several to analyze for perspectives on gender, race, and class. For example, you might analyze the Coppertone sunscreen ad from the 1950s, with its slogan "Don't be a Paleface" and "Tan—Don't Burn." The image of the dog tugging at the little girl's swimsuit bottoms became a national symbol of summertime fun for families. What treatment of race, class, or gender in these older ads, like the Coppertone ad, contributed to making them culturally acceptable at the time and would make them unacceptable now?

FIGURE 10.17 Recent "Priceless: MasterCard" Ad

FIGURE 10.18 Recent American Express Card Ad

WRITING PROJECT

Analysis of Two Visual Texts

Choose two documentary/news photographs, two paintings, or two print advertisements to analyze in a closed-form essay. Your two visual texts should have enough in common to facilitate meaningful comparisons. Show these images in your essay, but also describe your two visual texts in detail to highlight what you want viewers to see and to provide a foundation for your analysis. For this closed-form analysis, choose several key points of contrast as the focus. Your thesis statement should make a claim about key differences in the way that your chosen visual texts establish their purposes and achieve their persuasive effects.

Exploring and Generating Ideas for Your Analysis

For the subject of your analysis, your instructor may allow you to choose your own images or may provide them for you. If you choose your own, be sure to follow your instructor's guidelines. In choosing your visual texts, look for some important commonality that will enable you to concentrate on similarities and differences in your analysis:

- ***Documentary or news photographs.*** Analyze two photographs of an event from magazines with different political biases; two news photographs from articles addressing the same story from different angles of vision; or two images on Web sites presenting different perspectives on a recent controversial issue such as industrial farming or the war against terrorists.
- ***Paintings.*** Find two paintings with similar subject matter but different dominant impressions or emotional impacts.
- ***Print ads.*** Look for two ads for the same product (for example, cars, perfume, watches, shampoo) that are aimed at different target audiences or that make appeals to noticeably different value systems.

No matter what type of visual texts you are using, we suggest that you generate ideas and material for your analysis by using the question-asking strategies presented earlier in this chapter (see the strategies charts on pp. 246–249 and 261–263).

To help you generate more ideas, go detail by detail through your images, asking how the rhetorical effect would be different if some detail were changed:

- How would this documentary photo have a different effect if the homeless man were lying on the sidewalk instead of leaning against the doorway?
- Why did the artist blur images in the background rather than make them more distinct?
- What if the admakers had chosen a poodle rather than a black Lab? What if this model were a person of color rather than white?

FIGURE 10.19 Framework for an Analysis of Two Visuals

Introduction	• Hooks readers' interest; • Gives background on the two visual texts you are analyzing; • Sets up the similarities; • Poses the question your paper will address; • Ends with initial mapping in the form of a purpose or thesis statement.
General description of your two visual texts (ads, photographs, paintings)	• Describes each visual text in turn.
Analysis of the two visual texts	• Analyzes and contrasts each text in turn, using the ideas you generated from your observations, question asking, and close examination.
Conclusion	• Returns to the big picture for a sense of closure; • Makes final comments about the significance of your analysis.

Shaping and Drafting Your Analysis

Your closed-form essay should be fairly easy to organize at the big-picture level, but each part will require its own organic organization depending on the main points of your analysis. At the big-picture level, you can generally follow a structure like the one shown in Figure 10.19.

If you get stuck, we recommend that you write your rough draft rapidly, without worrying about gracefulness or correctness, merely trying to capture your initial ideas. Many people like to begin with the description of the two visual texts and then write the analysis before writing the introduction and conclusion. After you have written your draft, put it aside for a while before you begin revising.

Revising

Most experienced writers make global changes in their drafts when they revise, especially when they are doing analytical writing. The act of writing a rough draft generally leads to the discovery of more ideas. You may also realize that some of your original ideas aren't clearly developed or that the draft feels scattered or disorganized.

We recommend that you ask your classmates for a peer review of your draft early in the revising process to help you enhance the clarity and depth of your analysis.

Questions for Peer Review

In addition to the generic peer review questions explained in Skill 16.4, ask your peer reviewers to address these questions:

1. How well do the title, introduction, and thesis set up an academic analysis?
2. Where does the writer capture your interest and provide necessary background information? How might the writer more clearly pose the question to be addressed and map out the analysis?
3. Where could the writer describe the visual texts more clearly so that readers can "see" them?
4. How has the writer established the complexity of the texts and their commonalities and differences?
5. How well has the writer used the questions about angle of vision, artistic techniques, and compositional features presented in this chapter to achieve a detailed and insightful analysis of the texts? Where could the writer add more specific details about settings, props, furniture, posing of characters, facial expressions, manners of dress, and so forth?
6. In what ways could the writer improve this analysis by clarifying, deepening, expanding, or reorganizing the analysis? How has the writer helped you understand something new about these two texts?

Our first two readings argue different perspectives on the ethics of documentary photography, specifically, the photographing of victims of the massive Haiti earthquake of January 2010. The first reading, an op-ed piece by Clark Hoyt, Public Editor of the *New York Times*, appeared on January 23, 2010. For background, you may want to do a Web search of photographs of the Haiti disaster as well as explore the *New York Times'* gallery of photos.

Clark Hoyt

Face to Face with Tragedy

1 It was hard to look at some of the pictures of suffering and death caused by the earthquake in Haiti—and impossible to turn away.

2 The top of one front page in the *Times* was dominated by a woman, her hand to her cheek, as if in shock, walking past partially covered corpses lined up along a dirty curb. The next day, an even larger photograph at the top of page 1 showed a man covered in gray dust, lying alone, dead, statue-like, on a stretcher made from a piece of tattered cardboard spread over a crude ladder. Inside that same paper, the Friday after the disaster, was a gruesome scene from the central morgue in Port-au-Prince: a man mourning the death of his 10-month-old daughter, lying in her diaper atop a pile of bodies.

3 Some readers were offended at these scenes and even more graphic pictures on the paper's Web site, calling them exploitive and sensationalistic. "The numerous photographs printed in the *Times* showing the dead strewn about the streets of Port-au-Prince are unnecessary, unethical, unkind and inhumane," wrote Randy Stebbins of Hammond, La. Christa Robbins of Chicago said, "I feel that the people who have suffered the most are being spectacularized by your blood-and-gore photographs, which do not at all inform me of the relief efforts, the political stability of the region or the extent of damage to families and infrastructure." She spoke for several readers when she added, "If this had happened in California, I cannot imagine a similar depiction of half-clothed bodies splayed out for the camera. What are you thinking?"

4 But other readers were grateful for the shocking pictures, even as they were deeply troubled by them. Mary Louise Thomas of Palatka, Fla., said a different photo of the baby, lying on her dead mother, caused her to cry out, "Oh, my God!" and to sob for an hour. "But run from it? Never," she said. People repelled by such images "should really try staring truth in the face occasionally and try to understand it," she wrote.

5 Mary Claire Carroll of Richmond, Vt., asked, "How else can you motivate or inspire someone like me to donate money" to help out in Haiti? Her son, she added, thinks Americans "are too sheltered and protected from the real world."

6 Every disaster that produces horrific scenes of carnage presents photographers and their editors with the challenge of telling the unsanitized truth without crossing into the offensive and truly exploitive. In 2004, when a giant undersea earthquake unleashed a tsunami that killed tens of thousands along Indian Ocean coastlines, the *Times* ran a dramatic front-page photo of a woman overcome with grief amid rows of dead children, including her own. Some readers protested, but the newspaper's first public editor, Daniel Okrent, concluded that the paper was right to publish the picture. It told the story of the tsunami, he said.

7 I asked Kenneth Irby, leader of the visual journalism group at the Poynter Institute in Florida, for his assessment of the pictures from Haiti. Irby brings unusual perspectives to the task. He is a veteran photojournalist and an ordained minister, the pastor of an African Methodist Episcopal church in Palmetto, Fla. His wife's best friend is Haitian, and her family was still unaccounted for when we talked last week. "I think the *Times* coverage has been raw, truthful and tasteful," he told me, defending even the most graphic images.

8 Irby, who has been in touch with photographers in Haiti, said survivors want the world to see what has happened. "The actual loved ones, the bereaved, implore the journalists to tell their stories," he said.

9 That is exactly what Damon Winter told me. He is the *Times* photographer who took the pictures that elicited most of the protests to me and much praise on the paper's Web site. Winter, who won a Pulitzer Prize last year for his coverage of the Obama presidential campaign, was the first *Times* staff photographer on the scene, flying from New York to the Dominican Republic and then into Haiti aboard a chartered helicopter. He had never been to Haiti or covered a natural disaster.

10 "I have had so many people beg me to come to their home and photograph the bodies of their children, brothers, sisters, mothers, fathers," he said. "There are so many times that I have to apologize and say that I cannot, that I have photographed so many bodies already, and I think it breaks their hearts because they so desperately want people to know what has happened to them, what tremendous pain they are in, and that they desperately need help." Winter said it was important "that I do whatever I can to try and make our readers understand just how dire the situation is here."

11 Jessie De Witt, an international photo editor, said Winter sent the paper 26 pictures on his first day in Haiti, including the picture of the bodies along the curb that wound up on the front page. He sent 65 the next day, including the mourning father and the dead man on the stretcher. De Witt and her colleagues think carefully about photo selections. A picture of a dog eyeing a corpse is out, as are stacks of bodies without context. And they think about juxtaposition: an Armageddon-like scene of people scrambling for supplies from a ruined store was played against a quieter picture of people waiting patiently for medical treatment.

12 Michele McNally, the assistant managing editor in charge of photography, said she was going through all the photos from all sources, and Winter's photos of the single dead man and the grieving father "stopped me in my tracks." Bill Keller, the executive editor, said editors considered both for the front page, but chose the lone body, played big, because it was dramatic and there was "an intimacy that causes people to pause and dwell on the depth of the tragedy." Looking at one person, instead of many, "humanizes it," he said.

13 I asked McNally about Robbins's contention that such pictures would not appear in the paper if the victims were somewhere in the United States. If such pictures existed, she said, she would run them. When Hurricane Katrina hit New Orleans, the *Times* did publish a front-page picture of a body floating near a bridge where a woman was feeding her dog. But despite Katrina's toll, there were relatively few such images in the paper. Irby said that authorities in the United States are generally quick to cordon off disaster scenes.

14 Just as a picture of a grieving mother told the story of the tsunami in 2004, the disturbing images of the last two weeks have been telling the story of Haiti, and the *Times* is right to publish them. As Patricia Lay-Dorsey, a reader from Detroit, put it, Winter's "camera was my eye as much as it was his. And every one of his photos told the truth."

THINKING CRITICALLY
about "Face to Face with Tragedy"

1. According to Clark Hoyt, what are the ethical and rhetorical problems that photojournalists face in photographing disasters like the Haiti earthquake? Who are the different stakeholders in this controversy?
2. On page 246 in this chapter, we discussed the importance of the photographer's purpose and of the cultural, social, historical and political context of the photograph. What claims does Hoyt make for the purpose and context of the published images of human suffering in Haiti?
3. Research the coverage of the Haiti earthquake in one of the prominent general news commentary sources such as *Newsweek, Time, USA Today* or a leading newspaper's or online news site's archives. What images appear the most often? How did the captions for these images shape your impression of them?
4. What intellectual and emotional impact did these images have on you?

Our second reading, an op-ed piece by Manoucheka Celeste, a doctoral candidate in the Department of Communication at the University of Washington, was published in the *Seattle Times* on January 26, 2010.

Manoucheka Celeste

Disturbing Media Images of Haiti Earthquake Aftermath Tell Only Part of the Story

1 As a Haitian, former journalist and media scholar, [I found] the earthquake in Haiti . . . both personally devastating and intellectually challenging.

2 The first earthquake to hit Haiti in more than 200 years was unbelievable, unexpected and unprecedented. The devastation is clear with more than 200,000 lives lost. The damage is real. As we saw, people around the world responded quickly and generously.

3 This catastrophe presented an opportunity for media to respond in an unprecedented way. Some news outlets arrived before relief workers and doctors. We watched the horrors as they happened. I hoped that this was the moment when those of us trained in journalism would do something remarkable: Bring news of an unimaginable

event in a way that disrupted the sensational and stereotypical ways that people in the "Third World" are represented.

4 What we got instead was much less humane. Videos of dead bodies, including children and the elderly, filled our television screens. For those of us who tuned in for information about friends and families, it was and is unbearable and despicable. Coverage went from sensational to ridiculous as CNN compared the literacy rates of Haiti and the United States. This was irrelevant as it continued to represent Haiti as a failed state.

5 The focus on poverty, with the repeated tagline "the poorest country in the Western Hemisphere" and references to crime and unrest, make it hard for viewers to imagine any other aspect of life in Haiti. People were called looters for taking food from collapsed buildings after not having eaten for days, framing their survival as a crime. The humanity needed in this moment is clearly missing.

6 Media scholars have long connected media coverage with public opinion, cultivating our attitudes and creating and reinforcing stereotypes. It is predominantly people of color who are shown negatively in news and entertainment. While the images mobilized some to help, they are damaging in the long term as they become ingrained in how we imagine Haitians. For many this is the first and last contact they will have with this population. The images matter as Haitians are shown as less than human. In mass media when images of Haiti and various countries in the African continent are shown, blackness becomes associated with helplessness, danger, poverty and hopelessness.

7 In the most disgusting moment in broadcast history, Pat Robertson proclaimed that Haiti had it coming because of its "deal with the devil," linking Haiti to "godlessness." What Robertson didn't consider was that "godlessness" was used as an excuse to kill and colonize peoples throughout history in the name of God, including Haiti, which, incidentally, is a heavily Christian country.

8 The question that plagues me and hopefully all audiences is: Who is able to die with dignity? In recent media history, there are few, but increasing instances where dead Americans are shown. From Columbine to Sept. 11, we rightfully protect the dead and rarely dare show them on television or in newspapers. Yet, the increasing presence of graphic and emotionally charged images, especially in broadcast media makes it seem normal or desirable.

9 This earthquake, despite the amazing pain that it has caused to so many, presents an unprecedented opportunity. Viewers and readers can demand that in people's darkest hour or once they lose their lives that they are treated with dignity.

10 We want the story without sensationalism and reinforcement of stereotypes. We want the media to value the lives of people who are "not us." As I waited for eight days to hear that my own mother and grandmother in Port-au-Prince are safe, I wanted to hold on to good memories of the person who brought me into the world and the one who taught me to be generous and tenacious. Let's seize the opportunity of this horrific tragedy to demand better from our news sources: dignity for everyone.

THINKING CRITICALLY

about "Disturbing Media Images of Haiti Earthquake Aftermath Tell Only Part of the Story"

1. In her criticism of the media's use of "graphic and emotionally charged images," how does Manoucheka Celeste argue against the main perspective that Hoyt endorses?
2. Celeste's op-ed piece examines the role of viewers' knowledge, values, and assumptions in interpreting photos in news stories. What historical, political, and racial elements does Celeste underscore?
3. For the photographs of the Haiti disaster that you located and viewed, argue that they either simplified and distorted the issues or pushed them toward complexity and depth. In your mind, what does it mean to treat the human subjects of photographs with "dignity"?

Our final reading is student Lydia Wheeler's analytical essay written for the writing project in this chapter. It analyzes two documentary photos focused on economic hardship and displacement. One photo, taken by photographer Stephen Crowley, accompanied a *New York Times* story about a mother and her daughters in the 2008 recession caused by the collapse of the housing bubble in the United States. The subject, Isabel Bermudez, was subsisting on food stamps at the time of the story, unable to find a job; previously she had supported her daughters with a six-figure salary. Then the market collapsed, she lost her job, and shortly afterward she lost her house. The second photo is a famous image taken in 1936 in Nipoma, California, during the Great Depression. The photo is part of the *Migrant Mother* series by photographer Dorothea Lange. Lydia decided to examine the original newspaper contexts for these photographs and to approach them as depictions of women's experiences of economic crisis.

Lydia Wheeler (student)

Two Photographs Capture Women's Economic Misery

1 During economic crises, the hardship of individuals is often presented to us as statistics and facts: number of bankruptcies, percentage of the population living below the poverty line, and foreclosures or unemployment rates. Although this numerical data can be shocking, it usually remains abstract and impersonal. In contrast, photographers such as Stephen Crowley and Dorothea Lange help us visualize the human suffering involved in the economic conditions, skillfully evoking the emotional, as well as the physical, reality of their subjects. Crowley's color photograph, first published January 2, 2010, in a *New York Times* article titled "Living on Nothing but Food Stamps," is captioned "Isabel Bermudez, who has two daughters and no cash income." Lange's black and white photograph was commissioned by the Resettlement Agency to document Americans living in the Great Depression; she

originally captioned it *Destitute pea pickers in California; a 32 year old mother of seven children. February 1936.* However, in March of the same year, the *San Francisco Times* published Lange's photograph in an article demanding aid for workers like Florence Owens Thompson, the central subject of the picture. Once published, the photograph became famous and was nicknamed *Migrant Mother.* A close look at these two photos shows that through their skillful use of photographic elements such as focus, framing, orientation, and shape, Stephen Crowley and Dorothea Lange capture the unique emotional and physical realities of their subjects, eliciting compassion and admiration, respectively.

2 Stephen Crowley's photograph of a mother sitting in a room, perhaps the dining room of her house, and her young daughter standing and reaching out to comfort her sets up contrasts and tensions that underscore loss and convey grief. The accompanying article explains that Isabel Bermudez, whose income from real estate once amply supported her family, now has no income or prospect for employment and relies entirely on food stamps. A careful examination of Crowley's photograph implies this loss by hinting that Bermudez's wealth is insecure.

3 The framing, distance, and focus of Crowley's photograph emphasize this vanished wealth and the emotional pain. The image is a medium close up with its human subjects to the side, surrounding them with empty space and hints of expensive furnishings. While part of the foreground is sharply focused, the background is blurry and unfocused. There is a suggestion that the room is spacious. Further, the high, decorative backs of the room's chairs, the repetitive design decorating the bookshelf on

Isabel Bermudez, who has two daughters and no cash income, by Stephen Crowley

Destitute pea pickers in California; a 32 year old mother of seven children [*Migrant Mother*] by Dorothea Lange

the frame's left, and the houseplant next to the bookshelf show that the room is well furnished, even luxurious. Bermudez and her daughter match their surroundings in being elegantly dressed. Bermudez looks across the room as if absorbed in her troubles; her daughter looks intently at her. Viewers' eyes are drawn to Bermudez's dark dress and her pearl necklace and earrings. However, the ostensible comfort of Bermudez and her surroundings starkly contrasts with her grief.

4 Crowley heightens this contrast and tension through the subjects' orientation and the space between them. The space between Bermudez and her daughter is one of the

photograph's dominant features, but it contains only out-of-focus objects in the background. Neither figure is centered in the photo; neither looks at the camera. Consequently, the viewers' attention moves back and forth between them, creating a sense of uneasiness. The meaning of this photo is focused not on what Bermudez has but on what she has lost.

5 Crowley also evokes sympathy and compassion for his subjects with his choice of angle, scale, and detail. The photograph's slightly high angle makes viewers look down—literally—on Bermudez, making her appear vulnerable and powerless and reinforcing the pathos. The most striking bid for compassion is the tears streaming down Bermudez's well made-up face. The contrast between her tidy appearance and the tear tracks on her face suggest overwhelming sadness. The poignancy of her apparent breakdown is heightened by her somber daughter's attempt to wipe away the tears on her mother's face. Crowley's decisions regarding *Isabel's* composition create an image that is highly disturbing.

6 In contrast to Crowley's photograph, Lange's *Migrant Mother*—through its content, focus, frame, rhythm, and angle—conveys long-standing poverty. Yet through this image of inescapable poverty pressing upon its subjects, it evokes admiration for this mother.

7 Lange's frame and focus generate much of the intensity of *Migrant Mother.* This photo is also a medium close up, but Lange's frame is tight with no open space. The lack of this openness cramps Lange's subjects and creates a claustrophobic feel intensified by the number of subjects shown—four to *Isabel's* two. There is almost no background. The subjects filling the foreground are crowded and sharply focused. The contrast between crowded foreground and empty background exaggerates the former and adds a touch of loneliness to *Migrant Mother;* this mother has no resources besides herself. Additionally, the subjects of *Migrant Mother* almost epitomize poverty: their hair is messy and uncombed, their skin dirt-stained. Even their clothes are worn—from the hem of Thompson's frayed sleeve to the smudges on her baby's blanket, Lange's photograph shows that Thompson can barely afford functional items.

8 *Migrant Mother's* circular lines also create a sense of sameness, stagnation, and hopelessness. Thompson's face draws viewers' eyes as the dominant feature, and Lange has ringed it with several arcs. The parentheses of her standing children's bodies, the angle of her baby in its blanket, and the arc of her dark hair form a ring that hems Thompson in and creates a circular path for the eyes of viewers. Seen with the obvious destitution of Lange's subjects, this repetition is threatening and grimly promises that it will be difficult, if not impossible, for this family to escape its poverty.

9 Like Crowley's *Isabel*, the impact of Lange's *Migrant Mother* derives from both the tragedy of her subjects' situation and their reactions. Lange uses angle and scale to generate sympathy and admiration for Thompson's strength. Once again we see a slightly high angle highlighting the subjects' vulnerability, which Lange reinforces with the slender necks of Thompson's children and a glimpse of her brassiere. However, Lange then contrasts this vulnerability with Thompson's strength, fostering viewers' admiration rather than compassion. *Migrant Mother's* scale, for example, exaggerates rather than diminishes Thompson's size: the photograph's frame focuses viewers' attention on the mother, who looks large, compared to her children. Additionally, Lange's subject

literally supports the bodies of the children surrounding her. Unlike Bermudez, Thompson sits tall as a pillar of strength for her vulnerable children. Even her expression—worried but dry eyed—fosters admiration and respect in viewers. By juxtaposing Thompson's vulnerability with her strength, Lange creates a photograph that conveys both its subjects' poverty and their stoicism in facing the Great Depression.

10 Lange and Crowley guide viewer's reactions to their photographs through careful control of the elements that influence our emotional responses to their work. Though they both show women in economic crises, these artists are able to convey the distinct realities of their subjects' situations and consequently send viewers away in different emotional states: one of compassion, one of admiration. The fame and veneration of Lange's *Migrant Mother* is a testament to her ability to evoke desired emotions. The photograph was exhibited at the Museum of Modern Art in 1941 and again in 1955, and was co-opted by countless movements since it was first published. Whether Crowley's *Isabel* will achieve similar fame for epitomizing this generation's economic crisis remains to be seen, but both photographs certainly succeed in delivering strong, lasting emotional statements.

THINKING CRITICALLY

about "Two Photographs Capture Women's Economic Misery"

1. What photographic elements has Lydia chosen to emphasize in her analysis of each of these photos?
2. What parts of Lydia's analysis help you see and understand these photos with greater insight? Do you agree with her choice of important elements and her analysis of their effects?
3. If you were analyzing these photos, what features would you choose to compare and stress?

PEARSON mycomplab For support in learning this chapter's content, follow this path in **MyCompLab**: Resources ⇒ Writing ⇒ Writing and Visuals. Review the Instruction and Multimedia resources, then complete the Exercises and click on Gradebook to measure your progress.

11 ANALYZING A SHORT STORY

You've no doubt had more than one experience analyzing literature. For some students, such analysis is fun. It gives you a welcome break from densely packed textbook pages while stimulating your imagination. For others, the very word *literary* might trigger memories of mystifying class discussions and teachers' seemingly arbitrary decrees about the "hidden meaning" of something. Our goal in this chapter is to demonstrate that analyzing literature need not be either mystifying or arbitrary. In fact, analyzing literature is quite similar to analyzing just about any type of text or event: asking questions that you think will intrigue your reader as well as yourself and studying the text to find what answers it provides. What's different about literary analysis is that it opens up imaginative possibilities that can entertain and delight readers as well as inform them.

To begin understanding literary analysis, try to think of literature not so much as a collection of great books to be read, but rather as a way of reading. Or, put another way, you can choose to read anything literally or literarily. When you read something *literally*, you attempt to reduce its meaning to one clear set of statements and disregard other possible ways of reading the text. When you read something *literarily*, you read it playfully and openly, trying to see in it a wide range of possible meanings.

To help you understand the distinction we're drawing, consider the following analogy: A literal reading of an imaginative text is like a packaged bus tour of an unfamiliar city. In contrast, a literary understanding of a text, or a city, involves getting off the bus and opening yourself up to the otherness of a text the way travelers on foot open up to the sights and sounds of a new place.

This chapter introduces you to a common genre encountered in English and literature courses, the literary analysis or critical interpretive essay.

In this chapter, you will learn to:

- pose an interpretive question about a literary text
- offer an answer to the question supported by evidence from the text and your own critical analysis

Exploring Literary Analysis

As we have noted, any sort of text can be read either literally or literarily. However, texts do tend to invite one kind of reading over another. The following Navajo legend contains several signals that invite us to read literarily rather than literally. As you read this piece, note where those signals occur.

Retold by Evelyn Dahl Reed

The Medicine Man

1 There is a telling that, in the beginning, when the animals first came up from the darkness to live above the ground, Coyote was sent ahead by Thought Woman to carry a buckskin pouch far to the south.

2 "You must be very careful not to open the pouch," she told him, "or you will be punished."

3 For many days, Coyote ran southward with the pouch on his back. But the world was new, and there was nothing to eat along the way, so he grew very hungry. He wondered if there might be food in the pouch. At last, he took it from his back and untied the thongs. He looked inside and saw nothing but stars. Of course, as soon as he opened the pouch the stars all flew up into the sky, and there they are to this day.

4 "Now look what you've done," said Thought Woman. "For now you shall always get into trouble everywhere you go."

5 And because Coyote disobeyed, he was also made to suffer with the toothache. When the other animals were asleep, he could only sit and howl at the stars. Thus, he has been crying ever since the beginning of the world.

6 Sometimes he would ask the other animals to cure him, but they would only catch the toothache from him, and they, too, would cry.

7 One day he met Mouse, who lived in a little mound under the chaparral bush. "Friend Mouse," begged Coyote, "can you cure me of this toothache?"

8 Now it happened that while digging underground, as is his habit, Mouse had come upon a sweet-smelling root and had put it with the other herbs in the pouch he always carried. He was said to be very wise in the use of herbs.

9 "I don't know," said Mouse, "but I have just found a new root, and it may be that it will help you." He rubbed the root on Coyote's swollen cheek, and in a little while the toothache was gone.

10 This is how it happened that coyotes never hunt or kill field mice.

THINKING CRITICALLY

about "The Medicine Man"

1. List the signals in the text that led you to read this story literarily as opposed to literally. Summarize the most important differences between how you read this story and how you read the introduction to this chapter.
2. Devise questions about the legend that you think might produce different responses among your classmates. For example: Why is the woman named Thought Woman? Why is Thought Woman a female and not a male?
3. Explain why you think these questions will evoke different responses.

Understanding Literary Analysis

The Truth of Literary Events

"The Medicine Man" is immediately recognizable as literary; it's difficult, if not impossible, to read it literally. Animals can't talk, and galaxies can't be carted about in a buckskin pouch. We either make a leap of faith and license the author to play fast and loose with our conventional understanding of reality, or we put the story down, dismayed that anyone could think we'd be gullible enough to buy this twaddle.

The events of the story are presented to us as if they actually happened. We know better, but we go along with the ruse in order to enjoy the story. We know that when we read these sorts of texts, we can't demand a one-to-one correspondence between the words we read and the things, persons, and events to which they supposedly refer. We must read instead with what the poet Coleridge called "a Willing Suspension of Disbelief."

Suspending disbelief does not mean erasing it. While we're reading literarily, we are to some degree consciously suppressing skepticism and nagging doubts, leftovers of our literal-minded selves. Both ways of looking at the story—literal and literary—are open to us, and we consciously choose one over the other. While we're reading "The Medicine Man," we never really forget that coyotes can't talk. But if coyotes could talk, we can imagine them talking as this coyote talks.

The both/and principle allows us to become engrossed in the events in a fictional story, while at the same time standing back from the story to analyze how it works.

Writing (about) Literature

We put "about" in parentheses in this heading because in a sense, to write about literature is to write literature. When you read literarily you are an active cocreator of the text just as a musician is a cocreator of a concerto. The literary reader anticipates having to create meaning, which then must be justified to other readers and modified by them. Meaning is like a quilt constructed from bits and pieces of the text by many people who consult and argue and admire each other's skill and change each other's minds about which pieces to include and where to put them.

To participate in the reading process actively, to "write" your version of a text, you need to know the kinds of questions you might ask of it. To help you, we briefly summarize five critical elements of a literary text and the kinds of questions each element suggests.

For additional discussion of these elements and of open-form writing in general, refer to Chapter 6 and Chapter 18.

Asking Questions about Plot **Plot** refers to the sequence of critical events in the story. The key term here is *critical.* A plot summary does not include everything that happens in a story; it focuses on the elements that most directly move the action of the story forward. One method of analyzing the plot is to begin by identifying what you see as the most critical single event or moment in a story. What is the most pivotal point, the one that prior events lead up to and that subsequent events derive from? Different readers are apt to pick different moments, indicating differences in the way they read the story. Your task is to identify your own choice and to be prepared to defend it. Remember, you are *performing* the story, not trying to figure out some unambiguous right meaning. As long as you have a rationale for your decision, you are acting as a literary critic.

Asking Questions about Setting Although a **setting** is sometimes little more than a backdrop, like a black curtain behind a speaker on a stage, it can also serve to amplify or help explain the events and motivations of a story. Sometimes the setting acts as a symbol or serves the same function in a story that theme music serves in a movie, underscoring the text's primary themes and moods. A story could be set at the edge of a dark forest, on an ascent up a mountain, or in an inner city, with action moving back and forth between remote vacant lots and a warm kitchen. Sometimes setting plays an active role in the text, functioning almost as a character. A setting could thwart the protagonist's efforts to bring about change or to survive; for example, the collapse of a bridge could prevent a character from crossing a river. Does setting play a role in the story you are analyzing? If so, how would you characterize that role? Could you picture the events of the text taking place in a significantly different setting? Why or why not?

Asking Questions about Characters **Characters** are the people who make the decisions that forward the plot and whose fortunes change as a result of the plot. You can understand characters in a text only in relationship to each other and to the direction of change in the text. The major character, sometimes called the *protagonist*, is typically the one most responsible for forwarding the plot. In action stories, these characters are pretty static: Dirty Harry or Batman may undergo occasional physical changes and disguises, but their characters tend not to grow or deepen. In other kinds of stories, the major character may change significantly in terms of fortune, insight, or understanding. Which characters change in the story you are examining? How do they change? Which characters do not change? Why do the characters change or not change?

To examine the characters' relationships with each other, you might start with the protagonist and consider the other characters according to how they help or hinder the protagonist. Characters may contribute to the plot by overt action or inaction, by recognizing or failing to recognize something of significance, or by adapting to the situation of the story or being inflexible. They can guide or misguide the protagonist, be a friend or foe, share or threaten the protagonist's values or beliefs, and so forth. What tensions, contrasts, and differing points of view do you see among the characters?

Asking Questions about Point of View Perhaps the toughest element to perceive in a fictional work is point of view. It does not exist out there on the page as do character and plot. **Point of view** is the filter through which the reader views the action of a story. In some cases the impact of point of view on your perception of a character or event is obvious; in other cases it is not. The point of view can trick you into seeing an event in a particular way that you will have to revise when you realize that the narrator's perspective was limited, biased, or ironic. Often the narrator's values and perceptions are different from those of the author; you should never assume that the narrator of the story and the author are the same.

The two primary elements of point of view are time and person. Most stories are told in the past tense, a significant number in the present tense, and a few in the future tense. An almost equal number of stories are told in the first person (in which case the narrator is usually an actor in the story, although not always the main character) as in the third person (in which case the narrator tells the story from a position outside the tale). All choices of tense and person affect the reader's perception of a story. For example, a story told in the first-person present tense ("We ride back from the hunt at dusk") has an immediacy that a story told in the third-person past ("They rode back from the hunt at dusk") does not have. You learn about a first-person narrator both from what the narrator does or says in the plot and from how the narrator tells the story—what he or she includes or omits, the sentence structure, tone, or figures of speech that he or she adopts, and so forth. A third-person narrator may be objective (the narrator sees only the external actions of characters) or omniscient (the narrator can enter the minds and feelings of various characters). Sometimes a third-person narrator is omniscient with respect to one character but objective toward others.

Narrators can provide a full and complete sense of a given character (by entering that character's mind as an omniscient narrator) or a partial view only (by observing the character from the outside). Some stories feature multiple points of view through multiple narrators. For example, one character may discover a journal written by another character or may listen to a story told by another character.

The surest path to understanding point of view is to start with your feelings and attitudes toward characters and events and then to examine the extent to which point of view contributes to those attitudes. Do you trust the narrator? Do you like the narrator? Has the narrator loaded the dice, causing you to see characters or events in strongly slanted ways? Is the narrator scrupulously objective or ironic to the point that you're not quite sure what to make of his or her observations?

To ask questions about point of view, begin by asking whether the narrative is first or third person. Then ask whether the narrator's perspective is omniscient or limited. Does the narrator reveal bias or irony? Do you feel that there is more to the story than the narrator is telling you? What does the narrator leave out? How are the narrator's perceptions different from your own?

Asking Questions about Theme If a plot is what happens in a story, then **theme** is the significance of what happens. Your response to the question, "So what?" after reading a story represents your notion of the story's theme. Sometimes, a theme is obvious—the main characters might discuss it, or the author might even state it outright. Often, however, a theme is veiled, and you have to infer it from the words and deeds of the characters.

One way to discover theme is simply to reflect on your immediate responses to characters or on passages that affected you particularly strongly. Consider questions such as these: How did this story change your view of something or the way you feel about something? Is this story trying to reveal something about racism? About endurance in a time of trial? About growth from one phase of life to another? About appearance versus reality? About conflicts between the individual and family? About exterior loss and interior gain? About rebellion from society? About what's really valuable versus what appears to be valuable? About establishing values in a confusing world?

You can often gain valuable insights into a story's theme by examining the connections among the various literary elements we have been discussing. These points of intersection may also help you generate significant interpretive questions.

An Analysis of a Short Story

WRITING PROJECT

Your writing project for this chapter has two parts—a formal essay analyzing a short story and a series of reading log entries that will prepare you to write your essay. Your entries in your reading log will give you an opportunity to explore your own understanding of the story, pose questions about it, and then compare your ways of reading and responding to it with your classmates' experiences of it. This process of writing about and discussing the story will help you find places in the text where readers' understandings differ, where ambiguities lead to uncertainties about some aspect of the story. These places will prompt *interpretive questions*—that is, questions for which the text contains evidence that supports more than one good thesis regarding, for example, events, motives, or meaning. Such questions are the perfect starting points for an interpretive paper like the one called for in the following assignment.

Pose an interpretive question about a short story and respond to it analytically, showing your readers where and how the text of the story supports your interpretation. In the introduction to your essay, pose an interesting, problematic, and significant question about the story, one that can be answered several different ways according to the evidence in the text. Look for a question that might lead to differences in opinion among your classmates and that offers readers new insights into the story. Your task in this assignment is not to discover the right way to interpret the text, but to explain *your* way of reading some aspect of it.

For help choosing or framing such questions, review Chapter 1, Concept 2, about posing interesting, problematic, and significant questions.

Using a closed-form structure, present your thesis about the story and your supporting arguments. Before you give your thesis, make clear just what question you are putting to the text and why. It is this question that will engage your readers' interest and make them look forward to your analysis. Then, in the body of your paper, explain your own responses to this question, contrasting your answer with other possible interpretations that have been proposed by your classmates or that you yourself have considered. Without disputing the alternative interpretations, concentrate on showing your readers how you arrived at *your* interpretation and why you think that that interpretation is valuable. Use details from the story for support.

Reading the Story and Using Reading Logs

To help you settle on a good question for your paper and to develop and share ideas, we have prepared a series of reading log questions for you to use in exploring the story. Your reading log will help you the most if you write in response to each freewriting task.

The reading log entries will help you pose a good question about your assigned short story. Good literary questions call attention to problematic details of the text, stimulate conversation, and provoke readers to return to the text to reread and rethink. You know you have a good question if your classmates disagree about the answer and contribute their own differing views to the conversation. Sharing your reading log entries with classmates will help you generate and sustain a productive discussion about the short story.

Reading the First Time

We ask you now to read the short story your instructor has designated for this assignment. Task 1 asks you to stop several times along the way as you read. Tasks 2 and 3 should be written immediately after you finish reading.

Reading Log Task 1: As you read your assigned story, stop at several points and predict what you think will happen in the rest of the story. Make your first stop fairly early in the story, choose a second stopping place in the middle, and stop a third time near the end. In each case, predict what is going to happen next and note what in the text causes you to make your prediction. Freewrite for three or four minutes each time you stop.

Reading Log Task 2: As soon as you finish your reading, write down your immediate responses to the text—how it made you feel or think, what emotions it triggered, what issues it raised. Freewrite for five minutes.

Reading Log Task 3: Write down (a) what most interested you about the story and (b) the most important question you're left with after reading the text. Freewrite for a couple of minutes after several minutes of reflecting.

FOR WRITING AND DISCUSSION

Impressions and Questions

As a whole class or in small groups, share your responses to the reading log tasks. Because you need to begin your formal essay for this assignment with a problematic question, pay particular attention to your classmates' responses to (b) in Task 3—the most important question raised by the story. Perhaps you have a tentative answer that you would like to propose to someone else's question.

Analyzing the Plot

Reading Log Task 4: What is the single most important moment or event in your assigned story? Why do you see this moment as important or crucial? Freewrite for about ten minutes.

FOR WRITING AND DISCUSSION

Plot

As a whole class or in small groups, share your responses to Task 4. Which events did you choose and what are your arguments for selecting them? Take notes about how your classmates' interpretations differ.

Analyzing the Setting and Characters

Reading Log Task 5: What is worth noting about your assigned story's setting? What is the setting? How does it change? Consider multiple aspects of time, location, atmosphere, and so forth, to discern the role that setting plays in the unfolding events. Freewrite for ten minutes on your ideas about the importance of setting in the story.

Reading Log Task 6: Who do you think is the most important character in the story? How does this character change or grow as the story progresses? How do the other characters promote or inhibit change in the main character? How do they help you see and understand the changes? Freewrite for ten to fifteen minutes.

FOR WRITING AND DISCUSSION

Setting and Characters

Share your reading log entries for Tasks 5 and 6 and note differences in the interpretations of various members of the class. Remember that you are not seeking the one right answer to these questions. You are trying to determine how *you* read this story.

Analyzing Point of View

Reading Log Task 7: What is the story's point of view? What is the narrator's role in the unfolding of events? How do the narrator's perceptions filter your understanding of the story? Do you consider the narrator's perceptions reliable, or does the text suggest alternative understandings? Is the narrator's way of seeing part of what the story is about? Freewrite for ten minutes on ideas you generate by contemplating the story's point of view.

FOR WRITING AND DISCUSSION

Point of View

Share your reading log entry for Task 7 with your class and note differences in interpretations.

Revisiting the Story

Reading Log Task 8: Reread your response to Task 2, your first attempt to articulate ideas related to the story's theme. Then complete one of the following statements: (a) After further reflection on my assigned story, I think the author is trying to say something to readers about ________________. (b) Here is what this story makes me think about and see: ________________. Freewrite for ten minutes.

Reading Log Task 9: Look again at the place in the story that you identified in Task 4 as its most important moment or event. (a) What role do the elements of *character* that you identified in Task 6 play in this crucial passage? (b) Do elements of the story's *setting* contribute to your understanding of the importance of this passage? How do these details add to its impact? (c) How does *point of view* contribute to a reader's sense of the importance of the events and/or description in this passage? (d) Does your analysis of the interconnections of these literary elements give you new ideas or raise new questions for you about the story's *theme*? Freewrite for ten minutes.

FOR WRITING AND DISCUSSION

Theme and Critical Elements

Share your responses to Reading Log Tasks 8 and 9 with your class and note differences in the ways members of the class read this story.

The reading log entries you've completed in conjunction with your assigned story should help you considerably when you plan your essay. Begin that planning by writing out the question you will pose and explore in your paper. As we have seen, a good question, one that is problematic and significant, is one that promotes engaged conversation and differing points of view. To help you decide on a question, the reading log tasks in this section ask you to freewrite in response to several different "starter questions." After you decide on a question, you will need to explore ways to answer it, using textual details for support.

Generating and Exploring Ideas

To help you settle on a good problematic question for the introduction of your formal essay, we list several starter questions that focus on *turning points*—major changes in a story's characters, plot, language, and point of view. You may want to begin with one of these questions and then refine it to make it more specific to the story.

After reviewing these questions, complete the two reading log tasks that follow.

Turning-Point Starter Questions about a Short Story

1. Changes in characters
   a. How do circumstances change for each character? What sets each change of circumstance in motion?
   b. How does each character's understanding or knowledge change?
   c. How does your attitude toward each character change?
   d. How does each character's relationship to other characters change?

2. Changes in language
   a. How does the dialogue change? Do characters talk to each other differently at any point?
   b. How does the tone of the language change? Does it become lighter or darker at given points?
   c. How do the metaphors and similes change? Is there a pattern to that change?
3. Changes in point of view
   a. How does the narrator's attitude toward the characters and events change? Does the narrator move closer or farther away from characters and events at any point?
   b. How trustworthy or credible is the narrator? If the narrator is not credible, at what point do you first suspect him or her of unreliability?
4. Changes in setting
   a. How does the time or place depicted in the text change? How are other changes in the text related to these changes?

Reading Log Task 10: Using the turning-point starter questions to stimulate your thinking, pose five or six specific turning-point questions about your assigned story.

Reading Log Task 11: Choose one of your turning-point questions and explore your own answer to it.

Looking at turning points is not the only way to pose questions about a text. A second list of starter questions focuses on other considerations, such as theme, values, and characters. Review the questions and then complete the two reading log tasks that follow.

Additional Starter Questions

1. How does the story's title contribute to your understanding of the story?
2. What does each of the major characters seek and want? What are each character's values?
3. Which character's beliefs and values are closest to your own? How so?
4. What are the main conflicts in the story? What or who blocks the characters from reaching their goals (remember, sometimes what blocks them may be inside them), and how much control do they have over achieving their ends?
5. How successful are the characters in achieving their goals and how do they respond to the outcome?
6. Among all the characters, who seems to best understand what happens and why?

Reading Log Task 12: Use these additional starter questions to pose two or three specific questions about your assigned story.

Reading Log Task 13: Choose one of your questions and explore your responses to it.

Choosing Your Problematic Question and Exploring Your Answer

You're now ready to choose the question that will initiate your essay and to explore your answer. For the final reading log tasks, freewrite rapidly to spill your ideas onto the paper and avoid writer's block. Before you begin, read over what you have written so far in your reading log to help you get the juices flowing.

Reading Log Task 14: Write out the question that you want to ask in your essay about your assigned short story. What makes this an interesting and significant question? Why don't you and your classmates immediately agree on the answer?

Reading Log Task 15: Freewriting as rapidly as you can, explore your answer to the question you asked in Task 14. Use textual details and your own critical thinking to create an argument supporting your answer.

Shaping, Drafting, and Revising

Reading Log Tasks 14 and 15 give you a head start on a rough draft. The best way to organize your literary analysis is to follow the problem-thesis pattern of closed-form prose, as shown in the Framework for a Literary Analysis Essay (Figure 11.1).

After you have produced a good rough draft, let it sit for a while. Then try it out on readers, who can follow the Questions for Peer Review. Based on your readers' advice, begin revising your draft, making it as clear as possible for your readers. Remember to start with the big issues and major changes and then work your way down to the smaller issues and minor changes.

FIGURE 11.1 Framework for a Literary Analysis Essay

Introduction (one to several paragraphs)	• Poses your question about the text • Shows why your question is interesting, problematic, and significant • Presents relevant background about the story • Presents your thesis statement—a one-sentence answer to your question
Body (several paragraphs)	• Develops and supports your thesis using textual details and quotations and argument • Summarizes and responds to alternative interpretations (if not done in the introduction)
Conclusion	• Returns to your question and suggests why your answer is significant • Addresses the larger implications of your interpretation

Questions for Peer Review

In addition to the generic peer review questions provided in Skill 16.4, ask your peer reviewers to address these questions:

INTRODUCTION:

1. Does the title arouse interest and forecast the problem to be addressed? How might the author improve the title?
2. How does the introduction capture your interest, explain the question to be addressed, and suggest why it is both problematic and significant?
3. Does the introduction conclude with the writer's thesis? Is the thesis surprising? How might the author improve the introduction?

ANALYSIS AND INTERPRETATION:

1. How has the writer shown that his or her thesis is in conflict with alternative interpretations or views?
2. How is the essay organized? Does the writer helpfully forecast the whole, place points before particulars, use transitions, and follow the old/new contract as explained in Chapter 17? How might the author improve or clarify the organization?
3. Where does the author quote from the story (or use paraphrase or other specific references to the text)? How are each of the author's points grounded in the text? What passages not cited might better support the argument? What recommendations do you have for improving the author's use of supporting details?
4. Where do you disagree with the author's analysis? What aspects of the story are left unexplained? What doesn't fit?

Readings

Here is a short story to test your analytical skills. In addition, we include a student essay written for this chapter's writing project.

The first reading is "Everyday Use (For Your Grandmama)" by African-American writer Alice Walker. It was written in 1973.

Alice Walker

Everyday Use (For Your Grandmama)

1 I will wait for her in the yard that Maggie and I made so clean and wavy yesterday afternoon. A yard like this is more comfortable than most people know. It is not just a yard. It is like an extended living room. When the hard clay is swept clean as a floor and the fine sand around the edges lined with tiny, irregular grooves, anyone can come and sit and look up into the elm tree and wait for the breezes that never come inside the house.

2 Maggie will be nervous until after her sister goes: she will stand hopelessly in corners, homely and ashamed of the burn scars down her arms and legs, eying her sister with a mixture of envy and awe. She thinks her sister has held life always in the palm of one hand, that "no" is a word the world never learned to say to her.

3 You've no doubt seen those TV shows where the child who has "made it" is confronted, as a surprise, by her own mother and father, tottering in weakly from backstage. (A pleasant surprise, of course: What would they do if parent and child came on the show only to curse out and insult each other?) On TV mother and child embrace and smile into each other's faces. Sometimes the mother and father weep; the child wraps them in her arms and leans across the table to tell how she would not have made it without their help. I have seen these programs.

4 Sometimes I dream a dream in which Dee and I are suddenly brought together on a TV program of this sort. Out of a dark and soft-seated limousine I am ushered into a bright room filled with many people. There I meet a smiling, gray, sporty man like Johnny Carson who shakes my hand and tells me what a fine girl I have. Then we are on the stage and Dee is embracing me with tears in her eyes. She pins on my dress a large orchid, even though she has told me once that she thinks orchids are tacky flowers.

5 In real life I am a large, big-boned woman with rough, man-working hands. In the winter I wear flannel nightgowns to bed and overalls during the day. I can kill and clean a hog as mercilessly as a man. My fat keeps me hot in zero weather. I can work outside all day, breaking once to get water for washing; I can eat pork liver cooked over the open fire minutes after it comes steaming from the hog. One winter I knocked a bull calf straight in the brain between the eyes with a sledge hammer and had the meat hung up to chill before nightfall. But of course all this does not show on television. I am the way my daughter would want me to be: a hundred pounds lighter, my skin like an uncooked barley pancake. My hair glistens in the hot bright lights. Johnny Carson has much to do to keep up with my quick and witty tongue.

6 But that is a mistake. I know even before I wake up. Who ever knew a Johnson with a quick tongue? Who can even imagine me looking a strange white man in the

eye? It seems to me I have talked to them always with one foot raised in flight, with my head turned in whichever way is farthest from them. Dee, though. She would always look anyone in the eye. Hesitation was no part of her nature.

7 "How do I look, Mama?" Maggie says, showing just enough of her thin body enveloped in pink skirt and red blouse for me to know she's there, almost hidden by the door.

8 "Come out into the yard," I say.

9 Have you ever seen a lame animal, perhaps a dog run over by some careless person rich enough to own a car, sidle up to someone who is ignorant enough to be kind to him? That is the way my Maggie walks. She has been like this, chin on chest, eyes on ground, feet in shuffle, ever since the fire that burned the other house to the ground.

10 Dee is lighter than Maggie, with nicer hair and a fuller figure. She's a woman now, though sometimes I forget. How long ago was it that the other house burned? Ten, twelve years? Sometimes I can still hear the flames and feel Maggie's arms sticking to me, her hair smoking and her dress falling off her in little black papery flakes. Her eyes seemed stretched open, blazed open by the flames reflected in them. And Dee. I see her standing off under the sweet gum tree she used to dig gum out of; a look of concentration on her face as she watched the last dingy gray board of the house fall in toward the red-hot brick chimney. Why don't you do a dance around the ashes? I'd wanted to ask her. She had hated the house that much.

11 I used to think she hated Maggie, too. But that was before we raised the money, the church and me, to send her to Augusta to school. She used to read to us without pity; forcing words, lies, other folks' habits, whole lives upon us two, sitting trapped and ignorant underneath her voice. She washed us in a river of make-believe, burned us with a lot of knowledge we didn't necessarily need to know. Pressed us to her with the serious way she read, to shove us away at just the moment, like dimwits, we seemed about to understand.

12 Dee wanted nice things. A yellow organdy dress to wear to her graduation from high school; black pumps to match a green suit she'd made from an old suit somebody gave me. She was determined to stare down any disaster in her efforts. Her eyelids would not flicker for minutes at a time. Often I fought off the temptation to shake her. At sixteen she had a style of her own: and she knew what style was.

13 I never had an education myself. After second grade the school was closed down. Don't ask me why: in 1927 colored asked fewer questions than they do now. Sometimes Maggie reads to me. She stumbles along good-naturedly but can't see well. She knows she is not bright. Like good looks and money, quickness passed her by. She will marry John Thomas (who has mossy teeth in an earnest face) and then I'll be free to sit here and I guess just sing church songs to myself. Although I never was a good singer. Never could carry a tune. I was always better at a man's job. I used to love to milk till I was hooked in the side in '49. Cows are soothing and slow and don't bother you, unless you try to milk them the wrong way.

14 I have deliberately turned my back on the house. It is three rooms, just like the one that burned, except the roof is tin; they don't make shingle roofs any more. There are no real windows, just some holes cut in the sides, like the portholes in a ship, but not round and not square, with rawhide holding the shutters up on the outside. This

house is in a pasture, too, like the other one. No doubt when Dee sees it she will want to tear it down. She wrote me once that no matter where we "choose" to live, she will manage to come see us. But she will never bring her friends. Maggie and I thought about this and Maggie asked me, "Mama, when did Dee ever *have* any friends?"

15 She had a few. Furtive boys in pink shirts hanging about on washday after school. Nervous girls who never laughed. Impressed with her they worshipped the well-turned phrase, the cute shape, the scalding humor that erupted like bubbles in lye. She read to them.

16 When she was courting Jimmy T she didn't have much time to pay to us, but turned all her faultfinding power on him. He *flew* to marry a cheap city girl from a family of ignorant flashy people. She hardly had time to recompose herself.

17 When she comes I will meet—but there they are!

18 Maggie attempts to make a dash for the house, in her shuffling way, but I stay her with my hand. "Come back here," I say. And she stops and tries to dig a well in the sand with her toe.

19 It is hard to see them clearly through the strong sun. But even the first glimpse of leg out of the car tells me it is Dee. Her feet were always neat-looking, as if God himself had shaped them with a certain style. From the other side of the car comes a short, stocky man. Hair is all over his head a foot long and hanging from his chin like a kinky mule tail. I hear Maggie suck in her breath. "Uhnnnh," is what it sounds like. Like when you see the wriggling end of a snake just in front of your foot on the road. "Uhnnnh."

20 Dee next. A dress down to the ground, in this hot weather. A dress so loud it hurts my eyes. There are yellows and oranges enough to throw back the light of the sun. I feel my whole face warming from the heat waves it throws out. Earrings gold, too, and hanging down to her shoulders. Bracelets dangling and making noises when she moves her arm up to shake the folds of the dress out of her armpits. The dress is loose and flows, and as she walks closer, I like it. I hear Maggie go "Uhnnnh" again. It is her sister's hair. It stands straight up like the wool on a sheep. It is black as night and around the edges are two long ponytails that rope about like small lizards disappearing behind her ears.

21 "Wa-su-zo-Tean-o!" she says, coming in on that gliding way the dress makes her move. The short stocky fellow with the hair to his navel is all grinning and he follows up with "Asalamalakim, my mother and sister!" He moves to hug Maggie but she falls back, right up against the back of my chair. I feel her trembling there and when I look up I see the perspiration falling off her chin.

22 "Don't get up," says Dee. Since I am stout it takes something of a push. You can see me trying to move a second or two before I make it. She turns, showing white heels through her sandals, and goes back to the car. Out she peeks next with a Polaroid. She stoops down quickly and lines up picture after picture of me sitting there in front of the house with Maggie cowering behind me. She never takes a shot without making sure the house is included. When a cow comes nibbling around the edge of the yard she snaps it and me and Maggie *and* the house. Then she puts the Polaroid in the back seat of the car, and comes up and kisses me on the forehead.

23 Meanwhile Asalamalakim is going through the motions with Maggie's hand. Maggie's hand is as limp as a fish, and probably cold, despite the sweat, and she keeps trying to pull it back. It looks like Asalamalakim wants to shake hands but wants to do

it fancy. Or maybe he don't know how people shake hands. Anyhow, he soon gives up on Maggie.

24 "Well," I say. "Dee."

25 "No, Mama," she says. "Not 'Dee,' Wangero Leewanika Kemanjo!"

26 "What happened to 'Dee'?" I wanted to know.

27 "She's dead," Wangero said. "I couldn't bear it any longer, being named after the people who oppress me."

28 "You know as well as me you was named after your aunt Dicie," I said. Dicie is my sister. She named Dee. We called her "Big Dee" after Dee was born.

29 "But who was she named after?" asked Wangero.

30 "I guess after Grandma Dee," I said.

31 "And who was she named after?" asked Wangero.

32 "Her mother," I said, and saw Wangero was getting tired. "That's about as far back as I can trace it," I said. Though, in fact, I probably could have carried it back beyond the Civil War through the branches.

33 "Well," said Asalamalakim, "there you are."

34 "Uhnnnh," I heard Maggie say.

35 "There I was not," I said, "before 'Dicie' cropped up in our family, so why should I try to trace it that far back?"

36 He just stood there grinning, looking down on me like somebody inspecting a Model A car. Every once in a while he and Wangero sent eye signals over my head.

37 "How do you pronounce this name?" I asked.

38 "You don't have to call me by it if you don't want to," said Wangero.

39 "Why shouldn't I?" I asked. "If that's what you want us to call you, we'll call you."

40 "I know it might sound awkward at first," said Wangero.

41 "I'll get used to it," I said. "Ream it out again."

42 Well, soon we got the name out of the way. Asalamalakim had a name twice as long and three times as hard. After I tripped over it two or three times he told me to just call him Hakim-a-barber. I wanted to ask him was he a barber, but I didn't really think he was, so I didn't ask.

43 "You must belong to those beef-cattle peoples down the road," I said. They said "Asalamalakim" when they met you, too, but they didn't shake hands. Always too busy: feeding the cattle, fixing the fences, putting up salt-lick shelters, throwing down hay. When the white folks poisoned some of the herd the men stayed up all night with rifles in their hands. I walked a mile and a half just to see the sight.

44 Hakim-a-barber said, "I accept some of their doctrines, but farming and raising cattle is not my style." (They didn't tell me, and I didn't ask, whether Wangero (Dee) had really gone and married him.)

45 We sat down to eat and right away he said he didn't eat collards and pork was unclean. Wangero, though, went on through the chitlins and corn bread, the greens and everything else. She talked a blue streak over the sweet potatoes. Everything delighted her. Even the fact that we still used the benches her daddy made for the table when we couldn't afford to buy chairs.

46 "Oh, Mama!" she cried. Then turned to Hakim-a-barber. "I never knew how lovely these benches are. You can feel the rump prints," she said, running her hands

underneath her and along the bench. Then she gave a sigh and her hand closed over Grandma Dee's butter dish. "That's it!" she said. "I knew there was something I wanted to ask you if I could have." She jumped up from the table and went over in the corner where the churn stood, the milk in it clabber by now. She looked at the churn and looked at it.

47 "This churn top is what I need," she said happily. "Didn't Uncle Buddy whittle it out of a tree you all used to have?"

48 "Yes," I said.

49 "Uh huh," she said happily. "And I want the dasher, too."

50 "Uncle Buddy whittle that, too?" asked the barber.

51 Dee (Wangero) looked up at me.

52 "Aunt Dee's first husband whittled the dash," said Maggie so low you almost couldn't hear her. "His name was Henry, but they called him Stash."

53 "Maggie's brain is like an elephant's," Wangero said, laughing. "I can use the churn top as a centerpiece for the alcove table," she said, sliding a plate over the churn, "and I'll think of something artistic to do with the dasher."

54 When she finished wrapping the dasher the handle stuck out. I took it for a moment in my hands. You didn't even have to look close to see where hands pushing the dasher up and down to make butter had left a kind of sink in the wood. In fact, there were a lot of small sinks; you could see where thumbs and fingers had sunk into the wood. It was beautiful light yellow wood, from a tree that grew in the yard where Big Dee and Stash had lived.

55 After dinner Dee (Wangero) went to the trunk at the foot of my bed and started rifling through it. Maggie hung back in the kitchen over the dishpan. Out came Wangero with two quilts. They had been pieced by Grandma Dee and then Big Dee and me had hung them on the quilt frames on the front porch and quilted them. One was in the Lone Star pattern. The other was Walk Around the Mountain. In both of them were scraps of dresses Grandma Dee had worn fifty and more years ago. Bits and pieces of Grandma Jarrell's Paisley shirts. And one teeny faded blue piece, about the size of a penny matchbox, that was from Great Grandpa Ezra's uniform that he wore in the Civil War.

56 "Mama," Wangero said sweet as a bird. "Can I have these old quilts?"

57 I heard something fall in the kitchen, and a minute later the kitchen door slammed.

58 "Why don't you take one or two of the others?" I asked. "These old things was just done by me and Big Dee from some tops your grandma pieced before she died."

59 "No," said Wangero. "I don't want those. They are stitched around the borders by machine."

60 "That'll make them last better," I said.

61 "That's not the point," said Wangero. "These are all pieces of dresses Grandma used to wear. She did all this stitching by hand. Imagine!" She held the quilts securely in her arms, stroking them.

62 "Some of the pieces, like those lavender ones, come from old clothes her mother handed down to her," I said, moving up to touch the quilts. Dee (Wangero) moved back just enough so that I couldn't reach the quilts. They already belonged to her.

63 "Imagine!" she breathed again, clutching them closely to her bosom.

64 "The truth is," I said, "I promised to give them quilts to Maggie, for when she marries John Thomas."

65 She gasped like a bee had stung her.

66 "Maggie can't appreciate these quilts!" she said. "She'd probably be backward enough to put them to everyday use."

67 "I reckon she would," I said. "God knows I been saving 'em for long enough with nobody using 'em. I hope she will!" I didn't want to bring up how I had offered Dee (Wangero) a quilt when she went away to college. Then she had told me they were old-fashioned, out of style.

68 "But they're *priceless!*" she was saying now, furiously; for she has a temper. "Maggie would put them on the bed and in five years they'd be in rags. Less than that!"

69 "She can always make some more," I said. "Maggie knows how to quilt."

70 Dee (Wangero) looked at me with hatred. "You just will not understand. The point is these quilts, *these* quilts!"

71 "Well," I said, stumped. "What would *you* do with them?"

72 "Hang them," she said. As if that was the only thing you *could* do with quilts.

73 Maggie by now was standing in the door. I could almost hear the sound her feet made as they scraped over each other.

74 "She can have them, Mama," she said, like somebody used to never winning anything, or having anything reserved for her. "I can 'member Grandma Dee without the quilts."

75 I looked at her hard. She had filled her bottom lip with checkerberry snuff and it gave her face a kind of dopey, hangdog look. It was Grandma Dee and Big Dee who taught her how to quilt herself. She stood there with her hands hidden in the folds of her skirt. She looked at her sister with something like fear but she wasn't mad at her. This was Maggie's portion. This was the way she knew God to work.

76 When I looked at her like that something hit me in the top of my head and ran down to the soles of my feet. Just like when I'm in church and the spirit of God touches me and I get happy and shout. I did something I never had done before: hugged Maggie to me, then dragged her on into the room, snatched the quilts out of Miss Wangero's hands and dumped them into Maggie's lap. Maggie just sat there on my bed with her mouth open.

77 "Take one or two of the others," I said to Dee.

78 But she turned without a word and went out to Hakim-a-barber.

79 "You just don't understand," she said, as Maggie and I came out to the car.

80 "What don't I understand?" I wanted to know.

81 "Your heritage," she said. And then she turned to Maggie, kissed her, and said, "You ought to try to make something of yourself, too, Maggie. It's really a new day for us. But from the way you and Mama still live you'd never know it."

82 She put on some sunglasses that hid everything above the tip of her nose and her chin.

83 Maggie smiled; maybe at the sunglasses. But a real smile, not scared. After we watched the car dust settle I asked Maggie to me bring me a dip of snuff. And then the two of us sat there just enjoying, until it was time to go in the house and go to bed.

The following student essay on Walker's "Everyday Use (For Your Grandmama)" was written in response to this chapter's assignment. What questions and comments would you have for its writer if you were in a peer review session?

Betsy Weiler (student)

Who Do You Want to Be?

Finding Heritage in Walker's "Everyday Use"

"You just don't understand."
"What don't I understand?"
"Your heritage" (297).*

1 Whose heritage is Dee talking about? Is it her family's heritage or her ethnic heritage?

2 This exchange takes place near the end of Alice Walker's short story "Everyday Use" when Dee is saying goodbye to her mother and her sister Maggie after a brief visit and an argument about some quilts. That visit was almost like a treasure hunt for Dee. It seems that Dee, who now has the name Wangero Leewanika Kemanjo, came to visit because she wants to try to identify herself with the past. She wants to take parts of a butter churn and some family quilts back home with her, but Mama says "no" about the quilts because she promised them to Maggie. Dee thinks that Maggie can't "appreciate" the quilts and is "backward enough to put them to everyday use" (297). This confrontation over the quilts suggests that Dee may have learned a lot in college about her ethnic background as an African American, but she does not understand or appreciate her own family's heritage.

3 At first, a reader might think that Dee/Wangero has come home to express her appreciation for her family's heritage. While Mama is waiting for her, she expects that Dee will want to tear down the family house because it is just like the one that burned down when she was a child there. Dee hated that house. But when Dee arrives, before she even tells her mother her new name, she begins taking "picture after picture" of her mother and Maggie, "making sure the house is included" in every one (294). It seems that Dee is proud to include the house in her heritage—but is it her ethnic heritage or her family heritage? What will she do with the pictures? Are they something to remember her family with or are they something "artistic" that she will use to display her ethnic heritage?

4 When Dee explains her new name to her mother, she seems to have forgotten part of her family heritage. Wangero says that "Dee" is "dead" because "I couldn't bear it any longer, being named after the people who oppress me" (295). After her mother explains that she is actually named after Aunt Dee and Grandma Dee, Wangero Leewanika Kemanjo may gain some appreciation of the family tradition because she says that Mama doesn't have to call her the new name "if you don't want to." But Mama shows her own respect for her own daughter by saying "I'll get used to it."

*Numbers in parentheses indicate page numbers on which the quotation is found (in this case, page numbers in this text). This parenthetical citation system follows the MLA format. See Chapter 22.

5 When the treasure hunt part of the visit begins after the dinner, Dee's concern for ethnic heritage becomes clear. Dee wants items from the past that she identifies with her ethnic heritage. She jumps up from the table and declares that she needs the churn top. She asks, "Didn't Uncle Buddy whittle it [the churn] out of a tree you all used to have?" (296). She is talking about the churn top in terms of family heritage, but when she says that she intends to use it as a centerpiece on an alcove table, the reader understands that for Dee the churn is more significant for the ethnic heritage it represents. Many blacks could not afford to buy butter, so they had to make it themselves. (In fact, her mother is still using that churn to make butter.) She also wants the dasher from the churn. For Maggie and Mama, it is a tool in the present that represents family history. Maggie explains that Aunt Dee's first husband, Stash, whittled it; when Mama (the narrator) looks it over she notices the "small sinks" in the wood from the hands of people who had used it (including her own, no doubt). There is a strong contrast between their attitude toward the heirloom and Dee/Wangero's. She laughs at Maggie's story (family heritage), saying Maggie has a "brain ... like an elephant's" and announces that she herself will "think of something artistic to do with the dasher" (296). For all of them, the dasher represents the hard work blacks have had to struggle through, but for Mama and Maggie, it is a tool made by a family member to help with that work today. For Wangero it is an ethnic heritage object to display.

6 The final two items that Dee wants are the hand-stitched quilts that she digs out of Mama's trunk. They represent family heritage because they contain pieces of her ancestors' clothing, including a tiny piece from the blue uniform of a great-grandfather who fought in the Civil War. That family heritage is very strong for Mama, who was planning to give the quilts to Maggie as a wedding present. She remembers, but doesn't say anything, that Dee/Wangero had refused to take a quilt with her to college because they were old fashioned. Dee loses her temper over the idea of Maggie using the quilts on a bed because "in five years they'd be in rags" (297). Mama says that then Maggie would make new ones. But Dee wants "*these* quilts," the ones with pieces of her own family's clothing. This may appear to be an appreciation of family heritage, but since Dee/Wangero wants to hang the quilts on the wall, not use them for a practical purpose, it seems that she wants to display a heritage that she doesn't want to live anymore.

7 Maggie is willing to give up the quilts, saying she can remember Grandma Dee without them, but Mama grabs the quilts back from Dee. The conflict here is not only about remembering but also about how to remember. Although Dee wants to preserve the original quilts with their antique pieces, she keeps separating herself from the family heritage that created them.

8 As Dee gets into the car to leave, she puts on a pair of sunglasses that hide "everything above the tip of her nose and her chin" (297). If, as the saying goes, the eyes are the windows to the soul, then Dee is hiding her soul. By wearing the sunglasses, Dee is hiding who she truly is and just wants to be identified with the color of her skin, her ethnic heritage. She tells Maggie that "[i]t's really a new day for us" although "from the way you ... live, you'd never know it" (297).

9 Mama and Maggie may live in a very old-fashioned setting, using old-fashioned tools every day, but Dee/Wangero's attitude about her family and its heirlooms shows that actually she is the person who does not understand her heritage.

Thinking Critically

about "Who Do You Want to Be? Finding Heritage in Walker's 'Everyday Use'"

1. The assignment for this chapter asks for an essay built around a problematic and significant interpretive question. Do you think that Betsy Weiler adequately addresses the assignment? Has she been successful in articulating a problematic question and indicating its importance for our understanding of the story?
2. Does Weiler's thesis statement respond adequately to the question? Does she supply enough details to support her analysis? Would the paper be better with more analysis of literary elements? What should she add or cut?
3. What alternative answers to Weiler's interpretive question occur to you besides the ones she brings up? What evidence do you find in the text to support your analysis and interpretation?
4. What recommendations would you have for improving this essay?

For support in learning this chapter's content, follow this path in **MyCompLab**: Resources ⇒ Writing ⇒ Writing Purposes ⇒ Writing to Analyze. Review the Instruction and Multimedia resources, then complete the Exercises and click on Gradebook to measure your progress.

ANALYZING AND SYNTHESIZING IDEAS

12

In many college courses, you'll be asked to explore connections and contradictions among groups of texts. Distilling main points from more than one text, seeing connections among texts, commenting on meaningful relationships, and showing how the texts have influenced your own thinking on a question are all part of the thinking and writing involved in synthesis.

Synthesis, which is a way of seeing and coming to terms with complexities, is a counterpart to **analysis**. When you analyze something, you break it down into its parts to see the relationships among them. When you synthesize, you take one more step, putting parts together in some new fashion. The cognitive researcher Benjamin Bloom schematized "synthesis" as the fifth of six levels of thinking processes, ranked in order of complexity and challenge: knowledge, comprehension, application, analysis, *synthesis*, and evaluation. Bloom defined synthesis in these terms: "putting together of constituent elements or parts to form a whole requiring original creative thinking."* Synthesis drives those lightbulb moments when you exclaim, "Ah! Now I see how these ideas are related!"

A second useful way to think of synthesis is as a dialectical thinking process. Throughout this text, we have explained that college writing involves posing a significant question that often forces you to encounter clashing or contradictory ideas. Such conflicts intrigued the German philosopher Hegel, who posited that thinking proceeds dialectically when a thesis clashes against an antithesis, leading the thinker to formulate a synthesis encompassing dimensions of both the original thesis and the antithesis. When you write to synthesize ideas, your thinking exemplifies this dialectical process.

This Hegelian view is also discussed in Chapter 7, p. 156.

Synthesis is an especially important component of academic research writing, where you use synthesis to carve out your own thinking space on a question while sifting through the writings of others. Synthesis, then, is the skill of wrestling with ideas from different texts or sources, trying to forge a new whole out of potentially confusing parts. It is the principal way you enter into a conversation on a social, civic, or scholarly issue.

This chapter introduces you to an important academic genre, the synthesis essay. By writing a synthesis essay, you will learn to:

- interact with a group of texts
- explore their alternative perspectives on an issue
- present a new, enlarged perspective of your own

*Benjamin Bloom, *Taxonomy of Educational Objectives: Handbook I: Cognitive Domain* (New York: David McKay, 1956).

Exploring the Analysis and Synthesis of Ideas

To introduce you to some of the essential thinking moves involved in analyzing and synthesizing, we offer this exercise, which asks you to read two articles on the question, "What effect are cell phones having on our lives as American citizens?" The first reading, "Mobile Phone Tracking Scrutinized" by Nikki Swartz, was published in the *Information Management Journal* for March/April 2006. This journal bills itself as "the leading source of information on topics and issues central to the management of records and information worldwide." The second reading, "Reach Out and Track Someone" by Terry J. Allen, appeared in the May 2006 edition of *In These Times*, a publication "dedicated to informing and analyzing popular movements for social, environmental and economic justice." Read these pieces carefully and then do the exercises that follow.

Nikki Swartz

Mobile Phone Tracking Scrutinized

1 Nearly 200 million Americans have cell phones, but many of them are not aware that wireless technology companies, as well as the U.S. government, track their movements through signals emitted by their handsets.

2 Cellular providers, including Verizon Wireless and Cingular Wireless, know, within about 300 yards, the location of their subscribers whenever a phone is turned on. Even if the phone is not in use, it still communicates with cell tower sites, and the wireless provider keeps track of the phone's position as it travels. These companies are marketing services that turn handsets into even more precise global positioning devices for driving or allowing parents to track the whereabouts of their children.

3 In recent years, law enforcement officials have used cellular technology as a tool for easily and secretly monitoring the movements of suspects. But this kind of surveillance, which investigators have been able to conduct with easily obtained court orders, has now come under tougher legal scrutiny.

4 The *New York Times* reports that, in the last four months of 2005, three federal judges denied prosecutors the right to get cell phone tracking information from wireless companies without first showing "probable cause" that a crime has been or is being committed—the same standard applied to requests for search warrants.

5 The rulings, issued by magistrate judges in New York, Texas, and Maryland, underscore the growing debate over privacy rights and government surveillance in the digital age. Wireless providers keep cell phone location records for varying lengths of time, from several months to years, and have said that they turn over cell location information when presented with a court order to do so.

6 Prosecutors argue that having such data is crucial to finding suspects, corroborating their whereabouts with witness accounts, or helping build a case for a wiretap on the phone. The government has routinely used records of cell phone calls and caller locations to show where a suspect was at a particular time, with access to those records obtainable under a lower legal standard.

7 But it is unclear how often prosecutors have asked courts for the right to obtain cell-tracking data as a suspect is moving. And the government is not required to report publicly when it makes such requests.

8 Prosecutors, while acknowledging that they must get a court order before obtaining real-time cell-site data, argue that a 1994 amendment to the 1986 Stored Communications Act—a standard that calls for the government to show "specific and articulable facts" that demonstrate that the records sought are "relevant and material to an ongoing investigation"—is actually lower than the probable-cause hurdle. In the cell-tracking cases, some legal experts say that the Stored Communications Act refers only to records of where a person has been—historical location data—but does not address live tracking.

9 Prosecutors in the recent cases also unsuccessfully argued that the expanded police powers under the USA PATRIOT Act could be read as allowing cell phone tracking.

10 The magistrate judges, however, ruled that surveillance by cell phone because it acts like an electronic tracking device that can follow people into homes and other personal spaces must meet the same high legal standard required to obtain a search warrant to enter private places.

11 "The distinction between cell site data and information gathered by a tracking device has practically vanished," wrote Stephen W. Smith, a magistrate in Federal District Court in the Southern District of Texas, in his ruling. He added that when a phone is monitored, the process is usually "unknown to the phone users, who may not even be on the phone."

12 In a digital era, the stream of data that carries a telephone conversation or an e-mail message contains a great deal of information, including when and where the communications originated. And that makes it harder for courts to determine whether a certain digital surveillance method invokes Fourth Amendment protections against unreasonable searches.

Terry J. Allen

Reach Out and Track Someone

1 If you are one of the more than 200 million Americans with a cell phone nestled in your pocket, authorities may be able to find you any time day or night—even if you never make or receive a call.

2 You know the Verizon ad where a lockstep crowd personifies the network that accompanies its customer everywhere? Well, within that seemingly friendly horde, a hightech Big Brother is lurking.

3 Most people know that when they make a mobile call—during a 911 emergency, for example—authorities can access phone company technology to pin down their location, sometimes to within a few feet.

4 A lesser-known fact: Cell phone companies can locate you any time you are in range of a tower and your phone is on. Cell phones are designed to work either with

global positioning satellites or through "pings" that allow towers to triangulate and pinpoint signals. Any time your phone "sees" a tower, it pings it.

5 That is what happened last month when a New York City murder highlighted the existence of the built-in capability of phones to locate people even when they aren't making calls.

6 The case of Imette St. Guillen captivated the New York City media as only the murder of a young, attractive, middle-class, white female can. One piece of evidence leading to the arrest of Darryl Littlejohn, the bouncer at the club where St. Guillen was last seen, was what police called "cell phone records." In fact, it was not an actual call that placed Littlejohn at the crime scene. Instead, according to the *New York Daily News*, police traced Littlejohn's route the day of the murder by tracking the "pings" of his cell phone, which were "stored" in a tower and "later retrieved from T-Mobile by cops."

7 Telecom companies and government are not eager to advertise that tracking capability. Nor will companies admit whether they are archiving the breadcrumb trail of pings from a cell phone so that they—or authorities—can trace back, after the fact, where the customer had been at a particular time. "Of course, there is that capability," says Bruce Schneier, chief technical officer with Counterpane Internet Security. "Verizon and the other companies have access to that information and the odds are zero that they wouldn't sell it if it is legal and profitable. This is capitalism after all."

8 But legality can be so tricky to pin down, especially when national security and corporate profits are involved. Communications companies and government have been repeatedly caught collaborating in highly questionable practices. Warrantless wiretapping, now sparking cries for Bush's impeachment, was implemented by the NSA* accessing the "gateway" switches that route calls around the globe. Most of these switches are controlled by AT&T, MCI and Sprint.

9 Recently, the Electronic Frontier Foundation (EFF) said it had internal AT&T documents and a sworn statement by retired AT&T technician Mark Klein showing that the company's use of a "dragnet surveillance" was "diverting Internet traffic into the hands of the NSA wholesale."

10 It is likely that authorities are also accessing cell phone call records and conducting real-time tracing of hapless Palestinians who donated to clinics and liberal activists who dared march for peace. And if the administration's record is a guide, it is interpreting privacy protection laws relating to cell phones in ways that bend and perhaps batter the Constitution.

11 "I think there's a substantial worry that location information about cell phone users is being released without a court order," EFF Staff attorney Kevin Bankston told CNN.

12 Echoing the Bush administration's rationale for warrantless wiretapping, the Justice Department argues that time lost justifying a search warrant can mean dangerous delays. Several judges around the country have disagreed. Citing officials' failure to show probable cause, they have denied government requests for cell phone tracking. According to EFF, a New York magistrate revealed that "the Justice Department had routinely been using a baseless legal argument to get secret authorizations from a number of courts, probably for many years."

*National Security Agency

13 "Justice Department officials countered that courts around the country have granted many such orders in the past without requiring probable cause," the Oct. 28 *Washington Post* reported.

14 Real-time tracking technology also opens disturbing entrepreneurial opportunities. Anyone who provides their kids, spouse or employees with a software-readied cell phone can secretly monitor them on the web. Wherify.com "locates loved ones within feet/meters in about a minute," and allows subscribers to "view location on both street and aerial mapping, to include date/time stamp, lat/long and block address" and "set breadcrumb schedule for periodic locates." Another Internet business promises to sell you the calling records for any phone number you provide. (Note to readers: If you have Karl Rove's number, I'll cough up the $100 fee to get a look.)

15 But as far as invasiveness goes, the ability of the government to secretly track and find you anywhere, anytime, ranks right up with a pelvic exam in Times Square.

INDIVIDUAL TASKS

1. How would you describe each writer's perspective or angle of vision on cell phones? In one or two sentences, summarize each writer's main points in these passages.
2. List ideas that these pieces have in common.
3. List any contradictions or differences you see in these pieces.
4. Freewrite your own response to these readings for five minutes, exploring what questions they raise for you or personal experiences that they might remind you of.

GROUP OR WHOLE-CLASS TASKS

1. Working in small groups or as a whole class, try to reach consensus answers to questions 1, 2, and 3.
2. Share your individual responses to question 4. What are the major questions and issues raised by your group or the whole class? What different views of cell phones in particular and technology in general emerged?

Understanding Analysis and Synthesis

Posing a Synthesis Question

As we have shown throughout this text, most academic and professional writing begins with the posing of a problem. Writing a synthesis essay follows the same principle. The need to synthesize ideas usually begins when you pose a problematic question that sends you off on an intellectual journey through a group of texts. The synthesis or focusing question directs you to look for ways that a group of texts are connected and ways that they differ in their approaches to a particular problem or issue. A synthesis question helps you zero in on a problem that these texts address or that you are trying to solve through exploring these texts. Your goal is to achieve your own informed view on that question, a view that reflects your intellectual wrestling with the ideas in your sources and in some way integrates ideas from these sources with your own independent thinking.

Although synthesis writing appears in college courses across the curriculum, how these assignments are set up varies widely. Sometimes instructors will specify the texts and the questions that you are to explore whereas at other times you will be asked to choose your texts and articulate your own synthesis questions. The following examples show typical synthesis assignments that you might encounter in different disciplines, with both the texts and synthesis questions provided in each case.

Environmental Politics Course

Texts to Be Analyzed	Synthesis Questions
Garrett Hardin's essay on overpopulation, "The Tragedy of the Commons," from *Science* (1968)	Are there any common assumptions about the world's environment in these readings?
Kenneth E. Boulding's essay "Economics of the Coming Spaceship Earth" (1966)	What problems and solutions appear in these readings?
A chapter from Ron Bailey's *The True State of the Planet* (1995)	What direction would you take in proposing a solution?
A chapter from Al Gore's *An Inconvenient Truth* (2006)	

American Literature Survey Course

Texts to Be Analyzed	Synthesis Questions
Selections from the *Lowell Offering*, a publication produced in Lowell, Massachusetts, in the 1840s, featuring the writings of young female factory workers	What common questions about changes in women's social roles in the 1800s emerge in these texts?
Historian Gerda Lerner's essay "The Lady and the Mill Girl: Changes in the Status of Women in the Age of Jackson 1800–1840" (1969)	Which text gives you the clearest understanding of the problems with women's changing roles and why?
Herman Melville's short story "The Paradise of Bachelors and the Tartarus of Maids" (1835)	

Synthesis Writing as an Extension of Summary/ Strong Response Writing

In Chapter 5, we introduced you to writing summaries of texts and responding strongly to them through critique of their rhetorical strategies and ideas. It is helpful to think of synthesis writing as an extension of those skills. In writing a synthesis essay, you use both with-the-grain and against-the-grain thinking. You listen carefully to texts as you summarize them to determine their main points. You also conduct—at least informally in your exploratory stages—a critique of both the rhetorical features and the ideas of these texts. This analysis builds the platform from which you create a synthesis of ideas—that is, from which you begin your own independent thinking based on the synthesis question that ties your texts together.

A synthesis essay differs from a summary/strong response essay in that a synthesis extends the process to more texts with the aim of bringing them into conversation with each other. A synthesis essay shows how you have taken apart, made sense of, assessed, and recombined the ideas of these texts. A synthesis essay most likely incorporates the following features:

TYPICAL FEATURES OF A SYNTHESIS ESSAY

- A statement of the synthesis question that shows your interest in the texts and presents this question as problematic and significant
- Short summaries of these texts to give your readers a sense of the readings you are working with
- A thesis that indicates how you have analyzed and synthesized the readings to arrive at a new perspective
- Your analysis of key points in these texts, determined in part by the synthesis question
- Your new view, which combines ideas gathered from readings with your own independent ideas

To review summary/strong response writing, see Chapter 5.

Student Example of a Synthesis Essay

Before we move to the writing project for this chapter—and to the idea-generating strategies of student writers who are analyzing and synthesizing texts—we show you a student example of a synthesis essay. This example, by student writer Kate MacAulay, was written for the writing project for this chapter and addresses the assigned question, "What effect is technology having on humanity and the quality of life in the twenty-first century?" The texts she was asked to analyze and synthesize are these two:

- George Ritzer, "The Irrationality of Rationality: Traffic Jams on Those 'Happy Trails.'" This is a chapter from Ritzer's widely discussed book *The McDonaldization of Society*. New Century Edition (Thousand Oaks, CA: Pine Forge Press, 2000).
- Sherry Turkle, "Who Am We?" published in the magazine *Wired* 4.1 (January 1996): 148–52, 194–99.

We have not reprinted these two lengthy texts; however, later in this chapter, we include students' summaries of both articles and the informal and analytical exploratory pieces of another student writer, Kara Watterson, in order to show you helpful steps in writing synthesis essays.

Kate MacAulay (student)

Technology's Peril and Potential

Introduces focusing questions and context

Introduces the texts to be analyzed

Brief summary of Ritzer's text

Brief summary of Turkle's text

Thesis statement with analytical points and synthesis points

Recently in English class, we have been focusing on the question, What effect is technology having on humanity and the quality of life in the twenty-first century? We have had heated discussions about the use of cell phones, palm pilots, beepers, e-mail, chat rooms, texting, and the Web. As part of my investigation of this question, I read two texts: a chapter from George Ritzer's book *The McDonaldization of Society*, entitled "The Irrationality of Rationality: Traffic Jams on Those 'Happy Trails,'" and an article published in the magazine *Wired* entitled "Who Am We?", by Sherry Turkle. In his chapter, Ritzer, a sociology professor, explains how technology has rationalized businesses and many facets of society following the McDonald's model. He argues that modern technology is causing loss of quality products, time, and relationships. In the McDonaldized system, where everything is designed logically for economy and convenience, things have become more artificial, and our relationships have become more superficial. In her article "Who Am We?", Sherry Turkle, a psychology professor at MIT, shows how computers and the Internet are transforming our views of ourselves and the way we interact socially. Focusing on computers' capacities for simulation and promoting interaction, Turkle has explored MUDs (multiuser domains), which allow people to create virtual identities. MUDs, Turkle believes, contribute to the formation of postmodern multiple selves and raise new questions about personal identity and morality. Although both Turkle and Ritzer identify problems in technology's influence and in society's responses to it, Turkle sees more potential and gain where Ritzer sees mostly peril and loss. Both articles made me question how we define our values and morality in this postmodern, technologically advanced world and persuaded me of the need for caution in embracing technology.

Analytical point: compares and contrasts Ritzer's and Turkle's ideas

Analyzes and elaborates on Ritzer's ideas

Although Ritzer and Turkle both see technology as having some negative effects on human relations and the quality of life, they disagree about exactly where the most interesting and serious problems lie. Ritzer believes that the problems caused by technology are not problems within the individual, but problems imposed on the individual by McDonaldized systems. For example, Ritzer claims that fast-food restaurants encourage us to eat unhealthy food quickly and also contribute to "the disintegration of the family" (141) by taking away family time. He also believes that rationalized systems create illusions of fun, reality, and friendliness. He talks about the "scripted interactions" (138) that employees are supposed to have with customers, where they are told exactly what to say to every customer, making interactions less real. Further, rationalized systems are dehumanizing in the kinds of jobs they create that "don't offer much in the way of satisfaction or stability" (137), benefiting only stockholders, owners, and employers.

Analyzes, contrasts, and elaborates on Turkle's ideas

In contrast, Turkle responds to technology's threat by focusing inward on technology's effect on the self and on relationships. While she is clearly intrigued by such Internet capabilities as multiuser domains, she acknowledges that this potential for multiple simultaneous identities threatens the wholeness of individuals, possibly damaging our emotional and psychological selves. Her concern is that people become addicted to these games because in the virtual world it is easy to create better "selves," to be what you wish you were. Turkle shows that people can lose themselves between the real world and the virtual world and be "imprisoned by the screens" (199). Although the virtual world is exciting and fun, she notes that "[o]ur experiences there are serious play" (199). She also examines cases of virtual characters who get into relationships with other characters, including cyber-sex relationships. She ponders the issue of cyber-sex immorality and adultery.

Despite Turkle and Ritzer's agreement that technology can damage us as a society, they disagree on their overall outlook and on our power to respond positively to technology's influence. I find Ritzer's views almost entirely negative. He believes that we are irreversibly damaged by technological advances because we are completely caught up in the McDonaldized system, with few parts of society left unchanged. Almost all of the family-owned neighborhood restaurants or mom-and-pop grocery stores have been taken over by franchises like Red Robin or Safeway. The costs of these rationalized systems, he says, are "inefficiency, illusions of various types, disenchantment, dehumanization, and homogenization" (124). In this chapter of his book, Ritzer doesn't mention any ways that our lives could be improved by these systems; he gives only examples of the way we are misled and damaged by them.

Analytical point: compares and contrasts Ritzer's and Turkle's ideas

Analyzes and elaborates on Ritzer's ideas

Presents writer's independent thinking

Turkle's approach strikes me as much more positive and balanced than Ritzer's. Optimistically, she explains that MUDs can give people self-knowledge that they can apply to real life: "[t]he anonymity of MUDs gives people the chance to express multiple and often unexplored aspects of the self, to play with their identity and to try out new ones" (152). Turkle sees an opportunity for us to grow as individuals and to learn to use technology in a positive way: "If we can cultivate awareness of what stands behind our screen personae, we are more likely to succeed in using virtual experience for personal transformation" (199). I think Turkle's views are more complex than Ritzer's. She believes that we have to take responsibility for our own habits and psychological responses to technology. She encourages us to be aware of how we interact with technology and believes that we can grow as individuals using this technology.

Analyzes, contrasts, and elaborates on Turkle's ideas

Presents writer's independent thinking

After reading these articles, I have realized how the continuing advancement of technology raises new moral questions. In a McDonaldized system, where everything is designed for convenience, there seem to be many places for morals to be left out of the picture. For example, is it okay for us to exchange real human interaction for convenience and saving time? Is there something wrong with our ethics when interesting and fulfilling jobs are eliminated by machines or replaced by dead-end, low-paying Mcjobs? Turkle too shows us how virtual worlds pose new moral questions for us. In MUDs, people can form virtual relationships, even cyber-sex relationships. The people behind the characters are real people, even if they are acting as someone else. If a married person has a cyber-sex relationship on a MUD, is he or she cheating? If a person commits a virtual assault or other crime that has no real-world, physical effects, should he or she feel guilty or sinful for the intention? Ritzer and Turkle have made me see how important these questions are.

Transition to writer's synthesis. Synthesis point discusses writer's own view

Elaborates on the connections the writer is making

Reading the articles made me strongly believe that we must use this technology in moderation in order to preserve individual qualities and our relationships. From our class discussions, I remember what Scott said about the way that the Internet connects people. He said that people like his uncle, who was severely injured on the job, use the

Synthesis point discusses writer's own view

Internet as a way of "getting out" to meet people and socialize. He pointed out how the Microsoft Gaming Zone has brought his uncle into an ongoing backgammon tournament through which he has made friends. Meanwhile his aunt has gotten a lot of pleasure out of playing and problem solving in the world of MUDs.

Synthesis point discusses writer's own view

But my own experience has left me concerned about the danger we face as emotional, social beings in the face of technology. The other night at a family gathering, one of my cousins, after discussing car buying with some of the relatives, got the urge to research new car prices. He left the room, logged onto the Internet, and spent the rest of the evening looking at cars and prices. We saw him only once the whole evening when he came out to get a slice of pie. My cousin's withdrawal from the conversation made me think about Ritzer's and Turkle's concerns that technology decreases real interactions among people.

Transition and final connections

Conclusion

Ritzer and Turkle offer us a warning that technology can be damaging if we don't recognize and overcome its dangers. I would encourage us not to let ourselves become dominated by technology, not to let it take our full attention just because it is there, and not to overlook the complex moral questions that technology poses. The convenience that technology offers—our e-mail, cell phones, and debit cards—should help us save time that can be spent in nurturing our relationships with other people. The real challenge is to find ways to become even better people because of technology.

Complete citation of articles in MLA format

Works Cited

Ritzer, George. *The McDonaldization of Society*. Thousand Oaks, CA: Pine Forge, 2000. Print.

Turkle, Sherry. "Who Am We?" *Wired* Jan. 1996: 148+. Print.

WRITING PROJECT: A Synthesis Essay

Write a synthesis essay that meets the following criteria:

- Addresses a synthesis question that your instructor provides or that you formulate for yourself
- Summarizes and analyzes the views of at least two writers on this question
- Shows how you have wrestled with different perspectives on the question and have synthesized these ideas to arrive at your own new view of the question.

Ideas for Synthesis Questions and Readings

The writing project for this chapter draws on the kinds of texts you will typically be asked to synthesize in your college courses. This text provides a number of options from which your instructor can choose. Some instructors may assign both the readings and the synthesis questions. Others may assign the readings but invite students to pose their own questions. Still others may leave both the questions and the readings up to the students. The following list of questions and readings found in this text gives you options for subject matter and focus for synthesis essays.

Reading Options for This Assignment

Synthesis Questions	Possible Readings
How have cell phones affected the lives of American citizens?	• Nikki Swartz, "Mobile Phone Tracking Scrutinized," pp. 302–303 • Terry J. Allen, "Reach Out and Track Someone," pp. 303–305
What are the biggest obstacles in managing the problem of undocumented immigrants? What should the United States do to make progress in solving this problem?	Two or more of the excerpts from blogs collected in the Readings section of this chapter, pp. 324–330
What should be our attitude toward outsourcing of American jobs? What is the most reasonable approach to solving problems caused by outsourcing?	• Thomas L. Friedman, "30 Little Turtles," pp. 124–125 • David Horsey, "Today's Economic Indicator" (editorial cartoon) p. 128 • Mike Lane, "Labor Day Blues" (editorial cartoon), p. 129 • Froma Harrop, "New Threat to Skilled U.S. Workers," pp. 130–131
Should the United States increase its production of electricity by building more nuclear power plants or by pursuing some other form of energy?	• David Rockwood, "A Letter to the Editor," pp. 6–7 • William Sweet, "Why Uranium Is the New Green," pp. 362–365 • Stan Eales, "Welcome to Sellafield" (editorial cartoon), p. 366 • Editorial from the *Los Angeles Times*, "No to Nukes," pp. 367–369

Using Learning Logs

In our view, a productive way to generate ideas for your synthesis essay is to break your process into a series of incremental thinking steps that take you gradually from summaries of your chosen texts to an analysis of them and finally to a synthesis of their ideas with your own. The five learning log tasks in the sections that follow will guide you through this process. On several occasions you will have an opportunity to share your learning log explorations with classmates and to use these logs to generate further discussion of ideas. Your instructor will specify whether completion of these learning log tasks will be a requirement for this assignment. In our view, the learning log tasks work best if you keep your writing informal and exploratory with an emphasis on idea generation rather than on corrections and polish.

Exploring Your Texts through Summary Writing

Learning Log Task 1: Write a 200–250-word summary of each of the main texts you will use in your final paper.

Instructions on how to write a summary are found on pp. 99–102.

As a starting point for grappling with a writer's ideas, writing careful summaries prompts you to read texts with the grain, adopting each text's perspective and walking in each author's shoes. When you summarize a text, you try to achieve an accurate, thorough understanding of it by stating its main ideas in a tightly distilled format.

Instructions on how to use attributive tags are found in Skill 21.3.

What follows are student Kara Watterson's summary of the book chapter by Ritzer and student Kate MacAulay's summary of Turkle's article—the two readings they will use in their synthesis essays. Notice how they use attributive tags to show that they are representing Ritzer's and Turkle's ideas as objectively as they can and that these ideas belong to Ritzer or Turkle, not to them.

KARA'S SUMMARY OF RITZER'S CHAPTER

In "The Irrationality of Rationality," the seventh chapter in *The McDonaldization of Society*, sociologist George Ritzer identifies a major sociological and economic problem: in an effort to find the most efficient way to run a business (what Ritzer calls "rationalizing"), more and more companies are following the franchise model pioneered by McDonald's. Although McDonaldization is efficient and economical for the companies, Ritzer argues it can be irrational, inconvenient, inefficient, and costly for consumers who often stand in long lines at fast-food restaurants and supermarkets. Ritzer also claims that McDonaldized systems cause people to forfeit real fun for manufactured fun and illusion. He cites the example of fake international villages at amusement parks and the fake friendliness of the "scripted interactions" (138) that employees are supposed to have with customers. Ritzer explains that our McDonaldized society has begun focusing more on quantity than quality. He believes that McDonaldized systems are dehumanizing: jobs "don't offer much in the way of satisfaction or stability" (137) and families hardly ever eat together any more, a situation that is contributing to the "disintegration of the family" (141). Ritzer also argues that by franchising everywhere, we are losing cultural distinctions. Whether you are in Japan or the United States, products are beginning to look the same. Finally, Ritzer shows that when companies become rationalized, they limit the possibility of connection between human beings. Citing examples from fast-food restaurants to hospitals, he states that there are many serious drawbacks to "our fast-paced and impersonal society" (140).

KATE'S SUMMARY OF TURKLE'S ARTICLE

In her *Wired* article "Who Am We?" psychologist and MIT professor Sherry Turkle explores how computers and the Internet are transforming our views of ourselves and the way we interact socially. Turkle believes that the Internet is moving us toward a "decentered" (149) sense of the self. She says that computers used to be thought of as "calculating machines" (149), but they are increasingly now seen as intelligent objects capable of interaction and simulation. She uses children's interactive computer games to illustrate how some people now think of computers as having personalities and psyches, which make them "fitting partners for dialog and relationship" (150). In the second half of her article, she argues that virtual life raises new moral issues. She uses the example of MUDs (multiuser domains), which allow people to create multiple and often simultaneous virtual identities by playing different characters. She presents examples of the relationships of cyber characters—often cyber-sex—that raise the question of whether cyber-sex is an act of real-life infidelity or adultery. Turkle concludes that it is easy for people to lose themselves between the real world and these virtual worlds. Because we have the ability to create better "selves" in the virtual world, it is possible to become addicted to virtual life and be "imprisoned by the screens" (199). According to Turkle, we are moving toward a "postmodernist culture of simulation" (149), and she cautions that it is more important than ever that we are very self-aware.

FOR WRITING AND DISCUSSION

Summarizing Your Texts

Working in small groups or as a whole class, share your summaries of your two chosen or assigned readings. What important main ideas does your group agree must be included in a summary of each text? What points are secondary and can be left out?

Exploring Your Texts' Rhetorical Strategies

Learning Log Task 2: Analyze the rhetorical strategies used in each of your texts (for example, the way your texts handle purpose; audience; genre; angle of vision; appeals to *logos, ethos*, and *pathos*, and use of evidence).

Explanations of these terms and concepts are found in Concepts 3, 8, and 9.

In order to analyze a text and synthesize its ideas, you need to consider the text rhetorically. To whom is the author writing and why? Do you see how the genre of each text influences some of the author's choices about language and structure? What angle of vision shapes each text and accounts for what is included and excluded? Do you share the values of the author or of his or her intended audience?

In the next sections, we show examples of Kara's exploratory thinking. Here is Kara's learning log entry exploring the rhetorical contexts of the Ritzer and Turkle texts:

Instructions on how to write a rhetorical critique of a text are found in Chapter 5 on pp. 104–106.

KARA'S RESPONSE TO LEARNING LOG TASK 2

Although both George Ritzer and Sherry Turkle are scholars, their texts are not really written for scholarly audiences. Both would fall in the category of nonfiction books (articles) written for general audiences and both are written to raise audience awareness of sociological/cultural problems—in this case, the way that technological advances and the fast-food model of business are affecting the quality of life and the way that the Internet is affecting our sense of ourselves and our relationships.

Both Ritzer and Turkle have chosen to write in accessible language so that their ideas can easily be understood by a general audience, and both use many examples to build credibility. Still, because I had no previous personal background with multiuser domains, I found it challenging to imagine some of Turkle's descriptions of the virtual world of MUDs, but I did have previous experience with all of Ritzer's examples so I never felt in over my head while reading his chapters.

From Ritzer's angle of vision, McDonaldization has had a damaging and irreversible effect on the quality of contemporary life, and he is trying to prompt people to slow down this destructive process. His approach is quite one-sided, though. He does admit that "we undoubtedly have gained much from the rationalization of society in general" (132), but he does not develop this idea any further. He refuses to make any further concessions to the rationalization he is fighting. Instead of acknowledging contradicting ideas, Ritzer hammers his point strongly with example after example. By the end of the chapter, the reader is left with a glazed-over feeling, not really taking in the information.

Kara defines "rationalization" in the opening sentences of her summary of Ritzer, p. 312.

Turkle's angle of vision seems to include curiosity and exploration as well as concern about the way computers are transforming society. She seems to analyze more than argue. She is trying to get across her notion that the Internet lets people adopt many different characters and have multiple selves, for example when they play in MUDs and simulation games. So maybe, in claiming that computers are no longer calculating machines, Turkle, like Ritzer, is only presenting one limited view of her subject, the view that interests her as a psychologist who has written many books and articles on computers, and our changing sense of identity and community.

FOR WRITING AND DISCUSSION

Examining the Rhetorical Strategies of Your Texts

Working in small groups or as a whole class, share what each of you discovered in Learning Log Task 2. Try to reach consensus on the most important rhetorical features of each of the texts you are using for your synthesis essay.

Exploring Main Themes and Similarities and Differences in Your Texts' Ideas

Learning Log Task 3: Identify main issues or themes in your assigned or chosen texts. Then explore the similarities and differences in their ideas.

This learning log task asks you to identify main issues, ideas, or themes that surface in your texts as preparation for looking for similarities and differences among your texts. This process of thinking—comparison and contrast—will help you clarify your understanding of each reading and promote analysis of the underlying values, assumptions, and ideas of each author. Here are some questions that can guide your learning log writing at this stage of your thinking:

QUESTIONS TO HELP YOU GRAPPLE WITH SIMILARITIES AND DIFFERENCES IN YOUR TEXTS

- What main ideas or themes related to your synthesis question do you see in each text?
- What similarities and differences do you see in the way the authors choose to frame the issues they are writing about? How do their theses (either implied or stated) differ?

- What are the main similarities and differences in their angles of vision?
- What commonalities and intersections related to your synthesis question do you see in their ideas? What contradictions and clashes do you see in their ideas?
- What similarities and differences do you see in the authors' underlying values and assumptions?
- What overlap, if any, is there in these authors' examples and uses of terms?
- On the subject of your synthesis question, how would Author A respond to Author B?

Here is an excerpt from Kara's learning log, showing her exploratory analyses of Ritzer's and Turkle's texts. Note how she begins to organize comparisons by points, to make analytical connections among them, and to push herself to think out exactly where these authors agree and differ.

EXCERPT FROM KARA'S RESPONSE TO LEARNING LOG TASK 3

Both Ritzer and Turkle make strong comments about health problems that may be caused by the particular type of technology they are dealing with. For Ritzer, the dangers that arise from McDonaldization can most easily be seen in fast-food restaurants and their fatty, unhealthy foods: "such meals are the last things many Americans need, suffering as they do from obesity, high cholesterol levels, high blood pressure, and perhaps diabetes" (133). He also considers the high level of stress created by our high-speed society that can cause heart attacks, panic attacks, maybe nervous breakdowns. Turkle, too, is concerned about the effects of technology on people's health, but her focus is people's psyches and minds. One person in her research study who creates different identities on the Internet thinks that "MUDding has ultimately made him feel worse about himself" (196). For Turkle, the Internet can be dangerous for what it can do to a person's psyche.

Both authors agree that technological advances are causing a loss of real human connection. McDonaldization fosters fake contact; employees are given guidelines about how to interact with customers and are programmed with what to say and what not to say: "rule Number 17 for Burger King workers is 'Smiles at all times'" (Ritzer 130). Quick sales, not real customer relations, are the main concern. For Turkle too, this loss of human contact is a dilemma. MUDs are not places where you truly get to know a person; they are places where people are acting out characters. These are not real friends that can aid you when you are feeling ill or down. Also, people are spending vast quantities of time logging on, spending time with a computer screen instead of family and friends. . . .

FOR WRITING AND DISCUSSION

Generating Points about Themes, Shared Ideas, and Differences

Working as a whole class or in small groups, share your analyses of similarities and differences in your chosen or assigned texts. Pay close attention to these two overarching questions: How are the texts similar and different? How do each author's assumptions, beliefs, purposes, and values account for these similarities and differences?

Generating Ideas of Your Own

Learning Log Task 4: In light of what you have read and thought about so far, explore your own views on the original synthesis question that has guided your probing of the texts.

One of your biggest challenges in writing a synthesis essay is to move beyond analysis to synthesis. A successful synthesis essay incorporates ideas from your texts and yet represents your own independent thinking, showing evidence of the dialectic process. You need to think about how the differing perspectives of Texts A and B have led you to new realizations that will let you enter the conversation of these texts. As you begin to formulate your synthesis views, you will also need to reassert your personal/intellectual investment in the conversation of the texts. You will need to take ownership of the ideas and to emerge with a clearer sense of your own views. You may also want to consider which text—in your mind—makes the most significant contribution to the question you are exploring. You may want to evaluate the texts to determine which has influenced your thinking the most and why. The following questions should help you use Learning Log Task 4 to generate ideas of your own.

QUESTIONS TO HELP YOU DEVELOP YOUR OWN VIEWS

- What do I agree with and disagree with in the texts I have analyzed?
- How have these texts changed my perception and understanding of an issue, question, or problem? (You might want to use these prompts: "I used to think ________________, but now I think ________________." "Although these texts have persuaded me that ________________, I still have doubts about ________________.")
- Related to my synthesis question, what new, significant questions do these texts raise for me?
- What do I now see as the main controversies?
- What is my current view on the focusing question that connects my texts and that all my texts explore?
- How would I position myself in the conversation of the texts?
- If I find one author's perspective more valid, accurate, interesting, or useful than another's, why is that?

To illustrate this learning log task, we show you an excerpt from Kara's exploration.

EXCERPT FROM KARA'S RESPONSE TO LEARNING LOG TASK 4

When I was in Puerto Rico one spring break, I remember how excited my friend and I were to go to a burger place for dinner one night. It was so nice to have American food after days of eating fajitas and enchiladas. At the time, I did not think about how this American restaurant got to Puerto Rico; I was just glad it was there. However, after reading "The Irrationality of Rationality" by George Ritzer, I began to take a closer look at this experience. Both this article and "Who Am We?" have caused me to take a closer look at our society. ... What is it that causes people to surf the Internet for hours on end, to chat with people they have never met? What is this doing to our culture? Are we losing the distinctions evident when you travel from one region to the next, from one country to another? ...

Taking Your Position in the Conversation: Your Synthesis

Learning Log Task 5: Reread your first four learning logs and consider how your own views on the synthesis question have evolved and emerged. Think about the risky, surprising, or new views that you can bring to your readers. In light of your reading and thinking, explore what you want to say in your own voice to show the connections you have made and the new insights you now have.

After you have discovered what you think about the texts you have analyzed—what ideas you accept and reject, what new questions you have formulated, how your ideas have been modified and transformed through your reading experience—you need to find a way to pull your ideas together. Your synthesis view should be the fruit of your intellectual work, a perspective that you have come to after reading the ideas of other writers, pondering them reflectively and keenly. Here are some questions that can help you articulate the points that you want to develop in your essay:

QUESTIONS TO HELP YOU FORMULATE AND DEVELOP YOUR SYNTHESIS VIEWS

- What discoveries have I made after much thought?
- What are the most important insights I have gotten from these readings?
- What is my intellectual or personal investment with the synthesis question at this point?
- Where can I step out on my own, even take a risk, in my thinking about the ideas discussed in these texts?
- What new perspective do I want to share with my readers?

What follows is an excerpt from Kara's learning log. Note how she is beginning to find her stance on the synthesis question of whether technology enriches or dehumanizes our lives.

EXCERPT FROM KARA'S RESPONSE TO LEARNING LOG TASK 5

What is technology doing to our relationships with one another? Both Ritzer and Turkle seem to be urging us away from dependency on technology, and these authors have made me aware of my complacence in accepting technology, but still I see value in technology that these writers don't discuss. ...

I find myself questioning these writers' views. Ritzer seems to believe that families go to McDonald's rather than eat family meals together. He doesn't consider that it is when people are on the road or out already that these restaurants are visited, not when they are sitting at home deciding what is for dinner. Turkle also speaks of the loss of connection that can arise from people constantly at their computers. She raises some very important questions about what technology is doing to our relationships and self-image, but I think she focuses too much on MUDs. How many people actually are doing this MUDding? Also, there are some valid things that come out of relationships on the Internet. I know of several examples of people who have met their future spouses through chat rooms and Online Social Networks. When I left for college, I was not sure whom I would stay in touch with, but because of the Internet, I am able to stay connected to people I would have drifted away from otherwise.

Also, while we note the dangers of technology, I think we need to remember the benefits as well. I agree that cell phones are overused, but how often have cell phones saved people in emergencies or aided people stranded on the road with car problems? I hope to be a doctor. I have great appreciation for the way that cameras can see inside a patient as surgeons are operating and thus reduce the risk of many surgeries. . . .

FOR WRITING AND DISCUSSION

Generating Your Synthesis Points

Prior to the start of this task, work individually to write two or three main points that you want to make in the synthesis portion of your final essay. Working in small groups or as a whole class, share your short list of main points. Briefly explain to your group or to the whole class why these points interest you. Take notes on group ideas.

At this point, you might want to reread Kate MacAulay's synthesis essay (pp. 308–310), which shows evidence of the ideas discovered in the exploratory thinking she did in her learning logs. You can see how she selected, organized, and developed particular points that probably appeared as kernels in her exploratory writing, just as Kara's learning logs show her emerging ideas.

Shaping and Drafting

Your main project in shaping and drafting your synthesis essay is to move from the kernels of good ideas that you generated in your learning logs to a focused, fully developed, and logically organized discussion of these ideas. Focusing and organizing your ideas for a synthesis essay are both challenging writing tasks. We offer some suggestions for developing the analysis and synthesis sections of your essay and then for formulating a thesis that will direct and hold together your essay.

For the analysis part of your essay, identify the points in Learning Log Tasks 2 and 3 that strike you as the most interesting, lively, profound, or significant. The following strategies will help you focus and develop these ideas.

Strategies for Shaping the Analytical Section of Your Essay	
What to Consider in Planning the Analysis Section of Your Essay	**Questions and Decisions**
• Your analysis section lays the foundation for your synthesis. • The analysis section usually forms about one-half to two-thirds of your essay. • This section discusses several ways that your texts relate to your synthesis question.	• How many analytical points do you want to develop? • What are these points?
• Your analysis section should show that you have wallowed in the complexity of your texts. • It may include points about the rhetorical features of your texts (as in a rhetorical critique), and it may include points about the ideas (as in an ideas critique). • It should map out and explain a number of important similarities and differences in your texts.	Consider developing answers to these questions: • How do your texts frame the problem? How do they present different angles of vision? Where do they intersect in their perspectives and approaches? How do they argue and support their views with evidence? • How rhetorically effective are these texts? • What do the authors do to make their readers think?

For the synthesis part of your essay, use the following strategies to develop points that emerged for you from Learning Log Tasks 4 and 5.

Strategies for Shaping the Synthesis Section of Your Essay	
What to Consider in Planning the Synthesis Section of Your Essay	**Questions and Decisions**
• Your essay should build to your synthesis section. • Typically your synthesis ideas form at least one-third of your essay.	• How can you best show where the texts and their authors promote your own independent thinking? • What synthesis points do you want to explore and discuss?
• The synthesis section of your essay should show your informed, independent thinking. • It should show how you have worked your way to a new understanding.	• What new insights have you developed through studying these texts? • What new perspectives have you gained through the contrast and/or clash of different ideas? • How much or how little have these texts changed your views and why?

Writing a Thesis for a Synthesis Essay

In a synthesis essay, your thesis statement is particularly important and challenging to write. It sets up your readers' expectations, promising an illuminating view of the texts you have worked with. It should reflect earnest intellectual work, promise insights achieved through serious reflection, be your own original connection of ideas, and contain some element of risk and newness. Avoid bland, noncontestable thesis statements such as "These articles have both good and bad points."

For a full explanation of thesis statements, purpose statements, and mapping statements, see Skill 17.2.

See Chapter 2, Concept 5, for a discussion of how to avoid unsurprising, noncontestable thesis statements.

You will probably want to work back and forth between formulating your thesis statement and drafting the analysis and synthesis sections of your essay. We recommend that you map out a rough thesis, draft your essay, and then revise and sharpen your thesis. For a synthesis essay, it is sometimes difficult to write a one-sentence, high-level thesis statement that encompasses both your analysis and your synthesis points. In such cases, you can write two lower-level, more specific thesis statements—one for your analysis section and one for your synthesis section—and simply join them together. What is important is that your thesis forecasts your main analysis and synthesis points and creates a map for your reader. The following examples illustrate these different options.

LOW-LEVEL, TWO-SENTENCE THESIS

Lower-level thesis for analysis

Lower-level thesis for synthesis

Whereas Ritzer focuses on the way high-tech society makes us homogeneous and superficial, Turkle focuses on how the Internet unsettles traditional views of the self. Although I agree with Ritzer's argument that McDonaldization is dehumanizing, I think that role-playing in MUDs is actually a healthy way to oppose McDonaldization and expresses human desire to be creative, to develop the self, and to make human connections.

HIGH-LEVEL, ONE-SENTENCE THESIS

Writer chooses high-level, one-sentence thesis rather than two lower-level theses

Ritzer's attack on technological society and Turkle's more optimistic belief that it offers opportunity for growth and discovery have together forced me to consider the superficiality and vulnerability of human relationships in our high-tech society.

Organizing a Synthesis Essay

The biggest organizational decision you have to make in writing a synthesis essay is how much to summarize your texts and how to incorporate these summaries into your essay. Your decision should be guided by your audience's familiarity with the texts you are discussing and the complexity of the points you are making. Two ways of organizing a synthesis essay are shown in Figure 12.1.

Revising

As you revise your synthesis essay, make sure that you have set up the synthesis question effectively. Then work on clarifying and developing your analytical points while striving for an engaging style. Also consider how to make your synthesis views more clearly reflect your own wrestling with the texts' ideas. Think about finding the most interesting ways to show how these texts have enlarged and deepened your own views.

FIGURE 12.1 Two Frameworks for a Synthesis Essay

Framework 1

Introduction and summary of both texts (several paragraphs)	• Presents the synthesis question and hooks readers • Summarizes the texts (unless your instructor posits that readers have already read the texts, in which case you can omit the summaries or reduce them to one or two sentences each) • Presents your thesis, which maps out your main analytical and synthesis points (Your thesis might come at the end of the paragraphs with your summaries or in a mini-paragraph of its own.)
Analytical section	• Includes paragraphs discussing and developing your analytical points
Synthesis section	• Includes paragraphs discussing and developing your synthesis points
Concluding paragraph	• Reiterates the values and limitations of the texts you have analyzed • Pulls together your new insights • Leaves readers thinking about your views

Framework 2

Introduction	• Presents the synthesis question and hooks readers • Presents your thesis, which maps out your main analytical and synthesis points
Summary/analysis of first text	• Summarizes the first text • Analyzes the first text
Summary/analysis of second text	• Summarizes the second text • Analyzes the second text
Synthesis section	• Develops several main synthesis points
Concluding paragraph	• Reiterates values and limitations of the texts you have analyzed • Pulls together your new insights • Leaves readers thinking about your views

Questions for Peer Review

In addition to the generic peer review questions explained in skill 16.4, ask your peer reviewers to address these questions:

INTRODUCTION, SUMMARIES OF THE TEXT, AND THESIS

1. What works well about the writer's presentation of the synthesis question that connects the texts under examination? How could the writer better show this question's significance and problematic nature?

2. Where could the writer's summaries of the texts be expanded, condensed, or clarified? Where would the summaries be better located in the essay to help readers?
3. How could the thesis be made more focused, risky, and clear in setting up the writer's analytical and synthesis points?

ANALYTICAL SECTION OF THE ESSAY

1. How could the analytical points more clearly compare and contrast the authors' values, assumptions, angles of vision, or rhetorical strategies in addressing the synthesis question?
2. What further textual evidence could the writer add to develop these analytical points and make them more interesting or comprehensive?

SYNTHESIS SECTION OF THE ESSAY

1. How could the writer's synthesis points more clearly demonstrate the writer's thoughtful interaction with these texts?
2. What examples or other specifics could the writer include to develop these synthesis points more effectively?
3. How could the writer conclude this essay more effectively to leave readers with a new perspective on the texts and on the underlying question?

The readings in this chapter immerse you in a network of issues about illegal immigration and immigration reform, which continue to be volatile and contested. (Also connected to this issue is the exercise on news photographs in Chapter 10, pp. 241–243.) These issues cut across political parties and continue to perplex citizens, policymakers, and immigrants. Experts estimate that eleven to twelve million people have illegally crossed the border between the United States and Mexico and are currently living and working in the United States. What caused these persons to risk the dangers of border crossing in order to work in the United States? What questions about human rights and domestic security does this problem raise? What forces are interfering with effective policy discussions and decision making to solve these problems?

For this chapter's readings, we present five blogs on these issues. ("Blog" is an abbreviation for "Web log.") Blogging has become a popular arena for political discourse worldwide as well as for discourse on any subject ranging from hobbies to sports to conspiracy theories. The blogosphere constitutes a new and rapidly evolving rhetorical context open to anyone who desires to create a blogsite or respond to postings on someone else's site. Persons often blog under online pseudonyms. Because a blogger tends to attract persons with similar interests and views, a blogsite serves as a "virtual café" for like-minded people to exchange views. Consequently, blogs often have an uncomfortable "insider feel" for persons trying to enter a blog conversation for the first time. They are also often characterized by informal, colloquial, and occasionally obscene language that wouldn't be encountered in print media. Some widely known and highly influential sites—such as the Daily Kos on the left or MichelleMalkin or Little Green Footballs on the right—are major players in United States political debate. Many people now think that skilled and knowledgeable bloggers play a more important "free press" investigative role in our democracy than do major newspapers dominated by corporate interests.

To avoid influencing your own analysis of these readings, we omit the discussion questions that typically follow in other chapters. However, as you read each blog, consider the particular blogsite that is hosting this piece (mentioned in the headnote) and also think about these general questions: How does the writer frame the issue? What is the writer's main argument? What types of evidence are included? What is distinctive about the way the writer expresses his or her ideas?

Our first blog is by a Mexican-American woman who identifies herself only as "Dee." According to her blogsite, Dee is a United States citizen with a Hispanic ethnicity. She holds a mid-level management position in a large corporation. Upset by the divisive discourse over immigration, Dee started her own blogsite called "Immigration Talk with a Mexican American: Truth, Honesty, and the American Way." In the blog reprinted below (posted on August 7, 2007), she sums up her placement of blogosphere views of immigration in two categories: the PROs (those who support comprehensive immigration reform) and the ANTIs (those who oppose it). She places herself firmly among the PROs. In this brief blog, her reference to the 12M stands for the estimated twelve million undocumented workers currently in the United States. Her use of abbreviations suggests the insider audience characteristic of blog discourse.

Dee

Comprehensive Immigration Reform: PROs and ANTIs

http://immigrationmexicanamerican.blogspot.com/2007/08/comprehensive-immigration-reform-pros.html

1 Our country is divided on how to resolve our Immigration issues in our country. Comprehensive Immigration Reform (CIR) is needed. Who is for CIR? PROs. Who is against CIR? ANTIs. What are their perspectives?

2 Pro Profile: There are many, many PRO groups. Each group has a different motivation and they rarely rally together. The largest group is Hispanic Americans. The ethnicities vary and include: Mexican, Central and South American, Cuban, Puerto Rican and more. The majority of PROs who post on the internet are from this group. Other Minority groups include Asian, Southern European, Middle Eastern, African. I only see their posts when I search the international sites. Other PRO groups who also rarely post include: Churches and Humanitarian groups, Businesses that prosper from sales to the 12M (e.g. Banks, Insurance Companies, Retail, etc.), Businesses experiencing Labor Shortages that hire the 12M (e.g. Farming, IT, Construction, Contractors, Retail, etc), Politicians with reasons to support the 12M (e.g. enhance Globalization, running for office, etc). And, of course, the illegal immigrants themselves. The majority of PROs who do post tend to have the following views: They advocate secure borders, sanctioning employers and comprehensive immigration reform (because the current program is broken). The biggest difference between the ANTIs and the PROs is, the PROs advocate a path to citizenship for the 12M, particularly since most of the 12M have worked and contributed to this country for + 5–20 years.

3 ANTI Profile: American. The majority are Anglos. (Anglos = white, Northern European ethnicity). Viewpoint: The majority advocate Deportation (mass or self) of the illegal immigrants in this country. Anything short of Deportation is termed Amnesty by the ANTIs. Many call for a 2000 mile southern border fence. They advocate for restrictive Official English laws even though English is already the National Language. They advocate for changing the 14th amendment and birthright citizenship, hoping to end, what they term "Anchor Babies." There are a few legal immigrants and minorities within their groups, but not many. There are a few politicians that support them, not many. There are hundreds of ANTI websites across the internet. There are hundreds of ANTI radio shows across the country. ANTIs tend to be very angry. They try their darndest to get African Americans to join forces with them citing their uncorroborated claim [that] the 12M drag down the minimum wage. The ANTIs tend to forget the deep alliances between the two ethnic groups which were forged over the previous four decades when they marched together for civil rights. Some of the Worst Terms the ANTIs use: 3rd World Country, Mexifornia, return to American Values.

Our next reading is a blog by Byron Williams, an African-American syndicated columnist. According to his online biography, the Reverend Byron Williams is "a writer, theologian, and activist [who] fuses theology with public policy to bring a fresh social justice perspective to the public arena." He serves as pastor of the Resurrection Community Church in Oakland, California. This blog was posted on The Huffington Post on May 9, 2006.

Byron Williams

Immigration Frenzy Points Out Need for Policy Debate

http://www.huffingtonpost.com/byron-williams/immigration-frenzy-points_b_20717.html

1 As a child I recall Thanksgiving with mixed emotions. I enjoyed the big family feast with relatives I had not seen since the previous Thanksgiving, but I dreaded the days after. It was turkey ad nauseam. By the sixth day my father would make what he called "Turkey a la King," which was turkey remnants along with whatever else he could find to put in the pot.

2 As emotions flare on both sides of the immigration debate it has morphed into "Immigration a la King." But unlike my father's mysterious concoction, the ingredients are well known. It consists of one part legitimate public policy, one part ethnocentrism, and one part political pandering.

3 There is no doubting we need a legitimate public policy conversation around illegal immigration. The porous nature of America's borders coupled with the post 9/11 climate does warrant national concern.

4 If, however, we remove the legitimate public policy aspect, what's left? What's left is ugly, reactionary fear-based hatred symbolizing America at its worst.

5 With 9/11 approaching its 5th anniversary, why are we just getting around to dealing with immigration? Like a wounded, cornered animal, the Republican-led Congress and the president conveniently fan the flames of one of America's greatest tragedies, resurfacing fear, in order to gain short-term political points.

6 It is hard to embrace the concept that at this late date the administration and Congress are worried about Al Qaeda members coming across the border in man made tunnels or in the back of trucks when you consider the 9/11 attackers entered the country legally.

7 They have successfully created a climate where vigilantes known as the Minutemen—who do a disservice to the brave individuals who fought during the Revolutionary War by embracing the name—are viewed as patriotic by taking the law into their own hands allegedly protecting America's borders.

8 How many poor white southerners willingly accepted a death sentence by fighting for the Confederacy to protect a "southern way of life" in which they did not participate? They were seductively lured, in part, by the notion that all hell would break loose if emancipated African slaves were elevated to their same impoverished status.

9 The ethnocentrism and political pandering has sadly infected parts of the African American community. If one removes the veil of objecting to the comparisons between the civil rights movement and Hispanic immigration demonstrations, which a number of African Americans hide behind, they would discover the same fear that plagues the dominant culture.

10 This does not dismiss the obvious concerns about the plight of low-skilled African Americans who find themselves competing with immigrants for certain entry-level employment. But again, this is part of the much needed public policy debate that is submerged under the current political frenzy.

11 Freely throwing around words such [as] "illegal" and "Al Qaeda" opens the door to dehumanization. And once an individual has been dehumanized that individual can be taken advantage of.

12 Even those who compassionately advocate for a guest worker program, forget that the last such program that existed on a large scale in this country was struck down by Abraham Lincoln on September 22, 1863.

13 There are legitimate concerns on both sides of this issue. But history has shown us there is something wrong when marginalized groups are systematically pitted against each other.

14 For all of the cries to protect the borders and the loss of job opportunities for low-skilled Americans, I doubt there would be 11 million undocumented individuals in the country if no one was hiring. There can be no legitimate immigration debate that does not hold the business community equally accountable for hiring undocumented individuals while paying less than a living wage.

15 Each individual must come to his or her decision as to how they feel about immigration. But the only way to have an authentic policy is to have an authentic policy debate—one that does not include the unnecessary ingredients that ultimately lead to dehumanization.

Our third reading, by Victor Davis Hanson, is a posting to Roundup: Historians' Take, a spot for "historians writing about the news," on the History News Network site. Victor Davis Hanson, a former professor of classics and now a Senior Fellow at the Hoover Institution, is known as a military historian, a political essayist, and a regular conservative columnist for the *National Review* and Tribune Media Services. He has published numerous books and his writing has appeared frequently in such well-known newspapers and journals as the *New York Times*, the *Wall Street Journal*, and the *American Spectator.* He also blogs regularly at Pajamas Media. This posting appeared on Wednesday, June 6, 2007.

Victor Davis Hanson

The Global Immigration Problem

http://hnn.us/roundup/entries/39776.html

1 Thousands of aliens crossing our 2,000-mile border from an impoverished Mexico reflect a much larger global one-way traffic problem.

2 In Germany, Turkish workers—both legal and illegal—are desperate to find either permanent residence or citizenship.

3 "Londonstan" is slang for a new London of thousands of unassimilated Pakistani nationals.

4 In France, there were riots in 2005 because many children of North African immigrants are unemployed—and unhappy.

5 Albanians flock to Greece to do farm work, and then are regularly deported for doing so illegally.

6 The list could go on.

7 So why do millions of these border-crossers head to Europe, the United States or elsewhere in the West?

8 Easy. Stable democracies and free markets ensure economic growth, rising standards of living and, thus, lots of jobs, while these countries' birth rates and native populations fall.

9 Employers may console themselves that they pay better than what the immigrants earned back at home. This might be true, but the wages are never enough to allow such newcomers to achieve parity with their hosts.

10 Naturally, immigrants soon get angry. And rather than showing thanks for a ticket out of the slums of Mexico City or Tunis, blatant hypocrisy can follow: the once thankful, but now exhausted, alien may wave the flag of the country he would never return to while shunning the culture of the host county he would never leave.

11 In the second generation—as we see from riots in France or gangs in Los Angeles—things can get even worse.

12 The moment illegal immigrants arrive, a sort of race begins: can these newcomers become legal, speak the host language and get educated before they age, get hurt or lose their job? If so, then they assimilate and their children are held up as models of diversity. If not, the end of the story can be welfare or jail.

13 Hypocrisy abounds on all sides. Free-marketers claim they must have cheap workers to stay competitive. Yet they also count on public subsidies to take care of their former employees when old, sick or in trouble.

14 Governments in countries such as Mexico and Morocco usually care far more about their emigrants once they are long gone. Then these poor are no longer volatile proof of their own failures, but victims of some wealthy foreign government's indifference. And these pawns usually send cash home.

15 The lower middle classes complain most about massive immigration, but then they have to compete with aliens for jobs, often live among them and don't use their services. The wealthier, who hire immigrants for low wages and see them only at work, often think mass immigration, even if illegal, is wonderful.

16 The lasting solution is not the status quo—or even walls, fines, deportation, amnesty or guest-worker programs. Instead, failed societies in Latin America, Africa and much of the Middle East must encourage family planning and get smarter about using their plentiful natural wealth to keep more of their own people home.

17 The remedy for the richer West?

18 It is past time to remember that paying our own poorer laborers more, doing some occasional physical work and obeying the laws—the immigration ones especially—are not icky or a bummer. Rather, this is the more ethical and, in the long run, cheaper approach.

19 There is a final irony. The more Western elites ignore their own laws, allow unassimilated ethnic ghettos and profit from an exploitive labor market, the more their own nations will begin to resemble the very places immigrants fled from.

Our final two pieces focus on disagreements over the "temporary guest worker" program that was part of an immigration reform bill considered (and ultimately rejected) by Congress in 2007. One provision of the bill would have allowed currently illegal immigrants to stay in the United States legally for up to six years as guest workers. In this excerpt from a posting on The Hill Blog, Republican Senator Mike Crapo from Idaho explains why he supported the guest worker provision of the bill, although he eventually voted against the bill for other reasons.

Senator Mike Crapo

Excerpt from "Immigration Policy Must Help Economy While Preserving Ideals"

http://blog.thehill.com/2007/07/07/immigration-policy-must-help-economy-while-preserving-ideals-sen-mike-crapo/

A robust economy hinges on having a temporary guest worker program to fill jobs that are not filled by American citizens. U.S.-based businesses need economic incentives to keep operations stateside. If they have a dependable labor pool at all skill levels, incentives to move operations overseas are greatly decreased. We appreciate consumer goods and agriculture products "Made in America." We can keep things that way by approaching immigration rationally and sensibly. Whatever the skill level, any temporary guest worker system must be enforceable and reliable for the worker and employer. Once Americans have been given "first right" to jobs, employers such as the agriculture industry must have access to a system that's cost-effective, not bureaucratic, and doesn't carry the risk of prosecution while employers are trying to comply with the law. Congress understands the urgency of reaching a workable solution and is moving in the right direction.

Our last piece is an excerpt from "The Progressive Case Against the Immigration Bill," which appeared in the liberal blog The Daily Kos on June 25, 2007. It gives a different view of the temporary guest worker program than that expressed by Senator Mike Crapo. The author of this piece is "Trapper John," the online identity for Jake McIntyre, who is a contributing editor for The Daily Kos.

Trapper John

Excerpt from "The Progressive Case Against the Immigration Bill"

http://www.dailykos.com/story/2007/6/25/73229/6647

1 This immigration bill is an historically bad bill, one that will undermine wage markets and which will permanently cripple skills training in vital sectors of the

economy. … [T]he fatal flaw in this bill isn't "amnesty"—it's the euphemistically termed "temporary worker program."

2 The temporary worker program has nothing to do with immigration policy. To the contrary—it is a guaranteed cheap labor program grafted on to an immigration bill. When most people think of "immigration" to the US, they think of people coming to America to build a new life for themselves and their families, just as their ancestors did. But the temporary worker program has nothing to do with building American families and American dreams. Under the program, *400,000–600,000 guest workers would enter the country every year* on two-year visas. Although the visas can be renewed twice, recipients would be denied any path to permanent residency or citizenship. In fact, the guest workers would be precluded from even applying for permanent residency while here on temporary visas.

3 In short, the "temporary workers" will be just that—"temporary," and "workers." Not "immigrants." And they can never be "Americans." Instead, we will have created a permanent caste of non-citizens with no hope of ever becoming citizens. A class of over half-a-million workers without a voice in the political process, here at the sole sufferance of their employers. And those employers won't have to pay their new indentured servants any more than the minimum wage. See, unlike the existing H-2B visa—the visa that governs most "unskilled" temporary workers in the US today—the proposed temporary worker program contains no requirements that employers pay their temporary help the federally determined "prevailing wage" for their occupation and the geographic area. Today, if a contractor can't find a qualified electrician to work on a project in Chicago, the contractor can apply for an H-2B visa. But the contractor is required to pay any foreign electrician entering the US on the H-2B no less than $53.57 per hour, including benefits. That's the prevailing wage for an electrician in Chicago, according to the Department of Labor. And by requiring H-2B sponsors to pay their foreign help the prevailing wage, the H-2B program limits the ability of employers to use guest workers as a tool to undermine wage markets. The proposed temporary worker plan changes all that.

4 Under the proposed plan, there is no wage floor. If the Chicago contractor can't find an electrician in the US to work on his project for $20 per hour, he can import a temporary worker who will. The result will be a swift collapse of wage markets in many industries populated by skilled non-professional workers, like construction. And all of a sudden, we'll be hearing that the work of an electrician is one of those "jobs Americans won't do," like fruit picking. The truth, of course, is that there is no job that an American won't do for the right price. But by creating a steady flow of temporary workers with no ability to stay in the country for more than a couple years, and no practical ability to fight for better wages, the number of jobs that "Americans won't do" will grow dramatically. And they include a host of the jobs that sustain and nourish the middle class. The construction trades. Cosmetology. Culinary arts. These are jobs that take years to master, and consequently pay quite well, because not just anybody can do them. But by busting open the labor markets for these jobs, and opening them with no restrictions to folks from countries with much lower costs of living, we will strangle the middle class lives of the millions of Americans who have proudly earned their paychecks with their skills. …

5 There's no question that we need immigration reform in this country. We need to find a way to bring the millions of immigrants laboring in the shadows into the light, and into our American family. And to the extent that we have bona fide labor shortages in this country, we need to address them through an expansion of legal immigration. But the price of immigration reform cannot be a temporary worker program that exploits foreign workers, limits real immigration, and guts wages for American workers.

WRITING A CLASSICAL ARGUMENT

13

The need for argument arises whenever members of a community disagree on an issue. Classical rhetoricians believed that the art of arguing is essential for good citizenship. If disputes can be resolved through exchange of perspectives, negotiation of differences, and flexible seeking of the best solutions to a problem, then nations won't have to resort to war or individuals to fisticuffs.

The writing project for this chapter introduces you to a classical way of arguing. Your goal is to persuade your audience to adopt your position or at least to regard it more openly or favorably.

In this chapter, you will learn to:

- take a stand on an issue
- offer reasons and evidence in support of your position
- summarize and respond to alternative views

What Is Argument?

The study of argumentation involves two components: truth seeking and persuasion:

- By *truth seeking,* we mean a diligent, open-minded, and responsible search for the best course of action or solution to a problem, taking into account all the available information and alternative points of view.
- By *persuasion,* we mean the art of making a claim* on an issue and justifying it convincingly so that the audience's initial resistance to your position is overcome and they are moved toward your position.

These two components of argument seem paradoxically at odds: Truth seeking asks us to relax our certainties and be willing to change our views; persuasion asks us to be certain, to be committed to our claims, and to get others to change their views. We can overcome this paradox if we dispel two common but misleading views of argument. The most common view is that argument is a fight as in "I just got into a horrible argument with my roommate." This view of argument as a fist-waving, shouting match in which you ridicule anyone who disagrees with you (popularized by radio and television talk shows and the Internet) entirely disregards argument as truth seeking, but it also misrepresents

*By long-standing tradition, the thesis statement of an argument is often called its "claim."

argument as persuasion because it polarizes people, rather than promoting understanding, new ways of seeing, and change.

Another common but misleading view is that argument is a pro/con debate modeled after high school or college debate matches. Although debating can be an excellent way to develop critical thinking skills, it misrepresents argument as a two-sided contest with winners and losers. Because controversial issues involve many different points of view, not just two, reducing an issue to pro/con positions distorts the complexity of the disagreement. Instead of thinking of *both* sides of an issue, we need to think of *all* sides. Equally troublesome, the debate image invites us to ask, "Who won the debate?" rather than "What is the best solution to the question that divides us?" The best solution might be a compromise between the two debaters or an undiscovered third position. The debate image tends to privilege the confident extremes in a controversy rather than the complex and muddled middle.

From our perspective, the best image for understanding argument is neither "fight" nor "debate" but the deliberations of a committee representing a wide spectrum of community voices charged with finding the best solution to a problem. From this perspective, argument is both a *process* and a *product.* As a process, argument is an act of inquiry characterized by fact-finding, information gathering, and consideration of alternative points of view. As a product, it is someone's contribution to the conversation at any one moment—a turn taking in a conversation, a formal speech, or a written position paper such as the one you will write for this chapter. The goal of argument as process is truth seeking; the goal of argument as product is persuasion. When members of a diverse committee are willing to argue persuasively for their respective points of view but are simultaneously willing to listen to other points of view and to change or modify their positions in light of new information or better arguments, then both components of argument are fully in play.

We cannot overemphasize the importance of both truth seeking and persuasion to your professional and civic life. Truth seeking makes you an informed and judicious employee and a citizen who delays decisions until a full range of evidence and alternative views are aired and examined. Persuasion gives you the power to influence the world around you, whether through letters to the editor or blogs on political issues or through convincing position papers for professional life. Whenever an organization needs to make a major decision, those who can think flexibly and write persuasively can wield great influence.

Exploring Classical Argument

An effective way to appreciate argument as both truth seeking and persuasion is to address an issue that is new to you and then watch how your own views evolve. Your initial position will probably reflect what social scientists sometimes call your personal *ideology*—that is, a network of basic values, beliefs, and assumptions that tend to guide your view of the world. However, if you adopt a truth-seeking attitude, your initial position may evolve as the conversation progresses. In fact, the conversation may even cause changes in some of your basic beliefs, since ideologies aren't set in stone and since many of us have unresolved allegiance to competing ideologies that may be logically inconsistent (for example, a belief in freedom of speech combined with a belief that hate speech should be banned). In this exercise we ask you to keep track of how your views change and to note what causes the change.

The case we present for discussion involves ethical treatment of animals.

> Situation: A bunch of starlings build nests in the attic of a family's house, gaining access to the attic through a torn vent screen. Soon the eggs hatch, and every morning at sunrise the family is awakened by the sound of birds squawking and wings beating against rafters as the starlings fly in and out of the house to feed the hatchlings. After losing considerable early morning sleep, the family repairs the screen. Unable to get in and out, the parent birds are unable to feed their young. The birds die within a day. Is this cruelty to animals?

1. Freewrite your initial response to this question. Was the family's act an instance of cruelty to animals (that is, was their act ethically justifiable or not)?
2. Working in small groups or as a whole class, share your freewrites and then try to reach a group consensus on the issue. During this conversation (argument as process), listen carefully to your classmates' views and note places where your own initial views begin to evolve.
3. So far we have framed this issue as an after-the-fact yes/no question: Is the family guilty of cruelty to animals? But we can also frame it as an open-ended, before-the-fact question: "What should the family have done about the starlings in the attic?" Suppose you are a family member discussing the starlings at dinner, prior to the decision to fix the vent screen. Make a list of your family's other options and try to reach class consensus on the two or three best alternative solutions.
4. At the end of the discussion, do another freewrite exploring how your ideas evolved during the discussion. What insights did you get about the twin components of argument, truth seeking and persuasion?

Understanding Classical Argument

Having introduced you to argument as both process and product, we now turn to the details of effective argumentation. To help orient you, we begin by describing the typical stages that mark students' growth as arguers.

Stages of Development: Your Growth as an Arguer

We have found that when we teach argument in our classes, students typically proceed through identifiable stages as their argumentative skills increase. While these stages may or may not describe your own development, they suggest the skills you should strive to acquire.

- ***Stage 1: Argument as personal opinion.*** At the beginning of instruction in argument, students typically express strong personal opinions but have trouble justifying their opinions with reasons and evidence and often create short, undeveloped arguments that are circular, lacking in evidence, and insulting to those who disagree. The following freewrite, written by a student first confronting the starling case, illustrates this stage:

> The family shouldn't have killed the starlings because that is really wrong! I mean that act was disgusting. It makes me sick to think how so many people are just willing to kill something for no reason at all. How are these parents going to teach their children values if they just go out and kill little birds for no good reason?!! This whole family is what's wrong with America!

This writer's opinion is passionate and heartfelt, but it provides neither reasons nor evidence why someone else should hold the same opinion.

- ***Stage 2: Argument structured as claim supported by one or more reasons.*** This stage represents a quantum leap in argumentative skill because the writer can now produce a rational plan containing point sentences (the reasons) and particulars (the evidence). The writer who produced the previous freewrite later developed a structure like this:

  The family's act constituted cruelty to animals

  - because the starlings were doing minimal harm.
  - because other options were available.
  - because the way they killed the birds caused needless suffering.

- ***Stage 3: Increased attention to truth seeking.*** In stage 3 students become increasingly engaged with the complexity of the issue as they listen to their classmates' views, conduct research, and evaluate alternative perspectives and stances. They are often willing to change their positions when they see the power of other arguments.
- ***Stage 4: Ability to articulate the unstated assumptions underlying their arguments.*** As we show later in this chapter, each reason in a writer's argument is based on an assumption, value, or belief (often unstated) that the audience must accept if the argument is to be persuasive. Often the writer needs to state these assumptions explicitly and support them. At this stage students identify and analyze their own assumptions and those of their intended audiences. Students gain increased skill at accommodating alternative views through refutation or concession.
- ***Stage 5: Ability to link an argument to the values and beliefs of the intended audience.*** In this stage students are increasingly able to link their arguments to their audience's values and beliefs and to adapt structure and tone to the resistance level of their audience. Students also appreciate how delayed-thesis arguments or other psychological strategies can be more effective than closed-form arguments when addressing hostile audiences.

The rest of this chapter helps you progress through these stages. Although you can read the remainder in one sitting, we recommend that you break your reading into sections, going over the material slowly and applying it to your own ideas in progress. Let the chapter's concepts and explanations sink in gradually, and return to them periodically for review. This section on "Understanding Classical Argument" comprises a compact but comprehensive course in argumentation.

Creating an Argument Frame: A Claim with Reasons

Somewhere in the writing process, whether early or late, you need to create a frame for your argument. This frame includes a clear question that focuses the argument, your claim, and one or more supporting reasons. Often your reasons, stated as *because* clauses, can be attached to your claim to provide a working thesis statement.

Finding an Arguable Issue At the heart of any argument is an **issue,** which we can define as a question that invites more than one reasonable answer and thus leads to perplexity or disagreement. This requirement excludes disagreements based on personal tastes, where no shared criteria can be developed ("Baseball is more fun than soccer"). It also excludes purely private questions because issues arise out of disagreements in communities.

Issue questions are often framed as yes/no choices, especially when they appear on ballots or in courtrooms: Should gay marriage be legalized? Should the federal government place a substantial tax on gasoline to elevate its price? Is this defendant guilty of armed robbery? Just as frequently, they can be framed openly, inviting many different possible answers: What should our city do about skateboarders in downtown pedestrian areas? How can we best solve the energy crisis?

It is important to remember that framing an issue as a yes/no question does not mean that all points of view fall neatly into pro/con categories. Although citizens may be forced to vote yes or no on a proposed ballot initiative, they can support or oppose the initiative for a variety of reasons. Some may vote happily for the initiative, others vote for it only by holding their noses, and still others oppose it vehemently but for entirely different reasons. To argue effectively, you need to appreciate the wide range of perspectives from which people approach the yes/no choice.

How you frame your question necessarily affects the scope and shape of your argument itself. In our exploratory exercise we framed the starling question in two ways: (1) Was the family guilty of cruelty to animals? and (2) What should the family have done about the starlings? Framed in the first way, your argument would have to develop criteria for "cruelty to animals" and then argue whether the family's actions met those criteria. Framed in the second way, you could argue for your own solution to the problem, ranging from doing nothing (waiting for the birds to grow up and leave, then fixing the screen) to climbing into the attic and drowning the birds so that their deaths are quick and painless. Or you could word the question in a broader, more philosophical way: When are humans justified in killing animals? Or you could focus on a subissue: When can an animal be labeled a "pest"?

FOR WRITING AND DISCUSSION

Identifying Arguable Issues

1. Working individually, make a list of several communities that you belong to and then identify one or more questions currently being contested within those communities. (If you have trouble, check your local campus and city newspapers or an organizational newsletter; you'll quickly discover a wealth of contested issues.) Then share your list with classmates.
2. Pick two or three issues of particular interest to you, and try framing them in different ways: as broad or narrow questions, as open-ended or yes/no questions. Place several examples on the chalkboard for class discussion.

Stating a Claim Your **claim** is the position you want to take on the issue. It is your brief, one-sentence answer to your issue question:

> The family was not ethically justified in killing the starlings.
> The city should build skateboarding areas with ramps in all city parks.
> The federal government should substantially increase its taxes on gasoline.

You will appreciate argument as truth seeking if you find that your claim evolves as you think more deeply about your issue and listen to alternative views. Be willing to rephrase your claim to soften it or refocus it or even to reverse it as you progress through the writing process.

Articulating Reasons

Your claim, which is the position you take on an issue, needs to be supported by reasons and evidence. A **reason** (sometimes called a "premise") is a subclaim that supports your main claim. In speaking or writing, a reason is usually linked to the claim with such connecting words as *because, therefore, so, consequently,* and *thus.* In planning your argument, a powerful strategy for developing reasons is to harness the grammatical power of the conjunction *because;* think of your reasons as *because* clauses attached to your claim. Formulating your reasons in this way allows you to create a thesis statement that breaks your argument into smaller parts, each part devoted to one of the reasons.

For advice on how much of your supporting argument you should summarize in your thesis statement, see Skill 17.4 on effective introductions.

Suppose, for example, that you are examining the issue "Should the government legalize hard drugs such as heroin and cocaine?" Here are several different points of view on this issue, each expressed as a claim with *because* clauses:

ONE VIEW

Cocaine and heroin should be legalized

- because legalizing drugs will keep the government out of people's private lives.
- because keeping these drugs illegal has the same negative effects on our society that alcohol prohibition did in the 1920s.

ANOTHER VIEW

Cocaine and heroin should be legalized

- because taking drug sales out of the hands of drug dealers would reduce street violence.
- because decriminalization would cut down on prison overcrowding and free police to concentrate on dangerous crime rather than on finding drug dealers.
- because elimination of underworld profits would change the economic structure of the underclass and promote shifts to socially productive jobs and careers.

STILL ANOTHER VIEW

The government should not legalize heroin and cocaine

- because doing so will lead to an increase in drug users and addicts.
- because doing so will send the message that it is okay to use hard drugs.

Although the yes/no framing of this question seems to reduce the issue to a two-position debate, many different value systems are at work here. The first pro-legalization argument, libertarian in perspective, values maximum individual freedom. The second argument—although it too supports legalization—takes a community perspective valuing the social benefits of eliminating the black market drug-dealing culture. In the same way, individuals could oppose legalization for a variety of reasons.

FOR WRITING AND DISCUSSION

Generating *Because* Clauses

Working in small groups or as a whole class, generate a list of reasons for and against one or more of the following yes/no claims. State your reasons as *because* clauses. Think of as many *because* clauses as possible by imagining a wide variety of perspectives on the issue.

1. The school year for grades 1 through 12 should be lengthened to eleven months.
2. The federal government should place a substantial tax on gasoline.
3. The United States should adopt a single-payer, government-financed health system like that of Canada.
4. Playing violent video games is a harmful influence on teenage boys. [or] Women's fashion and style magazines (such as *Glamour* or *Seventeen*) are harmful influences on teenage girls.
5. The war on terror requires occasional use of "enhanced interrogation techniques" on some detainees.

Articulating Underlying Assumptions

So far, we have focused on the frame of an argument as a claim supported with one or more reasons. Shortly, we will proceed to the flesh and muscle of an argument, which is the evidence you use to support your reasons. But before turning to evidence, we need to look at another crucial part of an argument's frame: its *underlying assumptions.*

What Do We Mean by an Underlying Assumption? Every time you link a claim with a reason, you make a silent assumption that may need to be articulated and examined. Consider this argument:

> The family was justified in killing the starlings because starlings are pests.

To support this argument, the writer would first need to provide evidence that starlings are pests (examples of the damage they do and so forth). But the persuasiveness of the argument rests on the underlying assumption that it is okay to kill pests. If an audience doesn't agree with that assumption, then the argument flounders unless the writer articulates the assumption and defends it. The complete frame of the argument must therefore include the underlying assumption.

Claim: The family was justified in killing the starlings.

Reason: Because starlings are pests.

Underlying assumption: It is ethically justifiable to kill pests.

It is important to examine the underlying assumption that connects any reason to its claim *because you must determine whether your audience will accept that assumption. If not, you need to make it explicit and support it.* Think of the underlying assumption as a general principle, rule, belief, or value that connects the reason to the claim. It answers your reader's question, "Why, if I accept your reason, should I accept your claim?"†

Here are a few more examples:

Claim with reason: Women should be allowed to join combat units because the image of women as combat soldiers would help society overcome gender stereotyping.

Underlying assumption: It is good to overcome gender stereotyping.

Claim with reason: The government should not legalize heroin and cocaine because doing so will lead to an increase in drug users.

Underlying assumption: It is bad to increase the number of drug users.

Claim with reason: The family was guilty of cruelty to animals in the starling case because less drastic means of solving the problem were available.

Underlying assumption: A person should choose the least drastic means to solve a problem.

*Our explanation of argument structure is influenced by the work of philosopher Stephen Toulmin, who viewed argument as a dynamic courtroom drama where opposing attorneys exchange arguments and cross-examinations before a judge and jury. Although we use Toulmin's strategies for analyzing an argument structure, we have chosen not to use his specialized terms, which include *warrant* (the underlying assumption connecting a reason to a claim), *grounds* (the evidence that supports the claim), *backing* (the evidence and subarguments that support the warrant), *conditions of rebuttal* (all the ways that skeptics could attack an argument or all the conditions under which the argument wouldn't hold), and finally *qualifier* (an indication of the strength of the claim). However, your instructor may prefer to use these terms and in that case may provide you with more explanation and examples.

FOR WRITING AND DISCUSSION

Identifying Underlying Assumptions

Identify the underlying assumptions in each of the following claims with reasons.

1. Cocaine and heroin should be legalized because legalizing drugs will keep the government out of people's private lives.
2. The government should raise gasoline taxes because the higher price would substantially reduce gasoline consumption.
3. The government should not raise gasoline taxes because the higher price would place undo hardship on low-income people.
4. The government should not raise gasoline taxes because other means of reducing gasoline consumption would be more effective.
5. The government is justified in detaining suspected terrorists indefinitely without charging them with a crime because doing so may prevent another terrorist attack.

Using Evidence Effectively

Inside your arguments, each of your reasons (as well as any underlying assumptions that you decide to state explicitly and defend) needs to be supported either by subarguments or by evidence. By "evidence" we mean facts, examples, summaries of research articles, statistics, testimony, or other relevant data that will persuade your readers to accept your reasons. Note that evidence always exists within a rhetorical context; as a writer you select and shape the evidence that will best support your position, knowing that skeptics may point to evidence that you did not select. Evidence is thus not the same as "proof"; used ethically, evidence presents the best case for your claim without purporting to be the whole truth.

Evidence can sometimes come from personal experience, but in most cases it comes from your own field or library research. The kinds of evidence most often used in argument are the following:

Factual Data Factual data can provide persuasive support for your arguments. (Keep in mind that writers always select their facts through an angle of vision, so the use of facts doesn't preclude skeptics from bringing in counterfacts.) Here is how evolutionary biologist Olivia Judson used factual data to support her point that malaria-carrying mosquitoes cause unacceptable harm to human lives and wealth.

> Each year, malaria kills at least one million people and causes more than 300 million cases of acute illness. For children worldwide, it's one of the leading causes of death. The economic burden is significant too: malaria costs Africa more than $12 billion in lost growth each year. In the United States, hundreds of millions of dollars are spent every year on mosquito control.

Examples An example from personal experience can often be used to support a reason. Here is how student writer Ross Taylor used personal experience to argue that paintball is safe even though accidents can happen. (You can read his complete essay on pp. 359–361.)

> I admit that paintball can be dangerous and that accidents do happen. I personally had a friend lose an eye after inadvertently shooting himself in the eye from a very close range. The fact of the matter is that he made a mistake by looking down the barrel of a loaded gun and the trigger malfunctioned. Had he been more careful or worn the proper equipment, he most likely would have been fine. During my first organized paintball experience I was hit in the goggles by a very powerful gun and felt no pain. The only discomfort came from having to clean all the paint off my goggles after the game. When played properly, paintball is an incredibly safe sport.

Besides specific examples like this, writers sometimes invent hypothetical examples, or *scenarios,* to illustrate an issue or hypothesize about the consequences of an event. (Of course, you must tell your reader that the example or scenario is hypothetical.)

Summaries of Research Another common way to support an argument is to summarize research articles. Here is how a student writer, investigating whether menopausal women should use hormone replacement therapy to combat menopausal symptoms, used one of several research articles in her paper. The student began by summarizing research studies showing possible dangers of hormone replacement therapy. She then made the following argument:

> Another reason not to use hormone replacement therapy is that other means are available to ease menopausal symptoms such as hot flashes, irritability, mood changes, and sleep disturbance. One possible alternative treatment is acupuncture. One study (Cohen, Rousseau, and Carey) revealed that a randomly selected group of menopausal women receiving specially designed acupuncture treatment showed substantial decreases in menopausal symptoms as compared to a control group. What was particularly persuasive about this study was that both the experimental group and the control group received acupuncture, but the needle insertion sites for the experimental group were specifically targeted to relieve menopausal symptoms whereas the control group received acupuncture at sites used to promote general well-being. The researchers concluded that "acupuncture may be recommended as a safe and effective therapy for reducing menopausal hot flushes as well as contributing to the reduction in sleep disruptions" (299).*

Statistics Another common form of evidence is statistics. Here is how one writer used statistics to argue that the federal government should raise fuel-efficiency standards placed on auto manufacturers:

> There is very little need for most Americans to drive huge SUVs. One recent survey found that 87 percent of four-wheel-drive SUV owners had never taken their SUVs off-road (Yacobucci). . . . By raising fuel-efficiency standards, the government would force vehicle manufacturers to find a way to create more earth-friendly vehicles that would lower vehicle emissions and pollution. An article entitled "Update: What You Should Know Before Purchasing a New Vehicle" states that for

*The examples in this section use the MLA (Modern Language Association) style for documenting sources. See Chapter 22 for full explanations of how to use both the MLA and APA (American Psychological Association) systems for citing and documenting sources. The complete bibliographic information for this article would be found in the "Works Cited" pages alphabetized under "Cohen."

> every gallon of gasoline used by a vehicle, 20 to 28 pounds of carbon dioxide are released into the environment. This article further states that carbon dioxide emissions from automobiles are responsible for 20 percent of all carbon dioxide released into the atmosphere from human causes.

Just as writers select facts, examples, and research studies according to their angle of vision, so do they select and shape numerical data. In the above example, the writer focuses on the environmental harm caused by vehicles, especially SUVs. But you must always read statistics rhetorically. For example, the same statistical "fact" can be framed in different ways. There is a difference in focus and feel between these two ways of using the same data:

- "20 percent of human-caused CO_2 emissions come from automobiles" [puts automobiles in the foreground]
- "Although cars do cause some pollution, a full 80 percent of human-caused CO_2 emissions come from sources other than cars." [puts automobiles in the background]

Testimony Writers can also use expert testimony to bolster a case. The following passage from a student essay arguing in favor of therapeutic cloning uses testimony from a prominent physician and medical researcher. Part of the paragraph quotes this expert directly; another part paraphrases the expert's argument.

> As Dr. Gerald Fischbach, Executive Vice President for Health and Biomedical Sciences and Dean of Medicine at Columbia University, said in front of a United States Senate subcommittee: "New embryonic stem cell procedures could be vital in solving the persistent problem of a lack of genetically matched, qualified donors of organs and tissues that we face today." Fischbach goes on to say that this type of cloning could also lead to the discovery of cures for diseases such as ALS, Parkinson's disease, Alzheimer's disease, diabetes, heart disease, cancer, and possibly others.

Rather than provide direct research evidence that stem cell cloning might one day lead to cures for diseases, the writer draws on testimony from the dean of a prestigious medical school. Opponents of stem cell research might draw on other experts, selecting those who are skeptical of this claim.

Subarguments Sometimes writers support reasons not directly through data but through sequences of subarguments. Sometimes these subarguments develop a persuasive analogy, hypothesize about consequences, or simply advance the argument through a chain of connected points. In the following passage, taken from a philosophic article justifying torture under certain conditions, the author uses a subargument to support one of his main points—that a terrorist holding victims hostage has no "rights":

> There is an important difference between terrorists and their victims that should mute talk of the terrorist's "rights." The terrorist's victims are at risk unintentionally, not having asked to be endangered. But the terrorist knowingly initiated his actions. Unlike his victims, he volunteered for the risks of his deed. By threatening to kill for profit or idealism, he renounces civilized standards, and he can have no complaint if civilization tries to thwart him by whatever means necessary.

Rather than using direct empirical evidence, the author supports his point with a subargument showing how terrorists differ from victims and thus relinquish their claim to rights.

Evaluating Evidence: The STAR Criteria

To make your arguments as persuasive as possible, apply to your evidence what rhetorician Richard Fulkerson calls the STAR criteria (**S**ufficiency, **T**ypicality, **A**ccuracy, and **R**elevance),* as shown in the chart on this page.

It is often difficult to create arguments in which all your evidence fully meets the STAR criteria. Sometimes you need to proceed on evidence that might not be typical, verifiable, or as up-to-date as you would like. In such cases, you can often increase the effectiveness of your argument by qualifying your claim. Consider the difference between these two claims:

- **Strong claim:** Watching violent TV cartoons increases aggressive play behavior in boys.
- **Qualified claim:** Watching violent TV cartoons can increase aggressive play behavior in some boys.

To be made persuasive, the strong claim requires substantial evidence meeting the STAR criteria. In contrast, the qualified claim requires less rigorous evidence, perhaps only an example or two combined with the results of one study.

The STAR Criteria for Evaluating Evidence

STAR Criteria	Implied Question	Comments
Sufficiency	Is there enough evidence?	If you don't provide enough evidence, skeptical audiences can dismiss your claim as a "hasty generalization." To argue that marijuana is not a harmful drug, you would probably need more evidence than the results of one study or the testimony of a healthy pot smoker.
Typicality	Are the chosen data representative and typical?	If you choose extreme or rare-case examples, rather than typical and representative ones, your audience might accuse you of cherry-picking your data. Testimony from persons whose back pain was cured by yoga may not support the general claim that yoga is good for back pain.
Accuracy	Are the data accurate and up-to-date?	Providing recent, accurate data is essential for your own *ethos* as a writer. Data from 1998 on homelessness or inaccurately gathered data may be ineffective for a current policy argument.
Relevance	Are the data relevant to the claim?	Even though your evidence is accurate, up-to-date, and representative, if it's not pertinent to the claim, it will be ineffective. For example, evidence that nuclear waste is dangerous is not relevant to the issue of whether it can be stored securely in Yucca Mountain.

*Richard Fulkerson, *Teaching the Argument in Writing,* Urbana: National Council of Teachers of English, 1996, pp. 44–53. In this section we are indebted to Fulkerson's discussion.

As you gather evidence, consider also its source and the extent to which your audience will trust that source. While all data must be interpreted and hence are never completely impartial, careful readers are aware of how easily data can be skewed. Newspapers, magazines, blogs, and journals often have political biases and different levels of respectability. Generally, evidence from peer-reviewed scholarly journals is more highly regarded than evidence from secondhand sources. Particularly problematic is information gathered from Internet Web sites, which can vary widely in reliability and degree of bias.

See Skill 20.2 for advice on evaluating sources for reliability and bias. See Skill 20.3 for help on evaluating Web sites.

Addressing Objections and Counterarguments

Having looked at the frame of an argument (claim, reasons, and underlying assumptions) and at the kinds of evidence used to flesh out the frame, let's turn now to the important concern of anticipating and responding to objections and counterarguments. In this section, we show you an extended example of a student's anticipating and responding to a reader's objection. We then describe a planning schema that can help you anticipate objections and show you how to respond to counterarguments, either through refutation or concession. Finally, we show how your active imagining of alternative views can lead you to qualify your claim.

Anticipating Objections: An Extended Example In our earlier discussions of the starling case, we saw how readers might object to the argument "The family was justified in killing the starlings because starlings are pests." What rankles these readers is the underlying assumption that it is okay to kill pests. Imagine an objecting reader saying something like this:

> It is *not* okay to get annoyed with a living creature, label it a "pest," and then kill it. This whole use of the term *pest* suggests that humans have the right to dominate nature. We need to have more reverence for nature. The ease with which the family solved their problem by killing living things sets a bad example for children. The family could have waited until fall and then fixed the screen.

Imagining such an objection might lead a writer to modify his or her claim. But if the writer remains committed to that claim, then he or she must develop a response. In the following example in which a student writer argues that it is okay to kill the starlings, note (1) how the writer uses evidence to show that starlings are pests; (2) how he summarizes a possible objection to his underlying assumption that killing pests is morally justified; and (3) how he supports his assumption with further arguments.

STUDENT ARGUMENT DEFENDING REASON AND UNDERLYING ASSUMPTION

The family was justified in killing the starlings because starlings are pests. Starlings are nonindigenous birds that drive out native species and multiply rapidly. When I searched "starlings pests" on Google, I discovered thousands of Web sites dealing with starlings as pests. Starlings are hated by farmers and gardeners because huge flocks of them devour newly planted seeds in spring as well as fruits and berries at harvest. A flock of starlings can devastate a cherry orchard in a few days. As invasive nesters, starlings can also damage attics by tearing up insulation and defecating

Claim with reason

Evidence that starlings are pests

on stored items. Many of the Web site articles focused on ways to kill off starling populations. In killing the starlings, the family was protecting its own property and reducing the population of these pests.

Summary of a possible objection

Many readers might object to my argument, saying that humans should have a reverence for nature and not quickly try to kill off any creature they label a pest. Further, these readers might say that even if starlings are pests, the family could have waited until fall to repair the attic or found some other means of protecting their property without having to kill the baby starlings. I too would have waited until fall if the birds in the attic had been swallows or some other native species without starlings' destructiveness and propensity for unchecked population growth. But starlings should be compared to rats or mice. We set traps for rodents because we know the damage they cause when they nest in walls and attics. We don't get sentimental trying to save the orphaned rat babies. In the same way, we are justified in eliminating starlings as soon as they begin infesting our houses.

Response to the objection

In the preceding example, we see how the writer uses evidence to support his reason and then, anticipating readers' objection to his underlying assumption, summarizes that objection and provides a response to it. One might not be convinced by the argument, but the writer has done a good job of trying to support both his reason (starlings are pests) and his underlying assumption (it is morally justifiable to kill at least some pests).

Using a Planning Schema to Anticipate Objections In the previous example, the student's arguing strategy was triggered by his anticipation of reader objections. Note that a skeptical audience can attack an argument by attacking either a writer's reasons or a writer's underlying assumptions. This knowledge allows us to create a planning schema that can help writers develop a persuasive argument. This schema encourages writers to articulate their argument frame (claim, reason, and underlying assumption) and then to imagine what kinds of evidence or arguments could be used to support both the reason and the underlying assumption. Equally important, the schema encourages writers to anticipate counterarguments by imagining how skeptical readers might object to the writer's reason or underlying assumption or both. To create the schema, simply make a chart with slots for each of these elements. Here is how another student writer used this schema to plan an argument on the starling case:

CLAIM WITH REASON

The family showed cruelty to animals because the way they killed the birds caused needless suffering.

UNDERLYING ASSUMPTION

If it is necessary to kill an animal, then the killing should be done in the least painful way possible.

EVIDENCE TO SUPPORT REASON

First I've got to show how the way of killing the birds (starving them slowly) caused the birds to suffer. I've also got to show that this way of killing was needless since other means were available such as calling an exterminator who would remove the birds and either relocate them or kill them painlessly. If no other alternative was available, someone should have crawled into the attic and found a painless way to kill the birds.

EVIDENCE/ARGUMENTS TO SUPPORT UNDERLYING ASSUMPTIONS

I've got to convince readers it is wrong to make an animal suffer if you don't have to. Humans have a natural antipathy to needless suffering—our feeling of unease if we imagine cattle or chickens caused to suffer for our food rather than being cleanly and quickly killed. If a horse is incurably wounded, we put it to sleep rather then let it suffer. We are morally obligated to cause the least pain possible.

WAYS SKEPTICS MIGHT OBJECT

How could a reader object to my reason? A reader might say that the starlings didn't suffer much (baby birds don't feel pain). A reader might also object to my claim that other means were available: They might say there was no other way to kill the starlings. Poison may cause just as much suffering. Cost of exterminator is prohibitive.

How could a reader object to my underlying assumption? Perhaps the reader would say that my rule to cause the least pain possible does not apply to animal pests. In class, someone said that we shouldn't worry about the baby starlings any more than we would worry about killing baby rats. Laws of nature condemn millions of animals each year to death by starvation or by being eaten alive by other animals. Humans occasionally have to take their place within this tooth-and-claw natural system.

How many of the ideas from this schema would the writer use in her actual paper? That is a judgment call based on the writer's analysis of the audience. If this student's target audience includes classmates who think it is morally okay to kill pests by the most efficient means possible, then she should summarize her classmates' argument fairly and then try to convince them that humans are ethically called to rise above tooth-and-claw nature.

FOR WRITING AND DISCUSSION

Creating Argument Schemas

Working individually or in small groups, create a planning schema for the following arguments. For each claim with reason: (a) imagine the kinds of evidence needed to support the reason; (b) identify the underlying assumption; (c) imagine a strategy for supporting the assumption; and (d) anticipate possible objections to the reason and to the assumption.

1. ***Claim with reason:*** We should buy a hybrid car rather than an SUV with a HEMI engine because doing so will help the world save gasoline. (Imagine this argument aimed at your significant other, who has his or her heart set on a huge HEMI-powered SUV.)
2. ***Claim with reason:*** Gay marriage should be legalized because doing so will promote faithful, monogamous relationships among lesbians and gay men. (Aim this argument at supporters of traditional marriage.)
3. ***Claim with reason:*** The war in Iraq was justified because it rid the world of a hideous and brutal dictator. (Aim this argument at a critic of the war.)

Responding to Objections, Counterarguments, and Alternative Views

We have seen how a writer needs to anticipate alternative views that give rise to objections and counterarguments. Surprisingly, one of the best ways to approach counterarguments is to summarize them fairly. Make your imagined reader's best case against your argument. By resisting the temptation to distort a counterargument, you demonstrate a willingness to consider the issue from all sides. Moreover, summarizing a counterargument reduces your reader's tendency to say, "Yes, but have you thought of ... ?" After you have summarized an objection or counterargument fairly and charitably, you must then decide how to respond to it. Your two main choices are to rebut it or concede to it.

Rebutting Opposing Views When rebutting or refuting an argument, you can question the argument's reasons and supporting evidence or the underlying assumptions or both. In the following student example, the writer summarizes her classmates' objections to abstract art and then analyzes shortcomings in their argument.

> Some of my classmates object to abstract art because it apparently takes no technical drawing talent. They feel that historically artists turned to abstract art because they lacked the technical drafting skills exhibited by Remington, Russell, and Rockwell. Therefore these abstract artists created an art form that anyone was capable of and that was less time consuming, and then they paraded it as artistic progress. But I object to the notion that these artists turned to abstraction because they could not do representative drawing. Many abstract artists, such as Picasso, were excellent draftsmen, and their early pieces show very realistic drawing skill. As his work matured, Picasso became more abstract in order to increase the expressive quality of his work. *Guernica* was meant as a protest against the bombing of that city by the Germans. To express the terror and suffering of the victims more vividly, he distorted the figures and presented them in a black and white journalistic manner. If he had used representational images and color—which he had the skill to do—much of the emotional content would have been lost and the piece probably would not have caused the demand for justice that it did.

Conceding to Opposing Views In some cases, an alternative view can be very strong. If so, don't hide that view from your readers; summarize it and concede to it.

Making concessions to opposing views is not necessarily a sign of weakness; in many cases, a concession simply acknowledges that the issue is complex and that your position is tentative. In turn, a concession can enhance a reader's respect for you and invite the reader to follow your example and weigh the strengths of your own argument charitably. Writers typically concede to opposing views with transitional expressions such as the following:

admittedly	I must admit that	I agree that	granted
even though	I concede that	while it is true that	

After conceding to an opposing view, you should shift to a different field of values where your position is strong and then argue for those new values. For example, adversaries of drug legalization argue plausibly that legalizing drugs would increase the number of users and addicts. If you support legalization, here is how you might deal with this point without fatally damaging your own argument:

> Opponents of legalization claim—and rightly so—that legalization will lead to an increase in drug users and addicts. I wish this weren't so, but it is. Nevertheless, the other benefits of legalizing drugs—eliminating the black market, reducing street crime, and freeing up thousands of police from fighting the war on drugs—more than outweigh the social costs of increased drug use and addiction, especially if tax revenues from drug sales are plowed back into drug education and rehabilitation programs.

The writer concedes that legalization will increase addiction (one reason for opposing legalization) and that drug addiction is bad (the underlying assumption for that reason). But then the writer redeems the case for legalization by shifting the argument to another field of values (the benefits of eliminating the black market, reducing crime, and so forth).

Qualifying Your Claim The need to summarize and respond to alternative views lets the writer see an issue's complexity and appreciate that no one position has a total monopoly on the truth. Consequently, writers often need to qualify their claims—that is, limit the scope or force of a claim to make it less sweeping and therefore less vulnerable. Consider the difference between the sentences "After-school jobs are bad for teenagers" and "After-school jobs are often bad for teenagers." The first claim can be refuted by one counterexample of a teenager who benefited from an after-school job. Because the second claim admits exceptions, it is much harder to refute. Unless your argument is airtight, you will want to limit your claim with qualifiers such as the following:

perhaps	maybe
in many cases	generally
tentatively	sometimes
often	usually
probably	likely
may *or* might (*rather than* is)	

You can also qualify a claim with an opening *unless* clause ("*Unless* your apartment is well soundproofed, you should not buy such a powerful stereo system").

Seeking Audience-Based Reasons

Much of the advice that we have presented so far can be consolidated into a single principle: Seek "audience-based reasons." By **audience-based reasons**, we mean reasons that depend on underlying assumptions, values, or beliefs that your targeted audience already holds. In such cases, you won't need to state and defend your underlying assumptions because the audience already accepts them. A good illustration comes from civil engineer David Rockwood's argument against wind power that we used in Chapter 1 (pp. 6–7). Rockwood's targeted readers are environmentalists who have high hopes for wind-generated electricity. Rockwood's final reason opposing wind power is that constructing thousands of wind towers will damage the pristine mountain environment. To environmentalists, this reason is powerful because its underlying assumption ("Preserving the environment is good") appeals to their values.

When you plan your argument, seek audience-based reasons whenever possible. Suppose, for example, that you are advocating the legalization of heroin and cocaine. If you know that your audience is concerned about street crime, then you can argue that legalization of drugs will make the streets safer.

We should legalize drugs *because doing so will make our streets safer:* It will cut down radically on street criminals seeking drug money, and it will free up narcotics police to focus on other kinds of crime.	Audience-based reason: Underlying assumption is that making our streets safer is a good thing—a value the audience already holds.

For another group of readers—those concerned about improving the quality of life for youths in inner cities—you might argue that legalization of drugs will lead to better lives for people in poor neighborhoods.

We should legalize drugs *because doing so will improve the lives of inner-city youth* by eliminating the lure of drug trafficking that tempts so many inner-city youth into crime.	Audience-based reason: Its underlying assumption is that it is good to improve the lives of inner-city youth.

Or if your audience is concerned about high taxes and government debt, you might say:

We should legalize drugs *because doing so will help us balance federal and state budgets*: It will decrease police and prison costs by decriminalizing narcotics; and it will eliminate the black market in drugs, allowing us to collect taxes on drug sales.	Audience-based reason: Assumes that it is a good thing to balance federal and state budgets.

In contrast, if you oppose legalizing drugs, you could appeal to those concerned about drug addiction and public health by using the following audience-based reason:

We should not legalize drugs *because doing so will increase the number of drug addicts and make drug use seem socially acceptable.*	Audience-based reason: Appeals to the underlying assumption that increasing the number of drug addicts and making drugs socially acceptable are bad things.

In each case, you move people toward your position by connecting your argument to their beliefs and values.

Appealing to *Ethos* and *Pathos*

When the classical rhetoricians examined ways that orators could persuade listeners, they focused on three kinds of proofs: *logos,* the appeal to reason; *ethos,* the appeal to the speaker's character; and *pathos,* the appeal to the emotions and the sympathetic imagination. We introduced you to these appeals in Chapter 3, Concept 9, because they are important rhetorical considerations in any kind of writing. Understanding how arguments persuade through *logos, ethos,* and *pathos* is particularly helpful when your aim is persuasion. So far in this chapter we have focused on *logos.* In this section we examine *ethos* and *pathos.*

***Appeals* to Ethos** A powerful way to increase the persuasiveness of an argument is to gain your readers' trust. You appeal to *ethos* whenever you present yourself as credible and trustworthy. For most readers to accept your argument, they must perceive you as knowledgeable, trustworthy, and fair. In the following chart, we suggest ways to enhance your argument's *ethos:*

Strategies for Enhancing Your Argument's *Ethos*

What to Do	Explanation
Be knowledgeable by doing your homework.	Your credibility is enhanced when readers are convinced that you know your subject thoroughly.
Use evidence responsibly.	If you cherry-pick your evidence, you may be perceived as a propagandist rather than as a thoughtful arguer who recognizes complexity.
Be fair to alternative views.	If you scorn or misrepresent opposing views, you will win favor only with those who already agree with you. If you are a good listener to others, they will be more apt to listen to you.
Search for values and assumptions you can share with your audience.	You will build bridges toward skeptical readers, rather than alienate them, if you can highlight shared assumptions or values. Use audience-based reasons where possible.
Show that you care about your issue; show also why your readers should care about it.	By showing why the issue matters both to you and your readers, you portray yourself as a person of integrity rather than as someone playing an argumentative game.

***Appeals* to Pathos** Besides appealing to *logos* and *ethos,* you might also appeal to what the Greeks called *pathos.* Sometimes *pathos* is interpreted narrowly as an appeal to the emotions and is therefore devalued on the grounds that arguments should be rational rather than emotional. Although appeals to *pathos* can sometimes be irrational and irrelevant ("If you don't give me at least a B in this course, I will lose my scholarship and break my ill grandmother's heart"), they can also arouse audience interest and deepen understanding of an argument's human dimensions. The following chart suggests ways to increase *pathos* in your arguments:

Strategies for Enhancing Your Argument's *Pathos*

What to Do	Explanation	Example
Include storylike anecdotes.	Specific stories often create more emotional appeal than abstract statistics or generalizations.	In promoting health care reform, President Obama often told stories of persons made bankrupt by an illness or deprived of care because of a pre-existing condition. On many occasions, he spoke of his own mother's fight with insurance companies as she lay dying of cancer.
Choose words with emotional or values-laden connotations.	Connotations of words often carry heavy emotional impact.	Opponents of health care reform talked about the Democrats' bill as "being jammed down people's throats"; supporters used words like "safety net," "compassion," or "care for children in poverty."
Where appropriate, use vivid language low on the ladder of abstraction.	Specific words paint pictures that have emotional appeal.	"The homeless man is huddled over the sewer grate, his feet wrapped in newspapers. He blows on his hands, then tucks them under his armpits and lies down on the sidewalk with his shoulders over the grate, his bed for the night." *[creates sympathy for the homeless]*"Several ratty derelicts drinking wine from a shared sack caused shoppers to avoid going into the store." *[creates sympathy for shoppers rather than the homeless]*
If the genre permits, include visuals with emotional impact.	Photographs or other visuals, including dramatic graphs or charts, can have a strong emotional appeal.	Articles promoting the environment often include photographs of smoke-belching factories or of endangered animals (often emphasizing their beauty or cuteness); often charts can have emotional appeals—such as a graph portraying dramatic increases in coal-fired electricity plants.

A Brief Primer on Informal Fallacies

We'll conclude our explanation of classical argument with a brief overview of the most common informal fallacies. Informal fallacies are instances of murky reasoning that can cloud an argument and lead to unsound conclusions. Because they can crop up unintentionally in anyone's writing, and because advertisers and hucksters often use them intentionally to deceive, it is a good idea to learn to recognize the more common fallacies.

Post Hoc, Ergo Propter Hoc *("After This, Therefore Because of This")* This fallacy involves mistaking sequence for cause. Just because one event happens before another event doesn't mean the first event caused the second. The connection may be coincidental, or some unknown third event may have caused both of these events.

Example When the New York police department changed its policing tactics in the early 1990s, the crime rate plummeted. But did the new police tactics cause the decline in crime? (Many experts attributed the decline to other causes.) Persons lauding the police tactics ("Crime declined because the NYPD adopted new tactics") were accused of the *post hoc* fallacy.

Hasty Generalization Closely related to the *post hoc* fallacy is the hasty generalization, which refers to claims based on insufficient or unrepresentative data. Generally, persuasive evidence should meet the STAR criteria that we explained on page 342. Because the amount of evidence needed in a given case can vary with the audience's degree of skepticism, it is difficult to draw an exact line between hasty and justified generalizations.

Example The news frequently carries stories about vicious pit bulls. Therefore all pit bills must be vicious. [or] This experimental drug has been demonstrated safe in numerous clinical trials [based on tests using adult subjects]. Therefore this drug is safe for children.

False Analogy Arguers often use analogies to support a claim. (We shouldn't go to war in Iraq because doing so will lead us into a Vietnam-like quagmire.) However, analogical arguments are tricky because there are usually significant differences between the two things being compared as well as similarities. (Supporters of the war in Iraq argued that the situation in Iraq in 2002 was very different from that in Vietnam in 1964.) Although it is hard to draw an exact line between a false analogy and an acceptable one, charges of false analogy are frequent when skeptical opponents try to refute arguments based on analogies.

Example Gun control will work in the United States because it works in England. [or] It's a mistake to force little Johnnie to take piano lessons because you can't turn a reluctant child into a musician any more than you can turn a tulip into a rose.

Either/Or Reasoning This fallacy occurs when a complex, multisided issue is reduced to two positions without acknowledging the possibility of other alternatives.

Example Either you are pre-choice on abortion or you are against the advancement of women in our culture.

Ad Hominem *("Against the Person")* When people can't find fault with an argument, they sometimes attack the arguer, substituting irrelevant assertions about that person's character for an analysis of the argument itself.

Example We should discount Senator Jones's argument against nuclear power because she has huge holdings in oil stock.

Appeals to False Authority and Bandwagon Appeals These fallacies offer as support the fact that a famous person or "many people" already support it. Unless the supporters are themselves authorities in the field, their support is irrelevant.

Example Buy Freeble oil because Joe Quarterback always uses it in his fleet of cars. [or] How can abortion be wrong if millions of people support a woman's right to choose?

Non Sequitur *("It Does Not Follow")* This fallacy occurs when there is no evident connection between a claim and its reason. Sometimes a *non sequitur* can be repaired by filling in gaps in the reasoning; at other times, the reasoning is simply fallacious.

Example I don't deserve a B for this course because I am a straight-A student.

Circular Reasoning This fallacy occurs when you state your claim and then, usually after rewording it, you state it again as your reason.

Example Marijuana is injurious to your health because it harms your body.

Red Herring This fallacy refers to the practice of raising an unrelated or irrelevant point deliberately to throw an audience offtrack. Politicians often employ this fallacy when they field questions from the public or press.

Example You raise a good question about my support of companies' outsourcing jobs to find cheaper labor. Let me tell you about my admiration for the productivity of the American worker.

Slippery Slope The slippery slope fallacy is based on the fear that one step in a direction we don't like inevitably leads to the next step with no stopping place.

Example If we allow embryonic stem cells to be used for medical research, we will open the door for full-scale reproductive cloning.

A Classical Argument

WRITING PROJECT

Write a position paper that takes a stand on a controversial issue. Your introduction should present your issue, provide background, and state the claim you intend to support. In constructing your claim, strive to develop audience-based reasons. The body of your argument should summarize and respond to opposing views as well as present reasons and evidence in support of your own position. You will need to choose whether to summarize and refute opposing views before or after you have made your own case. Try to end your essay with your strongest arguments. Try also to include appeals to *pathos* and to create a positive, credible *ethos.*

We call this assignment a "classical" argument because it is patterned after the persuasive speeches of ancient Greek and Roman orators. A framework chart showing the generic structure of a classical argument is shown in Figure 13.1. Although there are many other ways to persuade audiences, the classical approach is a particularly effective introduction to persuasive writing.

FIGURE 13.1 Framework for a Classical Argument

INTRODUCTION	• Attention-grabber (often a memorable scene) • Explanation of issue and needed background • Writer's thesis (claim) • Forecasting passage
PRESENTATION OF WRITER'S POSITION	• Main body of essay • Presents and supports each reason in turn • Each reason is tied to a value or belief held by the audience
SUMMARY OF OPPOSING VIEWS	• Summary of views differing from writer's (should be fair and complete)
RESPONSE TO OPPOSING VIEWS	• Refutes or concedes to opposing views • Shows weaknesses in opposing views • May concede to some strengths
CONCLUSION	• Brings essay to closure • Often sums up argument • Leaves strong, lasting impression • Often calls for action or relates topic to a larger context of issues

Generating and Exploring Ideas

The tasks that follow are intended to help you generate ideas for your argument. Our goal is to help you build up a storehouse of possible issues, explore several of these possibilities, and then choose one for deeper exploration before you write your initial draft.

Finding an Issue

If you are having trouble finding an arguable issue for this writing project, consider the following strategies:

Strategies for Finding an Arguable Issue

What to Do	Explanation
Make an inventory of various communities you belong to.	See the exercise on page 355. Communities can range from the local (family, dorm, campus) to the state, nation, and world.
Brainstorm contested issues in these communities.	Start off with a fairly large list and then narrow it down according to your personal interest, current knowledge level, and degree of engagement.
On a few of these issues, explore the causes of disagreement.	Ask questions like these: What is at the heart of the disagreement? Disagreement about facts? About beliefs and values? About benefits versus costs?
Then explore your own point of view.	Ask: What is my position on the issue and why? What are alternative points of view? What is at stake?
Determine how much research you'll need to do.	If your issue requires research (check with your instructor), do a bibliographic search and enough skim reading to determine the kinds of arguments surrounding your issue, the kinds of evidence available, and the alternative views that people have taken.
Choose your issue and begin your research.	Your goal is to "wallow in complexity" in order to earn your thesis and create a knowledgeable *ethos*. Note: Some issues allow you to argue from personal experience (see Ross Taylor's argument on paintball, pp. 359–361). Again, check with your instructor.
Brainstorm claims and reasons on various sides of the issue.	State your own claim and possible *because* clause reasons in support of your claim. Do the same thing for one or more opposing or alternative claims.

Conduct an In-Depth Exploration Prior to Drafting

The following set of tasks is designed to help you explore your issue in depth. Most students take one or two hours to complete these tasks; the time will pay off, however, because most of the ideas that you need for your rough draft will be on paper.

1. Write out the issue your argument will address. Try phrasing your issue in several different ways, perhaps as a yes/no question and as an open-ended question. Try making the question broader, then narrower. Finally, frame the question in the way that most appeals to you.
2. Now write out your tentative answer to the question. This will be your beginning thesis statement or claim. Put a box around this answer. Next, write out one or more different answers to your question. These will be alternative claims that a neutral audience might consider.
3. Why is this a controversial issue? Is there insufficient evidence to resolve the issue, or is the evidence ambiguous or contradictory? Are definitions in dispute? Do the parties disagree about basic values, assumptions, or beliefs?
4. What personal interest do you have in this issue? How does the issue affect you? Why do you care about it? (Knowing why you care about it might help you get your audience to care about it.)
5. What reasons and evidence support your position on this issue? Freewrite everything that comes to mind that might help you support your case. This freewrite will eventually provide the bulk of your argument. For now, freewrite rapidly without worrying whether your argument makes sense. Just get ideas on paper.
6. Imagine all the counterarguments your audience might make. Summarize the main arguments against your position and then freewrite your response to each of the counterarguments. What are the flaws in the alternative points of view?
7. What kinds of appeals to *ethos* and *pathos* might you use to support your argument? How can you increase your audience's perception of your credibility and trustworthiness? How can you tie your argument to your audience's beliefs and values?
8. Why is this an important issue? What are the broader implications and consequences? What other issues does it relate to? Thinking of possible answers to these questions may prove useful when you write your introduction or conclusion.

See the discussion of issue questions on p. 335.

Shaping and Drafting

Once you have explored your ideas, create a plan. Here is a suggested procedure:

Begin your planning by analyzing your intended audience. You could imagine an audience deeply resistant to your views or a more neutral, undecided audience acting like a jury. In some cases, your audience might be a single person, as when you petition your department chair to waive a requirement in your major. At other times, your audience might be the general readership of a newspaper, church bulletin, or magazine. When the audience is a general readership, you need to imagine from the start the kinds of readers you particularly want to sway. Here are some questions you can ask:

- ***How much does your audience know or care about your issue?*** Will you need to provide background? Will you need to convince them that your issue is important? Do you need to hook their interest? Your answers to these questions will particularly influence your introduction and conclusion.
- ***What is your audience's current attitude toward your issue?*** Are they deeply opposed to your position? If so, why? Are they neutral and undecided? If so, what other views will they be listening to?
- ***How do your audience's values, assumptions, and beliefs differ from your own?*** What aspects of your position will be threatening to your audience? Why? How does your position on the issue challenge your imagined reader's worldview or identity? What objections will your audience raise toward your argument? Your answers to these questions will help determine the content of your argument and alert you to the extra research you may have to do to respond to audience objections.
- ***What values, beliefs, or assumptions about the world do you and your audience share?*** Despite your differences with your audience, where can you find common links? How might you use these links to build bridges to your audience?

Your next step is to plan an audience-based argument by seeking audience-based reasons or reasons whose underlying assumptions you can defend. Here is a process you can use:

1. Create a skeleton, tree diagram, outline, or flowchart for your argument by stating your reasons as one or more *because* clauses attached to your claim. Each *because* clause will become the head of a main section or *line of reasoning* in your argument.
2. Use the planning schema on pages 337–338 to plan each line of reasoning. If your audience accepts your underlying assumption, you can concentrate on supporting your reason with evidence. However, if your audience is apt to reject the underlying assumption for one of your lines of reasoning, then you'll need to state it directly and argue for it. Try to anticipate audience objections by exploring ways that an audience might question either your reasons or your underlying assumptions.
3. Using the skeleton you created, finish developing an outline or tree diagram for your argument. Although the organization of each part of your argument will grow organically from its content, the main parts of your classical argument should match the framework chart shown on page 353 (Figure 13.1).

This classical model can be modified in numerous ways. A question that often arises is where to summarize and respond to objections and counterarguments. Writers generally have three choices: One option is to handle opposing positions before you present your own argument. The rationale for this approach is that skeptical audiences may be more inclined to listen attentively to your argument if they have been assured that you understand their point of view. A second option is to place this material after you have presented your argument. This approach is effective for neutral audiences who don't start off with strong opposing views. A final option is to intersperse opposing views throughout your argument at appropriate moments. Any of these possibilities, or a combination of all of them, can be effective.

Another question often asked is, "What is the best way to order one's reasons?" A general rule of thumb when ordering your own argument is to put your strongest reason last and your second-strongest reason first. The idea here is to start and end with your most powerful arguments. If you imagine a quite skeptical audience, build bridges to your audience by summarizing alternative views early in the paper and concede to those that are especially strong. If your audience is neutral or undecided, you can summarize and respond to possible objections after you have presented your own case.

Revising

As you revise your argument, you need to attend both to the clarity of your writing (all the principles of closed-form prose described in Chapter 17) and also to the persuasiveness of your argument. As always, peer reviews are valuable, and especially so in argumentation if you ask your peer reviewers to role-play an opposing audience.

Questions for Peer Review

In addition to the generic peer review questions explained in Skill 16.4, ask your peer reviewers to address these questions:

INTRODUCTION

1. How could the title be improved so that it announces the issue, reveals the writer's claim, or otherwise focuses your expectations and piques interest?
2. What strategies does the writer use to introduce the issue, engage your interest, and convince you that the issue is significant and problematic? What would add clarity and appeal?
3. How could the introduction more effectively forecast the argument and present the writer's claim? What would make the statement of the claim more focused, clear, or risky?

ARGUING FOR THE CLAIM

1. Consider the overall structure: What strategies does the writer use to make the structure of the paper clear and easy to follow? How could the structure of the argument be improved?
2. Consider the support for the reasons: Where could the writer provide better evidence or support for each line of reasoning? Look for the kinds of evidence for each line of reasoning by noting the writer's use of facts, examples,

statistics, testimony, or other evidence. Where could the writer supply more evidence or use existing evidence more effectively?

3. Consider the support for the underlying assumptions: For each line of reasoning, determine the assumptions that the audience needs to grant for the argument to be effective. Are there places where these assumptions need to be stated directly and supported with arguments? How could support for the assumptions be improved?
4. Consider the writer's summary of and response to alternative viewpoints: Where does the writer treat alternative views? Are there additional alternative views that the writer should consider? What strategies does the writer use to respond to alternative views? How could the writer's treatment of alternative views be improved?

CONCLUSION

1. How might the conclusion more effectively bring completeness or closure to the argument?

Our first reading, by student writer Ross Taylor, aims to increase appreciation of paintball as a healthy sport. An avid paintballer, Ross was frustrated by how many of his friends and acquaintances didn't appreciate paintball and had numerous misconceptions about it. The following argument is aimed at those who don't understand the sport or those who condemn it for being dangerous and violent.

Ross Taylor (student)

Paintball:

Promoter of Violence or Healthy Fun?

1 Glancing out from behind some cover, I see an enemy soldier on the move. I level my gun and start pinching off rounds. Hearing the incoming fire, he turns and starts to fire, but it is far too late. His entire body flinches when I land two torso shots, and he falls when I hit his leg. I duck back satisfied with another good kill on my record. I pop up again, this time to scan for more enemy forces. Out of the corner of my eye I see some movement and turn to see two soldiers peeking out from behind a sewer pipe. I move to take cover again, but it's futile. I feel the hits come one by one hitting me three times in the chest and once on the right bicep before I fall behind the cover. I'm hit. It's all over—for me at least. The paintball battle rages on as I carefully leave the field to nurse my welts, which are already showing. Luckily, I watch my three remaining teammates trample the two enemy soldiers who shot me to win the game. This is paintball in all its splendor and glory.

2 Paintball is one of the most misunderstood and generally looked down upon recreational activities. People see it as rewarding violence and lacking the true characteristics of a healthy team sport like ultimate Frisbee, soccer, or pickup basketball. Largely the accusations directed at paintball are false because it is a positive recreational activity. Paintball is a fun, athletic, mentally challenging recreational activity that builds teamwork and releases tension.

3 Paintball was invented in the early 1980s as a casual activity for survival enthusiasts, but it has grown into a several hundred million dollar industry. It is, quite simply, an expanded version of tag. Players use a range of CO_2 powered guns that fire small biodegradable marbles of paint at approximately 250–300 feet per second. The result of a hit is a small splatter of oily paint and a nice dark bruise. Paintball is now played nationwide in indoor and outdoor arenas. Quite often variants are played such as "Capture the Flag" or "Assassination." In "Capture the Flag" the point is to retrieve the heavily guarded flag from the other team and return it to your base. The game of "Assassination" pits one team of "assassins" against the "secret service." The secret service men guard an unarmed player dubbed the "president." Their goal is get from point A to point B without the president's getting tagged. Contrary to popular belief, the games are highly officiated and organized. There is always a referee present. Barrel plugs are required until just before a game begins and must be reinserted as soon as the game ends. No hostages may be taken. A player catching another off guard at close range must first give the player the opportunity to surrender. Most importantly there is no physical contact between players. Punching, pushing, or butt-ending with the gun

is strictly prohibited. The result is an intense game that is relatively safe for all involved.

4 The activity of paintball is athletically challenging. There are numerous sprint and dives to avoid being hit. At the end of a game, typically lasting around 20 minutes, all the players are winded, sweaty, and ultimately exhilarated. The beginning of the game includes a mad dash for cover by both teams with heavy amounts of fire being exchanged. During the game, players execute numerous strategic moves to gain a tactical advantage, often including quick jumps, dives, rolls, and runs. While undercover, players crawl across broad stretches of playing field often still feeling their bruises from previous games. These physical feats culminate in an invigorating and physically challenging activity good for building muscles and coordination.

5 In addition to the athletic challenge, paintball provides strong mental challenge, mainly the need for constant strategizing. There are many strategic positioning methods. For example, the classic pincer move involves your team's outflanking an opponent from each side to eliminate his or her mobility and shelter. In the more sophisticated ladder technique, teammates take turns covering each other as the others move onward from cover to cover. Throughout the game, players' minds are constantly reeling as they calculate their positions and cover, their teammates' positions and cover, and their opponents' positions and strength. Finally, there is the strong competitive pull of the individual. It never fails to amaze me how much thought goes into one game.

6 Teamwork is also involved. Paintball takes a lot of cooperation. You need special hand signals to communicate with your teammates, and you have to coordinate, under rapidly changing situations, who is going to flank left or right, who is going to charge, and who is going to stay back to guard the flag station. The importance of teamwork in paintball explains why more and more businesses are taking their employees for a day of action with the intent of creating a closer knit and smooth-functioning workplace. The value of teamwork is highlighted on the Web site of a British Columbia facility, Action and Adventure Paintball, Ltd, which says that in paintball,

> as in any team sport, the team that communicates best usually wins. It's about thinking, not shooting. This is why Fortune 500 companies around the world take their employees to play paintball together.

An advantage of paintball for building company team spirit is that paintball teams, unlike teams in many other recreational sports, can blend very skilled and totally unskilled players. Women like paintball as much as men, and the game is open to people of any size, body type, and strength level. Since a game usually takes no more than seven to ten minutes, teams can run a series of different games with different players to have lots of different match-ups. Also families like to play paintball together.

7 People who object to paintball criticize its danger and violence. The game's supposed danger gets mentioned a lot. The public seems to have received the impression that paintball guns are simply eye-removing hardware. It is true that paintball can lead to eye injuries. An article by medical writer Cheryl Guttman in a trade magazine for ophthalmologists warns that eye injuries from paintball are on the rise. But the fact is that Guttman's article says that only 102 cases of eye injuries from paintballs were

reported from 1985 to 2000 and that 85 percent of those injured were not wearing the required safety goggles. This is not to say that accidents don't happen. I personally had a friend lose an eye after inadvertently shooting himself in the eye from a very close range. The fact of the matter is that he made a mistake by looking down the barrel of a loaded gun and the trigger malfunctioned. Had he been more careful or worn the proper equipment, he most likely would have been fine. During my first organized paintball experience I was hit in the goggles by a very powerful gun and felt no pain. The only discomfort came from having to clean all the paint off my goggles after the game. When played properly, paintball is an incredibly safe sport.

8 The most powerful argument against paintball is that it is inherently violent and thus unhealthy. Critics claim paintball is simply an accepted form of promoting violence against other people. I have anti-war friends who think that paintball glorifies war. Many new parents today try to keep their kids from playing cops and robbers and won't buy them toy guns. These people see paintball as an upgraded and more violent version of the same antisocial games they don't want their children to play. Some people also point to the connections between paintball and violent video games where participants get their fun from "killing" other people. They link paintball to all the other violent activities that they think lead to such things as gangs or school shootings. But there is no connection between school shootings and paintball. As seen in Michael Moore's *Bowling for Columbine*, the killers involved there went bowling before the massacre; they didn't practice their aim by playing paintball.

9 What I am trying to say is that, yes, paintball is violent to a degree. After all, its whole point is to "kill" each other with guns. But I object to paintball's being considered a promotion of violence. Rather, I feel that it is a healthy release of tension. From my own personal experience, when playing the game, the players aren't focused on hurting the other players; they are focused on winning the game. At the end of the day, players are not full of violent urges, but just the opposite. They want to celebrate together as a team, just as do softball or soccer teams after a game. Therefore I don't think paintball is an unhealthy activity for adults. (The only reason I wouldn't include children is because I believe the pain is too intense for them. I have seen some younger players cry after being shot.) Paintball is simply a game, a sport, that produces intense exhilaration and fun. Admittedly, paintball guns can be used in irresponsible manners. Recently there have been some drive-by paintballings, suggesting that paintball players are irresponsible and violent. However, the percentage of people who do this sort of prank is very small and those are the bad apples of the group. There will always be those who misuse equipment. For example, baseball bats have been used in atrocious beatings, but that doesn't make baseball a violent sport. So despite the bad apples, paintball is still a worthwhile activity when properly practiced.

10 Athletic and mentally challenging, team-building and fun—the game of paintball seems perfectly legitimate to me. It is admittedly violent, but it is not the evil activity that critics portray. Injuries can occur, but usually only when the proper safety equipment is not being used and proper precautions are ignored. As a great recreational activity, paintball deserves the same respect as other sports. It is a great way to get physical exercise, make friends, and have fun.

Thinking Critically

about "Paintball: Promoter of Violence or Healthy Fun?"

1. Before reading this essay, what was your own view of paintball? To what extent did this argument create for you a more positive view of paintball? What aspects of the argument did you find particularly effective or ineffective?
2. How effective are Ross's appeals to *ethos* in this argument? Does he create a persona that you find trustworthy and compelling? How does he do so or fail to do so?
3. How effective are Ross's appeals to *pathos*? How does he appeal to his readers' values, interests, and emotions in trying to make paintball seem like an exhilarating team sport? To what extent does he show empathy with readers when he summarizes objections to paintball?
4. How effective are Ross's appeals to *logos*? How effective are Ross's reasons and evidence in support of his claim? How effective are Ross's responses to opposing views?
5. What are the main strengths and weaknesses of Ross's argument?

Our next three readings focus on the issue of nuclear power—specifically, whether the United States should increase its production of electricity by building more nuclear power plants. The first of these readings, by electrical engineer and science writer William Sweet, appeared in the "Better Planet" section of the science magazine *Discover* in August 2007. Under the title "Why Uranium Is the New Green," it presents arguments in favor of greatly expanding our nuclear-generating capacity. William Sweet, a graduate of the University of Chicago and Princeton University, is the author of *Kicking the Carbon Habit: Global Warming and the Case for Nuclear and Renewable Energy* (Columbia University Press, 2006).

William Sweet

Why Uranium Is the New Green

1 ExxonMobil has thrown in the towel, terminating its campaign to convince the public that global warming is a hoax concocted by some pointy-headed intellectuals. All three major Democratic candidates for president, and some of the top Republican contenders as well, have promised serious action. Leading members of Congress have introduced a half dozen bills that would impose some kind of carbon regulation, and even the president now concedes that climate change is important.

2 Using coal to make electricity accounts for about a third of America's carbon emissions. As a result, tackling emissions from coal-fired power plants represents our best opportunity to make sharp reductions in greenhouse gases.

3 Fortunately, we already have the technology to do that. Unfortunately, right now the United States is addicted to coal, a cheap, abundant power source. Burning coal

produces more than half the country's electricity, despite its immense human and environmental costs. Particulates and other air pollutants from coal-fired power plants cause somewhere between 20,000 and 30,000 premature deaths in the United States *each year.* Fifty tons of mercury—one-third of all domestic mercury emissions—are pumped into the atmosphere annually from coal plants. In addition, the extraction of coal, from West Virginia to Wyoming, devastates the physical environment, and its processing and combustion produce gigantic volumes of waste.

4 For the last decade, coal-burning utilities have been fighting a rearguard action, resisting costly antipollution measures required by environmental legislation. At the same time, they have been holding out the prospect of "clean coal"—in which carbon is captured and stored as coal is burned. But clean-coal technologies have yet to be demonstrated on a large scale commercially, and by the admission of even the president's own climate-technology task force, clean coal doesn't have any prospect of making a big dent in the climate problem in the next 15 to 20 years.

5 By comparison, nuclear and wind power are proven technologies whose environmental risks and costs are thoroughly understood and which can make an immediate difference for the better.

6 The first thing to be appreciated about reactors in the United States is that they are essentially immune to the type of accident that occurred at Chernobyl in April 1986. Put simply, because of fundamental design differences, U.S. reactors cannot experience a sudden and drastic power surge, as happened at Chernobyl's Unit Number 4, causing it to explode and catch fire. In addition, the reliability of U.S. nuclear plants has been constantly improving. In 1980, American nuclear power plants were generating electricity only 56 percent of the time because they frequently needed special maintenance or repair. By 2004, reactor performance had improved to the point of generating electricity over 90 percent of the time.

7 Our regulatory regime, which was enormously strengthened in the wake of the 1979 Three Mile Island accident (during which no one was hurt, by the way), is indisputably much better than the Soviet system, which bred endemic incompetence. Management of U.S. nuclear power plants has improved dramatically since Three Mile Island, and security has been tightened significantly since 9/11 (though more remains to be done). By comparison with other tempting terrorist targets like petrochemical complexes, reactors are well fortified.

8 What about the problem of storing radioactive waste? It is overrated from an engineering standpoint and pales in comparison with the challenges associated with the permanent sequestration of immense quantities of carbon, as required by clean-coal systems. Though the wastes from nuclear power plants are highly toxic, their physical quantity is surprisingly small—barely more than 2,000 tons a year in the United States. The amount of carbon dioxide emitted by our coal plants? Nearly 2 *billion* tons.

9 Let us say it plainly: Today coal-fired power plants routinely kill tens of thousands of people in the United States each year by way of lung cancer, bronchitis, and other ailments; the U.S. nuclear economy kills virtually no one in a normal year.

10 Perhaps the most serious concern about increasing our reliance on nuclear power is whether it might lead to an international proliferation of atomic bombs. Contrary to a stubborn myth, however, countries do not decide to build nuclear weapons because

they happen to get nuclear reactors first; they acquire nuclear reactors because they want to build nuclear weapons. This was true of France and China in the 1950s, of Israel and India in the '60s and '70s, and it's true of Korea and Iran today. Does anybody honestly think that whether Tehran or Pyongyang produces atomic bombs depends on how many reactors the United States decides to build in the next 10 to 20 years?

11 Ultimately, the replacement of old, highly polluting coal-fired power plants by nuclear reactors is essentially no different from deciding, after putting sentimental considerations aside, to replace your inexpensive and reliable—but obsolete—1983 Olds Omega with a 2007 Toyota Camry or BMW 3 Series sedan.

12 All that said, it's important to be clear about nuclear energy's limits. It's likely that the construction of at least one new nuclear power plant will be initiated by the end of this year, ending a two-decade drought in new nuclear plant construction. But by its own estimates, the U.S. nuclear industry can handle only about two new nuclear reactor projects annually at its present-day capacity.

13 Obviously, given these limits, a lot of new wind generation, conservation, and improvements in energy use will also be needed. Wind is especially important because, despite the hopes of many, solar power just isn't going to cut it on a large scale in the foreseeable future. Right now, on a dollar per megawatt basis, solar installations are six or seven times as expensive as wind.

14 Wind turbines already generate electricity almost as inexpensively as fossil fuels. Thanks to a two cents per kiolwatt-hour production incentive from the U.S. government, they are being built at a rate that will increase the amount of wind-generated electricity by nearly three gigawatts a year. Taking into account that wind turbines produce electricity only about a third of the time, that's roughly the equivalent of building one standard one-gigawatt nuclear power plant a year.

15 Currently, nuclear and wind energy (as well as clean coal) are between 25 and 75 percent more expensive than old-fashioned coal at current prices (not including all the hidden health and environmental costs of coal), so it will take a stiff charge on coal to induce rapid replacement of obsolete plants. A tax or equivalent trading scheme that increases the cost of coal-generated electricity by, say, 50 percent would stimulate conservation and adoption of more efficient technologies throughout the economy and prompt replacement of coal by some combination of wind, nuclear, and natural gas. Proceeds from the tax or auctioned credits could (and should) be used to compensate regions and individuals most adversely affected by the higher costs, like the poor.

16 For the last six years, the U.S. government, with well-orchestrated support from industry, has told the American people that we can't afford to attack global warming aggressively. That's nonsense. We're the world's richest country, and we use energy about twice as extravagantly as Europe and Japan. It's no surprise that we account for a quarter of the globe's greenhouse-gas emissions.

17 What the United States needs to do is get in step with the Kyoto Protocol, both to establish its bona fides with the other advanced industrial countries and to give countries like India and China an incentive to accept mandatory carbon limits. That implies cutting U.S. carbon emissions by 25 percent as soon as possible.

18 The United States could do that by simply making the dirtiest and most inefficient coal plants prohibitively expensive by means of the carbon tax or trading systems mentioned above.

19 All we need to move decisively on carbon reduction is a different kind of political leadership at the very top. Surprisingly, it's the muscle-bound action-movie star who runs California who has best captured the spirit of what's needed. Last September, the day Arnold Schwarzenegger signed a bill committing his state to a program of sharp greenhouse-gas reductions, he told an ABC interviewer that climate change kind of "creeps up on you. And then all of a sudden it is too late to do something about it. We don't want to go there."

Thinking Critically
about "Why Uranium Is the New Green"

1. This article includes most of the features typically associated with classical argument—a claim with supporting reasons, a summary of alternative or opposing views, and responses to those views.
   a. What are the chief reasons that Sweet supports nuclear-generated electricity?
   b. What arguments against nuclear-generated electricity does Sweet mention or summarize?
   c. Where and how does he respond to those alternative views or opposing arguments?

2. From the perspective of *logos,* what reasons and evidence in favor of nuclear-generated power do you find most effective in Sweet's argument? Are there weaknesses in his argument? Where and how?

3. How, and to what effect, does Sweet appeal to *pathos* and *ethos*?

4. One of the chief arguments against nuclear power is the problem of storing nuclear waste. How would you analyze rhetorically Sweet's method of responding to that objection? How effective is his response?

Making a case against nuclear power, our next reading is a cartoon by Stan Eales, one of the most prominent cartoonists working in Europe today. Eales was born in 1962 and has a degree in graphic design from Auckland, New Zealand. Sellafield is a famous nuclear power site in England with a long, controversial history. It was the home of the world's first commercial nuclear power plant and is currently a storage site for radioactive waste as well as a major research facility on nuclear power. Sellafield has been the subject of numerous documentaries and protest rallies, including a famous 1992 Greenpeace rally that featured bands such as U2, Public Enemy, and Kraftwerk.

Stan Eales

Welcome to Sellafield

Thinking Critically
about "Welcome to Sellafield"

1. Translate Eales's cartoon into a verbal argument by finishing this sentence: "Nuclear energy is bad because _______________."
2. Cartoons get their power from their ability to encapsulate a complex argument in a striking visual image. In your own words, explain how this cartoon uses *logos, pathos,* and *ethos* to create its persuasive effect.
3. How would William Sweet (previous reading) respond to this cartoon?

Our last nuclear power reading is an editorial appearing in the *Los Angeles Times* on July 23, 2007. It responds to a growing public reassessment of nuclear power as a possible solution to global warming. Its immediate context is the July 2007 earthquake in Japan that damaged a nuclear power plant, causing leakage of a small amount of contaminated water.

Editorial from the *Los Angeles Times*

No to Nukes

1 Japan sees nuclear power as a solution to global warming, but it's paying a price. Last week, a magnitude 6.8 earthquake caused dozens of problems at the world's biggest nuclear plant, leading to releases of radioactive elements into the air and ocean and an indefinite shutdown. Government and company officials initially downplayed the incident and stuck to the official line that the country's nuclear plants are earthquake-proof, but they gave way in the face of overwhelming evidence to the contrary. Japan has a sordid history of serious nuclear accidents or spills followed by cover-ups.

2 It isn't alone. The U.S. government allows nuclear plants to operate under a level of secrecy usually reserved for the national security apparatus. Last year, for example, about nine gallons of highly enriched uranium spilled at a processing plant in Tennessee, forming a puddle a few feet from an elevator shaft. Had it dripped into the shaft, it might have formed a critical mass sufficient for a chain reaction, releasing enough radiation to kill or burn workers nearby. A report on the accident from the Nuclear Regulatory Commission was hidden from the public, and only came to light because one of the commissioners wrote a memo on it that became part of the public record.

3 The dream that nuclear power would turn atomic fission into a force for good rather than destruction unraveled with the Three Mile Island disaster in 1979 and the Chernobyl meltdown in 1986. No U.S. utility has ordered a new nuclear plant since 1978 (that order was later canceled), and until recently it seemed none ever would. But rising natural gas prices and worries about global warming have put the nuclear industry back on track. Many respected academics and environmentalists argue that nuclear power must be part of any solution to climate change because nuclear power plants don't release greenhouse gases.

4 They make a weak case. The enormous cost of building nuclear plants, the reluctance of investors to fund them, community opposition and an endless controversy over what to do with the waste ensure that ramping up the nuclear infrastructure will be a slow process—far too slow to make a difference on global warming. That's just as well, because nuclear power is extremely risky. What's more, there are cleaner, cheaper, faster alternatives that come with none of the risks.

Glowing Pains

5 Modern nuclear plants are much safer than the Soviet-era monstrosity at Chernobyl. But accidents can and frequently do happen. The Union of Concerned Scientists cites 51 cases at 41 U.S. nuclear plants in which reactors have been shut down for more than a year as evidence of serious and widespread safety problems.

6 Nuclear plants are also considered attractive terrorist targets, though that risk too has been reduced. Provisions in the 2005 energy bill required threat assessments at nuclear plants and background checks on workers. What hasn't improved much is the risk of spills or even meltdowns in the event of natural disasters such as earthquakes, making it mystifying why anyone would consider building reactors in seismically unstable places like Japan (or California, which has two, one at San Onofre and the other in Morro Bay).

7 Weapons proliferation is an even more serious concern. The uranium used in nuclear reactors isn't concentrated enough for anything but a dirty bomb, but the same labs that enrich uranium for nuclear fuel can be used to create weapons-grade uranium. Thus any country, such as Iran, that pursues uranium enrichment for nuclear power might also be building a bomb factory. It would be more than a little hypocritical for the U.S. to expand its own nuclear power capacity while forbidding countries it doesn't like from doing the same.

8 The risks increase when spent fuel is recycled. Five countries reprocess their spent nuclear fuel, and the Bush administration is pushing strongly to do the same in the U.S. Reprocessing involves separating plutonium from other materials to create new fuel. Plutonium is an excellent bomb material, and it's much easier to steal than enriched uranium. Spent fuel is so radioactive that it would burn a prospective thief to death, while plutonium could be carried out of a processing center in one's pocket. In Japan, 200 kilograms of plutonium from a waste recycling plant have gone missing; in Britain, 30 kilograms can't be accounted for. These have been officially dismissed as clerical errors, but the nuclear industry has never been noted for its truthfulness or transparency. The bomb dropped on Nagasaki contained six kilograms.

9 Technology might be able to solve the recycling problem, but the question of what to do with the waste defies answers. Even the recycling process leaves behind highly radioactive waste that has to be disposed of. This isn't a temporary issue: Nuclear waste remains hazardous for tens of thousands of years. The only way to get rid of it is to put it in containers and bury it deep underground—and pray that geological shifts or excavations by future generations that have forgotten where it's buried don't unleash it on the surface.

10 No country in the world has yet built a permanent underground waste repository, though Finland has come the closest. In the U.S., Congress has been struggling for decades to build a dump at Yucca Mountain in Nevada but has been unable to overcome fierce local opposition. One can hardly blame the Nevadans. Not many people would want 70,000 metric tons of nuclear waste buried in their neighborhood or transported through it on the way to the dump.

11 The result is that nuclear waste is stored on-site at the power plants, increasing the risk of leaks and the danger to plant workers. Eventually, we'll run out of space for it.

Goin' Fission?

12 Given the drawbacks, it's surprising that anybody would seriously consider a nuclear renaissance. But interest is surging; the NRC expects applications for up to 28 new reactors in the next two years. Even California, which has a 31-year-old ban on construction of nuclear plants, is looking into it. Last month, the state Energy Commission held a hearing on nuclear power, and a group of Fresno businessmen plans a ballot measure to assess voter interest in rescinding the state's ban.

13 Behind all this is a perception that nuclear power is needed to help fight climate change. But there's little chance that nuclear plants could be built quickly enough to make much difference. The existing 104 nuclear plants in the U.S., which supply roughly 20% of the nation's electricity, are old and nearing the end of their useful lives. Just to replace them would require building a new reactor every four or five

months for the next 40 years. To significantly increase the nation's nuclear capacity would require far more.

14 The average nuclear plant is estimated to cost about $4 billion. Because of the risks involved, there is scarce interest among investors in putting up the needed capital. Nor have tax incentives and subsidies been enough to lure them. In part, that's because the regulatory process for new plants is glacially slow. The newest nuclear plant in the U.S. opened in 1996, after having been ordered in 1970—a 26-year gap. Though a carbon tax or carbon trading might someday make the economics of nuclear power more attractive, and the NRC has taken steps to speed its assessments, community opposition remains high, and it could still take more than a decade to get a plant built.

15 Meanwhile, a 2006 study by the Institute for Energy and Environmental Research found that for nuclear power to play a meaningful role in cutting greenhouse gas emissions, the world would need to build a new plant every one to two weeks until mid-century. Even if that were feasible, it would overwhelm the handful of companies that make specialized parts for nuclear plants, sending costs through the roof.

16 The accelerating threat of global warming requires innovation and may demand risk-taking, but there are better options than nuclear power. A combination of energy-efficiency measures, renewable power like wind and solar, and decentralized power generators are already producing more energy worldwide than nuclear power plants. Their use is expanding more quickly, and the decentralized approach they represent is more attractive on several levels. One fast-growing technology allows commercial buildings or complexes, such as schools, hospitals, hotels or offices, to generate their own electricity and hot water with micro-turbines fueled by natural gas or even biofuel, much more efficiently than utilities can do it and with far lower emissions.

17 The potential for wind power alone is nearly limitless and, according to a May report by research firm Standard & Poor's, it's cheaper to produce than nuclear power. Further, the amount of electricity that could be generated simply by making existing non-nuclear power plants more efficient is staggering. On average, coal plants operate at 30% efficiency worldwide, but newer plants operate at 46%. If the world average could be raised to 42%, it would save the same amount of carbon as building 800 nuclear plants.

18 Nevertheless, the U.S. government spends more on nuclear power than it does on renewables and efficiency. Taxpayer subsidies to the nuclear industry amounted to $9 billion in 2006, according to Doug Koplow, a researcher based in Cambridge, Mass., whose Earth Track consultancy monitors energy spending. Renewable power sources, including hydropower but not ethanol, got $6 billion, and $2 billion went toward conservation.

19 That's out of whack. Some countries—notably France, which gets nearly 80% of its power from nuclear plants and has never had a major accident—have made nuclear energy work, but at a high cost. The state-owned French power monopoly is severely indebted, and although France recycles its waste, it is no closer than the U.S. to approving a permanent repository. Tax dollars are better spent on windmills than on cooling towers.

Thinking Critically
about "No to Nukes"

1. This article, like William Sweet's, includes the typical elements associated with classical argument.
   a. What are the editorial writer's chief arguments against nuclear power?
   b. What arguments in favor of nuclear power does this editorial mention or summarize?
   c. How and where does the editorial writer respond to these alternative views?
2. From the perspective of *logos,* what reasons and evidence opposing nuclear-generated power do you find most effective in this editorial? Are there weaknesses in the editorial's arguments? Where and how?
3. In what ways, and with what effectiveness, does the editorial appeal to *pathos* and *ethos*?
4. Both Sweet and the editorial writer have high hopes for wind energy. In fact, the editorial writer concludes by saying, "Tax dollars are better spent on windmills than on cooling towers." How would David Rockwood (see Rockwood's letter to the editor in Chapter 1, pp. 6–7) respond to both writers?
5. Where do you place yourself on the spectrum from "strong support of nuclear power" to "strong opposition to nuclear power"? What new research evidence would be required to persuade you to move in one direction or the other along this spectrum?

Our next reading changes pace, moving from the global issue of nuclear energy to the family issue of how we should discipline our children. "Spare the Rod, Spoil the Parenting" is an op-ed piece by *Miami Herald* columnist Leonard Pitts, Jr. In this editorial, Pitts jumps into the ongoing controversy over corporal punishment, children's rights, childrearing practices, and spanking. Leonard Pitts, one of the nation's foremost African-American opinion writers, won the Pulitzer Prize for commentary in 2004. He is the author of *Becoming Dad: Black Men and the Journey to Fatherhood.*

Leonard Pitts, Jr.

Spare the Rod, Spoil the Parenting

1 I hate to tell you this, but your kid is spoiled. Mine aren't much better.

2 That, in essence, is the finding of a recent Time/CNN poll. Most of us think most of our kids are overindulged, materialistic brats.

3 If you're waiting for me to argue the point, you're in the wrong column.

4 No, I only bring it up as context to talk about a controversial study released late last month. It deals with corporal punishment—spanking—and it has outraged those who oppose the practice while rearming those who support it.

5 It seems that Dr. Diana Baumrind, a psychologist at the University of California at Berkeley, followed 164 middle-class families from the time their children were in preschool until they reached their 20s. She found that most used some form of corporal punishment. She further found that, contrary to what we've been told for years, giving a child a mild spanking (defined as open-handed swats on the backside, arm or legs) does not leave the child scarred for life.

6 Baumrind, by the way, opposes spanking. Still, it's to her credit as an academic that her research draws a distinction other opponents refuse to. That is, a distinction between the minor punishments practiced by most parents who spank and the harsher variants practiced by a tiny minority (shaking and blows to the head or face, for example).

7 Yes, children whose parents treat them that severely are, indeed, more likely to be maladjusted by the time they reach adolescence. And, yes, the parents themselves are teetering dangerously close to child abuse.

8 But does the same hold true in cases where corporal punishment means little more than swatting a misbehaving backside?

9 For years, the official consensus from the nation's child-rearing experts was that it did. Maybe that's about to change. We can only hope.

10 For my money, there was always something spurious about the orthodoxy that assured us all corporal punishment, regardless of severity, was defacto abuse. Nevertheless, we bought into it, with the result being that parents who admitted to spanking were treated as primitive dolts and heaped with scorn. They were encouraged to negotiate with misbehaving children in order to nurture their self-esteem.

11 But the orthodoxy was wrong on several fronts.

12 In the first place, it's plainly ridiculous—and offensive—to equate a child who has been swatted on the butt with one who has been stomped, scalded or punched. In the second, the argument that reasonable corporal punishment leads inevitably to mental instability always seemed insupportable and has just been proven so by Baumrind's study. And in the third, have you ever tried to "negotiate" with a screaming 5-year-old? It may do wonders for the child's self-esteem, but, I promise, it's going to kill yours. Your sanity, too.

13 Don't get me wrong, contrary to what its proponents sometimes claim, corporal punishment is not a panacea for misbehavior. Rearing a child requires not just discipline, but also humor, love and some luck.

14 Yet the very fact that spanking must be exonerated by a university study suggests how far afield we've wandered from what used to be the central tenet of family life: parents in charge. Ultimately, it probably doesn't matter whether that tenet is enforced by spanking or other corrective measures, so long as it is enforced.

15 I've seen too many children behave with too grand a sense of entitlement to believe that it is. Heard too many teachers tell horror stories of dealing with kids from households where parents are not sovereign, adult authority not respected. As a culture, we seem to have forgotten that the family is not a democracy, but a benign dictatorship.

16 Small wonder our kids are brats.

17 So the pertinent question isn't: To spank or not to spank? Rather, it's: Who's in charge here? Who is teaching whom? Who is guiding whom?

18 The answer used to be obvious. It's obvious no more. And is it so difficult to see where that road leads? To understand that it is possible to be poisoned by self-esteem, and that a spoiled child becomes a self-centered adult ill-equipped to deal with the vagaries and reversals of life?

19 Some folks think it's abuse when you swat a child's backside. But maybe, sometimes, it's abuse when you don't.

Thinking Critically
about "Spare the Rod, Spoil the Parenting"

1. In the introductory paragraphs of this op-ed piece, Leonard Pitts, Jr., mentions the rhetorical situation that has called forth his argument. What contemporary research is prompting Pitts's column?
2. Pitts's argument takes a stand on the issue question, "Is spanking a good childrearing practice?" What claim does he make in this argument? What reasons and evidence does he offer to support this claim?
3. Where does Pitts acknowledge and respond to opposing views?
4. To understand the intensity of the social controversy on this issue, we suggest that you search the keywords "spanking" and "corporal punishment" using an online database and the Web. What different positions do you find represented in articles and by advocacy Web sites such as the site for the Center for Effective Discipline? How would these sources challenge Pitts's position and evidence?

The last reading is by student writer A. J. Chavez, who wrote this paper for the classical argument assignment in this chapter. In proposing the legalization of gay marriage, A. J. Chavez draws on personal knowledge and experience, some Internet research, and information from an anthropology course he was taking simultaneously with first-year composition.

A. J. Chavez (student)
The Case for (Gay) Marriage

1 "What if it was a gay world? And you were straight?" a recent TV spot asks (the ad can be viewed at commercialcloset.org—see "Human Rights Campaign" in Works Cited). The camera pans across a hospital waiting room, filled with gay and lesbian couples. There, a middle-aged man sits, waiting. "Your partner's in a coma. She's not responding," a young male doctor says to him. "Unfortunately, since the state doesn't recognize your marriage, I can't grant you spousal visitation. If she were to wake, or a family member gave consent—I wish there was more I could do. I'm sorry." After that, the camera quickly zooms out from the man's heartbroken face. The scene blurs, and a female voiceover reads the fact that appears on the screen: "hospital visitation: just one

of over 1000 rights granted to a legally married couple." Next, the scene fades into a black screen with a blue rectangle that has a yellow equal sign on it. The female voiceover continues, "Support equality for all Americans. Millionformarriage.org." This spot, sponsored by the Human Rights Campaign, the largest queer political organization in the United States, shows a scenario that undoubtedly happens every day in America, just with the tables turned. According to a report from the United States General Accounting Office, released after the passage of the federal Defense of Marriage Act of 1996, there are at least 1,049 federal laws in the U.S. code that relate to rights specific to marriage (2). Some are obvious, like Social Security or Veterans' Administration benefits upon the death of a spouse for the surviving spouse and children. Others are not so obvious, but equally important, such as the federally guaranteed right of an employee to take time off from work to care for an ill spouse or the so-called "spousal privilege" of not having to testify against a husband or wife in court. Currently, marriage rights are denied to a small, but still significant group in America—gays and lesbians, a group of which I am a part. We are denied the same rights enjoyed by straight people, simply because we are attracted to and love members of our own sex and have chosen to live open, honest lives, instead of closeted ones.

2 In opposition to the current Congressional proposal to amend the Constitution by defining marriage as a union between a man and a woman, I am proposing the nationwide legalization of same-sex marriage. First of all, gay marriage is the easiest way to ensure equality for all. Civil unions can only go part of the way. Secondly, the government must define marriage through a secular framework that respects the spirit of laws already in place, not a religious one that would violate separation between church and state. Third, the costs to taxpayers for legalizing gay marriage would be negligible. Some studies even suggest it would save taxpayer money. Finally, anthropological evidence exists for the existence of what we would refer to today as "gay marriage" across a long time span and wide range of cultures, demonstrating that it is not abnormal or perverted.

3 There are many arguments against gay marriage. Some are definitional, such as "Marriage is between a man and a woman." Other claims against gay marriage stem from concern for the well-being of children raised by gay or lesbian couples from previous straight marriages, adoption, or reproductive assistance. Still others arise out of respect for the Hebrew and Christian scriptures, the moral code from which most of Western civilization has lived by for thousands of years—certain passages in them prohibit homosexual relations. Another objection is that marriage is reserved for procreation, and that gay marriage, obviously, cannot serve this end. Additionally, there is the argument that legal options already exist for gay couples that offer some of the benefits of marriage, such as power of attorney or living will. Some politicians claim that marriage is something that should be left to the states to decide how to define and deal with individually. Furthermore, there is the argument that the legalization of gay marriage will open the doors to the legalization of more radical unions, such as adult-child unions or polygamy. Last, some members of America's queer community oppose gay marriage because they see it as just an attempt to copy and live a hetero lifestyle.

4 My first reason for legalizing gay marriage is that it is the easiest and most effective way to ensure equal rights for all in this country. Currently, sexual minorities receive no explicit protection from federal anti-discrimination acts, such as Title VII from the Civil Rights Act of 1964, which only prohibits discrimination in employment based on "race, color, religion, sex, or national origin." Employers are not required to offer the same benefits to the significant others of gay employees as they do to straight employees. With gay marriage, they would be obliged under laws that protect the rights of married couples to do so. Civil unions relegate gays and lesbians to second-class status. Civil unions or domestic partnerships are offered only by a few states, but can be disregarded by neighboring anti-gay states because of the federal Defense of Marriage Act. Civil unions can guarantee protections only at the state level, and at that, only the state they were issued in. Gay marriage, with its protections, would help prevent discrimination toward sexual minorities from prejudiced individuals. Here, it becomes clear that marriage laws should not just be left to the states, as some politicians who would rather not take a stand on the issue suggest, because if they are, patchwork laws will continue to develop across the nation. Some states will prohibit same-sex marriages and civil unions, while others will provide civil unions, and, perhaps in the future, gay marriage. A clear, federal standard for the inclusion of gay marriage will also prevent possible loopholes in marriage or civil union laws for inappropriate unions between adults and children or among more than two partners.

5 Second, for public policy, marriage, like all other things, needs to be defined through a non-religious, secular framework. The separation of church and state has always been an important tenet in American government. Allowing religious dogma to define marriage violates this tenet, setting up a dangerous precedent for further unification of church and state. If gay marriage were legalized, religions would still be allowed to distinguish what they do and do not see as "marriage." The Human Rights Campaign Web site provides the example of the Catholic church, which does not bless second marriages after divorce. Yet people can still file for divorce and then remarry if they see fit. In this case, the state recognizes a legal marriage that is not officially sanctioned by the church ("I Believe God Meant"). Also, while certain passages of the Bible prohibit sexual relationships between members of the same sex, others condone slavery and polygamy—both practices that would not be approved in American society today. Clearly, appeals to the Bible cannot be used to determine public policy. We would not only violate the important principle of separation between church and state, but by strict Biblical interpretation of morality, we could theoretically have a polygamous, slave-owning society.

6 Another compelling reason for legalizing same-sex marriage is the money that could actually be *saved* in state budgets every year. The FAQ section on marriage on the Human Rights Campaign Web site explains how government savings could add up through increased reliance between gay and lesbian couples on each other, reducing reliance on government assistance programs such as Temporary Assistance to Needy Families (welfare), Supplemental Security Income (disability), food stamps and Medicaid. The Web site cites two economic studies by professors at UCLA and the University of Massachusetts, Amherst, who examined possible savings to state governments in California and New Jersey if domestic benefits were extended to

same-sex couples. According to these studies, the savings were projected to be $10.6 million in California and $61 million in New Jersey ("Won't This Cost"). Additionally, the legalization of gay marriage would provide medical insurance benefits for thousands of currently uninsured children. While gay and lesbian couples obviously cannot conceive children on their own, plenty raise children from previous, heterosexual marriages, adopt children, or use reproductive assistance such as surrogate mothers or assisted insemination to bear their own children. The fact that many gay and lesbian partners are raising children shows the fallacy in claiming that gays should not be allowed to marry because they can't procreate. If we used the logic of procreation in determining whether to grant marriage rights, we would have to ban marriage between elderly couples, between sterile straight couples, and between those who plan to use birth control to prevent pregnancy. Of course, we would never ban such marriages because we recognize the value of having a life partner. Extending marriage benefits to gay partners brings the same benefits to them, with the additional benefit to the states of reducing reliance on state assistance programs and bringing medical insurance to many children.

7 My final reason for the legalization of gay marriage is that same-sex unions have existed across all cultures and times. This is important to recognize, because Judeo-Christian societies like ours tend to discount the legitimacy or even existence of such unions, and of so-called "sexual minorities." Such disregard can be explained by the histories of Judaism and Christianity, says Ted Fortier, Ph.D., a cultural anthropologist at Seattle University. In early Jewish societies, largely due to problems with underpopulation, he notes, any sexual activity without procreative power was considered taboo. Also, in Christian medieval Europe, disease and famine required that the people have all the labor possible to produce food. Again, all nonprocreative sex was labeled taboo. For anthropological purposes, Fortier defines marriage as "a union between a woman and another person." This definition, however, can be quite broad, he says. The "woman" can actually be a man playing a feminine role. He explains that in our culture, we look at gender as a biological concept, instead of a socially determined one. He gives examples of different cultures that distinguish certain men who take on womanly roles as being a third gender, such as that of Tahiti, where every village has a man that takes on the role of a woman, or the Native American *berdache* role, another womanly role played by a man. These men raise children just like the other adults. For the most part, Fortier claims, throughout all societies and cultures marriage has always been about securing resources and property—known as "alliance theory" in anthropology. Looking at our own society with this concept in mind, we see that marriage is utilized in the same way—as a stabilizing combination of tangible and intangible resources that leads to benefits to society, often including the raising of children. Law professor Mark Strasser, in an essay entitled "State Interests in Recognizing Same-Sex Marriage," mentions that "there is no evidence that children will not thrive when raised by same-sex parents and, indeed, some evidence that children may be better off in certain ways when they are raised by same-sex parents than when they are raised by different-sex parents" (37). Strasser refers to the increased tolerance and appreciation of differences that children of gays and lesbians typically have and the innumerable studies over the years that show these children grow up

just as well-adjusted and are no more likely to be homosexual than children living with straight parents. The government, therefore, should recognize and extend marriage protections to same-sex couples as well. While there are some gay/lesbian/bisexual/transgender people who think gay marriage is just a futile attempt to copy mainstream, straight society, and that the government should not bother legalizing it, entering into any union is based on the mutual choice of two individuals. GLBT persons who find the institution of marriage unsavory would still not be forced by the government to marry if gay marriage were legalized.

8 The case for gay marriage is a strong one indeed, similar to earlier struggles for interracial marriage, which was legalized only relatively recently in American history. Gay marriage will result in an unprecedented addition of formal protections to America's last marginalized minority—the queer community. Studies suggest that it will save individual states millions of dollars in revenue on an annual basis. Gay marriage is not sick or a perversion—it exists across all cultures and times in one form or another and was stigmatized in Judeo-Christian traditions for the practical purpose of achieving as high of a population as possible. It is impossible to turn on a television set or open a newspaper now without seeing a reference to gay marriage. Legalizing gay marriage affirms both the "liberal" ideal of equality and the "conservative" value of community stability and individual rights. It also affirms the dignity of all of mankind.

Works Cited

Fortier, Ted. Personal interview. 26 Feb. 2004.

Human Rights Campaign. Advertisement. *The Commercial Closet.* Commercial Closet Association, 2004. Web. 2 Mar. 2004.

"I Believe God Meant Marriage for Men and Women." *Human Rights Campaign.* Human Rights Campaign, 20 Feb. 2004. Web. 15 Mar. 2004.

Strasser, Mark. "State Interests in Recognizing Same-Sex Marriage." *Marriage and Same Sex Unions: A Debate.* Ed. Lynn D. Wardle et al. Westport: Praeger, 2003. Print.

United States. General Accounting Office. *Categories of Laws Involving Marital Status.* Letter of transmittal. By Barry R. Bedrick. 31 Jan. 1997. Web. 16 Mar. 2004.

"Won't This Cost Taxpayers Too Much Money?" *Human Rights Campaign.* Human Rights Campaign, 2004. Web. 15 Mar. 2004.

Thinking Critically
about "The Case for (Gay) Marriage"

1. In classical arguments there is often an overlap between the reasons used to support one's own claim and the reasons used to rebut opposing views. In such cases the distinction between support and rebuttal can become blurred (not a problem so long as the argument remains clear). In this essay, where does A. J. Chavez summarize the arguments opposing the legalization of gay marriage? How many of these arguments does he respond to as the argument proceeds? Where does he add supporting reasons in favor of gay marriage that aren't initially framed as rebuttals?

2. How effectively does A. J. create appeals to *ethos* in this argument? How would you characterize his persona based on tone, reasonableness, and empathy for opposing views?

3. On the gay marriage issue, opponents of gay marriage can range from conservative audiences with strong religious arguments against same-sex marriage to very liberal gay audiences who believe that gays shouldn't imitate heterosexual relationships. How well does A. J. use appeals to *pathos* to connect with his imagined readers at both ends of this spectrum? How does he appeal to the values, beliefs, and emotions of his audiences? Point out specific passages where you think he is successful or unsuccessful.

4. How would you assess the appeals to *logos* in this argument? Are A. J.'s uses of reasons and evidence persuasive?

5. What do you see as the major strengths and weaknesses of this argument?

PEARSON mycomplab

For support in learning this chapter's content, follow this path in **MyCompLab**: Resources ⇒ Writing ⇒ Writing Purposes ⇒ Writing to Argue or Persuade. Review the Instruction and Multimedia resources, then complete the Exercises and click on Gradebook to measure your progress.

14 MAKING AN EVALUATION

In our personal lives, we make evaluations all the time: What computer should I buy? Which is the best diet plan? What career is best for me? Evaluations usually involve a two-step critical thinking process: (1) deciding on the appropriate criteria and (2) deciding whether a particular case meets the criteria. Thus when you decide what courses to take next term, you must first decide the criteria you will apply, such as your interest in the subject, the reputation of the instructor, the required workload, or the time of day. Once you establish criteria, you will probably rank-order them and then begin seeing what available courses best meet them.

Often, both in college and in your career, you will be called upon to turn informal evaluations into written evaluation arguments. According to a study by Barbara Walvoord and Lucille McCarthy, college assignments often take the form of "good/better/best" questions. For example, in a history course you might be asked: "Was Queen Elizabeth I of England a good ruler?" In a communications course, you might be asked: "Is Twitter or Facebook the better technology for promoting citizen participation in current public issues?" Or in a political science course, you might be asked to evaluate several proposals for increasing voter turnout among college students and to argue for the best approach.

Evaluation arguments typically have a persuasive rather than a purely informational aim and thus differ from, say, a movie or restaurant review that simply notes the good points and bad points of the thing being evaluated. As you will see, an evaluation argument can be considered a specific kind of classical argument—one focused on an evaluation question. Because evaluation arguments help communities make choices about actions, beliefs, or values, they are among the most important kinds of arguments to understand.

In this chapter's writing project, you will learn to:

- determine criteria for an evaluation
- write an evaluation argument for an audience of skeptical readers who have some degree of initial resistance to your evaluation

Exploring Evaluative Writing

To introduce you to evaluative thinking, we ask you to explore a provocative evaluative question:

> **Situation:** You are a member of a student group planning a workshop on the dangers of binge drinking. Universities around the country are trying to address this problem, which has been shown to have dangerous short-range and long-range consequences. The goals of your workshop are (1) to raise awareness of the consequences of binge drinking and other forms of alcohol abuse; (2) to work toward changing the "culture of drinking" that exists on college campuses across the country; and (3) to promote responsible, safe, and legal behavior regarding alcohol. Your particular committee is in charge of creating a poster for displaying around campus to promote student interest in the workshop. Your committee is choosing among four possible visuals (shown in Figures 14.1–14.4) to use in this poster. You want to choose the "best" visual for your poster in order to reach a range of students from your particular college or university. You'll need to consider not only the design and subject matter of each visual but also its suitability for reaching students on your particular campus, given its size, location, culture, and mission.

1. After studying Figures 14.1–14.4, freewrite your initial responses to them. What is striking or memorable about each? What is confusing? What message does each convey? How well do the dominant impression and message of each visual fit with the purpose of your workshop on binge drinking and with your academic institution?
2. Working in small groups or as a whole class, create the best argument that you can for selecting one of these visuals for your poster. Frame each argument as a claim with reasons, stating each reason as a *because* clause (for example, "The graph using the beer glasses is best because . . . , because . . . ," etc.).

FIGURE 14.1 Graph Correlating Alcohol Consumption and Academic Performance

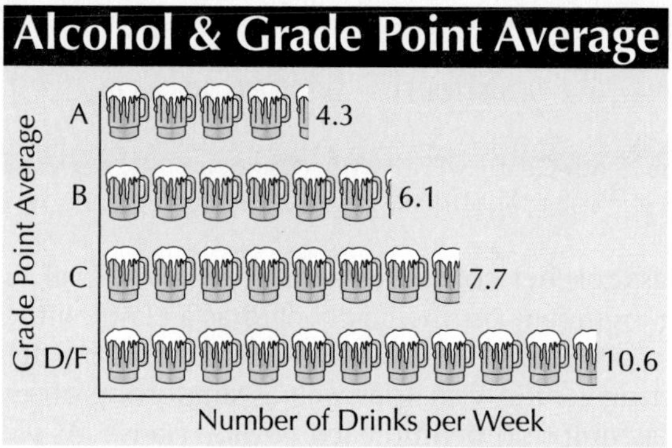

FIGURE 14.2 Nineteenth-Century Prohibition Cartoon

3. When the class reaches consensus about the best visual, write the frame of the justifying argument on the chalkboard as a claim with *because* clauses. If you wish, you can also write a dissenting argument on the board or list reasons for rejecting certain visuals as well as supporting others. Then articulate the unstated assumption behind each *because* clause. As we will show in the next section, these unstated assumptions are the criteria for your evaluation argument.

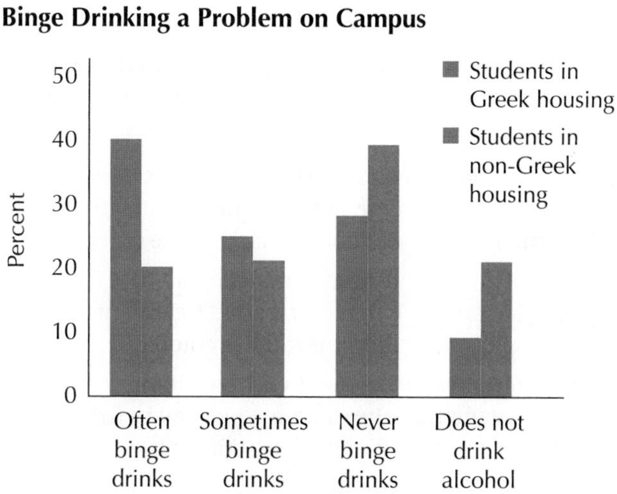

FIGURE 14.3 Graphic Showing Percentage of Students Reporting Substance Abuse by Housing Type

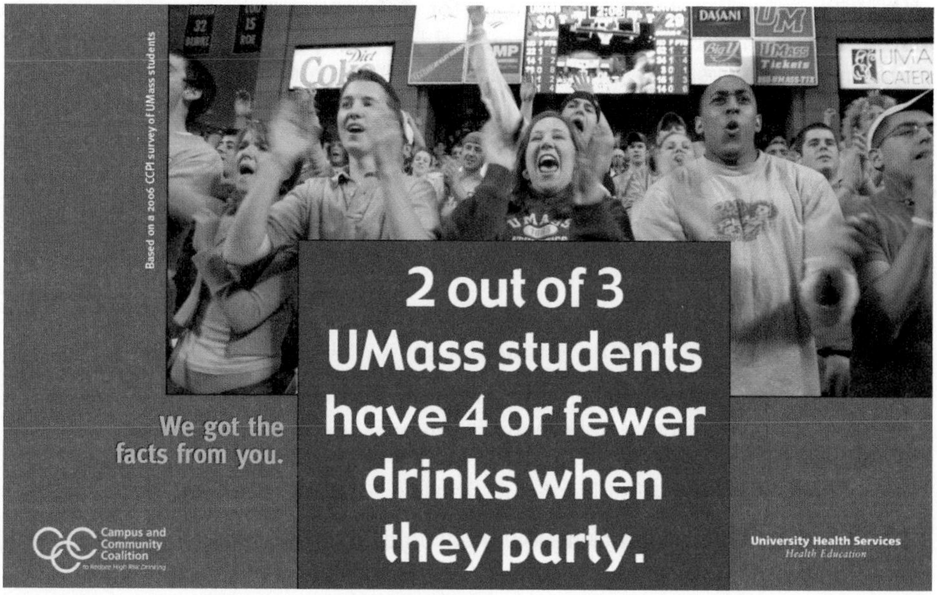

FIGURE 14.4 A Social Norms Campaign Poster

Understanding Evaluation Arguments

Now that you have been introduced to evaluative thinking, we'll explain in more detail how to think and write about evaluation issues.

The Criteria-Match Process

Evaluation arguments involve what we call a criteria-match process. The first step in this process is to establish criteria; the second step is to show how well your subject matches these criteria. Here are several examples:

- Which students should be awarded the prestigious presidential scholarship?
  Criteria task: What are the criteria for the presidential scholarship?
  Match task: Which of the candidates best meet the criteria?
- Is hospitalization a good treatment for anorexia?
  Criteria task: What are the criteria for a good treatment for anorexia?
  Match task: Does hospitalization meet these criteria?
- Is a carbon tax a good way to combat climate change?
  Criteria task: What are the criteria for a good way to fight climate change?
  Match task: Does a carbon tax meet these criteria?
- Which is the best visual for the poster advertising this school's workshop on the dangers of binge drinking?
  Criteria task: What are the criteria for the best visual in this context?
  Match task: Which visual best meets the criteria?

In each of these cases, it is possible to articulate criteria while anticipating that different stakeholders might argue for different criteria or consider certain criteria more important than others and thus weight the criteria differently. For example, on the poster issue, one group of designers might argue this way:

ARGUMENT FOR CHOOSING A VISUAL WITH NUMERIC GRAPHS

One of the two numeric graphs is the best visual for our poster ...

- because a graph succinctly highlights the problem of binge drinking.
- because it takes a factual approach.
- because it stimulates intelligent questions.

The unstated assumptions behind these reasons are the criteria for this argument. In other words, the argument states that a good visual should meet these criteria:

1. It should highlight the problem of binge drinking;
2. It should take a factual approach (as opposed to an imaginative or emotional approach); and
3. It should stimulate intelligent questions.

Based on these criteria, Figure 14.1 or 14.3 would be the best choice. (The argument would then need to be refined further to choose the better of these two options.)

But other poster designers might present a different argument:

ARGUMENT FOR CHOOSING A VISUAL WITH IMAGES

One of the two visuals with images is the best visual for our poster ...

- because these images are eye-catching and dramatic.
- because they have emotional and imaginative appeal.
- because they have a personal, immediate impact.

The unstated assumptions behind this argument set up a different set of criteria. For these poster designers, a good visual is:

1. eye-catching;
2. emotionally appealing; and
3. personal and immediate.

Based on these criteria, the social norms campaign poster with the photo of the college students cheering or the nineteenth-century Prohibition cartoon would be more effective. (Again, a further argument would be needed to narrow the choice to one.)

The preceding argument focuses on disagreements over the criteria. Evaluation arguments can also focus on disagreements over the match. For example, consider a family deciding what used car to buy. They might agree on the criteria—let's say, (1) low cost, (2) safety, and (3) reliability. But they might disagree whether a specific car meets the criteria. In terms of cost, Car A may be initially cheaper than Car B but may get lower gas mileage and have a higher frequency-of-repair record. In this match argument, the family would be arguing over whether Car A or Car B best meets the low-cost criterion.

FOR WRITING AND DISCUSSION

Establishing and Applying Criteria

Whenever you evaluate something, you first need to establish criteria—that is, for any given class of items, you have to determine the qualities, traits, behaviors, or features that constitute excellence for members of that class. Then you need to match those criteria to a single member of that class—the thing you are evaluating. The following simple exercise will give you practice in thinking in this systematic, two-stage way:

1. Working individually, make a list of criteria that are important to you in choosing a career. These criteria are apt to differ from person to person. Some people might place "high income" at the top of their list, while others might put "prestige," "leadership opportunities," "adventure," "being outdoors," or "time for family and leisure" at the top. Then rank your criteria from highest to lowest priority.
2. Share your criteria lists in small groups or as a whole class. Then write on the chalkboard two or three representative lists of criteria.
3. Finally, write several different careers on the board and match them to the lists of criteria. Which possible careers come out on top for you? Which ones come out on top based on the criteria lists placed on the board? Possible careers to consider include these: grade school/high school teacher, lawyer, auto mechanic, airplane pilot, bus driver, military officer, hedge fund manager, engineer, computer technician, insurance salesperson, accountant, small business owner, plumber, commercial artist, homemaker, nurse/physician/dentist, chiropractor/optometrist, social worker, police officer.
4. When disagreements arise, try to identify whether they are disagreements about criteria or disagreements about the facts of a given career.

The Role of Purpose and Context in Determining Criteria

Ordinarily, criteria are based on the purpose of the class to which the thing being evaluated belongs. For example, if you asked a professor to write a recommendation for you, he or she would need to know what you were applying for—A scholarship? Internship in a law office? Peace Corps volunteer? Summer job in a national park? The qualities of a successful law office intern differ substantially from those of a successful Peace Corps worker in Uganda. The recommendation isn't about you in the abstract but about you fulfilling the purposes of the class "law office intern" or "Peace Corps volunteer." Similarly, if you were evaluating a car, you would need to ask, "a car for what purpose?"—Reliable family transportation? Social status (if so, what social group?)? Environmental friendliness?

Decisions about purpose are often affected by context. For example, a union member, in buying a car, might specify an American-made car while a subscriber to *Mother Jones* magazine might specify high gas mileage and low pollution. To see how context influences criteria, consider a recent review of Seattle's soup kitchens appearing in a newspaper produced by homeless people. In most contexts, restaurant reviews focus on the quality of food. But in this review the highest criterion was the sense of dignity and love extended to homeless people by the staff.

FOR WRITING AND DISCUSSION

Working with Purpose and Criteria

1. Working in small groups or as a whole class, decide how you would evaluate a local eatery as a place to study. How would you evaluate it as a place to take a date, a place to hang out with friends, or a place to buy a nutritious meal?
2. As a whole class or in small groups, discuss how this individual exercise helped you realize how criteria for excellence vary when you place the same item into different classes with different purposes.

Special Problems in Establishing Criteria

Establishing the criteria for evaluation arguments can entail other considerations besides purpose and context. Sometimes it is difficult to establish criteria because of special problems connected to evaluation. The following chart explains four typical kinds of problems and their solutions.

Problems and Solutions in Establishing Criteria

Problem	Explanation	Solution
Different classes: Apples and oranges	It is harder to establish criteria for a good fruit than it is for a good apple or a good orange.	Comparative evaluations should focus on members of the same class. So, compare one kind of apple against another kind, but not against oranges or bananas. Compare Kobe Bryant to other basketball players, not to golfers or swimmers. Even better, compare him to other basketball guards.

Problem	Explanation	Solution
Competing standards: The ideal versus the doable/achievable	This problem is illustrated by the aphorism "Don't let the perfect be enemy to the good." Sometimes we have to evaluate something highly if it is "good enough" or "better than what we have now" rather than ideal.	Clarify whether you are using an ideal standard or the lesser standard of "good enough." Democrats who supported the Obama health care reform bill argued that it was better than doing nothing. Democrats who opposed the bill argued that it fell short of the ideal. (Meanwhile, Republicans applied different criteria and rejected the bill entirely.)
Seductive empirical measures: The power of numbers	We may be tempted to evaluate something based on traits that can be quantified: highest GPA or SAT scores for scholarships; the amount of revenue generated for the best tax policy. Because numbers rank-order themselves, they can hold huge sway in evaluations.	Although numbers can be persuasive, they often don't measure the nonquantifiable things that we really value. Always ask what the numbers do *not* measure and seek ways to evaluate the traits that might be more important.
Tyranny of cost: Can we afford it?	Sometimes the things we evaluate highest simply cost too much. (Note: Cost may be measured by money, time, emotional stress, or other factors.)	You may have to eliminate the top choices in your evaluation because they cost too much. Recognize the inhibiting factor of cost from the start. You may need to evaluate only those items in your cost range.

Distinguishing Necessary, Sufficient, and Accidental Criteria

Still another factor in establishing criteria is recognizing that some criteria are more important than others. Suppose you said, "I will be happy with any job as long as it puts food on my table and gives me time for my family." In this case the criteria "adequate income" and "time for family," taken together, are **sufficient**, meaning that once these criteria are met, the job being rated meets your standard for excellence. Suppose you said instead, "I am hard to please in my choice of a career, which must meet many criteria. But I definitely will reject any career that doesn't put enough food on my table or allow me time for my family." In this case the criteria of "adequate income" and "time for family" are **necessary but not sufficient**, meaning that these two criteria have to be met for a career to meet your standards, but that other criteria must be met also.

Besides necessary and sufficient criteria, there are **accidental** criteria, which are added bonuses but not essential. For example, you might say, "Although it's not essential, having a career that would allow me to be outside a lot would be nice." In this case "being outside" is an accidental criterion (nice but not required).

Using a Planning Schema to Develop Evaluation Arguments

In Chapter 13, we showed you how to use a planning schema to develop ideas for an argument (pp. 344–345). The schema encourages writers to articulate their argument frame (each reason and the underlying assumption that links the reason back to the claim) and then to imagine what kinds of evidence could be used to support both the reason and the underlying assumption. Equally important, the schema encourages writers to anticipate counterarguments by imagining how skeptical readers might object to the writers' reasons or underlying assumptions or both.

Let's say that you are the student member of a committee to select a professor for an outstanding teaching award. Several members of the committee want to give the award to Professor M. Mouse, a popular sociology professor at your institution. You are opposed. One of your lines of reasoning is that Professor Mouse's courses aren't rigorous. Here is how you could develop this line of reasoning using the planning schema explained in Chapter 13.

CLAIM WITH REASON

Professor Mouse does not deserve the teaching award because his courses aren't rigorous.

EVIDENCE TO SUPPORT THE REASON

I need to provide evidence that his courses aren't rigorous. From the dean's office records, I have discovered that eighty percent of his students get As or high Bs; a review of his syllabi shows that he requires little outside reading and only one short paper; he has a reputation in my dorm of being fun and easy.

UNDERLYING ASSUMPTION (CRITERION)

Having rigorous academic standards is a necessary criterion for the university teaching award.

EVIDENCE/ARGUMENTS TO SUPPORT THE ASSUMPTION

I need to show why I think rigorous academic standards are necessary. Quality of teaching should be measured by the amount that students learn. Good teaching is more than a popularity contest. Good teachers draw high-level performance from their students and motivate them to put time and energy into learning. High standards lead to the development of skills that are demanded in society.

WAYS SKEPTICS MIGHT OBJECT

How could someone attack my reason and evidence? Might a person say that Mouse has high standards? Could someone show that students really earned the high grades? Are the students I talked to not representative? Could someone say that Mouse's workload and grading patterns meet or exceed the commonplace behavior of faculty in his department?

How could someone attack my underlying assumption? Could someone argue that rigorous academic standards aren't as important as other criteria—that this is an accidental not a necessary criterion? Could a person say that Mouse's goal—to inspire interest in sociology—is best achieved by not loading students down with too many papers and too much reading, which can appear to be busywork? (I'll need to refute this argument.) Could someone say that the purpose of giving the university teaching award is public relations and it is therefore important to recognize widely popular teachers who will be excellent speakers at banquets and other public forums?

Conducting an Evaluation Argument: An Extended Example

Now that we have explored some potential difficulties in establishing and defending criteria for an evaluation, let's consider in more detail the process of making an evaluation argument.

The student examples in this section focus on the evaluation of a rock and roll museum in Seattle, Washington, called Experience Music Project (EMP). Designed by architect Frank Gehry (who is known for his creation of the Guggenheim Museum in Bilbao, Spain, the Aerospace Hall in Los Angeles, and other famous buildings around the world), EMP was sponsored by Microsoft cofounder Paul Allen as a tribute to rock singer Jimi Hendrix and to rock music itself. In Figure 14.5, you can see this innovative structure, which sparked much controversy (is it a wonder or an eyesore?). Sharing some characteristics with the Rock and Roll Hall of Fame and Museum in Cleveland, Ohio, EMP features some permanent exhibits—the Hendrix Gallery, the Guitar Gallery (tracing the development of guitars from the 1500s to the electric guitars of today), Milestones (including displays from rhythm and blues to hip-hop and current rap artists), and Northwest Passage (focusing on popular music in Seattle, from jazz and rhythm and blues to heavy metal, punk, grunge, and the contemporary music scene). EMP also includes Sound Lab (where visitors can play instruments using interactive technology), On Stage (where visitors can pretend to be rock stars

FIGURE 14.5 Experience Music Project, Seattle, Washington

playing before a cheering crowd), Artist's Journey (a ride involving motion platform technology), three restaurants, and a store. (To see for yourself what EMP is and how it looks on the inside, you can go to its Web site.)

Let's now turn to the specific steps of making an evaluation argument.

Step 1: Determining the Class to Which X Belongs and the Purposes of That Class When you conduct an evaluation argument, you must first assign your person/object/phenomenon (the X you are evaluating) to a category or class and then determine the purposes of that class. Often people disagree about an evaluation because they disagree about the arguer's choice of category for X. EMP, as students soon discovered, could be placed in several different categories, leading to different criteria for evaluation. Here are typical classes proposed by students:

- A tourist attraction (for an audience of visitors to Seattle)
- A museum of rock history (for people interested in the development of rock as an art form)
- A rock and roll shrine (for rock fans who want to revere their favorite artists and feel part of the rock scene for a day)

Clearly these classes have different purposes. The purpose of a tourist attraction is to offer a unique, fun place to spend the day during a visit to Seattle. The purpose of a rock museum is to teach about the history of its subject in an informative, interesting, and accessible way. The purpose of a rock and roll shrine is to honor famous rock stars, bring visitors into their lives and work, and let them experience the music scene.

Step 2: Determining and Weighting Criteria The criteria for your evaluation are directly connected to the purposes of the class to which X belongs. The following lists show typical criteria chosen by different students for each of the classes listed in Step 1:

A good *tourist attraction* should
- be entertaining and enjoyable.
- be affordable and worth the price, not simply out to gouge tourists' wallets.
- be unique—something tourists wouldn't find in another city.

A good *museum of rock history* should
- have a clear, well-organized layout that is easy to navigate.
- display objects of clear aesthetic or historical significance.
- teach the public by providing clear, meaningful information about rock music.
- arouse interest in rock as an art form and encourage the public's appreciation and involvement.

A good *rock and roll shrine* should
- take fans up close and personal into the lives of major artists.
- encourage fans to appreciate the complexity of rock and the skills of artists.
- help fans experience the rock scene and fantasize about being rock stars themselves.

In addition to identifying criteria, you should arrange them in order of importance so that you build to your most important criterion. In each of the preceding examples, students placed their most important criterion last.

Step 3: Determining the Extent to Which X Meets Your Criteria for the Class A third step in constructing an evaluation argument is to make your match argument: To what extent does X meet or not meet the criteria you have formulated? The following examples show how three students framed the match part of their evaluation arguments on EMP. Note how each student matches EMP to the specific criteria he or she has selected.

Experience Music Project is a tourist trap rather than an attraction because
- the headphones and heavy computerized MEGs (Museum Exhibit Guides) keep everyone isolated, making companionship difficult.
- the arrangement of exhibits is chaotic, leading to frustration and repetition of the same experiences.
- it doesn't give any substance, just endless music trivia.
- it's too expensive and commercial, leaving the tourist feeling ripped-off.

Experience Music Project is a good museum of rock and roll history because
- it covers a range of popular music styles from jazz and blues to reggae, punk, grunge, and hip-hop.
- it provides interesting information on musicians, musical styles, and key moments in popular music history.
- it makes people excited about popular music and its history through the museum's interactive exhibits and technologically advanced museum guide devices.

For rock fans, Experience Music Project is a good rock and roll shrine because
- it gives illuminating insights into the lives and artistry of many rock musicians.
- it gives an in-depth look at some of the greats like Jimi Hendrix and helps fans really appreciate the talent of these musicians.
- the "onstage" room lets fans fulfill a fantasy by pretending they are rock stars.

Step 4: Determining What Alternative Views You Must Respond to in Your Evaluation Argument Finally, in constructing your evaluation argument you need to determine whether your intended audience is likely to object to (1) the class in which you have placed your object; (2) the criteria you have developed for assessing your object; or (3) the degree to which your object matches the criteria you have chosen. You have numerous options for accommodating your audience's doubts or objections. For example, if your proposed class is controversial, you might choose to justify it in your introduction. If your criteria might be controversial, you could address objections before you start the match part of your argument. If you think your match argument will raise doubts, you could intersperse alternative views throughout or treat them separately near the end of your argument. Any of these methods can work.

In the Readings section of this chapter, we include a student writer's complete evaluation argument on the Experience Music Project.

FOR WRITING AND DISCUSSION

Responding to Objections

Consider how student writer Katie Tiehen confronts and responds to alternative views. After reading this typical passage from her argument, answer the questions that follow:

> ... Some may challenge my contention that EMP is an ineffective museum of rock history by arguing that a day spent at EMP is entertaining and fun. I'll be the first to admit that EMP is fun. From a rock and roll fan's perspective, EMP is nonstop entertainment, a musical paradise. I felt like a five-year-old on Christmas morning when I saw Eric Clapton's guitar, Jimi Hendrix's personal journals, and walls plastered in punk memorabilia. These items, coupled with video documentaries and hands-on activities, provided hours of enjoyment. Because of the fun factor, it's easy for people to jump to EMP's defense. However, it is not the entertainment value of EMP that I am questioning. There's no doubt that it is a fun and amusing place to visit. The problem arises when one tries to classify EMP as an historical museum, which should provide visitors with access to objects of lasting historical significance. Some entertainment is fine, but not to the point that it clouds the true purpose of the museum as it does in EMP's case. After two visits, I still couldn't tell you where rock and roll originated, but I could tell you that the line to play the drums in Sound Lab is really long. Entertainment is the main purpose of EMP and it shouldn't be.

1. What objections to her argument does Katie anticipate (doubts about her proposed class for EMP, her criteria, or her match argument)?
2. How does Katie respond to alternative views—by conceding points and shifting back to her own perspective or by refuting alternative views with counterreasons and counterexamples?

WRITING PROJECT

An Evaluation Argument

Write an argument in which you use evaluative thinking to persuade your audience to see the value (or lack of value) of the person, place, thing, event, or phenomenon that you are evaluating. The introduction to your argument should hook your audience's interest in your evaluation question. The body of your argument should establish criteria for evaluating your chosen subject, and then show how your subject meets or does not meet those criteria. Depending on the degree of controversy surrounding your subject, follow the procedure for other arguments by summarizing alternative views and responding to them through either concession or refutation.

For this assignment you need to pose an evaluative question that is important to your audience and invites multiple views. In some cases, you may choose to evaluate a controversial person, event, thing, or phenomenon—something that engenders lively disagreement within a particular community. (For example: Is "Nimbletoes" Nelson a good quarterback? Is establishing a national ID system or profiling airline passengers a good way to combat terrorism?) When your subject is controversial, you need to consider alternative evaluations and show why yours is better.

In other cases, you may choose to evaluate something that is not itself controversial. Your purpose might be to help a specific audience determine how to spend their time or money. For example, is taking an art gallery walk a good way for students to spend a Saturday afternoon in your city? Or, you might consider writing your evaluation for a specific forum. For example, you might write a review for a parents' magazine or Web site evaluating whether the *Twilight* movies are good family films. Or you might write an editorial for your school newspaper explaining why tutoring with the local children's literacy project is a good experience for education majors.

Generating and Exploring Ideas

For your evaluation essay, you will try either to change your readers' assessment of a controversial person, event, thing, or phenomenon or help your readers decide whether an event or thing is worth their time or money.

If you have not already chosen an evaluation issue, try thinking about evaluative questions within the various communities to which you belong:

Local civic community: evaluative questions about transportation, land use, historical monuments, current leaders, political bills or petitions, housing, parking policies, effectiveness of police

National civic community: evaluative questions about public education, environmental concerns, economic policies, responses to terrorism, Supreme Court decisions, foreign policies, political leaders

Your university community: evaluative questions about academic or sports programs, campus life programs, first-year or transfer student orientation, clubs, dorm life, campus facilities, financial-aid programs, campus security, parking, cultural programs

Your scholarly community or disciplinary community in your major: evaluative questions about internships, study abroad programs, general studies programs, course requirements, first-year studies, major curriculum, advising, course sequences, teaching methods, homework requirements, academic standards, recent books or articles, new theories in a field, library resources, laboratory facilities, Web site sources of primary documents or numerical data in a field

Culture and entertainment issues within your social or family communities: evaluative questions about restaurants, movies, plays, museums, TV shows, musicians, video games, entertainment Web sites, concerts, books, paintings, sports figures, buildings

Consumer issues within your social or family communities: evaluative questions about computer systems, CDs, cars, clothing brands, stores, products, e-commerce

Work communities: evaluative questions about supervisors or subordinates, office efficiency, customer relations, advertising and marketing, production or sales, record keeping and finance, personnel policies

Another good strategy for finding a topic is to think about a recent review or critique with which you disagree—a movie or restaurant review, a sportswriter's assessment of a team or player, an op-ed column or blog assessing a government official or proposed legislation. How would you evaluate this controversial subject differently?

Once you have chosen a possible controversial topic, use the following strategies to help you explore and develop ideas for your evaluation argument.

Strategies for Developing an Evaluative Claim

Strategies	Questions to Ask and Steps to Follow
Place the X you will evaluate in the smallest and most meaningful category for your intended audience.	For the audience you have in mind, what is the smallest, most relevant class in which to place your X? For example, Is Super Eye 2000 a good digital camera *for novices on a low-cost budget* (not simply, is it a good digital camera)?
Determine the criteria you will use to make your evaluation meaningful and helpful to your audience.	What are the purposes of the class in which you have placed your subject? Use freewriting or idea mapping to explore the qualities a member of that class needs to have to achieve those purposes.
Think about the objections to your criteria your audience might raise.	How will you justify your criteria? What reasoning and evidence will you use?
Think about how you will weight or rank your criteria.	Which of your criteria is most important and why?
Evaluate your subject by matching it to each of your criteria.	Why does your subject match or not match each of the criteria? Freewrite to find examples and counterexamples.

Shaping and Drafting

In drafting your evaluation argument, you have two key developmental and organizational questions to consider: (1) Will you have to defend your choice of criteria as well as complete the match part of your argument? (2) Where should you locate and respond to alternative views? Your answers to these questions will depend on your specific evaluation claim and on your audience. In the readings at the end of this chapter, you will notice that student writers Jackie Wyngaard (pp. 394–395) and Teresa Filice (pp. 398–400) chose different approaches to handling alternative views.

FIGURE 14.6 Framework for an Evaluation Argument

Introduction	• Presents your issue • Shows why evaluating X is problematic or controversial • Presents your evaluation claim and your criteria
Argument	• States criterion 1 and defends it if necessary • Shows that X meets/does not meet criterion 1 • States criterion 2 and defends it if necessary • Shows that X meets/does not meet criterion 2 • Continues with additional criteria and match arguments
Treatment of alternative or opposing views	• Summarizes objections to your criteria or your match • Responds to these objections
Conclusion	• Sums up your evaluation

Although there are many ways to organize an evaluation argument, the framework chart shown in Figure 14.6 is a good place to start.

Revising

As you revise, think of ways that you can make your evaluation clearer and more useful for your audience. Consider ways to sharpen your criteria and build up the match part of your argument to make your evaluation more persuasive.

Questions for Peer Review

In addition to the generic peer review questions explained in Skill 16.4, ask your peer reviewers to address these questions:

INTRODUCTION

1. How well do the title and introduction capture your interest, provide needed background, identify the controversy, and show importance of the subject?
2. How well has the writer established the evaluative question, the claim, and the criteria? How could these be improved?

THE CRITERIA-MATCH ARGUMENT

3. How fitting and persuasive is the writer's choice of criteria for evaluating this subject? How could the writer support or defend his/her criteria and the weighting of those criteria more clearly or persuasively?
4. How does the writer support and develop the match part of the argument? What evidence helps readers see that the X being evaluated meets or fails to meet each criterion? How could the writer improve the match argument?
5. Where does the writer summarize and address alternative views? How could this treatment of alternative views be improved?

Readings

The first reading is a student essay by Jackie Wyngaard evaluating the Experience Music Project in Seattle, Washington.

Jackie Wyngaard (student)

EMP:

Music History or Music Trivia?

1 Along with other college students new to Seattle, I wanted to see what cultural opportunities the area offers. I especially wanted to see billionaire Paul Allen's controversial Experience Music Project (known as EMP), a huge, bizarre, shiny, multicolored structure that is supposed to resemble a smashed guitar. Brochures say that EMP celebrates the creativity of American popular music, but it has prompted heated discussions among architects, Seattle residents, museumgoers, and music lovers, who have questioned its commercialism and the real value of its exhibits. My sister recommended this museum to me because she knows I am a big music lover and a rock and roll fan. Also, as an active choir member since the sixth grade, I have always been intrigued by the history of music. I went to EMP expecting to learn more about music history from exhibits that showed a range of popular musical styles, that traced historical connections and influences, and that enjoyably conveyed useful information. However, as a museum of rock history, EMP is a disappointing failure.

2 EMP claims that it covers the history of rock and roll from its roots to the styles of today, but it fails at this task because it isolates musicians and styles without explaining historical progressions or cultural influences. For instance, the museum doesn't show how Elvis Presley's musical style was influenced by his predecessors like Chuck Berry and Muddy Waters. It doesn't show how early folk and blues influenced Bob Dylan's music. It doesn't show how early jazz paved the way for rock and roll. How are these isolated and separate EMP exhibits connected? How did rock and roll progress from the '50s "Let's Go to the Hop" beats to the laid-back guitar riffs of the '60s and '70s? How did '70s music become the heavy metal, head-banger rock of the '80s and '90s? How did these styles lead to rap? The exhibits show the existence of these different styles, but they don't help viewers understand the historical developments or historical context. While it is interesting to see a peace patch once owned by Janis Joplin, this exhibit does not explain either the social and political events of the time or Joplin's political views.

3 Another fault of EMP is that it omits many influential groups and musicians, particularly women. For example, there is no display about the Beatles, the Rolling Stones, Led Zeppelin, or the Doors. The exhibits also exclude many major female artists who made substantial contributions to popular music. I found nothing about Joan Baez, Ella Fitzgerald, Aretha Franklin, Carly Simon, or Joni Mitchell. I was also surprised that there were few women mentioned in the Northwest Passage exhibit. Weren't more women involved in the Seattle music scene? As a woman interested in music, I felt left out by EMP's overall neglect of women musicians.

4 Perhaps most frustrating about EMP is the way exhibits are explained through the awkward, difficult-to-use handheld computer called a Museum Exhibit Guide (MEG).

The explanations are hard to access and then disappointing in their content. I wanted to hear a landmark song that an artist wrote or an interesting analysis of the artist's musical style. Instead, I listened to "how Elvis made the leather jacket famous" and other random trivia. The MEG also offers too many choices for each exhibit, like a Web page with a dozen links. But after all the time and effort, you learn nothing that increases your understanding or stimulates your thinking about music history. The MEGs themselves are very heavy, clunky, and inconvenient. If you don't point this gadget exactly at the activator, nothing happens. It took me a good ten minutes to figure out how to get the device to play information for me, and many of my classmates had to keep going back to the booth to get new batteries or other repairs. The museum would be much more effective if visitors had the option of just reading about the displays from plaques on the walls.

5 I know that many people will disagree with my assessment of EMP. They'll point to the fun of the interactive exhibits and the interesting collection of album covers, crushed velvet costumes, concert clips, famous guitars, and old jukeboxes. But a good museum has to be more than a display of artifacts and an array of hands-on activities. Pretending you're a rock star by performing on stage with instruments doesn't tell you how a certain style of music came about. Displaying trivial information about Elvis's leather jacket or Janis Joplin's feather boa doesn't help you appreciate the importance of their music. Devoting half an exhibit to punk rock without any analysis of that style doesn't teach you anything. In short, the museum displays frivolous trivia tidbits without educational substance.

6 Music lovers hoping for an educational experience about the rock and roll era of musical history will be disappointed by EMP. And this is without the additional insult of having to shell out $19.95 to get in the door. Speaking for serious music lovers and students of music history, I have to say that EMP is a failure.

THINKING CRITICALLY
about "EMP: Music History or Music Trivia?"

1. What strategies particularly appropriate for evaluation arguments does Jackie Wyngaard use in her introduction?
2. How has Jackie chosen to classify Experience Music Project? What criteria does she choose?
3. In the match part of her argument, what evidence does Jackie use to support her assessment of Experience Music Project?
4. What alternative views does she acknowledge and where in her argument does she choose to treat them? Does she anticipate objections to her criteria or to the match part of her argument? What other objections might people raise to her argument?
5. What do you find persuasive about her arguments? How might this evaluation argument be improved?

The second reading aims at changing its readers' assessment of the children's television program *Sesame Street.* It posits just one criterion—a good children's program should not be sexist—and then focuses exclusively on demonstrating that *Sesame Street* is sexist. Its authors are both attorneys and mothers of young children.

Diane Helman and Phyllis Bookspan

Sesame Street:

Brought to You by the Letters M-A-L-E

1 A recent report released by the American Association of University Women, "How Schools Shortchange Women," finds that teachers, textbooks, and tests are, whether intentionally or unintentionally, giving preferential treatment to elementary-school boys. As a result, girls who enter school with equal or better academic potential than their male counterparts lose confidence and do not perform as well.

2 An earlier study about law students, published in the *Journal of Legal Education,* found a similar disparity. "Gender Bias in the Classroom" found that male law students are called upon in class more frequently than females, speak for longer periods of time, and are given more positive feedback by law professors.

3 The article raised some disturbing questions about whether women and men receive truly equal education in American law schools.

4 Unfortunately, this insidious gender bias appears long before our children enter school and pervades even the television show *Sesame Street.* Yes, *Sesame Street* is sexist! But, just as in the story of the emperor and his new clothes, many of us do not notice the obvious.

5 The puppet stars of the show, Bert and Ernie, and all the other major *Sesame Street* animal characters—Big Bird, Cookie Monster, Grover, Oscar the Grouch, Kermit the Frog, and Mr. Snuffleupagus—are male. Among the secondary characters, including Elmo, Herry Monster, Count VonCount, Telly Monster, Prairie Dawn, and Betty Lou, only a very few are girls.

6 The female Muppets always play children, while the males play adult parts in various scenes. In a recently aired skit "Squeal of Fortune," this disparity is evident when the host of the show introduces the two contestants. Of Count VonCount of Transylvania the host asks, "What do you do for a living?" to which the count responds authoritatively, "I count!" Of Prairie Dawn, he inquires, "And how do you spend your day?" Sure, it would be silly to ask a schoolgirl what she does for a living. But none of the female Muppets on *Sesame Street* are even old enough to earn a living.

7 Further, almost all the baby puppet characters on *Sesame Street* are girls. For example, Snuffie's sibling is Baby Alice; in books, Grover's baby cousin is a girl, and when Herry Monster's mother brings home the new baby—it's a girl. Since babies are totally dependent and fairly passive, the older (male) relatives take care of them and provide leadership.

8 Also, the female Muppets almost never interact with each other. In sharp contrast, consequential and caring friendships have been fully developed between male

Muppets: Ernie and Bert; Big Bird and Snuffie; even Oscar the Grouch and his (male) worm, Squirmy.

9 Any parent of toddlers or preschoolers can testify that the "girls" on *Sesame Street* are not very popular. Children ask their parents for Bert and Ernie dolls, not Baby Alice. Is this just because the girls are not marketed via books, tapes, placemats and toy dolls the same way the boys are? Or is it that the *Sesame Street* writers simply have not developed the girls into the same types of lovable, adorable personalities that belong to the main characters?

10 Interestingly and peculiarly, the minor "girls" look more human than most of the well-loved animal roles. They are not physically cuddly, colorful or bizarre, as are the more important male characters. Prairie Dawn has ordinary blonde hair and brown eyes—nothing even remotely similar to Big Bird's soft yellow feathers or Cookie Monster's wild, bright blue, mane.

11 Yes, we believe that *Sesame Street* is one of the best shows on television for small children. Our children—boys and girls—are regular viewers. In addition to its educational value, lack of violence and emphasis on cooperation, the adult characters on the show are admirably balanced in terms of avoiding sexual stereotypes.

12 But even the best of the bunch has room for improvement. Just as elementary through professional school educators must learn to be more sensitive to subtle and unintentional gender bias, so too should the folks at Children's Television Network. We can stop sexism from seeping into our children's first "formal" educational experience.

13 The message was brought to you by the letter F: fairness for females.

THINKING CRITICALLY
about "Sesame Street"

1. This essay spends no time on the criteria part of the argument ("Sexism is bad") and all its time on the match argument ("*Sesame Street* exhibits sexism"). Why do the authors feel no need to defend the criterion?
2. Do the authors convince you that *Sesame Street* is sexist?
3. If you agree with the argument that *Sesame Street* is sexist, should that criterion be sufficient for undermining the popular assessment of *Sesame Street* as a model educational program for children?

The final reading, an essay by student writer Teresa Filice, uses the criteria for evaluating Web sites found in Skill 20.3—authority, objectivity or clear disclosure of advocacy, coverage, accuracy, and currency—to evaluate the site Parents: The Anti-Drug (www.theantidrug.com). Although an evaluation of material on the Internet could focus on the home page or even on one link of a Web site, Teresa has chosen to examine whether this advocacy site as a whole accomplishes its purposes effectively.

Teresa Filice

Parents: The Anti-Drug:

A Useful Site

1 The United States' War on Drugs seems to make little progress, and the drug use of American teenagers remains a rampant problem; however, positive, forward-thinking groups have risen to the occasion and sought to meet the challenge, as anyone who listens to radio ads or reads popular news magazines will testify. While the Reagan-sponsored "Just say no" mantra toward drugs still prevails in some households, some anti-drug organizations are promoting open and honest communication between parents and their teens. These groups offer information and fresh perspectives on helping parents talk to their children about illegal substances. In my exploration of how the Web has been enlisted in this campaign against teen drug use, I chose to analyze the site of *Parents: The Anti-Drug* to determine if it is a good advocacy Web site. My evaluation employed the following well-accepted criteria: the breadth of coverage, the accuracy and currency of the information provided, and the site's openness about its mission, goals, and supporters. Despite some strong misgivings in the disclosure area of the Web site, I concluded that it is still a worthwhile advocacy site on the topic of teens and drug prevention, specifically in regards to the current, extensive information it provides on teens and drug use.

2 Initially, I had difficulty discovering what organizations and special interest groups were sponsoring this site, so the site failed to meet the criterion of clear disclosure of advocacy or objectivity. After clicking on the "About Us" link (which was fairly difficult to find), I found out that the site jumps to another Web site for the *Media Campaign*, sponsored by the Office of National Drug Control Policy (http://www.mediacampaign.org). The Office of National Drug Control Policy is a government-sponsored organization, and the Media Campaign site contains links to the White House Web site. Though *Parents: The Anti-Drug* and the *Media Campaign* Web sites are not outrightly politically biased, further scrutiny reveals glimpses of the current conservative political administration in both sites. There is an entire section of *Parents: The Anti-Drug* dedicated to faith leaders and faith-based activities to keep teens away from illegal substances.

3 In addition, I noticed that this advocacy organization's site speaks about and to parents and teens in a traditional, middle-class family setting and therefore limits its coverage and usefulness. Most of the advice the site offers is based on the fact that teens will have parents with enough time (which often means money as well) to spend with them. While most parents may want to spend quality time with their children, many American parents literally cannot afford time for their children. The site also constantly refers to life in the suburbs and suburban values. One of the boys in the Prescription video states, "I couldn't be a drug addict ... I'm from the suburbs." In addition, some of the advice given to parents seems simplistic and unrealistic. For example, the site offers somewhat unrealistic suggestions for "summer activities" for parents to keep their children out of dangerous situations where drugs might be present: "Encourage them to write a song, and then let them record it; build, and

maintain a birdfeeder; encourage them to paint a mural; and make homemade ice cream together" (http://www.theantidrug.com/SchoolsOut/activity_checklist.asp?action=form). This site seems to be imagining a specific, limited audience with somewhat old-fashioned values.

4 Despite these flaws and this one area of narrowness, *Parents: The Anti-Drug* has a wide range of information and appears committed to transmitting important factual material to viewers. The site provides an extensive breadth of coverage and accurate information on teen behavior, recreational drugs, and motivating factors for teen drug use. The home page of the site is divided into three panels: "Learn," "Evaluate," and "Take Action," each of which offers numerous links such as "Signs & Symptoms," "Hear Real Stories and Advice," and "Find Help Locally." The "Drug Information" page (http://www.theantidrug.com/drug_info/), which is easily accessible from the home page, offers comprehensive information on a wide variety of drugs, including more recent offenders such as prescription drugs and Ecstasy. In each subsequent section, the site presents basic drug information, the health risks, and the signs that a person might be using that drug. Additionally, each link for the various drugs offers further links with specifics about that drug. The site also has specific "Feature Articles" on topics such as "Keep Your Teen Athlete Drug-Free" and "Teens, Drugs, and Violence." The section on "Teens, Drugs, and Violence" contains documented scientific and social development statistics on the rates of teen drug use and violence. It also has links to other advocacy sites that target gang activity and bullying at school. The "Studies and Research" section (http://www.theantidrug.com/news/studies-and-research.aspx) lists several articles from well-respected medical journals such as the *Journal of Preventative Medicine* and the *American Journal of Public Health*, as well as presenting the authors' credentials. I concluded that the entire site provides well-documented sources for the statistics it uses.

5 *Parents: The Anti-Drug* also shows its worth by meeting the important criterion of currency. The site is surprisingly current and exemplifies a fairly progressive attitude toward and direct approach to drug prevention. *Parents: The Anti-Drug* favors discussion and open communication with teens, as opposed to criticizing their beliefs. The "Teens Today" section cheekily reminds parents that "teens today are less likely to drink, smoke, commit a crime, or get pregnant or drop out of school, compared to their parents' generation" (http://www.theantidrug.com/advice/inside-teens-today.asp). The "Kids Eye View" section provides a voice for the teens themselves, offers a glimpse as to why certain teenagers choose to engage in this activity, and includes video diaries. The site also uses videos to give it a sense of immediacy. For example, on the "Prescription Drug Abuse" video, a teenage girl with brown curly hair comes into focus on the screen. Her name is Sara and she is nineteen years old. She recalls for the camera her path toward prescription drug addiction that began in her own home. She says, "I could find them [prescriptions] in my kitchen cupboard ... My parents wouldn't notice it, without the smell of marijuana" (http://www.theantidrug.com/drug_info/prescription_video.asp). Most parents never want to see their children share this young woman's struggles with addiction, rehab, and the subsequent consequences of both. With material like these videos, this site shows its relevance and awareness of the urgency of the problem and offers helpful advice.

6 Although the site *Parents: The Anti-Drug* has some weaknesses, its strengths compensate well for these deficiencies. I spent many hours poring over the *Parents: The Anti-Drug* Web site. It bothered me greatly that the site emphasized middle-class values and did not fully disclose its government sponsorship. However, after taking some time away from viewing the Web site, I decided to imagine what a visit to this site would mean to parents desperate to communicate with their child. This Web site provides numerous valuable recommendations and, most importantly, provides credible and ample information on a subject that many parents need to understand. Though the site may appear unrealistic in places to older teens, I think it does effectively reach its target group and does qualify as a good advocacy Web site.

Work Cited

Parents: The Anti-Drug. The National Youth Anti-Drug Media Campaign, n.d. Web. 20 May 2007.

THINKING CRITICALLY

about "*Parents: The Anti-Drug*: A Useful Site"

1. In her evaluation argument, Teresa Filice evaluates the advocacy site Parents: The Anti-Drug for its usefulness for parents. How might her evaluation criteria vary if she were evaluating this site for a different audience—for example, teens or the medical profession?
2. What opposing views does Teresa Filice acknowledge in her argument? How does she respond to them?
3. Where do examples work well to support the match part of her argument?
4. From your own use of advocacy Web sites, what evaluation criteria would you add to the typical ones listed here in the headnote, applied in this argument, and presented in more detail in Skill 20.3?

PEARSON mycomplab For support in learning this chapter's content, follow this path in **MyCompLab**: Resources ⇒ Writing ⇒ Writing Purposes ⇒ Writing to Evaluate. Review the Instruction and Multimedia resources, then complete the Exercises and click on Gradebook to measure your progress.

PROPOSING A SOLUTION

15

Proposal arguments call an audience to action. They make a claim that some action should or ought to be taken. Sometimes referred to informally as *should arguments,* proposals are among the most common kinds of arguments that you will write or read.

Practical proposals focus on local, practical problems and generally target a specific audience (usually the person with the power to act on the proposal). For example, Lucy Morsen's proposal in this chapter (pages 423–426) advocates banning laptops and cell phones in classrooms. In the work world, many individuals and businesses generate new revenues by writing competitive proposals to solve a prospective client's practical problem.

Another kind of proposal, a **policy proposal,** addresses public policy issues with the aim of swaying public support toward the writer's proposed solution. Student writer Dylan Fujitani's proposal against using civilian contractors in military roles (pages 429–433) illustrates a researched policy proposal.

The power of proposal arguments is often enhanced with images, which can appeal to both *logos* and *pathos.* In fact, proposal arguments sometimes take the form of striking visual-verbal texts such as posters or **advocacy advertisements** calling an audience to action. Additionally, proposal arguments can be delivered as **oral presentations** when, for example, a citizen presents a proposal at an open-mike public hearing.

The writing projects for this chapter cover the range of genres just described—a written proposal, an advocacy ad or poster, and a speech with visual aids. No matter what genre you choose, you must make the problem vivid to your audience before proposing and justifying a course of action.

In this chapter, by writing a proposal argument, you will learn to:

- convince your audience that a serious problem exists
- persuade them that some action should be taken to resolve it

Exploring Proposal Writing

The following activity introduces you to the thinking processes involved in writing a proposal argument.

1. In small groups, identify and list several major problems facing students in your college or university.

2. Decide among yourselves which problems are most important and rank them in order of importance.
3. Choose your group's number-one problem and explore answers to the following questions. Group recorders should be prepared to present answers to the class as a whole.
   a. Why is the problem a problem?
   b. For whom is the problem a problem?
   c. How will these people suffer if the problem is not solved? Give specific examples.
   d. Who has the power to solve the problem?
   e. Why hasn't the problem been solved up to this point?
   f. How can the problem be solved? Create a proposal for a solution.
   g. What are the probable benefits of acting on your proposal?
   h. What costs are associated with your proposal?
   i. Who will bear these costs?
   j. Why should this proposal be enacted?
   k. What makes this proposal better than alternative proposals?
4. As a group, draft an outline for a proposal argument in which you:
   a. Describe the problem and its significance.
   b. Propose your solution to the problem.
   c. Justify your proposal by showing how the benefits outweigh the costs.
5. Recorders for each group should write the group's outline on the board and be prepared to present the group's argument orally to the class.

Understanding Proposal Writing

All proposals have one feature in common—they offer a solution to a problem. For every proposed solution, there are always alternative solutions, including doing nothing. Your task therefore is to convince readers that the problem is worth solving, that your proposed solution will actually work, and that the benefits outweigh the costs. Accordingly, a proposal argument typically has three main parts:

1. ***Description of the problem.*** You must first demonstrate that a significant problem exists. Your goal is to make the problem vivid and real for your readers. Who is affected by the problem? What are its causes? Why hasn't it been solved before? What are the negative consequences of not solving the problem?
2. ***Proposal for a solution.*** This section describes your solution with enough detail to show how it would work and what it would cost. If you don't have a solution, you may choose to generate a planning proposal calling for a committee to propose solutions at a later date.
3. ***Justification.*** Here you persuade your audience that your proposal should be enacted. Typically you show that the benefits of your proposal outweigh the costs. You also need to show why your proposed solution is better than alternative solutions. Point out why other possible approaches would not solve the problem, would provide fewer benefits, or would cost significantly more than your proposed solution.

In the following sections, we examine the special challenges of proposal arguments and then show you a powerful strategy for developing the justification section of a proposal.

Special Challenges of Proposal Arguments

To get your readers to take action—the ultimate purpose of a proposal—you must overcome some difficult challenges. In the following chart, we examine the special difficulties people encounter when writing proposal arguments and offer strategies for overcoming them.

Strategies for Overcoming the Special Challenges of Proposal Arguments

Challenge	Explanation	What to Do
Giving the problem presence	To convince readers that a problem exists, you must make them *see* and *feel* the problem—give the problem *presence*.	• Use anecdotes or examples of people suffering from the problem. • Provide startling facts or statistics to dramatize the problem. • Include a photograph or other image that conveys the problem. • Use other appeals to *pathos*.
Appealing to the interests and values of decision makers	A proposal that benefits one group often creates costs for others. Decision makers may not share the sufferers' perspective on a problem. Solving your problem may simply cause more problems for the decision maker.	• Show decision makers how acting on your proposal will benefit *them* directly. • Use audience-based reasons. • If appropriate, appeal to idealism and principle (do the right thing, even if it will cause temporary grief). • Show how benefits to the sufferers outweigh costs to others.
Overcoming inherent conservatism	People are inherently resistant to change, often willing to live with a flawed but bearable situation rather than risk change that could make the situation worse. "Better the devil you know than the one you don't know."	• Emphasize the seriousness of the problem (give it *presence*). • Stress the benefits of solving the problem. • Emphasize the lost potential in not acting. • Show that the risks are minimal. • Show that negative consequences are unlikely.

(*continued*)

Challenge	Explanation	What to Do
Predicting consequences	Often readers distrust the proposal writer's rosy scenario. They doubt that the predicted benefits will occur, or they fear negative consequences.	• Take care not to overpromise benefits. • Persuade readers that your predictions are realistic—show how the links in the chain lead directly from the solution to the benefits. • Cite cases where a similar proposal led to real benefits.
Evaluating consequences	Any solution that benefits one group may bring costs to another group. It is difficult to establish a common principle of measurement for weighing costs against benefits.	• In some cases, you can use money as measurement—the savings from this proposal will be more than the initial costs. • In other cases, emphasize that the benefits of increased happiness, less suffering, or saved time outweigh the initial dollar costs. • Emphasize the greatest good for the greatest number (more people will have benefits; fewer will bear costs). • Emphasize idealism and principle (this is the right thing to do despite the cost).

With these particular challenges in mind, we now set forth some strategies for making proposals as effective as possible.

Developing an Effective Justification Section

The distinctions between proposals and other kinds of arguments invite particular kinds of support for proposals. Writers often develop support for their proposals by using the three-strategy approach, which focuses sequentially on principles, consequences, and precedents or analogies, as explained here.

Strategies for Developing a Justification Section

Strategies	What to Do	Templates and Comments	Examples
Argument from principle	Argue that an action should (should not) be taken because it is right (wrong) according to some value, assumption, principle, or belief you share with your audience.	We should (should not) do (this action) because (this action) is ____________. Fill in the blank with a belief or value that the audience holds: *good, honest, fair,* and so on.	"We should create publicly financed jobs for poor people because doing so is both charitable and just."

Strategies	What to Do	Templates and Comments	Examples
Argument from consequence	Argue that an action should (should not) be taken because doing so will lead to consequences that you and your audience think are good (bad).	We should (should not) do (this action) because (this action) will lead to these good (bad) consequences: ________, ________, and ________. Use consequences that your audience will agree are good or bad, as needed.	"We should create publicly financed jobs for poor people because doing so will provide them with money for food and housing, promote a work ethic, and produce needed goods and services."
Argument from precedent or analogy	Argue that an action should (should not) be taken because doing so is similar to what was done in another case, which turned out well (badly).	We should (should not) do (this action) because doing (this action) is like ________, which turned out to be good (bad). Use precedents or analogies that are similar to your proposed action and that will have good (bad) associations for your audience.	*Precedent:* "We should create publicly financed jobs for poor people because doing so will alleviate poverty just as a similar program has helped the poor in Upper Magnesia." *Analogy:* " . . . because doing so is like teaching the poor how to fish rather than giving them fish."

Each of these argumentation strategies was clearly evident in a public debate in Seattle, Washington, over a proposal to raise county sales taxes to build a new baseball stadium. Those favoring the stadium put forth arguments such as these:

> We should build the new stadium because preserving our national pastime for our children is important (*argument from principle*), because building the stadium will create new jobs and revitalize the adjacent Pioneer Square district (*argument from consequence*), and because building the stadium will have the same beneficial effects on the city that building Camden Yards had in Baltimore (*argument from precedent*).

Those opposing the stadium created arguments using the same strategies:

> We should not build the stadium because it is wrong to subsidize rich owners and players with tax dollars (*argument from principle*), because building a stadium diverts tax money from more important concerns such as low-income housing (*argument from consequence*), and because Toronto's experience with Skydome shows that once the novelty of a new stadium wears off, attendance declines dramatically (*argument from precedent*).

FOR WRITING AND DISCUSSION

Using Different Strategies to Develop Support

Working individually or in small groups, use the strategies of principle, consequence, and precedent/analogy to create *because* clauses that support (or oppose) the following proposals. Try to have at least one *because* clause from each of the strategies, but generate as many reasons as possible.

Example:

Claim	Spanking children should be made illegal.
Principle	Because it is wrong to cause bodily pain to children.
Consequence	Because it teaches children that it is okay to hit someone out of anger; because it causes children to obey rules out of fear rather than respect; because it can lead children to be abusive parents.
Precedent/analogy	Because spanking a child is like throwing dishes or banging your fists against a wall—it relieves your anger but turns the child into an object.

1. The school year for grades K–12 should/should not be extended to eleven months.
2. "Enhanced interrogation techniques" (such as sleep deprivation, stressful positions, or water boarding) should/should not be used on suspected terrorists.
3. An impenetrable fence should/should not be built between the United States and Mexico.
4. Marijuana should/should not be legalized.
5. The federal government should/should not enact a substantially increased tax on gasoline.

Proposals as Visual Arguments and PowerPoint Presentations

Proposal arguments are often enhanced by photographs, drawings, graphs, or other images. Frequently we encounter proposal arguments as condensed, attention-grabbing verbal-visual texts such as posters or flyers, paid advertisements in newspapers or magazines, brochures, or Web pages in advocacy Web sites. Their creators know the arguments must work fast to capture our attention, give presence to a problem, advocate a solution, and enlist our support. These advocacy ads frequently use photographs, images, or icons that are arresting or in some way memorable and that appeal to a reader's emotions and imagination.

As an example of a one-page advocacy ad, consider Figure 15.1, which is sponsored by the organization Common Sense for Drug Policy. Note how the advocacy advertisement makes its view of the problem real and urgent to readers by using disturbing black-and-white drawings, varied type sizes and fonts, and powerful lists of evidence. It also gains credibility through its documentation of sources, presented at the bottom of the page.

WHITE KIDS ARE MUCH MORE LIKELY TO BE USING (AND SELLING) DRUGS!

According to the federal Centers for Disease Control, he's 4 times more likely than his African-American classmate to be a regular cocaine user.

White high-school students who are current users of cocaine: 4.1%[1]

Chance of a white person ever trying an illicit drug in their lifetime: 42%[2]

Percent of felony drug defendants in state courts who are white: 37%[3]

Percent of white drug felons given probation or nonincarceration sentence by state courts: 32%[4]

Percent of white drug felons sentenced to prison by state courts each year: 27%[5]

According to the Justice Department, if he's arrested on drug charges, he's 1-1/2 times more likely than his white classmate to be sent to prison.

African-American high-school students who are current users of cocaine: 1.1%[1]

Chance of an African-American person ever trying an illicit drug in their lifetime: 37.7%[2]

Percent of felony drug defendants in state courts who are black: 61%[3]

Percent of black drug felons given probation or nonincarceration sentence by state courts: 25%[4]

Percent of black drug felons sentenced to prison by state courts each year: 43%[5]

BLACK KIDS ARE MORE LIKELY TO GO TO PRISON!

Note:
According to the US Justice Department and the Office of National Drug Control Policy, drug users typically buy their drugs from sellers of their own racial or ethnic background. Research of Ethnicity & Race of Drug Sellers and Users: US Dept. of Justice National Institute of Justice & the Office of National Drug Control Policy, "Crack, Powder Cocaine, and Heroin: Drug Purchase and Use Patterns in Six U.S. Cities, " December 1997, p.1, 16, and p. 15, Table 16.

Sources:

1 Data on drug use by high-school students: Youth Risk Behavior Survey 1999, Centers for Disease Control, reported in Morbidity and Mortality Weekly Report, Vol. 49, No. SS-5, p. 66, Table 24.

2 Data on lifetime prevalence of drug use: US Dept. of HHS Substance Abuse and Mental Health Services Administration, "Summary of Findings from the 1999 National Household Survey on Drug Abuse," August 2000, p. G-13, Table G-13.

3 Demogaphic data on felony drug defendants in state courts: US Dept. of Justice Bureau of Justice Statistics. "Felony Defendants in Large Urban Counties, 1996," October 1999, p.4, Table 3

4 Demographic data on felony drug defendants in state courts: US Dept. of Justice Bureau of Justice Statistics, "State Court Sentencing of Convicted Felons, 1996," February 2000, p. 13, Table 2.5

5 Demographic data on felony drug defendants in state courts: US Dept. of Justice Bureau of Justice Statistics, "State Court Sentencing of Convicted Felons, 1996," February 2000, p. 13, Table 2.5

Kevin B. Zeese, President, Common Sense for Drug Policy
3220 "N" Street, NW, #141, Washington, D.C. 20007 * 703-354-9050 * fax 703-354-5695 * info@csdp.org
For more information, visit www.csdp.org and www.drugwarfacts.org

FIGURE 15.1 A One-Page Advocacy Advertisement from a Magazine

For a somewhat different approach to a visual proposal argument, consider the part opener image shown on page 607. This advocacy ad, sponsored by the American Indian College Fund, uses striking portrait and landscape photography and simple but powerful claims to make appeals for financial support for tribal colleges. Note how this ad employs familiar images of the West (the grassy plain and towering rock formation) yet resists stereotypes in the contemporary figure of the young Navajo woman. For a visual proposal argument that relies even more heavily on visual impact, consider the part opener image shown on page 637. This poster, "If You Are Not Using It ... Turn It Off," produced by Energy Conservation Awareness Products, employs a striking symbolic image and a vivid use of color to underscore its simple, forceful message.

Since proposal arguments are often delivered orally rather than visually as ads, speakers frequently create visual aids with presentation software like PowerPoint.* Although effectively designed slides can enhance the impact of a speech, PowerPoint presentations are controversial among communication experts. Used poorly, PowerPoint can detract from an argument rather than enhance it. A Web search reveals wonderfully satirical diatribes against PowerPoint—including Lincoln's Gettysburg address imagined as a PowerPoint presentation, complete with Lincoln's mumbling, grumbling, off-the-cuff remarks as he tries to connect his laptop to the projector. Despite all the ways that PowerPoint can go wrong, using it to produce effective visual aids can enhance an argument's appeals to *logos, pathos,* and *ethos*. In the last writing project for this chapter, we offer advice on powerful ways to use PowerPoint in support of a proposal speech.

WRITING PROJECT

A Proposal Argument

Call your audience's attention to a problem, propose a solution to that problem, and present a justification for your solution. You have two choices (or your instructor may limit you to just one): (a) create a practical proposal, with a letter of transmittal, proposing a nuts-and-bolts solution to a local problem; or (b) write a more general policy proposal, addressing a public issue, in the form of a feature editorial for a particular (state, local, or college) newspaper. If you choose (b), your instructor might ask you to do research and model your proposal after a magazine or journal article.

*PowerPoint, which is a registered trademark of Microsoft, has become the common name for all kinds of computer-created and -projected slides. However, other companies also make presentation software. We use the term "PowerPoint presentation" because its use has become ubiquitous in business and industry. We intend the term to include any kind of oral presentation supported by visual aids developed on presentation software. Most businesses and professions now expect new management-level hires to be adept at using presentation software in oral presentations.

Generating and Exploring Ideas

If you have trouble thinking of a proposal topic, try making an idea map of local problems you would like to see solved. Consider some of the following starting points:

Finding a Proposal Issue

Problems at your university: parking, registration system, absence of recycling options, hours of cafeterias and eating facilities, too many activities on campus during the week, poor school spirit, problems with residence halls, availability of internships

Problems in your city or town: lack of bike paths, inadequate lighting, unattractive public parks or lack of public parks, zoning problems, inadequate support for public education, need for public transportation, conservation of water

Problems at your place of work: flow of customer traffic, inadequate staffing during peak times, unclear division of responsibilities, no policies for raises or training new employees, health care coverage, safety issues

Social problems and problems related to other aspects of your life: problems with credit card debt, need for financial literacy, physical fitness in the public schools, aid for victims of disasters, employment opportunities for college students, media consumption and awareness of current events

Another approach is to freewrite your response to these trigger statements:

I would really like to solve the problem of ______________.
I believe that X should ______________. (Substitute for X words such as *my instructor, the president, the school administration, Congress, my boss,* and so forth.)

Note that the problem you pose for this paper can be personal, but shouldn't be private; that is, others should be able to benefit from a solution to your personal problem. For example, your inability to find child care for your daughter is a private problem. But if you focus your proposal on how zoning laws discourage development of in-home day care—and propose a change in those zoning laws to permit more in-home day care centers—then your proposal will benefit others.

Using Stock Issues to Explore Your Problem

Once you have decided on a proposal issue, explore it by freewriting your responses to the following questions. These questions are often called *stock issues,* since they represent generic, or stock, questions that apply to almost any kind of proposal.

1. Is there a problem here that has to be solved?
2. Will the proposed solution really solve this problem?
3. Can the problem be solved in a simpler way without disturbing the status quo?
4. Is the proposed solution practical enough that it really stands a chance of being implemented?
5. What will be the positive and negative consequences of the proposal?

You might also try freewriting your responses to the questions in the exploratory exercise on page 402. Although these questions cover much the same territory as the stock issues, their different presentation might stimulate additional thought.

Finally, try thinking of justifications for your solution by using the three-strategy approach described on pages 404–405.

Avoiding Presupposing Your Solution in Your Problem Statement

A common mistake of inexperienced proposal writers is to write problem statements that presuppose their solutions. As a restaurant server, suppose you notice that customers want coffee refills faster than servers can provide them. To solve this problem, you propose placing carafes of hot coffee at each table. When describing your problem, don't presuppose your solution: "The problem is that we don't have carafes of hot coffee at the tables." Rather, describe the problematic situation itself: annoyed customers clamoring for coffee and harassed servers trying to bring around refills. Only by giving presence to the original problem can you interest readers in your proposed solution, which readers will compare to other possible approaches (including doing nothing).

Here is another example:

> **Weak:** The problem is that the Student Union doesn't stay open late enough at night.
>
> **Better:** The problem is that students who study late at night don't have an attractive, convenient place to socialize or study; off-campus coffee houses are too far to walk to at night; dorm lounges aren't attractive or conducive to studying; late-nighters make noise in the dorms instead of going to a convenient place.

Shaping and Drafting

In Figure 15.2, we show a typical organizational plan for a proposal argument that you might use if you get stuck while composing the first draft of your essay.

FIGURE 15.2 Framework of a Proposal Argument

Introduction	• Presents and describes a problem that needs solving, giving it presence • Gives background including previous attempts to solve the problem • Argues that the problem is solvable (optional)
Presentation of the proposed solution	• States the solution succinctly • Explains the specifics of the solution
Justification	• Persuades readers that the proposal should be implemented • Presents and develops Reasons 1, 2, and so forth • Reasons to support the proposed solution may be arguments from principle, consequence, and precedent or analogy
Summary and rebuttal of opposing views	*Policy proposal:* • Presents opposing view(s) • Rebuts opposing view(s) *Practical proposal:* • Presents alternative solution(s) • Explains why alternative solution(s) are inferior
Conclusion	• Asks readers to act (sometimes incorporated into the last sentences of the final supporting reason)

Revising

After you have completed your first draft and begun to clarify your argument for yourself, you are ready to start making your argument clear and persuasive for your readers. Use the strategies for clear closed-form prose outlined in Chapter 17. At this stage, feedback from peer readers can be very helpful.

Questions for Peer Review

In addition to the generic peer review questions explained in Skill 16.4, ask your peer reviewers to address these questions:

INTRODUCTION AND STATEMENT OF PROBLEM:

1. How could the title more effectively focus the paper and pique your interest?
2. Where does the writer convince you that a problem exists and that it is significant (worth solving) and solvable? Where does the writer give the problem presence? How could the writer improve the presentation of the problem?

PROPOSED SOLUTION:

3. Does the writer's thesis clearly propose a solution to the problem? Could the thesis be made more precise?
4. Could the writer give you more details about the solution so that you can understand it and see how it works? How could the writer make the solution clearer?

JUSTIFICATION:

5. In the justification section, how could the writer provide stronger reasons for acting on the proposal? Where could the reasons be better supported with more details and evidence? How could the reasons appeal more to the values and beliefs of the audience?
6. Can you help the writer think of additional justifying arguments (arguments from principle, from consequences, from precedent or analogy)? How else could the writer improve support for the proposal?
7. Where does the writer anticipate and address opposing views or alternative solutions? How does the writer convince you that the proposed solution is superior to alternative solutions?
8. Has the writer persuaded you that the benefits of this proposal will outweigh the costs? Who will pay the costs and who will get the benefits? What do you think the gut reaction of a typical decision maker would be to the writer's proposal?
9. Can you think of other, unforeseen costs that the writer should acknowledge and address? What unforeseen benefits could the writer mention?
10. How might the writer improve the structure and clarity of the argument? Where might the writer better apply the principles of clarity from Chapter 17?

WRITING PROJECT

Advocacy Ad or Poster

Create a one-page advocacy ad or poster that presents a controversial public problem and calls for action and support. Consider how you will use all the features of visual arguments—type sizes and fonts, layout, color, and images and graphics—to grab the attention of your audience, construct a compelling sketch of the problem, and inform your audience what course of action you want them to take. In this advocacy piece, you need to capture your proposal argument in a highly condensed form, while making it visually clear and memorable. Your instructor might ask you instead to create a longer brochure-length handout or a Web page.

Using Document Design Features

To interpret and drive home the problem presented in photos or drawings, advocacy ads employ different type sizes and fonts. Large-type text in these documents frequently takes the form of slogans or condensed thesis statements written in an arresting style. Here are some examples of large boldfaced copy from advocacy literature that the authors of this text have encountered recently:

- "Abstinence: It works every time. ... " (from a newspaper advocacy ad sponsored by Focus on the Family, asking readers to donate money to promote abstinence education)
- "Educating, Organizing, Fighting to end the barbarism, racism, unfairness, and shame of judicial homicide in our lifetime" (from an advocacy ad in the *Progressive* asking readers to donate money to Death Penalty Focus to end capital punishment)
- "Expectant Mothers Deserve Compassionate Health Care—Not Prison!" (an advocacy advertisement from Common Sense for Drug Policy; this one appeared in the *National Review*)

To outline and justify their solutions, creators of advocacy ads often put main supporting reasons in bulleted lists and sometimes enclose carefully selected facts and quotations in boxed sidebars. To add an authoritative *ethos,* the ads often include footnotes and bibliographies in fine print.

Another prominent feature of these condensed, highly visual arguments is their direct call for a course of action: Go to an advocacy Web site to find out more information on how to support a cause; cut out a postcard-like form to send to a decision maker; vote for or against the proposition or the candidate; write a letter to a political representative; or donate money to a cause.

Exploring and Generating Ideas

The first stage of your invention process should be the same as that for a longer proposal argument. Choose a controversial public issue that needs immediate attention or a neglected issue about which you want to arouse public passion. As with a longer proposal argument, consider your audience in order to identify the values and beliefs on which you will base your appeal.

Shaping and Drafting

When you construct your argument, the limited space available puts high demands on you, the writer, to be efficient in your choice of words and in your use of document design. Your goal is to have a memorable impact on your readers in order to promote the action you advocate. When creating a condensed advocacy ad, we suggest that you consider the following question-asking strategies to help you design your ad:

Strategies for Choosing Design Features for an Advocacy Ad

Features and Strategies to Consider	Questions to Ask
Medium: Choose the most appropriate medium for your rhetorical purpose.	Will your advocacy argument be a poster, a flyer, a one-page advertisement in a newspaper or magazine, a brochure, or a Web page?
Giving Presence to the Problem: Choose the most effective visual features to create appeals to *pathos*.	What would be the best means to establish the urgency and importance of the problem: graphic elements, cartoon images, photos?
Presenting the Core of the Proposal: Decide on how you will condense your argument and convey it clearly.	What type size, font, and layout will be the most powerful in presenting your claim and justifying your reasons to your intended audience? How much verbal text do you want to use?
Accentuating Key Phrases: Decide what key phrases could highlight the parts or the main points of this argument.	What memorable phrases or slogans could you use to convey your argument? How condensed or detailed should your argument be?
Clarifying the Call for Action: Decide what you are asking your audience to do.	How can document design clarify the course of action and the direct demand on the audience that this argument is proposing?
Using Color for Impact: Decide whether you will use color. Note: For some media, color might be cost-prohibitive.	If color is an option, how could you use color to enhance the overall impact of your advocacy argument? How could you use black-and-white images effectively?

Revising

Because visual elements are subject to personal and varied interpretations even more so than verbal text, you will want to try out your advocacy ad on a group of readers who can role-play your intended audience. Ask your readers to focus on the messages that your advocacy piece sends, the emotional impact of the piece, and the credibility and professionalism it conveys.

Questions for Peer Review

In addition to the generic peer review questions explained in Skill 16.4, ask your peer reviewers to address these questions:

1. How clear is the argument of this advocacy ad? Where could the presentation of the problem, the claim, and the reasons be clearer?
2. What design features (type, layout, images and graphics, and color) work particularly well in this advocacy ad? Where could the designer make improvements?
3. To what course of action is the ad calling the audience? How could this appeal to take action be clearer and more powerful?
4. How could the designer enhance his/her credibility and authority? How could the designer make this advocacy argument more compelling and memorable in this medium?

WRITING PROJECT

Proposal Speech with Visual Aids

Deliver a proposal argument as a prepared but extemporaneous speech of approximately five to eight minutes supported with visual aids created on presentation software such as PowerPoint or through other means. Your speech should present a problem, propose a solution, justify the solution with reasons and evidence, and defend it against objections or alternative solutions. As you deliver your speech, use appropriate visual aids to give presence to the problem, highlight points, provide memorable data or evidence, or otherwise enhance appeals to *logos, ethos,* and *pathos*. Although the following explanations focus on PowerPoint (or equivalent presentation software), low-tech means of using visual aids (for example, overhead transparencies or flip charts) can also be effective. Follow the guidelines provided by your instructor.

As you contemplate this project, consider its three different components: creating the speech itself, designing the visuals, and delivering the speech. As you create your proposal argument, think *aurally* by imagining your audience listening to a speech rather than reading a written text and think *visually* by considering how visual aids can increase the clarity and persuasive power of your argument.

Developing, Shaping, and Outlining Your Proposal Speech

This project asks you to deliver your proposal speech extemporaneously. To speak extemporaneously means to spend ample time preparing the speech, but not to read it from a script or to recite it from memory. Instead, the speaker talks directly to the audience with the aid of an outline or note cards.

Long before the delivery of the speech, the speaker should have engaged in the same sort of composing process that precedes a finished essay, including giving attention to both subject-matter and rhetorical problems. Effective speakers typically spend an hour of preparation time per minute of speaking time. Much of this work focuses on creating a well-developed sentence outline for the speech. Finding the balance between a speech that is too impromptu and one that is too "scripted," and therefore begs for an audience of readers, is a main consideration in creating a speech.

One way to accommodate the needs of listeners is to make your speech even more closed form than are closed-form essays. To help an audience grasp an argument aurally, speakers need to forecast their points and provide aural signals. The most common formula for a speech is sometimes called the "tell 'em rule." It says: Tell 'em what you are about to say, say it, and then tell 'em what you just said. This redundancy greatly enhances an audience's ability to follow a spoken argument without a text. This "tell 'em rule" serves audience-based needs for unity and coherence, for receiving old information before new information, and for forecasting and fulfillment. Another important way to help your audience follow your speech is to use attributive tags to indicate who and when you are quoting: "According to Pat Miller, a clinical psychologist at Children's Hospital, ... " These attributive tags signal a quotation and also indicate why the quoted material is important.

In developing the content for your speech, follow the suggestions for idea generation and development covered in the first writing project for this chapter, pages 409–410. Also try the following strategies:

Strategies for Creating Effective Speech Outlines

Strategies	Rationales and Explanations of How They Work
Plan the structure and content of your speech with the needs of your audience in mind.	How can you make the problem come alive for your audience and make your solution understandable and persuasive? What background information or defined terms does your audience need? What kinds of evidence will you need to show the seriousness of the problem and to support your reasons for enacting the proposal? What objections will your listeners be apt to raise? How can you motivate action?

(continued)

Strategies	Rationales and Explanations of How They Work
Create a complete-sentence outline of your argument; use parallel structures, coordination, and subordination to clarify relationships among ideas.	See Skill 17.3 for advice about different kinds of outlines, particularly the advantage of complete-sentence outlines, which state meanings rather than topics. Since you won't be writing out the complete argument in prose, this outline will be the written frame for your speech.
Build into your outline places for explicit signposting to help the audience follow your speech.	Indicate where you are in your speech: "My second reason is that. . . . " "As I stated earlier. . . . "
Early on, practice saying your speech in a normally paced speaking voice to determine its length.	Often speeches can cover much less ground than a written argument. By timing the speech when it is still in its rough draft stage, you will know whether you must cut or add material.

Designing Your Visual Aids

If you use presentation software such as PowerPoint to design your visual aids, focus on making your argument clear and persuasive rather than on demonstrating your technical wizardry.* A common mistake with PowerPoint presentations—in addition to producing boring or jumbled slides—is to make too many slides, to overdesign them, or to become enamored with special effects rather than with the ideas in the speech.

Using Points, Not Topics, as Slide Titles

Many communication researchers object to Microsoft's default PowerPoint template, which encourages short topic phrases for the title of a slide. The "title" box uses a large (for example, Arial 44-point bold) font that limits the number of words at the top of the slide. Dissatisfied with this approach, many researchers argue that points (stated in complete sentences) are more effective than topic phrases for conveying meanings, and they recommend writing complete-sentence assertions at the top of the slide. To do so, however, one has to override the PowerPoint default to use a smaller font. Professor Michael Alley recommends using an Arial 28-point bold font for slide headlines. This font is large enough to be seen throughout the room, but small enough to allow a two-line complete sentence for the headline.

*Our discussion of visual aids designed on PowerPoint is indebted to advice from our rhetorician colleague, Professor Jeffrey Philpott in the Department of Communication at Seattle University. We are also indebted to the work of Professor Michael Alley of Virginia Technical University. Alley's Web site at http://writing.eng.vt.edu/slides.html provides an overview of rhetorical objections to PowerPoint and shows the value of an assertion-evidence design for slides rather than a topic-subtopic design.

Here are some examples of the differences between a topic and a point for a slide:

Topics Versus Points for Slide Title

Slide Title as Topic	Slide Title as Point
Gender Stereotypes in Children's Birthday Cards	95 percent of children's birthday cards revealed gender stereotyping.
Wage Comparison: CEO Versus Worker	In 2008, the average CEO of a large corporation earned 300 times more than the average worker.

We recommend the point approach wherever possible. When the title of a slide makes a point, the body of the slide can then either provide evidence supporting the point (through a graph or bullet points) or reinforce the point with a photograph, drawing, or diagram.

Given this background, we offer the following strategies for creating your visual aids.

Strategies for Creating Effective Visual Aids

Strategies	Rationales and Explanations of How They Work
Make sure each visual aid (slide) is graphically interesting, relevant, functional, and directly connected to the points of your speech.	Visual aids (slides) should be visual and integral to your presentation. Create your speech first and then create visuals.
Use meaningful features as visual aids; don't use cutesy bells and whistles.	PowerPoint has special effects like exploding figures, words circling into position, and little buses wheeling across the screen. Using these special effects can distract the audience from the content of your speech, creating the *ethos* of a technical whiz rather than a serious presenter of a proposal.
Use slides as a way to visually enhance meaning or impact. Do not use them as index cards of talking points.	If you convert your outline into slides, you simply replicate rather than enhance the speech. Use images (rather than words) wherever possible. Think visually.
Make slides simple, neat, and big enough for everyone to see.	PowerPoint wisely limits the number of words in a line. Include no more than eight to ten lines of text per slide. Don't create slides that need to be read as text.

(*continued*)

Strategies	Rationales and Explanations of How They Work
Where appropriate, follow a point-evidence design, rather than a topic-subtopic design. Titles (headlines) should be complete sentences that state a point.	The point-evidence design promotes audience understanding by emphasizing meanings. (See examples on p. 417.) Note: You'll need to change the PowerPoint title font to 28-point Arial bold.
Use different font sizes and spacing to indicate hierarchy.	The title font should be the largest font on the slide. Subordinate points should be in a smaller font size.
Limit the number of visual aids you use.	Communication experts advise speakers to use no more than one visual aid per minute of presentation. In many parts of the speech, the screen can be blank.

Student Example of a Speech Outline and Slides

To illustrate how slides can be effectively integrated into a speech, we offer the example of student Sam Rothchild, who created a speech (5–8 minutes) proposing an increase in income tax rates on the nation's wealthiest households. Here is Sam's sentence outline for his speech.

SAM'S SPEECH OUTLINE

Reward Work Not Wealth:
A Proposal to Increase Income Tax Rates for the Richest 1 Percent of Americans

PROBLEM

1. Since 1980 the gap between rich and poor has increased enormously.
   a. Statistical evidence demonstrates the gap.
      (i) The rich have gotten richer.
      (ii) The poor have gotten poorer.
      (iii) The middle class are treading water.
   b. A primary cause of the income gap is the Bush-era tax cuts that benefited the rich more than the poor.
   c. Income gap leads to an unhealthy middle class and increased poverty, hurting all Americans.

SOLUTION

2. The solution is to raise the income tax rates on the ultra-rich back to 1980 levels.

REASONS TO SUPPORT THIS PROPOSAL

3. A more progressive income tax structure promotes a more just society.
   a. Sales taxes and payroll taxes (Social Security, Medicare) take a high percentage chunk out of low income salaries and a tiny percentage out of high income salaries.
   b. Progressive income tax balances the regressive effect of sales taxes and payroll taxes.
4. Reducing the gap between rich and poor creates a stronger middle class and reduces poverty.

5. Increasing tax rates on the very rich will not hurt the incentive to work or the entrepreneurial spirit.
6. The ultra rich will still be ultra rich.

CONCLUSION

After Sam had completed his argument outline, he began designing PowerPoint slides aimed at enhancing the impact of his proposal. He limited himself to eight slides and turned off the screen during part of his speech. He displayed a slide only when he felt it increased the impact of his speech. His slides can be placed into three design categories:

- Slides using images to enhance *pathos*
- Slides using a graph for evidence
- Slides using bulleted subpoints for evidence (all text)

In all cases, Sam used "points" for the slide titles (making an assertion) rather than a topic phrase. Six of Sam's slides, illustrating the first two of the above categories, are shown in Figures 15.3–15.8.

In a reflection paper accompanying his speech, Sam explained his thinking process in designing the slides. At the start of his speech, Sam wanted to give "presence" to the income gap problem—to have the audience feel the huge gap between ultra-rich Americans and the poor or middle class. For his title slide (Figure 15.3), he selected a stock photo of a construction worker in order to emphasize the social contribution of blue-collar laborers, who undertake difficult, often dangerous, yet important jobs. The upward angle of the camera suggested to Sam the dignity and value of the hard hat worker dangerously walking on a high beam. Likewise, in Figure 15.4 Sam chose the image of an out-of-work-American in an unemployment line, a photograph that highlights the man's humanity and courage and invites empathy. Sam thought that both these images made strong appeals to *pathos*.

Figures 15.5 and 15.6 represent a different thought process. Sam wanted to emphasize the gap between ordinary Americans' conception of wealth and the unimaginably larger actual wealth of the ultra-rich. Most Americans, Sam felt, would consider a person "really wealthy" if he or she could afford a Ferrari (Figure 15.5). But Sam made his own back-of-the-envelope calculations and found that the ultra-rich could afford five Ferraris a day every day of the week. He photoshopped the image in Figure 15.6 to make this point humorously.

Finally, Figures 15.7 and 15.8 show two slides using graphs for evidence. The title of each slide is a complete-sentence "point." During his speech, Sam spent several minutes on the slide shown in Figure 15.7. He pointed out that for the very rich, the vertical axis (annual income) starts at $5,000,000 and then goes skyward. For the "median earner," however, the vertical axis starts at $24,000. He also explained the meaning of "median"—half of all American workers have incomes above the median line and half have incomes below it. The half below the line are the ones most suffering from the declining wealth of the middle class.

Our takeaway message in this section is that Sam first placed emphasis on the content of his speech and then designed PowerPoint slides to enhance the impact of the speech. He did not employ any of the bells and whistles of PowerPoint software, nor did he use the slides simply to display the section-by-section outline of his speech.

FIGURE 15.3 Sam's Title Slide Using an Image for *Pathos*

FIGURE 15.4 Slide Using an Image for Pathos

FIGURE 15.5 First of a Two-Slide Sequence Using Images to Illustrate Income Gap

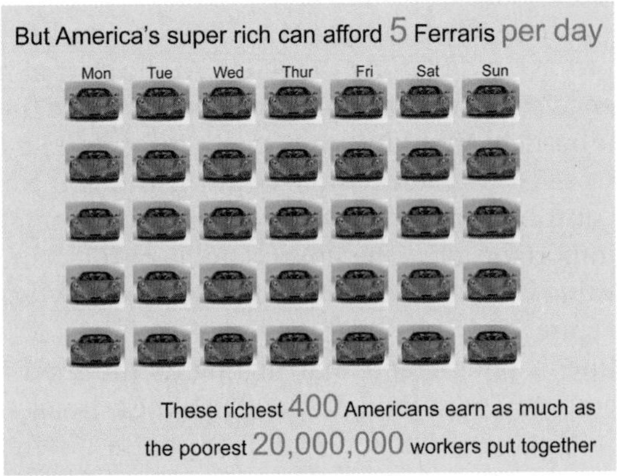

FIGURE 15.6 Second Slide in Sequence, Designed by Sam to Dramatize Wealth

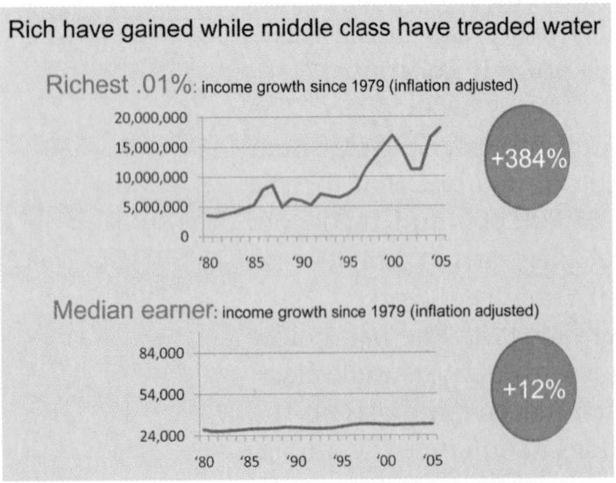

FIGURE 15.7 Slide with Point Title and Graphics for Evidence

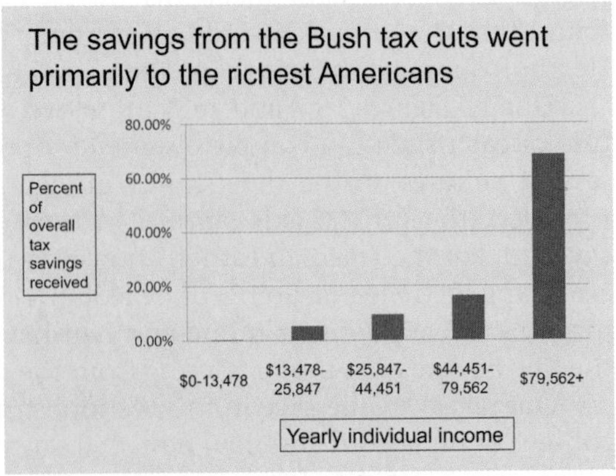

FIGURE 15.8 Another Slide with Point Title and Graphics for Evidence

Delivering Your Speech

Adapting your argument to be delivered orally as a speech requires some special considerations. First, it is important that you allow plenty of time to practice delivering your speech. You can practice before a mirror, with a recorder, or in front of friends until you are confident about the length of your speech and your ability to deliver it with minimal prompting from your notes. In addition, you should think about these important strategies for successful speechmaking.

Strategies for Successfully Delivering Speeches

Strategies	What to Do
Control your volume and pace.	• Speak loudly enough to be heard and add emphasis by speaking louder or softer. • Speed up to get through details quickly and slow down for points you want to stress.
Use posture and gestures to your advantage.	• Stand straight and tall to help your breathing and projection. • Use natural gestures or a few carefully planned ones. • Avoid distracting or nervous gestures.
Maintain eye contact with your audience and look at every member of your audience.	• Know your speech well enough that you can look at your audience, not read your note cards. • Make steady and even eye contact with your audience.
Show enthusiasm and passion for the issue of your speech.	• Make your audience care about your issue through your own enthusiasm. • Show your audience that your issue is important by the energy you put into your delivery. • Also, use your enthusiasm to help you control nervousness.
Use note cards, PowerPoint slides, visual aids, and handouts effectively.	• Control the flow of ideas and information that comes through your slides and visual aids. • Keep your audience listening to you rather than reading handouts or the projector screen.
Overcome nervousness by controlling your hands, your breathing, and the volume of your voice.	• Take deep breaths and speak slightly louder than usual to help your body relax. • Use a podium if one is available.

Revising

After practicing your speech on your own or in front of an informal audience, think about ways you can improve the clarity of your message, your use of visual aids, and your delivery. After you make these improvements, practice the final outline of your speech a number of times to develop familiarity and confidence.

Questions for Peer Review

In addition to the generic peer review questions explained in Skill 16.4, many of which will pertain to your outlined speech, ask your informal audience/reviewers to address these questions:

CONTENT OF THE SPEECH:

1. How well does this speech follow the problem-solution-justification-opposing views-rebuttal structure? How could the speaker improve the clarity of these parts of the speech?
2. How has the speaker tailored the speech to the audience? What could make the speech more lively and easier to follow?
3. Does this speech fit the time limit specified by the assignment? If not, what changes could develop or condense the speech?

USE OF VISUAL AIDS:

4. How functional, simple, clear, and illustrative are the visual aids? Which visual aids enhance the impact of the speech? If any are unclear or distracting, what could improve them?
5. How well do the visual aids support the message of the speech? Where could the speaker more effectively employ the strategies for using PowerPoint or other visual aids?

DELIVERY:

6. Where could the speaker improve his/her volume, enunciation, eye contact, posture, and gestures?
7. How well does the speaker maintain control of his/her material, visual aids, and manner? What suggestions do you have for the speaker to improve his or her enthusiasm and composure?

Our first reading, by student writer Lucy Morsen, is a practical proposal entitled "A Proposal to Improve the Campus Learning Environment by Banning Laptops and Cell Phones from Class." Because practical proposals are aimed at a specific audience, they are often accompanied by a letter of transmittal that introduces the writer, sets the context, and summarizes the proposal. We reproduce here Lucy's transmittal letter followed by her proposal. We also show you the appearance of her title page.

April 26, 2010

Professor Ralph Sorento
Chair, Faculty Senate
____________ University
Street
City, State, Zip

Dear Professor Sorento:

1 Enclosed is a proposal that I hope you will present to the Faculty Senate. It asks the university to ban all laptops and cell phones from classes in consideration of those many students like myself whose educational experience is diminished by classmates who surf the Web or send text messages during lectures or class discussion. As I try to show in this proposal, the effect of laptops and cell phones in class is distracting to many students and may hurt the academic performance of students who think they can multitask without any negative effects. I use both personal experience and recent research reports on multitasking as support for my argument.

2 Banning laptops and cell phones from class would deepen students' engagement with course material and make for more lively and energetic class discussions. I argue that an outright campus ban would be more effective than leaving the decision up to individual instructors.

3 Thank you for considering my proposal. I am happy that this university has a Faculty Senate that welcomes ideas from students on how to make teaching and learning more effective.

Sincerely,
Lucy Morsen,
First-Year Student

A PROPOSAL TO IMPROVE THE CAMPUS LEARNING ENVIRONMENT
BY BANNING LAPTOPS AND CELL PHONES FROM CLASS

Submitted to Professor Ralph Sorento
Chair of the Faculty Senate

Lucy Morsen
First-Year Student, Williamson Hall

If this were the actual proposal, it would begin on a new page following the cover page.

1 Although I am generally happy as a first-year student at this university, I wish to call the Faculty Senate's attention to a distracting problem: classmates' frequent use of laptops and cell phones during class. In many classes more than half the students have open laptops on their desks or are openly text-messaging on cell phones. Inevitably, laptop users multitask between taking notes and checking email, perusing Facebook, surfing the Web, looking at YouTube videos, playing a game, or working on an assignment for another class. (I have yet to see a student use his or her laptop solely for note-taking.) Even though I try to focus on class lectures and discussion, I find myself missing key points and ideas as my eyes are drawn to the animations and flashing colors on neighboring laptop screens. Other distractions come from the clicking of cell phone keypads—or the momentary vibration of a phone on a desktop—which can seem surprisingly loud in an otherwise quiet environment. When the person next to me continually picks up and sets down her phone to send and receive text messages, she not only distracts me from the lecture but also lets me know that she is not engaged in class, and seemingly has no interest in being so. My annoyance at my classmates and my frustration at not being able to focus undercut my enjoyment of class.

2 Given the extensive use of laptops and cell phones in class, I question the academic motivation of my classmates. As a student, I most enjoy classes when I and my classmates are actively interested and engaged in class lecture and discussion. Collective interest has a way of feeding on itself. I mean, we as students do not operate in isolation from one another, but instead we affect and influence one another in gross and subtle ways. Together with our professor we create a collective environment in the classroom, and just as we as individuals affect this collective environment, this collective environment influences us as individuals. The broad effects and consequences of this dynamic interplay should not be underestimated. Humans are highly social beings; we have the power to influence each other in both positive and negative ways. I believe that the distracting nature of laptops and cell phones is negatively affecting classroom environments. Any steps we can take collectively to help each other learn and succeed should be considered.

3 To address this problem, I propose a campus-wide ban on laptops and cell phones during class. I believe a campus-wide ban would be more effective than more limited measures some institutions have adopted, such as blocking wireless access from classrooms or allowing each professor to choose whether or not to ban laptops in his or her classroom. Blocking wireless access does not address the problem of cell phones or non-Web-based laptop distractions (such as computer games or other class work). Leaving the decision up to professors creates an added difficulty for them. I can imagine that professors, fearing resentment and poor evaluations from their students, would be reluctant to enforce a ban in their classrooms, even if they feel it would improve the classroom experience.

4 A campus-wide ban, on the other hand, would be easy to enforce, and students would more easily establish new habits—namely, not using laptops and cell phones during class. Over time, this could become the new campus norm.

5 Although many students might at first object to a ban, the decision to ban all laptops and cell phones in class would bring benefits not only to distracted students like me but also to current users of laptops and cell phones as well as to professors.

6 For one thing, the banning of laptops and cell phones would improve the learning atmosphere of a classroom. These technologies simply create too many distractions for students, and the negative consequences of these distractions are significant enough to call for institutional intervention. While some of my classmates may begrudge the ban, I believe they would quickly get used to it and notice improvements in their own classroom interest and performance. Many of my classmates may actually welcome the ban because they—like myself—are aware of the negative distractions laptops and cell phones create. In fact, an informal survey by a Georgetown University law professor who bans laptops in his classroom indicated that 70% of his students welcomed the ban (Cole, 2008).

7 Second, a ban might directly improve academic performance of current users of laptops and cell phones. A recent study at the University of Winona (Fried, 2008) found that laptop use in the classroom had a significant negative effect on class performance. In Fried's study, students who brought laptops to class received lower grades than their classmates who did not bring laptops to class. Moreover, those who brought laptops to class reported using their laptops for non-class purposes for nearly a quarter of class time.

8 Many of my classmates will likely argue that this study doesn't apply to them. They believe that they are skilled multitaskers who can continue to pay attention to a lecture while also engaging in these other activities. There is empirical evidence that they are in fact mistaken about their ability to multitask. A study by three Stanford University researchers found that persons who self-reported being heavy multitaskers were *more* easily distracted from a primary task than those who reported themselves as light multitaskers (Ophir, Nass, & Wagner, 2009). The researchers conducted this study in a lab by giving multitasking tasks to a group of self-identified heavy multitaskers and then to a group of light multitaskers. This study suggests that a person's own perception of how well he or she multitasks may not be reliable. Moreover it suggests that large amounts of daily multitasking may actually decrease a person's ability to concentrate on a single task and suppress irrelevant information.

9 A handful of students will likely argue that they only use their laptops for class-related purposes, and that an outright ban on laptops in the classroom would be unfair because they would be prohibited from using them for note-taking. However, I am skeptical of any claims that students make of only using laptops for class-related purposes. I personally have never seen any evidence of this, and research is indicating that multitasking is overwhelmingly the common norm among laptop users in the classroom. In a study by Benbunan-Fich and Truman (2009), student laptop use was monitored for 28 classroom sessions of 80 minutes (with students' permission). The researchers analyzed how often the students toggled between screens, and whether the screens were class-related or non-class-related. They found that 76% of the time students toggled between screens that were non-class-related. On average, students toggled between computer-based activities 37.5 times per 80-minute session. This research suggests that the temptations of non-class-related activities are simply too

great for students *not* to engage in multitasking in class—it is just too easy to do a brief check of email or a quick Facebook scan with a swift click of a mouse.

10 University institutions may feel reluctant to propose a campus-wide ban on laptops and cell phones in the classroom for fear of seeming overly authoritative and unnecessarily limiting student freedom. After all, students might rightly claim that they have a right to do whatever they want in the classroom as long as they aren't harming anyone else. (I have already shown they actually are harming others.) While I believe that individual rights are an important concern—in general I believe university institutions should allow for a great amount of autonomy for their students—I think that laptop use has too many negative consequences to be allowed simply in the name of student freedom. (Of course, a professor can always allow laptop use for students with special needs.)

11 For these reasons, I propose that a campus-wide ban on laptops and cell phones in the classroom should be considered. A campus-wide ban would help to create more positive, cohesive classroom experiences, and it would provide a reprieve for students from the myriad of distractions this modern technological age presents us. A campus-wide ban would be easier on professors to enforce, and it would help to establish a new (and improved) norm.

References

Benbunan-Fich, R., & Truman, G. E. (2009). Multitasking with laptops during meetings. *Communications of the ACM, 52*(2), 139–141. doi:10.1145/1461928.1461963

Cole, D. (2008, October 23). Why I ban laptops in my classroom [Web log post]. Retrieved from http://www.britannica.com/blogs/2008/10/why-i-ban-laptops-in-my-classroom

Fried, C. B. (2008). In-class laptop use and its effects on student learning. *Computers and Education, 50*, 906–914. Retrieved from www.elsevier.com

Ophir, E., Nass, C., & Wagner, A. D. (2009). Cognitive control in media multitaskers. *Proceedings of the National Academy of Sciences.* PNAS Early Edition. Retrieved from www.pnas.org

THINKING CRITICALLY

about "A Proposal to Improve the Campus Learning Environment by Banning Laptops and Cell Phones from Class."

1. What strategies does Lucy Morsen use to convince the Faculty Senate that a problem exists?
2. What strategies does Lucy employ to persuade the Faculty Senate that her proposal is worth enacting and that it is more effective than alternative solutions?
3. How does Lucy tie her proposal to the values and beliefs of her audience—college professors who are members of the Faculty Senate?
4. How effective is Lucy's use of research evidence to support her proposal?
5. If you were a faculty member, how effective would you find Lucy's proposal? How effective do you find it as a student? What are its chief strengths and weaknesses?

Our second reading, an op-ed piece from the *New York Times* (February 20, 2004), proposes that competitive cheerleading be recognized as a varsity sport. It was written by Jennifer Allen, the daughter of former Washington Redskins football coach George Allen. She has also written a memoir about growing up female in a football family, *Fifth Quarter: The Scrimmage of a Football Coach's Daughter.*

Jennifer Allen

The Athlete on the Sidelines

1 It's midseason in cheer nation. This winter, thousands of girls will travel on college all-star teams to take part in competitions across the country. Practicing more than 20 hours a week, they will refine a routine of back flips, handsprings, round-offs and splits—all perfectly synchronized and timed to an Olympic second. Their goal: first place. Their game: competitive cheerleading, one of the fastest-growing sports for women in America.

2 Last year, the University of Maryland became the first Division I N.C.A.A. institution to recognize competitive cheerleading as a varsity sport. That means team members are accorded the same benefits as other campus athletes—a coaching and medical staff; locker rooms; help with academics; help dealing with the press. By the 2005–06 academic year, Maryland will provide 12 full scholarships to competitive cheerleaders. The question is this: What took so long?

3 (Time out for a definition. Competitive cheerleading overlaps with but is not identical to the spirit squads you see, say, on the sidelines of a Saturday afternoon college football game. The teams we're talking about do cheer at school games, but they also compete against other schools in cheerleading competitions where they perform high-risk routines under high-pressure circumstances.)

4 For too many years, cheerleading has been the subject of derision. *Sports Illustrated* has lampooned it. Many Americans fail to distinguish it from the sideline shows the Dallas Cowboys cheerleaders put on. Back when I was a cheerleader in high school in the late 70s, we were called a sideshow. In those days, we performed at every sporting event—football, basketball and baseball. We practiced three days a week; purchased our own uniforms (skirts, sweaters, trunks, socks, saddle shoes) and were responsible for our own steady supply of bandages. Ace bandages. There were plenty of injuries, mostly to ligaments. After a big game, my knee would swell. My dad would offer a diagnosis—water on the knee—bandage it up, and then prescribe 50 reps on the knee machine. But cheerleaders weren't allowed in the school weight room.

5 Today, more than 200,000 high-school and college students attend cheerleading camps each year; at least 15 percent of them participate in competitions. The Universal Cheerleading Association feeds its competitions to ESPN for lively weekend fare. When these events were televised last year, they drew an average audience of 334,000 homes.

6 For all its popularity, though, the sport is governed—or not governed—by a patchwork of entities. Schools may treat cheerleaders as athletes—but they don't have to. Some offer little more than a uniform and a game-day parking pass; others offer scholarships; none offer the full range of support and benefit that Maryland does for

competitive cheerleading. What's more, cheerleading is not even recognized by the N.C.A.A. as a sport.

7 Given the nature of competitive cheerleading, this seems like a risky proposition. Think about it: in what other sport is an athlete tossed more than 30 feet in the air—smiling—before spiraling down into the arms of a trusted teammate? Lifts and tosses and catches are the mainstay of competitive cheerleading. "Fliers" do not wear hip pads or kneepads or helmets. There is little to protect a cheerleader from awkward or poor landings on the gym floor.

8 Not surprisingly, cheerleading is the No. 1 cause of serious sports injuries to women, according to the National Center for Catastrophic Sport Injury Research, ahead of gymnastics and track. From 1980 to 2001, emergency room visits for cheerleading injuries rose fivefold.

9 Pushing colleges to recognize competitive cheerleading as a sport will surely help to cut down on injuries. Right now, the American Association of Cheering Coaches and Advisers publishes a manual and administers a safety certification program, but only a fraction of coaches have been certified. Many cheerleaders try dangerous stunts without proper training, coaching and supervision.

10 Of course, convincing other schools to make competitive cheerleading an official sport won't be easy. According to Deborah Yow, Maryland's athletic director, it took more than a year to make sure that the university's cheerleading squad would meet all the guidelines set forth by the Department of Education's Office of Civil Rights. While the department does not define what is or is not a "sport," it does determine whether a university's given activity—such as cheerleading—can be considered a sport in order to comply with Title IX.

11 Is Maryland's action entirely altruistic? Probably not. It doubtless relieves some Title IX pressure. But what's wrong with that? And would it be so wrong to ask the N.C.A.A. to sponsor and govern the sport? After all, when the big collegiate cheerleading competitions begin next month, hundreds of thousands of people will tune in, acknowledging the importance of cheerleading. More N.C.A.A. colleges would be wise to follow suit.

THINKING CRITICALLY

about "The Athlete on the Sidelines"

1. As in most proposal arguments, Allen's first task is to convince readers that a problem exists. She has to persuade readers to take competitive cheerleading seriously and to show them why it is problematic for competitive cheerleaders not to be granted varsity sport status. What are her strategies for convincing us that a problem exists? How effective is she?

2. How does Allen justify her claim that cheerleading should be recognized as a sport? According to her argument, what are the benefits that will come from making cheerleading a varsity sport? What costs does she acknowledge? What additional costs might you point to if you were skeptical of her claim?

3. Overall, how persuasive is her argument? In your response to this question, focus on the strengths and weaknesses of her appeals to *logos*, *ethos*, and *pathos*.

4. If you are persuaded by her argument and if you are attending an institution where competitive cheerleading could exist, how might you persuade the administration on your campus to make cheerleading a varsity sport? (Who are the decision makers for this issue? What arguments would most motivate them? What are the constraints that must be overcome?)

Our last reading, by student writer Dylan Fujitani, is a researched policy argument that addresses the problem of civilian contractors taking military roles in Iraq.

Dylan Fujitani (student)

"The Hardest of the Hardcore":

Let's Outlaw Hired Guns in Contemporary American Warfare

1 On March 31, 2004, America was shocked by the news that four civilians had been brutally killed, mutilated, and hung up on a bridge in Falluja, Iraq. This horrific event publicized the little-known role of civilian "contractors" in the Iraq war. The public's unawareness that some of these contractors are armed to the teeth is hardly surprising, however, because the language used to refer to non-military personnel in Iraq is often so vague that one can scarcely tell whether a reference to a contractor means a truck driver working for Halliburton or a South African mercenary with a history of killing blacks under the apartheid government working for a private security company. These personnel are often referred to using such broad and mundane terms as "security consultants" or simply "civilian contractors." But in reality, the jobs involved and the kinds of people doing them vary so greatly that these catchall labels are inaccurate. Persons referred to as "civilian contractors" are often well-armed ex-military personnel who took an early retirement to double their pay by working for one of many private security firms hired by the Pentagon. With their obvious training and heavy weaponry, these contractors bear a striking resemblance to soldiers, but one enormous difference sets them apart from the regular troops of the U.S. military: They are actually civilians who can be hired without even the symbolic approval of Congress. Without the need for approval, contractors give the Pentagon the flexibility of outsourcing certain military jobs to private security companies. Despite being paid much more than regular troops, contractors may actually cost less when military benefits and retirement are taken into account.

2 Soldiers for hire have historically been called mercenaries. A case could be made that this term is inapplicable in Iraq because contractors in Iraq are being hired to *support* the military's operations, not to fight the war itself. It is true that many of these civilians are support personnel who should not be called mercenaries—for example, highly specialized technicians or drivers of supply trucks—even though these persons may carry a weapon in case of an attack. But some of these personnel replace soldiers in combat roles historically filled by the military. According to Joshua Hammer of the *New Republic*, these jobs include guarding the Baghdad airport, protecting oil fields, escorting convoys, training local police, and serving as prison interrogators (18). The use of these mercenaries circumvents public and congressional scrutiny of some aspects of war. Their non-military status gives virtual legal immunity to heavily

armed individuals who often have questionable backgrounds, who profit from violent conflict, and who ultimately have responsibility to no one but their employers. In light of these dangerous developments, the use of mercenary soldiers must be halted or brought under intense congressional scrutiny.

3 Using mercenaries in war is problematic for six major reasons. First, the deployment of mercenaries disguises the true cost of war to the American public. According to *New York Times* reporter David Barstow, there are roughly 20,000 mercenaries on the ground in Iraq supporting U.S. military operations, and these numbers are not included in reports of the number of American soldiers in Iraq. These 20,000 private contractors make up the second largest contingent in Iraq, surpassing even the British deployment ("Privatizing Warfare"), yet they have received relatively little media attention even as their numbers continue to increase. The use of contractors enables the Pentagon to get by with a smaller number of actual troops through outsourcing to private military companies. Only the deployments of actual troops are reported, so the Pentagon appears to have done more with less. According to a Baghdad-based security consultant, "If you're going to keep the number of troops down, this is the way to do it. … The expense is the same or more. But politically it's much less expensive" (qtd. in Daragahi). The use of mercenaries in Iraq blurs the high cost of war in the public eye, both in terms of dollars and in terms of human lives. Contractors have suffered casualties, yet the public scarcely hears of their death toll unless they are mutilated and publicly exhibited. Furthermore, with the service of a civilian mercenary in Iraq costing as much as $1,500 a day ("Privatizing Warfare"), contractor use is consuming an enormous portion of the funding allocated for reconstruction. *New York Times* reporter David Barstow asserts that "security costs could claim up to 25 percent of the $18 billion budgeted for reconstruction," diverting capital from important reconstruction projects like school and road construction. Thus, the use of mercenaries in Iraq makes it more difficult for the American public to determine the true cost of war.

4 The second major problem with use of mercenaries is that as a group they have no national loyalties and ultimately answer to their employers, not the armed forces. According to the Brookings Institution's P. W. Singer, "during the Persian Gulf War, a 'very small number' of private contractors working at an air base in Saudi Arabia fled from fear that chemical weapons might be used" (qtd. in Bredemeier). In using mercenaries, the Pentagon is outsourcing what the *New York Times* calls its "core responsibilities" ("Privatizing Warfare"), and despite the importance of these tasks, the jobs are being assigned to people who can basically leave whenever they want to. As P. W. Singer has pointed out, a soldier faces a court-martial for refusing to face battle, whereas a contractor merely loses his job (Bredemeier). In addition, the mercenaries and regular military personnel sometimes have poor working relationships. Since contractors are not required to abide by normal military procedures, mercenaries can pretty much operate any way they want, sometimes to the armed forces' disliking. Writing in the *New Republic*, Joshua Hammer explains the attitudes of the Marines who had been with the four contractors killed in Falluja the day before their deaths. Quoting a Marine officer, Hammer writes, "We would have told them not to do it [take an unauthorized shortcut through Baghdad]." According to Hammer, the officer "angrily called the contractors 'cowboys' and said they had failed to inform anyone

on the base of their plans, a direct violation of military policy" (19). Relying on such a large number of poorly supervised and unaccountable mercenaries to fill crucial roles leaves the United States dangerously vulnerable to the future uncertainties of war.

5 Another problem with the use of mercenaries is their civilian status, creating legal ambiguity and making discipline extremely difficult if not impossible. Phillip Carter, a former U.S. Army officer, writing for the e-magazine *Slate*, commented that the involvement of private contractors in the Abu Ghraib prison abuse scandal brought the issue of discipline to the forefront ("How to Discipline"). According to Carter, mercenaries don't fit the Geneva convention definition of "non-combatants" (since they are armed), or of "lawful combatants" (since they don't wear uniforms or fit within a military chain of command). Rather, "they fall into an international legal gray zone" ("Hired Guns"). This problem is highlighted in an editorial from the *Economist*, which pointed out that the "great sanction on wrongdoing—the law—does not really operate. Regular soldiers are subject to courts-martial or international law. But it is not clear what law applies to private security firms" ("Dangerous Work"). Borzou Daragahi, in a piece for the *Post-gazette.com*, wrote that contractors are not subject to the Uniform Code of Military Justice and that there are military personnel who are very uncomfortable with their seemingly untouchable status. Contractors' fuzzy legal status with regard to military justice and international law is highly problematic.

6 Some have argued against these claims of virtual immunity, saying that in reality a lot can be done to discipline law-breaking private contractors. Carter says that possible disciplinary measures include termination of contracts, prohibition from bidding for future contracts, criminal prosecution, and civil suits ("How to Discipline"). All of these penalties, however, are at "the discretion of the agency that issued the original contract," or in this case, presumably the Pentagon. Although Carter effectively makes the point that contractors are not entirely immune from discipline, many of these forms of punishment ultimately amount to nothing more than loss of the job. Carter admits that government contractors are "shielded" from civil suits by a legal doctrine called the "government contractor" defense. Under the current circumstances in Iraq where offensive and defensive roles are becoming increasingly muddied, the only form of punishment contractors are concerned with is financial. This virtual legal immunity is striking considering the strict rules that govern the actions of military personnel. The threat of mere financial punishment cannot be expected to deter mercenaries from possible abusive and criminal behavior. Their legal status must be clarified as soon as possible in both domestic and international law.

7 The fourth major problem with mercenaries is that private military companies frequently hire employees with questionable backgrounds. Inadequate governmental oversight has allowed private companies to hire known war criminals who have been or continue to be paid with American taxpayer dollars. According to journalist Louis Nevaer, writing for the *National Catholic Reporter*, roughly 1,500 South African mercenaries are now in Iraq, many of them former Apartheid-era mercenaries, some of whom have even confessed to killing blacks. Nevaer states that there are "terrorists ... and war criminals on the payrolls of companies contracted by the Pentagon." He gives the example of a former South African police officer who was "a member of the Vlakplass death squad that terrorized blacks under apartheid." Not only are the

personal histories of the mercenaries questionable, but their motivations are also dubious. Joshua Hammer in his *New Republic* article "Cowboy Up" describes what he observed of these private contractors in Baghdad:

> [M]ost of the contractors are the hardest of the hard core—veterans of such elite outfits as the U.S. Special Forces; the Rhodesian Selous Scouts, the former special forces of the Rhodesian white regime; and Executive Outcomes, the now-disbanded South African mercenary army that fought in Sierra Leone and Angola. These men thrive on the danger of working in war zones. (19)

Given the current uncertainly about the legal status of private contractors, and given the fact that actual American military personnel could be targeted in retaliation for the behavior of mercenaries, Congress must quickly act to regulate hiring practices of private military companies to screen against the hiring of terrorists, war criminals, or anyone who would potentially misrepresent the United States.

8 The fifth problem with the use of mercenaries is that the growth of the private security industry entices many of America's most experienced soldiers to leave the military for higher paying contractor jobs. Eric Schmitt and Tom Shanker, writing in the *New York Times*, explain the lure of contractors' salaries:

> Senior enlisted members of the Army Green Berets or Navy Seals with 20 years or more experience now earn about $50,000 in base pay, and can retire with a $23,000 pension. But private security companies ... are offering salaries of $100,000 to nearly $200,000 a year to the most experienced of them.

The military is losing some of its finest soldiers to the private sector where their expertise goes to the highest bidder. The use of mercenaries must be swiftly restrained and eventually halted lest the military be gradually stripped of its edge and become further reliant upon the expertise of private military companies.

9 Finally, the sixth major problem regarding the use of mercenaries is that the rapid increase in their numbers is creating large international interest groups who will *want war* in the long run. For mercenaries, war means fortune and excitement, and peace means a boring period of unemployment. The creation of such groups who thrive off violent conflict is dangerous on a very fundamental level. In the interests of peace, mercenaries and any other war profiteers must not be encouraged through governmental employment. The business of war has proven lucrative, and the free market must not be allowed to encourage war any more than it already does.

10 The expanded use of mercenaries in American warfare has given rise to numerous problems that must be addressed immediately. Among the obvious, their use hides the true cost of war from the American people; contractors' backgrounds and loyalties are questionable; and they have been given a great reason to hope for war in the world. These problems must be addressed swiftly and immediately, particularly by Congress. Mercenaries are used because they are cheaper, both economically and politically, but they also serve the critical purpose of circumventing the scrutiny of Congress and the people of the United States. Action must be taken now to disable this circumvention of democracy and to protect legitimate uses of war from market forces, lawlessness, and the abuse of power.

Works Cited

Barstow, David. "Security Companies: Shadow Soldiers in Iraq." *New York Times* 19 Apr. 2004: A1+. *LexisNexis*. Web. 19 May 2004.

Bredemeier, Kenneth. "Thousands of Private Contractors Support U.S. Forces in Persian Gulf." *Washington Post*. Washington Post, 3 Mar. 2003: E01. Web. 19 May 2004.

Carter, Phillip. "Hired Guns: What to Do about Military Contractors Run Amok." *Slate* 9 Apr. 2004. Web. 12 June 2004.

—. "How to Discipline Private Contractors." *Slate* 4 May 2004. Web. 19 May 2004.

"Dangerous Work." *Economist* 10 Apr. 2004: 22–23. *Academic Search Premier*. Web. 23 May 2004.

Daragahi, Borzou. "In Iraq, Private Contractors Lighten Load on U.S. Troops." *Post-gazette.com*. PG Publishing, 28 Sept. 2003. Web. 19 May 2004.

Hammer, Joshua. "Cowboy Up." *New Republic* 24 May 2004: 18–19. *Academic Search Premier*. Web. 23 May 2004.

Nevaer, Louis. "Many Hired Guns in Iraq Have War Crimes Pasts." *National Catholic Reporter* 14 May 2004: 10. Print.

"Privatizing Warfare." Editorial. *New York Times* 21 Apr. 2004: A22. *LexisNexis*. Web. 19 May 2004.

Schmitt, Eric, and Tom Shanker. "Big Pay Luring Military's Elite to Private Jobs." *New York Times* 30 Mar. 2004: A1+. *LexisNexis*. Web. 19 May 2004.

THINKING CRITICALLY

about "'The Hardest of the Hardcore': Let's Outlaw Hired Guns in Contemporary American Warfare"

1. Many people are unaware that a problem might exist with civilian contractors in Iraq. Dylan's major rhetorical task, therefore, is to persuade readers that a problem exists. To what extent do you think he convinces readers that the use of civilian contractors to fulfill military roles constitutes a problem? Point to passages that you think are or are not persuasive in building his case.

2. The structure of Dylan's paper is almost entirely devoted to showing that a problem exists. However, his proposed solution is vague: either to eliminate the use of contractors in military roles entirely or to demand more congressional oversight. Dylan's strategy is typical for "planning proposals" (see p. 402) where the writer points out a problem but is unable to propose a clear plan for solving it. Does this strategy work for you? Do you think Dylan needs to propose a more specific solution, or is it enough that he identifies a problem?

3. Overall, how would you evaluate the *logos* of this argument? How effective is Dylan's use of reasons and evidence to convince you that the continued use of civilian contractors in military roles is a problem that requires some action?

4. How effective are Dylan's appeals to *ethos* and *pathos*? To what extent does Dylan project a credible and trustworthy persona? To what extent does he connect his argument to the values and beliefs of his audience, appealing to readers' emotions and sympathies as well as to their minds?

PEARSON mycomplab

For support in learning this chapter's content, follow this path in **MyCompLab:** Resources ⇒ Writing ⇒ Writing Purposes ⇒ Writing to Argue or Persuade.

PART 3

A GUIDE TO COMPOSING AND REVISING

This ad for the United States Army, which first appeared in a general news commentary magazine, highlights qualities traditionally associated with patriotic military service to the country: respect, honor, and courage. Note that this poster does not depict soldiers in uniform on a battlefield or in the midst of a drill. Consider the way the images of the father and daughter and the words in this ad connect character-building, family relationships, the Army, and success. Think about how gender functions in this ad by focusing on the young woman's long hair, tasteful makeup, and earnest manner. This advertisement is part of a For Writing and Discussion exercise in Chapter 10.

YOU TAUGHT HER ABOUT RESPECT, HONOR AND COURAGE.
IS IT ANY SURPRISE THAT NOW SHE WANTS TO USE THEM?
She'll experience the most challenging training, use the latest technology and get the strongest support. Every drill and every mission will reinforce in her that character always leads to success. Encourage her to consider becoming a Soldier – AN ARMY OF ONE.®
GOARMY.COM
U.S.ARMY
AN ARMY OF ONE®
©2004. Paid for by the United States Army. All rights reserved.

PART 3 **A GUIDE TO COMPOSING AND REVISING**

Part 3 addresses the following outcomes for first-year composition from the Council of Writing Program Administrators.

RHETORICAL KNOWLEDGE	• Focus on a purpose (Ch. 17, 18) • Respond to the needs of different audiences (Skills 17.1, 18.3) • Respond appropriately to different kinds of rhetorical situations (Ch. 17, 18) • Use conventions of format and structure appropriate to the rhetorical situation (Ch. 17, 18) • Adopt appropriate voice, tone, and level of formality (Skills 18.5, 18.6) • Understand how genres shape reading and writing (Ch. 17, 18)
PROCESSES	• Be aware that it usually takes multiple drafts to create and complete a successful text (Skill 16.1) • Develop flexible strategies for generating, revising, editing, and proof-reading (Skills 16.2 and 16.33) • Understand writing as an open process that permits writers to use later invention and re-thinking to revise their work (Skills 16.2 and 16.3) • Understand the collaborative and social aspects of writing processes (Skill 16.4) • Learn to critique their own and others' works (Skill 16.4) • Learn to balance the advantages of relying on others with the responsibility of doing their part (Skill 16.3)
KNOWLEDGE OF CONVENTIONS	• Learn common formats for different kinds of texts (Ch. 17, 18) • Develop knowledge of genre conventions ranging from structure and paragraphing to tone and mechanics (Ch. 17, 18)
COMPOSING IN ELECTRONIC ENVIRONMENTS	• Understand and exploit the differences in the rhetorical strategies and in the affordances available for both print and electronic composing processes and texts (Skill 16.1)

WRITING AS A PROBLEM-SOLVING PROCESS

16

I rewrite as I write. It is hard to tell what is a first draft because it is not determined by time. In one draft, I might cross out three pages, write two, cross out a fourth, rewrite it, and call it a draft. I am constantly writing and rewriting. I can only conceptualize so much in my first draft—only so much information can be held in my head at one time; my rewriting efforts are a reflection of how much information I can encompass at one time. There are levels and agenda which I have to attend to in each draft.*

—*Description of Revision by an Experienced Writer*

I read what I have written and I cross out a word and put another word in; a more decent word or a better word. Then if there is somewhere to use a sentence that I have crossed out, I will put it there.*

—*Description of Revision by an Inexperienced Writer*

Blot out, correct, insert, refine,
Enlarge, diminish, interline;
Be mindful, when invention fails,
To scratch your head, and bite your nails.

—*Jonathan Swift*

Throughout this text, we have emphasized writing as a critical thinking process requiring writers to "wallow in complexity." This opening chapter of Part 3 explains how experienced writers use multiple drafts to manage the complexities of writing.

In this chapter, you will learn to improve your own writing processes:

- **SKILL 16.1** Follow the experts' practice of using multiple drafts.
- **SKILL 16.2** Revise globally as well as locally.
- **SKILL 16.3** Develop ten expert habits to improve your writing processes.
- **SKILL 16.4** Use peer reviews to help you think like an expert.

*From Nancy Sommers, "Revision Strategies of Student Writers and Experienced Adult Writers," *College Composition and Communication* 31 (October 1980): 291–300.

SKILL 16.1 Follow the experts' practice of using multiple drafts.

We begin this chapter with a close look at why expert writers use multiple drafts to move from an initial exploration of ideas to a finished product. As composition theorist Peter Elbow has asserted about the writing process, "meaning is not what you start out with" but "what you end up with." In the early stages of writing, experienced writers typically discover, deepen, and complicate their ideas before they can clarify them and arrange them effectively. Only in the last drafts will expert writers be in sufficient control of their ideas to shape them elegantly for readers.

What most distinguishes expert from novice writers is the experts' willingness to keep revising their work until they feel it is ready to go public. They typically work much harder at drafting and revising than do novice writers, taking more runs at their subject. Expert writers also make more substantial alterations in their drafts during revision—what we call "global" rather than "local" revision. This difference between expert and novice writers might seem counterintuitive. One might think that novices would need to revise more than experts. But decades of research on the writing process of experts reveals how extensively experts revise. Compare the first two quotations that open this chapter—one from an experienced and one from an inexperienced writer. The experienced writer crosses out pages and starts over while the inexperienced writer crosses out a word or two. The experienced writer feels cognitive overload while drafting, having to attend to many different "levels and agendas" at once. In contrast, the inexperienced writer seems to think only of replacing words or adding an occasional transition. Learning to revise extensively is thus a hallmark of a maturing writer.

Figure 16.1 shows how a first-year college student demonstrates expert writing behavior when she makes a substantial revision of an early draft. Note that she crosses out several sentences at the end of one paragraph, creates a new topic sentence for the next paragraph, and moves a detail sentence so that it follows the topic sentence.

Why Expert Writers Revise So Extensively

Our emphasis on experts' substantial revision might have surprised you. If the experts are such good writers, why do they need multiple drafts? Why don't they get it right the first time? Our answer is simply this: Expert writers use multiple drafts to break a complex task into manageable subtasks. Let's look more closely at some of the functions that drafting and revising can perform for writers.

- ***Multiple drafts help writers overcome the limits of short-term memory.*** Cognitive psychologists have shown that working memory—often called short-term memory—has remarkably little storage space. You can picture short-term memory as a small tabletop surrounded by filing cabinets (long-term memory). As you write, you can place on your tabletop (working memory) only a few chunks of material at any given moment—a few sentences of a draft or several ideas in an outline. The remaining portions of your draft-in-progress

First Draft with Revisions

sticks of our favorite flavors in the bottom of the bag. That discovery was, by far, the best discovery that could ever be made, week after week. So, as you can probably guess, my opinion of farmer's markets has always been very high as they were what fulfilled my sugar fix.

~~However, another important point can come out of that story. That point being about~~ the man who sold us our precious honey sticks. He was kind, patient, and genuinely happy to have our business. In contrast to ~~Not quite the same vibe that one would expect to get from~~ the supermarket employee who often doesn't ~~even really~~ know what isle you need in order to find the peanut butter. Another ~~A~~ huge selling point of farmer's markets, for me, is that you can go and talk to people who know about the food they are selling. It is so refreshing to go

Revised Draft

sticks of our favorite flavors in the bottom of the bag.

Another huge selling point of farmer's markets, for me, is that you can go and talk to people who know about the food they are selling. The man who sold us our precious honey sticks was kind, patient, and genuinely happy to have our business, in contrast to the supermarket employee who often doesn't ~~even really~~ know what aisle you need in order to find the peanut butter.

FIGURE 16.1 A First-Year Student's Substantial Revisions

fall off the table without getting stored in long-term memory. (Think of your horror when your computer eats your draft—proof that you can't rely on long-term memory to restore what you wrote.) Writing a draft captures and stores your ideas as your working memory develops them. When you reread these stored ideas, you can then see your evolving ideas whole, note problem areas, develop more ideas, see material that doesn't fit, recall additional information, and begin extending or improving the draft.

- ***Multiple drafts help accommodate shifts and changes in the writer's ideas.*** Early in the writing process, expert writers often are unsure of where their ideas are leading; they find that their ideas shift and evolve as their drafts progress. An expert writer's finished product often is radically different from the first draft—not simply in form and style but also in actual content.
- ***Multiple drafts help writers clarify audience and purpose.*** While thinking about their subject matter, experienced writers also ask questions

about audience and purpose: What do my readers already know and believe about my subject? How am I trying to change their views? In the process of drafting and revising, the answers to these questions may evolve so that each new draft reflects a deeper or clearer understanding of audience and purpose.

- ***Multiple drafts help writers improve structure and coherence for readers.*** Whereas the ideas in early drafts often follow the order in which writers conceived them, later drafts are often restructured—sometimes radically—to meet readers' needs. Writing teachers sometimes call this transformation a movement from writer-based to reader-based prose.* The composing and revising skills taught in Chapter 17 will help you learn how to revise your drafts from a reader's perspective.
- ***Multiple drafts let writers postpone worrying about correctness.*** Late in the revision process, experienced writers turn their energy toward fixing errors and revising sentences for increased cohesion, conciseness, and clarity. Focusing on correctness too soon can shut down the creative process.

An Expert's Writing Processes Are Recursive

Given this background on why expert writers revise, we can see that for experts, the writing process is recursive rather than linear. Writers continually cycle back to earlier stages as their thinking evolves. Sometimes writers develop a thesis statement early in the writing process. But just as frequently, they formulate a thesis during an "aha!" moment of discovery later in the process, perhaps after several drafts. ("So *this* is my point! Here is my argument in a nutshell!") Even very late in the process, while checking usage and punctuation, experienced writers are apt to think of new ideas, thus triggering more revision.

SKILL 16.2 Revise globally as well as locally.

To think like an expert writer, you need to appreciate the difference between "global" and "local" revision. You revise **locally** whenever you make changes to a text that affect only the one or two sentences that you are currently working on. In contrast, you revise **globally** when a change in one part of your draft drives changes in other parts of the draft. Global revision focuses on the big-picture concerns of ideas, structure, purpose, audience, and genre. It often involves substantial rewriting, even starting over in places with a newly conceived plan. For example, your revising part of the middle of your essay might cause you to rewrite the whole introduction or to change the tone or point of view throughout the essay.

*The terms "writer-based" and "reader-based" prose come from Linda Flower, "Writer-Based Prose: A Cognitive Basis for Problems in Writing." College English, 1979, 41.1, 19–37.

What follows are some on-the-page strategies that you can adopt to practice the global and local revision strategies of experts:*

On-the-Page Strategies for Doing Global and Local Revision	
Strategies to Use on the Page	**Reasons**
Throw out the whole draft and start again.	• Original draft helped writer discover ideas and see the whole territory. • New draft needs to be substantially refocused and restructured.
Cross out large chunks and rewrite from scratch.	• Original passage was unfocused; ideas have changed. • New sense of purpose or point meant that the whole passage needed reshaping. • Original passage was too confused or jumbled for mere editing.
Cut and paste; move parts around; (then write new transitions, mapping statements, and topic sentences).	• Parts didn't follow in logical order. • Parts occurred in the order writer thought of them rather than the order needed by readers. • Conclusion was clearer than introduction; part of conclusion had to be moved to introduction. • Revised thesis statement required different order for parts.
Add/revise topic sentences of paragraphs; insert transitions.	• Reader needs signposts to see how parts connect to previous parts and to whole. • Revision of topic sentences often requires global revision of paragraph.
Make insertions; add new material.	• Supporting particulars needed to be added: examples, facts, illustrations, statistics, other evidence (usually added to bodies of paragraphs). • New section was needed or more explanation was needed for a point. • Gaps in argument needed to be filled in.
Delete material.	• Material is no longer needed or is irrelevant. • Deleted material may have been good but went off on a tangent.

(continued)

*We have chosen to say "on the page" rather than "on the screen" because global revision is often facilitated by a writer's working off double-spaced hard copy rather than a computer screen. See pages 443–444 for our advice on using hard copy for revision.

Strategies to Use on the Page	Reasons
Recast sentences (cross out and rewrite portions; combine sentences; rephrase sentences; start sentences with a different grammatical structure).	• Passage violated old/new contract (see Skill 17.7). • Passage was wordy/choppy or lacked rhythm or voice. • Grammar was tangled, diction odd, or meaning confused. • Passage lost focus of topic sentence of paragraph.
Edit sentences to correct mistakes.	• Writer found comma splices, fragments, dangling modifiers, nonparallel constructions, or other problems of grammar and usage. • Writer found spelling errors, typos, repeated or omitted words.

FOR WRITING AND DISCUSSION

Revising a Paragraph Globally

Choose an important paragraph in the body of a draft you are currently working on. Then write your answers to these questions about that paragraph.

1. Why is this an important paragraph?
2. What is its main point?
3. Where is that main point stated?

Now—as an exercise only—write the main point at the top of a blank sheet of paper, put away your original draft, and, without looking at the original, write a new paragraph with the sole purpose of developing the point you wrote at the top of the page.

When you are finished, compare your new paragraph to the original. What have you learned that might help you revise your original?

Here are some typical responses of writers who have tried this exercise:

> I recognized that my original paragraph was unfocused. I couldn't find a main point.
>
> I recognized that my original paragraph was underdeveloped. I had a main point but not enough particulars supporting it.
>
> I began to see that my draft was scattered and that I had too many short paragraphs.
>
> I recognized that I was making a couple of different points in my original paragraph and that I needed to break it into separate paragraphs.
>
> I recognized that I hadn't stated my main point (or that I had buried it in the middle of the paragraph).
>
> I recognized that there was a big difference in style between my two versions and that I had to choose which version I liked best. (It's not always the "new" version!)

SKILL 16.3 Develop ten expert habits to improve your writing processes.

Now that you understand why experts revise more extensively than novices and what they do on the page, we describe in Skill 16.3 the habitual ways of thinking and acting that experts use when they write. Our hope is that this description will help you develop these same habits for yourself. Because one of the best ways to improve your writing process is to do what the experts do, we offer you the following ten habits of experienced writers, expressed as advice:

1. ***Use exploratory writing and talking to discover and clarify ideas.*** Don't let your first draft be the first occasion when you put your ideas into writing. Use exploratory strategies such as freewriting and idea mapping to generate ideas (see Chapter 2, Concept 4). Also seek out opportunities to talk about your ideas with classmates or friends in order to clarify your own thinking and appreciate alternative points of view.
2. ***Schedule your time.*** Don't begin your paper the night before it is due. Plan sufficient time for exploration, drafting, revision, and editing. Recognize that your ideas will shift, branch out, and even turn around as you write. Allow some time off between writing the first draft and beginning revision. For many writers, revision takes considerably longer than writing the first draft. If your institution has a writing center, consider scheduling a visit.
3. ***Discover what methods of drafting work best for you.*** Some people compose rough drafts directly on the computer; others write longhand. Some make outlines first; others plunge directly into drafting and make outlines later. Some revise extensively on the computer as they are drafting; others plough ahead until they have a complete draft before they start revising. Some people sit at their desk for hours at a time; others need to get up and walk around every couple of minutes. Some people need a quiet room; others work best in a coffee shop. Discover the methods that work best for you.
4. ***Think about audience and purpose from the start.*** Early on, think about the effect you want your writing to have on readers. In formulating a thesis, look to change your readers' view of your subject. ("Before reading my paper, my readers will think X. But after reading my paper, my readers will think Y.")
5. ***For the first draft, reduce your expectations.*** Many novice writers get blocked by trying to make their first draft perfect. In contrast, expert writers expect the first draft to be an unreadable mess. (They often call it a "zero draft" or a "garbage draft" because they don't expect it to be good.) They use the first draft merely to get their ideas flowing, knowing they will revise later. If you get blocked, just keep writing. Get some ideas on paper.
6. ***Revise on double- or triple-spaced hard copy.*** Although many experienced writers revise on the screen without going through paper drafts, there are powerful advantages in printing occasional paper drafts. Research suggests that writers are more apt to make global changes in a draft if they work from hard copy because they can see more easily how the parts connect to the whole. They can refer quickly to page two while revising page six without having to scroll back and forth. We suggest that you occasionally print out a double- or triple-spaced hard copy of your draft and then mark it up aggressively. (See again Figure 16.1, which shows how a first-year student learned the benefits of revising off hard copy.) When your draft gets too messy, keyboard your changes into your computer and begin another round of revision.
7. ***As you revise, think increasingly about the needs of your readers.*** Experts use first drafts to help them clarify their ideas for themselves but not necessarily for readers. In many respects, writers of first drafts are talking to

themselves. Through global revision, however, writers gradually convert "writer-based prose" to "reader-based prose." Writers begin to employ consciously the skills of reader-expectation theory that we explain in detail in Chapter 17.

8. ***Exchange drafts with others.*** Get other people's reactions to your work in exchange for your reactions to theirs. Experienced writers regularly seek critiques of their drafts from trusted readers. Later in this chapter we explain procedures for peer review of drafts.
9. ***Save correctness for last.*** To revise productively, concentrate first on the big questions: Do I have good ideas in this draft? Am I responding appropriately to the assignment? Are my ideas adequately organized and developed? Save questions about exact wording, grammar, mechanics, and documentation style for later. These concerns are important, but they cannot be efficiently attended to until after higher-order concerns are met. Your first goal is to create a thoughtful, richly developed draft.
10. ***To meet deadlines and bring the process to a close, learn how to satisfice.*** Our description of the writing process may seem formidable. Technically, it seems, you could go on revising forever. How can you ever know when to stop? There is no ready answer to that question, which is more a psychological than a technical problem. Expert writers have generally learned how to **satisfice**, a term coined by influential social scientist Herbert Simon from two root words, *suffice* and *satisfy*. It means to do the best job you can under the circumstances considering your time constraints, the pressures of other demands on you, and the difficulty of the task. Expert writers begin the writing process early and get as far as they can before their deadline looms. Then they let the deadline give them the energy for intensive revision. From lawyers preparing briefs for court to engineers developing design proposals, writers have used deadlines to help them put aside doubts and anxieties and to conclude their work, as every writer must. "Okay, it's not perfect, but it's the best I can do for now."

FOR WRITING AND DISCUSSION

Analyzing Your Own Writing Process

When you write, do you follow a process resembling the one we just described? Have you ever

- had a writing project grow out of your engagement with a problem or question?
- explored ideas by talking with others or by doing exploratory writing?
- made major changes to a draft because you changed your mind or otherwise discovered new ideas?
- revised a draft from a reader's perspective by consciously trying to imagine and respond to a reader's questions, confusions, and other reactions?
- road tested a draft by trying it out on readers and then revising it as a result of what they told you?

Working in groups or as a whole class, share stories about previous writing experiences that match or do not match the description of experienced writers' processes. To the extent that your present process differs, what strategies of experienced writers might you like to try?

SKILL 16.4 **Use peer reviews to help you think like an expert.**

One of the best ways to become a better reviser is to see your draft from a *reader*'s rather than a *writer*'s perspective. As a writer, you know what you mean; you are already inside your own head. But you need to see what your draft looks like to readers—that is, to people who are not inside your head.

A good way to learn this skill is to practice reading your classmates' drafts and have them read yours. In this section we offer advice on how to respond candidly to your classmates' drafts and how to participate in peer reviews.

Becoming a Helpful Reader of Classmates' Drafts

When you respond to a writer's draft, learn to make *readerly* rather than *writerly* comments. For example, instead of saying, "Your draft is disorganized," say, "I got lost when . . . . " Instead of saying, "This paragraph needs a topic sentence," say, "I had trouble seeing the point of this paragraph." In other words, describe your mental experience in trying to understand the draft rather than use technical terms to point out problem areas or to identify errors.

When you help a writer with a draft, your goal is both to point out where the draft needs more work and to brainstorm with the writer possible ways to improve the draft. Begin by reading the draft all the way through at a normal reading speed. As you read, make mental notes to help focus your feedback. We recommend that you also mark passages that you find confusing. Write "G!" for "Good" next to parts that you like. Write "?" next to places where you want to ask questions.

After you have read the draft, use the following strategies for making helpful responses, either in writing or in direct conversation with the writer.

Strategies for Responding Helpfully to a Classmate's Draft

Kinds of Problems Noted	Helpful Responses
If the ideas in the draft seem thin or undeveloped, or if the draft is too short	• Help the writer brainstorm for more ideas. • Help the writer add more examples, better details, more supporting data or arguments.
If you get confused or lost in some parts of the draft	• Show the writer where you got confused or miscued in reading the draft ("I started getting lost here because I couldn't see why you were giving me this information" or "I thought you were going to say X, but then you said Y"). • Have the writer talk through ideas to clear up confusing spots.

(*continued*)

Kinds of Problems Noted	Helpful Responses

If you get confused or lost at the "big-picture" level	• Help the writer sharpen the thesis: suggest that the writer view the thesis as the answer to a controversial or problematic question; ask the writer to articulate the question that the thesis answers.
	• Help the writer create an outline, tree diagram, or flowchart (see Skill 17.3).
	• Help the writer clarify the focus by asking him or her to complete these statements about purpose:
	  • The purpose of this paper is ______.
	  • The purpose of this section (paragraph) is ______.
	  • Before reading my paper, my reader will think X. But after reading my paper, my reader will think Y.

If you can understand the sentences but can't see the point	• Help the writer articulate the meaning by asking "So what?" questions, making the writer bring the point to the surface. ("I can understand what you are saying here but I don't quite understand why you are saying it. What do these details have to do with the topic sentence of the paragraph? Or what does this paragraph have to do with your thesis?") • Help the writer create transitions, new topic sentences, or other means of making points clear.
If you disagree with the ideas or think the writer has avoided alternative points of view	• Play devil's advocate to help the writer deepen and complicate ideas. • Show the writer specific places where you had queries or doubts.

Using a Generic Peer Review Guide

When participating in peer reviews, writers and reviewers often appreciate a list of guiding questions or checkpoints. What follows is a list of generic questions that can be used for peer-reviewing many different kinds of drafts. In each assignment chapter for Part 2 of this text, we have created additional peer review questions tailored specifically to that chapter's rhetorical aim and genres. For any given peer review session, your instructor may specify which generic or assignment-specific questions you are to use for the peer review.

Generic Peer Review Guide

For the writer

Prepare two or three questions you would like your peer reviewer to address while responding to your draft. The questions can focus on some aspect of your draft that you are uncertain about, on one or more sections where you particularly seek help or advice, on some feature that you particularly like about your draft, or on some part you especially wrestled with. Write out your questions and give them to your peer reviewer along with your draft.

For the reviewer

Basic overview: Read the draft at a normal reading speed from beginning to end. As you read do the following:

- Mark a "?" next to any passages that you find confusing, that somehow slow down your reading, or that raise questions in your mind.
- Mark a "G" next to any passages where you think the writing is particularly good, strong, or interesting.

Going into more depth: Prior to discussion with the writer, complete the following tasks:

- Identify at least one specific place in the draft where you got confused. Make notes for why you got confused, using readerly rather than writerly comments.
- Identify one place in the draft where you think the ideas are thin or need more development. Make discussion notes.
- Identify one place where you might write "So what?" after the passage. These are places where you don't understand the significance or importance of the writer's points. These are also places where you can't see how certain sentences connect to a topic sentence or how certain paragraphs or sections connect to the thesis statement.
- Identify at least one place where you could play devil's advocate or otherwise object to the writer's ideas. Make notes on the objections or alternative views that you will raise with the writer.

Evaluating the writer's argument: Look at the draft's effectiveness from the perspective of the classical rhetorical appeals:

- *Logos:* How effectively does the writer use reasons and evidence to support his or her claim? How effectively does the writer use details, particulars, examples, and other means as evidence to support points? How logical are the points and how clearly are they connected?
- *Ethos:* What kind of image does the writer project? How effective is the tone? How trustworthy, reliable, knowledgeable, and fair does this writer seem?
- *Pathos:* How effectively does the writer engage the audience's interest? How effectively does the writer tie into the audience's beliefs and values? To what extent does the writer make the reader care about the topic?

Noting problems of grammar and editing: Mark the draft wherever you notice problems in grammar, spelling, punctuation, documentation form, or other issues of mechanics.

Summing up: Create a consolidated summary of your review:

- Sum up the strengths of the draft.
- Identify two or three main weaknesses or problem areas.
- Make two or three suggestions for revision.

FOR WRITING AND DISCUSSION

Practicing a Peer Review

Background: In the following exercise, we invite you to practice a peer review by responding to a student's draft ("Should the University Carpet the Dorm Rooms?" below) or to another draft provided by your instructor. The "Carpets" assignment asked students to take a stand on a local campus issue. Imagine that you have exchanged drafts with this student and that your task is to help this student improve the draft through both global and local revision.

Individual task: Read the draft carefully following the instructions in the "Generic Peer Review Guide." Write out your responses to the bulleted items under "Going into more depth," "Evaluating the writer's argument," and "Summing up."

Small group or whole class: Share your responses. Then turn to the following additional tasks:

1. With the instructor serving as a guide, practice explaining to the writer where or how you got confused while reading the draft. Readers often have difficulty explaining their reading experience to a writer. Let several class members role-play being the reader. Practice using language such as "I like the way this draft started because . . . ." "I got confused when . . . ." "I had to back up and reread when . . . ." "I saw your point here, but then I got lost again because . . . ." Writing theorist Peter Elbow calls such language a "movie of your mind."
2. Have several class members role-play being devil's advocates by arguing against the writer's thesis. Where are the ideas thin or weak?

SHOULD THE UNIVERSITY CARPET THE DORM ROOMS?

Tricia, a university student, came home exhausted from her work-study job. She took a blueberry pie from the refrigerator to satisfy her hunger and a tall glass of milk to quench her thirst. While trying to get comfortable on her bed, she tipped her snack over onto the floor. She cleaned the mess, but the blueberry and milk stains on her brand-new carpet could not be removed.

Tricia didn't realize how hard it was to clean up stains on a carpet. Luckily this was her own carpet.

A lot of students don't want carpets. Students constantly change rooms. The next person may not want carpet.

Some students say that since they pay to live on campus, the rooms should reflect a comfortable home atmosphere. Carpets will make the dorm more comfortable. The carpet will act as insulation and as a soundproofing system.

Paint stains cannot be removed from carpets. If the university carpets the rooms, the students will lose the privilege they have of painting their rooms any color. This would limit students' self-expression.

The carpets would be an institutional brown or gray. This would be ugly. With tile floors, the students can choose and purchase their own carpets to match their taste. You can't be an individual if you can't decorate your room to fit your personality.

According to Rachel Jones, Assistant Director of Housing Services, the cost will be $300 per room for the carpet and installation. Also the university will have to buy more vacuum cleaners. But will vacuum cleaners be all that is necessary to keep the carpets clean? We'll need shampoo machines too.

What about those stains that won't come off even with a shampoo machine? That's where the student will have to pay damage deposit costs.

There will be many stains on the carpet due to shaving cream fights, food fights, beverage parties, and smoking, all of which can damage the carpets.

Students don't take care of the dorms now. They don't follow the rules of maintaining their rooms. They drill holes into the walls, break mirrors, beds, and closet doors, and leave their food trays all over the floor.

If the university buys carpets our room rates will skyrocket. In conclusion, it is a bad idea for the university to buy carpets.

Participating in Peer Review Workshops

If you are willing to respond candidly to a classmate's draft—in a readerly rather than a writerly way—you will be a valuable participant in peer review workshops. In a typical workshop, classmates work in groups of two to six to respond to each other's rough drafts and offer suggestions for revisions. These workshops are most helpful when group members have developed sufficient levels of professionalism and trust to exchange candid responses. A frequent problem in peer review workshops is that classmates try so hard to avoid hurting each other's feelings that they provide vague, meaningless feedback. Saying, "Your paper's great. I really liked it. Maybe you could make it flow a little better" is much less helpful than saying, "Your issue about environmental pollution in the Antarctic is well defined in the first paragraph, but I got lost in the second paragraph when you began discussing penguin coloration."

Responsibilities of Peer Reviewers and Writers Learning to respond conscientiously and carefully to others' work may be the single most important thing you can do to improve your own writing. When you review a classmate's draft, you are not acting as a teacher, but simply as a fresh reader. You can help the writer appreciate what it's like to encounter his or her text for the first time. Your primary responsibility is to articulate your understanding of what the writer's words say to you and to identify places where you get confused, where you need more details, where you have doubts or queries, and so on.

When you play the role of writer during a workshop session, your responsibilities parallel those of your peer reviewers. You need to provide a legible rough draft, preferably typed and double-spaced, that doesn't baffle the reader with hard-to-follow corrections and confusing pagination. Your instructor may ask you to bring copies of your draft for all group members. During the workshop, your primary responsibility is to *listen,* taking in how others respond to your draft without becoming defensive. Many instructors also ask writers to formulate two or three specific questions about their drafts—questions they particularly want their reviewers to address. These questions might focus on something writers particularly like about their drafts or on specific problem areas or concerns.

Responding to Peer Reviews

After you and your classmates have gone over each other's papers and walked each other through the responses, everyone should identify two or three things about his or her draft that particularly need work. Before you leave the session, you should have some notion about how you want to revise your paper.

You may get mixed or contradictory responses from different reviewers. One reviewer may praise a passage that another finds confusing or illogical. Conflicting advice is a frustrating fact of life for all writers, whether students or professionals. Such disagreements reveal how readers cocreate a text with a writer: Each brings to the text a different background, set of values, and way of reading.

It is important to remember that you are in charge of your own writing. If several readers offer the same critique of a passage, then no matter how much you love that passage, you probably need to follow their advice. But when readers disagree, you have to make your own best judgment about whom to heed.

Once you have received advice from others, reread your draft again slowly and then develop a revision plan, allowing yourself time to make sweeping, global changes if needed. You also need to remember that you can never make your draft perfect. Plan when you will bring the process to a close so that you can turn in a finished product on time and get on with your other classes and your life.

PEARSON mycomplab For support in learning this chapter's content, follow this path in MyCompLab: Resources ⇒ Writing ⇒ Writing Process ⇒ Drafting and Revising. Review the Instruction and Multimedia resources about drafting and revising, and then complete the Exercises and click on Gradebook to measure your progress.

COMPOSING AND REVISING CLOSED-FORM PROSE

17

Form is an arousing and fulfillment of desires. A work has form insofar as one part of it leads a reader to anticipate another part, to be gratified by the sequence.

—Kenneth Burke, Rhetorician

Chapter 16 presents strategies for improving your revising process. In Chapter 17 we focus specifically on strategies for composing and revising closed-form prose. To help you avoid information overload, we recommend that you don't try to read this whole chapter in one sitting. The skills taught in this chapter are presented in ten self-contained lessons that can be read comfortably in half an hour or less. You will benefit most from these lessons if you focus on one skill at a time and then return to the lessons periodically as you progress through the term. Each lesson's advice will become increasingly meaningful and relevant as you gain experience as a writer. The first lesson (Skill 17.1) is intended as a theoretical overview to the rest of the chapter. The remaining lessons can then be assigned and read in any order your instructor desires.

In this chapter, you will learn how these skills can improve your writing:

• **SKILL 17.1**	Understand reader expectations.
• **SKILL 17.2**	Convert loose structures into thesis/support structures.
• **SKILL 17.3**	Plan and visualize your structure.
• **SKILL 17.4**	Set up reader expectations through effective titles and introductions.
• **SKILLS 17.5–17.7**	Keep readers on track through the use of topic sentences, transitions, and the old/new contract.
• **SKILL 17.8**	Learn four expert moves for organizing and developing ideas.
• **SKILL 17.9**	Use effective tables, graphs, and charts to present numeric data.
• **SKILL 17.10**	Write effective conclusions.

Together these lessons will teach you strategies for making your closed-form prose reader-friendly, well structured, clear, and persuasive.

SKILL 17.1 **Understand reader expectations.**

In this opening lesson, we show you how to think like a reader. Imagine for a moment that your readers have only so much *reader energy*, which they can use either to follow your ideas or to puzzle over confusing passages.* In order to follow your ideas, skilled readers continually make predictions about where a text is heading based on cues provided by the writer. When readers get lost, the writer has often either failed to provide cues or has given misleading cues. "Whoa, you lost me on the turn," a reader might say. "How does this passage relate to what you just said?" In this lesson we explain what readers of closed-form prose expect from writers in order to predict where a text is heading. Specifically we show you that readers expect three things in a closed-form text:

- They expect unity and coherence.
- They expect old information before new information.
- They expect forecasting and fulfillment.

Let's look at each in turn.

Unity and Coherence

Together the terms *unity* and *coherence* are defining characteristics of closed-form prose:

- **Unity** refers to the relationship between each part of an essay and the larger whole.
- **Coherence** refers to the relationship between adjacent sentences, paragraphs, and parts.

The following thought exercise will explore your own expectations for unity and coherence:

THOUGHT EXERCISE 1

Read the following two passages and try to explain why each fails to satisfy your expectations as a reader:

A. Recent research has given us much deeper—and more surprising—insights into the father's role in childrearing. My family is typical of the east side in that we never had much money. Their tongues became black and hung out of their mouths. The back-to-basics movement got a lot of press, fueled as it was by fears of growing illiteracy and cultural demise.

B. Recent research has given us much deeper—and more surprising—insights into the father's role in childrearing. Childrearing is a complex process that is frequently investigated by psychologists. Psychologists have also investigated sleep patterns and dreams. When we are dreaming, psychologists have shown, we are often reviewing recent events in our lives.

*For the useful term *reader energy*, we are indebted to George Gopen and Judith Swan, "The Science of Scientific Writing," *American Scientist* 78 (1990): 550–559. In addition, much of our discussion of writing in this chapter is indebted to the work of Joseph Williams, George Gopen, and Gregory Colomb. See especially Gregory G. Colomb and Joseph M. Williams, "Perceiving Structure in Professional Prose: A Multiply Determined Experience," in Lee Odell and Dixie Goswamie (eds.), *Writing in Nonacademic Settings* (New York: The Guilford Press, 1985), pp. 87–128.

If you are like most readers, Passage A comically frustrates your expectations because it is a string of random sentences. Because the sentences don't relate to each other or to a larger point, Passage A is neither unified nor coherent.

Passage B frustrates expectations in a subtler way. If you aren't paying attention, Passage B may seem to make sense because each sentence is linked to the one before it. But the individual sentences don't develop a larger whole: The topics switch from a father's role in childrearing to psychology to sleep patterns to the function of dreams. This passage has coherence without unity.

To fulfill a reader's expectations, then, a closed-form passage must be both unified and coherent:

> C. (*Unified and coherent*) Recent research has given us much deeper—and more surprising—insights into the father's role in childrearing. It shows that in almost all of their interactions with children, fathers do things a little differently from mothers. What fathers do—their special parenting style—is not only highly complementary to what mothers do but is by all indications important in its own right. [The passage continues by showing the special ways that fathers contribute to childrearing.]

This passage makes a unified point—that fathers have an important role in childrearing. Because all the parts relate to that whole (unity) and because the connections from sentence to sentence are clear (coherence), the passage satisfies our expectations: It makes sense.

Because achieving unity and coherence is a major goal in revising closed-form prose, we'll refer frequently to these concepts in later lessons.

Old before New

One dominant way that readers process information and register ideas is by moving from already known (old) information to new information. In a nutshell, this concept means that new material is meaningful to a reader only if it is linked to old material that is already meaningful. To illustrate this concept, consider the arrangement of names and numbers in a telephone directory. Because we read from left to right, we want people's names in the left column and the telephone numbers in the right column. A person's name is the old, familiar information we already know and the number is the new, unknown information that we seek. If the numbers were in the left column and the names in the right, we would have to read backward.

You can see the same old-before-new principle at work in the following thought exercise:

THOUGHT EXERCISE 2

You are a passenger on an airplane flight into Chicago and need to transfer to Flight 16 to Memphis. As you descend into Chicago, the flight attendant announces transfer gates. Which of the following formats is easier for you to process? Why?

Option A		**Option B**	
To Atlanta on Flight 29	Gate C12	Gate C12	Flight 29 to Atlanta
To Dallas on Flight 35	Gate C25	Gate C25	Flight 35 to Dallas
To Memphis on Flight 16	Gate B20	Gate B20	Flight 16 to Memphis

If you are like most readers, you prefer Option A, which puts old information before new. In this case, the old/known information is our destination (cities arranged alphabetically) and perhaps our flight number (To Memphis on Flight 16). The new/unknown information is Gate B20. Option B causes us to expend more energy than does Option A because it forces us to hold the number of each gate in memory until we hear its corresponding city and flight number. Whereas Option A allows us to relax until we hear the word "Memphis," Option B forces us to concentrate intensely on each gate number until we find the meaningful one.

Old before New at the Essay Level The principle of old before new has great explanatory power for writers. At the level of the whole essay, this principle helps writers establish the main structural frame and ordering principle of their argument. An argument's frame derives from the writer's purpose to change some aspect of the reader's view of the topic. The reader's original view of the topic—what we might call the common, expected, or ordinary view—constitutes old/known/familiar material. The writer's surprising view constitutes the new/unknown/unfamiliar material. The writer's hope is to move readers from their original view to the writer's new and different view. By understanding what constitutes old/familiar information to readers, the writer can determine how much background to provide, how to anticipate readers' objections, and how to structure material by moving from the old to the new. We treat these matters in more depth in Skill 17.4, on writing effective titles and introductions.

Old before New at the Sentence Level At the sentence level, the principle of old before new also helps writers create coherence between adjacent parts and sentences. Most sentences in an essay should contain both an old element and a new element. To create coherence, the writer begins with the old material, which links back to something earlier, and then puts the new material at the end of the sentence. (See the discussion of the old/new contract in Skill 17.7.)

Forecasting and Fulfillment

Finally, readers of closed-form prose expect writers to forecast what is coming and then to fulfill those forecasts. To appreciate what we mean by forecasting and fulfillment, try one more thought exercise:

THOUGHT EXERCISE 3

Although the following paragraph describes a simple procedure in easy-to-follow sentences, most readers still scratch their heads in bewilderment. Why? What makes the passage difficult to understand?

The procedure is actually quite simple. First, you arrange things into different groups. Of course, one pile may be sufficient depending on how much there is to do. If you have to go somewhere else due to lack of facilities, that is the next step; otherwise, you are pretty well set. Next you operate the machines according to the instructions. After the procedure is completed, one arranges the materials into different groups again. Then they can be put in their appropriate places. Eventually, they will be used once more and the whole cycle will have to be repeated. However, that is part of life.

Most readers report being puzzled about the paragraph's topic. Because the opening sentence doesn't provide enough context to tell them what to expect, the paragraph makes no forecast that can be fulfilled. Now try rereading the paragraph, but this time substitute the following opening sentence:

> The procedure for washing clothes is actually quite simple.

With the addition of "for washing clothes," the sentence provides a context that allows you to predict and understand what's coming. In the language of cognitive psychologists, this new opening sentence provides a schema for interpretation. A *schema* is the reader's mental picture of a structure for upcoming material. The new opening sentence allows you as reader to say mentally, "This paragraph will describe a procedure for washing clothes and argue that it is simple." When the schema proves accurate, you experience the pleasure of prediction and fulfillment. In the language of rhetorician Kenneth Burke, the reader's experience of form is "an arousing and fulfillment of desires."

What readers expect from a closed-form text, then, is an ability to predict what is coming as well as regular fulfillment of those predictions. Writers forecast what is coming in a variety of ways:

- by writing effective titles
- by writing effective introductions with forecasting cues
- by placing topic sentences near the beginning of paragraphs
- by creating effective transitions and mapping statements
- by using effective headings and subheadings if appropriate for the genre.

To meet their readers' needs for predictions and fulfillment, closed-form writers start and end with the big picture. They tell readers where they are going before they start the journey, they refer to this big picture at key transition points, and they refocus on the big picture in their conclusion.

SKILL 17.2 **Convert loose structures into thesis/support structures.**

In Skill 17.1 we described readers' expectations for unity and coherence, old information before new, and forecasting and fulfillment. In academic contexts, readers also expect closed-form prose to have a thesis/support structure. As we explained in Chapter 2, most closed-form academic writing—especially writing with the aim of analysis or persuasion—is governed by a contestable or risky thesis statement. Because developing and supporting a thesis is complex work requiring much critical thought, writers sometimes retreat into loose structures that are easier to compose than a thesis-based argument with points and particulars.

In this lesson we help you better understand thesis-based writing by contrasting it with prose that looks like thesis-based writing but isn't. We show you three common ways in which inexperienced writers give the appearance of writing thesis-based prose while actually retreating from the rigors of making and developing an argument. Avoiding the pitfalls of these loose structures can go a long way toward improving your performance on most college writing assignments.

Avoiding *And Then* Writing, or Chronological Structure

Chronological structure, often called "narrative," is the most common organizing principle of open-form prose. It may also be used selectively in closed-form prose to support a point. But sometimes the writer begins recounting the details of a story and chronological order takes over, driving out the thesis-based structure of points and particulars.

To a large degree, chronological order is the default mode we fall into when we aren't sure how to organize material. For example, if you were asked to analyze a fictional character, you might slip into a plot summary instead. In much the same way, you might substitute historical chronology ("First A happened, then B happened ...") for historical analysis ("B happened because A happened ..."); or you might give a chronological recounting of your research ("First I discovered A, then I discovered B ...") instead of organizing your material into an argument ("I question A's account of this phenomenon on the grounds of my recent discovery of B ...").

The tendency toward loose chronological structure is revealed in the following example from a student's essay on Shakespeare's *The Tempest*. This excerpt is from the introduction of the student's first draft:

PLOT SUMMARY—*AND THEN* WRITING

> Prospero cares deeply for his daughter. In the middle of the play Prospero acts like a gruff father and makes Ferdinand carry logs in order to test his love for Miranda and Miranda's love for him. In the end, though, Prospero is a loving father who rejoices in his daughter's marriage to a good man.

Here the student seems simply to retell the play's plot without any apparent thesis. (The body of her rough draft primarily retold the same story in more detail.) However, during an office conference, the instructor discovered that the student regarded her sentence about Prospero's being a loving father as her thesis. In fact, the student had gotten in an argument with a classmate over whether Prospero was a good person or an evil one. The instructor helped her convert her draft into a thesis/support structure:

REVISED INTRODUCTION—THESIS/SUPPORT STRUCTURE

> Many persons believe that Prospero is an evil person in the play. They claim that Prospero exhibits a harsh, destructive control over Miranda and also, like Faust, seeks superhuman knowledge through his magic. However, I contend that Prospero is a kind and loving father.

Chapter 2, Concept 5, discusses this principle in depth: "A strong thesis statement surprises readers with something new or challenging."

This revised version implies a problem (What kind of father is Prospero?), presents a view that the writer wishes to change (Prospero is harsh and hateful), and asserts a contestable thesis (Prospero is a loving father). The body of her paper can now be converted from plot summary to an argument with reasons and evidence supporting her claim that Prospero is loving.

This student's revision from an *and then* to a thesis/support structure is typical of many writers' experience. Because recounting events chronologically is a natural way to organize, many writers—even very experienced ones—lapse into long stretches of *and then* writing in their rough drafts. However, experienced writers have learned to recognize these *and then* sections in their drafts and to rework this material into a closed-form, thesis-based structure.

Avoiding *All About* Writing, or Encyclopedic Structure

Whereas *and then* writing turns essays into stories by organizing details chronologically, *all about* writing turns essays into encyclopedia articles by piling up details in heaps. When *all about* writing organizes these heaps into categories, it can appear to be well organized: "Having told you everything I learned about educational opportunities in Cleveland, I will now tell you everything I learned about the Rock and Roll Hall of Fame." But the categories do not function as points and particulars in support of a thesis. Rather, like the shelving system in a library, they are simply ways of arranging information for convenient retrieval, not a means of building a hierarchical structure.

An Example of "All About" Structure To illustrate the differences between *all about* writing and thesis-based writing, consider the case of two students choosing to write term papers on the subject of female police officers. One student is asked simply to write "all about" the topic; the other is asked to pose and investigate some problem related to female police officers and to support a thesis addressing that problem. In all likelihood, the first student would produce an initial outline with headings such as the following:

I. History of women in police roles
  A. Female police or soldiers in ancient times
  B. 19th century (Calamity Jane)
  C. 1900s–1960
  D. 1960–present
II. How female police officers are selected and trained
III. A typical day in the life of a female police officer
IV. Achievements and acts of heroism of female police officers
V. What the future holds for female police officers

Such a paper is a data dump that places into categories all the information the writer has uncovered. It is riskless, and, except for occasional new information, surpriseless. In contrast, when a student focuses on a significant question—one that grows out of the writer's own interests and demands engagement—the writing can be quite compelling.

Conversion to Problem-Thesis Structure Consider the case of a student, Lynnea, who wrote a research paper entitled "Women Police Officers: Should Size and Strength Be Criteria for Patrol Duty?" Her essay begins with a group of male police officers complaining about being assigned to patrol duty with a new female officer, Connie Jones (not her real name), who is four feet ten inches tall and weighs ninety pounds. Here is the rest of the introduction to Lynnea's essay.

FROM LYNNEA'S INTRODUCTION

Connie Jones has just completed police academy training and has been assigned to patrol duty in _______________. Because she is so small, she has to have a booster seat in her patrol car and has been given a special gun, since she can barely manage to pull the trigger of a standard police-issue .38 revolver. Although she passed the physical requirements at the academy, which involved speed and endurance running, situps, and monkey bar tests, most of the officers in her department doubt her ability to perform competently as a patrol officer. But nevertheless she is on patrol because men and women receive equal assignments in most of today's police forces. But is this a good policy? Can a person who is significantly smaller and weaker than her peers make an effective patrol officer?

Lynnea examined all the evidence she could find—through library and field research (interviewing police officers)—and arrived at the following thesis: "Because concern for public safety overrides all other concerns, police departments should set stringent size and strength requirements for patrol officers, even if these criteria exclude many women." This thesis has plenty of tension because it sets limits on equal rights for women. Because Lynnea considers herself a feminist, it caused her considerable distress to advocate setting these limits and placing public safety ahead of gender equity. The resulting essay was engaging precisely because of the tension it creates and the controversy it engenders.

Avoiding *Engfish* Writing, or Structure without Surprise

Unlike the chronological story and the *all about* paper, the **engfish** essay has a thesis.* But the thesis is a riskless truism supported with predictable reasons—often structured as the three body paragraphs in a traditional five-paragraph theme. It is fill-in-the-blank writing: "The food service is bad for three reasons. First, it is bad because the food is not tasty. Blah, blah, blah about tasteless food. Second, it is bad because it is too expensive. Blah, blah, blah about the expense." And so on. The writer is on autopilot and is not contributing to a real conversation about a real question. In some situations, writers use *engfish* intentionally: bureaucrats and politicians may want to avoid saying something risky; students may want to avoid writing about complex matters that they fear they do not fully understand. In the end, using *engfish* is bad not because what you say is *wrong*, but because what you say couldn't *possibly be* wrong. To avoid *engfish*, stay focused on the need to surprise your reader.

*The term *engfish* was coined by the textbook writer Ken Macrorie to describe a fishy kind of canned prose that bright but bored students mechanically produce to please their teachers. See Ken Macrorie, *Telling Writing* (Rochelle Park, NJ: Hayden Press, 1970).

FOR WRITING AND DISCUSSION

Developing a Thesis/Support Structure

As a class, choose a topic from popular culture such as reality TV shows, Twitter, rap, fad diets, legalizing marijuana, or a topic similar to these.

1. Working as a whole class or in small groups, give examples of how you might write about this topic in an *and then* way, an *all about* way, and an *engfish* way.
2. Then develop one or more questions about the topic that could lead to thesis/support writing. What contestable theses can your class create?

SKILL 17.3 **Plan and visualize your structure.**

As we explained in Skill 17.2, closed-form writing supports a contestable thesis through a hierarchical network of points and particulars. One way to visualize this structure is to outline its skeleton, an exercise that makes visually clear that not all points are on equal levels. The highest-level point is an essay's thesis statement, which is usually supported by several main points that are in turn supported by subpoints and sub-subpoints, all of which are supported by their own particulars. In this lesson we show you how to create such a hierarchical structure for your own papers and how to visualize this structure through an outline, tree diagram, or flowchart.

At the outset, we want to emphasize that structural diagrams are not rigid molds, but flexible planning devices that evolve as your thinking shifts and changes. The structure of your final draft may be substantially different from your initial scratch outline. In fact, we want to show you how your evolving outlines or diagrams can help you generate more ideas and reshape your structure.

With this background, we now proceed to a sequence of steps you can take to plan and visualize a structure.

Making Lists of "Chunks" and a Scratch Outline Early in the Writing Process

Early in the writing process, before you know how to organize your material, you know that you have certain ideas, sections, parts, or "chunks" that you want to include somewhere. Just making a list of these chunks will help you get started. Here is a list of chunks by student writer James Gardiner early in his process of writing a researched argument on online social networks:

We first introduced James's research problem in Chapter 2, p. 30; James's final paper is shown in Chapter 22, pp. 590–598.

CHUNKS THAT I WANT TO INCLUDE SOMEWHERE IN MY PAPER

- Section on the popularity of online social networks (OSNs)
- Tamyra Pierce article that OSNs can lead to bad grades
- Examples of athletes embarrassing team by putting drinking pictures on Facebook
- One of my research article's argument about OSNs and narcissism
- Danah Boyd's argument that OSNs are positive and provide a place to experiment with identity

- Story of college student who posted a revealing picture of herself as Catwoman and was later embarrassed
- The term "Facebook trance"

Once you make a list of chunks, you can begin thinking about which of them are high-level points and which are details in support of a point. Before writing a rough draft, many writers like to make a brief scratch outline to help with planning. Here is James's initial scratch outline.

JAMES'S INITIAL SCRATCH OUTLINE

- Attention-grabber (maybe story of my watching friends use Facebook or some kind of statistic)
- Evidence of popularity of OSNs
- Show the good side of OSNs (Boyd's argument, statements from my friends)
- Then move to bad side (use term "Facebook trance")
  - Narcissism
  - Embarrassing cases (Catwoman, athletes)
  - Lower grades

"Nutshelling" Your Argument as an Aid to Finding a Structure

As you begin drafting, you will find your ideas gradually becoming clearer and more structured. You can accelerate this process through the following short exercise that will help you "nutshell" your argument. The six prompts in this exercise invite you to look at your argument from different perspectives. We recommend that you write your responses to each prompt as a preliminary step in helping you visualize your structure.

EXERCISE FOR NUTSHELLING YOUR ARGUMENT

1. What puzzle or problem initiated your thinking about X?
2. *Template: Many people think X, but I am going to argue Y.*

   Before reading my paper, my readers will think X: [specify what you imagine your readers initially think about your topic] ______________________.

   But after reading my paper, my readers will think Y: [specify the new or different way readers will think after finishing your paper] ______________________.
3. The purpose of my paper is ______________________.
4. My paper addresses the following question: ______________________.
5. My one-sentence summary answer to this question is this: ______________________.
6. A tentative title for my paper is this: ______________________.

Here are James Gardiner's responses to these prompts:

1. I was initially puzzled why so many students used online social networks. I didn't have a profile on Facebook or MySpace and wondered what the advantages and disadvantages of OSNs might be.
2. Before reading my paper, my readers will believe that OSNs have few detrimental consequences. After reading my paper, my readers will appreciate the potential dangers of OSNs.

3. The purpose of this paper is to point out potential negative consequences of OSNs.
4. What are the possible negative consequences of OSNs?
5. Overuse of OSNs can contribute to a decline in grades, to a superficial view of relationships, to an increase in narcissism, and to possible future embarrassment.
6. Some Dangers of Online Social Networks

Articulating a Working Thesis with Main Points

Once you have nutshelled your argument, you are ready to create a working thesis statement that includes main supporting points. These supporting points help you visualize an emerging structure. Here is James Gardiner's working thesis statement.

> Despite the benefits of online social networks such as MySpace or Facebook, these networks can have negative consequences such as a decline in grades, a superficial view of relationships, an increase in narcissism, and possible future embarrassment.

Chapter 2, Concept 5, explains in detail how a thesis statement needs to surprise readers with something new or challenging.

Using Complete Sentences in Outlines to Convey Meanings

An effective working outline helps you organize *meanings*, not topics. Note that in the outline, tree diagram, and flowchart that follow, James Gardiner uses *complete sentences* rather than phrases in the high-level slots. Because sentences have both subjects and verbs, they can make a point, which asserts a meaning, unlike a phrase, which identifies a topic but doesn't make an assertion about it. Here are examples:

> **Phrase:** Lower grades
> **Sentence:** OSNs can have a negative effect on grades.
>
> **Phrase:** OSNs and narcissism
> **Sentence:** OSNs may contribute to a rise in narcissism among today's young people.

Any point—whether a thesis, a main point, or a subpoint—is a contestable assertion that requires its own particulars for support. By using complete sentences rather than phrases in an outline, the writer is forced to articulate the point of each section of the emerging argument.

Sketching Your Structure Using an Outline, Tree Diagram, or Flowchart

Once you have created a working thesis statement, you can sketch your structure to show how points, subpoints, and particulars can be arranged to support your thesis. We offer you three different ways to visualize your argument: outlines, tree diagrams, and flowcharts. Use whichever strategy best fits your way of thinking and perceiving.

Outlines The most common way of visualizing structure is the traditional outline, which uses letters and numerals to indicate levels of points, subpoints, and particulars. If you prefer outlines, we recommend that you use the outlining feature of your word processing program, which allows you to move and insert material and change heading levels with great flexibility.

Figure 17.1 shows the first half of James Gardiner's detailed outline for his argument. Note that, except in the introduction, James uses complete sentences rather than phrases for each level.

FIGURE 17.1 James Gardiner's Outline for First Half of Paper

Thesis: Despite the benefits of online social networks like MySpace or Facebook, these networks can have negative consequences such as a decline in grades, a superficial view of relationships, an increase in narcissism, and possible future embarrassment.

I Introduction
- A Attenion-grabber about walking into any computer lab
- B Media evidence shows a large increase in the popularity of OSNs among young people.
- C The term "Facebook Trance" indicates possible harms of OSNs.
- D Thesis paragraph

II Admittedly, OSNs have positive benefits.
- A They provide a way to stay in close contact with friends and family.
- B Researcher Danah Boyd says that OSNs give young people a place to experiment with identities and voices.
- C They provide a way to get quick additional information about someone you've met in class or at a party.

III Despite these benefits, OSNs have potential negative consequences.
- A They can have a negative effect on grades.
  - 1 Researcher Tamyra Pierce found that high school students with MySpace accounts were more likely to report a decline in grades than those without accounts.
  - 2 Her data show heavy use of OSNs among as many as 59 percent of students, taking time away from school, work, and sleep.
  - 3 Other writers apply the high school study to college.
- B OSNs have a tendency to promote superficial relationships.
  - 1 A study by Chou, Condron, and Belland shows that for some users, online relationships can result in problems with real-life interpersonal relationships.
  - 2 Another researcher, Matsuba, found that online relationships might hinder some people from developing an adult identity.
  - 3 A possible contributing factor to the superficiality of online relationships might be the absence of nonverbal communication.
- C O[illegible] migh[illegible] also co[illegible]tribut[illegible] a rise [illegible] arci[illegible]

Tree Diagrams A tree diagram displays a hierarchical structure visually, using horizontal and vertical space instead of letters and numbers. Figure 17.2 shows James's argument as a tree diagram. His thesis is at the top of the tree. His main reasons, written as point sentences, appear as branches beneath his claim. Supporting evidence and arguments are subbranches beneath each reason.

Unlike outlines, tree diagrams allow us to *see* the hierarchical relationship of points and particulars. When you develop a point with subpoints or particulars, you move down the tree. When you switch to a new point, you move across the tree to make a new branch. Our own teaching experience suggests that for many writers, this visual/spatial technique produces fuller, more detailed, and more logical arguments than does a traditional outline.

Flowcharts A flowchart presents the sequence of sections as separate boxes, inside which (or next to which) the writer notes the material needed to fill each box. A flowchart of James's essay is shown in Figure 17.3.

FIGURE 17.2 James's Tree Diagram

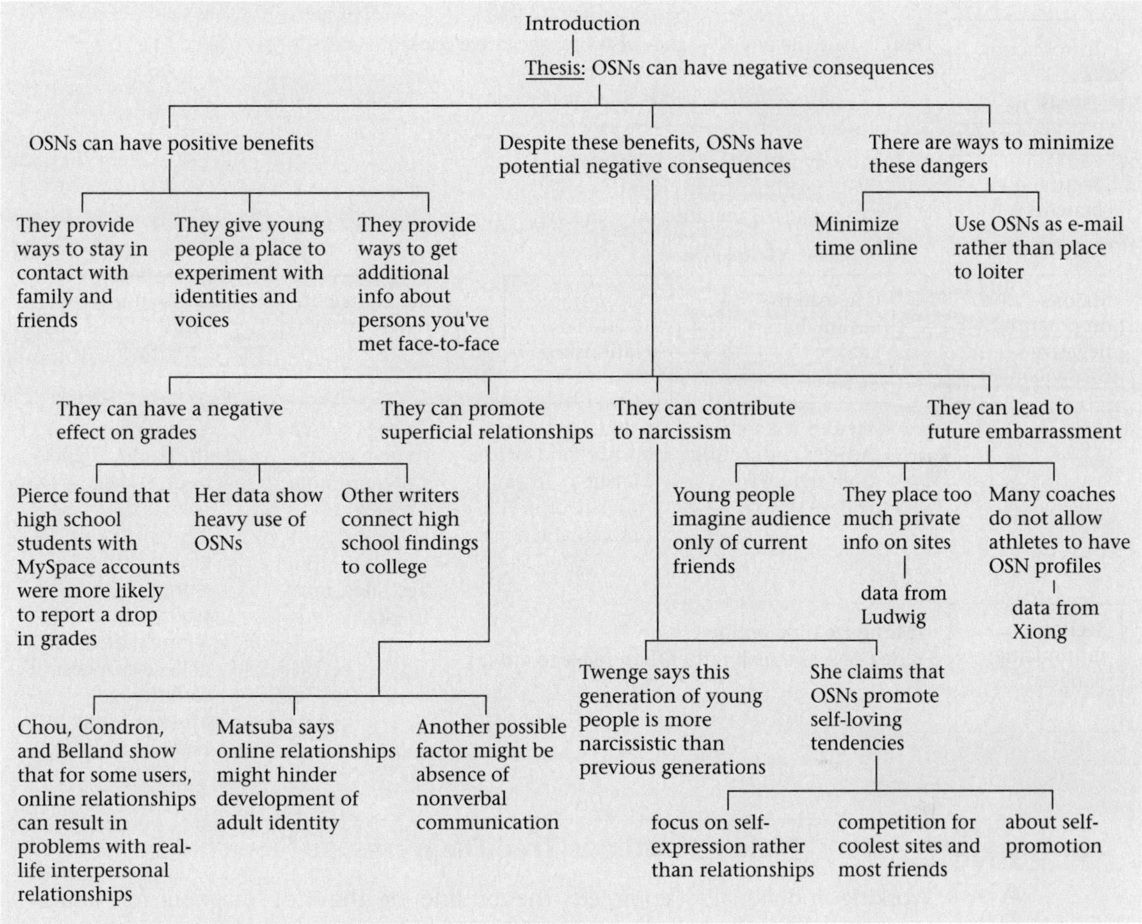

Letting the Structure Evolve

Once you have sketched out an initial structural diagram, use it to generate ideas. Tree diagrams are particularly helpful because they invite you to place question marks on branches to "hold open" spots for new points or supporting particulars. If you have only two main points, for example, you could draw a third main branch and place a question mark under it to encourage you to think of another supporting idea. Likewise, if a branch has few supporting particulars, add question marks beneath it. The trick is to think of your structural diagrams as evolving sketches rather than rigid blueprints. As your ideas grow and change, revise your structural diagram, adding or removing points, consolidating and refocusing sections, moving parts around, or filling in details.

FIGURE 17.3 James's Flowchart

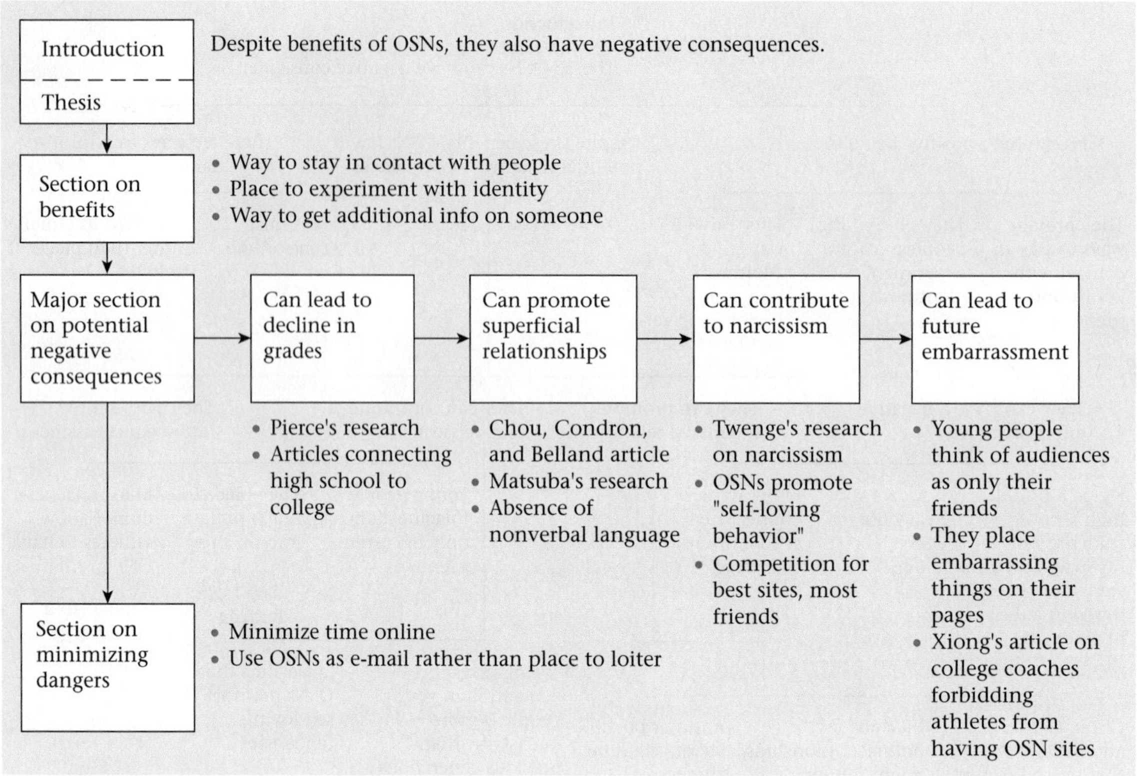

FOR WRITING AND DISCUSSION

Making Outlines, Tree Diagrams, or Flowcharts

Working individually, complete the outline or the tree diagram for James Gardiner's researched argument (pp. 590–598). Use complete sentences in the outline. Then convene in small groups to compare your outlines. Finally, share points of view on which method of representing structure—outlines, tree diagrams, or flowcharts—works best for different members of the class.

SKILL 17.4 Set up reader expectations through effective titles and introductions.

Because effective titles and introductions give readers a big-picture overview of a paper's argument, writers often can't compose them until they have finished one or more drafts. But as soon as you know your essay's big picture, you'll find that writing titles and introductions follows some general principles that are easy to learn.

Avoiding the "Topic Title" and the "Funnel Introduction"

Some students have been taught an opening strategy, sometimes called the "funnel," that encourages students to start with broad generalizations and then narrow down to their topics. This strategy often leads to a "topic title" (which names the topic area but doesn't forecast the problem being addressed or the surprise the writer will bring to readers) and vapid generalizations in the opening of the introduction, as the following example shows:

B. F. SKINNER

Since time immemorial people have pondered the question of freedom. The great philosophers of Greece and Rome asked what it means to be free, and the question has echoed through the ages up until the present day. One modern psychologist who asked this question was B. F. Skinner, who wanted to study whether humans had free will or were programmed by their environment to act the way they did. . . .

Here the writer eventually gets to his subject, B. F. Skinner, but so far presents no sense of what the point of the essay will be or why the reader should be interested. A better approach is to hook your readers immediately with an effective title and a problem-posing introduction.

Hooking Your Reader with an Effective Title

Good titles follow the principle of old before new information that we introduced in Skill 17.1. A good title needs to have something old (a word or phrase that hooks into a reader's existing interests) and something new (a word or phrase that forecasts the writer's problematic question, thesis, or purpose). Here are examples of effective titles from two student essays in this textbook:

"Why Facebook Might Not Be Good for You"
"Paintball: Promoter of Violence or Healthy Fun?"

The old information in these titles ("Facebook" and "Paintball") ties into readers' preexisting knowledge or interests. But the titles also indicate each essay's direction or purpose—the new information that promises to expand or challenge the readers' views. The first writer will argue that Facebook might be harmful in some way; the second writer will explore the problem of violence versus fun in paintball.

As these examples show, your title should provide a brief overview of what your paper is about. Academic titles are typically longer and more detailed than are titles in popular magazines. There are three basic approaches that academic writers take, as shown in the following strategies chart.

Strategies for Writing Titles of Academic Papers

What to Do	Examples
State or imply the question that your essay addresses.	Will Patriarchal Management Survive Beyond the Decade? The Impact of Cell Phones on Motor Vehicle Fatalities [Implied question: What is the impact . . . ?]

(continued)

What to Do	Examples
State or imply, often in abbreviated form, your essay's thesis.	The Writer's Audience Is Always a Fiction How Foreign Aid Can Foster Democratization in Authoritarian Regimes
Use a two-part title separated by a colon: • On the left, present key words from your essay's issue or problem or a "mystery phrase" that arouses interest. • On the right, place the essay's question, thesis, or summary of purpose.	Deep Play: Notes on a Balinese Cockfight Coping with Hurricane Katrina: Psychological Stress and Resilience among African-American Evacuees

Such titles might seem overly formal to you, but they indicate how much an academic writer wishes to preview an article's big picture. Although the titles in popular magazines may be more informal, they often use these same strategies. Here are some titles from popular magazines such as *Redbook* and *Forbes*:

> "Is the Coffee Bar Trend About to Peak?" (question)
> "A Man *Can* Take Maternity Leave—And Love It" (abbreviated thesis)
> "Feed Your Face: Why Your Complexion Needs Vitamins" (two parts linked by colon)

Composing a title for your essay can help you find your focus when you get bogged down in the middle of a draft. Thinking about your title forces you to *nutshell* your ideas by seeing your project's big picture. It causes you to reconsider your purpose and to think about what's old and what's new for your audience.

From Old to New: The General Principle of Closed-Form Introductions

Just as effective titles present something old and something new, so do dynamic and powerful introductions. Old information is something your readers already know and find interesting before they start reading your essay. New information is the surprise of your argument, the unfamiliar material that you add to your readers' understanding.

In this section, we elaborate on the rhetorical concept introduced in Chapter 2, Concept 6: "In closed-form prose, an introduction starts with the problem, not the thesis."

Because the writer's thesis statement forecasts the new information the paper will present, a thesis statement for a closed-form essay typically comes *at the end of the introduction.* What precedes the thesis is typically the problem or question that the thesis addresses—the old information that the reader needs in order to understand the conversation that the thesis joins. A typical closed-form introduction has the following shape:

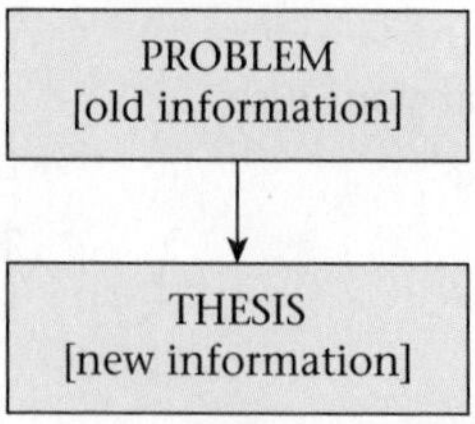

The length and complexity of your introduction is a function of how much your reader already knows and cares about the question or problem your paper addresses. The function of an introduction is to capture the reader's interest in the first few sentences, to identify and explain the question or problem that the essay addresses, to provide any needed background information, and to present the thesis. You can leave out any of the first three elements if the reader is already hooked on your topic and already knows the question you are addressing. For example, in an essay exam you can usually start with your thesis statement because you can assume the instructor already knows the question and finds it interesting.

To illustrate how an effective closed-form introduction takes the reader from the question to the thesis, consider how the following student writer revised his introduction to a paper on Napster.com:

ORIGINAL INTRODUCTION (CONFUSING)

Napster is all about sharing, not stealing, as record companies and some musicians would like us to think. Napster is an online program that was released in October of '99. Napster lets users easily search for and trade mp3s—compressed, high-quality music files that can be produced from a CD. Napster is the leading file sharing community; it allows users to locate and share music. It also provides instant messaging, chat rooms, an outlet for fans to identify new artists, and a forum to communicate their interests.

Thesis statement

Background on Napster

Most readers find this introduction confusing. The writer begins with his thesis statement before the reader is introduced to the question that the thesis addresses. He seems to assume that his reader is already a part of the Napster conversation, and yet in the next sentences, he gives background on Napster. If the reader needs background on Napster, then the reader also needs background on the Napster controversy. In rethinking his assumptions about old-versus-new information for his audience, this writer decided he wants to reach general newspaper readers who may have heard about a lawsuit against Napster and are interested in the issue but aren't sure of what Napster is or how it works. Here is his revised introduction:

REVISED INTRODUCTION (CLEARER)

Several months ago the rock band Metallica filed a lawsuit against Napster.com, an online program that lets users easily search for and trade mp3s—compressed, high-quality music files that can be produced from a CD. Napster.com has been wildly popular among music lovers because it creates a virtual community where users can locate and share music. It also provides instant messaging, chat rooms, an outlet for fans to identify new artists, and a forum to communicate their interests. But big-name bands like Metallica, alarmed at what they see as lost revenues, claim that Napster.com is stealing their royalties. However, Napster is all about sharing, not stealing, as some musicians would like us to think.

Triggers readers' memory of lawsuit

Background on Napster

Clarification of problem (Implied question: Should Napster be shut down?)

Thesis

This revised introduction fills in the old information the reader needs in order to recall and understand the problem; then it presents the thesis.

Typical Elements of a Closed-Form Introduction

Now that you understand the general principle of closed-form introductions, let's look more closely at its four typical features or elements:

1. ***An opening attention-grabber.*** If you aren't sure that your reader is already interested in your problem, you can begin with an attention-grabber (what journalists call the "hook" or "lead"), which is typically a dramatic vignette, a startling fact or statistic, an arresting quotation, an interesting scene, or something else that taps into your reader's interests. Attention-grabbers are uncommon in academic prose (where you assume your reader will be initially engaged by the problem itself) but frequently used in popular prose.
2. ***Explanation of the question to be investigated.*** If your reader already knows about the problem and cares about it, then you need merely to summarize it. This problem or question is the starting point of your argument. If you aren't sure whether your audience fully understands the question or fully cares about it, then you need to explain it in more detail, showing why it is both problematic and significant.
3. ***Background information.*** In order to understand the conversation you are joining, readers sometimes need background information such as a definition of key terms, a summary of events leading up to the problem, factual details needed for explaining the context of the problem, and so forth. In academic papers, this background often includes a review of what other scholars have said about the problem.
4. ***A preview of where your paper is heading.*** The final element of a closed-form introduction sketches the big picture of your essay by previewing the kind of surprise or challenge readers can expect and giving them a sense of the whole. This preview is initially new information for your readers (this is why it comes at the end of the introduction). Once stated, however, it becomes old information that readers will use to locate their position in their journey through your argument. By predicting what's coming, this preview initiates the pleasurable process of forecasting/fulfillment that we discussed in Skill 17.1. Writers typically forecast the whole by stating their thesis, but they can also use a purpose statement or a blueprint statement to accomplish the same end. These strategies are the subject of the next section.

Forecasting the Whole with a Thesis Statement, Purpose Statement, or Blueprint Statement

The most succinct way to forecast the whole is to state your thesis directly. Student writers often ask how detailed their thesis statements should be and whether it is permissible, sometimes, to delay revealing the thesis until the conclusion—an open-form move that gives papers a more exploratory, mystery-novel feel. It is useful, then, to outline briefly some of your choices as a writer. To illustrate a writer's options for forecasting the whole, we use James Gardiner's research paper on online social networks.

To see the choices James Gardiner actually made, see his complete essay on pp. 590–598.

Strategies for Forecasting the Whole Paper

Options	What to Do	Examples
Short thesis	State claim without summarizing your supporting argument or forecasting your structure.	Online social networks can have negative consequences.
Detailed thesis	Summarize whole argument; may begin with an *although* clause that summarizes the view you are trying to change.	Despite the benefits of online social networks like MySpace or Facebook, these networks can have negative consequences such as a decline in grades, a superficial view of relationships, an increase in narcissism, and possible future embarrassment.
Purpose statement	State your purpose or intention without summarizing the argument. A purpose statement typically begins with a phrase such as "My purpose is to . . ." or "In the following paragraphs I wish to . . ."	My purpose in this essay is to show the potential negative consequences of online social networks.
Blueprint or mapping statement	Describe the structure of your essay by announcing the number of main parts and describing the function or purpose of each one.	After discussing briefly the positive benefits of online social networks, I will describe four potential negative consequences. Finally I will suggest ways to avoid these consequences by using OSNs wisely.
Combination of elements	Include two or more of these elements. In long essays, academic writers sometimes have a purpose statement followed by a detailed thesis and blueprint statement.	[James's essay is not long enough nor complex enough to need an extensive multisentence overview.]
Thesis question only *[Implies a reflective or exploratory paper rather than an argument]*	State the question only, without initially implying your answer. This open-form strategy invites the reader to join the writer in a mutual search.	Although online social networks are widely popular, something about them makes me feel uncomfortable. I am wondering if there are unappreciated risks as well as benefits associated with OSNs.

Which of these options should a writer choose? There are no firm rules to help you answer this question. How much you forecast in the introduction and where you reveal your thesis is a function of your purpose, audience, and genre. The more you forecast, the clearer your argument is and the easier it is to read quickly. You minimize the demands on readers' time by giving them the gist of your argument in the introduction, making it easier to skim your essay if they don't have time for a thorough reading. The less you forecast, the more demands you make on readers' time: You invite them, in effect, to accompany you through the twists and turns of your own thinking process, and you risk losing them if they become confused, lost, or bored. For these reasons, academic writing is generally closed form and aims at maximum clarity. In many rhetorical contexts, however, more open forms are appropriate.

Chapter 1, Concept 1, gives more advice on when to choose closed or open forms.

If you choose a closed-form structure, we can offer some advice on how much to forecast. Readers sometimes feel insulted by too much forecasting, so include only what is needed for clarity. For short papers, readers usually don't need to have the complete supporting argument forecast in the introduction. In longer papers, however, or in especially complex ones, readers appreciate having the whole argument forecast at the outset. Academic writing in particular tends to favor explicit and often detailed forecasting.

FOR WRITING AND DISCUSSION

Revising a Title and Introduction

Individual task: Choose an essay you are currently working on or have recently completed and examine your title and introduction. Ask yourself these questions:

- What audience am I imagining? What do I assume are my readers' initial interests that will lead them to read my essay (the old information I must hook into)? What is new in my essay?
- Do I have an attention-grabber? Why or why not?
- Where do I state or imply the question or problem that my essay addresses?
- Do I explain why the question is problematic and significant? Why or why not?
- For my audience to understand the problem, do I provide too much background information, not enough, or just the right amount?
- What strategies do I use to forecast the whole?

Based on your analysis of your present title and introduction, revise as appropriate.

Group task: Working with a partner or in small groups, share the changes you made in your title or introduction and explain why you made the changes.

SKILL 17.5 **Create effective topic sentences for paragraphs.**

In our lesson on outlining (Skill 17.3) we suggested that you write complete sentences rather than phrases for the high-level slots of the outline in order to articulate the *meaning* or *point* of each section of your argument. In this lesson we show you how to place these points where readers expect them: near the beginning of the sections or paragraphs they govern.

When you place points before particulars, you follow the same principle illustrated in our old-before-new exercise (Skill 17.1) with the flight attendant announcing the name of the city before the departure gate (the city is the old information, the departure gate the new information). When you first state the point, it is the new information that the next paragraph or section will develop. Once you have stated it, it becomes old information that helps readers understand the meaning of the particulars that follow. If you withhold the point until later, the reader has to keep all the particulars in short-term memory until you finally reveal the point that the particulars are supposed to support or develop.

Placing Topic Sentences at the Beginning of Paragraphs

Readers of closed-form prose need to have point sentences (usually called "topic sentences") at the beginnings of paragraphs. However, writers of rough drafts often don't fulfill this need because, as we explained in Chapter 16, drafting is an exploratory process in which writers are often still searching for their points as they compose. Consequently, in their rough drafts writers often omit topic sentences entirely or place them at the ends of paragraphs, or they write topic sentences that misrepresent what the paragraphs actually say. During revision, then, you should check your body paragraphs carefully to be sure you have placed accurate topic sentences near the beginning.

What follow are examples of the kinds of revisions writers typically make. We have annotated the examples to explain the changes the writer has made to make the paragraphs unified and clear to readers. The first example is from a later draft of the essay on the dorm room carpets from Chapter 16 (pp. 448–449).

Revision–Topic Sentence First

Another reason for the university not to buy carpets is the cost.
^According to Rachel Jones, Assistant Director of Housing Services, the initial purchase and installation of carpeting would cost $300 per room. Considering the number of rooms in the three residence halls, carpeting amounts to a substantial investment. Additionally, once the carpets are installed, the university would need to maintain them through the purchase of more vacuum cleaners and shampoo machines. This money would be better spent on other dorm improvements that would benefit more residents, such as expanded kitchen facilities and improved recreational space. ~~Thus carpets would be too expensive.~~

Topic sentence placed first

In the original draft, the writer states the point at the end of the paragraph. In his revision he states the point in an opening topic sentence that links back to the thesis statement, which promises "several reasons" that the university should not buy carpets for the dorms. The words "Another reason" thus link the topic sentence to the argument's big picture.

Revising Paragraphs for Unity

In addition to placing topic sentences at the heads of paragraphs, writers often need to revise topic sentences to better match what the paragraph actually says, or revise the paragraph to better match the topic sentence. Paragraphs have unity when all their sentences develop the point stated in the topic sentence. Paragraphs in rough drafts are often not unified because they reflect the writer's shifting, evolving, thinking-while-writing process. Consider the following paragraph from an early draft of an argument against euthanasia by student writer Dao Do. Her peer reviewer labeled it "confusing." What makes it confusing?

We look at more examples from Dao's essay later in this chapter.

Early Draft–Confusing

First, euthanasia is wrong because no one has the right to take the life of another person. Some people say that euthanasia or suicide will end suffering and pain. But what proofs do they have for such a claim? Death is still mysterious to us; therefore, we do not know whether death will end suffering and pain or not. What seems to be the real claim is that death to those with illnesses will end *our* pain. Such pain involves worrying over them, paying their medical bills, and giving up so much of our time. Their deaths end our pain rather than theirs. And for that reason, euthanasia is a selfish act, for the outcome of euthanasia benefits us, the nonsufferers, more. Once the sufferers pass away, we can go back to our normal lives.

The paragraph opens with an apparent topic sentence: "Euthanasia is wrong because no one has the right to take the life of another person." But the rest of the paragraph doesn't focus on that point. Instead, it focuses on how euthanasia benefits the survivors more than the sick person. Dao had two choices: to revise the paragraph to fit the topic sentence or to revise the topic sentence to fit the paragraph. Here is her revision, which includes a different topic sentence and an additional sentence midparagraph to keep particulars focused on the opening point. Dao unifies this paragraph by keeping all its parts focused on her main point: "Euthanasia … benefits the survivors more than the sick person."

Revision for Unity

Revised topic sentence better forecasts focus of paragraph

Keeps focus on "sick person"

First, euthanasia is wrong because it benefits the survivors more than the sick person.
~~First, euthanasia is wrong because no one has the right to take the life of another person.~~ Some people say that euthanasia or suicide will end *the sick person's* suffering and pain. But what proofs do they have for such a claim? Death is still

mysterious to us; therefore, we do not know whether death will end suffering and pain or not. *Moreover, modern pain killers can relieve most of the pain a sick person has to endure.* What seems to be the real claim is that death to those with illnesses will end *our* pain. Such pain involves worrying over them, paying their medical bills, and giving up so much of our time. Their deaths end our pain rather than theirs. And for that reason, euthanasia is a selfish act, for the outcome of euthanasia benefits us, the nonsufferers, more. Once the sufferers pass away, we can go back to our normal lives.

Concludes subpoint about sick person

Supports subpoint about how euthanasia benefits survivors

A paragraph may lack unity for a variety of reasons. It may shift to a new direction in the middle, or one or two sentences may simply be irrelevant to the point. The key is to make sure that all the sentences in the paragraph fulfill the reader's expectations based on the topic sentence.

Adding Particulars to Support Points

Just as writers of rough drafts often omit point sentences from paragraphs, they also sometimes leave out the particulars needed to support a point. In such cases, the writer needs to add particulars such as facts, statistics, quotations, research summaries, examples, or further subpoints. Consider how adding additional particulars to the following draft paragraph strengthens a student writer's argument opposing the logging of old-growth forests.

DRAFT PARAGRAPH: PARTICULARS MISSING

One reason that it is not necessary to log old-growth forests is that the timber industry can supply the world's lumber needs without doing so. For example, we have plenty of new-growth forest from which timber can be taken (Sagoff 89). We could also reduce the amount of trees used for paper products by using other materials besides wood for paper pulp. In light of the fact that we have plenty of trees and ways of reducing our wood demands, there is no need to harvest old-growth forests.

REVISED PARAGRAPH: PARTICULARS ADDED

One reason that it is not necessary to log old-growth forests is that the timber industry can supply the world's lumber needs without doing so. For example, we have plenty of new-growth forest from which timber can be taken as a result of major reforestation efforts all over the United States (Sagoff 89). In the Northwest, for instance, Oregon law requires every acre of timber harvested to be replanted. According to Robert Sedjo, a forestry expert, the world's demand for industrial wood could be met by a widely implemented tree farming system (Sagoff 90). We could also reduce the amount of trees used for paper products by using a promising new innovation called Kenaf, a fast-growing annual herb which is fifteen feet tall and is native to Africa. It has been used for making rope for many years, but recently it was found to work just as well for paper pulp. In light of the fact that we have plenty of trees and ways of reducing our wood demands, there is no need to harvest old-growth forests.

Added particulars support subpoint that we have plenty of new-growth forest

Added particulars support second subpoint that wood alternatives are available

FOR WRITING AND DISCUSSION

Revising Paragraphs for Points-First Structure

Individual task: Bring to class a draft-in-progress for a closed-form essay. Pick out several paragraphs in the body of your essay and analyze them for "points-first" structure. For each paragraph, ask the following questions:

- Does my paragraph have a topic sentence near the beginning?
- If so, does my topic sentence accurately forecast what the paragraph says?
- Does my topic sentence link to my thesis statement or to a higher-order point that my paragraph develops?
- Does my paragraph have enough particulars to develop and support my topic sentence?

Group task: Then exchange your draft with a partner and do a similar analysis of your partner's selected paragraphs. Discuss your analyses of each other's paragraphs and then help each other plan appropriate revision strategies. If time permits, revise your paragraphs and show your results to your partner. [Note: Sometimes you can revise simply by adding a topic sentence to a paragraph, rewording a topic sentence, or making other kinds of local revisions. At other times, you may need to cross out whole paragraphs and start over, rewriting from scratch after you rethink your ideas.]

SKILL 17.6 **Guide your reader with transitions and other signposts.**

As we have explained, when readers read closed-form prose, they expect each new sentence, paragraph, and section to link clearly to what they have already read. They need a well-marked trail with signposts signaling the twists and turns along the way. They also need resting spots at major junctions where they can review where they've been and survey what's coming. In this lesson, we show you how transition words as well as summary and forecasting passages can keep your readers securely on the trail.

Using Common Transition Words to Signal Relationships

Transitions are like signposts that signal where the road is turning and limit the possible directions that an unfolding argument might take. Consider how the use of "therefore" and "nevertheless" limits the range of possibilities in the following examples:

> While on vacation, Suzie caught the chicken pox. Therefore, ________________.
> While on vacation, Suzie caught the chicken pox. Nevertheless, ________________.

"Therefore" signals to the reader that what follows is a consequence. Most readers will imagine a sentence similar to this one:

> Therefore, she spent her vacation lying in bed itchy, feverish, and miserable.

In contrast, "nevertheless" signals an unexpected or denied consequence, so the reader might anticipate a sentence such as this:

> Nevertheless, she enjoyed her two weeks off, thanks to a couple of bottles of calamine lotion, some good books, and a big easy chair overlooking the ocean.

Here is a list of the most common transition words and phrases and what they signal to the reader:*

Words or Phrases	What They Signal
first, second, third, next, finally, earlier, later, meanwhile, afterward	*sequence*—First we went to dinner; then we went to the movies.
that is, in other words, to put it another way, — (dash), : (colon)	*restatement*—He's so hypocritical that you can't trust a word he says. To put it another way, he's a complete phony.
rather, instead	*replacement*—We shouldn't use the money to buy opera tickets; rather, we should use it for a nice gift.
for example, for instance, a case in point	*example*—Mr. Carlyle is very generous. For example, he gave the janitors a special holiday gift.
because, since, for	*reason*—Taxes on cigarettes are unfair because they place a higher tax burden on the working class.
therefore, hence, so, consequently, thus, then, as a result, accordingly, as a consequence	*consequence*—I failed to turn in the essay; therefore I flunked the course.
still, nevertheless	*denied consequence*—The teacher always seemed grumpy in class; nevertheless, I really enjoyed the course.
although, even though, granted that (*with* still)	*concession*—Even though the teacher was always grumpy, I still enjoyed the course.
in comparison, likewise, similarly	*similarity*—Teaching engineering takes a lot of patience. Likewise, so does teaching accounting.
however, in contrast, conversely, on the other hand, but	*contrast*—I disliked my old backpack immensely; however, I really like this new one.
in addition, also, too, moreover, furthermore	*addition*—Today's cars are much safer than those of ten years ago. In addition, they get better gas mileage.
in brief, in sum, in conclusion, finally, to sum up, to conclude	*conclusion or summary*—In sum, the plan presented by Mary is the best choice.

FOR WRITING AND DISCUSSION

Using Transitions

This exercise is designed to show you how transition words govern relationships between ideas. Working in groups or on your own, finish each of the following statements using ideas of your own invention. Make sure what you add fits the logic of the transition word.

1. Writing is difficult; therefore ________________.
2. Writing is difficult; however, ________________.

(*continued*)

*Although all the words on the list serve as transitions or connectives, grammatically they are not all equivalent, nor are they all punctuated the same way.

3. Writing is difficult because ________________.
4. Writing is difficult. For example, ________________.
5. Writing is difficult. To put it another way, ________________.
6. Writing is difficult. Likewise, ________________.
7. Although writing is difficult, ________________.

In the following paragraph, various kinds of linking devices have been omitted. Fill in the blanks with words or phrases that would make the paragraph coherent. Clues are provided in brackets.

> Writing an essay is a difficult process for most people. ________________ [contrast] the process can be made easier if you learn to practice three simple techniques. ________________ [sequence] learn the technique of nonstop writing. When you are first trying to think of ideas for an essay, put your pen to your paper and write nonstop for ten or fifteen minutes without letting your pen leave the paper. Stay loose and free. Let your pen follow the waves of thought. Don't worry about grammar or spelling. ________________ [concession] this technique won't work for everyone, it helps many people get a good cache of ideas to draw on. A ________________ [sequence] technique is to write your rough draft rapidly without worrying about being perfect. Too many writers try to get their drafts right the first time. ________________ [contrast] by learning to live with imperfection, you will save yourself headaches and a wastepaper basket full of crumpled paper. Think of your first rough draft as a path hacked out of the jungle—as part of an exploration, not as a completed highway. As a ________________ [sequence] technique, try printing out a triple-spaced copy to allow space for revision. Many beginning writers don't leave enough space to revise. ________________ [consequence] these writers never get in the habit of crossing out chunks of their rough draft and writing revisions in the blank spaces. After you have revised your rough draft until it is too messy to work from anymore, you can ________________ [sequence] enter your changes into your word processor and print out a fresh draft, again setting your text on triple-space. The resulting blank space invites you to revise.

Writing Major Transitions between Parts

In long closed-form pieces, writers often put *resting places* between major parts—transitional passages that allow readers to shift their attention momentarily away from the matter at hand to get a sense of where they've been and where they're going. Often such passages sum up the preceding major section, refer back to the essay's thesis statement or opening blueprint plan, and then preview the next major section. Here are three typical examples:

> So far I have looked at a number of techniques that can help people identify debilitating assumptions that block their self-growth. In the next section, I examine ways to question and overcome these assumptions.

> Now that the difficulty of the problem is fully apparent, our next step is to examine some of the solutions that have been proposed.

> These, then, are the major theories explaining why Hamlet delays. But let's see what happens to Hamlet if we ask the question in a slightly different way. In this next section, we shift our critical focus, looking not at Hamlet's actions, but at his language.

Signaling Major Transitions with Headings

In many genres, particularly scientific and technical reports, government documents, business proposals, textbooks, and long articles in magazines or scholarly journals, writers conventionally break up long stretches of text with headings and subheadings. Headings are often set in different type sizes and fonts and mark transition points between major parts and subparts of the argument.

SKILL 17.7 **Bind sentences together by placing old information before new information.**

The previous skill focused on marking the reader's trail with transitions. This skill will enable you to build a smooth trail without potholes or washed-out bridges.

The Old/New Contract in Sentences

A powerful way to prevent gaps is to follow the old/new contract—a writing strategy derived from the principle of old before new that we explained and illustrated in Skill 17.1. Simply put, the old/new contract asks writers to begin sentences with something old—something that links to what has gone before—and then to end sentences with new information.

To understand the old/new contract more fully, try the following thought exercise. We'll show you two passages, both of which explain the old/new contract. One of them, however, follows the principle it describes; the other violates it.

THOUGHT EXERCISE

Which of these passages follows the old/new contract?

VERSION 1

The old/new contract is another principle for writing clear closed-form prose. Beginning your sentences with something old—something that links to what has gone before—and then ending your sentences with new information that advances the argument is what the old/new contract asks writers to do. An effect called *coherence,* which is closely related to *unity,* is created by following this principle. Whereas the clear relationship between the topic sentence and the body of the paragraph and between the parts and the whole is what *unity* refers to, the clear relationship between one sentence and the next is what *coherence* relates to.

VERSION 2

Another principle for writing clear closed-form prose is the old/new contract. The old/new contract asks writers to begin sentences with something old—something that links to what has gone before—and then to end sentences with new information that advances the argument. Following this principle creates an effect called *coherence,* which is closely related to unity. Whereas *unity* refers to the clear relationship between the body of a paragraph and its topic sentence and between the parts and the whole, *coherence* refers to the clear relationship between one sentence and the next, between part and part.

If you are like most readers, you have to concentrate much harder to understand Version 1 than Version 2 because Version 1 violates the old-before-new way that our minds normally process information. When a writer doesn't begin a sentence with old material, readers have to hold the new material in suspension until they have figured out how it connects to what has gone before. They can stay on the trail, but they have to keep jumping over the potholes between sentences.

To follow the old/new contract, place old information near the beginning of sentences in what we call the **topic position** and place new information that advances the argument in the predicate or **stress position** at the end of the sentence. We associate topics with the beginnings of sentences simply because in the standard English sentence, the topic (or subject) comes before the predicate—hence the notion of a "contract" by which we agree not to fool or frustrate our readers by breaking with the "normal" order of things. The contract says that the old, backward-linking material comes at the beginning of the sentence and that the new, argument-advancing material comes at the end.

FOR WRITING AND DISCUSSION

Practicing the Old/New Contract

Here are two more passages, one of which obeys the old/new contract while the other violates it. Working in small groups or as a whole class, reach consensus on which of these passages follows the old/new contract. Explain your reasoning by showing how the beginning of each sentence links to something old.

PASSAGE A

Play is an often-overlooked dimension of fathering. From the time a child is born until its adolescence, fathers emphasize caretaking less than play. Egalitarian feminists may be troubled by this, and spending more time in caretaking may be wise for fathers. There seems to be unusual significance in the father's style of play. Physical excitement and stimulation are likely to be part of it. With older children more physical games and teamwork that require the competitive testing of physical and mental skills are also what it involves. Resemblance to an apprenticeship or teaching relationship is also a characteristic of fathers' play: Come on, let me show you how.

PASSAGE B

An often-overlooked dimension of fathering is play. From their children's birth through adolescence, fathers tend to emphasize play more than caretaking. This emphasis may be troubling to egalitarian feminists, and it would indeed be wise for most fathers to spend more time in caretaking. Yet the fathers' style of play seems to have unusual significance. It is likely to be both physically stimulating and exciting. With older children it involves more physical games and teamwork that require the competitive testing of physical and mental skills. It frequently resembles an apprenticeship or teaching relationship: Come on, let me show you how.

How to Make Links to the "Old"

To understand how to link to "old information," you need to understand more fully what we mean by "old" or "familiar." In the context of sentence-level coherence, we mean everything in the text that the reader has read so far. Any upcoming sentence is new information, but once the reader has read it, it becomes old information. For example, when a reader is halfway through a text, everything previously read—the title, the introduction, half the body—is old information to which you can link to meet your readers' expectations for unity and coherence.

In making these backward links, writers have three targets:

1. They can link to a key word or concept in the immediately preceding sentence (creating coherence).
2. They can link to a key word or concept in a preceding point sentence (creating unity).
3. They can link to a preceding forecasting statement about structure (helping readers map their location in the text).

Writers have a number of textual strategies for making these links. In Figure 17.4 our annotations show how a professional writer links to old

FIGURE 17.4 How a Professional Writer Follows the Old/New Contract

Recent research has given us much deeper—and more surprising—insights into the father's role in childrearing. It shows that in almost all of their interactions with children, fathers do things a little differently from mothers. What fathers do—their special parenting style—is not only highly complementary to what mothers do but is by all indications important in its own right.

For example, an often-overlooked dimension of fathering is play. From their children's birth through adolescence, fathers tend to emphasize play more than caretaking. This may be troubling to egalitarian feminists, and it would indeed be wise for most fathers to spend more time in caretaking.

Yet the fathers' style of play seems to have unusual significance. It is likely to be both physically stimulating and exciting. With older children it involves more physical games and teamwork that require the competitive testing of physical and mental skills. It frequently resembles an apprenticeship or teaching relationship: Come on, let me show you how.

David Popenoe, "Where's Papa?" from *Life Without Father: Compelling New Evidence that Fatherhood and Marriage Are Indispensable for the Good of Children and Society.*

Refers to "research" in previous sentence

Refers to "fathers" in previous sentence

Rephrases idea of "childrearing"

Repeats "fathers" from previous sentence

Transition tells us new paragraph will be an example of previous concept

Rephrases concept in previous paragraph

Refers to "fathers"

New information that becomes topic of this paragraph

Pronoun sums up previous concept

Repeats words "father" and "play" from the topic sentence of the preceding paragraph

"It" refers to fathers' style of play

information within the first five or six words of each sentence. What follows is a compendium of these strategies:

Strategies for Linking to the "Old"

What to Do	Example Shown in Figure 17.4
Repeat a key word from the preceding sentence or an earlier point sentence.	Note the number of sentences that open with "father," "father's," or "fathering." Note also the frequent repetitions of "play."
Use a pronoun to substitute for a key word.	In our example, the second sentence opens with the pronouns "It," referring to "research," and "their," referring to "fathers." The last three sentences open with the pronoun "It," referring to "father's style of play."
Summarize, rephrase, or restate earlier concepts.	In the second sentence, "interactions with children" restates the concept of childrearing. Similarly, the phrase "an often-overlooked dimension" sums up a concept implied in the preceding paragraph—that recent research reveals something significant and not widely known about a father's role in childrearing. Finally, note that the pronoun "This" in the second paragraph sums up the main concept of the previous two sentences. (But see our warning on p. 481 about the overuse of "this" as a pronoun.)
Use a transition word such as *first . . . , second . . . , third . . . ,* or *therefore* or *however* to cue the reader about the logical relationship between an upcoming sentence and the preceding ones.	Note how the second paragraph opens with "For example," indicating that the upcoming paragraph will illustrate the concept identified in the preceding paragraph.

These strategies give you a powerful way to check and revise your prose. Comb your drafts for gaps between sentences where you have violated the old/new contract. If the opening of a new sentence doesn't refer back to an earlier word, phrase, or concept, your readers could derail, so use what you have learned to repair the tracks.

FOR WRITING AND DISCUSSION

Applying the Old/New Contract to Your Own Draft

Individual task: Bring to class a draft-in-progress for a closed-form essay. On a selected page, examine the opening of each sentence. Place a vertical slash in front of any sentence that doesn't contain near the beginning some backward-looking element that links to old, familiar material. Then revise these sentences to follow the old/new contract.

Group task: Working with a partner, share the changes you each made on your drafts. Then on each other's pages, work together to identify the kinds of links made at the beginning of each sentence. (For example, does the opening of a sentence repeat a key word, use a pronoun to substitute for a key word, rephrase or restate an earlier concept, or use a transition word?)

As we discussed in Skill 17.1, the principle of old before new has great explanatory power in helping writers understand their choices when they compose. In this last section, we give you some further insights into the old/new contract.

Avoiding Ambiguous Use of "This" to Fulfill the Old/New Contract

Some writers try to fulfill the old/new contract by frequent use of the pronoun *this* to sum up a preceding concept. Occasionally such usage is effective, as in our example passage on fathers' style of play when the writer says: "*This* may be troubling to egalitarian feminists." But frequent use of *this* as a pronoun creates lazy and often ambiguous prose. Consider how our example passage might read if many of the explicit links were replaced by *this*:

LAZY USE OF *THIS* AS PRONOUN

> Recent research has given us much deeper—and more surprising—insights into **this.** It shows that in doing **this,** fathers do things a little differently from mothers. **This** is not only highly complementary to what mothers do but is by all indications important in its own right.
>
> For example, an often-overlooked dimension of **this** is play.

Perhaps this passage helps you see why we refer to *this* (used by itself as a pronoun) as "the lazy person's all-purpose noun-slot filler."*

SKILL 17.8 Learn four expert moves for organizing and developing ideas.

Writers of closed-form prose often employ a conventional set of moves to organize parts of an essay. In using the term *moves,* we are making an analogy with the "set moves" or "set plays" in such sports as basketball, volleyball, and soccer. For example, a common set move in basketball is the "pick," in which an offensive player without the ball stands motionless in order to block the path of a defensive player who is guarding the dribbler. Similarly, certain organizational patterns in writing occur frequently enough to act as set plays for writers. These patterns set

*It's acceptable to use *this* as an adjective, as in "this usage"; we refer here only to *this* used by itself as a pronoun.

up expectations in the reader's mind about the shape of an upcoming stretch of prose, anything from a few sentences to a paragraph to a large block of paragraphs. As you will see, these moves also stimulate the invention of ideas. Next, we describe four of the most powerful set plays.*

The *For Example* Move

Perhaps the most common set play occurs when a writer makes an assertion and then illustrates it with one or more examples, often signaling the move explicitly with transitions such as *for example, for instance,* or *a case in point is* . . . . Here is how student writer Dao Do used the *for example* move to support her third reason for opposing euthanasia:

***FOR EXAMPLE* MOVE**

Topic sentence

Transition signaling the move

Extended example supporting point

My third objection to euthanasia is that it fails to see the value in suffering. Suffering is a part of life. We see the value of suffering only if we look deeply within our suffering. For example, I never thought my crippled uncle from Vietnam was a blessing to my grandmother until I talked to her. My mother's little brother was born prematurely. As a result of oxygen and nutrition deficiency, he was born crippled. His tiny arms and legs were twisted around his body, preventing him from any normal movements such as walking, picking up things, and lying down. He could only sit. Therefore, his world was very limited, for it consisted of his own room and the garden viewed through his window. Because of his disabilities, my grandmother had to wash him, feed him, and watch him constantly. It was hard, but she managed to care for him for forty-three years. He passed away after the death of my grandfather in 1982. Bringing this situation out of Vietnam and into Western society shows the difference between Vietnamese and Western views. In the West, my uncle might have been euthanized as a baby. Supporters of euthanasia would have said he wouldn't have any quality of life and that he would have been a great burden. But he was not a burden on my grandmother. She enjoyed taking care of him, and he was always her company after her other children got married and moved away. Neither one of them saw his defect as meaningless suffering because it brought them closer together.

This passage uses a single, extended example to support a point. You could also use several shorter examples or other kinds of illustrating evidence such as facts or statistics. In all cases the *for example* move creates a pattern of expectation and fulfillment. This pattern drives the invention of ideas in one of two ways: It urges the writer either to find examples to develop a generalization or to formulate a generalization that shows the point of an example.

*You might find it helpful to follow the set plays we used to write this section. This last sentence is the opening move of a play we call "division into parallel parts." It sets up the expectation that we will develop four set plays in order. Watch for the way we chunk them and signal transitions between them.

Practicing the *For Example* Move

FOR WRITING AND DISCUSSION

Working individually or in groups, develop a plan for supporting one or more of the following generalizations using the *for example* move:

1. Another objection to state sales taxes is that they are so annoying.
2. Although assertiveness training has definite benefits, it can sometimes get you into real trouble.
3. Sometimes effective leaders are indecisive.

The *Summary/However* Move

This move occurs whenever a writer sums up another person's viewpoint in order to qualify or contradict it or to introduce an opposing view. Typically, writers use transition words such as *but, however, in contrast,* or *on the other hand* between the parts of this move. This move is particularly common in academic writing, which often contrasts the writer's new view with prevailing views. Here is how Dao uses a *summary/however* move in the introduction of her essay opposing euthanasia:

***SUMMARY/HOWEVER* MOVE**

> Should euthanasia be legalized? My classmate Martha and her family think it should be. Martha's aunt was blind from diabetes. For three years she was constantly in and out of the hospital, but then her kidneys shut down and she became a victim of life support. After three months of suffering, she finally gave up. Martha believes this three-month period was unnecessary, for her aunt didn't have to go through all of that suffering. If euthanasia were legalized, her family would have put her to sleep the minute her condition worsened. Then, she wouldn't have had to feel pain, and she would have died in peace and with dignity. However, despite Martha's strong argument for legalizing euthanasia, I find it wrong.

Issue over which there is disagreement

Summary of opposing viewpoint

Transition to writer's viewpoint

Statement of writer's view

The first sentence of this introduction poses the question that the essay addresses. The main body of the paragraph summarizes Martha's opposing view on euthanasia, and the final sentence, introduced by the transition "However," presents Dao's thesis.

Practicing the *Summary/However* Move

FOR WRITING AND DISCUSSION

For this exercise, assume that you favor development of wind-generated electricity. Use the *summary/however* move to acknowledge the view of civil engineer David Rockwood, whose letter opposing wind-generated electricity you read in Chapter 1 (p. 6). Assume that you are writing the opening paragraph of your own essay. Follow the pattern of Dao's introduction: (a) begin with a one-sentence issue or question; (b) summarize Rockwood's view in approximately one hundred words; and (c) state your own view, using *however* or *in contrast* as a transition. Write out your paragraph on your own, or work in groups to write a consensus paragraph. Then share and critique your paragraphs.

The *Division-into-Parallel-Parts* Move

Among the most frequently encountered and powerful of the set plays is the *division-into-parallel-parts* move. To initiate the move, a writer begins with an umbrella sentence that forecasts the structure and creates a framework. (For example, "Freud's theory differs from Jung's in three essential ways" or "The decline of the U.S. space program can be attributed to several factors.") Typical overview sentences either specify the number of parts that follow by using phrases such as "two ways," "three differences," or "five kinds," or they leave the number unspecified, using words such as *several, a few,* or *many.* Alternatively, the writer may ask a rhetorical question that implies the framework: "What are some main differences, then, between Freud's theory and Jung's? One difference is. . . . "

To signal transitions from one part to the next, writers use two kinds of signposts in tandem. The first is a series of transition words or bullets to introduce each of the parallel parts. Here are typical series of transition words:

First . . . Second . . . Third . . . Finally . . .
First . . . Another . . . Still another . . . Finally . . .
One . . . In addition . . . Furthermore . . . Also . . .

The second kind of signpost, usually used in conjunction with transitions, is an echolike repetition of the same grammatical structure to begin each parallel part.

> I learned several things from this course. First, *I learned that* [development]. Second, *I learned that* [development]. Finally, *I learned that* [development].

The *division-into-parallel-parts* move can be used within a single paragraph, or it can control larger stretches of text in which a dozen or more paragraphs may work together to complete a parallel series of parts. (For example, you are currently in the third part of a parallel series introduced by the mapping sentence on p. 482: "Next, we describe four of the most powerful set plays.") Here is an example of a student paragraph organized by the *division-into-parallel-parts* move.

DIVISION-INTO-PARALLEL-PARTS MOVE

Mapping statement forecasts "move"

Transition to first parallel part

Transition to second parallel part

Transition to third parallel part

Final transition completes "move"

In this paper I will argue that political solutions to homelessness must take into account four categories of homeless people. A first category is persons who are out of work and seek new jobs. Persons in this category may have been recently laid off, unable to meet their rental payments, and forced temporarily to live out of a car or van. They might quickly leave the ranks of the homeless if they can find new jobs. A second category includes the physically disabled or mentally ill. Providing housing addresses only part of their problems since they also need medical care and medication. For many, finding or keeping a job might be impossible. A third category is the street alcoholic or drug addict. These persons need addiction treatment as well as clothing and shelter and will not become productive citizens until they become sober or drug free. The final category includes those who, like the old railroad "hobo," choose homelessness as a way of life.

Instead of transition words, writers can also use bullets followed by indented text:

USE OF BULLETS TO SIGNAL PARALLEL PARTS

The Wolf Recovery Program is rigidly opposed by a vociferous group of ranchers who pose three main objections to increasing wolf populations:

- They perceive wolves as a threat to livestock. [development]
- They fear the wolves will attack humans. [development]
- They believe ranchers will not be compensated by the government for their loss of profits. [development]

FOR WRITING AND DISCUSSION

Practicing the *Division-into-Parallel-Parts* Move

Working individually or in small groups, use the *division-into-parallel-parts* move to create, organize, and develop ideas to support one or more of the following point sentences.

1. To study for an exam effectively, a student should follow these [specify a number] steps.
2. Why do U.S. schoolchildren lag so far behind European and Asian children on standardized tests of mathematics and science? One possible cause is ... [continue].
3. Constant dieting is unhealthy for several reasons.

The *Comparison/Contrast* Move

A common variation on the *division-into-parallel-parts* move is the *comparison/contrast* move. To compare or contrast two items, you must first decide on the points of comparison (or contrast). If you are contrasting the political views of two presidential candidates, you might choose to focus on four points of comparison: differences in their foreign policy, differences in economic policy, differences in social policy, and differences in judicial philosophy. You then have two choices for organizing the parts: the *side-by-side pattern,* in which you discuss all of candidate A's views and then all of candidate B's views; or the *back-and-forth pattern,* in which you discuss foreign policy, contrasting A's views with B's views, then move on to economic policy, then social policy, and then judicial philosophy. Figure 17.5 shows how these two patterns would appear on a tree diagram.

There are no cut-and-dried rules that dictate when to use the *side-by-side pattern* or the *back-and-forth pattern.* However, for lengthy comparisons, the *back-and-forth pattern* is often more effective because the reader doesn't have to store great amounts of information in memory. The *side-by-side pattern* requires readers to remember all the material about A when they get to B, and it is sometimes difficult to keep all the points of comparison clearly in mind.

FIGURE 17.5 Two Ways to Structure a Comparison or Contrast

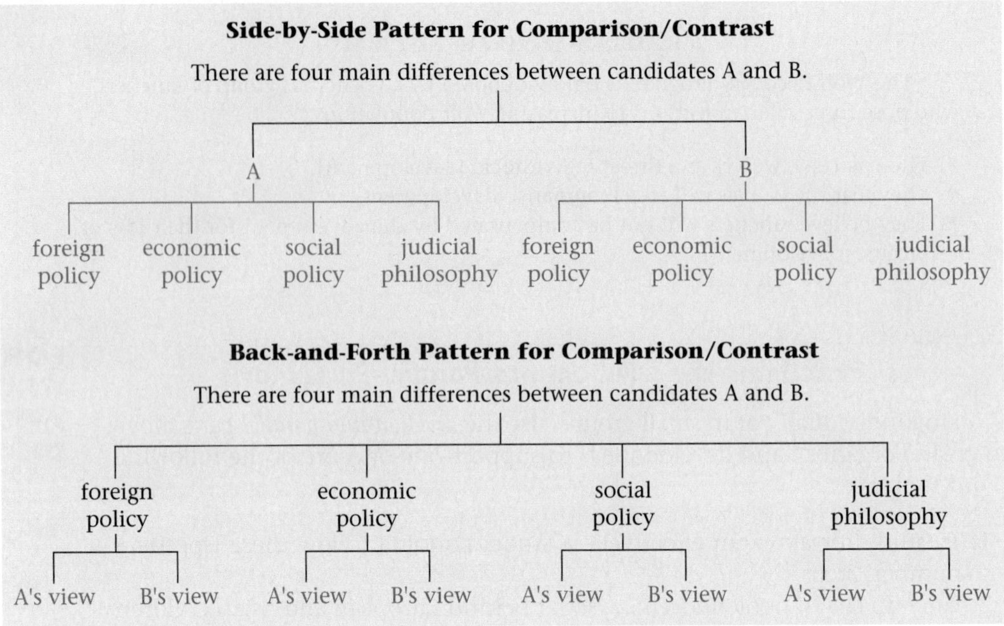

FOR WRITING AND DISCUSSION

Practicing the *Comparison/Contrast* Move

Working individually or in groups, create tree diagrams for stretches of text based on one or more of the following point sentences, all of which call for the *comparison/contrast* move. Make at least one diagram follow the *back-and-forth pattern* and at least one diagram follow the *side-by-side pattern.*

1. To understand U.S. politics, an outsider needs to appreciate some basic differences between Republicans and Democrats.
2. Although they are obviously different on the surface, there are many similarities between the Boy Scouts and a street gang.
3. There are several important differences between closed-form and open-form writing.

SKILL 17.9 Use effective tables, graphs, and charts to present numeric data.

In contemporary analyses and arguments, writers often draw on quantitative data to support their points. Writers can make numbers speak powerfully by means of reader-effective graphics including tables, graphs, and charts. Generally, quantitative data displayed in tables invite the reader to tease out many different stories that the numbers might tell. In contrast, line graphs, bar graphs, or pie charts focus vividly on one story.

How Tables Tell Many Stories

Data displayed in tables usually have their origins in raw numbers collected from surveys, questionnaires, observational studies, scientific experiments, and so forth. These numbers are then consolidated and arranged in tables where they can be analyzed for potentially meaningful patterns. Consider, for example, Table 17.1, produced by the National Center for Education Statistics. It shows the number of postsecondary degrees earned by men and women from 1960 to 2007.

This process is explained more fully in Chapter 9 on analyzing field research data.

Reading a Table Tables are read in two directions: from top to bottom and from left to right. To read a table efficiently, begin with the title, *which always includes elements from both the vertical and horizontal dimensions of the table.* Note how this rule applies to Table 17.1.

- The table's horizontal dimension is indicated in the first part of the title: "Earned Degrees Conferred by Level and Sex." Reading horizontally, we see the names of the degrees (associate's, bachelor's, and so forth) with subcategories indicating male and female.
- The table's vertical dimension is indicated in the second part of the title: "1960 to 2007." Reading vertically, we see selected years between 1960 and 2007.

Beneath the title are further instructions: Numbers represent thousands except for one column labeled "percent."

We are now prepared to read specific information from the table. In 1994, for example, colleges and universities in the United States conferred 2,206,000 degrees, of which 45.1 percent were earned by men. In that same year, 532,000 men and 637,000 women earned bachelors's degrees while 27,000 men and 17,000 women earned doctoral degrees.

Discovering Stories in the Data You need to peruse the table carefully before interesting patterns begin to emerge. Among the stories the table tells are these:

- The percent of women receiving postsecondary degrees rose substantially between 1960 and 2007 (with a corresponding fall for men).
- This increased percentage of degrees given to women is more dramatic for associate's and bachelor's degrees than it is for master's, first professional, or doctoral degrees.

As we show in the next section, these two stories, which must be teased out of this table, can be told more dramatically with graphs.

Using a Graphic to Tell a Story

Whereas tables can embed many stories and invite detailed examination of the numbers, a graph or chart makes one selected story immediately visible.

Line Graph A line graph converts numerical data to a series of points on a grid and connects them to create flat, rising, or falling lines. The result gives us a picture of the relationship between the variables represented on the horizontal and vertical axes.

TABLE 17.1 Earned Degrees Conferred by Level and Sex: 1960 to 2007

[In thousands (477 represents 477,000), except percent. Based on survey; see Appendix III]

Year ending	All degrees		Associate's		Bachelor's		Master's		First professional		Doctoral	
	Total	Percent male	Male	Female	Male	Female	Male	Female	Male	Female	Male	Female
1960[1]	477	65.8	(NA)	(NA)	254	138	51	24	(NA)	(NA)	9	1
1970	1,271	59.2	117	89	451	341	126	83	33	2	26	4
1975	1,666	56.0	191	169	505	418	162	131	49	7	27	7
1980	1,731	51.1	184	217	474	456	151	147	53	17	23	10
1985	1,828	49.3	203	252	483	497	143	143	50	25	22	11
1990	1,940	46.6	191	264	492	560	154	171	44	27	24	14
1991	2,025	45.8	199	283	504	590	156	181	44	28	25	15
1992	2,108	45.6	207	297	521	616	162	191	45	29	26	15
1993	2,167	45.5	212	303	533	632	169	200	45	30	26	16
1994	2,206	45.1	215	315	532	637	176	211	45	31	27	17
1995	2,218	44.9	218	321	526	634	179	219	45	31	27	18
1996[2]	2,248	44.2	220	336	522	642	179	227	45	32	27	18
1997[2]	2,288	43.6	224	347	521	652	181	238	46	33	27	19
1998[2]	2,298	43.2	218	341	520	664	184	246	45	34	27	19
1999[2]	2,323	42.7	218	342	519	682	186	254	44	34	25	19
2000[2]	2,385	42.6	225	340	530	708	192	265	44	36	25	20
2001[2]	2,416	42.4	232	347	532	712	194	274	43	37	25	20
2002[2]	2,494	42.2	238	357	550	742	199	283	43	38	24	20
2003[2]	2,621	42.1	253	380	573	775	211	301	42	39	24	22
2004[2]	2,755	41.8	260	405	595	804	230	329	42	41	25	23
2005[2]	2,850	41.6	268	429	613	826	234	341	44	43	27	26
2006[2]	2,936	41.3	270	443	631	855	238	356	44	44	29	27
2007[2]	3,007	41.2	275	453	650	875	238	366	45	45	30	30

NA Not available.

[1] First-professional degrees are included with bachelor's degrees.

[2] Beginning 1996, data reflect the new classification of institutions.

Source: U.S. National Center for Education Statistics, *Digest of Education Statistics*, annual.

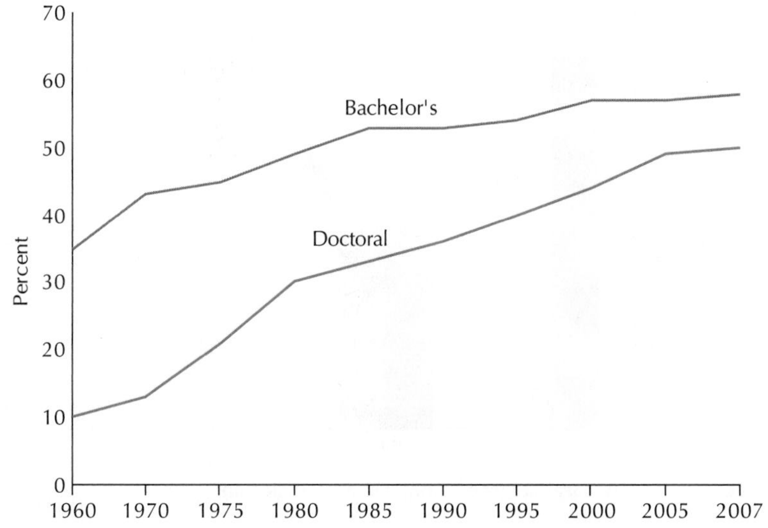

FIGURE 17.6 Percentage of Bachelor's and Doctoral Degrees Conferred on Females: 1960–2007

Suppose you wanted to tell the story of the increasing percentage of women receiving bachelor's and doctoral degrees from 1960 to 2007. Using Table 17.1 you can calculate these percentages yourself and display them in a line graph as shown in Figure 17.6. To determine what a graph tells you, you need to clarify what's represented on the two axes. By convention, the horizontal axis of a graph contains the predictable, known variable that has no surprises, such as time or some other sequence—in this case, the years 1960 to 2007 in predictable chronological order. The vertical axis contains the unpredictable variable that tells the graph's story—in this case, the percent of degrees conferred on women in each year on the graph. The ascending lines tell the stories at a glance.

Bar Graph Bar graphs use bars of varying lengths, extending either horizontally or vertically, to contrast two or more quantities. To make the story of women's progress in earning doctoral degrees particularly vivid (the same story told in the "doctoral" line in Figure 17.6), you could use a bar graph as shown in Figure 17.7. To read a bar graph, note carefully the title and the axes to see what is compared to what. Bars are typically distinguished from each other by use of different colors, shades, or patterns of cross-hatching. The special power of bar graphs is that they can help you make quick comparisons. Figure 17.7 tells you at a glance that in 1960, women received far fewer doctoral degrees than men but that in 2007 they received an equal percentage.

Pie Chart A pie chart, also called a circle graph, depicts the different percentages of a total (the pie) represented by variously sized slices. Suppose you wanted to know the most popular undergraduate majors in American colleges and universities. These statistics, which are available in table format from the National Center for Education Statistics, can be quickly converted into a pie chart as

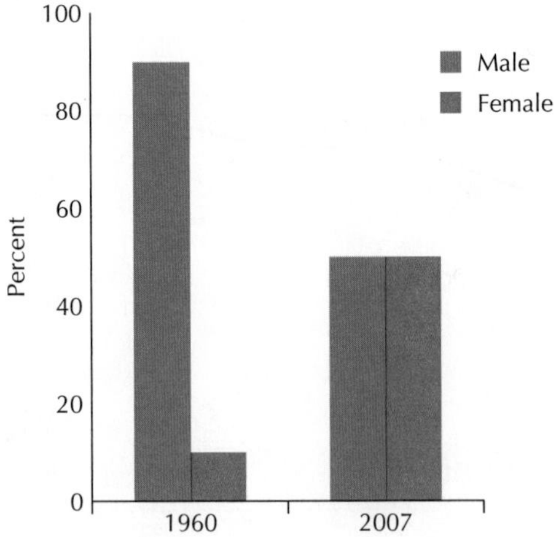

FIGURE 17.7 Percentage of Doctoral Degrees Conferred on Males and Females: 1960 and 2007

shown in Figure 17.8. As you can see, a pie chart shows at a glance how the whole of something is divided into segments. In 2007, for example, 7 percent of graduating seniors majored in education while 22 percent majored in business. The effectiveness of pie charts diminishes as you add more slices. In most cases, you begin to confuse readers if you include more than five or six slices.

Incorporating a Graphic into Your Essay

Today, most word processing programs, often integrated with a spreadsheet, easily allow you to create a graphic and insert it into your document. In some cases,

FIGURE 17.8 Distribution of Bachelor's Degrees by Majors, 2007

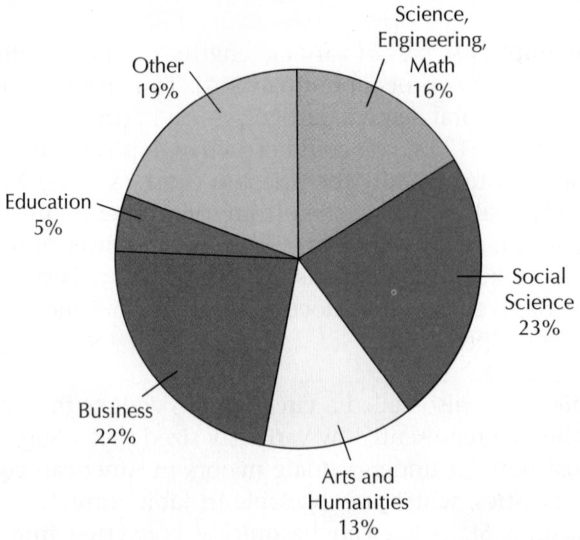

your instructor may give you permission to make a graphic with pen or pencil and paste it into your document.

Designing Your Graphic In academic manuscripts, graphics are designed conservatively without bells and whistles such as three-dimensional effects or special fonts and patterns. Keep the graphic as simple and uncluttered as possible. Also in academic manuscripts, do not wrap text around the graphic. In contrast, in popular published work, writers often use flashy fonts, three dimensions, text wrapping, and other effects that would undermine your *ethos* in an academic setting.

Numbering, Labeling, and Titling the Graphic In newspapers and popular magazines, writers often include graphics in boxes or sidebars without specifically referring to them in the text. However, in academic manuscripts or scholarly works, graphics are always labeled, numbered, titled, and referred to in the text. Tables are listed as "Tables," while line graphs, bar graphs, pie charts, or any other kinds of drawings or photographs are labeled as "Figures." By convention, the title for tables goes above the table, while the title for figures goes below.

Referencing the Graphic in Your Text Academic and professional writers follow a referencing convention called independent redundancy. The graphic should be understandable without the text; the text should be understandable without the graphic. In other words, the text should tell in words the same story that the graphic displays visually. An example is shown in Figure 17.9.

FIGURE 17.9 Example of a Student Text with a Referenced Graph

In the decades following the 1960s feminist movement, women have made remarkable progress in higher education. As shown in Figure 1, in 1960 women received 35 percent of bachelor's degrees awarded in the United States and only 10 percent of doctoral degrees. However, in 2007 women received 59 percent of bachelor's degrees and 50 percent of doctorates. These numbers suggest the substantial impact of the women's movement.

Writer's point
References figure
Tells same story as graph

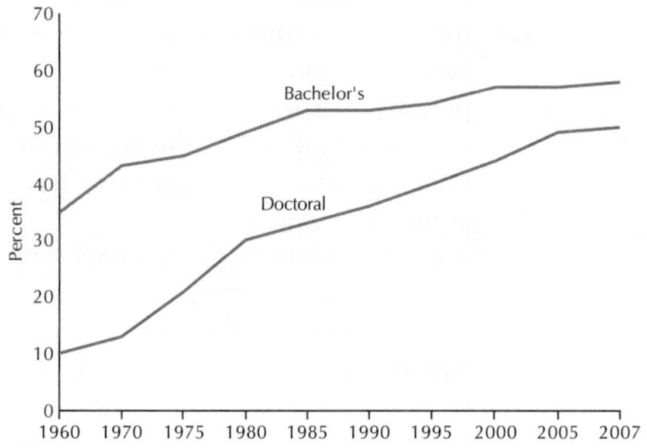

Fig. 1. Percentage of Bachelor's and Doctoral Degrees Conferred on Females: 1960–2007

Figure number
Figure title

SKILL 17.10 Write effective conclusions.

Conclusions can best be understood as complements to introductions. In both the introduction and the conclusion, writers are concerned with the essay as a whole more than with any given part. In a conclusion, the writer attempts to bring a sense of completeness and closure to the profusion of points and particulars laid out in the body of the essay. The writer is particularly concerned with helping the reader move from the parts back to the big picture and to understand the importance or significance of the essay.

Because many writers find conclusions challenging to write, we offer six possible strategies for ending an essay.

Strategies for Concluding an Essay

Strategies	What to Do	Comments
***Simple summary* conclusion**	Recap what you have said.	This approach is useful in a long or complex essay or in an instructional text that focuses on concepts. However, in a short, easy-to-follow essay, a summary conclusion can be dull and even annoying to readers. A brief summary followed by a more artful concluding strategy can sometimes be effective.
***Larger significance* conclusion**	Draw the reader's attention to the importance or the applications of your argument.	The conclusion is a good place to elaborate on the significance of your problem by showing how your proposed solution to a question leads to understanding a larger, more significant question or brings practical benefits to individuals or society. If you posed a question about values or about the interpretation of a confusing text or phenomenon, you might show how your argument could be applied to related questions, texts, or phenomena.
***Proposal* conclusion**	Call for action.	Often used in analyses and arguments, a *proposal* conclusion states the action that needs to be taken and briefly

Strategies	What to Do	Comments
		explains its advantages over alternative actions or describes its beneficial consequences. If your paper analyzes the negative consequences of shifting from a graduated to a flat-rate income tax, your conclusion may recommend an action such as modifying or opposing the flat tax.
	Call for future study.	A *call-for-future-study* conclusion indicates what else needs to be known or resolved before a proposal can be offered. Such conclusions are especially common in scientific writing.
***Scenic* or *anecdotal* conclusion**	Use a scene or brief story to illustrate the theme without stating it explicitly.	Often used in popular writing, a scene or anecdote can help the reader experience the emotional significance of the topic. For example, a paper favoring public housing for the homeless may end by describing an itinerant homeless person collecting bottles in a park.
***Hook and return* conclusion**	Return to something mentioned at the beginning of the essay.	If the essay begins with a vivid illustration of a problem, the conclusion can return to the same scene or story but with some variation to indicate the significance of the essay.
***Delayed-thesis* conclusion**	State the thesis for the first time at the end of the essay.	This strategy is effective when you are writing about complex or divisive issues and you don't want to take a stand until you have presented all sides. The introduction of the essay merely states the problem, giving the essay an exploratory feel.

FOR WRITING AND DISCUSSION

Writing Conclusions

Choose a paper you have just written and write an alternative conclusion using one of the strategies discussed in this lesson. Then share your original and revised conclusions in groups. Have group members discuss which one they consider most effective and why.

PEARSON mycomplab

For support in learning this chapter's content, follow this path in MyCompLab: Resources ⇒ Writing ⇒ Writing Process ⇒ Planning and Drafting. Review the Instruction and Multimedia resources about planning and drafting, and then complete the Exercises and click on Gradebook to measure your progress.

COMPOSING AND REVISING OPEN-FORM PROSE

18

Good writing is supposed to evoke sensation in the reader—not the fact that it's raining, but the feel of being rained upon.

—E. L. Doctorow, Novelist

Although much of this book focuses on closed-form prose, there are many kinds of good writing, and we probably all share the desire at times to write in ways other than points-first, thesis-governed prose. In our epigraph, novelist E. L. Doctorow suggests another way to think of "good writing": Writing that evokes sensations, that triggers in the reader's imagination the very feel of the rain.

In this chapter, we shift our attention to open-form writing, which, because it uses literary strategies such as story, plot, characterization, setting, and theme, is often called *literary nonfiction*. Of course, it should be remembered that writing exists on a continuum from closed to open forms and that many features of open-form prose can appear in primarily closed-form texts. In fact, many of the example essays in this book combine elements of both open and closed styles. At the extremes of the continuum, closed- and open-form writing are markedly different, but the styles can be blended in pleasing combinations.

For more on plot, characterization, setting, and theme, see Chapter 6.

Our goal in this chapter is to give you some practical lessons on how to write effective open-form prose. But we need to acknowledge at the outset that, whereas closed-form prose is governed by a few widely accepted conventions, one of the main features of open-form prose is its freedom to play with conventions in a bewildering variety of ways. Consequently, our discussion of open-form writing seeks more to introduce you to guiding principles rather than to treat open-form writing exhaustively.

In this chapter, you will learn these skills for open-form writing:

- SKILL 18.1 Make your narrative a story, not an *and then* chronology.
- SKILL 18.2 Write low on the ladder of abstraction.
- SKILL 18.3 Disrupt your reader's desire for direction and clarity.
- SKILL 18.4 Tap the power of figurative language.
- SKILL 18.5 Expand your repertoire of styles.
- SKILL 18.6 Use open-form elements to create "voice" in closed-form prose.

Key Features of Open-Form Prose

As we have discussed throughout this text, writing at the closed end of the spectrum seeks to be efficient and reader-friendly. By forecasting what's coming, placing points first, and putting old information before new, closed-form writers try to convey complex ideas in as clear a way as possible, enabling readers to grasp ideas quickly. In contrast, open-form writers, by violating or simply stretching those same conventions, set up a different kind of relationship with readers. They often provide more pleasure in reading, but just as often demand more patience, more tolerance of ambiguity, and more openness to a range of meanings and nuance. They are likely to take readers backstage to share the process of their thinking. They often cast themselves in the role of narrators or characters reporting all the coincidences, disappointments, and confusion they experienced during their quest for understanding. In this process of sharing, they make readers codiscoverers of ideas and insights.

Open-form prose is also characterized by its emphasis on an aesthetic use of language—that is, language used to please and entertain. Without the benefit of a thesis or points appearing first to convey meaning, open-form prose depends on the very specificity of words—the ability of words to create mental pictures, to appeal to readers' senses and emotions, and to conjure up memories.

SKILL 18.1 Make your narrative a story, not an *and then* chronology.

We have said that open-form prose is narrative based and uses the strategies of a story. In this first section we want you to think more deeply about the concept of a story—particularly how a story differs from an *and then* chronology. Both a story and an *and then* chronology depict events happening in time. But there are important differences between them. In the following exercise, we'd like you to try your own hand at articulating the differences between a story and an *and then* chronology.

FOR WRITING AND DISCUSSION

And Then Chronology Versus Story

Individual task:

1. Read the student autobiographical narrative "No Cats in America?" by Patrick José in Chapter 6, pages 148–149.
2. Then read the following autobiographical narrative entitled "The Stolen Watch," which was submitted by a student as a draft for an assignment on narrative writing.

THE STOLEN WATCH

Last fall and winter I was living in Spokane with my brother, who during this time had a platonic girlfriend come over from Seattle and stay for a weekend. Her name was Karen, and we became interested in each other and I went over to see her at the first of the year. She then invited me to, supposedly, the biggest party of the year, called the Aristocrats' Ball. I said sure and made my way back to Seattle in February. It started out bad on Friday, the day my brother and I left Spokane. We left town an hour late, but what's new. Then my brother had to stop along the way and pick up some parts; we stayed there for an hour trying to find this guy. It all started out bad because we arrived in Seattle and I forgot to call Karen. We were staying at her brother's house and after we brought all our things in, we decided to go to a few bars. Later that night we ran into Karen in one of the bars, and needless to say she was not happy with me. When I got up the next morning I knew I should have stayed in Spokane, because I felt bad vibes. Karen made it over about an hour before the party. By the time we reached the party, which drove me crazy, she wound up with another guy, so her friends and I decided to go to a few bars. The next morning when I was packing, I could not find my watch and decided that someone had to have taken it. We decided that it had to have been the goon that Karen had wound up with the night before, because she was at her brother's house with him before she went home. So how was I going to get my watch back?

We decided the direct and honest approach to the problem would work out the best. We got in contact and confronted him. This turned out to be quite a chore. It turned out that he was visiting some of his family during that weekend and lived in Little Harbor, California. It turned out that Karen knew his half brother and got some information on him, which was not pretty. He had just been released by the army and was trained in a special forces unit, in the field of Martial Arts. He was a trained killer! This information did not help matters at all, but the next bit of information was just as bad if not worse. Believe it or not, he was up on charges of attempted murder and breaking and entering. In a way, it turned out lucky for me, because he was in enough trouble with the police and did not need any more. Karen got in contact with him and threatened him that I would bring him up on charges if he did not return the watch. His mother decided that he was in enough trouble and sent me the watch. I was astounded, it was still working and looked fine. The moral of the story is don't drive 400 miles to see a girl you hardly know, and whatever you do, don't leave your valuables out in the open.

Group task: Share your responses to the following questions:

1. How does your experience of reading "No Cats in America?" differ from your experience of reading "The Stolen Watch"? Try to articulate the different ways you reacted to the two pieces while in the process of reading them.
2. Based on the differences between these two pieces, how would you define a "story"? Begin by brainstorming all the ways that the two pieces differ. Then try to identify the essential differences that make one a "story" and the other an *and then* chronology.

Now that you have tried to define a story for yourselves, we would like to explain our own four criteria for a story: (1) depiction of events through time, (2) connectedness, (3) tension, and (4) resolution. If we combine these criteria into a sentence, it would read like this: A story depicts events that are connected causally or thematically to create a sense of tension that is resolved through action, insight, or understanding. These four criteria occurring together turn a chronology into a story.

Depiction of Events through Time

The essence of storytelling is the depiction of events through time. Whereas thesis-based writing descends from problem to thesis to supporting reasons and evidence, stories unfold linearly, temporally, from event to event. You may start in the middle of the action and then jump backward and forward, but you always encounter some sequence of events happening in time. This temporal focus creates a sense of "onceness." Things that happen at a point in time happen only once, as the classic fairy-tale opening "Once upon a time" suggests. When you compose and revise a narrative, you want to try to capture the "onceness" of that experience. As the essayist E. B. White once advised a young writer, "Don't write about Man but about a man."

Consider how Val Plumwood, a professor of women's studies and author of the book *Feminism and the Mastery of Nature*, depicts the events leading up to a disturbing encounter with a crocodile. (Later in the story, the reader sees how this encounter shapes her understanding of humans' place in the food chain and the need for a respectful, rather than a dominating, attitude toward other animals.)

> In the early wet season, Kakadu's paper-bark wetlands are especially stunning, as the water lilies weave white, pink, and blue patterns of dreamlike beauty over the shining thunderclouds reflected in their still waters. Yesterday, the water lilies and the wonderful bird life had enticed me into a joyous afternoon's idyll as I ventured onto the East Alligator Lagoon for the first time in a canoe lent by the park service. "You can play about on the backwaters," the ranger had said, "but don't go onto the main river channel. The current's too swift, and if you get into trouble, there are the crocodiles. Lots of them along the river!" I followed his advice and glutted myself on the magical beauty and bird life of the lily lagoons, untroubled by crocodiles.
>
> Today, I wanted to repeat the experience despite the drizzle beginning to fall as I neared the canoe launch site. I set off on a day trip in search of an Aboriginal rock art site across the lagoon and up a side channel. The drizzle turned to a warm rain within a few hours, and the magic was lost. The birds were invisible, the water lilies were sparser, and the lagoon seemed even a little menacing. I noticed now how low the 14-foot canoe sat in the water, just a few inches of fiberglass between me and the great saurian, close relatives of the ancient dinosaurs. . . .
>
> After hours of searching the maze of shallow channels in the swamp, I had not found the clear channel leading to the rock art site, as shown on the ranger's sketch map. When I pulled my canoe over in driving rain to a rock outcrop for a hasty, sodden lunch, I experienced the unfamiliar sensation of being watched. Having never been one for timidity, in philosophy or in life, I decided, rather than return defeated to my sticky trailer, to explore a clear, deep channel closer to the river I had traveled the previous day.
>
> The rain and wind grew more severe, and several times I pulled over to tip water from the canoe. The channel soon developed steep mud banks and snags. Farther on, the channel opened up and was eventually blocked by a large sandy

bar. I pushed the canoe toward the bank, looking around carefully before getting out of the shallow and pulling the canoe up. I would be safe from crocodiles in the canoe—I had been told—but swimming and standing or wading at the water's edge were dangerous. Edges are one of the crocodile's favorite food-capturing places. I saw nothing, but the feeling of unease that had been with me all day intensified.

In this example of literary nonfiction, Plumwood persuades readers to appreciate the beauties of the exotic Australian rain forest as well as its dangers. Note how her method includes the depicting of events that happen once in time—her wondrous first day of exploration, the ranger's warning to stay away from the main river, her second day's unsuccessful search by canoe for a site of Aboriginal rock art, and then her emerging discovery that in the increasing intensity of the rainstorm, she had reached the junction with the main river. Plumwood's powerful narrative becomes the basis for a profound concluding reflection on what she calls humans' "ecological identity."

Connectedness

The events of a story must also be connected, not merely spatially or sequentially, but causally or thematically. When discussing "The Stolen Watch" in the previous exercise, you might have asked yourselves, "What does all that stuff about forgetting to call Karen and stopping for parts, etc., have to do with the stolen watch? Is this story about the watch or about confronting a potential killer?" If so, you instinctively understood the concept of connectedness. Stories are more than just chronicles of events. Novelist E. M. Forster offered the simplest definition of a story when he rejected "The king dies and then the queen died," but accepted "The king died and then the queen died ... of grief." The words "of grief" connect the two events to each other in a causal relationship, converting a series of events into a patterned, meaningfully related sequence of events. Now examine this passage to see the connections the writer establishes between the scenes.

THEMATIC AND CAUSAL CONNECTEDNESS

I have been so totally erased from nature lately, like a blackboard before school starts, that yesterday when I was in the Japanese section of San Francisco, Japantown, I saw the sidewalk littered with chocolate wrappers.

There were hundreds of them. Who in the hell has been eating all these chocolates? I thought. A convention of Japanese chocolate eaters must have passed this way.

Then I noticed some plum trees on the street. Then I noticed that it was autumn. Then I noticed that the leaves were falling as they will and as they must every year. Where had I gone wrong?

—Richard Brautigan, "Leaves"

Brautigan's narrative becomes a story only when you realize that the "chocolate wrappers" are really plum leaves; the two images are connected by the writer's changed perception, which illuminates the thematic question raised at the beginning and end: Why has he become "so totally erased from nature"? As you write, connect the elements of your narrative causally and thematically.

Tension or Conflict

The third criterion for a story—tension or conflict—creates the anticipation and potential significance that keep the reader reading. In whodunit stories, the tension follows from attempts to identify the murderer or to prevent the murderer from doing in yet another victim. In many comic works, the tension is generated by confusion or misunderstanding that drives a wedge between people who would normally be close. Tension always involves contraries, such as those between one belief and another, between opposing values, between the individual and the environment or the social order, between where I am now and where I want to be or used to be. In the following passage, notice how the contraries create dramatic tension that engages readers.

DRAMATIC TENSIONS

> Straddling the top of the world, one foot in China and the other in Nepal, I cleared the ice from my oxygen mask, hunched a shoulder against the wind, and stared absently down at the vastness of Tibet. I understood on some dim, detached level that the sweep of earth beneath my feet was a spectacular sight. I'd been fantasizing about this moment, and the release of emotion that would accompany it, for many months. But now that I was finally here, actually standing on the summit of Mount Everest, I just couldn't summon the energy to care.
>
> It was early in the afternoon of May 10, 1996. I hadn't slept in fifty-seven hours. The only food I'd been able to force down over the preceding three days was a bowl of ramen soup and a handful of peanut M&M's. Weeks of violent coughing had left me with two separated ribs that made ordinary breathing an excruciating trial. At 29,028 feet up in the troposphere, so little oxygen was reaching my brain that my mental capacity was that of a slow child. Under the circumstances, I was incapable of feeling much of anything except cold and tired.
>
> —Jon Krakauer, *Into Thin Air*

Notice how this passage presents several contraries or conflicts: the opposition between the narrator's expectation of what it would be like to stand on the top of Mount Everest and the actuality once he's there; and the opposition between the physical strength and stamina of the climber and the extreme danger of climbing this mountain. The reader wonders how Krakauer reached the summit with no sleep, almost no food, and a violent and agonizing cough; more important, the reader wonders why he kept on climbing. We can ask this important query of any narrative: What conflicts and tensions are prompting readers' ongoing questions and holding their interest?

Resolution, Recognition, or Retrospective Interpretation

The final criterion for a story is the resolution or retrospective interpretation of events. The resolution may be stated explicitly or implied. Fables typically sum up the story's significance with an explicit moral at the end. In contrast, the interpretation of events in poetry is almost always implicit. Note how the following haiku collapses events and resolution.

RESOLUTION

A strange old man
stops me,
Looking out of my deep mirror.

—Hitomaro, *One Hundred Poems from the Japanese*

In this tiny story, two things happen simultaneously. The narrator is stopped by a "strange old man" and the narrator looks into a mirror. The narrator's *recognition* is that he is that same old man. This recognition—"That's me in the mirror; when I wasn't looking, I grew old!"—in turn ties the singular event of the story back to more universal concerns and the reader's world.

The typical direction of a story, from singular event(s) to general conclusion, reverses the usual points-first direction of closed-form essays. Stories force readers to read inductively, gathering information and looking for a pattern that's confirmed or unconfirmed by the story's resolution. This resolution is the point *toward* which readers read. It often drives home the significance of the narrative. Typically, a reader's satisfaction or dissatisfaction with a story hinges on how well the resolution manages to explain or justify the events that precede it. Writers need to ask: How does my resolution grow out of my narrative and fit with the resolution the reader has been forming?

FOR WRITING AND DISCUSSION

Identifying Criteria for "Story"

1. Working as a whole class or in small groups, return to Patrick José's essay "No Cats in America?" and explain how it qualifies as a story rather than an *and then* chronology. How does it meet all four of the criteria: depiction of events through time, connectedness, tension, and resolution?
2. Consider again "The Stolen Watch." It seems to meet the criterion of "depiction of events through time," but it is weak in connectedness, tension, and resolution. How could the writer revise the chronology to make it a story? Brainstorm several different ways that this potentially exciting early draft could be rewritten.
3. If you are working on your own open-form narrative, exchange drafts with a classmate. Discuss each other's draft in light of this lesson's focus on story. To what extent do your drafts exhibit the features of a story rather than those of an *and then* chronology? Working together, develop revision plans that might increase the story elements in your narratives.

SKILL 18.2 **Write low on the ladder of abstraction.**

In Chapter 4 we introduced the concept of "ladder of abstraction," in which words can be arranged from the very abstract (living creatures, clothing) down to the very specific (our dog Charley with the floppy ears; my hippie Birkenstocks with the saltwater stains; see Chapter 4, Concept 11). In this lesson we show why and how open-form writers stay low on the ladder of abstraction through their use of concrete words, revelatory words, and memory-soaked words.

Concrete Words Evoke Images and Sensations

To appreciate the impact of specific, concrete language, look again at the opening sentence of Val Plumwood's narrative about her encounter with crocodiles (p. 498):

> In the early wet season, Kakadu's paper-bark wetlands are especially stunning, as the water lilies weave white, pink, and blue patterns of dreamlike beauty over the shining thunderclouds reflected in their still waters.

Here is how that same passage might sound if rewritten a level higher on the ladder of abstraction:

> In the early wet season the Kakadu landscape is especially stunning, as the water plants weave their colorful patterns of dreamlike beauty over the clouds reflected in the water's surface.

This is still quite a nice sentence. But something is lost when you say "landscape" rather than "paper-bark wetlands," "clouds" rather than "thunderclouds," or "colorful" rather than "white, pink, and blue." The lower you write on the ladder of abstraction, the more you tap into your readers' storehouse of particular memories and images.

The power of concrete words has been analyzed by writer John McPhee in a widely quoted and cited interview. When asked why he wrote the sentence "Old white oaks are rare because they had a tendency to become bowsprits, barrel staves, and queen-post trusses" instead of a more generic sentence such as, "Old white oaks are rare because they were used as lumber," he responded in a way that reveals his love of the particular:

> There isn't much life in [the alternative version of the sentence]. If you can find a specific, firm, and correct image, it's always going to be better than a generality, and hence I tend, for example, to put in trade names and company names and, in an instance like this, the names of wood products instead of a general term like "lumber." You'd say "Sony" instead of "tape recorder" if the context made it clear you meant to say tape recorder. It's not because you're on the take from Sony, it's because the image, at least to this writer or reader, strikes a clearer note.

Some readers might complain that the particulars "bowsprits, barrel staves, and queen-post trusses" don't help readers' understanding, as do particulars in closed-form prose, but instead give most readers a moment's pause. Today most barrel staves and bowsprits are made of metal, not oak, and few contemporary readers encounter them on a regular basis no matter what they're made of. Furthermore, few readers at any time could readily identify "queen-post trusses," a technical term from the building trade. Instead of smoothly completing the reader's understanding of a point, McPhee's particulars tend to arrest and even sidetrack, sending the reader in pursuit of a dictionary.

But if McPhee's examples momentarily puzzle, it's the sort of puzzlement that can lead to greater understanding. Precisely because they are exotic terms, these words arouse the reader's curiosity and imagination. "Exotic language is of value," says McPhee. "A queen-post truss is great just because of the sound of the words and what they call to mind. The 'queen,' the 'truss'—the ramifications in everything."

For McPhee, the fact that these words trip up the reader is a point in their favor. If McPhee had said that old white oaks are rare these days because they became parts of "ships, barrels, and roofs," no one would blink or notice. If you were to visualize the items, you'd probably call up some ready-made pictures that leave little trace in your mind. You also wouldn't hear the sounds of the words. (In this regard, notice McPhee's emphasis on images sounding "a clearer note.") Your forward progress toward the point would be unimpeded, but what would be lost? A new glimpse into a lost time when oak trees were used to make exotic items that today exist mostly in old books and memories.

Another quality also recommends words that readers trip over, words such as *bowsprit, barrel stave,* and *queen-post truss:* their power to persuade the reader to believe in the world being described. Tripping over things, whether they're made of steel or words, forces the reader to acknowledge their independence, the reality of a world outside the reader's own head. For this reason, writers of formula fiction—thrillers, westerns, romances, and the like—will load their texts with lots of little details and bits of technical information from the time and place they describe. Because their stories are otherwise implausible (e.g., the description of the Evil Empire's doomsday machine), they need all the help they can get from their details (the size of the toggle bolts used to keep the machine in place while it's blasting out intergalactic death rays) to convince readers that the story is real.

Using Revelatory Words and Memory-Soaked Words

As we have seen, concrete language, low on the ladder of abstraction, can evoke imaginative experiences for readers. Two particularly powerful kinds of concrete language are revelatory words and memory-soaked words. By *revelatory* words we mean specific details that reveal the social status, lifestyle, beliefs, and values of people. According to writer Tom Wolfe, carefully chosen details can reveal a person's *status life*—"the entire pattern of behavior and possessions through which people express their position in the world or what they think it is or hope it to be." Wolfe favors writing that records "everyday gestures, habits, manners, customs, styles of furniture, clothing, decoration, styles of traveling, eating, keeping house, modes of behaving toward children, servants, superiors, inferiors, peers, plus the various looks, glances, poses, styles of walking and other symbolic details that might exist within a scene." Thus subtle differences in a person's status life might be revealed in details about fast food (a Big Mac versus a Subway turkey wrap), body piercing (pierced ears versus pierced tongue), a watch (a Timex versus a Rolex), or music (Kenny Chesney versus Busta Rhymes).

Another way to create powerful concrete language is through *memory-soaked* words. Such words trigger a whole complex of ideas, emotions, and sensations in readers who share memories from a particular era. People who grew up in the 1950s, for example, might have deep associations with 45-rpm records, the *Ed Sullivan Show,* or the words "duck tail" or "tail fins." For Vietnam veterans, Nancy

Sinatra's "These Boots Were Made for Walking" or the whirr of helicopter blades might evoke strong memories. Persons growing up in the 1970s or 1980s might remember "Cookie Monster," "Pez guns," or 8-track tapes. In recent years, our students have come up with these memory-soaked words from their own childhoods: American Girl dolls, Power Rangers, Ghostbuster action figures, Super Nintendo, Pokeman, *American Idol,* and The Sims.

FOR WRITING AND DISCUSSION

Working Low on the Ladder of Abstraction

1. Working in small groups or as a whole class, try your own hand at using revelatory words to reveal status life. Create a list of specific details that you might associate with each of the following: middle school girls at a slumber party; friends at a tailgate party before a football game; the kitchen of an upscale urban apartment of a two-profession couple who subscribe to *Gourmet* magazine; the kitchen of a middle-class, middle America family with three kids and a collection of *Good Housekeeping* magazines; the kitchen of an apartment shared by college students. (If you are describing kitchens, for example, consider the different *status life* signaled by ketchup versus stone-ground mustard or by an iceberg lettuce salad with ranch dressing versus an almond mandarin salad.)
2. Also try your hand at finding memory-soaked words. Make a list of specific words and names associated with your childhood that you now rarely hear or see. Share your list with others in your group and identify the items that have the strongest associations.
3. If you are working on your own open-form narrative, exchange drafts with a classmate and, working together, find specific examples where each of you has successfully used concrete, revelatory, or memory-soaked words. Then find passages that could be profitably revised by moving down a rung on the ladder of abstraction or by adding concrete details that follow the advice in this lesson.

SKILL 18.3 Disrupt your reader's desire for direction and clarity.

The epigraph to Chapter 17 by the philosopher Kenneth Burke speaks about form as "an arousing and fulfillment of desires." In closed-form prose, we can easily see this process at work: The writer previews what he or she is going to say, arousing the reader's desire to see the general outline fleshed out with specifics, and then fulfills that desire speedily through a presentation of pertinent points and particulars.

In more open-form prose, the fulfillment of desire follows a less straightforward path. Writers offer fewer overviews and clues, leaving readers less sure of where they're headed; or writers mention an idea and then put it aside for a while as they pursue some other point whose relevance may seem tenuous to the reader. Rather than establish the direction or point of their prose, writers suspend that direction, waiting until later in the prose to show how the ideas are meaningfully related. In other words, the period of arousal is longer and more drawn out; the fulfillment of desire is delayed until the end, when the reader finally sees how the pieces fit together.

Open-form prose gives you the opportunity to overlay your narrative core with other patterns of ideas—to move associatively from idea to idea, to weave a complex pattern of meaning in which the complete picture emerges later. Often the way you achieve these surprising twists and turns of structure and meaning is by playing with the conventions of closed-form prose. For example, in the autobiographical narrative "No Cats in America?", Patrick José breaks the cardinal closed-form rule that titles should forecast the essay's thesis: If José's essay were closed form, it should be about some kind of surprising decline of cats in America. However, José's title is metaphoric, and the reader doesn't completely comprehend its significance until the last lines of the essay. This delaying of meaning—requiring the reader to help cocreate the meaning—is typical of open-form prose. Here in this section we describe some of your open-form options for surprising your readers and delaying their fulfillment of desires.

Disrupting Predictions and Making Odd Juxtapositions

Open-form writers frequently violate the principle of forecasting and mapping that we stressed in Chapter 17. Consider the following introduction to an essay:

PASSAGE WITH DISRUPTED PREDICTIONS AND ODD JUXTAPOSITIONS

> I suppose their little bones have years ago been lost among the stones and winds of those high glacial pastures. I suppose their feathers blew eventually into the piles of tumbleweed beneath the straggling cattle fences and rotted there in the mountain snows, along with dead steers and all the other things that drift to an end in the corners of the wire. I do not quite know why I should be thinking of birds over the *New York Times* at breakfast, particularly the birds of my youth half a continent away. It is a funny thing what the brain will do with memories and how it will treasure them and finally bring them into odd juxtapositions with other things, as though it wanted to make a design, or get some meaning out of them, whether you want it or not, or even see it.
>
> —Loren Eisley, "The Bird and the Machine"

Whose bones? What feathers?

Birds? What birds?

What do birds have to do with how the brain works? Where is this writer going?

Note the sequence of ideas from bones to birds to breakfast over the *New York Times* to comments about the workings of the brain. In fact, in this essay it takes Eisley six full paragraphs in which he discusses mechanical inventions to return to the birds with the line: "... or those birds, I'll never forget those birds. ... "

Throughout these paragraphs, what drives the reader forward is curiosity to discover the connections between the parts and to understand the meaning of the essay's title, "The Bird and the Machine." Actually, Eisley's comment about the brain's "odd juxtapositions" of memories with "other things, as though it wanted to make a design, or get some meaning out of them" could be a description of this open-form technique we've called "disrupting predictions and making odd juxtapositions." Open-form writers can choose when "odd juxtapositions" are an appropriate strategy for inviting the reader to accompany the discovering, reflecting writer on a journey toward meaning.

Leaving Gaps

An important convention of closed-form prose is the old/new contract, which specifies that the opening of every sentence should link in some way to what has gone before. Open-form prose often violates this convention, leaving *gaps* in the text, forcing the reader to puzzle over the connection between one part and the next.

The following passage clearly violates the old/new contract. This example recounts the writer's thoughts after startling a weasel in the woods and exchanging glances with it.

Gap caused by unexplained or unpredicted shift from weasel to philosophic musing

PASSAGE WITH INTENTIONAL GAPS

What goes on in [a weasel's brain] the rest of the time? What does a weasel think about? He won't say. His journal is tracks in clay, a spray of feathers, mouse blood and bone: uncollected, unconnected, loose-leaf, and blown.

I would like to learn, or remember, how to live. I come to Hollins Pond not so much to learn how to live as, frankly, to forget about it.

—Annie Dillard, "Living Like Weasels"

Dillard suddenly switches, without transition, from musing about the mental life of a weasel to asserting that she would like to learn how to live. What is the connection between her encounter with the weasel and her own search for how to live? Dillard's open-form techniques leave these gaps for readers to ponder and fill in, inviting us to participate in the process of arriving at meaning. Just as open-form writers can deliberately avoid predicting or mapping statements, they also have the liberty to leave gaps in a text when it suits their purpose.

FOR WRITING AND DISCUSSION

Disrupting Reader Expectations

If you are currently working on an open-form narrative, exchange drafts with a classmate. Discuss in what way the strategies explained in this lesson might be appropriate for your purposes. Where might you currently "explain too much" and benefit by juxtaposing scenes without explanatory filler? Where might you use other strategies from this lesson?

SKILL 18.4 Tap the power of figurative language.

Open-form writers often use figurative language in situations in which closed-form writers would use literal language. In this brief section, we show you some of the power of figurative language.

When journalist Nicholas Tomalin describes a captured Vietnamese prisoner as young and slight, the reader understands him in a literal way, but when, a moment later, he compares the prisoner to "a tiny, fine-boned wild animal," the reader understands him in a different way; the reader understands not only what the subject looks like—his general physical attributes—but how that particular boy appears in that moment to those around him—fierce, frightened, trapped.

Metaphors abound when literal words fail. When writers encounter eccentric people or are overwhelmed by the strangeness of their experiences, they use *figurative language*—imaginative comparisons—to explain their situation and their reactions to it. Figurative language—similes, metaphors, and personifications—enables the writer to describe an unfamiliar thing in terms of different, more familiar things. The surprise of yoking two very unlike things evokes from the reader a perception, insight, or emotional experience that could not otherwise be communicated. The originality and vividness of the imaginative comparison frequently resonates with meaning for readers and sticks in their minds long afterward.

In the following passage, Isak Dinesen describes an experience that most of us have not had—seeing iguanas in the jungle and shooting one. After reading this passage, however, we have a striking picture in our minds of what she saw and a strong understanding of what she felt and realized.

PASSAGE USING FIGURATIVE LANGUAGE

In the Reserve I have sometimes come upon the Iguana, the big lizards, as they were sunning themselves upon a flat stone in a riverbed. They are not pretty in shape, but nothing can be imagined more beautiful than their coloring. They shine like a heap of precious stones or like a pane cut out of an old church window. When, as you approach, they swish away, there is a flash of azure, green and purple over the stones, the color seems to be standing behind them in the air, like a comet's luminous tail.

Similes heaped up

Simile

Once I shot an Iguana. I thought that I should be able to make some pretty things from his skin. A strange thing happened then, that I have never afterwards forgotten. As I went up to him, where he was lying dead upon his stone, and actually while I was walking a few steps, he faded and grew pale, all color died out of him as in one long sigh, and by the time that I touched him he was gray and dull like a lump of concrete. It was the live impetuous blood pulsating within the animal, which had radiated out all that glow and splendor. Now that the flame was put out, and the soul had flown, the Iguana was as dead as a sandbag.

Metaphor of dying applied to color

Simile

Metaphor

Simile

—Isak Dinesen, "The Iguana"

The figurative language in this passage enables readers to share Dinesen's experience. It also compacts a large amount of information into sharp, memorable images.

FOR WRITING AND DISCUSSION

Using Figurative Language

1. Figurative language can fall flat when it takes the form of clichés ("I stood transfixed like a bump on a log") or mixed metaphors ("Exposed like a caterpillar on a leaf, he wolfed down his lunch before taking flight"). But when used effectively, figurative language adds powerfully compressed and meaningful images to a passage. Working individually or in small groups, find examples of figurative language in one or more of the example

passages in this chapter or in Chapter 6 (pp. 132–152). See if you can reach consensus on what makes a particular instance of figurative language effective or ineffective.

2. If you are currently working on an open-form narrative, exchange drafts with a classmate. See if you can find instances of figurative language in your current drafts and analyze their effectiveness. Perhaps you can also discover places where figurative language could be profitably added to the text.

SKILL 18.5 Expand your repertoire of styles.

In Chapter 4, we introduced you to the concept of style, which is a combination of sentence structure, word choice, and rhythm that allows writers to vary their emphasis and tone in a variety of ways. In this section, we show you how to expand your repertoire of styles through a classic method of teaching in which you try to imitate other writers' styles. This rhetorical practice—called "creative imitation"—has a long history beginning with the rhetoricians of classical Greece and Rome. When you do creative imitation, you examine a passage from an expert stylist and try to emulate it. You substitute your own subject matter, but you try to imitate the exact grammatical structures, lengths and rhythms of the sentences, and the tones of the original passage. The long-range effect of creative imitation is to expand your stylistic choices; the more immediate effect is to increase your skill at analyzing a writer's style. Most practitioners find that creative imitation encourages surprising insights into their own subject matter (when seen through the lens of the original writer's style) as well as a new understanding of how a particular piece of writing creates its special effects.

See Chapter 4, Concept 11, for a discussion of style.

You begin a creative imitation by asking questions such as these: What is distinctive about the sentences in this passage of writing? How do choices about sentence length and complexity, kinds of words, figures of speech, and so forth create a writer's voice? After close examination of the passage, you then think of your own subject matter that could be appropriately adapted to this writer's style.

To help you understand creative imitation, we provide the following example. In this passage, the writer, Victoria Register-Freeman, is exploring how relations between young men and women today threaten to undo some of the twentieth century's progress toward gender equality. In the section of her article that precedes this passage, Register-Freeman explains how she, as a single mother, taught her boys to cook, sew, do laundry, and "carry their weight domestically." But then, as she explains in this passage, teenage girls undid her attempts at creating gender equality:

REGISTER-FREEMAN PASSAGE

> Then came puberty and hunkhood. Over the last few years, the boys' domestic skills have atrophied because handmaidens have appeared en masse. The damsels have driven by, beeped, phoned and faxed. Some appeared so frequently outside the front door they began to remind me of the suction-footed Garfields spread-eagled on car windows. While the girls varied according to height, hair color and basic body type, they shared one characteristic. They were ever eager to help the guys out.
>
> —Victoria Register-Freeman, "My Turn: Hunks and Handmaidens"

Register-Freeman's voice projects the image of a concerned mother and feminist social critic. Her tone includes a range of attitudes: serious, personal, factual, ironic, frustrated. Note how this passage begins and ends with short, clipped sentences. The second sentence states a problem that the next three sentences develop with various kinds of details. The third sentence includes a series of colorful verbs; the fourth uses a metaphor (the ever-present girls compared to Garfields on car windows). The fifth sentence builds to the point in the sixth sentence, which is delivered bluntly and simply.

Here is one writer's attempt at a creative imitation:

CREATIVE IMITATION OF REGISTER-FREEMAN

Then came prosperity and popularity. Over the last ten years, Seattle's special charms have faded because expansion has occurred too rapidly. Traffic has multiplied, thickened, amplified, and slowed. Traffic jams appeared so often on the freeways and arterials they began to remind me of ants swarming over spilled syrup. While the congestion varied according to time, seasons, and weather conditions, it had one dominant effect. It increasingly threatened to spoil the city's beauty.

FOR WRITING AND DISCUSSION

Practicing Style through Creative Imitation

1. Do your own creative imitation of the passage from Register-Freeman.
2. Choose one or both of the following passages for creative imitation. Begin by jotting down all the specific observations you can make about the stylistic features of the passage. Then choose a topic that matches the topic of the original in its degree of lightness or seriousness and its depth. Explore your topic by presenting it using the sentence structures and kinds of words used in the original. Try to imitate the original phrase by phrase and sentence by sentence. You may find it helpful to use a dictionary and thesaurus.
   a. Africa is mystic; it is wild; it is a sweltering inferno; it is a photographer's paradise, a hunter's Valhalla, an escapist's Utopia. It is what you will, and it withstands all interpretations. It is the last vestige of a dead world or the cradle of a shiny new one. To a lot of people, as to myself, it is just "home." It is all of these things but one thing—it is never dull.

      —Beryl Markham, "Flying Elsewhere," *West with the Night*

   b. The disease was bubonic plague, present in two forms: one that infected the bloodstream, causing the buboes and internal bleeding, and was spread by contact; and a second, more virulent pneumonic type that infected the lungs and was spread by respiratory infection. The presence of both at once caused the high mortality and speed of contagion. So lethal was the disease that cases were known of persons going to bed well and dying before they woke, of doctors catching the illness at bedside and dying before the patient.

      —Barbara Tuchman, "This Is the End of the World," *A Distant Mirror*

SKILL 18.6 **Use open-form elements to create "voice" in closed-form prose.**

So far we have been talking about features of open-form prose in its purer forms. Sometimes, however, writers wish simply to loosen basically closed-form prose by combining it with some features of open-form prose. If, for example, an academic wanted to share new developments in a field with a popular audience, he or she would be well-advised to leaven his or her prose with some elements of open-form writing. In this final section, we offer several pieces of advice for loosening up closed-form prose.

Introducing Some Humor

Humor is rare in tightly closed prose because humor is nonfunctional—it doesn't *have* to be there for a writer to make a point—and closed-form prose values efficiency, saying what you have to say in the most economical fashion.

Humor is particularly valuable in that it can make imposing subjects more manageable for readers. Formal, abstract language can put readers off, estranging them from the subject; humor has the power to "de-strange" a subject, to allow the audience to look at it long enough to understand it. Many popular books on science and many of the best instructional books on car repair, cooking, money management, and others of life's drearier necessities use a humorous style to help their phobic readers get on with life.

To appreciate the effect of humor, consider the following passages from two different instructional books on how to operate the database program Paradox. The first passage, from *Windows in 21 Days*, uses a clear, humor-free, closed-form style.

> In this book, you learn by following detailed step-by-step exercises based on real-world problems in database application design. Every exercise leads you further into the power of "Paradox for Windows" as you develop the components of an automated application. This section does the following: explains the assumptions and conventions used in this book; lists the hardware and software requirements and setup needed to run Paradox for Windows and use this book efficiently; and offers some suggestions for strategies to get the most from this book. The step-by-step exercises make it easy.

Now note the different effect produced by the following passage from one of the hugely popular *For Dummies* books:

> Welcome to *Paradox for Windows for Dummies*, a book that's not afraid to ask the tough questions like "When's lunch?" and "Who finished the cookie dough ice cream?" If you're more interested in food (or Australian Wombats, for that matter) than you are in Paradox for Windows, this book is for you. If you're more interested in Paradox for Windows, please get some professional help before going out into society again.
>
> My goal is to help you get things done despite the fact that you're using Paradox. Whether you're at home, in your office, or at home in your office (or even if you just *feel* like you live at work) *Paradox for Windows for Dummies* is your all-in-one guidebook through the treacherous, frustrating, and appallingly technical world of the relational database.

Thinking about Humor

FOR WRITING AND DISCUSSION

1. Which of these two instructional books would you prefer to read?
2. The second passage says that the world of relational databases is "treacherous, frustrating, and appallingly technical," whereas the first stresses that the "step-by-step exercises [in the book] make it easy." Why do you suppose the humorous passage stresses the difficulty of databases whereas the humorless passage stresses the ease of a step-by-step approach? Is it good strategy for the humorous writer to stress the difficulty of Paradox?
3. Under what rhetorical circumstances are humorous instructions better than strictly serious instructions? When is a strictly serious approach better?

Using Techniques from Popular Magazines

Writers who publish regularly for popular audiences develop a vigorous, easy-reading style that differs from the style of much academic writing. The effect of this difference is illustrated by the results of a famous research study conducted by Michael Graves and Wayne Slater at the University of Michigan. For this study, teams of writers revised passages from a high school history textbook.* One team consisted of linguists and technical writers trained in producing closed-form texts using the strategies discussed in Chapter 17 (forecasting structure, putting points first, following the old/new contract, using transitions). A second team consisted of two *Time-Life* book editors.

Whereas the linguists aimed at making the passages clearer, the *Time-Life* writers were more concerned with making them livelier. The result? One hundred eleventh-grade students found the *Time-Life* editors' version both more comprehensible and more memorable. The problem with the original textbook wasn't lack of clarity but rather dryness. According to the researchers, the *Time-Life* editors did not limit themselves

> to making the passages lucid, well-organized, coherent, and easy to read. Their revisions went beyond such matters and were intended to make the texts interesting, exciting, vivid, rich in human drama, and filled with colorful language.

To see how they achieved this effect, let's look at their revision. Here is a passage about the Vietnam War taken from the original history text:

ORIGINAL HISTORY TEXT

> The most serious threat to world peace developed in Southeast Asia. Communist guerrillas threatened the independence of the countries carved out of French Indo-China by the Geneva conference of 1954. In South Vietnam, Communist guerrillas (the Viet Cong) were aided by forces from Communist North Vietnam in a struggle to overthrow the American-supported government. ...

*The study involved three teams, but for purposes of simplification we limit our discussion to two.

Shortly after the election of 1964, Communist gains prompted President Johnson to alter his policy concerning Vietnam. American military forces in Vietnam were increased from about 20,000 men in 1964 to more than 500,000 by 1968. Even so, North Vietnamese troops and supplies continued to pour into South Vietnam.

Here is the *Time-Life* editors' revision:

HISTORY PRESENTED IN POPULAR MAGAZINE STYLE

In the early 1960s the greatest threat to world peace was just a small splotch of color on Kennedy's map, one of the fledgling nations sculpted out of French Indo-China by the Geneva peacemakers of 1954. It was a country so tiny and remote that most Americans had never uttered its name: South Vietnam. ...

Aided by Communist North Vietnam, the Viet Cong guerrillas were eroding the ground beneath South Vietnam's American-backed government. Village by village, road by road, these jungle-wise rebels were waging a war of ambush and mining: They darted out of tunnels to head off patrols, buried exploding booby traps beneath the mud floors of huts, and hid razor-sharp bamboo sticks in holes. ...

No sooner had Johnson won the election than Communist gains prompted Johnson to go back on his campaign promise. The number of American soldiers in Vietnam skyrocketed from 20,000 in 1964 to more than 500,000 by 1968. But in spite of GI patrols, leech-infested jungles, swarms of buzzing insects, and flash floods that made men cling to trees to escape being washed away—North Vietnamese troops streamed southward without letup along the Ho Chi Minh Trail.

What can this revision teach you about invigorating closed-form prose? What specifically are the editors doing here?

First, notice how far the level of abstraction drops in the revision. The original is barren of sensory words; the revision is alive with them ("South Vietnam" becomes a "small splotch of color on Kennedy's map"; "a struggle to overthrow the American-supported government" becomes "[They] buried exploding booby traps beneath the mud floors of huts, and hid razor-sharp bamboo sticks in holes").

Second, notice how much more dramatic the revision is. Actual scenes, including a vision of men clinging to trees to escape being washed away by flash floods, replace a chronological account of the war's general progress. According to the editors, such scenes, or "nuggets"—vivid events that encapsulate complex processes or principles—are the lifeblood of *Time-Life* prose.

Finally, notice how the revision tends to delay critical information for dramatic effect, moving information you would normally expect to find early on into a later position. In the first paragraph, the *Time-Life* writers talk about "the greatest threat to world peace" in the early 1960s for four lines before revealing the identity of that threat—South Vietnam.

Enlivening Closed-Form Prose with Open-Form Elements

FOR WRITING AND DISCUSSION

Here is a passage from a student argument opposing women's serving on submarines. Working individually or in small groups, enliven this passage by using some of the techniques of the *Time-Life* writers.

> Not only would it be very expensive to refit submarines for women personnel, but having women on submarines would hurt the morale of the sailors. In order for a crew to work effectively, they must have good morale or their discontent begins to show through in their performance. This is especially crucial on submarines, where if any problem occurs, it affects the safety of the whole ship. Women would hurt morale by creating sexual tension. Sexual tension can take many forms. One form is couples' working and living in a close space with all of the crew. When a problem occurs within the relationship, it could affect the morale of those directly involved and in the workplace. This would create an environment that is not conducive to good productivity. Tension would also occur if one of the women became pregnant or if there were complaints of sexual harassment. It would be easier to deal with these problems on a surface ship, but in the small confines of a submarine these problems would cause more trouble.

PART 4

A RHETORICAL GUIDE TO RESEARCH

This screen capture shows the home page of Women Against Gun Control (www.wagc.com), a grassroots organization dedicated to supporting women's right to defend themselves. This organization participates in pro-gun political activism, legislative research, media awareness, distribution of print resources, and gun-related education. The Web site itself uses color, images, other design features, and bold text to stake out its position in the complex controversy over women's role in the hotly contested, larger issue of gun control. This Web site home page is featured in a class discussion exercise in Chapter 20.

Ladies of High-Caliber

Protect Your Rights!

Join Now!

Click Here for the 10 Commandments of gun safety!

Home

WAGC Information

WAGC Features

WAGC Boycotts

WAGC Links

WAGC Site map

WAGC Contact

Get your pin in honor of WAGC!

Women Against Gun Control

"The Second Amendment IS the Equal

Click here to sign and read our new forum board!

WAGC sends amicus brief to the U.S. Supreme Court!

Click Here (Opens New Window)

Click here to read a press release regarding this hearing.

Click here for a special message from WAGC President, Janalee Tobias

Contact Us

Postal Address

- WAGC

PO Box 95357
South Jordan, UT
84095

Telephone

- 801-328-9660

E-Mail

- info@wagc.com
- State and Local Chapters
- webmaster

It's a Fact:

RECENT RESEARCH INDICATES THAT GUNS ARE USED DEFENSIVELY 2.5 MILLION TIMES PER YEAR.

It's not surprising then, that more women than ever want to keep their rights to own and carry a gun.
The reason is simple: Women **are** concerned about becoming victims of crime. Guns give women a fighting chance against crime.

Join Women Against Gun Control.
Take the Women Against Gun Control Pledge and you qualify for a membership in Women Against Gun Control, a grass roots volunteer organization dedicated to preserving our gun rights.

Join thousands of women (and men) in sending a powerful message throughout the world.

"Guns **SAVE** Lives. We do **NOT** support gun control. Gun Control does **NOT** control crime!"

2nd Amendment
A well regulated Militia being necessary to the security of a free State, the right of the people to keep and bear Arms shall not be infringed.

"The Second Amendment IS Homeland Security."

Special Article
Have gun, will not fear it anymore

Rosie O' Donnel

Hillary Clinton

Janet Reno

Diane Feinstein

Want Americans to believe all women support gun control...

Let's BLOW HOLES in this MYTH!

If women are disarmed, a rapist will never hear...

"STOP OR I'LL SHOOT!"

Looking for Pro-Second Amendment and Pro-Freedom Books? Check Out These Book Reviews and Help Support This Site!

THE UTAH GIRAFFE SOCIETY

Support WAGC Efforts with the Utah GIRAFFE Society!

PART 4 **A RHETORICAL GUIDE TO RESEARCH**

Part 4 addresses the following outcomes for first-year composition from the Council of Writing Program Administrators.

RHETORICAL KNOWLEDGE	• Focus on purpose (Skills 19.1, 21.1) • Use conventions of format and structure appropriate to the rhetorical situation (Skills 21.1-21.5, 22.1-22.4) • Understand how genres shape reading and writing (Skill 20.1)
CRITICAL THINKING, READING, AND WRITING	• Use writing and reading for inquiry, learning, thinking, and communicating (Skill 19.1, 20.1-20.3) • Understand a writing assignment as a series of tasks, including finding, evaluating, analyzing, and synthesizing appropriate primary and secondary sources (Skills 19.1-19.3, 20.1-20.3) • Integrate their own ideas with those of others (Skills 21.1-21.5) • Understand the relationships among language, knowledge, and power (Skills 20.2, 20.3, 21.5)
PROCESSES	• Understand the collaborative and social aspects of writing processes (Skill 21.5) • Learn to balance the advantages of relying on others with the responsibility of doing their part (Skills 19.1, 21.5)
KNOWLEDGE OF CONVENTIONS	• Learn common formats for different kinds of texts (Skills 21.2-21.4, 22.1-22.4) • Develop knowledge of genre conventions ranging from structure and paragraphing to tone and mechanics (Skill 20.1) • Practice appropriate means of documenting their work (Skills 22.1-22.4)
COMPOSING IN ELECTRONIC ENVIRONMENTS	• Locate, evaluate, organize, and use in research electronic sources, including web databases and informal networks, and intranet sources (Skills 19.2, 19.3) • Understand and exploit the differences in the rhetorical strategies and in the affordances available for both print and electronic composing processes and texts (Skills 19.2, 20.2, 20.3)

ASKING QUESTIONS, FINDING SOURCES

19

Our goal in Part 4 is to explain the skills you'll need for successful college-level research papers. In this opening chapter, we help you start on the right track as a college researcher. The remaining chapters in Part 4 show you how to evaluate research sources (Chapter 20), integrate sources into your own arguments and avoid plagiarism (Chapter 21), and create in-text citations and corresponding bibliographic citations to document your sources (Chapter 22).

In this chapter, you will learn these skills:

- **SKILL 19.1** Argue your own thesis in response to a research question.
- **SKILL 19.2** Understand differences among kinds of sources.
- **SKILL 19.3** Use purposeful strategies for searching libraries, databases, and Web sites.

An Overview of Research Writing

Although the research paper is a common writing assignment in college, students are often baffled by their professor's expectations. Many students think of research writing as finding information on a topic or as finding quotations to support a thesis rather than as wrestling with a question or problem. One of our colleagues calls these sorts of papers "data dumps": The student dumps a bucket of data on the professor's desk and says, "Here's what I found out about sweatshops, Professor Jones. Enjoy!" Another colleague calls papers full of long quotations "choo-choo train papers": big boxcars of indented block quotations coupled with little patches of a student's own writing.

Characteristics of a Good Research Paper

But a research paper shouldn't be a data dump or a train of boxcar quotations. Instead, it should follow the same principles of writing discussed throughout this text:

- A research paper should pose an interesting and significant problem.
- A research paper should respond to the problem with a contestable thesis.
- In a research paper, sources should be used purposefully and ethically.

An Effective Approach to Research

How does a writer develop a research paper with these characteristics? Early on, your goal is to develop a research question and, through your research process, to begin "wallowing in complexity." You become immersed in alternative points of view, clashing values, different kinds of evidence (often conflicting), and unresolved questions arising from gaps in current knowledge. Relying on your own critical thinking, you eventually refine your research question and begin to formulate your own thesis. In your completed research paper, some of your sources provide background information, others supply supporting evidence, and still others present alternative points of view that you are pushing against. Throughout, your research data should come from credible sources that are documented in a formal, academic style.

The Role of Documentation in College Research

Much of the writing you encounter in popular magazines or online journalism has the characteristics of a research paper—a thesis and support—but not the documentation that college professors expect. By **documentation**, we mean the in-text citations and accompanying bibliography that allow readers to identify and locate your sources for themselves. Such documentation makes all the difference because new knowledge is inevitably built on the work of others. In academic culture, authors who hope to gain acceptance for new findings and ideas must explain the roots of their work as well as show how they reached their conclusions. By documenting their sources according to appropriate conventions, research writers establish a credible *ethos* and provide a valuable resource for others who wish to locate the same sources.

Many of the writing projects in this text invite your use of research sources. In fact, your instructor may pair the material in Part 4 with specific writing projects from Part 2. As you study this material, keep in mind your twofold purpose in reading research sources:

1. To develop your own answer to your research question (your thesis) by bringing your critical thinking to bear on your research sources
2. To position yourself in a conversation with others who have addressed the same question

Throughout, you need to use your research sources responsibly in order to avoid plagiarism and to present yourself as an ethical apprentice scholar joining the academic community. As you begin your research project, make sure that you know your institution's and your teachers' policies on plagiarism and academic honesty. The four chapters in part 4 will explain fully the knowledge and skills needed for confident and ethical research.

SKILL 19.1 Argue your own thesis in response to a research question.

The best way to produce effective, engaged, and ethically responsible research papers is to begin with a good research question. A good question keeps you in charge of your writing. It reminds you that your task is to forge an answer to this question yourself, in your own voice, through your own critical thinking. This approach, which follows the principles of Concept 2 in Chapter 1 of this text ("Good writers address problems rather than topics"), helps you avoid the wrong paths of data dumping, strung-together quotations, and uncertainties about why and how you are using sources.

Topic Focus Versus Question Focus

To see the difference between a topic focus and a problem focus, suppose a friend asks you what your research paper is about. Consider differences in the following responses:

Topic Focus: I am doing a paper on eating disorders.

Question Focus: I'm trying to sort out what the experts say is the best way to treat severe anorexia nervosa. Is inpatient or outpatient treatment more effective?

Topic Focus: I am doing my paper on gender-specific toys for children.

Question Focus: I am puzzled about some of the effects of gender-specific toys. Do boys' toys, such as video games, toy weapons, and construction sets, develop intellectual and physical skills more than girls' toys do?

As these scenarios suggest, a topic focus invites you to collect information without a clear purpose—a sure road toward data dumping. In contrast, a question focus requires you to be a critical thinker who must assess and weigh data and understand multiple points of view. A topic focus encourages passive collection of information. A question focus encourages active construction of meaning. The more active your thinking, the more likely you will write in your own voice with no worries about purposeless uses of sources or possible plagiarism.

Formulating a Research Question

How do you arrive at a research question? The concepts discussed in Chapters 1 and 2 about question asking and wallowing in complexity apply to research writing. We invite you to look again at Table 1.1 on pages 13–14 ("How Writers Become Gripped by a Problem") and the strategies chart on pages 40–41 ("Strategies for Creating a Thesis with Tension or Surprise"). Good research questions can emerge from puzzles that you pose for yourself or from controversial questions already "out there" that are being actively debated by others. In most cases your initial research question will evolve as you do your research. You may make it broader or narrower, or refocus it on a newly discovered aspect of your original problem.

You can test the initial feasibility of your research question by considering the following prompts:

- Are you personally interested in this question?
- Is the question both problematic and significant?
- Is the question limited enough for the intended length of your paper?
- Is there a reasonable possibility of finding information on this question based on the time and resources you have available?
- Is the question appropriate for your level of expertise?

Establishing Your Role as a Researcher

After you have formulated your research question, you need to consider the possible roles you might play as a researcher. Your role is connected to the aim or purpose of your paper—to explore, to inform, to analyze, or to persuade. To appreciate your options, consider the following strategies based on typical roles researchers can play:

Strategies for Establishing Your Role as a Researcher

Aims and Roles	What to Do	Examples of Research Questions
Reporter of information that fills a knowledge gap	Find, synthesize, and report data related to an information question.	• How do Japan and France dispose of nuclear waste from nuclear power plants? • What attitude do elementary math teachers have toward the University of Chicago's *Everyday Math* curriculum?
Reporter of the current best thinking on a problem	Research the current thinking of experts on some important problem and report what the experts think.	• What are the views of experts on the causes of homosexuality? • What do researchers consider the possible dangers of online social networks?
Conductor of original field research in response to an empirical question	Pose a problem that requires field research, conduct the research, and present results in a scientific report. Often, include a "review of the literature" section.	• To what extent do pictures of party drinking appear on our students' Facebook profiles? • How do the study habits of humanities majors differ from those of science and engineering majors?
Reviewer of a controversy (primarily an informative aim)	Investigate and report differing arguments on various sides of a controversy.	• What are the arguments for and against granting amnesty and eventual U.S. citizenship to illegal immigrants? • What policy approaches have been proposed to the U.S. government for increasing fuel economy of automobiles?

Aims and Roles	What to Do	Examples of Research Questions
Advocate for a position in a controversy (primarily an analytic and persuasive aim)	Assert a position using research data for background, for support, or for alternative views.	• Should the United States grant amnesty and eventual citizenship to illegal immigrants? (Writer argues yes or no.) • What is the best way for the U.S. government to ensure that cars achieve higher fuel economy? (Writer argues for a specific approach.)
Analyzer of an interpretive or evaluative question who also positions himself or herself within a critical conversation	Do your own original analysis of a text, phenomenon, or data source, but also relate your views to what others have said about the same or similar questions.	• To what extent does the film *Avatar* present a Christian worldview? • How effective is microlending at alleviating poverty in third world countries?

FOR WRITING AND DISCUSSION

Using Research Roles to Generate Research Questions

Working individually or in small groups, develop research questions on a general topic such as music, health, sports, use of fossil fuels, a literary work, or some other topic specified by your instructor. Develop research questions that would be appropriate for each of the following roles:

1. Reporter of information to fill a knowledge gap
2. Reporter of the current best thinking of experts on a problem
3. Original field or laboratory researcher
4. Reviewer of a controversy
5. Advocate in a controversy
6. Critical thinker about an interpretive or evaluatve question in conversation with other thinkers
7. Miscellaneous (good questions that don't fit neatly into any of these other roles)

A Case Study: James Gardiner's Research on Online Social Networks

To illustrate how a student writer poses a research question and argues his own thesis, let's return to James Gardiner's investigation of online social networks (OSNs). We first introduced James's research in Chapter 2, where we reprinted his initial musings about OSNs in the form of a five-minute freewrite (p. 30).

James's original problem was his uncertainty about why OSNs are so popular and why he himself had chosen not to have a Facebook profile. In his original freewrite, he said, "I am a little hesitant to display personal information about myself on a website that can be viewed by anyone in the world." He also was afraid that joining an OSN would take up too much time.

Later in the course he decided to investigate OSNs for a major research project. His research process is narrated in his exploratory essay in Chapter 7, pages 169–173. As he began reading articles about OSNs, he noted that many researchers were highly favorable of OSNs, arguing that they provide new ways for teenagers to maintain relationships with friends, to explore their own self-images, and to practice constructing online identities. However, James remained somewhat skeptical of OSNs and, late in his initial research, he encountered the term "Facebook trance" and located an article on Internet addictions. He became more and more interested in exploring the negative aspects of OSNs. At the conclusion of his exploratory essay, James sums up the direction he would like to move in further research:

> As I continue with my research, I am not sure what thesis I will assert for my final project. I still want to do more research on the negative effects of OSNs. For example, I haven't found studies that explore the possible phoniness of Facebook relationships. I remember a passage from Copeland where one user labels Facebook interaction as "communication lean." According to this student, "It's all a little fake—the 'friends'; the profiles that can be tailored to what others find appealing; the 'groups' that exist only in cyberspace." I'm still thinking about that quotation. Do OSNs contribute to deeper, more meaningful relationships or do they promote a superficial phoniness? I hope to explore this issue further before writing my major paper.

James's exploratory research gave him a solid background on OSNs, enabling him to bring his own critical thinking to bear on his research sources. In order to convert his exploratory narrative into a closed-form research paper, he eventually created a thesis statement focused on potential dangers of OSNs. You can read his final paper in Chapter 22, pages 590–596.

FOR WRITING AND DISCUSSION

Following James Gardiner's Research Process

Working individually, read James's exploratory paper (pp. 169–173) and his final research paper (pp. 590–596). Then, working in small groups or as a whole class, try to reach consensus answers to the following questions:

1. Trace the steps in James's thinking from the time he first becomes interested in OSNs until he finally settles on their possible negative effects. What were the key moments that shaped his thinking? How did his thinking evolve?
2. We have used James's story as an example of a student in charge of his own writing. Where do you see James doing active critical thinking? Where do you see instances of what we have called "rhetorical reading"—that is, places where James asks questions about an author's purpose, angle of vision, and selection of evidence?
3. How is James's final paper different from a data dump or a choo-choo train paper? How does it demonstrate ethical use of sources?

SKILL 19.2 Understand differences among kinds of sources.

To be an effective researcher, you need to understand the differences among the many kinds of sources that you might use while doing your research. These can be classified in different ways, such as primary versus secondary sources (a scheme that focuses on how you'll use the source in your final paper) or as print versus Web sources (a scheme based on its medium of publication). In this section we'll explain a variety of ways to distinguish among different kinds of sources. Your payoff will be an increased ability to read sources rhetorically and to use them purposefully in your research writing.

Primary and Secondary Sources

Researchers often distinguish between primary and secondary sources. **Primary sources** are the original documents, artifacts, or data that you are actively analyzing; **secondary sources** are works by other people who have analyzed the same documents, artifacts, or data. In short, secondary sources comment upon or analyze primary sources. Table 19.1 presents some examples.

The distinction between primary and secondary sources is sometimes slippery and depends on context. In the media studies example from Table 19.1, the parenting Web site is a secondary source if your research question focuses on *South Park*. But if you are investigating the political biases of parenting Web sites, then this site becomes a primary source.

Some research projects use primary sources extensively, while others mainly or exclusively involve secondary sources. You may be asked, for example, to bring your critical thinking to bear on specific primary sources—for example, gender stereotypes in children's birthday cards, political views expressed in old *Archie*

TABLE 19.1 Examples of Primary and Secondary Sources

Field	Examples of Primary Sources	Examples of Secondary Sources
History	Diaries, speeches, newspaper accounts, letters, manuscripts, official records, old photographs, old news reels, archeological sites	• Scholarly book on European fascism in the 1930s • 1970s film about the rise of the Nazis in Germany
Media studies	Rap lyrics, advertisements, graffiti, episodes of *South Park*, bumper stickers, documentary photographs	• Scholarly journal article analyzing racism in *South Park* • Parenting Web site objecting to *South Park*
Nursing	Patient records, direct observation of patients, research findings on transmission of AIDS virus; public health data on swine flu	• Popular magazine article about nurses working in third world hospital • Blog site focusing on nursing issues

comic books, or legal requirements for "proof" in transcripts from witchcraft trials. In these cases, your secondary research would focus on what other scholars have said about these issues in scholarly books or articles. Modern libraries together with the Internet now make available a wealth of primary sources—government documents, historical archives, slide collections, population or ethnographic data, maps, health data, and so forth.

For other kinds of research projects, particularly those connected to civic issues, students often need to work mainly or exclusively with secondary sources. In trying to decide where you stand, say, on nuclear power plants, on a single-payer medical system, or on immigration policy, you will need to enter the civic conversation about these issues carried on in secondary sources. You'll also need to pay attention to what these secondary sources use as evidence in support of their arguments. Were they able to use primary sources for their evidence? Or does their evidence come from other secondary sources? In trying to evaluate each of these secondary sources, you'll need to employ all your rhetorical skills, as we begin to show in the next section.

Reading Secondary Sources Rhetorically

When you look at a secondary source—whether in stable print form or in often unstable Web form—you need to think rhetorically about the kind of source you are perusing and the original author's purpose in producing the source. In this section we'll look specifically at print sources, which are commonly classified either as books or as periodicals (magazines, newspapers, scholarly journals, and so forth), and contrast them with Web sources. Later, in Skill 20.3, we'll look specifically at ways to read Web sources rhetorically.

Table 19.2 shows how these sources can be analyzed according to genre, publisher, author credentials, and angle of vision. The last column in Table 19.2 identifies contextual clues that will help you recognize what category each of these sources belongs to. We suggest that you take a few moments now to peruse the information in these tables so that you can begin to appreciate the distinctions we are making among types of sources.

Print Sources Versus Web-Only Sources New researchers need to appreciate the differences in stability and reliability between print sources and Web-only sources. Print sources (books, journals, magazines, newspapers) are stable in contrast to materials published on Web sites, which might change hourly. If you work from print sources, you can be sure that others will be able to track down your sources for their own projects. Furthermore, print publications generally go through an editorial review process that helps ensure accuracy and reputability. In contrast, Web-only documents from individuals or small organizations may be unedited and thus unreliable. Because the cost of producing, distributing, and storing print materials is high, books and periodicals are now often published in electronic formats, complicating the distinction between print and Web sources.

TABLE 19.2 A Rhetorical Overview of Print Books and Periodicals

Genre and Publisher	Author and Angle of Vision	How to Recognize Them
Books		
SCHOLARLY BOOKS • University/academic presses • Nonprofit • Selected through peer review	**Author:** Professors, researchers **Angle of vision:** Scholarly advancement of knowledge	• University press on title page • Specialized academic style • Documentation and bibliography • Sometimes available as e-books
TRADE BOOKS (NONFICTION) • Commercial publishers (for example, Penguin Putnam) • Selected for profit potential	**Author:** Journalists, freelancers, scholars aiming at popular audience **Angle of vision:** Varies from informative to persuasive; often well researched and respected, but sometimes shoddy and aimed for quick sale	• Covers designed for marketing appeal • Popular style • Usually documented in an informal rather than an academic style • Sometimes available as e-books
REFERENCE BOOKS • Publishers specializing in reference material • For-profit through library sales	**Author:** Commissioned scholars **Angle of vision:** Balanced, factual overview	• Titles containing words such as *encyclopedia, dictionary,* or *guide* • Found in reference section of library or online through library Web site
Periodicals		
SCHOLARLY JOURNALS • University/academic presses • Nonprofit • Articles chosen through peer review • Examples: *Journal of Abnormal Psychology, Review of Metaphysics*	**Author:** Professors, researchers, independent scholars **Angle of vision:** Scholarly advancement of knowledge; presentation of research findings; development of new theories and applications	• Not sold on magazine racks • No commercial advertising • Specialized academic style • Documentation and bibliography • Cover often has table of contents • Often can be found in online databases
PUBLIC AFFAIRS MAGAZINES • Commercial, "for-profit" presses • Manuscripts reviewed by editors • Examples: *Harper's, Commonweal, National Review*	**Author:** Staff writers, freelancers, scholars for general audiences **Angle of vision:** Aims to deepen public understanding of issues; magazines often have political bias of left, center, or right	• Long, well-researched articles • Ads aimed at upscale professionals • Often has reviews of books, theater, film, and the arts • Often can be found in online databases or on the Web

(*continued*)

TABLE 19.2 *continued*

Genre and Publisher	Author and Angle of Vision	How to Recognize Them
	Periodicals (*continued*)	
TRADE MAGAZINES • Commercial, "for-profit" presses • Focused on a profession or trade • Examples: *Advertising Age, Automotive Rebuilder, Farm Journal*	**Author:** Staff writers, industry specialists **Angle of vision:** Informative articles for practitioners; advocacy for the profession or trade	• Title indicating trade or profession • Articles on practical job concerns • Ads geared toward a particular trade or profession
NEWSMAGAZINES AND NEWSPAPERS • Newspaper chains and publishers • Examples: *Time, Newsweek, Washington Post, Los Angeles Times*	**Author:** Staff writers and journalists; occasional freelance pieces **Angle of vision:** News reports aimed at balance and objectivity; editorial pages reflect perspective of editors; op-ed pieces reflect different perspectives	• Readily familiar by name, distinctive cover style • Widely available on newsstands, by subscription, and on the Web • Ads aimed at broad, general audience
POPULAR NICHE MAGAZINES • Large conglomerates or small presses with clear target audience • Focused on special interests of target audience • Examples: *Seventeen, People, TV Guide, Car and Driver, Golf Digest*	**Author:** Staff or freelance writers **Angle of vision:** Varies—in some cases content and point of view are dictated by advertisers or the politics of the publisher	• Glossy paper, extensive ads, lots of visuals • Popular, often distinctive style • Short, undocumented articles • Credentials of writer often not mentioned

These changes mean that when evaluating and citing sources, researchers must now pay attention to whether a source retrieved electronically was originally a print source made available electronically (by being posted to a Web site or contained in a database) or is in fact a Web-only source. You'll need to know this information in order to read the source rhetorically, evaluate its trustworthiness, and cite it properly. When you retrieve print sources electronically, be aware that you may lose important contextual clues about the author's purpose and angle of vision—clues that would be immediately apparent in the original print source. These clues come from such things as statements of editorial policy, other articles in the same magazine or journal, or advertisements targeting specific audiences. (The increasing availability of *.pdf* or *portable document format* files, which reproduce the appearance of the original print page, makes understanding publication contexts much easier. When .pdf format is available, take advantage of it.)

Scholarly Books and Journal Articles Versus Trade Books and Magazines Note in Table 19.2 the distinction between scholarly books or journal articles, which are peer-reviewed and published by nonprofit academic presses, and trade books or magazines, which are published by for-profit presses. By **peer review**, which is a highly prized concept in academia, we mean the selection process by which scholarly manuscripts get chosen for publication. When manuscripts are submitted to an academic publisher, the editor sends them for independent review to experienced scholars who judge the rigor and accuracy of the research and the significance and value of the argument. The process is highly competitive and weeds out much shoddy or trivial work.

In contrast, trade books and magazines are not peer-reviewed by independent scholars. Instead, they are selected for publication by editors whose business is to make a profit. Fortunately, it can be profitable for popular presses to publish superbly researched and argued material because college-educated people, as lifelong learners, create a demand for intellectually satisfying trade books or magazines written for the general reader rather than for the highly specialized reader. These can be excellent sources for undergraduate research, but you need to separate the trash from the treasure. Trade books and magazines are aimed at many different audiences and market segments and can include sloppy, unreliable, and heavily biased material.

Encyclopedias, Wikipedia, and Other Reference Books and Wikis Another kind of source is an encyclopedia or other kind of reference work. These are sometimes called "tertiary sources" because they provide distilled background information derived from primary and secondary sources. Encyclopedias and reference works are excellent starting places at the beginning of a research project. New researchers, however, should be aware of the difference between a commissioned encyclopedia article and an article in the online source *Wikipedia*. Professional encyclopedia companies such as *Encyclopedia Britannica* commission highly regarded scholars with particular expertise in a subject to write that subject's encyclopedia entry. Usually the entry is signed so that the author can be identified. In contrast, all forms of wikis—including *Wikipedia*—are communal projects using collaborative wiki software. *Wikipedia, the Free Encyclopedia* (its official name) is written communally by volunteers; anyone who follows the site's procedures can edit an entry. The entry's accuracy and angle of vision depend on collective revisions by interested readers.

Wikipedia is a fascinating cultural product that provides rapid overview information, but it is not a reliable academic source. It is often accused of inaccurate information, editorial bias, and shifting content because of constant revisions by readers. Most instructors will not accept *Wikipedia* as a factual or informative source.

FOR WRITING AND DISCUSSION

Identifying Types of Sources

Your instructor will bring to class a variety of sources—different kinds of books, scholarly journals, magazines, and downloaded material. Working individually or in small groups, try to decide which category in Table 19.2 each piece belongs to. Be prepared to justify your decisions on the basis of the cues you used to make your decision.

SKILL 19.3 Use purposeful strategies for searching libraries, databases, and Web sites.

In the previous section, we explained differences among the kinds of sources you may encounter in a research project. In this section, we explain how to find these sources by using your campus library's own collection, library-leased electronic databases, and Web search engines for finding material on the World Wide Web.

Checking Your Library's Home Page

We begin by focusing on the specialized resources provided by your campus library. Your starting place and best initial research tool will be your campus library's home page. This portal will lead you to two important resources: (1) the library's online catalog and (2) direct links to the periodicals and reference databases leased by the library. Here you will find indexes to a wide range of articles in journals and magazines and direct access to frequently used reference materials, including statistical abstracts, biographies, dictionaries, and encyclopedias. Furthermore, many academic library sites post lists of good research starting points, organized by discipline, including Web sites librarians have screened.

In addition to checking your library's home page, make a personal visit to your library to learn its features and especially to note the location of a researcher's best friend and resource: the reference desk. Make use of reference librarians—they are there to help you.

Searching Efficiently: Subject Searches Versus Keyword Searches At the start of a research project, researchers typically search an online catalog or database by subject or by keywords. Your own research process will be speedier if you understand the difference between these kinds of searches.

- ***Subject searches.*** Subject searches use predetermined categories published in the reference work *Library of Congress Subject Headings*. This work informs you that, for example, material on "street people" would be classified under the heading "homeless persons." If the words you use for a subject search don't yield results, seek help from a librarian, who can show you how to use the subject heading guide to find the best word or phrase.
- ***Keyword searches.*** Keyword searches are not based on predetermined subject categories. Rather, the computer locates the keywords you provide in titles,

abstracts, introductions, and sometimes bodies of text. Keyword searches in online catalogs are usually limited to finding words and phrases in titles. We explain more about keyword searches in the upcoming section on using licensed databases, whose search engines look for keywords in bodies of text as well as in titles.

Finding Print Articles: Searching a Licensed Database

For many research projects, useful sources are print articles immediately available in your library's periodical collection. You find these articles by searching licensed databases leased by your library.

What Is a Licensed Database? Electronic databases of periodical sources are produced by for-profit companies that index articles in thousands of periodicals and construct engines that can search the database by author, title, subject, keyword, date, genre, and other characteristics. In most cases the database contains an abstract of each article, and in many cases it contains the complete text of the article, which you can download and print. These databases are referred to by several different generic names: "licensed databases" (our preferred term), "periodicals databases," or "subscription services." Because access to these databases is restricted to fee-paying customers, they can't be searched through Web engines like Google. Most university libraries allow students to access these databases from a remote computer by using a password. You can therefore use the Internet to connect your computer to licensed databases as well as to the World Wide Web (see Figure 19.1).

Although the methods of accessing licensed databases vary from institution to institution, we can offer some widely applicable guidelines. Most likely your library has online one or more of the following databases:

- ***EBSCOhost:*** Includes citations and abstracts from journals in most disciplines as well as many full-text articles from thousands of journals.
- ***ProQuest:*** Gives access to full text of articles from magazines and journals in many subject areas; may include full-text articles from newspapers.

FIGURE 19.1 Licensed Database Versus Free-Access Portions of Internet

- ***FirstSearch Databases:*** Incorporates multiple specialized databases in many subject areas, including WorldCat, which contains records of books, periodicals, and multimedia formats from libraries worldwide.
- ***Lexis-Nexis Academic Universe:*** Is primarily a full-text database covering current events, business, and financial news; includes company profiles and legal, medical, and reference information.
- ***JSTOR:*** Offers full text of scholarly journal articles across many disciplines; you can limit searches to specific disciplines.

MLA and APA formats for citing information and texts retrieved from licensed electronic databases are presented in Skill 22.3 (MLA) and Skill 22.4 (APA).

Given the variability of these and many other resources, we once again refer you to your campus library's Web site and the librarians at the reference desk (who often answer questions by e-mail). There you will find the best advice about where to look for what. Then, when you decide to use a specific source for your research project, be sure to include in your notes the names of both the database and the database company because, as we explain in Chapter 22, you will need to include that information when you cite your sources.

More on Keyword Searching To use an online database, you need to be adept at keyword searching, which we introduced on page 528. When you type a word or phrase into a search box, the computer will find sources that contain the same words or phrases. If you want the computer to search for a phrase, put it in quotation marks. Thus if you type "*street people*" using quotation marks, the computer will search for those two words occurring together. If you type in *street people* without quotation marks, the computer will look for the word *street* and the word *people* occurring in the same document but not necessarily together. Use your imagination to try a number of related terms. If you are researching gendered toys and you get too many hits using the keyword *toys,* try *gender toys, Barbie, G.I. Joe, girl toys, boy toys, toys psychology,* and so forth. You can increase the flexibility of your searches by using Boolean terms to expand, narrow, or limit your search (see Table 19.3 for an explanation of Boolean searches).

TABLE 19.3 Boolean Search Commands

Command and Function	Research Example	What to Type	Search Result
X OR Y (Expands your search)	You are researching Barbie dolls and decide to include G.I. Joe figures.	"Barbie doll" OR "G.I. Joe"	Articles that contain either phrase
X AND Y (Narrows your search)	You are researching the psychological effects of Barbie dolls and are getting too many hits under *Barbie dolls.*	"Barbie dolls" AND psychology	Articles that include both the phrase "Barbie dolls" and the word *psychology*
X NOT Y (Limits your search)	You are researching girls' toys and are tired of reading about Barbie dolls. You want to look at other popular girls' toys.	"girl toys" NOT Barbie	Articles that include the phrase "girl toys" but exclude *Barbie*

Illustration of a Database Search

As an illustration of a database search, we'll use student writer James Gardiner's research on online social networks. Figure 19.2 shows the results from James's search using the keywords *online relationships* and *loneliness* on the database EBSCOhost. As the figure shows, EBSCOhost returned three articles from scholarly journals that deal in some way with online relationships and loneliness. The first article, "Searching for Self and Relationships Online," comes from an academic journal (*CyberPsychology & Behavior*) and a full text of the article is available online in .pdf format. To get more information, James clicked on the name of the article. The resulting screen, which is shown in Figure 22.1 (p. 584), gives an abstract of the article as well as complete data about when and where the article was published in print. (We placed this screen in Chapter 22 on documentation, rather than here, to show how it provides the information you'll need for your Works Cited list.) Based on the abstract, James downloaded the .pdf file and

FIGURE 19.2 Sample Results List from a Search Using EBSCOhost

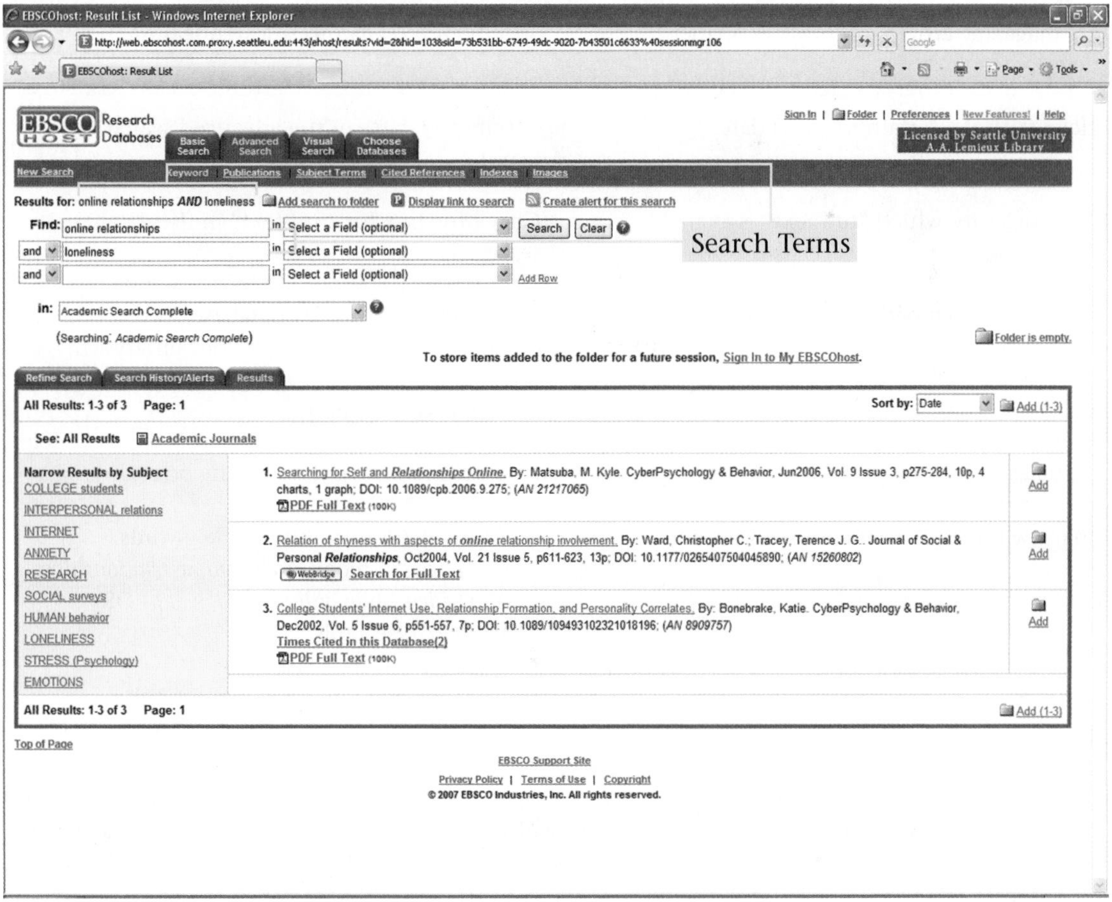

eventually used this article in his final research paper. (See the entry under "Matsuba" in his Works Cited list on p. 597.)

A particularly valuable feature of databases is the way that you can limit or expand your searches in a variety of useful ways. Here are some strategies for focusing, narrowing, or expanding your list of sources:

Strategies for Narrowing or Expanding Your Searches on Licensed Databases

What You Want	What to Do
Only scholarly articles in peer-reviewed journals	Check the box for "peer-reviewed" articles in the database search box (different databases have different procedures—ask a librarian).
Only short articles (or only long articles)	Specify length of articles you want in the advanced search feature.
Only magazine articles or only newspaper articles	Specify in the advanced search feature.
Articles within a certain range of dates	Specify the dates in the advanced search feature.
Only articles for which "full text" is available	Check the box for "full text" in the database search box.
Only articles from periodicals carried by your library	Check method used by database. (Most databases accessed through your library will indicate whether your library carries the magazine or journal.)
All articles	Don't check any of the limiting boxes.
To narrow (or expand) the focus of the search	• Experiment with different keywords. • Use Boolean techniques: *online relationships* AND *friendship*; *online relationships* OR *MySpace* (see Table 19.3). • Try different databases. • Ask your reference librarian for help.

After you've identified articles you'd like to read, locate physically all those available in your library's periodical collection. (This way you won't lose important contextual cues for reading them rhetorically.) For those unavailable in your library, print them from the database (if full text is provided), or order them through interlibrary loan.

Finding Cyberspace Sources: Searching the World Wide Web

Another valuable resource is the World Wide Web. To understand the logic of Web search engines, you need to know that the Internet is divided into restricted sections open only to those with special access rights and a "free-access" section. Web engines such as Google search only the free-access portion of the Internet. When you type keywords into a Web search engine, it searches for matches in material made available on the Web by all the users of the world's network of computers—government agencies, corporations, advocacy groups, information services, individuals with their own Web sites, and many others.

The following example will quickly show you the difference between a licensed database search and a Web search. When we entered the keywords *online relationships* and *loneliness* into EBSCOhost, we received three hits from scholarly journals (see Figure 19.2). In contrast, when we typed *online relationships loneliness* into Google, we received "about 1,670,000" hits. The first screen for this search is shown in Figure 19.3.

FIGURE 19.3 First Few Hits from Google

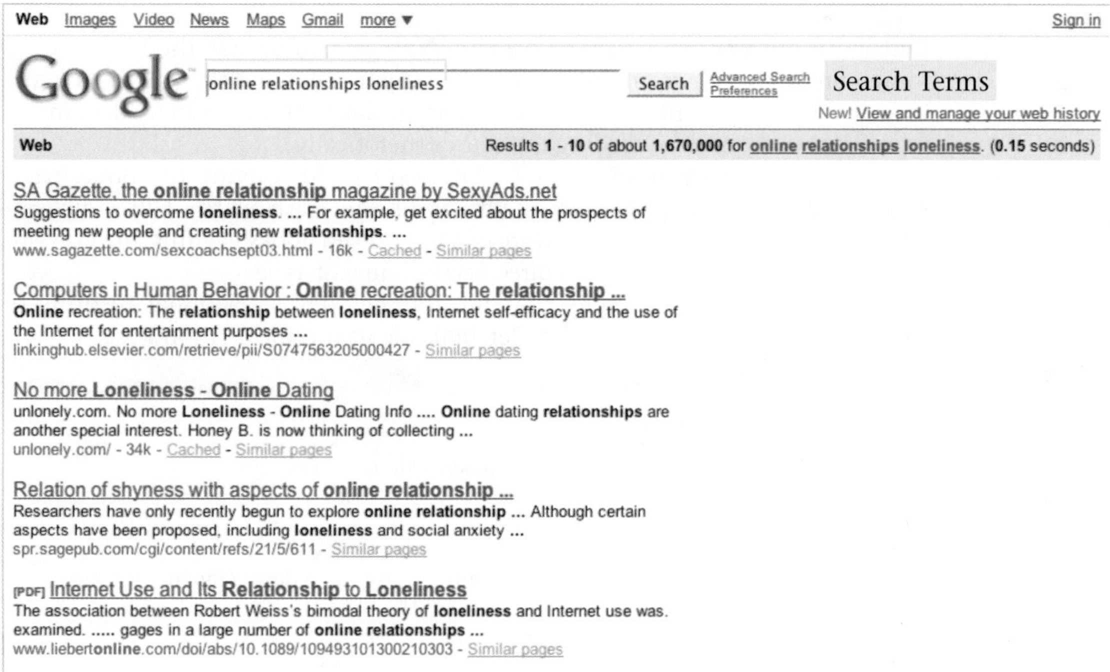

FOR WRITING AND DISCUSSION

Comparing a Licensed Database Search and a Web Search

Working in small groups or as a whole class, see if you can reach consensus on the following questions:

1. How does a licensed database search differ from a Web search? Explain what is being searched in each case.
2. There is no way that James or any other researcher could scroll through more than a million hits. However, just the first five hits on Google (see Figure 19.3) offer interesting possibilities for James's research. Which of these sites might be worth exploring and why? As you look at each hit, pay attention to the URL, as well as to the description, to see if you can predict the kind of organization that sponsors the site. (Skill 20.3 explains in detail how to analyze Web sites.)

Using Web Search Engines Different search engines search the Web in different ways, so it is important that you try a variety of search engines when you look for information. For example, a service offered by Google is "Google Scholar," with which you can limit a Web search to academic or scholarly sources. (But you will still need to turn to your library's collection or licensed databases for a full text of the source.) On campus, reference librarians and disciplinary experts can give you good advice about what has worked well in the past for particular kinds of searches. On the Web, an additional resource is NoodleTools.com, which offers lots of good advice for choosing the best search engine.

Determining Where You Are on the Web As you browse the Web looking for resources, clicking from link to link, try to figure out what site you are actually in at any given moment. This information is crucial, both for properly documenting a Web source and for reading the source rhetorically.

To know where you are on the Web, begin by identifying the home page, which is the material to the left of the first single slash in the URL (universal resource locator). The generic structure of a typical URL looks like this: http://www.servername.domain/directory/subdirectory/filename.filetype

Here is a specific example, the URL for the NINDS (National Institute of Neurological Disorders and Stroke) Cerebral Aneurysm Information Page:

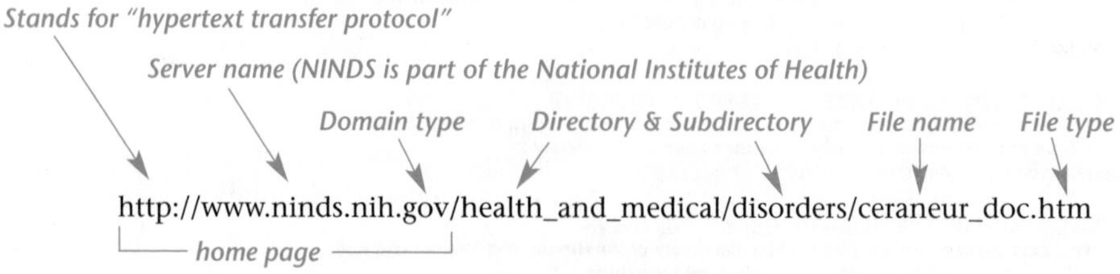

When you click on a link in one site, you may be sent to a totally different site. To determine the home page of this new site, simply note the root URL immediately following the "www."* To view the home page directly, delete the codes to the right of the initial home page URL in your computer's location window and hit Enter. You will then be linked directly to the site's home page, where you may be able to find an "About" link through which you can gather information about the purpose and sponsors of the page. As we discuss in later chapters, being able to examine a site's home page helps you read the site rhetorically and document it properly.

PEARSON mycomplab For support in learning this chapter's content, follow this path in MyCompLab: Resources ⇒ Research ⇒ The Research Assignment ⇒ Finding Sources. Review the Instruction and Multimedia resources about finding sources, and then complete the Exercises and click on Gradebook to measure your progress.

*Not all URLs begin with "www" after the first set of double slashes. Our description doesn't include variations of the most typical URL types. You can generally find the home page of a site by eliminating all codes to the right of the first slash mark after the domain or country name.

20 EVALUATING SOURCES

In Chapter 19, we explained the importance of posing a good research question, of understanding the different kinds of sources, and of using purposeful strategies for searching libraries, databases, and Web sites.

In this chapter, you will learn these additional research skills:

- **SKILL 20.1** Read sources rhetorically and take purposeful notes.
- **SKILL 20.2** Evaluate sources for reliability, credibility, angle of vision, and degree of advocacy.
- **SKILL 20.3** Use your rhetorical knowledge to evaluate Web sources.

SKILL 20.1 Read sources rhetorically and take purposeful notes.

Once you've located a stack of books and magazine or journal articles, it's easy to feel overwhelmed. How do you begin reading all this material? There is no one right answer to this question. At times you need to read slowly with analytical closeness. At other times you can skim a source, looking only for its gist or for a needed piece of information. In this section, we offer some advice on how to read your sources with rhetorical savvy and take notes that will help you write your final paper.

Reading with Your Own Goals in Mind

How you read a source depends to a certain extent on where you are in the research process. Early in the process, when you are in the thesis-seeking, exploratory stage, your goal is to achieve a basic understanding of your research area. You need to become aware of different points of view, learn what is unknown or controversial about your research question, see what values or assumptions are in conflict, and build up your store of background knowledge. As we saw in the case of James Gardiner, one's initial research question often evolves as one's knowledge increases and interests shift.

Given these goals, at the early stages of research you should select "overview" kinds of sources to get you into the conversation. In some cases, even an encyclopedia or specialized reference work can be a good start for getting general background.

As you get deeper into your research, your questions become more focused, and the sources you seek out become more specialized. Once you formulate a thesis and plan a structure for your paper, you can determine more clearly the sources you need. For example, after James Gardiner decided to focus on the negative aspects of online social networks, he began following up leads on Internet addiction, on OSNs as sites for narcissistic display, and on the possible superficiality of online relationships. At the same time he remained open-minded about the psychological and social benefits of OSNs.

Reading Your Sources Rhetorically

To read your sources rhetorically, you should keep two basic questions in mind:

1. What was the source author's purpose in writing this piece?
2. What might be my purpose in using this piece?

Let's begin with the first question. The following chart sums up the strategies you can use to read your sources rhetorically, along with research tips for answering some of the questions you've posed.

Strategies for Reading Your Sources Rhetorically

Questions to Ask	What to Do	Results
• Who is this author? • What are his or her credentials and affiliations?	• Look for the author's credentials at the end of the article or in the contributors' page. • Google the author's name. • In a database results list, click on the author's name for a list of other articles he/she has written.	• Helps you assess author's *ethos* and credibility. • Helps you establish author's angle of vision.
• What is this source's genre? • Who is the intended audience?	• If the source is downloaded, identify the original publication information. • If the source comes from a periodical, look at the print copy for clues about the audience (titles of other articles, ads, document design). • Use Table 19.2 for further clues about audience and genre. • If a Web-only source, see Skill 20.3.	• Helps you further determine the author's angle of vision as well as the source's reliability and credibility. • Helps explain rhetorical features of the source.

(*continued*)

Questions to Ask	What to Do	Results
• What is this author's purpose? • How is this author trying to change his/her audience's view of the topic?	• Determine whether the piece is primarily expressive, informational, analytical, or persuasive. • If the source comes from the Web, who is the site's sponsor? Read the "About us" material on the site's home page. • If it is a print source, determine the reputation and bias of the journal, magazine, or press (see Table 20.1, p. 542).	• Helps you evaluate the source for angle of vision and degree of advocacy. • Helps you decide how you might use the source in your own argument.
• What is this author's angle of vision or bias? • What facts, data, and other evidence does this author cite and what are the sources for the data? • What are this author's underlying values, assumptions, and beliefs? • What is omitted or censored from this text?	• Apply the rhetorical reading strategies explained in Chapter 5. • Evaluate the source for reliability, credibility, angle of vision, and degree of advocacy as explained in Skill 20.2. • If a Web source, evaluate it using strategies explained in Skill 20.3.	• Helps you bring your own critical thinking to bear on your sources. • Keeps your paper intellectually honest and interesting.

This chart reinforces a point we've made throughout this text: All writing is produced from an angle of vision that privileges some ways of seeing and filters out other ways. You should guard against reading your sources as if they present hard, undisputed facts or universal truths. For example, if one of your sources says that "Saint-John's-wort [an herb] has been shown to be an effective treatment for depression," some of your readers might accept that statement as fact; but many wouldn't. Skeptical readers would want to know who the author is, where his views have been published, and what he uses for evidence. Let's say the author is someone named Samuel Jones. Skeptical readers would ask whether Jones is relying on published research, and if so, whether the studies have been peer-reviewed in reputable, scholarly journals and whether the research has been replicated by other scientists. They would also want to know whether Jones has financial connections to companies that produce herbal remedies and supplements. Rather than settling the question about Saint-John's-wort as a treatment for depression, a quotation from Jones might open up a heated controversy about medical research.

Reading rhetorically is thus a way of thinking critically about your sources. It influences the way you take notes, evaluate sources, and shape your argument.

Taking Purposeful Notes

Many beginning researchers opt not to take notes—a serious mistake, in our view. Instead, they simply photocopy or printout articles, perhaps using a highlighter to mark passages. This practice, which experienced researchers almost never use, reduces your ability to engage the ideas in a source, to synthesize different sources, and to find your own voice in a conversation. When you begin drafting your paper, you'll have no bibliographic information, no notes to refer to, no record of your thinking-in-progress. Your only recourse is to revisit all your sources, thumbing through them one at a time—a practice that leads to passive cutting and pasting (and possible plagiarism).

Recording Bibliographic Information To take good research notes, begin by making a bibliographic entry for the source, following the documentation format assigned by your instructor—usually MLA (Modern Language Association) or APA (American Psychological Association). Although you may be tempted to put off doing this mechanical task ("Hey, boring, I can do this documentation stuff later"), there are two reasons to do it immediately:

Chapter 22 explains in detail how to make a bibliographic entry.

- Doing it now, while the source is in front of you, will save you time in the long run. Otherwise, you'll have to try to retrieve the source, in a late-night panic, just before the paper is due.
- Doing it now will make you look at the source rhetorically. Is this a peer-reviewed journal article? A magazine article? An op-ed piece? A blog? Making the bibliographic entry forces you to identify the source's genre.

Recording Ideas and Information and Responding to Each Source To take good research notes, follow the habits for "strong reading" discussed in Chapter 5 by weaving back and forth between two modes of writing:

- ***Your informational notes on each source:*** Summarize each source's argument and record useful information. To avoid the risk of plagiarizing later, make sure that you put quotation marks around any passages that you copy word for word (be sure to copy *exactly*). When you summarize or paraphrase passages, be sure to put the ideas entirely into your own words.
- ***Your own exploratory notes as you think of ideas:*** Write down your own ideas as they occur to you. Record your thinking-in-progress as you mull over and speak back to your sources.

For more on quoting, summarizing, and paraphrasing sources, see Skill 21.2.

An approach that encourages both modes of writing is to keep a dialectic or double-entry journal. Divide a page in half; enter your informational notes on one side and your exploratory writing on the other. If you use a computer, you can put your informational notes in one font and your own exploratory writing in another.

An example of double-entry notes appears in Chapter 7, pp. 159–160.

Taking effective notes is different from the mechanical process of copying out passages or simply listing facts and information. Rather, make your notes purposeful by imagining how you might use a given source in your research paper. The following chart shows the different functions that research sources might play in your argument and highlights appropriate note-taking strategies for each function.

Strategies for Taking Notes According to Purpose

Function that Source Might Play in Your Argument	Strategies for Informational Notes	Strategies for Exploratory Notes
Provides background about your problem or issue	• Summarize the information. • Record specific facts and figures useful for background.	• Speculate on how much background your readers will need.
Gives an alternative view that you will mention briefly	• Summarize the source's argument in a couple of sentences; note its bias and perspective. • Identify brief quotations that sum up the source's perspective.	• Jot down ideas on how and why different sources disagree. • Begin making an idea map of alternative views.
Provides an alternative or opposing view that you might summarize fully and respond to	• Summarize the article fully and fairly (see Chapter 5 on summary writing). • Note the kinds of evidence used.	• Speculate about why you disagree with the source and whether you can refute the argument, concede to it, or compromise with it. • Explore what research you'll need to support your own argument.
Provides information or testimony that you might use as evidence	• Record the data or information. • If using authorities for testimony, quote short passages. • Note the credentials of the writer or person quoted.	• Record new ideas as they occur to you. • Continue to think purposefully about additional research you'll need.

Function that Source Might Play in Your Argument	Strategies for Informational Notes	Strategies for Exploratory Notes
Mentions information or testimony that counters your position or raises doubts about your argument	• Note counterevidence. • Note authorities who disagree with you.	• Speculate how you might respond to counterevidence.
Provides a theory or method that influences your approach to the issue	• Note credentials of the author. • Note passages that sparked ideas.	• Freewrite about how the source influences your method or approach.

SKILL 20.2 **Evaluate sources for reliability, credibility, angle of vision, and degree of advocacy.**

When you read sources for your research project, you need to evaluate them as you go along. As you read each potential source, ask yourself questions about the author's reliability, credibility, angle of vision, and degree of advocacy.

Reliability

"Reliability" refers to the accuracy of factual data in a source. If you check a writer's "facts" against other sources, do you find that the facts are correct? Does the writer distort facts, take them out of context, or otherwise use them unreasonably? In some controversies, key data are highly disputed—for example, the frequency of date rape or the risk factors for many diseases. A reliable writer acknowledges these controversies and doesn't treat disputed data as fact. Furthermore, if you check out the sources used by a reliable writer, they'll reveal accurate and careful research—respected primary sources rather than hearsay or secondhand reports. Journalists of reputable newspapers (not tabloids) pride themselves on meticulously checking out their facts, as do editors of serious popular magazines. Editing is often minimal for Web sources, however, and they can be notoriously unreliable. As you gain knowledge of your research question, you'll develop a good ear for writers who play fast and loose with data.

Credibility

"Credibility" is similar to "reliability" but is based on internal rather than external factors. It refers to the reader's trust in the writer's honesty, goodwill, and trustworthiness and is apparent in the writer's tone, reasonableness, fairness in summarizing opposing views, and respect for different perspectives. Audiences differ in how much credibility they will grant to certain authors. Nevertheless, a writer can achieve a reputation for credibility, even among bitter political opponents, by applying to issues a sense of moral courage, integrity, and consistency of principle.

"Credibility" is synonymous with the classical term *ethos*. See pp. 58–59 and 348–349.

Angle of vision is discussed in detail in Chapter 3, Concept 8. See also Chapter 5, pp. 104–106, which shows how analyzing angle of vision helps you read a text with and against the grain.

Angle of Vision and Political Stance

By "angle of vision," we mean the way that a piece of writing is shaped by the underlying values, assumptions, and beliefs of its author, resulting in a text that reflects a certain perspective, worldview, or belief system. Of paramount importance are the underlying values or beliefs that the writer assumes his or her readers will share. You can get useful clues about a writer's angle of vision and intended audience by doing some quick research into the politics and reputation of the author on the Internet or by analyzing the genre, market niche, and political reputation of the publication in which the material appears.

Determining Political Stance Your awareness of angle of vision and political stance is especially important if you are doing research on contemporary cultural or political issues. In Table 20.1, we have categorized some well-known political commentators, publications, policy research institutes (commonly known as *think tanks*), and blogs across the political spectrum from left/liberal to right/conservative.

TABLE 20.1 Angles of Vision in U.S. Media and Think Tanks: A Sampling Across the Political Spectrum[1]

Commentators

Left	Left Center	Center	Right Center	Right
Barbara Ehrenreich	E. J. Dionne	David Ignatius	David Brooks	Charles Krauthammer
Bob Herbert	Leonard Pitts	Thomas Friedman	Peggy Noonan	Cal Thomas
Michael Moore (film-maker)	Eugene Robinson	Kathleen Hall Jamieson	Jonah Goldberg	Glenn Beck (radio/TV)
Bill Moyers (television)	Nicholas Kristof	Kevin Phillips	Andrew Sullivan	Rush Limbaugh (radio/TV)
Paul Krugman	Maureen Dowd	David Broder	George Will	Bill O'Reilly (radio/TV)
Thom Hartman (radio)	Mark Shields	William Saletan	Ruben Navarrette, Jr.	Kathleen Parker
Rachel Maddow (radio)	Frank Rich	Mary Sanchez		Thomas Sowell

Newspapers and Magazines[2]

Left/Liberal	Center	Right/Conservative
The American Prospect	*Atlantic Monthly*	*American Spectator*
Harper's	*Business Week*	*Fortune*
Los Angeles Times	*Commentary*	*National Review*
Mother Jones	*Commonweal*	*Reader's Digest*
The Nation	*Foreign Affairs*	*Reason*
New York Times	*New Republic*	*Wall Street Journal*
New Yorker	*Slate*	*Washington Times*
Salon	*Washington Post*	*Weekly Standard*
Sojourners		

TABLE 20.1 *continued*

Blogs

Liberal/Left	Center	Right/Conservative
americablog.com	donklephant.com	conservativeblogger.com
atrios.blogspot.com	newmoderate.blogspot.com	drudgereport.com
crooksandliars.com	politics-central.blogspot.com	instapundit.com
dailykos.com	rantingbaldhippie.com	littlegreenfootballs.com
digbysblog.blogspot.com	stevesilver.net	michellemalkin.com
firedoglake.com	themoderatevoice.com	polipundit.com
huffingtonpost.com	washingtonindependent.com	powerlineblog.com
mediamatters.com	watchingwashington.blogspot.com	sistertoldjah.com
talkingpointsmemo.com		redstate.com
wonkette.com		townhall.com

Think Tanks

Left/Liberal	Center	Right/Conservative
Center for American Progress	The Brookings Institution	American Enterprise Institute
Center for Media and Democracy (sponsors Disinfopedia.org)	Carnegie Endowment for International Peace	Cato Institute (Libertarian)
Institute for Policy Studies	Council on Foreign Relations	Center for Strategic and International Studies
Open Society Institute (Soros Foundation)	Jamestown Foundation	Heritage Foundation (sponsors Townhall.com)
Progressive Policy Institute	National Bureau of Economic Research	Project for the New American Century
Urban Institute		

[1] *For further information about the political leanings of publications or think tanks, ask your librarian about* Gale Directory of Publications and Broadcast Media *or* NIRA World Directory of Think Tanks.

[2] *Newspapers are categorized according to positions they take on their editorial page; any reputable newspaper strives for objectivity in news reporting and includes a variety of views on its op-ed pages. Magazines do not claim and are not expected to present similar breadth and objectivity.*

Although the terms *liberal* and *conservative* or *left* and *right* often have fuzzy meanings, they provide convenient shorthand for signaling a person's overall views about the proper role of government in relation to the economy and social values. Liberals, tending to sympathize with those potentially harmed by unfettered free markets (workers, consumers, plaintiffs, endangered species), are typically comfortable with government regulation of economic matters while conservatives, who tend to sympathize with business interests, typically assert faith in free markets and favor a limited regulatory role for government. On social issues, conservatives tend to espouse traditional family values and advocate laws that would maintain these values (for example, promoting a Constitutional amendment limiting marriage to a bond between a man and a woman). Liberals, on the other hand, tend to espouse individual choice regarding marital partnerships and a wide range of other issues. Some persons identify themselves as economic conservatives but social liberals; others side with workers' interests on economic issues but are conservative on social issues.

Finally, many persons regard themselves as "centrists." In Table 20.1 the column labeled "Center" includes commentators who seek out common ground between the left and the right and who often believe that the best civic decisions are compromises between opposing views. Likewise, centrist publications and institutes often approach issues from multiple points of view, looking for the most workable solutions.

Degree of Advocacy

By "degree of advocacy" we mean the extent to which an author unabashedly takes a persuasive stance on a contested position as opposed to adopting a more neutral, objective, or exploratory stance. For example, publications affiliated with advocacy organizations (the Sierra Club, the National Rifle Association) will have a clear editorial bias. When a writer has an ax to grind, you need to weigh carefully the writer's selection of evidence, interpretation of data, and fairness to opposing views. Although no one can be completely neutral, it is always useful to seek out authors who offer a balanced assessment of the evidence. Evidence from a more detached and neutral writer may be more trusted by your readers than the arguments of a committed advocate. For example, if you want to persuade corporate executives on the dangers of global warming, evidence from scholarly journals may be more persuasive than evidence from an environmentalist Web site or from a freelance writer for a leftist popular magazine such as *Mother Jones*.

SKILL 20.3 **Use your rhetorical knowledge to evaluate Web sources.**

In the previous section we focused on reading sources rhetorically by asking questions about a source's reliability, credibility, angle of vision, and degree of advocacy. In this section we focus on evaluating sources from the World Wide Web.

The Web as a Unique Rhetorical Environment

In addition to familiar entertainment and commercial sites, the Web can provide access to highly specialized data banks, historical archives, government documents, blogosphere commentary, scholarly portals useful for academic researchers, and much more. The Web is also a great vehicle for democracy, giving voice to the otherwise voiceless. Anyone with a cause and a rudimentary knowledge of Web design can create a site. The result is a rhetorical medium that differs in significant ways from print.

Consider, for example, the difference in the way writers attract readers. Magazines displayed on racks attract readers through interest-grabbing covers and teaser headlines inviting readers to look inside. Web sites, however, can't begin attracting readers until the readers have found them through links from another site or through a "hit" from a Web search. Research suggests that Web surfers stay connected to a site for no more than thirty seconds unless something immediately attracts their interest; moreover, they seldom scroll down to see the bottom of a page. The design of a home page—the arrangement and size of the print, the use of images and colors, the locations and labels of navigational buttons—must hook readers immediately and send a clear message about the purpose and contents of the site. If the home page is a confused jumble or simply a long, printed text, the average surfer will take one look and move on.

The biggest difference between the Web and print is the Web's hypertext structure. Users click from link to link rather than read linearly down the page. Users often "read" a Web page as a configuration of images and strategically arranged text that is interspersed with bullets, boxes, and hot links. Long stretches of linear text are usually found only deep within a site, usually through links to .pdf files or other archived or posted documents.

Criteria for Evaluating a Web Source

When you evaluate a Web source, we suggest that you ask five different kinds of questions about the site in which the source appeared, as shown in Table 20.2. These questions, developed by scholars and librarians as points to consider when

TABLE 20.2 Criteria for Evaluating Web Sites

Criteria	Questions to Ask
1. Authority	• Is the document author or site sponsor clearly identified? • Does the site identify the occupation, position, education, experience, or other credentials of the author? • Does the home page or a clear link from the home page reveal the author's or sponsor's motivation for establishing the site? • Does the site provide contact information for the author or sponsor such as an e-mail or organization address?
2. Objectivity or Clear Disclosure of Advocacy	• Is the site's purpose clear (for example, to inform, entertain, or persuade)? • Is the site explicit about declaring its point of view? • Does the site indicate whether the author is affiliated with a specific organization, institution, or association? • Does the site indicate whether it is directed toward a specific audience?
3. Coverage	• Are the topics covered by the site clear? • Does the site exhibit a suitable depth and comprehensiveness for its purpose? • Is sufficient evidence provided to support the ideas and opinions presented?
4. Accuracy	• Are the sources of information stated? • Do the facts appear to be accurate? • Can you verify this information by comparing this source with other sources in the field?
5. Currency	• Are dates included in the Web site? • Do the dates apply to the material itself, to its placement on the Web, or to the time the site was last revised and updated? • Is the information current, or at least still relevant, for the site's purpose? For your purpose?

you are evaluating Web sites, will help you determine the usefulness of a site or source for your own purposes.

See Chapter 14, pp. 398–400, for Teresa Filice's essay evaluating the advocacy site "Parents: The Anti-Drug."

As a researcher, the first question you should ask about a potentially useful Web source should be, Who placed this piece on the Web and why? You can begin answering this question by analyzing the site's home page, where you will often find navigational buttons linking to "Mission," "About Us," or other identifying information about the site's sponsors. You can also get hints about the site's purpose by asking, What kind of Web site is it? Different kinds of Web sites have different purposes, often revealed by the domain identifier following the server name:

- ***.com sites:*** These are commercial sites designed to promote a business's image, attract customers, market products and services, and provide customer service. Their angle of vision is to promote the view of the corporation or business. Often material has no identified author. (The sponsoring company is often cited as the author.)
- ***.org sites:*** These are sites for nonprofit organizations or advocacy groups. Some sites provide accurate, balanced information related to the organization's mission work (Red Cross, World Vision), while others promote political views (Heritage Foundation) or advocate a cause (Persons for the Ethical Treatment of Animals).
- ***.edu sites:*** These sites are associated with a college or university. Home pages aim to attract prospective students and donors and provide a portal into the site. Numerous subsites are devoted to research, pedagogy, libraries, and so forth. The angle of vision can vary from strong advocacy on issues (a student paper, an on-campus advocacy group) to the objective and scholarly (a university research site).
- ***.gov or .mil sites:*** These sites are sponsored by a government agency or military units. They can provide a range of basic data about government policy, bills in Congress, economic forecasts, census data, and so forth. Their angle of vision varies from objective informational sites to sites that promote the agency's agenda.

Analyzing Your Own Purposes for Using a Web Source

Besides analyzing a sponsor's purpose for establishing a Web site, you also need to analyze your own purpose for using the site. To illustrate strategies for evaluating a Web site, we'll use as examples two hypothetical student researchers who are interested in the civic controversy over gun control. In both cases, the students are particularly interested in women's concerns about gun control.

Our first student researcher asked the question, "How are women represented and involved in the public controversy over gun control?" She did an initial Google search using "women gun control" as keywords and found dozens of pro-gun and anti-gun sites sponsored by women or by women's organizations. The home page of one such site, sponsored by the organization Women Against Gun Control, is shown on the opening page of Part 4 (p. 515). Fascinated by the Annie Oakley–like image (gun-toting cowgirl) on this home page, our researcher decided to focus her project on the ways that women depict themselves on pro-gun and anti-gun sites and on the kinds of arguments they make. These Web sites thus became primary sources for this student's project.

Our second researcher was more directly interested in determining her own stance in the gun control debate. She was trying to decide, from a woman's perspective, whether to advocate for gun control laws or to oppose gun control—whether even to join the National Rifle Association (NRA) and perhaps buy a gun and learn to shoot. As a researcher, her dilemma was how much she could use data about guns, crime, firearm accidents, and violence against women obtained from these sites. The sites for her were mostly secondary rather than primary sources.*

Let's look at each student's research process in turn.

Researcher 1: Using Women and Guns Web Sites for Rhetorical Analysis Our first student quickly found herself immersed in a vigorous national conversation on gun control by women's groups and by traditionally male-dominated groups seeking support or membership from women. Her research goal was to analyze these sites rhetorically to understand the ways that women frame their interests and represent themselves. She discovered that the angle of vision of each kind of site—whether pro-gun or anti-gun—led to the filtering of evidence in distinctive ways. For example, anti-gun women's groups emphasized accidental deaths from guns (particularly of children), suicides from easy access to guns, domestic violence turned deadly, guns in schools, and gun-related crime (particularly juvenile crime). In contrast, pro-gun women's groups emphasized armed resistance to assaults and rapes, inadequate police responses to crime, the right of individuals to protect themselves and their families, and the Second Amendment right to keep and bear arms. (Women's pro-gun sites often framed the gun control issue as pro-self-defense versus anti-self-defense.) She also noted that most of these sites made powerful use of visual elements—icons, colors (bright pink in particular), and well-known symbols—to enhance their emotional appeals. For instance, pro-gun sites often had patriotic themes with images of waving American flags, stern-eyed eagles, and colonial patriots with muskets. Anti-gun sites often had pictures of young children, with an emphasis on innocence, childhood fun, and family.

Researcher 1 noted that many of these sites tailored their appeals directly to women. The most well-known of the anti-gun sites is the Million Mom March Organization, which describes itself (on the "About us" link) as "the nation's largest, non-partisan, grassroots organization leading the fight to prevent gun violence. ..." Its mission statement ends with these words; "With one loud voice, we will continue to cry out that we love our children more than the gun lobby loves its guns." In Figure 20.1, we have reproduced some images, text boxes for anecdotes, and "fact statements" from this site's home page.

*The terms *primary* and *secondary* sources are relative terms often used by researchers to differentiate between original data (primary sources) and data filtered through another researcher's perspective (secondary sources) (see pages 323–324). Thus the Women Against Gun Control site (p. 515) is a primary source for someone doing a rhetorical analysis of gun Web sites, but it is a secondary source for statistical data about gun violence.

FIGURE 20.1 Images, Anecdotes, and Fact Statements from the Million Mom March Home Page (www.millionmommarch.org)

For Researcher 1, it is evident that both this site and the Women Against Gun Control site, as well as other pro-gun or anti-gun sites, are useful and relevant for her purpose of analyzing rhetorically how women are portrayed in the Second Amendment debate.

FOR WRITING AND DISCUSSION

Analyzing the Rhetorical Elements of Two Home Pages

Working in small groups or as a whole class, try to reach consensus answers to the following questions about how Web sites seek to draw in readers. Use the illustrations on pages 515 and 548.

1. How are the images of women in the Women Against Gun Control site different from those on the Million Mom March page? How do pieces of text (such as "Ladies of High-Caliber" on the Women Against Gun Control site or one of the "facts" on the Million Mom March site) contribute to the visual-verbal effects of the home pages?
2. In the Women Against Gun Control (WAGC) page, what seems to be the Web designer's intention in the use of color, curved background lines, and images?
3. How does the home page for each site use *logos, ethos,* and *pathos* to sway readers toward its point of view?

Researcher 2: Using Women and Guns Web Sites for Data on Guns and Gun Violence Researcher 2 intends to create her own research-based argument on whether women should support or oppose gun control. Her dilemma is this: To what extent can she use "facts" appearing on these sites (such as the statement on the Women Against Gun Control site that "guns are used defensively 2.5 million times per year")?

She frequently encountered equivalent kinds of pithy statistical statements. In her initial Web search, she found an article entitled "Women Are the Real Victims of Handgun Control" by Kelly Ann Connolly, who was identified as the director of the Nevada State Rifle and Pistol Association. The site, www.armedandsafe.com, included a biographical note identifying Connolly as a public school teacher with a master's degree.

Connolly argues that a woman can walk confidently down any street in America if she is carrying a concealed weapon and is skilled in using it. She offers as support anecdotes of women who fought off rapists and cites numerous statistics, attributing the sources to "Bureau of Justice Statistics (1999)." Here are some examples from her article:

- 3 out of 4 American women will be a victim of violent crime at least once in their lifetime.
- 2 million women are raped each year, one every 15 seconds.
- Rapists know they have only a 1 in 605 chance of being caught, charged, convicted, and sentenced to serving time.

The purpose of these statistics is to increase women's anxiety about the prevalence of rape and other violent crimes and to reduce women's confidence in the police or justice system to protect them. The implied solution is to buy a pistol and learn how to use it.

How should our second researcher proceed in evaluating such an article for her own research purposes? Her first step is to evaluate the site itself. She found the home page by deleting extensions from the URL and looking directly at the home page (www.armedandsafe.com), which turned out to be the commercial site for a firing range that provided lessons in the use of rifles, pistols, and machine guns. The site obviously advocated Second Amendment rights and promoted gun ownership as a means of domestic and personal security. The images on the home page, showing a fierce eagle emerging from a collage of the American flag, the burning World Trade Center towers, and an aircraft carrier, were meant to reflect the patriotic sentiments that tend to dominate pro-gun Web sites. Researcher 2 could easily evaluate this site against the five criteria:

1. **Authority:** She could clearly tell that this was the commercial site of a firing range.
2. **Advocacy:** The site clearly advocated Second Amendment rights and gun ownership.
3. **Coverage:** The site did not cover gun-control issues in a complex way. Every aspect of the site was filtered to support its pro-gun vision.
4. **Accuracy:** At this point she was unable to check the accuracy of the site's data against other sources, but she assumed that all data would be rhetorically filtered and selected to promote the site's angle of vision.
5. **Currency:** Both anecdotal and statistical data were dated, taken primarily from the 1990s.

Based on this analysis, how might Researcher 2 use Connolly's article from this site? Our view is that the article could be very useful as one perspective on the gun-control controversy. It is a fairly representative example of the argument that guns can increase a woman's sense of confidence and well-being, and it clearly shows the kinds of rhetorical strategies such articles use—statistics on rape, descriptions of guns as equalizers in empowering women, and so forth. A summary of this article's argument could therefore be effective for presenting the pro-gun point of view.

As a source of factual data, however, the article is unusable. It would be irresponsible for her to claim that "3 out of 4 American women will be a victim of violent crime at least once in their lifetime" and to cite Connolly's article as an authoritative source. (Similarly, she would be irresponsible to claim that "a person is killed by a gun every 17 minutes in America" and give the Million Mom March site as a source.) Researcher 2 should instead look at primary data on crime statistics and guns compiled by trustworthy sources such as the Department of Justice, the FBI, state police departments, or peer-reviewed research by scholars (government statistics are all easily available from the Web). One purpose of reading sources rhetorically is to appreciate how much advocates for a given position will filter data. Trying to find the original data and to interpret it for yourself are two of the challenges of responsible research.

FOR WRITING AND DISCUSSION

Unpacking Factoids in Advocacy Web Sites

Consider the following two "factoids" from the sites we have just discussed:

Factoid 1: "3 out of 4 American women will be a victim of violent crime at least once in their lifetime." [from the Connolly article "Women Are the Real Victims of Handgun Control"]

Factoid 2: "A person is killed by a gun every 17 minutes in America." [from the Million Mom March home page]

Working individually or in small groups, try to reach consensus on the following questions. (When doing your own back-of-the-envelope calculations, consider the population of the United States to be 300 million people, with half of those being women.)

1. Based on the two primary sources shown here below, try to determine
   a. how these factoids were computed.
   b. how accurate they seem to be.

***SOURCE 1:* DATA ON VIOLENT CRIME RATES BY GENDER OF VICTIM, 1973–2003**

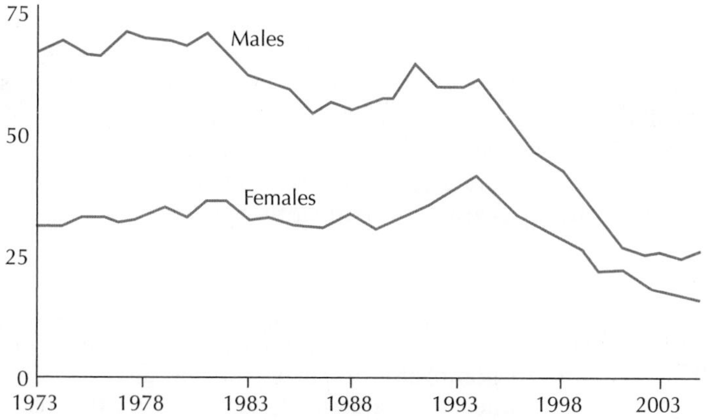

Adjusted victimization rate per 1,000 persons age 12 and over.
The violent crimes included are rape, robbery, aggravated and simple assault, and homicide.

Source: Bureau of Justice Statistics, Department of Justice (http://ojp.usdoj.gov/bjs/glance/vsx2.htm).

***SOURCE 2:* DATA ON DEATH BY FIREARMS**

Firearm—In 2003, 30,136 persons died from firearm injuries in the United States (. . .), accounting for 18.4 percent of all injury deaths in 2003. Firearm suicide and homicide, the two major component causes, accounted for 56.1 and 39.6 percent, respectively, of all firearm injury deaths in 2003. In 2003, the age-adjusted death rate for firearm injuries was 10.3 deaths per 100,000 U.S. standard population. Males had an age-adjusted rate that was 6.8 times that for females,

(*continued*)

the black population had a rate that was 2.1 times that of the white population, and the non-Hispanic population had a rate that was 1.3 times that of the Hispanic population (. . .). The decrease between 2002 and 2003 in the age-adjusted death rate for firearm injuries was not statistically significant (. . .).

Source: Centers for Disease Control and Prevention. "Deaths: Final Data for 2003." *National Vital Statistics Reports* 54.13 (2006). 2 Sept. 2007 <http://www.cdc.gov/nchs/data/nvsr/nvsr54/nvsr54_13.pdf>.

2. Why do the factoids on each site have a different rhetorical impact than the original data displayed in statistical graphs and tables would? How do the factoids spin raw data in favor of a certain angle of vision?
3. Why do we say that Researcher 2 would be irresponsible if she used either the Connolly article or the Million Mom March Web site as a source of data on gun issues?
4. Note in the graph on violent crime (Source 1 above) how sharply crime rates fell from 1993 to 2003. Scholars have debated extensively the causes of this decline. How does this graph suggest the importance of "currency" when evaluating evidence?

In this chapter we have focused on evaluating sources, particularly on reading sources rhetorically and taking purposeful notes; on evaluating sources for reliability, credibility, angle of vision, and degree of advocacy; and on using your rhetorical knowledge to evaluate Web sources. In the next chapters, we turn to the skills you will need to incorporate your sources into your own prose and to cite and document them according to academic conventions.

PEARSON mycomplab

For support in learning this chapter's content, follow this path in MyCompLab: Resources ⇒ Research ⇒ The Research Assignment ⇒ Evaluating Sources. Review the Instruction and Multimedia resources about evaluating sources, and then complete the Exercises and click on Gradebook to measure your progress.

INCORPORATING SOURCES INTO YOUR OWN WRITING

21

So far, we have covered strategies for finding and evaluating sources. Now we focus on the skills needed for incorporating sources into your own writing.

In this chapter, you will learn the following skills:

- **SKILL 21.1** Let your own argument determine your use of sources.
- **SKILL 21.2** Know when and how to use summary, paraphrase, and quotation.
- **SKILL 21.3** Use attributive tags to distinguish your ideas from a source's.
- **SKILL 21.4** Punctuate quotations correctly.
- **SKILL 21.5** Avoid plagiarism by following academic conventions for ethical use of sources.

Many of the examples in this chapter will be based on the following short article about violence in the Old West. This chapter will be most useful to you if you read the article first.

Roger D. McGrath

The Myth of Violence in the Old West*

1 It is commonly assumed that violence is part of our frontier heritage. But the historical record shows that frontier violence was very different from violence today. Robbery and burglary, two of our most common crimes, were of no great significance in the frontier towns of the Old West, and rape was seemingly nonexistent.

2 Bodie, one of the principal towns on the trans-Sierra frontier, illustrates the point. Nestled high in the mountains of eastern California, Bodie, which boomed in the late 1870s and early 1880s, ranked among the most notorious frontier towns of the Old West. It was, as one prospector put it, the last of the old-time mining camps.

*From Roger D. McGrath, "The Myth of Violence in the Old West," *Gunfighters, Highwaymen, and Vigilantes: Violence on the Frontier*. Regents of the University of California, 1984.

3 Like the trans-Sierra frontier in general, Bodie was indisputably violent and lawless, yet most people were not affected. Fistfights and gunfights among willing combatants—gamblers, miners, and the like—were regular events, and stagecoach holdups were not unusual. But the old, the young, the weak, and the female—so often the victims of crime today—were generally not harmed.

4 Robbery was more often aimed at stagecoaches than at individuals. Highwaymen usually took only the express box and left the passengers alone. There were eleven stagecoach robberies in Bodie between 1878 and 1882, and in only two instances were passengers robbed. (In one instance, the highwaymen later apologized for their conduct.)

5 There were only ten robberies and three attempted robberies of individuals in Bodie during its boom years, and in nearly every case the circumstances were the same: the victim had spent the evening in a gambling den, saloon, or brothel; he had revealed that he had on his person a significant sum of money; and he was staggering home drunk when the attack occurred.

6 Bodie's total of twenty-one robberies—eleven of stages and ten of individuals—over a five-year period converts to a rate of eighty-four robberies per 100,000 inhabitants per year. On this scale—the same scale used by the FBI to index crime—New York City's robbery rate in 1980 was 1,140, Miami's was 995, and Los Angeles's was 628. The rate for the United States as a whole was 243. Thus Bodie's robbery rate was significantly below the national average in 1980.

7 Perhaps the greatest deterrent to crime in Bodie was the fact that so many people were armed. Armed guards prevented bank robberies and holdups of stagecoaches carrying shipments of bullion, and armed homeowners and merchants discouraged burglary. Between 1878 and 1882, there were only thirty-two burglaries—seventeen of homes and fifteen of businesses—in Bodie. At least a half-dozen burglaries were thwarted by the presence of armed citizens. The newspapers regularly advocated shooting burglars on sight, and several burglars were, in fact, shot at.

8 Using the FBI scale, Bodie's burglary rate for those five years was 128. Miami's rate in 1980 was 3,282, New York's was 2,661, and Los Angeles's was 2,602. The rate of the United States as a whole was 1,668, thirteen times that of Bodie.

9 Bodie's law enforcement institutions were certainly not responsible for these low rates. Rarely were robbers or burglars arrested, and even less often were they convicted. Moreover, many law enforcement officers operated on both sides of the law.

10 It was the armed citizens themselves who were the most potent—though not the only—deterrent to larcenous crime. Another was the threat of vigilantism. Highwaymen, for example, understood that while they could take the express box from a stagecoach without arousing the citizens, they risked inciting the entire populace to action if they robbed the passengers.

11 There is considerable evidence that women in Bodie were rarely the victims of crime. Between 1878 and 1882 only one woman, a prostitute, was robbed, and there were no reported cases of rape. (There is no evidence that rapes occurred but were not reported.)

12 Finally, juvenile crime, which accounts for a significant portion of the violent crime in the United States today, was limited in Bodie to pranks and malicious mischief.

13 If robbery, burglary, crimes against women, and juvenile crime were relatively rare on the trans-Sierra frontier, homicide was not: thirty-one Bodieites were shot, stabbed, or beaten to death during the boom years, for a homicide rate of 116. No U.S. city today comes close to this rate. In 1980, Miami led the nation with a homicide rate of 32.7; Las Vegas was a distant second at 23.4. A half-dozen cities had rates of zero. The rate for the United States as a whole in that year was a mere 10.2.

14 Several factors contributed to Bodie's high homicide rate. A majority of the town's residents were young, adventurous, single males who adhered to a code of conduct that frequently required them to fight even if, or perhaps especially if, it could mean death. Courage was admired above all else. Alcohol also played a major role in fostering the settlement of disputes by violence.

15 If the men's code of conduct and their consumption of alcohol made fighting inevitable, their sidearms often made it fatal. While the carrying of guns probably reduced the incidence of robbery and burglary, it undoubtedly increased the number of homicides.

16 For the most part, the citizens of Bodie were not troubled by the great number of killings; nor were they troubled that only one man was ever convicted of murder. They accepted the killings and the lack of convictions because most of those killed had been willing combatants.

17 Thus the violence and lawlessness of the trans-Sierra frontier bear little relation to the violence and lawlessness that pervade American society today. If Bodie is at all representative of frontier towns, there is little justification for blaming contemporary American violence on our frontier heritage.

SKILL 21.1 Let your own argument determine your use of sources.

For effective college-level research, your own argument should govern your use of sources. How you incorporate a research source into your own paper—whether, for example, you summarize it fully or simply draw a few pieces of factual information from it—depends on your own purpose. As an illustration, consider how three hypothetical writers might use Roger D. McGrath's article "The Myth of Violence in the Old West." In each case, the writer's goal is not to reproduce McGrath's article but to use the article in support of the writer's own argument.

Writer 1: An Analytical Paper on Causes of Violence in Contemporary Society

The first writer is analyzing the causes of violence in contemporary U.S. society. She wants to reject one possible cause—that contemporary violence is a direct outgrowth of our violent past. To make this point, she summarizes McGrath's argument that the Old West was not as violent as most people think. This summary then becomes evidence for her own argument.

> *Identification of source*
> *Summary of McGrath's argument*
> *Page number of original material*
> *Writer 1's own argument*

Many people believe that our Wild West heritage is one of the causes of contemporary violence. But Roger McGrath, in his article "The Myth of Violence in the Old West," shows that today's violence is much different from frontier violence. He explains that in a typical frontier town, violence involved gunslingers who were "willing combatants," whereas today's typical victims—"the old, the young, the weak, and the female"—were unaffected by crime (554). Because the presence of an armed populace deterred robbery and burglary, theft was much less common in the Old West than today. On the other hand, McGrath explains, killings were fueled by guns, alcohol, and a code of conduct that invited fighting, so murders were much more frequent than in any U.S. city today (555). Thus, according to McGrath, there is little resemblance between violence on the frontier and violence in today's cities, so we cannot blame current violence on a tumultuous frontier past.

In this passage the author summarizes McGrath's argument in order to refute the violent frontier theory about the causes of contemporary violence. This author will proceed to other causes of violence and will not return to McGrath.

Writer 2: A Persuasive Paper Supporting Gun Control

In our next case, the writer uses McGrath's article to argue in favor of gun control. The writer wants to refute the popular pro-gun argument that law-abiding citizens need to be armed to protect themselves against criminals.

> *Identification of source*
> *Data from McGrath's article*
> *Page number in original*
> *Writer 2's own analysis of the data and his argument*

Opponents of gun control often argue that guns benefit society by providing protection against intruders. But such protection is deadly, as Roger McGrath shows in his study of violence in the frontier town of Bodie, California. Although guns reduced theft, as seen in the low rate of theft in the well-armed town of Bodie, the presence of guns also led to a homicide rate far above that of the most violent city in the U.S. today. The homicide rate in the frontier town of Bodie, California, for example, was 116 per 100,000, compared to the current national average of 10.2 per 100,000 (555). True, Bodie citizens reduced the theft rate by being heavily armed, but at a cost of a homicide rate more than ten times the current national average. To protect our consumer goods at the cost of so much human life is counter to the values of most Americans.

McGrath's article contains data (low rate of crimes against property, high homicide rate) that can be used on either side of the gun control debate. This writer acknowledges the evidence from Bodie showing that gun possession reduces theft and then works that potentially damaging information into an argument for gun control. How might you use the McGrath article to oppose gun control?

Writer 3: An Informative Paper Showing Shifting Definitions of Crime

The third writer summarizes part of McGrath's article to support her thesis that a community's definition of crime is constantly shifting.

> Our notion of criminal activity shifts over time. For example, only a short time ago on the American frontier, murder was often ignored by law enforcement. Roger McGrath, in his discussion of violence in the frontier town of Bodie, California, during the 1870s and 1880s, showed that the townspeople accepted homicides as long as both the murderer and the victim were "willing combatants" who freely participated in gunfights (554). These young males who were the "willing combatants" in Bodie share many characteristics with modern gang members in that they were encouraged to fight by a "code of conduct." According to McGrath, "A majority of the town's residents were young, adventurous, single males who adhered to a code of conduct that frequently required them to fight even if . . . it could mean death" (555). Today's gang members also follow a code of conduct that requires violence—often in the form of vengeance. Although joining a gang certainly makes youths "willing combatants," that status doesn't prevent prosecution in court. Today's "willing combatants" are criminals, but yesterday's "willing combatants" were not.

Identification of source

Partial summary of McGrath's article

Page number

Writer draws comparisons with modern criminals.

Quotation from McGrath's article

Writer extends her comparison.

This writer uses McGrath's article to make a point completely different from McGrath's. But by extending and applying information from McGrath's article to a new context, the writer gathers fuel for her own argument about shifting definitions of the word *criminal*.

FOR WRITING AND DISCUSSION

Using Sources for a Purpose

Each of the hypothetical writers uses McGrath's article for a different purpose. Working individually or in groups, answer the following questions.

1. What are the differences in the ways the writers use the original article?
2. How are these differences related to differences in each writer's purpose?

SKILL 21.2 Know when and how to use summary, paraphrase, and quotation.

For an explanation of plagiarism in academic writing and a summary of how to avoid plagiarism, see Skill 21.5. For making in-text citations, see Chapter 22.

As a research writer, you need to incorporate sources gracefully into your own prose so that you stay focused on your own argument. Depending on your purpose, you might (1) summarize all or part of a source author's argument, (2) paraphrase a relevant portion of a source, or (3) quote small passages from the source directly. Whenever you use a source, you need to avoid plagiarism by referencing the source with an in-text citation, by putting paraphrases and summaries entirely in your own words, and by placing quotation marks around quoted passages. The following strategies chart gives you an overview of summary, paraphrase, and quotation as ways of incorporating sources into your own prose.

Strategies for Incorporating Sources into Your Own Prose

Strategies	What to Do	When to Use These Strategies
Summarize the source.	Condense a source writer's argument by keeping main ideas and omitting details (see Chapter 5, pp. 99–104).	• When the source writer's whole argument is relevant to your purpose • When the source writer presents an alternative or opposing view that you want to push against • When the source writer's argument can be used in support of your own
Paraphrase the source.	Reproduce an idea from a source writer but translate the idea entirely into your own words; a paraphrase should be approximately the same length as the original.	• When you want to incorporate factual information from a source or to use one specific idea from a source • When the source passage is overly complex or technical for your targeted audience • When you want to incorporate a source's point in your own voice without interrupting the flow of your argument

Strategies	What to Do	When to Use These Strategies
Quote short passages from the source using quotation marks.	Work brief quotations from the source smoothly into the grammar of your own sentences (see Skill 21.4 on the mechanics of quoting).	• When you need testimony from an authority (state the authority's credentials in an attributive tag—see Skill 21.3) • In summaries, when you want to reproduce a source's voice, particularly if the language is striking or memorable • In lieu of paraphrase when the source language is memorable
Quote long passages from the source using the block method.	Results in a page with noticeably lengthy block quotations (see Skill 21.4)	• When you intend to analyze or critique the quotation—the quotation is followed by your detailed analysis of its ideas or rhetorical features • When the flavor and language of testimonial evidence is important

With practice, you'll be able to use all these strategies smoothly and effectively.

Summarizing

Detailed instructions on how to write a summary of an article and incorporate it into your own prose are provided in Chapter 5, "Reading Rhetorically" (pp. 99–104). Summaries can be as short as a single sentence or as long as a paragraph. Make the summary as concise as possible so that you don't distract the reader from your own argument. Writer 1's summary of the McGrath article is a good example of a graceful summary used in support of the writer's own thesis (see p. 556).

Paraphrasing

Unlike a summary, which is a condensation of a source's whole argument, a **paraphrase** translates a short passage from a source's words into the writer's own words. Writers often choose to paraphrase when the details of a source passage are particularly important or when the source is overly technical and needs to be simplified for the intended audience. When you paraphrase, be careful to avoid reproducing the original writer's grammatical structure and syntax. If you mirror the original sentence structure while replacing occasional words with synonyms or small structural changes, you will be doing what composition specialists call

"patchwriting"—that is, patching some of your language into someone else's writing.* Patchwriting is a form of academic dishonesty because you aren't fully composing your own sentences and thus misrepresent both your own work and that of the source writer. An acceptable paraphrase needs to be entirely in your own words. To understand patchwriting more fully, track the differences between unacceptable patchwriting and acceptable paraphrase in the following example.

ORIGINAL

There is considerable evidence that women in Bodie were rarely the victims of crime. Between 1878 and 1882 only one woman, a prostitute, was robbed, and there were no reported cases of rape. (There is no evidence that rapes occurred but were not reported.)

Finally, juvenile crime, which accounts for a significant portion of the violent crime in the United States today, was limited in Bodie to pranks and malicious mischief.

UNACCEPTABLE PATCHWRITING

Note phrases taken word for word from original.

According to McGrath, much evidence exists that women in Bodie were rarely the victims of crime. Between 1878 and 1882 only one woman was robbed, and she was a prostitute. There were no reported cases of rape and no evidence that unreported rapes occurred. Also juvenile crime, which occurs frequently in the United States today, was limited in Bodie to pranks and mischief.

ACCEPTABLE PARAPHRASE

Only one word-for-word phrase

Quotation marks around exact phrase

Page number of original

Violence in Bodie was different from violence today. According to McGrath, women in Bodie seldom suffered at the hands of criminals. No reported rapes occurred in Bodie between 1878 and 1882, and the only female robbery victim was a prostitute. Another difference, as McGrath points out, is that juvenile crime was rare except for occasional "pranks and malicious mischief" (554).

Both the patchwriting example and the acceptable paraphrase reproduce the same ideas as the original in approximately the same number of words. But the writer of the paraphrase has been more careful to change the sentence structure substantially and to focus more clearly on his own argument (differences between Bodie and the present). In the acceptable paraphrase, one unquoted phrase still mirrors the original: "between 1878 and 1882." But this phrase is short and carries little of the passage's meaning. The longer mirrored phrase is quoted exactly. In contrast, the patchwritten version contains longer strings of borrowed language without quotation marks.

*We are indebted to the work of Rebecca Moore Howard and others who have led composition researchers to reexamine the use of sources and plagiarism from a cultural and rhetorical perspective. See especially Rebecca Moore Howard, *Standing in the Shadow of Giants: Plagiarists, Authors, Collaborators*. Stamford, CT: Ablex Pub., 1999.

Among novice writers, the use of Web sources can particularly lead to patchwriting. It is all too easy to copy and paste a Web-based passage into your own draft and then attempt to revise it by changing some of the words. In contrast, patchwriting almost never occurs if you are generating your own language—that is, if you are converting information from a source into your own words in order to make your own argument.

When you first practice paraphrasing, you might try paraphrasing a passage twice to avoid patchwriting and achieve an acceptable paraphrase.

- The first time, read the passage carefully and put it into your own words, looking at the source as little as possible.
- The second time, paraphrase your own paraphrase. Then recheck your final version against the original to make sure you have eliminated similar sentence structure and word-for-word strings.

We'll return to the problem of patchwriting in our discussion of plagiarism (Skill 21.5).

Quoting

Besides summary and paraphrase, writers often choose to quote directly in order to give the reader the flavor and style of the source author's prose or to make a memorable point in the source author's own voice. Our previous example of an acceptable paraphrase includes such a quotation in the last sentence. Be careful not to quote a passage that you don't fully understand. (Sometimes novice writers quote a passage because it sounds impressive.) When you quote, you must reproduce the source author's original words exactly, without any changes, unless you indicate changes with ellipses or brackets. Also be careful to represent the author's intentions and meaning fairly; don't change the author's meaning by taking quotations out of context. Because the mechanics of quoting offers its own difficulties, we devote a separate section to it later in this chapter (Skill 21.4).

SKILL 21.3 Use attributive tags to distinguish your ideas from a source's.

Whenever you use sources in your writing, you need to signal to your reader which words and ideas come from your source and which are your own. There are generally two ways of doing so:

- ***State source author's name in an attributive tag.*** You can identify the source by using a short phrase (called an **attributive tag** or sometimes a **signal phrase** or **signal tag**) such as "according to McGrath," "McGrath says," "in McGrath's view," and so on. In the humanities, the source author's full name is commonly used the first time the author is mentioned. If the tag refers to a specific passage or quotation in the source, then a page number is placed in parentheses at the end of the quotation (see Skill 22.2).

Attributive tag

According to Roger D. McGrath, violence was not as common in the Wild West as most people think.

Attributive tag

Page number of quotation.

McGrath explains that "frontier violence was very different from violence today" (553).

- ***State source author's name in a parenthetical citation.*** You can identify a source by placing the author's name in parentheses at the end of the material taken from the source (called a **parenthetical citation**).

Source identified in parentheses

Page number of quotation.

Violence was not as common in the Wild West as most people think (McGrath).

"Frontier violence was very different from violence today" (McGrath 553).

Of these two methods, attributive tags are generally preferred, especially when you are writing for general rather than specialist audiences. The attributive tag method has three advantages:

- It signals where borrowed material starts and ends.
- It avoids ambiguities about what is "fact" and what is filtered through a source's angle of vision.
- It allows the writer to frame the borrowed material rhetorically.

Let's look at each of these in turn.

Attributive Tags Mark Where Source Material Starts and Ends

The parenthetical method requires readers to wait until the end of the writer's use of source material before the source is identified. Attributive tags, in contrast, identify the source from the moment it is first used. Here are excerpts from Writer 1's summary of McGrath, in which we have highlighted the attributive tags. Note the frequency with which the writer informs the reader that this material comes from McGrath. (The complete summary appears on p. 556.)

USE OF ATTRIBUTIVE TAGS IN WRITER 1'S SUMMARY

Many people believe that our Wild West heritage is one of the causes of contemporary violence. But Roger McGrath, in his article "The Myth of Violence in the Old West," shows that today's violence is much different from frontier violence. He explains that. . . . On the other hand, McGrath explains, killings were fueled. . . . Thus, according to McGrath, there is little resemblance between violence on the frontier and violence in today's cities. . . .

Here the attributive tags signal the use of McGrath's ideas throughout the summary. The reader is never confused about which words and ideas come from McGrath.

Attributive Tags Avoid Ambiguities that Can Arise with the Parenthetical Citations

Not only does the parenthetical method fail to mark where the source material begins, it also tends to imply that the source material is a "fact" rather than the view of the source author. In contrast, attributive tags always call attention to the source's angle of vision. Note this ambiguity in the following passage, where parenthetical citations are used without attributive tags:

AMBIGUOUS ATTRIBUTION

> There are many arguments in favor of preserving old-growth forests. First, it is simply unnecessary to log these forests to supply the world's lumber. We have plenty of new-growth forest from which lumber can be taken (Sagoff 89–90). Recently there have been major reforestation efforts all over the United States, and it is common practice now for loggers to replant every tree that is harvested. These new-growth forests, combined with extensive planting of tree farms, provide more than enough wood for the world's needs. Tree farms alone can supply the world's demand for industrial lumber (Sedjo 90).

When confronted with this passage, skeptical readers might ask, "Who are Sagoff and Sedjo? I've never heard of them." It is also difficult to tell how much of the passage is the writer's own argument and how much is borrowed from Sagoff and Sedjo. Is this whole passage a paraphrase? Finally, the writer tends to treat Sagoff's and Sedjo's assertions as uncontested facts rather than as professional opinions. Compare the preceding version with this one, in which attributive tags are added:

CLEAR ATTRIBUTION

> There are many arguments in favor of preserving old-growth forests. First, it is simply unnecessary to log these forests to supply the world's lumber. According to environmentalist Carl Sagoff, we have plenty of new-growth forest from which lumber can be taken (89–90). Recently there have been major reforestation efforts all over the United States, and it is common practice now for loggers to replant every tree that is harvested. These new-growth forests, combined with extensive planting of tree farms, provide more than enough wood for the world's needs. According to forestry expert Robert Sedjo, tree farms alone can supply the world's demand for industrial lumber (90).

We can now see that most of the paragraph is the writer's own argument, into which she has inserted the expert testimony of Sagoff and Sedjo, whose views are treated not as indisputable facts but as the opinions of authorities in this field.

Attributive Tags Frame the Source Material Rhetorically

When you introduce a source for the first time, you can use the attributive tag not only to introduce the source but also to shape your readers' attitudes toward the source. In the previous example, the writer wants readers to respect Sagoff and Sedjo, so she identifies Sagoff as an "environmentalist" and Sedjo as a "forestry expert." If the writer favored logging old-growth forests and supported the logging industry's desire to create more jobs, she might have used different tags: "Carl Sagoff, an outspoken advocate for spotted owls over people," or "Robert Sedjo, a forester with limited knowledge of world lumber markets."

When you compose an initial tag, you can add to it any combination of the following kinds of information, depending on your purpose, your audience's values, and your sense of what the audience already knows or doesn't know about the source:

Strategies for Modifying Attributive Tags to Shape Reader Response

Add to Attributive Tags	Examples
Author's credentials or relevant specialty (enhances credibility)	Civil engineer David Rockwood, a noted authority on stream flow in rivers
Author's lack of credentials (decreases credibility)	City Council member Dilbert Weasel, a local politician with no expertise in international affairs
Author's political or social views	Left-wing columnist Alexander Cockburn [has negative feeling]; Alexander Cockburn, a longtime champion of labor [has positive feeling]
Title of source if it provides context	In her book *Fasting Girls: The History of Anorexia Nervosa,* Joan Jacobs Brumberg shows that [establishes credentials for comments on eating disorders]
Publisher of source if it adds prestige or otherwise shapes audience response	Dr. Carl Patrona, in an article published in the prestigious *New England Journal of Medicine*
Historical or cultural information about a source that provides context or background	In his 1960s book popularizing the hippie movement, Charles Reich claims that
Indication of source's purpose or angle of vision	Feminist author Naomi Wolfe, writing a blistering attack on the beauty industry, argues that

Our point here is that you can use attributive tags rhetorically to help your readers understand the significance and context of a source when you first introduce it and to guide your readers' attitudes toward the source.

FOR WRITING AND DISCUSSION

Evaluating Different Ways to Use and Cite a Source

What follow are four different ways that a writer can use the same passage from a source to support a point about the greenhouse effect. Working in groups or as a whole class, rank the four methods from "most effective" to "least effective." Assume that you are writing a researched argument addressed to your college classmates.

1. ***Quotation with parenthetical citation***
   The greenhouse effect will have a devastating effect on the earth's environment: "Potential impacts include increased mortality and illness due to heat stress and worsened air pollution, as in the 1995 Chicago heat wave that killed hundreds of people. ... Infants, children and other vulnerable populations—especially in already-stressed regions of the world—would likely suffer disproportionately from these impacts" (Hall 19).
2. ***Quotation with attributive tag***
   The greenhouse effect will have a devastating effect on the earth's environment. David C. Hall, president of Physicians for Social Responsibility, claims the following: "Potential impacts include increased mortality and illness due to heat stress and worsened air pollution, as in the 1995 Chicago heat wave that killed hundreds of people. ... Infants, children and other vulnerable populations—especially in already-stressed regions of the world—would likely suffer disproportionately from these impacts" (19).
3. ***Paraphrase with parenthetical citation***
   The greenhouse effect will have a devastating effect on the earth's environment. One of the most frightening effects is the threat of diseases stemming from increased air pollution and heat stress. Infants and children would be most at risk (Hall 19).
4. ***Paraphrase with attributive tag***
   The greenhouse effect will have a devastating effect on the earth's environment. One of the most frightening effects, according to David C. Hall, president of Physicians for Social Responsibility, is the threat of diseases stemming from increased air pollution and heat stress. Infants and children would be most at risk (19).

SKILL 21.4 Punctuate quotations correctly.

In Skill 21.2, we explained your options for incorporating a source into your own paper—summary, paraphrase, and quotation. Whenever you quote, you must make nuts-and-bolts decisions about punctuation such as when and how to use quotation marks, commas, colons, brackets, and ellipses. When you learn these skills, you will know how to punctuate any quotation correctly, including how to make slight changes in the quotation to fit the grammar of your own sentence. This section answers the following mechanical question about quotations:

- How do I quote a complete sentence from my source?
- How do I insert quoted words and phrases into my own sentences?
- How do I indicate my own modifications to a quotation?
- How do I indicate that I have left something out of a quotation?
- How do I quote something that already has quotation marks in it?
- What if I want to use a long quotation?

These explanations will cover the big picture about the mechanics of quoting. Additional explanations covering variations and specific cases can be found in any good handbook.

Quoting a Complete Sentence

In some cases, you will want to quote a complete sentence from your source. Typically, you will include an attributive tag that tells the reader who is being quoted. At the end of the quotation, you usually indicate its page number in parentheses (see Skill 22.2).

ORIGINAL PASSAGE

It was the armed citizens themselves who were the most potent—though not the only—deterrent to larcenous crime. [found on p. 554 of source]

Because quotation is a complete sentence, it starts with capital letter.

WRITER'S QUOTATION OF THIS PASSAGE

According to McGrath, "It was the armed citizens themselves who were the most potent—though not the only—deterrent to larcenous crime" (554).

Final quotation mark goes before the parentheses.

Page number from source

Period comes after the parentheses.

Inserting Quoted Words and Phrases into Your Own Sentences

Instead of quoting a complete sentence, you often want to quote only a few words or phrases from your source and insert them into your own sentence. In these cases, make sure that the grammatical structure of the quotation fits smoothly into the grammar of your own sentence.

ORIGINAL PASSAGE

But the old, the young, the weak, and the female—so often the victims of crime today—were generally not harmed. [found on p. 554 of source]

Quotation marks show where quotation starts and ends.

QUOTED PHRASE INSERTED INTO WRITER'S OWN SENTENCE

McGrath contrasts frontier violence to crime today, pointing out that today's typical crime victims are "the old, the young, the weak, and the female" and showing that these groups were not molested in Bodie (554).

Period comes after parentheses.

Modifying a Quotation

Occasionally you may need to alter a quotation to make it fit your own context. Sometimes the grammar of a desired quotation doesn't match the grammar of your own sentence. At other times, the meaning of a quoted word is unclear because it is removed from its original context. In these cases, use brackets to modify the quotation's grammar or to add a clarifying explanation. Place your changes or additions in brackets to indicate that the bracketed material is not part of the original wording. You should also use brackets to show a change in capitalization.

ORIGINAL PASSAGES

The newspapers regularly advocated shooting burglars on sight, and several burglars were, in fact, shot at. [found on p. 554 of source]

Highwaymen, for example, understood that while they could take the express box from a stagecoach without arousing the citizens, they risked inciting the entire populace to action if they robbed the passengers. [found on p. 554 of source]

QUOTATIONS MODIFIED WITH BRACKETS

By "regularly advocat[ing] shooting burglars on sight," newspapers in Bodie helped an armed citizenry deter crime (McGrath 554).

Public sentiment influenced what laws were likely to be broken. According to McGrath, "[W]hile they [highwaymen] could take the express box from a stagecoach without arousing the citizens, they risked inciting the entire populace to action if they robbed the passengers" (554).

Brackets show change in quotation to fit grammar of writer's sentence.

Parenthetical method of identifying source

Attributive tag

Brackets show a lowercase letter changed to a capital letter.

Brackets show that writer has added a word to explain what "they" stands for.

Omitting Something from a Quoted Passage

Another way that writers modify quotations is to leave words out of the quoted passage. To indicate an omission, use three spaced periods called an **ellipsis** (. . .). Placement of the ellipsis depends on where the omission of material occurs. In the middle of a sentence, each of the periods should be preceded and followed by a space. When your ellipsis comes at the boundary between sentences, use an additional period to mark the end of the first sentence. When a parenthetical page number must follow the ellipsis, insert it before the final (fourth) period in the sequence.

ORIGINAL PASSAGES

Finally, juvenile crime, which accounts for a significant portion of the violent crime in the United States today, was limited in Bodie to pranks and malicious mischief. [found on p. 554 of source]

Bodie's law enforcement institutions were certainly not responsible for these low rates. Rarely were robbers or burglars arrested, and even less often were they convicted. Moreover, many law enforcement officers operated on both sides of the law. [found on p. 554 of source]

Three spaced periods mark omitted words in middle of sentence.

QUOTATIONS WITH OMITTED MATERIAL MARKED BY ELLIPSES

According to McGrath, "juvenile crime . . . was limited in Bodie to pranks and malicious mischief" (554).

This period ends the sentence.

These three periods form the ellipsis.

"Bodie's law enforcement institutions were certainly not responsible for these low rates. . . . Moreover, many law enforcement officers operated on both sides of the law" (McGrath 554).

Ellipsis marks omitted words before the end of the sentence.

Quotation mark shows where quotation ends.

This period ends the sentence.

"Bodie's law enforcement institutions were certainly not responsible for these low rates. Rarely were robbers or burglars arrested . . ." (McGrath 554).

Quoting Something That Already Contains a Quotation

Occasionally a passage that you wish to quote will already contain quotation marks. If you insert the passage within your own quotation marks, change the original double marks (") into single marks (') to indicate the quotation within the quotation. The same procedure works whether the quotation marks are used for quoted words or for a title. Make sure that your attributive tag signals who is being quoted. Because the McGrath article contains no internal quotation marks, we will use a different example to illustrate quotations within quotations.

ORIGINAL PASSAGE

And finally, we tend to stereotype because it helps us make sense out of a highly confusing world, a world which William James once described as "one great, blooming, buzzing confusion." [Passage from an article by Robert Heilbroner, who here quotes William James]

Regular quotation marks indicate the material quoted from Heilbroner.

Heilbroner's own attributive tag notes William James.

Single quotation marks indicate the material quoted from James.

USE OF SINGLE QUOTATION MARKS TO IDENTIFY A QUOTATION WITHIN A QUOTATION

Robert Heilbroner explains that people create stereotypes "because it helps us make sense out of a highly confusing world, a world which William James once described as 'one great, blooming, buzzing confusion'."

Using a Block Quotation for a Long Passage

If your quoted passage uses more than four lines in your own paper, use the block indentation method rather than quotation marks. Block quotations are generally introduced with an attributive tag followed by a colon. The indented block of text, rather than quotation marks, signals that the material is a direct quotation. Block quotations occur rarely in scholarly writing and are used primarily in cases where the writer intends to analyze the text being quoted. If you overuse block quotations, you produce a "choo-choo train" paper (see page 517) that is simply a collage of other people's voices.

ORIGINAL PASSAGE

Fistfights and gunfights among willing combatants—gamblers, miners, and the like—were regular events, and stagecoach holdups were not unusual. But the old, the young, the weak, and the female—so often the victims of crime today—were generally not harmed.

BLOCK QUOTATION

McGrath describes the people most affected by violence in the frontier town of Bodie:

> Fistfights and gunfights among willing combatants—gamblers, miners, and the like—were regular events, and stagecoach holdups were not unusual. But the old, the young, the weak, and the female—so often the victims of crime today—were generally not harmed. (554)

Block quotation introduced with a colon

No quotation marks

Block indented 1 inch on left.

Period and mark end of sentence.

Page number in parentheses after the closing period and space.

SKILL 21.5 Avoid plagiarism by following academic conventions for ethical use of sources.

In the next chapter, we proceed to the nuts and bolts of citing and documenting sources—a skill that will enhance your *ethos* as a skilled researcher and as a person of integrity. Unethical use of sources—called **plagiarism**—is a major concern not only for writing teachers but for teachers in all disciplines. To combat plagiarism, many instructors across the curriculum use plagiarism-detection software like turnitin.com. Their purpose, of course, is to discourage students from cheating. But sometimes students who have no intention of cheating can fall into producing papers that look like cheating. That is, they produce papers that might be accused of plagiarism even though the students had no intention of deceiving their readers.* Our goal in this section is to explain the concept of plagiarism more fully and to sum up the strategies needed to avoid it.

Why Some Kinds of Plagiarism May Occur Unwittingly

To understand how unwitting plagiarism might occur, consider Table 21.1, where the middle column—"Misuse of Sources"—shows common mistakes of novice writers. Everyone agrees that the behaviors in the "Fraud" column constitute deliberate cheating and deserve appropriate punishment. Everyone also agrees that good scholarly work meets the criteria in the "Ethical Use of Sources" column. Novice researchers, however, may find themselves unwittingly in the middle column until they learn the academic community's conventions for using research sources.

*See Rebecca Moore Howard, *Standing in the Shadow of Giants: Plagiarists, Authors, Collaborators.* Stamford, CT: Ablex Pub., 1999.

TABLE 21.1 Plagiarism and the Ethical Use of Sources

Plagiarism		Ethical Use of Sources
Fraud	**Misuse of Sources** ***(Common Mistakes Made by New Researchers)***	
The writer • buys paper from a paper mill • submits someone else's work as his own • copies chunks of text from sources with obvious intention of not being detected • fabricates data or makes up evidence • intends to deceive	The writer • copies passages directly from a source, references the source with an in-text citation, but fails to use quotation marks or block indentation • in attempting to paraphrase a source, makes some changes, but follows too closely the wording of the original ("patchwriting") • fails to indicate the sources of some ideas or data (often is unsure what needs to be cited or has lost track of sources through poor note taking) • in general, misunderstands the conventions for using sources in academic writing	The writer • writes paper entirely in her own words or uses exact quotations from sources • indicates all quotations with quotation marks or block indentation • indicates her use of all sources through attribution, in-text citation, and an end-of-paper list of works cited

You might appreciate these conventions more fully if you recognize how they have evolved from Western notions of intellectual property and patent law associated with the rise of modern science in the seventeenth and eighteenth centuries. A person not only could own a house or a horse, but also could own an idea and the words used to express that idea. You can see these cultural conventions at work—in the form of laws or professional codes of ethics—whenever a book author is disgraced for lifting words or ideas from another author or whenever an artist or entrepreneur is sued for stealing song lyrics, publishing another person's photographs without permission, or infringing on some inventor's patent.

This understanding of plagiarism may seem odd in some non-Western cultures where collectivism is valued more than individualism. In these cultures, words written or spoken by ancestors, elders, or other authority figures may be regarded with reverence and shared with others without attribution. Also in these cultures, it might be disrespectful to paraphrase certain passages or to document them in a way that would suggest the audience didn't recognize the ancient wisdom.

However, such collectivist conventions won't work in research communities committed to building new knowledge. In the academic world, the conventions separating ethical from unethical use of sources are essential if research findings are to win the community's confidence. Effective research can occur only within ethical and responsible research communities where people do not fabricate data and where current researchers respect and acknowledge the work of those who have gone before them.

Strategies for Avoiding Plagiarism

The following chart will help you review the strategies presented throughout Chapters 19 to 22 for using source material ethically and avoiding plagiarism.

Strategies for Avoiding Plagiarism or the Appearance of Plagiarism

What to Do	Why to Do It	Where to Find More Information
	At the beginning	
Read your college's policy on plagiarism as well as statements from your teachers in class or on course syllabi.	Understanding policies on plagiarism and academic integrity will help you research and write ethically.	Chapter 19, p. 518
Pose a research question rather than a topic area.	Arguing your own thesis gives you a voice, establishes your *ethos,* and urges you to write ethically.	Skill 19.1
	At the note-taking stage	
Create a bibliographic entry for each source.	This action makes it easy to create an end-of-paper bibliography and encourages rhetorical reading	Skill 20.1
When you copy a passage into your notes, copy word for word and enclose it with in quotation marks.	It is important to distinguish a source's words from your own words.	Skill 20.1
When you enter summaries or paraphrases into your notes, avoid patchwriting.	If your notes contain any strings of a source's original wording, you might later assume that these words are your own.	Skill 20.1 Skill 21.2
Distinguish your informational notes from your personal exploratory notes	Keeping these kinds of notes separate will help you identify borrowed ideas when it's time to incorporate the source material into your paper.	Skill 20.1

(*continued*)

What to Do	Why to Do It	Where to Find More Information
	When writing your draft	
Except for exact quotations, write the paper entirely in your own words.	This strategy keeps you from patchwriting when you summarize or paraphrase.	Skill 21.2
Indicate all quotations with quotation marks or block indentation. Use ellipses or brackets to make changes to fit your own grammar.	Be careful to represent the author fairly; don't change meaning by taking quotations out of context.	Skills 21.2 and 21.4
When you summarize or paraphrase, avoid patchwriting.	Word-for-word strings from a source must either be avoided or placed in quotation marks. Also avoid mirroring the source's grammatical structure.	Skill 21.2
Never cut and paste a Web passage directly into your draft. Paste it into a separate note file and put quotation marks around it.	Pasted passages are direct invitations to patchwrite.	Skill 21.2
Inside your text, use attributive tags or parenthetical citations to identify all sources. List all sources alphabetically in a concluding works cited or references list.	This strategy makes it easy for readers to know when you are using a source and where to find it.	Skill 21.3 Skill 22.1
Cite with attributive tags or parenthetical citations all quotations, paraphrases, summaries, and any other references to specific sources.	These are the most common in-text citations in a research paper.	Skills 22.1 and 22.2
Use in-text citations to indicate sources for all visuals and media such as graphs, maps, photographs, films, videos, broadcasts, and recordings.	The rules for citing words and ideas apply equally to visuals and media cited in your paper.	Skill 22.1
Use in-text citations for all ideas and facts that are not common knowledge.	Although you don't need to cite widely accepted and noncontroversial facts and information, it is better to cite them if you are unsure.	Skill 22.1

FOR WRITING AND DISCUSSION

Avoiding Plagiarism

Read the passage below. Unlike the ethical summary of McGrath's article produced by Writer 1 on page 556, the writer of the following passage would likely be accused of plagiarism.

SUMMARY OF McGRATH'S ARTICLE (AN EXAMPLE OF PLAGIARISM)

It is commonly assumed that violence is part of our Wild West heritage. But Roger McGrath, in his article "The Myth of Violence in the Old West," shows that frontier violence was very different from violence today. He explains that in a typical frontier town, violence involved gunslingers who were "willing combatants," whereas today's typical victims—the old, the young, the weak, and the female—were unaffected by crime (554). The greatest deterrent to crime in Bodie was the fact that so many people were armed. Armed guards prevented bank robberies and stagecoach holdups, and armed citizens stopped burglary. On the other hand, McGrath explains, Bodie had a high homicide rate. Most of the town's residents were young single males who adhered to a code of conduct that frequently required them to fight. Alcohol also played a major role. Therefore murders were much more frequent than in any U.S. city today (554). Thus, according to McGrath, there is little resemblance between violence on the frontier and violence in today's cities, so we cannot blame current violence on our tumultuous frontier past.

Working in small groups or as a whole class, respond to the following questions.

1. How does this passage cross the line into plagiarism? (You'll need to compare the passage to Writer 1's ethical summary on p. 556.)
2. The writer of this passage might say, "How can this be plagiarism? I cited my source and gave page numbers." How would you explain the problem to this writer?
3. Psychologically or cognitively, what may have caused this writer to misuse the source? How might this writer's note-taking process or composing process have differed from that of Writer 1 on page 556? In other words, what happened that got this writer into trouble?

PEARSON mycomplab

For support in learning this chapter's content, follow this path in MyCompLab: Resources ⇒ Research ⇒ The Research Assignment ⇒ Integrating Sources. Review the Instruction and Multimedia resources about integrating sources, then complete the Exercises and click on Gradebook to measure your progress.

22 CITING AND DOCUMENTING SOURCES

In the previous chapter we explained how to incorporate sources into your writing; in this chapter we focus on the nuts and bolts of documenting those sources in a way appropriate to your purpose, audience, and genre, using the systems of the Modern Language Association (MLA) and the American Psychological Association (APA).* Accurate documentation not only helps other researchers locate your sources but also contributes substantially to your own *ethos* as a writer.

Specifically, in this chapter you will learn the following skills:

- **SKILL 22.1** Know what needs to be cited and what doesn't.
- **SKILL 22.2** Understand the connection between in-text citations and the end-of-paper list of cited works.
- **SKILL 22.3** Cite and document sources using MLA style.
- **SKILL 22.4** Cite and document sources using APA style.

SKILL 22.1 Know what needs to be cited and what doesn't.

Beginning researchers are often confused about what needs to be cited and what doesn't. Table 22.1 will help you make this determination. If you are in doubt, it is better to cite than not to cite.

It is often difficult to determine when a given piece of information falls into the "common knowledge" column of Table 22.1. The answer depends both on your target audience's background knowledge and on your own ability to speak as an authority. Consider the statement "Twitter and Facebook are forms of social networking." That information is noncontroversial and well known and so doesn't require citation. But if you added, "Twitter is more popular with middle-aged adults than with teenagers," you would need to cite your source (some newspaper article or poll?) unless you are a teenager speaking with authority from your own experience, in which case you would provide personal-experience examples. If you are uncertain, our best advice is this: When in doubt, cite.

*Our discussion of MLA style is based on the *MLA Handbook for Writers of Research Papers*, 7th ed. (2009). Our discussion of APA style is based on the *Publication Manual of the American Psychological Association*, 6th ed. (2010).

TABLE 22.1 Determining What Needs to Be Cited

What Needs to Be Cited	What Does Not Need to Be Cited
You must cite all references to your research sources as well as any information that is not commonly known by your targeted audience: • Any quotation • Any passage that you paraphrase • Any passage or source that you summarize or otherwise refer to • Any image, photograph, map, drawing, graph, chart, or other visual that you download from the Web (or find elsewhere) and include in your paper • Any sound or video file that you use in a multimedia project • Any idea, fact, statistic, or other information that you find from a source and that is not commonly known by your targeted audience	You do not need to cite commonly shared, widely known knowledge that will be considered factual and noncontroversial to your targeted audience: • Commonly known facts (Water freezes at 32 degrees Fahrenheit.) • Commonly known dates (Terrorists flew airplanes into New York's World Trade Center on September 11, 2001.) • Commonly known events (Barack Obama defeated John McCain for the presidency.) • Commonly known historical or cultural knowledge (Twitter and Facebook are forms of social networking.)

SKILL 22.2 Understand the connection between in-text citations and the end-of-paper list of cited works.

The most common forms of documentation use what are called in-text citations that match an end-of-paper list of cited works (as opposed to footnotes or endnotes). An ***in-text citation*** identifies a source in the body of the paper at the point where it is summarized, paraphrased, quoted, inserted, or otherwise referred to. At the end of your paper you include a list—alphabetized by author (or by title if there is no named author)—of all the works you cited. Both the Modern Language Association (MLA) system, used primarily in the humanities, and the American Psychological Association (APA) system, used primarily in the social sciences, follow this procedure. In MLA, your end-of-paper list is called **Works Cited.** In APA it is called **References.**

Whenever you place an in-text citation in the body of your paper, your reader knows to turn to the Works Cited or References list at the end of the paper to get the full bibliographic information. The key to the system's logic is this:

- Every source in Works Cited or References must be mentioned in the body of the paper.
- Conversely, every source mentioned in the body of the paper must be included in the end-of-paper list.
- The first word in each entry of the Works Cited or References list (usually an author's last name) must also appear in the in-text citation. In other words, there must be a one-to-one correspondence between the first word in each entry in the end-of-paper list and the name used to identify the source in the body of the paper.

Suppose a reader sees this phrase in your paper: "According to Debra Goldstein. . . ." The reader should be able to turn to your Works Cited list and find an alphabetized entry beginning with "Goldstein, Debra." Similarly, suppose that in looking over your Works Cited list, your reader sees an article by "Guillen, Manuel." This means that the name "Guillen" has to appear in your paper in one of two ways:

For more on attributive tags, see Skill 21.3.

- As an attributive tag: Economics professor Manuel Guillen argues that. . . .
- As a parenthetical citation, often following a quotation: ". . . changes in fiscal policy" (Guillen 49).

Because this one-to-one correspondence is so important, let's illustrate it with some complete examples using the MLA formatting style:

If the body of your paper has this:	Then the Works Cited list must have this:
According to linguist Deborah Tannen, political debate in America leaves out the complex middle ground where most solutions must be developed.	Tannen, Deborah. *The Argument Culture: Moving from Debate to Dialogue*. New York: Random, 1998. Print.
In the 1980s, cigarette advertising revealed a noticeable pattern of racial stereotyping (Pollay, Lee, and Carter-Whitney).	Pollay, Richard W., Jung S. Lee, and David Carter-Whitney. "Separate, but Not Equal: Racial Segmentation in Cigarette Advertising." *Journal of Advertising* 21.1 (1992): 45–57. Print.
On its Web site, the National Men's Resource Center offers advice to parents on how to talk with children about alcohol and drugs ("Talking").	"Talking with Kids about Alcohol and Drugs." *Menstuff*. National Men's Resource Center, 1 Mar. 2007. Web. 26 June 2007.

How to format an MLA in-text citation and a Works Cited list entry is the subject of the next section. The APA system is similar except that it emphasizes the date of publication in both the in-text citation and the References entry. APA formatting is the subject of Skill 22.4.

SKILL 22.3 Cite and document sources using MLA style.

An in-text citation and its corresponding Works Cited entry are linked in a chicken-and-egg system: You can't cite a source in the text without first knowing how the source's entry will be alphabetized in the Works Cited list. However, since most Works Cited entries are alphabetized by the first author's last name, for convenience we start with in-text citations.

In-Text Citations in MLA Style

A typical in-text citation contains two elements: (1) the last name of the author and (2) the page number of the quoted or paraphrased passage. However, in some cases a work is identified by something other than an author's last name, and sometimes no page number is required. Let's begin with the most common cases.

Typically, an in-text citation uses one of these two methods:

- ***Parenthetical method.*** Place the author's last name and the page number in parentheses immediately after the material being cited.

  The Spanish tried to reduce the status of Filipina, women who had been able to do business, get divorced, and sometimes become village chiefs (Karnow 41).

- ***Attributive tag method.*** Place the author's name in an attributive tag at the beginning of the source material and the page number in parentheses at the end.

  According to Karnow, the Spanish tried to reduce the status of Filipina women, who had been able to do business, get divorced, and sometimes become village chiefs (41).

Once you have cited an author and it is clear that the same author's material is being used, you need cite only the page numbers in parentheses in subsequent citations. A reader who wishes to look up the source will find the bibliographic information in the Works Cited section by looking for the entry under "Karnow."

Let's now turn to the variations. Table 22.2 identifies the typical variations and shows again the one-to-one connection between the in-text citation and the Works Cited list.

TABLE 22.2 In-Text Citations in MLA Style

Type of Source	Works Cited Entry at End of Paper (Construct the entry while taking notes on each source.)	In-Text Citation in Body of Paper (*Use the first word of the Works Cited entry in parentheses or an attributive tag; add page number at end of quoted or paraphrased passage.*)
One author	Pollan, Michael. *The Omnivore's Dilemma: A Natural History of Four Meals.* New York: Penguin, 2006. Print.	...(Pollan 256). OR According to Pollan,...(256).
More than one author	Pollay, Richard W., Jung S. Lee, and David Carter-Whitney. "Separate, but Not Equal: Racial Segmentation in Cigarette Advertising." *Journal of Advertising* 21.1 (1992): 45–57. Print.	...race" (Pollay, Lee, and Carter-Whitney 52). OR Pollay, Lee, and Carter-Whitney have argued that "advertisers...race" (52). *For the in-text citation, cite the specific page number rather than the whole range of pages given in the Works Cited entry.*

(*continued*)

TABLE 22.2 *continued*

Type of Source	Works Cited Entry at End of Paper	In-Text Citation in Body of Paper (*Use the first word of the Works Cited entry in parentheses or an attributive tag; add page number at end of quoted or paraphrased passage.*)
Author has more than one work in Works Cited list	Dombrowski, Daniel A. *Babies and Beasts: The Argument from Marginal Cases*. Urbana: U of Illinois P, 1997. Print. ---. *The Philosophy of Vegetarianism.* Amherst: U of Massachusetts P, 1984. Print.	. . . (Dombrowski, *Babies* 207). . . . (Dombrowski, *Philosophy* 328). OR According to Dombrowski, . . . (*Babies* 207). Dombrowski claims that . . . (*Philosophy* 328). *Because author has more than one work in Works Cited, include a short version of title to distinguish between entries.*
Corporate author	American Red Cross. *Standard First Aid*. St. Louis: Mosby Lifeline, 1993. Print.	. . . (American Red Cross 102). OR Snake bite instructions from the American Red Cross show that . . . (102).
No named author (Work is therefore alphabetized by title.)	"Ouch! Body Piercing." *Menstuff.* National Men's Resource Center, 1 Feb. 2001. Web. 17 July 2004.	. . . ("Ouch!"). According to the National Men's Resource Center, . . . ("Ouch!"). • *Add "Ouch!" in parentheses to show that work is alphabetized under "Ouch!" not "National."* • *No page numbers are shown because Web site pages aren't stable.*
Indirect citation of a source that you found in another source *Suppose you want to use a quotation from Peter Singer that you found in a book by Daniel Dombrowski. Include Dombrowski but not Singer in Works Cited.*	Dombrowski, Daniel A. *Babies and Beasts: The Argument from Marginal Cases*. Urbana: U of Illinois P, 1997. Print.	Animal rights activist Peter Singer argues that . . . (qtd. in Dombrowski 429). • *Singer is used for the attributive tag, but the in-text citation is to Dombrowski.* • *"qtd. in" stands for "quoted in."*

When to Use Page Numbers in In-Text Citations When the materials you are citing are available in print or in .pdf format, you can provide accurate page numbers for parenthetical citations. If you are working with Web sources or HTML files, however, do not use the page numbers obtained from a printout because they will not be consistent from printer to printer. If the item has numbered paragraphs, cite them with the abbreviation *par.* or *pars.*—for example,

"(Jones, pars. 22–24)." In the absence of reliable page numbers for the original material, MLA says to omit page references from the parenthetical citation. The following chart summarizes the use of page numbers in in-text citations.

Include a page number in the in-text citation:	Do not include a page number:
If the source has stable page numbers (print source or .pdf version of print source): • If you quote something • If you paraphrase a specific passage • If you refer to data or details from a specific page or range of pages in the source	• If you are referring to the argument of the whole source instead of a specific page or passage • If the source does not have stable page numbers (articles on Web sites, HTML text, and so forth)

Works Cited List in MLA Style

In the MLA system, you place a complete Works Cited list at the end of the paper. The list includes all the sources that you mention in your paper. However, it does *not* include works you read but did not use. Entries in the Works Cited list follow these general guidelines:

- Entries are arranged alphabetically by author, or by title if there is no author.
- Each entry includes the medium of publication of the source you consulted—for example, *Print, Web, DVD, Performance, Oil on canvas,* and so on.
- If there is more than one entry per author, the works are arranged alphabetically by title. For the second and all additional entries, type three hyphens and a period in place of the author's name.

Dombrowski, Daniel A. *Babies and Beasts: The Argument from Marginal Cases.* Urbana: U of Illinois P, 1997. Print.

---. *The Philosophy of Vegetarianism.* Amherst: U of Massachusetts P, 1984. Print.

You can see a complete, properly formatted Works Cited list on the last pages of James Gardiner's paper (pp. 597–598).

The remaining pages in this section show examples of MLA citation formats for different kinds of sources and provide explanations and illustrations as needed.

MLA Citation Models

To see what citations look like when typed in a research paper, see James Gardiner's Works Cited list on pp. 597–598.

Print Articles in Scholarly Journals

General Format for Print Article in Scholarly Journal

Author. "Article Title." *Journal Title* volume number.issue number (year): page numbers. Print.

Note that all scholarly journal entries include both volume number and issue number, regardless of how the journal is paginated. For articles published in a scholarly Web journal, see page 586. For scholarly journal articles retrieved from an online database, see page 583.

One author

Herrera-Sobek, Maria. "Border Aesthetics: The Politics of Mexican Immigration in Film and Art." *Western Humanities Review* 60.2 (2006): 60–71. Print.

Two or three authors

Pollay, Richard W., Jung S. Lee, and David Carter-Whitney. "Separate, but Not Equal: Racial Segmentation in Cigarette Advertising." *Journal of Advertising* 21.1 (1992): 45–57. Print.

Four or more authors

Either list all the authors in the order in which they appear, or use "et al." (meaning "and others") to replace all but the first author.

Buck, Gayle A., et al. "Examining the Cognitive Processes Used by Adolescent Girls and Women Scientists in Identifying Science Role Models: A Feminist Approach." *Science Education* 92.4 (2008): 688–707. Print.

Print Articles in Magazines and Newspapers

If no author is identified, begin the entry with the title or headline. Distinguish between news stories and editorials by putting the word "Editorial" after the title. If a magazine comes out weekly or biweekly, include the complete date ("27 Sept. 2010"). If it comes out monthly, then state the month only ("Sept. 2010").

General Format for Magazines and Newspapers

Author. "Article Title." *Magazine Title* day Month year: page numbers. Print.

Note: If the article continues in another part of the magazine or newspaper, add "+" to the number of the first page to indicate the nonsequential pages.

Magazine article with named author

Snyder, Rachel L. "A Daughter of Cambodia Remembers: Loung Ung's Journey." *Ms.* Aug.–Sept. 2001: 62–67. Print.

Magazine article without named author

"Daddy, Daddy." *New Republic* 30 July 2001: 2–13. Print.

Review of book, film, or performance

Schwarz, Benjamin. "A Bit of Bunting: A New History of the British Empire Elevates Expediency to Principle." Rev. of *Ornamentalism: How the British Saw Their Empire,* by David Cannadine. *Atlantic Monthly* Nov. 2001: 126–35. Print.

Kaufman, Stanley. "Polishing a Gem." Rev. of *The Blue Angel,* dir. Josef von Sternberg. *New Republic* 30 July 2001: 28–29. Print.

Lahr, John. "Nobody's Darling: Fascism and the Drama of Human Connection in *Ashes to Ashes*." Rev. of *Ashes to Ashes*, by Harold Pinter. The Roundabout Theater Co. Gramercy Theater, New York. *New Yorker* 22 Feb. 1999: 182–83. Print.

Newspaper article

Henriques, Diana B. "Hero's Fall Teaches Wall Street a Lesson." *Seattle Times* 27 Sept. 1998: A1+. Print.

Page numbers in newspapers are typically indicated by a section letter or number as well as a page number. The "+" indicates that the article continues on one or more pages later in the newspaper.

Newspaper editorial

"Dr. Frankenstein on the Hill." Editorial. *New York Times* 18 May 2002, natl. ed.: A22. Print.

Letter to the editor of a magazine or newspaper

Tomsovic, Kevin. Letter. *New Yorker* 13 July 1998: 7. Print.

Print Books

General Format for Print Books

Author. *Title.* City of publication: Publisher, year of publication. Print.

One author

Pollan, Michael. *The Omnivore's Dilemma: A Natural History of Four Meals*. New York: Penguin, 2006. Print.

Two or more authors

Dombrowski, Daniel A., and Robert J. Deltete. *A Brief, Liberal, Catholic Defense of Abortion*. Urbana: U of Illinois P, 2000. Print.

Belenky, Mary, et al. *Women's Ways of Knowing: The Development of Self, Voice, and Mind.* New York: Basic, 1986. Print.

If there are four or more authors, you have the choice of listing all the authors in the order in which they appear on the title page or using "et al." (meaning "and others") to replace all but the first author. Your Works Cited entry and the parenthetical citation should match.

Second, later, or revised edition

Montagu, Ashley. *Touching: The Human Significance of the Skin.* 3rd ed. New York: Perennial, 1986. Print.

In place of "3rd ed.," you can include abbreviations for other kinds of editions: "Rev. ed." (for "Revised edition") or "Abr. ed." (for "Abridged edition").

Republished book (for example, a paperback published after the original hardback edition or a modern edition of an older work)

Hill, Christopher. *The World Turned Upside Down: Radical Ideas During the English Revolution*. 1972. London: Penguin, 1991. Print.

Wollstonecraft, Mary. *The Vindication of the Rights of Woman, with Strictures on Political and Moral Subjects*. 1792. Rutland: Tuttle, 1995. Print.

The date immediately following the title is the original publication date of the work.

Multivolume work

Churchill, Winston S. *A History of the English-Speaking Peoples*. 4 vols. New York: Dodd, 1956–58. Print.

Churchill, Winston S. *The Great Democracies*. New York: Dodd, 1957. Print. Vol. 4 of *A History of the English-Speaking Peoples*. 4 vols. 1956–58.

Use the first method when you cite the whole work; use the second method when you cite one individually titled volume of the work.

Article in familiar reference work

"Mau Mau." *The New Encyclopaedia Britannica*. 15th ed. 2002. Print.

Article in less familiar reference work

Ling, Trevor O. "Buddhism in Burma." *Dictionary of Comparative Religion*. Ed. S. G. F. Brandon. New York: Scribner's, 1970. Print.

Translation

De Beauvoir, Simone. *The Second Sex*. 1949. Trans. H. M. Parshley. New York: Bantam, 1961. Print.

Illustrated book

Jacques, Brian. *The Great Redwall Feast*. Illus. Christopher Denise. New York: Philomel, 1996. Print.

Graphic novel

Miyazaki, Hayao. *Nausicaa of the Valley of Wind*. 4 vols. San Francisco: Viz, 1995–97. Print.

Corporate author (a commission, committee, or other group)

American Red Cross. *Standard First Aid*. St. Louis: Mosby Lifeline, 1993. Print.

No author listed

The New Yorker Cartoon Album: 1975–1985. New York: Penguin, 1987. Print.

Whole anthology

O'Connell, David F., and Charles N. Alexander, eds. *Self Recovery: Treating Addictions Using Transcendental Meditation and Maharishi Ayur-Veda*. New York: Haworth, 1994. Print.

Anthology article

Royer, Ann. "The Role of the Transcendental Meditation Technique in Promoting Smoking Cessation: A Longitudinal Study." *Self Recovery: Treating Addictions Using Transcendental Meditation and Maharishi Ayur-Veda*. Ed. David F. O'Connell and Charles N. Alexander. New York: Haworth, 1994. 221–39. Print.

When you cite an individual article, give the inclusive page numbers for the article at the end of the citation, before the medium of publication.

Articles or Books from an Online Database

General Format for Material from Online Databases

Author. "Title." *Periodical Name* Print publication data including date and volume/issue numbers: pagination. *Database*. Web. Date of access.

Journal article from online database

Matsuba, M. Kyle. "Searching for Self and Relationships Online." *CyberPsychology and Behavior* 9.3 (2006): 275–84. *Academic Search Complete*. Web. 14 Apr. 2007.

To see where each element in this citation was found, see Figure 22.1, which shows the online database screen from which the Matsuba article was accessed. For articles in databases, follow the formats for print newspapers, magazines, or scholarly journals, as relevant. When the database text provides only the starting page number of a multipage article, insert a plus sign after the number, before the period.

Broadcast transcript from online database

Conan, Neal. "Arab Media." *Talk of the Nation*. With Shibley Telhami. 4 May 2004. Transcript. *LexisNexis*. Web. 31 July 2004.

The label "Transcript" after the broadcast date indicates a text (not audio) version.

E-book from online database

Hanley, Wayne. *The Genesis of Napoleonic Propaganda, 1796–1799*. New York: Columbia UP, 2002. *Gutenberg-e*. Web. 31 July 2010.

Machiavelli, Niccolo. *Prince*. 1513. *Bibliomania*. Web. 31 July 2009.

Information about the original print version, including a translator if relevant and available, should be provided.

Other Internet Sources

General Format for Web Sources Since Web sources are often unstable, MLA recommends that you download or printout your Web sources. The goal in

FIGURE 22.1 Article Downloaded from an Online Database, with Elements Identified for an MLA-Style Citation

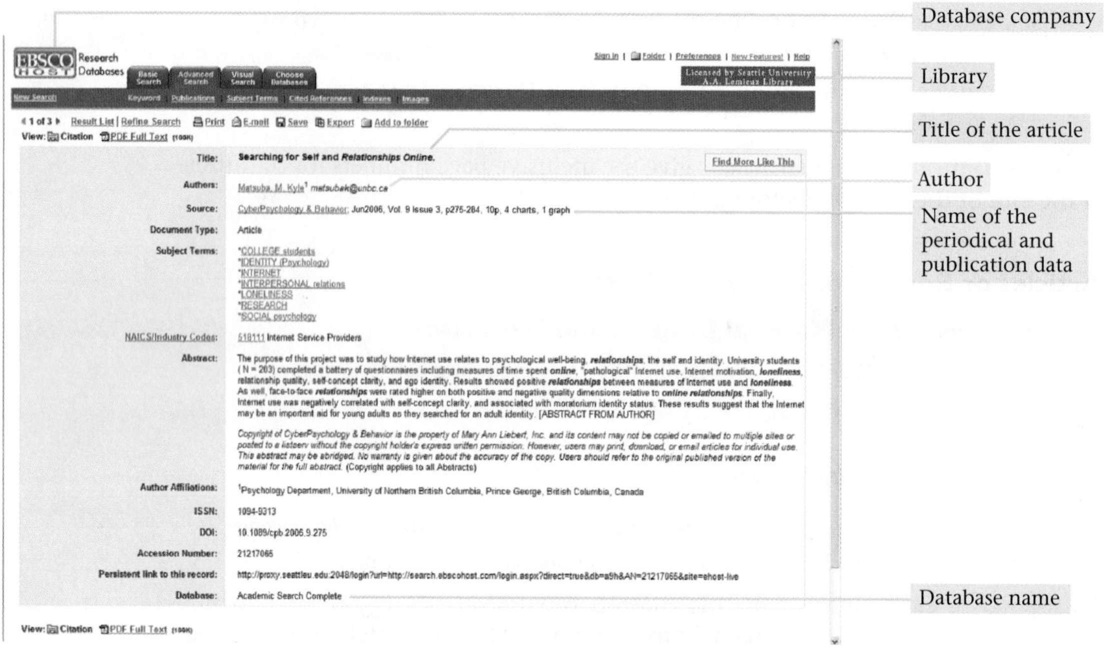

Matsuba, M. Kyle. "Searching for Self and Relationships Online." *CyberPsychology and Behavior* 9.3 (2006): 275–84. *Academic Search Complete*. Web. 14 Apr. 2007.

citing these sources is to enable readers to locate the material. To that end, use the basic citation model and adapt it as necessary.

Author, editor, director, narrator, performer, compiler, or producer of the work, if available. *Title of a long work, italicized.* OR "Title of page or document that is part of a larger work, in quotation marks." *Title of the overall site, usually taken from the home page, if this is different from the title of the work*. Publisher or sponsor of the site (if none, use N.p.), day Month year of publication online or last update of the site (if not available, use n.d.). Web. day Month year you accessed the site.

Saucedo, Robert. "A Bad Idea for a Movie." *theeagle.com*. Bryan College Station Eagle, 1 July 2010. Web. 7 July 2010.

To see where each element of the Saucedo citation comes from, see the Web article in Figure 22.2.

FIGURE 22.2 An Article Published on the Web, with Elements Identified for an MLA-Style Citation

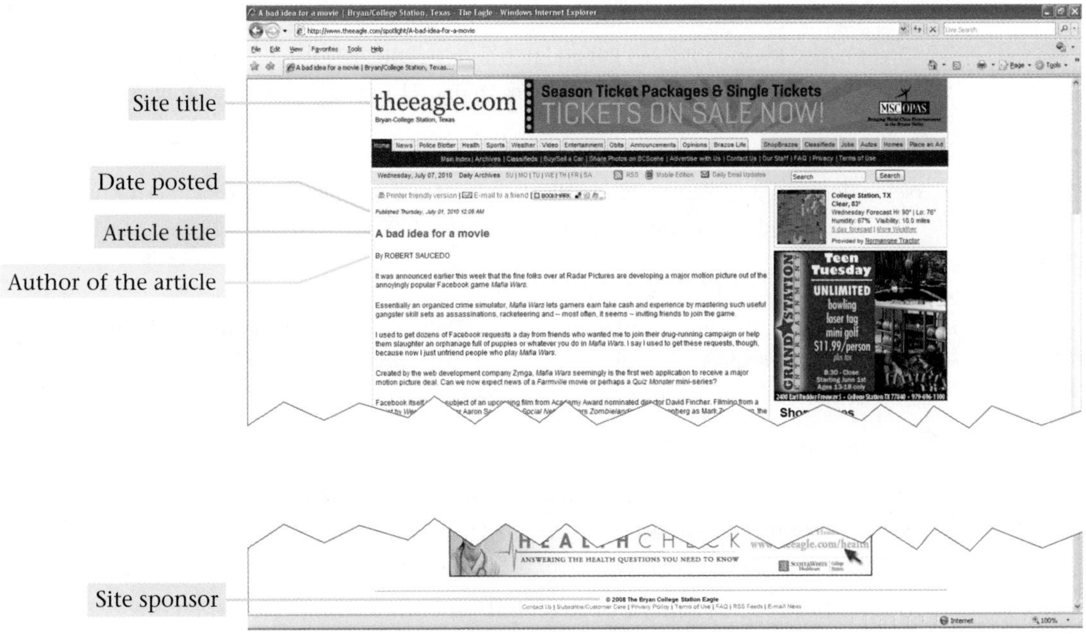

Saucedo, Robert. "A Bad Idea for a Movie." *theeagle.com.* Bryan College Station Eagle, 1 July 2010. Web. 7 July 2010.

MLA assumes that readers will use a search engine to locate a Web source, so do not include a URL *unless* the item would be hard to locate without it. If you do include a URL, it goes at the end of the citation, after the access date. Enclose it in angle brackets <> followed by a period. If you need to break the URL from one line to the next, divide it only after a slash. Do not hyphenate a URL. See the home page entries on page 586 for examples of citations with URLs.

Entire Web site

BlogPulse. Intelliseek, n.d. Web. 24 July 2010.

Padgett, John B., ed. *William Faulkner on the Web.* U of Mississippi, 26 Mar. 2007. Web. 25 June 2009.

Documents within a Web site

Marks, John. "Overview: Letter from the President." *Search for Common Ground.* Search for Common Ground, n.d. Web. 25 June 2007.

Gourlay, Alexander S. "Glossary." *The William Blake Archive.* Lib. of Cong., 2005. Web. 21 Jan. 2009.

"Ouch! Body Piercing." *Menstuff*. National Men's Resource Center, 1 Feb. 2001. Web. 17 July 2004. <http://www.menstuff.org/issues/byissue/fathersgeneral .html#bodypiercing>.

Article from a newspaper or newswire site

Bounds, Amy. "Thinking Like Scientists." *Daily Camera* [Boulder]. Scripps Interactive Newspaper Group, 26 June 2007. Web. 26 June 2007.

"Great Lakes: Rwanda Backed Dissident Troops in DRC-UN Panel." *IRIN*. UN Office for the Coordination of Humanitarian Affairs, 21 July 2004. Web. 31 July 2004.

Article from a scholarly e-journal

Welch, John R., and Ramon Riley. "Reclaiming Land and Spirit in the Western Apache Homeland." *American Indian Quarterly* 25.4 (2001): 5–14. Web. 19 Dec. 2001.

Broadcast transcript from a Web site

Woodruff, Judy, Richard Garnett, and Walter Dellinger. "Experts Analyze Supreme Court Free Speech Rulings." Transcript: background and discussion. *Online NewsHour*. PBS, 25 June 2007. Web. 26 June 2007.

Blog posting

Dyer, Bob, and Ella Barnes. "The 'Greening' of the Arctic." *Greenversations*. U.S. Environmental Protection Agency, 7 Oct. 2008. Web. 11 Oct. 2010. <http://blog.epa.gov/blog/2008/10/07/the-greening-of-the-artic/>.

To see where each element of this citation comes from, refer to Figure 22.3.

Podcast

"The Long and Winding Road: DNA Evidence for Human Migration." *Science Talk*. Scientific American, 7 July 2008. Web. 21 July 2010.

Web video

Beck, Roy. "Immigration Gumballs." *YouTube*. YouTube, 2 Nov. 2006. Web. 23 July 2009.

For films and DVDs, see page 588.

Home Pages

Agatucci, Cora. *Culture and Literature of Africa*. Course home page. Humanities Dept., Central Oregon Community College, Jan. 2007–May 2007. Web. 31 July 2007. <http://web.cocc.edu/cagatucci/classes/hum211/>.

African Studies Program. Home page. School of Advanced International Study, Johns Hopkins U, n.d. Web. 31 July 2007.

Sharpe, William F. Home page. May 2004. Web. 31 July 2004. <http://www.stanford.edu/~wfsharpe/>.

E-mail

Daffinrud, Sue. "Scoring Guide for Class Participation." Message to the author. 12 Dec. 2001. E-mail.

Use the subject line as the title of the e-mail. Use "E-mail" as the medium of publication and omit your access date.

FIGURE 22.3 A Blog Posting from the Web, with Citation Elements Identified

Dyer, Bob, and Ella Barnes. "The 'Greening' of the Arctic." *Greenversations*. U.S. Environmental Protection Agency, 7 Oct. 2008. Web. 11 Oct. 2008. <http://blog.epa.gov/blog/2008/10/07/the-greening-of-the-arctic/>.

Miscellaneous Sources

Television or radio program

Begin with the episode name, if any, in quotation marks, followed by the program name, italicized. Use "Television" or "Radio" as the medium of publication.

"Lie Like a Rug." *NYPD Blue*. Dir. Steven Bochco and David Milch. ABC. KOMO, Seattle. 6 Nov. 2001. Television.

If you accessed a program on the Web, give the basic citation information without the original medium of publication; then include the Web publication information with an access date.

Ashbrook, Tom. "Turf Wars and the American Lawn." *On Point*. Natl. Public Radio, 22 July 2008. Web. 23 July 2009.

For podcasts, see page 586.

Film or video recording

Shakespeare in Love. Dir. John Madden. Perf. Joseph Fiennes and Gwyneth Paltrow. Screenplay by Marc Norman and Tom Stoppard. Universal Miramax, 1998. Film.

Use "DVD" or "Videocassette" rather than "Film" as the medium of publication if that is the medium you consulted. If you accessed a film or video on the Web, omit the original medium of publication, include the Web site or database name (italicized), the sponsor and posting date, "Web" as medium of publication, and the date of access.

Shakespeare in Love. Dir. John Madden. Perf. Joseph Fiennes and Gwyneth Paltrow. Screenplay by Marc Norman and Tom Stoppard. Universal Miramax, 1998. *Netflix*. Netflix, n.d. Web. 9 Mar. 2010.

For videos published originally on the Web, see page 586.

Sound recording

Begin the entry with what your paper emphasizes—for example, the artist's, composer's, or conductor's name—and adjust the elements accordingly. List the medium—CD, LP, Audiocassette—last.

Dylan, Bob. "Rainy Day Women #12." *Blonde on Blonde*. Columbia, 1966. LP.

If you accessed the recording on the Web, drop the original medium of publication and include the Web site or database name (italicized), "Web" as the medium of publication, and the access date.

Dylan, Bob. "Rainy Day Women #12." *Blonde on Blonde*. Columbia, 1966. *Lala*. La La Media, n.d. Web. 10 Mar. 2010.

Cartoon or advertisement

Trudeau, Garry. "Doonesbury." Comic strip. *Seattle Times* 19 Nov. 2001: B4. Print.

Banana Republic. Advertisement. *Details* Oct. 2001: 37. Print.

Interview

Castellucci, Marion. Personal interview. 7 Oct. 2010.

Lecture, speech, or conference presentation

Sharples, Mike. "Authors of the Future." Conference of European Teachers of Academic Writing. U of Groningen. Groningen, Neth. 20 June 2001. Lecture.

Government publications

In general, follow these guidelines:

- Usually cite as author the government agency that produced the document. Begin with the highest level and then branch down to the specific agency:

  United States. Dept. of Justice. FBI.

  Idaho. Dept. of Motor Vehicles.

- Follow this with the title of the document, italicized.
- If a specific person is clearly identified as the author, you may begin the citation with that person's name, or you may list the author (preceded by the word "By") after the title of the document.
- Follow standard procedures for citing publication information for print sources or Web sources.

United States. Dept. of Justice. FBI. *The School Shooter: A Threat Assessment Perspective*. By Mary Ellen O'Toole. 2000. Web. 16 Aug. 2001.

James Gardiner (student), "Why *Facebook* Might Not Be Good for You" (MLA-Style Research Paper)

As an illustration of a student research paper written in MLA style, we present James Gardiner's paper on online social networks. James's process in producing this paper has been discussed in various places throughout the text.

MLA Style

Include your last name and page number on each page.

Gardiner 1

James Gardiner

Professor Johnson

Writing Seminar: Inquiry and Argument

15 May 2007

Center title.

Why *Facebook* Might Not Be Good for You:

Some Dangers of Online Social Networks

Indent paragraphs 5 spaces or 1/2 inch.

Walk into any computer lab located at any college campus across the country and you'll see dozens of students logged onto an online social network (OSN). In the last few years, the use of these networks has skyrocketed among Internet users, especially young adults. These new virtual communities are significantly influencing the way young people communicate and interact with one another. A report titled "E-Expectations: The Class of 2007" went so far as to label upcoming college freshmen "the Social-Networking Generation" (qtd. in Joly).

Double space all text.

In late 2006, the Pew Internet Project, a nonpartisan, nonprofit research group that examines the social impact of the Internet, reported that 55 percent of online teens have created a personal profile on OSNs and that 48 percent of teens visit social networking Web sites daily, with 22 percent visiting several times a day (Lenhart and Madden 2). The two most popular OSNs are *MySpace* and *Facebook*. *MySpace* is a general networking site that allows anyone to join, develop a profile, and display personal information. In less than four years of existence, *MySpace* has exploded to become the third most visited Web site on the Internet behind only *Google* and *Yahoo* ("Top Sites") with more than 100 million members (Joly). *Facebook* is geared more toward college students (until recently it required that a person attend a university to join the network) and is the number-one site accessed by 18- to 24-year-olds. According to research studies cited in an article in the *Toronto Star*, 90 percent of all undergraduates log on to *Facebook* and

Use 1-inch margins.

Italicize book and periodical titles and Web site names.

Gardiner 2

60 percent log on daily (George-Cosh W1). *Facebook* has also experienced unprecedented growth in its relatively short existence and now ranks as the seventh most visited site on the Internet ("Top Sites") and has a member base of more than 19 million (Joly).

With the use of OSNs increasing among young people, the term "Facebook trance" has emerged to describe a person who loses all track of time and stares at the screen for hours (Copeland). While "Facebook trance" might describe only an occasional and therefore harmless phenomenon, it gives rise to important questions: What are the possible negative consequences of OSNs? What should youthful users be watchful for and guard against? The purpose of this paper is to identify the possible harms of OSNs. I will suggest that overuse of OSNs can be a contributing factor to a decline in grades as well as to other problems such as a superficial view of relationships, an increase in narcissism, and possible future embarrassment.

I don't mean to deny that OSNs have positive consequences for young people. For one thing, they provide a "virtual hangout" that acts as a convenient and cost-effective way to stay in close contact with friends and family. According to the Pew survey, 91 percent of users use OSNs to keep in touch with their regularly seen friends, while 82 percent use the sites to stay in touch with distant friends (Lenhart and Madden). OSNs let young people regularly view their friends' profiles, leave short messages or comments, and share personal information. OSN researcher Danah Boyd also claims that these sites give young people a platform on which to experiment with identities, voice their opinions, and practice how they present themselves through personal data, pictures, and music placed in their profiles (Bowley). OSNs also assist them in learning more about people they've met offline. Used as an investigative tool, OSNs offer quick ways to get additional background information on someone. For example, a student could use an OSN to decide whom to partner with for

Gardiner 3

a class project, to learn more about a new roommate, or to find out more about someone he or she just met at a party, all by browsing classmates' profiles.

Use quotation marks for article titles.

Use "qtd. in" for a source quoted in another source.

Despite these benefits, OSNs have a downside. One potential harm is that OSNs could have a negative effect on grades. One study shows a direct connection between the amount of time spent on the networks and declining grades in school. A college newspaper article entitled "Research Links *MySpace* Use to Drop in Grades" reports a survey of high school students conducted by Fresno State University professor Tamyra Pierce. Pierce found that students with *MySpace* accounts were significantly more likely than students without *MySpace* accounts to report a decline in grades since the previous year. According to Pierce, "We can't know for sure that *MySpace* caused the lower grades, but when compared to other after-school activities (work, sports, video games, etc.), only *MySpace* showed significance" (qtd. in "Research Links"). Pierce's research also revealed that 42 percent of polled students said they often had *MySpace* open while doing homework, and 34 percent stated that they would delay homework to spend time on social networking sites. Pierce adds that 59 percent of students reported spending "between 30 minutes and six hours daily on *MySpace*." Such heavy usage significantly takes time away from school work, extracurricular activities, and sleep. Although this specific study focused on high school students, it would be safe to assume that the results would be generally similar for college students. In fact, the results of the Fresno State study were reported in other college newspapers (Scrabis; Jimenez); the writers for these college newspapers usually included anecdotes from their own campuses about college students obsessed with OSNs. One Penn State student said of *MySpace*, "I keep getting rid of it and then getting it back again because I'm addicted. It's like cocaine" (qtd. in Scrabis).

Another potential problem with OSNs is their tendency to promote superficial or unsatisfying relationships. According to Chou, Condron, and

Gardiner 4

Belland, for some users "over-dependence on online relationships may result in significant problems with real-life interpersonal and occupational functioning" (381). When logged on to the network, students may believe that they are "in touch" with people, when actually they are physically alone with their computers. In a controversial 1998 article cited by Matsuba, Kraut and his colleagues suggested that extensive Internet use "was associated with declines in participants' communication with family members in the household, declines in the size of their social circle, and increases in their depression and loneliness" (qtd. in Matsuba 275). Matsuba conducted an extensive study to test Kraut's conclusions. Matsuba found that persons who scored high on measures of loneliness spent more time on the Internet than persons who scored low on the loneliness measures. In another facet of his study, Matsuba found that for persons who established online friendships, these friendships did not seem "as rich and diverse in quality compared to face-to-face friendships" (283). Matsuba concludes that while online communication can be used to enhance relationships, it can become a problem when it begins to replace offline interaction. He found that face-to-face friendships scored higher for both positive and negative aspects of relationships than did online friendships. He then speculates, "While it is possible that the internet is helping [lonely] people in their search, the possibility remains that the internet is hindering them in facing life in the 'real' world and thus preventing them from developing an adult identity" (283).

Matsuba's finding that face-to-face friendships are more "rich and diverse in quality" than online friendships has led me to speculate that a possible problem with OSNs is the complete lack of nonverbal communication exchanged between users. According to communications professor Julia T. Woods, "Scholars estimate that nonverbal behaviors account for 65 percent to 93 percent of the total meaning of communication" (132). Since the people interacting on OSNs are unable to view each other, they are unable to gauge the other's subtle body language, facial expressions, and voice tones that are such vital ingredients of effective communication. Part of achieving the "adult identity" called for by Matsuba is learning to communicate nonverbally as well as verbally in an environment requiring real contact.

For me, a particularly interesting yet subtle danger of OSNs is their contribution to a rise in narcissism. In an article with the subtitle "Study Says Many Students Are Narcissists," journalist E. Hoover reports on the unpublished research of Jean M. Twenge, a psychology professor at San Diego State University, who says that new technologies such as OSNs have "stoked the self-loving tendencies of modern students" (qtd. in Hoover). Twenge's recent research shows that college kids today are more narcissistic than college kids were in the 1980s; she labels the current generation of youth as "the most narcissistic in recent history" (Hoover). According to Hoover, Twenge defines narcissism as "excessive vanity and a sense of entitlement." Narcissists, Hoover reports, "tend to lack empathy for others, behave aggressively when insulted, and ignore the needs of those around them."

According to Twenge, narcissism finds expression on OSNs in the way that young people on *MySpace* and *Facebook* compete with each other to be heard. In another article reporting Twenge's research, Melissa Ludwig states that OSNs have "gone beyond touching base with friends to an arena where people vie for the most digital friends, the best videos, the coolest sites, and the biggest audience" (A15). She then quotes Twenge: "Now it all becomes a competition, seeking attention and seeking status rather than a true connection between people, or a meaningful connection." The work of Twenge and others suggests that the popularity of OSNs is partly the result of young people's finding an online way to express their narcissistic tendencies. The sites may contribute to self-expression more than to connection and friendship.

Gardiner 6

A final danger of OSNs is that persons will place on their sites material that they will later regret. Young people tend to think that their audiences are only their like-minded friends and classmates. They often don't imagine their professors, their potential employers, or even their parents reading their sites. One journalist describes a *MySpace* profile in which a college student has posted photos of herself in "a skin-tight black leather Catwoman costume, two triangles of vinyl struggling to cover her silicone-enhanced breasts" (Ludwig A15). Ludwig continues:

> Much of the stuff floating around in cyberspace is tame, mundane even. But there also is plenty that's racy, embarrassing or squeamishly intimate. Bad or good, Generation Next is living out loud and doing it online, before a global audience, in a medium where digital archives may linger for a long, long time.... [Generation Nexters] still are too young to fully grasp the permanence of their online actions, and the possible consequences down the road. (A15)

Indent longer quotations 10 spaces or 1 inch.

Use ellipsis to show omitted words.

Use brackets when inserting explanatory words in quotation.

Cite page number after period.

One indication of this danger has already surfaced in the case of some sports teams. The University of Minnesota Duluth recently barred all athletes from creating profiles on *MySpace*, *Facebook*, and similar sites, a policy that, according to journalist Chao Xiong, aims to shield students and the school from bad press that might occur from the posting of inappropriate material. Xiong reports that athletic departments across the country are considering similar bans. One coach at the UM-Duluth campus said, "It was amazing to me how revealing people are with their lives on the Internet" (qtd. in Xiong 1A). (This coach had established her own *Facebook* profile in order to police the activities of her team members.) Xiong reports that across the country athletes have embarrassed their programs by posting pictures of themselves drinking blindfolded at parties or making disparaging comments about coaches or teammates. It is unclear whether coaches have the legal right to forbid their team members to place profiles on OSNs (some students are claiming violation of free speech rights). However, the fact that athletic programs are concerned about the impact of these social networks shows the potential negative consequence of posting embarrassing material on OSNs.

Although I don't support the banning of *Facebook* or *MySpace* profiles for athletes or other students, I do think that young people should be aware of some of the problems associated with them. Two of the problems I have noted here—decline in grades and narcissistic competition for the coolest sites—could be avoided by students' simply limiting their time online. Knowing that OSNs can promote a superficial view of friendships might encourage people to use OSNs to stay in touch face-to-face with friends rather than try to find online substitutes for real friendships. Finally, young people should be aware that the materials they post on their profiles might one day come back to haunt them. To gain the maximum benefits of online social networks and avoid the pitfalls associated with them, my advice to today's students would be to use them as an advanced e-mail-type communication tool rather than as a place to loiter and waste valuable hours that they will never get back.

Gardiner 8

Works Cited

Bowley, Graham. "The High Priestess of Internet Friendship." *Financial Times Weekend Magazine* 27 Oct. 2006. *LexisNexis Academic*. Web. 22 Feb. 2007.

Chou, Chien, Linda Condron, and John C. Belland. "A Review of the Research on Internet Addiction." *Educational Psychology Review* 17.4 (2005): 363–89. *Academic Search Complete.* Web. 22 Feb. 2007.

Copeland, Libby. "Click Clique: *Facebook's* Online College Community." *Washingtonpost.com*. Washington Post, 28 Dec. 2004. Web. 24 Feb. 2007.

George-Cosh, David. "Social Net: Thousands of Local Students Build Friendships on *Facebook*." *TheStar.com*. Toronto Star, 20 Jan. 2007. Web. 15 Apr. 2007.

Hoover, E. "Here's You Looking at You, Kid: Study Says Many Students Are Narcissists." *Chronicle of Higher Education* 53.29 (9 Mar. 2007): A41. *Academic Search Complete*. Web. 14 Apr. 2007.

Jimenez, Eddie. "*MySpace* Adds to Overload for Teens." *Fresno Bee* 9 Mar. 2007. *Newspaper Source*. Web. 14 Apr. 2007.

Joly, Karine. "*Facebook, MySpace*, and Co." *University Business*. Professional Media Group, Apr. 2007. Web. 5 May 2007.

Lenhart, Amanda, and Mary Madden. "Social Networking Websites and Teens: An Overview." *Pew Internet and American Life Project*. Pew Research Center, 3 Jan. 2007. Web. 19 Feb. 2007.

Ludwig, Melissa. "LOOK@ME: Generation Next Is Living Out Loud and Online." *MySanAntonio.com*. San Antonio Express News, 15 Mar. 2007. Web. 15 Apr. 2007.

Matsuba, M. Kyle. "Searching for Self and Relationships Online." *CyberPsychology and Behavior* 9.3 (2006): 275–84. *Academic Search Complete*. Web. 14 Apr. 2007.

Start Works Cited list on a new page.

Center heading.

List sources alphabetically.

Use day-month-year format for dates.

Italicize database names.

Italicize periodical titles.

Use quotation marks for article titles.

MLA Style

Gardiner 9

"Research Links *MySpace* Use to Drop in Grades." *FresnoStateNews.com*. California State U, 9 Mar. 2007. Web. 2 May 2007.

Scrabis, J. "*MySpace* Usage May Lower Grades in Both High School, College Students." *Daily Collegian*. Pennsylvania State U, 23 Mar. 2007. Web. 15 Apr. 2007.

"Top Sites for United States." *alexia.com*. N.p., n.d. Web. 2 May 2007. <http://www.alexia.com/site/ds/ top_sites?cc=US&ts_mode=country&lang=none>.

Woods, Julia T. *Interpersonal Communication*: *Everyday Encounters*. 5th ed. New York: Wadsworth, 2007. Print.

Xiong, Chao. "Not Their Space." *Minneapolis Star Tribune* 16 Apr. 2007. *LexisNexis*. Web. 2 May 2007.

Put URLs in angle brackets.

Italicize book titles.

Check that everything cited in paper is in Works Cited list.

SKILL 22.4 Cite and document sources using APA style.

In many respects, the APA style and the MLA style are similar and the basic logic is the same. In the APA system, the list where readers can find full bibliographic information is titled "References"; as in MLA format, it includes only the sources cited in the body of the paper. The distinguishing features of APA citation style are highlighted in the following sections.

For an example of a student paper in APA style, see the report by Campbell et al. on pp.231–238.

In-Text Citations in APA Style

A typical APA-style in-text citation contains three elements: (1) the last name of the author, (2) the date of the publication, and (3) the page number of the quoted or paraphrased passage. Table 22.3 identifies some typical variations and shows again the one-to-one connection between the in-text citation and the References list.

TABLE 22.3 In-Text Citations in APA Style

Type of Source	References Entry at End of Paper	In-Text Citation in Body of Paper
One author	Pollan, M. (2006). *The omnivore's dilemma: A natural history of four meals.* New York, NY: Penguin.	...(Pollan, 2006, p. 256). OR According to Pollan (2006), ... (p. 256).
Two authors	Kwon, O., & Wen, Y. (2010). An empirical study of the factors affecting social network service use. *Computers in Human Behavior, 26,* 254–263. doi:10.1016/j.chb.2009.04.011	...(Kwon & Wen, 2010, p. 262). OR Kwon and Wen (2010) claim that...(p. 262).
Three to five authors	Pollay, R. W., Lee, J. S., & Carter-Whitney, D. (1992). Separate, but not equal: Racial segmentation in cigarette advertising. *Journal of Advertising, 21*(1), 45–57.	...race" (Pollay, Lee, & Carter-Whitney, 1992, p. 52). OR Pollay, Lee, and Carter-Whitney have argued that "advertisers... race" (1992, p. 52). *For subsequent citations, use* Pollay et al. *For a quotation, use the specific page number, not the whole range of pages.*

(continued)

TABLE 22.3 *continued*

Type of Source	References Entry at End of Paper	In-Text Citation in Body of Paper
Author has more than one work in References list	Dombrowski, D. A. (1984). *The philosophy of vegetarianism.* Amherst, MA: University of Massachusetts Press. Dombrowski, D. A. (1997). *Babies and beasts: The argument from marginal cases.* Urbana: University of Illinois Press.	. . . (Dombrowski, 1984, p. 207). . . . (Dombrowski, 1997, p. 328). OR Dombrowski (1984) claims that . . . (p. 207). According to Dombrowski (1997), . . . (p. 328).
Indirect citation of a source that you found in another source *You use a quotation from Peter Singer from a book by Dombrowski. Include Dombrowski, not Singer, in References.*	Dombrowski, D. A. (1997). *Babies and beasts: The argument from marginal cases.* Urbana: University of Illinois Press.	Animal rights activist Peter Singer argues that . . . (as cited in Dombrowski, 1997, p. 429). *Singer is used for the attributive tag, but the in-text citation is to Dombrowski.*

References List in APA Style

The APA References list at the end of a paper presents entries alphabetically. If you cite more than one item for an author, repeat the author's name each time and arrange the items in chronological order, beginning with the earliest. In cases where two works by an author appeared in the same year, arrange them in the list alphabetically by title, and then add a lowercase "a" or "b" (etc.) after the date so that you can distinguish between them in the in-text citations:

A formatted References list appears on p. 238.

Smith, R. (1999a). *Body image in non-Western cultures, 1750–present.* London, England: Bonanza Press.

Smith, R. (1999b). Eating disorders reconsidered. *Journal of Appetite Studies, 45,* 295–300.

APA Citation Models

Print Articles in Scholarly Journals

General Format for Print Article in Scholarly Journal

Author. (Year of Publication). Article title. *Journal Title, volume number,* page numbers. doi: xx.xxxx/x.xxxx.xx

If there is one, include the **DOI** (digital object identifier), a number that is uniquely assigned to many journal articles. Note the style for capitalizing article titles and for italicizing the volume number.

One author

Herrera-Sobek, M. (2006). Border aesthetics: The politics of Mexican immigration in film and art. *Western Humanities Review, 60,* 60–71. doi:10.1016/j.chb.2009.04.011

Two to seven authors

Kwon, O., & Wen, Y. (2010). An empirical study of the factors affecting social network service use. *Computers in Human Behavior, 26*, 254–263.

When a source has more than seven authors, list the first six and the last one by name. Use ellipses (. . .) to indicate the authors whose names have been omitted.

Scholarly journal that restarts page numbering with each issue

Pollay, R. W., Lee, J. S., & Carter-Whitney, D. (1992). Separate, but not equal: Racial segmentation in cigarette advertising. *Journal of Advertising, 21*(1), 45–57.

Note that the issue number and the parentheses are *not* italicized.

Print Articles in Magazines and Newspapers

General Format for Print Article in Magazine or Newspaper

Author. (Year, Month Day). Article title. *Periodical Title, volume number*, page numbers.

If page numbers are discontinuous, identify every page, separating numbers with a comma.

Magazine article with named author

Hall, S. S. (2001, March 11). Prescription for profit. *The New York Times Magazine*, 40–45, 59, 91–92, 100.

Magazine article without named author

Daddy, daddy. (2001, July 30). *New Republic, 225*, 12–13.

Review of book or film

Schwarz, B. (2001, November). A bit of bunting: A new history of the British empire elevates expediency to principle [Review of the book *Ornamentalism: How the British saw their empire*]. *Atlantic Monthly, 288*, 126–135.

Kaufman, S. (2001, July 30). Polishing a gem [Review of the motion picture *The blue angel*]. *New Republic, 225*, 28–29.

Newspaper article

Henriques, D. B. (1998, September 27). Hero's fall teaches Wall Street a lesson. *Seattle Times*, pp. A1, A24.

Newspaper editorial

Dr. Frankenstein on the hill [Editorial]. (2002, May 18). *The New York Times*, p. A22.

Letter to the editor of a magazine or newspaper

Tomsovic, K. (1998, July 13). Culture clash [Letter to the editor]. *The New Yorker*, 7.

Print Books

General Format for Print Books

Author. (Year of publication). *Book title: Subtitle.* City, State [abbreviated]: Name of Publisher.

Brumberg, J. J. (1997). *The body project: An intimate history of American girls.* New York, NY: Vintage.

If the publisher's name indicates the state in which it is located, list the city but omit the state.

Reid, H., & Taylor, B. (2010). *Recovering the commons: Democracy, place, and global justice.* Champaign: University of Illinois Press.

Second, later, or revised edition

Montagu, A. (1986). *Touching: The human significance of the skin* (3rd ed.). New York, NY: Perennial Press.

Republished book (for example, a paperback published after the original hardback edition or a modern edition of an older work)

Wollstonecraft, M. (1995). *The vindication of the rights of woman, with strictures on political and moral subjects.* Rutland, VT: Tuttle. (Original work published 1792)

The in-text citation should read: (Wollstonecraft, 1792/1995).

Multivolume work

Churchill, W. S. (1956–1958). *A history of the English-speaking peoples* (Vols. 1–4). New York, NY: Dodd, Mead.

Citation for all the volumes together. The in-text citation should read: (Churchill, 1956–1958).

Churchill, W. S. (1957). *A history of the English-speaking peoples: Vol. 4. The great democracies.* New York, NY: Dodd, Mead.

Citation for a specific volume. The in-text citation should read: (Churchill, 1957).

Article in reference work

Ling, T. O. (1970). Buddhism in Burma. In S. G. F. Brandon (Ed.), *Dictionary of comparative religion.* New York, NY: Scribner's.

Translation

De Beauvoir, S. (1961). *The second sex* (H. M. Parshley, Trans.). New York, NY: Bantam Books. (Original work published 1949)

The in-text citation should read: (De Beauvoir, 1949/1961).

Corporate author (a commission, committee, or other group)

American Red Cross. (1993). *Standard first aid.* St. Louis, MO: Mosby Lifeline.

Anonymous author

The New Yorker cartoon album: 1975–1985. (1987). New York, NY: Penguin Books.

The in-text citation is (*New Yorker*, 1987).

Whole anthology

O'Connell, D. F., & Alexander, C. N. (Eds.). (1994). *Self recovery: Treating addictions using transcendental meditation and Maharishi Ayur-Veda.* New York, NY: Haworth Press.

Anthology article

Royer, A. (1994). The role of the transcendental meditation technique in promoting smoking cessation: A longitudinal study. In D. F. O'Connell & C. N. Alexander (Eds.), *Self recovery: Treating addictions using transcendental meditation and Maharishi Ayur-Veda* (pp. 221–239). New York, NY: Haworth Press.

Articles or Books from an Online Database

Article from database with digital object identifier (DOI)

Scharrer, E., Daniel, K. D., Lin, K.-M., & Liu, Z. (2006). Working hard or hardly working? Gender, humor, and the performance of domestic chores in television commercials. *Mass Communication and Society, 9*(2), 215–238. doi:10.1207/s15327825mcs0902_5

Omit the database name. If an article or other document has been assigned a digital object identifier (DOI), include the DOI at the end. To see where the information in the Scharrer citation came from, refer to Figure 22.4.

Article from database without DOI

Highland, R. A., & Dabney, D. A. (2009). Using Adlerian theory to shed light on drug dealer motivations. *Applied Psychology in Criminal Justice, 5*(2), 109–138. Retrieved from http://www.apcj.org

Omit the database name. Instead, use a search engine to locate the publication's home page, and cite that URL. If you need to break a URL at the end of a line, do not use a hyphen. Instead, break it *before* a punctuation mark or *after* http://.

Other Internet Sources

General Format for Web Documents

Author, editor, director, narrator, performer, compiler, or producer of the work, if available. (Year, Month Day of posting). *Title of web document, italicized.* Retrieved from Name of website if different from author or title: URL of home page

Barrett, J. (2007, January 17). *MySpace is a natural monopoly.* Retrieved from ECommerce Times website: http://www.ecommercetimes.com

FIGURE 22.4 Scholarly Journal Article with a Digital Object Identifier (DOI) with Elements Identified for an APA-Style Citation

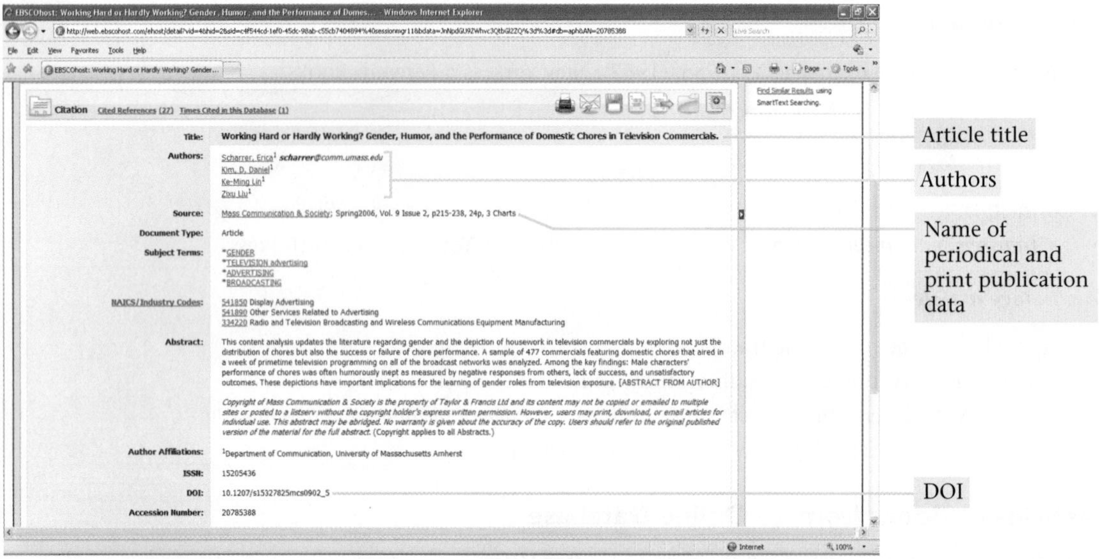

Scharrer, E., Daniel, K. D., Lin, K.-M., & Liu, Z. (2006). Working hard or hardly working? Gender, humor, and the performance of domestic chores in television commericals. *Mass Communication and Society*, *9*(2), 215–238. doi:10.1207/s15327825mcs0902_5

To see where each element of the Barrett citation comes from, refer to Figure 22.2.

If there is no posting date for the document you cite, use *n.d.* (for "no date").

Marks, J. (n.d.). "Overview: Letter from the president." Retrieved June 3, 2010, from the Search for Common Ground website: http://www.sfcg.org

Entire Web site

BlogPulse. (n.d.). Retrieved September 3, 2010, from the Intelliseek website: http://www.intelliseek.com

Article from a newspaper site

Bounds, A. (2007, June 26). Thinking like scientists. *Daily Camera* [Boulder]. Retrieved from http://www.dailycamera.com

Article from a scholarly e-journal

Welch, J. R., & Riley, R. (2001). Reclaiming land and spirit in the western Apache homeland. *American Indian Quarterly, 25*, 5–14. Retrieved from http://muse.jhu.edu/journals/american_indian_quarterly

Reference material

Cicada. (2004). In *Encyclopaedia Britannica*. Retrieved from http://www.britannica.com

E-book

Hoffman, F. W. (1981). *The literature of rock: 1954–1978.* Retrieved from http://www.netlibrary.com

E-mail, interviews, and personal correspondence

Cite personal correspondence in the body of your text, but not in the References list: "Daffinrud (personal communication, December 12, 2001) claims that. . . . "

Blog Posting

Dyer, B., & Barnes, E. (2008, October 7). The "greening" of the Arctic [Web log post]. Retrieved from http://blog.epa.gov/blog/2008/10/07/the-greening-of-the-arctic

To see where each element of this citation comes from, refer to Figure 22.3.

Web video

Beck, R. (2006, November 2). Immigration gumballs [Video file]. Retrieved from http://www.youtube.com/watch?v=n7WJeqxuOfQ

Podcast

Funke, E. (Host). (2007, June 26). *ArtScene* [Audio podcast]. National Public Radio. Retrieved from http://www.npr.org

Miscellaneous Sources

Television program

Bochco, S., & Milch, D. (Directors). (2001, November 6). Lie like a rug [Television series episode]. In *NYPD blue*. New York, NY: American Broadcasting Company.

Film

Madden, J. (Director). (1998). *Shakespeare in love* [Motion picture]. United States: Universal Miramax.

Sound recording

Dylan, B. (1966). Rainy day women #12. On *Blonde on blonde* [Record]. New York, NY: Columbia.

Government publications

O'Toole, M. (2000). *The school shooter: A threat assessment perspective*. Washington, DC: U.S. Federal Bureau of Investigation. Retrieved from http://www.fbi.gov/publications/school/school2.pdf

Student Example of an APA-Style Research Paper

An example of a paper in APA style is shown on pages 230–238.

PART 5

WRITING FOR ASSESSMENT

This advocacy ad, part of the ongoing "If I Stay on the Rez" campaign to raise money for tribal colleges, is sponsored by the American Indian College Fund. At the Web site www.collegefund.org, you can see the other campaign ads. Each ad spotlights a contemporary Native American man or woman against a striking landscape, briefly identifies the reservation and the tribal college, states a few persuasive facts and statistics about the success of these colleges, and provides contact information. Consider how these ads achieve the campaign's purpose "to shatter people's misconceptions about Indian people" (www.collegefund.org).

We refer to this ad in Chapter 15, page 408 in the discussion of proposals as visual arguments.

NAVAJO RESERVATION,
HOME OF DINÉ COLLEGE
If I stay on the rez
I'm eight times less likely to drop out of college.
BY STARTING THEIR ACADEMIC CAREERS AT A TRIBAL COLLEGE,
NINE IN TEN INDIAN STUDENTS WILL COMPLETE THEIR COURSE OF STUDY.
LEARN HOW THE TRIBAL COLLEGES PROVIDE QUALITY EDUCATION TO NATIVE AMERICANS. 1-800-776-FUND | COLLEGEFUND.ORG
AMERICAN INDIAN COLLEGE FUND
EDUCATING THE MIND AND SPIRIT

PART 5 WRITING FOR ASSESSMENT

Part 5 addresses the following outcomes for first-year composition from the Council of Writing Program Administrators.

RHETORICAL KNOWLEDGE	• Focus on a purpose (Ch. 23, 24) • Respond appropriately to different kinds of rhetorical situations (Ch. 23, 24) • Adopt appropriate voice, tone, and level of formality (Ch. 23)
CRITICAL THINKING	• Use writing and reading for inquiry, learning, thinking, and communicating (Ch. 23, 24) • Understand the relationships among language, knowledge, and power (Ch. 24)
PROCESSES	• Develop flexible strategies for generating, revising, editing, and proofreading (Ch. 23) • Learn to critique their own and others' work (Ch. 24)
KNOWLEDGE OF CONVENTIONS	• Develop knowledge of genre conventions ranging from structure and paragraphing to tone and mechanics (Ch. 23)
COMPOSING IN ELECTRONIC ENVIRONMENTS	• Use electronic environments for drafting, revising, reviewing, editing and submitting texts (Ch. 24)

ESSAY EXAMINATIONS

23

I'm pretty good at writing research essays, but when I have to write under pressure, I freeze. Last time I took an essay test, I wrote two pages before I realized that I'd left out an important piece of my argument. By the time I had scratched out, made additions, and drawn arrows all over the page, my paper was such a mess that I couldn't decipher it. Needless to say, the instructor couldn't either.

—*Student A*

For me, the worst thing about exams is trying to figure out what the professor wants. The final in my European literature course was a perfect example: There was only one question. It started with a difficult-to-follow quotation from an author we hadn't studied, which we were supposed to apply to a whole slew of questions about novels we had read during the semester. The question went on for half a page (single-spaced!) and had at least five or six subsections. By the time I finished reading it, I didn't have a clue about where to start or how to cover so much ground in a single essay.

—*Student B*

As these students' comments indicate, taking essay exams can be stressful and frustrating. When instructors give essay exams, they want to see how well you can restate, apply, and assess course material. Just as important, they want to see whether you can discuss what you have studied—whether you can participate in that discipline's discourse community. These twin demands make essay exams doubly challenging. Furthermore, not only must you master course material, but you must also write about it quickly.

In this chapter, you will learn to:

- plan and write an essay exam
- adapt to the unique requirements of in-class essay writing

How Essay Exams Differ from Other Essays

Essay exams do share similarities with other assignments. Most of the instructions in this book apply to exam writing. For instance, you have learned how to respond to rhetorical context—audience, purpose, and genre—as you write an essay. Your audience for an essay exam is your instructor, so you need to ask yourself what your instructor values and wants. Does your instructor stress analysis of material or application of roles? Does your instructor encourage individual interpretations? Just as analyzing an audience helps you focus an out-of-class essay, so too can analyzing your instructor's expectations help you focus an exam response.

You also know the importance of knowing what you're talking about. Even the most brilliant writers will stumble on a test if they haven't bothered to attend class regularly, take notes, participate in class discussions, and keep up with the reading. Familiarity with the material lays the groundwork for a successful exam performance, just as thorough research and exploratory writing grounds a good paper.

However, not all the writing strategies you use for papers will serve you well in a test situation. Writing researcher Randall Popken, after reviewing more than two hundred sample exams in various disciplines, identified three skills unique to essay exam writing:

1. The ability to store, access, and translate appropriate knowledge into an organized essay
2. The ability to analyze quickly the specific requirements of an exam question and formulate a response to those requirements
3. The ability to deal with time pressure, test anxiety, and other logistical constraints of the exam situation

We examine each of these skills in the next section.

Preparing for an Exam: Learning Subject Matter

Preparing for an exam involves finding efficient ways to organize, recall, and apply your knowledge so that you can easily construct an intelligent discussion on paper.

Identifying and Learning Main Ideas

No instructor will expect you to remember every single piece of information covered in class. Most instructors are happy if you can remember main ideas and theories, key terminology, and a few supporting examples. The best strategy when you study for an essay exam is to figure out what is most important and learn it first.

How do you determine the main ideas and key concepts? Sometimes they're obvious. Many professors outline their lectures on the board or distribute review sheets before each exam. If your professor does not provide explicit instructions, listen for a thesis statement, main points, and transitions in each lecture to determine the key ideas and relationships among them. For example,

> The *most important critics* of the welfare state are...
> *Four developments* contributed to the reemergence of the English after the Norman invasion...
> Hegel's dialectic was *most influenced by* Kant...

Look for similar signals in your textbook and pay special attention to chapter summaries, subheadings, and highlighted terms. If the course involves a lot of discussion or if your professor prefers informal remarks to highly structured lectures, you may have to work harder to identify major points. But streamlining and organizing your knowledge in this way will keep you from feeling overwhelmed when you sit down to study.

Skill 17.8 explains some of the main organizing moves writers use in the bodies of essays to clarify and develop their points.

Most instructors expect you to master more than the information they cover in class. Essay exams in humanities, social science, and fine arts courses often ask for an individual interpretation, argument, or critique. To prepare for such questions, practice talking back to course readings by developing your own positions on the viewpoints they express. If the professor has lectured on factors involved in mainstreaming schoolchildren with physical disabilities, look at your notes and try to define your own position on mainstreaming. If the textbook identifies salient features of Caravaggio's art, decide how you think his paintings compare to and differ from his contemporaries' work. Questioning texts and lectures in this way will help you personalize the material, expand your understanding, and take ownership of your education. Remember, though, that professors won't be impressed by purely subjective opinions; as you explore your views, search for evidence and arguments, not just from your own experience but from the course as well, that you can use to support your ideas in the exam.

For specific strategies to help you understand and respond to reading material, review Chapter 5 and Chapter 12.

Applying Your Knowledge

In business, science, social science, and education courses, professors may ask you to apply a theory or method to a new situation. For example, they might ask you to show how "first in, last out" accounting might work in bookkeeping for a machine parts factory or how you might use psychodynamic concepts to analyze a hypothetical case study.

If you suspect that such a question might appear, use some study time to practice this kind of thinking. Brainstorm two or three current situations to which you could apply the theories or concepts you've been learning. Check local newspapers or browse the Web for ideas. Then freewrite for a few minutes on how you might organize an essay that puts the theory to work. For instance, if you've studied federal affirmative action law in a public administration course, you might ask the following questions: How did the decision by the U.S. Supreme Court in regard to the University of Michigan's affirmative action policies affect the use of race as a factor in college admissions? How might it apply to a local college trying to attract a diverse student body? You won't be able to predict exactly what will appear on the exam, but you can become skilled at transferring ideas into new settings.

Making a Study Plan

Once you've identified crucial subject matter, you need to develop a study plan. If you're a novice at studying for a major exam, try following some tried-and-true approaches.

- Review your instructor's previous exams. Don't be afraid to ask your instructor for general guidelines about the type, length, and format of questions he or she normally includes on tests.
- Generate your own practice questions and compose responses.
- Organize group study sessions with two to four classmates. Meet regularly to discuss readings, exchange practice questions, test each other informally, and critique each other's essays.

Avoid study techniques that are almost universally ineffective: Don't waste time trying to reread all the material or memorize passages word for word (unless the exam will require you to produce specific formulas or quotations). Don't set an unreasonable schedule. You can seldom learn the material adequately in one or two nights, and the anxiety produced by cramming can hurt your performance even more. Most important, don't stay up all night studying. Doing so can be worse than not studying at all, since sleep deprivation impairs your ability to recall and process information.

No matter how you decide to study, remember that the point of developing exam-preparation strategies isn't simply to do well on a single test, but to become comfortable with learning difficult, complex material and to acquire a level of intellectual confidence that will help you grow as a writer.

Analyzing Exam Questions

Whereas paper assignments typically ask you to address broad problems that can be solved in numerous possible ways, essay exams usually require much more narrowly focused responses. Essay exams feature well-defined problems with a very narrow range of right answers. They require you to recall a particular body of information and present it in a highly specific way. However, what your instructors are asking you to recall and how they want it presented will not always be clear to you. Exam questions often require interpretation.

Although the language of essay exams varies considerably across disciplines, professors typically draw on a set of conventional moves when they write exam prompts. Consider the following question from an undergraduate course in the history of the English language:

> Walt Whitman once wrote that English was not "an abstract construction of dictionary makers" but a language that had "its basis broad and low, close to the ground." Whitman reminds us that English is a richly expressive language because it comes from a variety of cultural sources. One of these is African-American culture. Write an essay discussing the major ways in which African-American culture and dialect have influenced the English language in the United States. Identify and illustrate at least

three important influences: What were the historical circumstances? What important events and people were involved? What were the specific linguistic contributions?

This question presents an intimidating array of instructions, but it becomes manageable if you recognize some standard organizational features.

Understanding the Use of Outside Quotations

First, like many exam questions, this sample opens with a quotation from an author or work not covered in the course. Many students panic when they encounter such questions. "Whitman?! We didn't even study Whitman. What am I supposed to do now?" Don't worry. The primary function of such quotations is to encapsulate a general issue that the instructor wants you to address in your response. When you encounter an unfamiliar quotation, look carefully at the rest of the question for clues about what role the quotation should play in your essay. The point of the Whitman quotation is restated in the very next sentence—English is shaped by numerous cultural influences—and the function of the quotation is simply to reinforce that point. Because the rest of the question tells you specifically what kinds of cultural influences your response should address (African-American culture, three major linguistic contributions), you don't need to consider this quotation when you write your essay.

Sometimes professors will ask you to take a position on an unfamiliar quotation and support your argument with material covered in the course. Suppose that the question was, "What is your position on Whitman's view? Do you believe that English is enriched or corrupted by multicultural influences?" In this case the quotation is presented as the basis for a thesis statement, which you would then explain and support. A successful response might begin, "Whitman believes that multicultural influences make our language better, but this view is hopelessly naive for the following reasons..." or "Whitman correctly argues that the contributions of different cultures enrich our language. Take these three examples...."

Recognizing Organizational Cues

The question itself can show you the best way to organize your response. Questions tend to begin with general themes that often suggest a thesis statement. Subsequent divisions tell you how to organize the essay into sections and in what order to introduce supporting points. For example, a successful response that follows the organization of our sample might be arranged as follows:

- A thesis stating that several contributions from African-American language and culture have enriched English
- Three supporting paragraphs, each discussing a different area of influence by
  1. summarizing historical circumstances
  2. noting important people and events
  3. providing one or two examples of linguistic contributions

Interpreting Key Terms

As do all exam questions, this one asks you to write about a specific body of information in a specific way. When you encounter a lengthy question such as this, first pick out the *noun phrases* that direct you to specific areas of knowledge: "African-American culture," "major influences on the English language in the United States," "historical circumstances," "important events and people," "linguistic contributions." Pay careful attention to words that modify these noun phrases. Does the question tell you how many influences to discuss? What kinds of examples to cite? Does the instructor include conjunctions, such as *or*, to give you a choice of topics, or does he or she use words such as *and* or *as well as* that require you to address all areas mentioned? Words such as *who, what, where,* and *why* also point to particular kinds of information.

After you've determined the specific areas you need to address, look for *directive verbs* that tell you what to do: *discuss, identify,* or *illustrate*, for example. These verbs define the horizons of your response. The strategies chart below defines some key directives that frequently appear in essay exams and provides sample questions for each. Meanings vary somewhat according to the course, the context of the question, and the professor's expectations, but you'll feel more confident if you have basic working definitions.

Strategies for Responding to Common Essay-Question Verbs

Verbs	How to Respond	Example Questions
Analyze	Break an argument, concept, or approach into parts and examine the relations among them; discuss causes and effects; evaluate; or explain your interpretation. Look at the rest of the question to determine which strategies to pursue.	*Analyze* the various technical, acoustic, and aesthetic factors that might lead a musician to choose analog over digital recording for a live performance. Be sure to include the strengths and weaknesses of both methods in your discussion.
Apply	Take a concept, formula, theory, or approach and adapt it to another situation.	Imagine that you've been hired to reengineer the operations of a major U.S. automaker. How might you *apply* the principles of Total Quality Management in your recommendations?
Argue	Take a position for or against an issue and give reasons and evidence to support that position.	*Argue* whether or not cloning should be pursued as a method of human reproduction. Be sure to account for the relationship between cloning and mitosis in your discussion.

Verbs	How to Respond	Example Questions
Compare/ Contrast	Note the similarities (compare) or differences (contrast) between two or more objects or ideas.	*Compare* and *contrast* the leadership styles of Franklin Delano Roosevelt, John F. Kennedy, and Ronald Reagan, focusing on their uses of popular media and political rhetoric.
Construct	Assemble a model, diagram, or other organized presentation of your knowledge about a subject.	*Construct* a model of the writing process that illustrates the major stages writers go through when developing an idea into a finished text.
Critique	Analyze and evaluate an argument or idea, explaining both strengths and weaknesses.	Dinesh D'Souza's "Illiberal Education" sparked widespread controversy when it was published in 1991. Write an essay *critiquing* D'Souza's arguments against affirmative action, identifying both the strengths and weaknesses of his position. Use examples from the text, class discussion, and other class readings to illustrate your points.
Define	Provide a clear, concise, authoritative meaning for an object or idea. The response may include describing the object or idea, distinguishing it clearly from other objects or ideas, or providing one or more supporting examples.	How was "equality" *defined* by the Supreme Court in *Plessy v. Ferguson* (1896)? How did that definition influence subsequent educational policy in the United States?
Discuss	Comprehensively present and analyze important concepts, supported by examples or evidence. Cover several key points or examine the topic from several perspectives. Check the question for guidelines about what to include.	*Discuss* the controversy that surrounded Stanley Milgram's studies of authority and state your own position on the relevance and validity of the experiments.
Enumerate (or List)	List steps, components, or events pertaining to a larger phenomenon, perhaps briefly explaining and commenting on each item.	A two-year-old child falls from a swing on the playground and lies unconscious. As the head preschool teacher, *enumerate* the steps you would take from the time of the accident until the ambulance arrives.

(*continued*)

Verbs	How to Respond	Example Questions
Evaluate	Make a judgment about the worth of an object or idea, examining strengths and weaknesses.	*Evaluate* William Whyte's "Street Corner Society" as an ethnographic study. What are its methodological strengths and weaknesses? Do you believe the weaknesses make Whyte's research obsolete?
Explain	Clarify and state reasons to show how some object or idea relates to a more general topic.	*Explain* the relationship of centripetal force to mass and velocity and give an example to illustrate this relationship.
Identify	Describe some object or idea and explain its significance to a larger topic.	*Identify* the major phonetic characteristics of each of the following language groups of Africa, and provide illustrative examples: Koisan, Niger-Kordofanian, and Nilo-Saharan.
Illustrate	Give one or more examples, cases, or other concrete instances to clarify a general concept.	Define "monopoly," "public utility," and "competition," and give specific *illustrations* of each.
Prove	Produce reasons and evidence to establish that a position is logical, supportable, or factual.	Use your knowledge about the findings of the National Assessment of Educational Progress to *prove* that public schools either are or are not doing an adequate job of educating children to become productive U.S. citizens.
Review	Briefly survey or summarize something.	*Review* the major differences between Socrates' conception of ethics and the ethical theories of his contemporaries in the fifth century B.C.E.
Summarize	Lay out the main points of a theory, argument, or event in a concise and organized manner.	*Summarize* Mill's definition of justice and explain how it differs from Kant's. Which definition comes closest to your own, and why?
Trace	Explain chronologically a series of events or the development of an idea.	Write an essay that *traces* the pathway of a nerve impulse through the nervous system, being sure to explain neuron structure, action potential, and the production and reception of neurotransmitters.

Our thanks to Michael C. Flanigan, who suggested some of the terms for this table, in "Processes of Essay Exams," manuscript. University of Oklahoma, 1991.

In some questions, directives are implied rather than stated directly. If a question asks, "Discuss the effects of Ronald Reagan's tax policies on the U.S. economy during the 1980s," you'll need to summarize what those policies were before you can assess their effects. Before you can take a position on an issue, you have to define what the controversy is about. In general, when you answer any question, you should include sufficient background information about the topic to convince your instructor that you're making an informed argument, whether or not the question specifically asks for background information.

FOR WRITING AND DISCUSSION

Analyze Essay Questions

This exercise will hone your ability to analyze essay questions. The following student essay, which received an A, was a response to one of the four closely related questions that follow it. The essay may address issues raised in two or more questions, but it is an A response to only one of them. Your task is to figure out which question the essay answers best.

Decide on your answer independently; then compare answers in small groups. Try to come to a consensus, referring to the strategies chart on pages 614–616 to help resolve disagreements. As you discuss your responses, note any successful strategies that you may be able to adapt to your own writing.

FROM A BRITISH LITERATURE COURSE

Gulliver's Travels and *Frankenstein* portray characters whose adventures bring them face to face with the innate weaknesses and limitations of humankind. Victor Frankenstein and Lemuel Gulliver find out during their travels that humans are limited in reasoning capacity and easily corruptible, traits that cause even their best-intentioned projects to go awry. These characters reflect the critical view that Swift and Shelley take of human nature. Both believe that humans have a "dark side" that leads to disastrous effects.

In *Gulliver's Travels*, Gulliver's sea voyages expose him to the best and worst aspects of human civilization. Through Gulliver's eyes, readers come to share Swift's perception that no matter how good people's original intentions, their innate selfishness corrupts everything they attempt. All the societies Gulliver visits give evidence of this. For example, Lilliput has a system of laws once grounded on justice and morality, but that slowly were perverted by greedy politicians into petty applications. Even the most advanced society, Brobdingnag, has to maintain a militia even though the country is currently peaceful—since they acknowledge that because humans are basically warlike, peace can't last forever. By showing examples of varied cultures with common faults, Swift demonstrates what he believes to be innate human weaknesses. He seems to believe that no matter how much progress we make, human societies will eventually fall back into the same old traps.

Victor Frankenstein also experiences human limitations, this time in his own personality, as he pushes to gain knowledge beyond what any human has ever possessed. When he first begins his experiments to manufacture life in the laboratory, his goals are noble—to expand scientific knowledge and to help people. As

(continued)

he continues, he becomes more concerned with the power that his discovery will bring him. He desires to be a "god to a new race of men." Later, when the creature he creates wreaks havoc, Frankenstein's pride and selfishness keep him from confessing and preventing further deaths. Like the societies Gulliver observed, Frankenstein is a clear example of how human frailties corrupt potentially good projects.

Even though Swift and Shelley wrote during two different historical periods, they share a critical view of human nature. However, several unambiguously good characters in *Frankenstein*—including the old man and his daughter—suggest that Shelley feels more optimism that people are capable of overcoming their weaknesses, while Swift seems adamant that humans will eternally backslide into greed and violence. Basically, however, both works demonstrate vividly to readers the ever present flaws that prevent people and their societies from ever attaining perfection.

Which of the following questions does this essay address most successfully?

1. Contrast Swift's and Shelley's views of human nature, illustrating your points with specific examples from *Gulliver's Travels* and *Frankenstein.*
2. Analyze the use Swift and Shelley make of scientific knowledge to show the limits of human progress in *Gulliver's Travels* and *Frankenstein,* citing specific illustrations from each work.
3. Discuss the characters of Lemuel Gulliver in *Gulliver's Travels* and Victor Frankenstein in *Frankenstein:* What purpose does each serve in the text? How does each author use the character to illustrate important traits or concepts?
4. Many of the writers we've studied this semester explored the limitations of human potential in their work. Write an essay showing how any two of the following works deal with this idea: William Blake's *Songs of Innocence and Experience,* Jonathan Swift's *Gulliver's Travels,* Mary Shelley's *Frankenstein,* Percy Shelley's "Prometheus Unbound." Does each writer suggest a pessimistic or optimistic view of human nature? Be sure to support your argument with specific illustrations from each text.

Dealing with the Limits of the Test Situation

Suppose that you've organized the course material, studied faithfully, analyzed the exam questions, and know generally how you'll respond. You still need one more skill to succeed: the ability to thrive within the limits of a test situation. Here are some suggestions for handling the pressure.

Minimize Test Anxiety Many students feel anxious if a test question looks unfamiliar or difficult. Others freeze up if they lose their train of thought midway through an essay. Still others panic when time begins to run out. But you can learn to anticipate potential disasters and brainstorm ways to handle them. If you tend to panic when a test question looks impossible on first reading, make a deal with yourself to close your eyes and count to ten and then read it again and try to block off the parts that you don't have to consider. If you usually run out of time, set a time limit when writing some practice answers so that you can get used to performing under pressure. Finally, make sure that you're in top form to take the exam: organize your supplies—including extra exam booklets and scratch paper, pens, and any testing aids your instructor allows—the night before; get plenty of sleep; eat breakfast; arrive at class a few minutes early; give yourself a pep talk. These measures will increase your confidence and head off debilitating nerves.

Manage Your Time Lack of time when writing an essay exam is perhaps the hardest constraint for most people to deal with. Most writers produce their best work only after writing several drafts. You won't be able to compose a perfectly polished essay in an exam—there simply isn't time—so you will need to streamline your writing process through planning. After you have analyzed the exam question carefully, take a few minutes to jot down a quick outline or a list of key concepts you want to discuss. Exploratory writing techniques, such as tree diagrams and freewriting, can help you generate and arrange ideas. Prewriting gives you a sense of direction and helps you remember where the essay is going as you write.

For example, one undergraduate student jotted down this five-minute scratch outline in response to the following exam question in a Texas government course:

> What are the relative advantages and disadvantages of the district method versus the at-large method in municipal elections? Analyze the strengths and weaknesses of each and then either argue in favor of one method over the other or propose a different plan that avoids the limitations of both.

Thesis
District method
Advantages—history of discrimination and underrepresentation of minorities (examples)
  —race consciousness important for overcoming injustice
Disadvantages—encourages racial divisions
  —not necessary because much racism has been overcome; minorities may now be freely elected (ex. Sen. Barrientos, Ann Richards) BUT
At-large
Advantages—all citizens can work together for common good, not just concerned with narrow group interests
Disadvantages—majority rule may ignore important minority needs (ex. East Austin)
THESIS—B/c minorities have been and are still underrepresented in local government, the district method of local elections, while flawed, offers the best chance for these communities' voices to be heard.

Once you have a plan, you need to determine how much time to give to each answer. Many students' grades suffer because they blow all their time on the first question and then race through the rest of the exam. To determine how much time to allot each response, you need to solve a quick ratio problem. Divide the points assigned to a given question by the points for the whole exam; the result equals the percentage of time you should spend on that question. When you write your answer, follow the example of journalists and load critical information into your lead. Write a first paragraph that summarizes your whole answer (the student response in the For Writing and Discussion exercise on pp. 617–618 does this beautifully). Add examples and details to the extent that you have time, moving from more important to less important. If you can't finish a response in time, stop, but don't panic. You may have time to return to it later. If not, write a brief note directing the professor to your original notes or outline; let your professor know that you intended to write more but ran out of time. Many instructors will award partial credit for outlined responses.

Focus on the Important Things You can save time by focusing only on elements important to your grade. Instructors don't expect dramatic, polished introductions and conclusions or artistically constructed sentences in an exam. They would rather you provide a clear thesis statement and explain your main points fully. Most instructors also value organization, although some grade almost entirely on content.

Instructors differ in how they treat errors in grammar, spelling, and punctuation. Some believe it's unfair to expect students to edit their work thoroughly in a short time and don't penalize such errors unless they interfere with the argument (as do garbled or fragmented sentences, for example). Other instructors deduct points for grammatical errors on the grounds that correct usage is always important. If your instructor is a stickler for these details, you may want to save the last five or ten minutes of the exam period for proofreading.

Even if you know a lot about a question, avoid writing more than it asks—unless, perhaps, you know absolutely nothing about one question and want to demonstrate extreme depth of understanding about the others to compensate. Extraneous material may make it difficult for your instructor to find the core of your argument.

Producing an "A" Response

No matter how committed you are to studying, planning, analyzing exam questions, and managing time constraints, your worries about essay tests probably come down to a single, inevitable question: What does an "A" response look like? Research suggests that most professors want closed-form, thesis-based prose that develops key ideas fully, drawing on supporting facts and examples. Although your essay's shape will be influenced by your individual writing style and the particular rhetorical context, the following summary of the points covered in this chapter can serve as a template for a successful essay:

- ***Clear thesis statement.*** Show your professor that you understand the big picture that the question addresses by including a thesis statement early on. Many professors recommend that you state your thesis clearly, though not necessarily stylishly, in the very first sentence.
- ***Coherent organization.*** Although a few instructors will read your essay only to see whether you've included important facts and concepts, most expect a logical presentation. Each paragraph should develop and illustrate one main point. Use transition words and phrases to connect each paragraph clearly to the thesis of the essay: "Another factor that led to the economic decline of the South was..."; "In contrast to Hegel, Mill believed...." Show your instructor that you know where the essay's going, that you're developing your thesis.

- ***Support and evidence.*** When the question calls for supporting facts and examples, be specific. Don't assert or generalize unless you present names, dates, studies, examples, diagrams, or quotations from your reading as support.
- ***Independent analysis and argument.*** Your response should not be a pedestrian rehash of the textbook. When the question allows, present your own insights, criticisms, or proposals, making sure to support these statements with course material and relate them clearly to your thesis.
- ***Conclusion.*** Even if you're running short of time, write a sentence or two to tie together main points and restate your thesis. Your conclusion, even if brief, serves an important rhetorical function. It confirms that you've dealt adequately with the question and proved your point.

Clearly we can't teach you everything you need to know about exam writing in one chapter. Becoming comfortable with any genre of writing requires patience and experience. Practicing the suggestions in this chapter for preparing for essay exams, comprehending exam questions, and organizing your answers will help you build your mastery of this kind of writing.

FOR WRITING AND DISCUSSION

Take a Practice Exam

To gain some practical experience, your instructor may ask you to write an essay exam on one of the following topics. Use the preparation and prewriting strategies you've practiced in this chapter and any other strategies you find useful to prepare for the exam. Review the strategies for writing a successful response presented on pages 614–616 and, if possible, organize and conduct group study sessions with your classmates.

1. Imagine that you've been appointed to a campus committee charged with developing minimum requirements for writing assignments in undergraduate courses. Specifically, the committee is trying to decide whether to require professors to assign a final essay exam or a major research paper in core-curriculum courses. Write an essay in which you argue in favor of mandatory essay exams or mandatory research papers, using examples from your own experience and material from Chapters 1 through 4 and this chapter to support your position. You may want to consider some or all of the following questions in your discussion: Which kind of writing helps students learn the most? Which kind of writing most accurately gauges how well students know course material? Which kind of writing develops skills students are most likely to need in the future?
2. Explain the differences between closed-form and open-form prose as presented in Chapter 1 and Chapters 17 and 18. Illustrate your answer with examples taken from Ross Taylor's "Paintball" (pp. 359–361) and Patrick José's "No Cats in America?" (pp. 148–149). Why does Taylor choose to write near the closed end of the closed-to-open continuum, whereas José chooses to write near the open end?
3. Write an essay on a topic of your instructor's choice.

Chapter Summary

This chapter has discussed strategies for writing effective essay examinations under time pressure:

- Preparing for an exam involves identifying and learning main ideas, applying your knowledge, and following a study plan.
- Being able to analyze exam questions before writing is a key skill. You need to understand how quotations are used, recognize cues that will guide the organization of your essay, and interpret the key terms that indicate how you should approach answering the question.
- Overcoming anxiety and managing time are also important for success.
- An "A" response has a clear thesis statement, coherent organization, specific support and evidence, independent analysis and argument, and an effective conclusion.

PEARSON mycomplab For additional help with writing, go to **www.mycomplab.com**

PORTFOLIOS AND REFLECTIVE ESSAYS

24

Reflection becomes a habit of mind, one that transforms.

—*Kathleen Blake Yancey, Writing and Composition Theorist*

Being an adult student, returning after a twelve-year layoff, working full-time and taking a twelve-credit load, I found that I really had to make time to reinvent my writing. These were times of incredible discovery and frustration. Odd as it seems, frustration breeds discovery.

—*William Jensen, Student*

Assembling a portfolio of your writing for a composition course, in which you select and present the work that best shows your progress or the work that represents your best writing, engages you deeply in reflective self-evaluation. Sometimes this work includes rough drafts and informal writing such as freewrites and journal entries as well as polished, final drafts; at other times, it includes just the polished, final products. Just as architects select their best designs to put into a portfolio to show a potential employer, so, too, do student writers assemble their best writing to demonstrate to the instructor or portfolio readers what they have learned and accomplished during the term.

Typically, writing portfolios also include a reflective letter or essay in which you discuss your portfolio choices and the learning they represent. The role of the accompanying reflective letter or essay is to offer the author's perspective on the writing in the portfolio, to give a behind-the-scenes account of the thinking and writing that went into the work, and to assess the writer's struggles and achievements during the term. This type of reflective writing, called a **comprehensive reflection,** demonstrates what you have learned from your writing over the course of the term, in order to apply that learning to future writing situations.

Another type of reflective essay focuses on a particular piece of writing. The aim of this type of reflective writing, called a **single reflection,** is to learn about a particular piece of writing in order to understand and often to revise it in the present or near future. When you write a single reflection, you formulate your ideas primarily for yourself and perhaps for a friendly, nonjudgmental audience.

In this chapter, you will learn to:

- assemble a portfolio of your writing
- write a reflective essay

Understanding Portfolios

Portfolios offer many advantages to writers. You may have more time to revise before presenting your work for evaluation since many instructors who assign portfolios do not assign grades to individual drafts. Through your comprehensive reflection, you can assess and comment on your writing and learning before someone else passes judgment. Further, the portfolio process helps you develop insights about your thinking and writing processes, insights that you can apply to new writing situations. Finally, this experience can prepare you for work-related tasks because portfolios are increasingly required in job applications as well as in assessments for job promotions or merit-based increases.

Specific guidelines for preparing a writing portfolio vary from course to course, so you will need to check with each individual instructor for directions about what to include and how to organize your portfolio. You may be given a lot of leeway in what to include in your portfolio, or you may be required to submit a specific number of assignments or type of work. However, no matter what the specific requirements are, the following general suggestions can help you manage the portfolio process.

Collecting Work for Paper and Electronic Portfolios

Crucial to your success in assembling a portfolio is careful organization and collection of your work throughout the term. This way, you will avoid the headache and wasted time caused by trying to hunt down lost or misplaced work.

If you are in a non-computer-based course, we recommend that you purchase an accordion-type file folder to keep and organize all of your work for the course. You can use the dividers to separate your work for individual writing projects. Include everything that contributed to your work on a particular writing project: the original assignment sheet, process work, multiple drafts, peer response sheets, teacher comments, reflective writing about the project, research notes, photocopied research articles, and so on. In addition to careful organization and storage of your work, you need to date and label all work so that you can reconstruct your work on a particular project and identify which draft is second or third, which peer response goes with which draft, and so on.

If you are in a computer-based course where most of the work is submitted electronically, then your portfolio will take electronic form. In this case, you will need to develop an electronic storage system. Specifically, you will need to establish separate electronic folders and files for all work related to specific writing projects and to save and back up all of that work. You may also have hard copy you need to save—say, of in-class handwritten peer responses. If this is the case, you will need to scan this material and save it electronically or develop two storage systems.

Besides the practical need to keep track of all your work in order to review and select the writing that you will include in your portfolio, the process of saving and organizing your work will cause you to attend to writing processes throughout the term, one of the key goals of portfolio teaching.

Selecting Work for Your Portfolio

Even if you are given explicit instructions about the number and type of writing to include in your portfolio, you will still have important choices to make about which completed pieces to include or which pieces to revise for inclusion. We suggest three general guidelines to consider as you review your writing and select work for your portfolio presentation.

- ***Variety:*** One purpose of portfolio assessment is to give a fuller picture of a writer's abilities. Therefore, it is important that you choose work that demonstrates your versatility—your ability to make effective rhetorical choices according to purpose, audience, and genre. What combination of writing samples best illustrates your ability to write effectively for different rhetorical situations and in different genres and media?
- ***Course goals:*** A second consideration is course goals. The goals are likely to be stated in the course syllabus and may include such things as "ability to demonstrate critical thinking in writing"; "ability to use multiple strategies for generating ideas, drafting, revising, and editing"; and "ability to demonstrate control over surface features such as syntax, grammar, punctuation, and spelling." Which pieces of writing most clearly demonstrate the abilities given as your course's goals, or which pieces can be revised to offer such a demonstration?
- ***Personal investment:*** Finally, be sure to consider which pieces of writing best reflect your personal investment and interest. If you are going to be revising the selected pieces multiple times during the last few weeks of class, you will want to make sure you choose work that holds your interest and has ideas you care about. Which pieces are you proudest of? Which were the most challenging or satisfying to write? Which present ideas you'd like to explore further?

Understanding Reflective Writing

Broadly defined, reflective writing is writing that describes, explains, interprets, and evaluates any past performance, action, belief, feeling, or experience. To **reflect** is to turn or look back, to reconsider something thought or done in the past from the perspective of the present.

Whether or not you record your thinking on paper, you think reflectively all the time. Suppose you ask your boss for a raise and get turned down. An hour later, as you cool your anger over coffee and a doughnut, you think of a particular point you could have made more effectively. On a larger scale, this kind of informal reflective thinking can be made more formal, systematic, and purposeful. Consider, for example, a football team that systematically reviews game videos to evaluate their own and their opponents' strategies and patterns of play. The camera's eye offers players and coaches new perspectives on their performance; it enables them to isolate, analyze, and evaluate specific moves that were unconsciously performed in the heat of the game.

Similar ways of thinking can be applied to any past performance. Writing reflectively encourages you to train your own camera's eye, metaphorically speaking, on the past. The following example is from an e-mail message sent by a student writer to her writing instructor concerning his comments on a draft of a paper she had written about the causes of anorexia. On the draft, the instructor had puzzled over a confusing sentence and suggested a revised version. Here is her e-mail response:

EXCERPT FROM A STUDENT REFLECTION ON A DRAFT

> I think that your suggested revision changes what I intended. I'd like that sentence to read: "Perhaps anorexics don't pursue desirability but are rather avoiding it." I am arguing not that anorexics want to be "undesirable" (as your sentence suggests) but rather that they want to avoid the whole issue; they want to be neutral. Sexuality and desire can be tremendously scary if you're in a position that places the value of your body over the value of your self/personage; one can feel that, by entering the sexual world of mature adults, one will lose hold of one's essential self. This is the idea I'm trying to express. Perhaps I should try to draft it some more.... At any rate, thank you for pointing out the inadequacies of the topic sentence of this paragraph. I struggled with it, and I think your impulse is right: it needs to encompass more of a transition.

The synthesizing strategies in Chapter 12 for responding to multiple readings and arriving at your own enlarged views can also be applied to your own pieces of writing.

As this example suggests, reflection involves viewing your writing from different perspectives, looking back on the past from the present, achieving a critical distance. Just as light waves are thrown or bent back from the surface of a mirror, so, too, reflective writing throws our experience, action, or performance back to us, allowing us to see it differently.

This process resembles the kind of dialectical thinking introduced in Chapter 7 on exploratory writing, where we explained how juxtaposing one thesis against its opposite can lead to a synthesis that incorporates some aspects of each of the opposing views. Similarly, the process of reexamining one's writing from a new perspective yields new insights and an enriched, more complicated understanding of a particular action, question, problem, or choice.

FOR WRITING AND DISCUSSION

Reflecting on a Past Experience

Working individually, think of a past experience that you can evaluate reflectively. This experience could be your performance in a job; participation in a sport, play, music recital, or other activity; development of a skill (learning to play the piano, juggle a soccer ball, perform a complex dance movement); or problem with another person (a coach, your dorm resident assistant, a job supervisor). To encourage you to think about the past from the perspective of the present, try asking yourself the question, "How do I see the experience differently now from the way I saw it then?" Imagine that you are doing a debriefing of your participation in the experience. Working on your own for ten minutes, freewrite reflectively about your performance. What did you do well? What wasn't working for you? What could you have done better?

Then in groups or as a whole class, share what you have learned through your reflective freewrites. How did the process of looking back give you a new perspective on your experience? How might reflective writing help you bring about changes and improvements in future performances?

Why Is Reflective Writing Important?

According to learning theorists, reflective writing can substantially enhance both your learning and your performance.* Reflective writing helps you gain the insights needed to apply current knowledge to new situations. For example, one of our students recently reported that the most important thing she had learned in her first-year writing course was that research could be used in the service of her own argument. In high school, she had thought of research as merely assembling and reporting information she had found in various sources. Now she realized that writers must make their own arguments, and she saw how research could help her do so. Clearly, this new understanding of the relationship between argument and research will help this student do the kind of research writing expected in upper-level college courses.

Learning theorists call this kind of thinking **metacognition:** the ability to monitor consciously one's intellectual processes or, in other words, to be aware of how one "does" intellectual work. Reflection enables you to control more consciously the thinking processes that go into your writing, and it enables you to gain the critical distance you need to evaluate and revise your writing successfully.

Reflective Writing Assignments

In this section we describe the kinds of reflective writing that your instructors across the disciplines may ask of you.

Single Reflection Assignments

Single reflection assignments are usually informal, exploratory pieces, similar to other kinds of informal writing you have done. Like the exploratory writing described in Chapter 2, Concept 4, single reflections are conversational in tone, open in form, and written mainly for yourself and, perhaps, a friendly, nonjudgmental audience. However, single reflections differ from most other kinds of exploratory writing in timing, focus, and purpose.

Whereas exploratory writing helps you generate ideas early in the writing process, single reflection writing is usually assigned between drafts or after you have completed an essay. Its focus is your writing itself, both the draft and the processes that produced it. Its aim is critical understanding, usually for the

*Learning theorists who have made this general claim include J. H. Flavel, "Metacognitive Aspects of Problem-Solving," in L. B. Resnick (ed.), *The Nature of Intelligence* (Hillsdale, NJ: Erlbaum, 1976); Donald Schon, *Educating the Reflective Practitioner* (San Francisco: Jossey-Bass, 1987); and Stephen Brookfield, *Becoming a Critically Reflective Teacher* (San Francisco: Jossey-Bass, 1995). Throughout this chapter we are indebted to Kathleen Blake Yancey, *Reflection in the Writing Classroom* (Logan, UT: Utah State UP, 1998), who has translated and extended this work on reflection for writing instructors. We are also indebted to Donna Qualley, *Turns of Thought: Teaching Composition as Reflexive Inquiry* (Portsmouth, NH: Boynton/Cook, Heinemann, 1997), who draws on feminist and other critical theorists to argue for the value of reflexive approaches to writing instruction.

purpose of revision. In it, you think about what's working or not working in the draft, what thinking and writing processes went into producing it, and what possibilities you see for revising it. An example of a single reflection is Jaime Finger's essay in the Readings section at the end of this chapter (see p. 633).

Instructors use a variety of assignments to prompt single reflections. Some examples of assignments are the following:

- ***Process log:*** Your instructor asks you to keep a process log in which you describe the writing processes and decisions made for each essay you write throughout the term. In particular, you should offer a detailed and specific account of the problems you encountered (your "wallowing in complexity") and the rhetorical and subject-related alternatives considered and choices made.
- ***Writer's memo:*** Your instructor asks you to write a memorandum to turn in with your draft. In it, you answer a series of questions: How did you go about composing this draft? What problems did you encounter? What do you see as this draft's greatest strengths? What are its greatest weaknesses? What questions about your draft would you like the instructor to address?
- ***Companion piece:*** Less structured than a formal memorandum, a companion piece asks you to reflect briefly on one or two questions. A typical assignment might be this: "Please turn in (1) your draft and (2) an additional piece telling me what you would do with this draft if you had more time."
- ***Talk-to:*** In this type of companion piece, your instructor asks you to do four things: (1) believe this is the best paper you've ever written and explain why; (2) doubt that this paper is any good at all and explain why; (3) predict your instructor's response to this paper; and (4) agree or disagree with what you expect your instructor's response to be.
- ***Talk-back:*** In another type of companion piece, the instructor asks you to respond to his or her comments after you get the paper back: (1) What did I value in this text as a reader? (2) Do you agree with my reading? and (3) What else would you like for me to know?*

Guidelines for Writing a Single Reflection

If you are inexperienced with reflective writing, your tendency at first may be to generalize about your writing. That is, you may be tempted to narrate your writing process in generic, blow-by-blow procedural terms ("First I took some notes. Then I wrote a first draft and showed it to my roommate, who gave me some suggestions. Then I revised") or to describe your rhetorical choices in general, prescriptive terms ("I started with a catchy introduction because it's important to grab your reader's attention").

*We are indebted to Kathleen Blake Yancey and Donna Qualley for a number of the definitions, specific assignments, and suggestions for single and comprehensive reflection tasks that are discussed in the rest of this chapter. Yancey explains the "Talk-To" and "Talk-Back" assignments in her book *Reflection in the Writing Classroom* (Logan, UT: Utah State UP, 1998).

To write an effective single reflection, select only a few ideas to focus on, look at specific aspects of a specific paper, explore dialectically your past thinking versus your present thinking, and support your analysis with adequate details. We suggest the following questions as a guide to producing such reflections. But don't answer them all. Rather, pick out the two or three questions that best apply to your performance and text. (Try to select your questions from at least two different categories.) Your goal should be depth, not a broad survey. The key criteria are these: Be *selective*, be *specific*, show *dialectic thinking*, and include *adequate details*.

Process questions: What specific writing strategies did I use to complete this work?

- Which strategies were the most or least productive?
- Did this writing project require new strategies, or did I rely on past strategies?
- What was the biggest problem I faced in writing this piece, and how successful was I in solving that problem?
- What has been my major content-level revision so far?
- What were my favorite sentence- or word-level revisions?
- What did I learn about myself as a writer or about writing in general by writing this paper?

Subject-related questions: How did the subject of my writing cause me to "wallow in complexity"?

- What tensions did I encounter between my ideas/experiences and those of others? Between the competing ideas about the subject in my own mind?
- Did I change my mind or come to see something differently as a result of writing this work?
- What passages show my independent thinking about the subject? My unresolved problems or mixed feelings about it?
- What were the major content problems I had, and how successful was I in resolving them?
- What did writing about this subject teach me?

Rhetoric-related questions: How did the audience I imagined influence me in writing this paper?

- How did my awareness of genre influence my choices about subject matter and rhetorical features?
- What do I want readers to take away from reading my work?
- What rhetorical strategies please me most (my use of evidence, my examples, my delayed thesis, etc.)? What effect do I hope these strategies have on my audience?
- How would I describe my voice in this work? Is this voice appropriate? Similar to my everyday voice or to the voices I have used in other kinds of writing?
- Did I take any risks in writing this?
- What do readers expect from this genre of writing, and did I fulfill those expectations?

Self-assessment questions: What are the most significant strengths and weaknesses in this writing?

- Do I think others will also see these as important strengths or weaknesses? Why or why not?
- What specific ideas and plans do I have for revision?

Comprehensive Reflection Assignments

You may also be asked to write a final, comprehensive reflection on your development as a writer over a whole term. Although end-of-the-term reflective essays differ in scope and audience from single reflections, similar qualities are valued in both: selectivity, specificity, dialectical thinking, and adequate detail.

In some cases, the comprehensive reflective essay will introduce the contents of a final portfolio; in other cases, this will be a stand-alone assignment. Either way, your goal is to help your readers understand more knowledgeably how you developed as a writer. Most important, in explaining what you have learned from this review of your work, you also make new self-discoveries.

Guidelines for Writing a Comprehensive Reflection

Instructors look for four kinds of knowledge in comprehensive reflections: self-knowledge, content knowledge, rhetorical knowledge, and critical knowledge or judgment. Here we suggest questions that you can use to generate ideas for your comprehensive reflective letter or essay. Choose only a few of the questions to respond to, questions that allow you to explain and demonstrate your most important learning in the course. Also, choose experiences to narrate and passages to cite that illustrate more than one kind of knowledge.

Self-Knowledge By *self-knowledge,* we mean your understanding of how you are developing as a writer. Think about the writer you were, are, or hope to be. You can also contemplate how the subjects you have chosen to write about (or the way you have approached your subjects) relate to you personally beyond the scope of your papers. Self-knowledge questions you might ask are the following:

- What knowledge of myself as a writer have I gained from the writing I did in this course?
- What changes, if any, have occurred in my writing practices or my sense of myself as a writer?
- What patterns or discontinuities can I identify between the way I approached one writing project versus the way I approached another?
- How can I best illustrate and explain through reference to specific writing projects the self-knowledge I have gained?

Content Knowledge *Content knowledge* refers to what you have learned by writing about various subjects. It also includes the intellectual work that has gone into the writing and the insights you gained from considering multiple points of view and grappling with your own conflicting ideas. Perhaps you have grasped ideas about your subjects that you have not shown in your papers. These questions about content knowledge can prod your thinking:

- What kinds of content complexities did I grapple with this term?
- What *earned insights** did I arrive at through confronting clashing ideas?

*Thomas Newkirk, in *Critical Thinking and Writing: Reclaiming the Essay* (Urbana, IL: NCTE, 1989), coined the phrase "earned insights," a phrase that Donna Qualley also refers to in *Turns of Thought: Teaching Composition as Reflexive Inquiry* (Portsmouth, NH: Boynton/Cook, Heinemann, 1997), pp. 35–37.

- What new perspectives did I gain about particular subjects from my considerations of multiple or alternate viewpoints?
- What new ideas or perspectives did I gain that may not be evident in the writings themselves?
- What passages from various papers best illustrate the critical thinking I did in my writing projects for this course?

Rhetorical Knowledge Our third category, *rhetorical knowledge,* focuses on your awareness of your rhetorical decisions—how your contemplation of purpose, audience, and genre affected your choices about content, structure, style, and document design. The following questions about rhetorical choices can help you assess this area of your knowledge:

- What important rhetorical choices did I make in various works to accomplish my purpose or to appeal to my audience? What parts of my various works best illustrate these choices? Which of these choices are particularly effective and why? About which choices am I uncertain and why?
- What have I learned about the rhetorical demands of audience, purpose, and genre, and how has that knowledge affected my writing and reading practices?
- How do I expect to use this learning in the future?

Critical Knowledge or Judgment A fourth area of knowledge, *critical knowledge or judgment,* concerns your awareness of significant strengths and weaknesses in your writing. This area also encompasses your ability to identify what you like or value in various pieces of writing and to explain why. You could ask yourself these questions about your critical knowledge:

- Of the works in my portfolio, which is the best and why? Which is the weakest and why?
- How has my ability to identify strengths and weaknesses changed during this course?
- What role has peer, instructor, or other reader feedback had on my assessments of my work?
- What improvements would I make in these works if I had more time?
- How has my writing changed over the term? What new abilities will I take away from this course?
- What are the most important things I still have to work on as a writer?
- What is the most important thing I have learned in this course?
- How do I expect to use what I've learned from this course in the future?

Guidelines for Writing a Comprehensive Reflective Letter

Because the letter (sometimes an essay) that you write to introduce your portfolio shows your insights not only about your writing abilities but also about your abilities as a reflective learner, it may be one of the most important pieces of writing you do for a writing course. Here we offer some additional suggestions geared specifically toward introducing your writing portfolio:

- Review the single reflections you have written about specific writing projects during the term. As you reread these process log entries, writer's memos, companion pieces, and so on, what do you discover about yourself as a writer?
- Consider key rhetorical concepts that you have learned in this course. Use the detailed table of contents of Chapters 1 through 4 to refresh your memory about these concepts. How can you show that you understand these concepts and have applied them in your writing?
- Take notes on your own writing as you review your work and reconstruct your writing processes for particular writing projects. What patterns do you see? What surprises you? How can you show the process behind the product? How can you show your growth as a writer through specific examples?
- Be honest. Identifying weaknesses is as important as identifying strengths. How can you use this opportunity to discover more about yourself as a writer or learner?

Our first reading is a single reflection by student Jaime Finger. She writes about what she sees as the strengths and weaknesses of an exploratory essay in which she was asked to pose a question raised but not clearly answered in a collection of essays on issues of race and class. (She posed the question, "What motivates people to behave as they do?") She was then asked to investigate various perspectives on the question that were offered by the readings, to consider other perspectives drawn from her own knowledge and experience, and to assess the strengths and weaknesses of differing points of view.

Jaime Finger (student)

A Single Reflection on an Exploratory Essay

1 Although this paper was harder than the first one, I believe I have a good opening question. I like how I divided her [the author of the essays] ideas about motivation into two parts—individual and social. I also like how I used examples from many different essays (this proves I really read the whole book!). Another thing I like about this essay is how I include some examples of my own, like the Michael Jordan example of how he did not make the basketball team in his freshman year and that motivated him to practice every day for a year before making the team his sophomore year. I wonder if he ever would have been as good as he is if he had made the team his freshman year? I wish I could or would have added more of my own examples like this one.

2 What I'm not sure about is if I later ask too many other questions, like when I ask, "If someone is doing something because of society's pressures, is he responsible for that behavior?" and "How much are we responsible to other people like the homeless?" I felt that I piled up questions, and also felt I drifted from my original questions. The paper was confusing for me to write, and I feel that it jumps around. Maybe it doesn't, but I don't know.

3 Since *Alchemy* [the title of the essay collection] was such a hard book, I'm kind of happy with my paper (although after hearing some of the others in my peer group, I don't know if it's up to par!!).

THINKING CRITICALLY

about "A Single Reflection on an Exploratory Essay"

1. To what extent does this reflection show that Jaime has deepened her thinking about the question, "What motivates people to behave as they do?"
2. Where does Jaime show an awareness of audience and purpose in her self-reflection on her essay?
3. To what extent does Jaime show us that she can identify strengths and weaknesses of her essay?
4. What are Jaime's most important insights about her essay?

5. How would you characterize Jaime's voice in this reflection? Does this voice seem appropriate for this kind of reflective writing? Why or why not?
6. What are the greatest strengths and weaknesses in Jaime's single reflection?

Our second reading is the draft of a comprehensive reflective letter written by a student, Bruce Urbanik, for a second-semester composition course that involved a large-scale portfolio assessment. Bruce's portfolio as a whole will be read and scored (Pass or Fail) by two outside readers (and a third if the first two disagree). The contents of Bruce's portfolio include two essays written outside of class and revised extensively and one essay written in class under test conditions. As his letter suggests, his two out-of-class essays were classical arguments (see Chapter 13) written in response to the nonfiction texts that his class read during the semester. The assignment he was given for this comprehensive reflection is similar to the one on pages 629–632.

Bruce Urbanik (student)

A Comprehensive Reflective Letter

Dear Portfolio Reader:

1 This is my first college course in five years. I left school for financial reasons and a career opportunity that I couldn't pass up. I thought of contesting the requirement of this course because I had completed its equivalent five years ago. But, as I reflected on the past few years, I realized that the only books I have read have been manuals for production machinery. My writing has consisted of shorthand, abbreviated notes that summarize a shift's events. Someday, after I finish my degree and move up in my company, I'm going to have to write a presentation to the directors on why we should spend millions of dollars on new machinery to improve productivity. I need this course if I expect to make a persuasive case.

2 I was very intimidated after I read the first book in the course, *No Contest: The Case Against Competition*, by Alfie Kohn. The author used what seemed to me a million outside sources to hammer home his thesis that competition is unhealthy in our society and that cooperation is the correct route. I felt very frustrated with Kohn and found myself disagreeing with him although I wasn't always sure why. I actually liked many of his ideas, but he seemed so detached from his argument. Kohn's sources did all the arguing for him. I tried to take a fresh perspective by writing about my own personal experience. I also used evidence from an interview I conducted with a school psychologist to back up my argument about the validity of my own experiences with cooperative education. The weakness of this paper is my lack of opposing opinions.

3 For my second essay, on Terry Tempest Williams's *Refuge: An Unnatural History of Family and Place*, I certainly could not use any personal experience. Williams, a Mormon woman, writes about the deaths of her mother, grandmother, and other female relatives from breast cancer, believed to be caused by the atomic testing in Utah. I argued that the author, Williams, unfairly blamed men and the role women play in the

Mormon religion for the tragic death of her mother and other relatives. She thinks that if the Mormon Church had not discouraged women from questioning authority, maybe some of them would have protested the nuclear testing. But I think this reasoning ignores the military and government pressures at the time and the fact that women in general didn't have much power back in the '50s. Since I didn't know anything about the subject, I asked a Mormon woman that I know to comment on these ideas. Also, my critique group in class was comprised of myself and three women. I received quite a bit of verbal feedback from them on this essay. I deal with men at work all day. This change, both for this essay and the entire semester, was welcome.

4 In-class, timed essay writing was my biggest downfall. I have not been trained to develop an idea and present support for it on the fly. Thoughts would race through my head as I tried to put them on paper. I thought I was getting better, but the in-class essay in this portfolio is just awful. I really wish I could have had more practice in this area. I'm just not comfortable with my writing unless I've had lots of time to reflect on it.

5 A few weeks ago, I found a disk that had some of my old papers from years ago stored on it. After reading some of them, I feel that the content of my writing has improved since then. I know my writing has leaped huge steps since my first draft back in September. As a student not far from graduation, I know I will value the skills practiced in this course.

THINKING CRITICALLY
about "A Comprehensive Reflective Letter"

1. What kinds of self-knowledge does Bruce display in his reflective letter?
2. Does Bruce demonstrate dialectical thinking about himself as a writer? If so, where? What multiple writing selves does Bruce identify in his letter?
3. What has Bruce learned from writing about *No Contest* and *Refuge*? What specific examples does he give of "earned insights" or dialectical thinking regarding his subjects?
4. Does Bruce demonstrate his ability to make judgments about his essays' strengths and weaknesses?
5. What learning from this course do you think Bruce is likely to use in the future?
6. Which of the four kinds of writer's knowledge would you like Bruce to address more closely in revising this reflective letter? What kinds of questions does he overlook? Which points could he build up more? Where could his comments be more text-specific and adequately detailed?

PART 6

A GUIDE TO EDITING

This energy poster is part of a series produced by Energy Conservation Awareness Products (www.energyconservationposters.com). These posters are intended to make people conscious of energy consumption and waste and of alternative energy sources that can lessen the use of fossil fuels. Consider how the poster's words, the features of this image, and the use of color all work together to attract viewers and make them think about their energy habits. This poster relates to various readings on energy and various For Writing and Discussion exercises throughout Parts 1 and 2 of this text.

IF YOU ARE NOT USING IT...
TURN IT OFF!
OFF
ON

PART 6 **A GUIDE TO EDITING**

Part 6 addresses the following outcomes for first-year composition from the Council of Writing Program Administrators.

RHETORICAL KNOWLEDGE	• Respond appropriately to different kinds of rhetorical situations (Handbook 1, 5) • Use conventions of format and structure appropriate to the rhetorical situation (Handbook 6) • Adopt appropriate voice, tone, and level of formality (Handbook 5)
CRITICAL THINKING, READING, AND WRITING	• Understand the relationships among language, knowledge, and power (Handbook 5)
PROCESSES	• Be aware that it usually takes multiple drafts to create and complete a successful text (Handbook 1) • Develop flexible strategies for generating, revising, editing, and proof-reading (Handbook 1) • Learn to critique their own and others' works (Handbook 1)
KNOWLEDGE OF CONVENTIONS	• Learn common formats for different kinds of texts (Handbook 6) • Control such surface features as syntax, grammar punctuation, and spelling (Handbook 2, 3, 4, 6)
COMPOSING IN ELECTRONIC ENVIRONMENTS	• Use electronic environments for drafting, reviewing, revising, editing, and sharing texts (Handbook 1) • Understand and exploit the differences in the rhetorical strategies and in the affordances available for both print and electronic composing processes and texts (Handbook 1)

IMPROVING YOUR EDITING SKILLS

1

Why Editing Is Important

In our discussion of the writing process in Chapter 16, we recommend saving editing for last. We do so not because editing is unimportant but because fine-tuning a manuscript requires that the main features of the text—its ideas and organization—be relatively stable. There is no point in correcting mistakes in a passage that is going to be deleted or completely rewritten.

This late-stage concern for clarity and correctness is a crucial part of the writing process because editing and proofreading errors reflect directly on your *ethos*, that is, on the reader's image of you as a writer. The problem with sentence-level errors is that they inevitably show up to embarrass us whenever we let our guard down. If you're writing something with real-world consequences—a job application letter, a grant proposal, a letter to a client, a field report for your boss—then typos, misspellings, sentence fragments, and dangling participles are like a piece of lettuce between your teeth. Instead of focusing on your message, your readers may not even take you seriously enough to finish reading what you have written.

Another reason to edit is more existential than rhetorical. It has to do with the care we devote to the details of something that matters to us. In Robert Pirsig's philosophical novel about writing, *Zen and the Art of Motorcycle Maintenance*, editing and proofreading belong to the "motorcycle maintenance" side of writing, not to the Zen side. For Pirsig, motorcycle maintenance is a metaphor for the unglamorous but essential aspect of any thoughtful enterprise. It requires discipline; you must give yourself up to the object before you, whether it is a motorcycle, a philosophical system, or the draft of an essay. Editing and proofreading, like motorcycle maintenance, require us to focus painstakingly on the parts. It can seem unrelentingly, oppressively nitpicky, but in a complex engine or complex essay, misfires and mistakes among the parts keep the whole from realizing its full potential. Even if you are the only one aware of these failures, you gain an innate satisfaction in making the parts function perfectly—the sort of satisfaction that carries over into larger pursuits.

In this chapter, you will learn to:

- improve your editing processes.

Improving Your Editing and Proofreading Processes

You can become a more attentive editor and proofreader of your own prose if you practice the kinds of editing strategies we suggest in this section.

Keep a List of Your Own Characteristic Errors

When one of your papers is returned, look carefully at the kinds of sentence-level errors noted by your instructor. A paper with numerous errors might actually contain only two or three *kinds* of errors repeated several times. For example, some writers consistently omit apostrophes from possessives or add them to plurals; others regularly create comma splices when they use such words as *therefore* or *however* at the beginning of an independent clause. Try to classify the kinds of errors you made on the paper, and then try to avoid these errors on your next paper.

Do a Self-Assessment of Your Editing Knowledge

Look over the detailed table of contents for this editing guide and note the various topics covered. Which of these topics are familiar to you from previous instruction? In which areas are you most confident? In which areas are you most shaky? We generally recommend that students study the topics in Handbook 3 early in a course because the chapter explains the main punctuation Rules that help you avoid fragments and comma splices and that help you make decisions about comma placement within a sentence. The remaining handbook chapters can function as handy references when specific questions arise. Become familiar with the organization of this guide so that you can find information rapidly.

Read Your Draft Aloud

A key to good editing is noting every word. An especially helpful strategy is to read your paper aloud—really aloud, not half-aloud, mumbling to yourself, but at full volume, as if you were reading to a room full of people. When you stumble over a sentence or have to go back to fit sound to sense, mark the spot. Something is probably wrong there and you will want to return to it later. Make sure that the words you read aloud are actually on the page. When reading aloud, people often unconsciously fill in missing words or glide over mispunctuated passages, so check carefully to make sure that what you say matches what you wrote. Some writers like to read aloud into a tape recorder and then reread their draft silently while playing back the recording. If you haven't tried the tape recorder technique, consider doing so at least once; it is a surprisingly powerful way to improve your editing skills.

Read Your Draft Backward

Another powerful editing technique—strange as it might seem—is to read your paper backward, word by word, from end to beginning. When you read forward, you tend to focus on meaning and often read right past mistakes. Reading backward estranges you from the paper's message and allows you to focus on the details of the essay—the words and sentences. As you read backward, keep a dictionary and this handbook close by. Focus on each word, looking for typos, spelling errors, misused apostrophes, pronoun case errors, and so forth, and attend to each sentence unit, making sure that it is a complete sentence and that its boundaries have been properly marked with punctuation.

See Handbook 3.

Use a Spell-Checker and (Perhaps) Other Editing Programs

With spell-checkers, you have almost no excuse for including misspelled words or typos in a formal paper. Become a skilled operator of your computer's spell-checker, and always run the program before printing your final draft.

Be aware, however, that a spell-checker isn't foolproof. These programs match strings of letters in a document against strings stored in memory. A spell-checker may not contain some of the specialized words you use (authors' names or special course terms), nor can it tell whether a correctly spelled word is used correctly in context (*it's, its; their, there,* or *they're; to, too,* or *two*).

Many writers use "grammar" checkers, also called "style" or "usage" checkers. We place "grammar" in quotation marks because these programs do not really check grammar. They can perform only countable or matchable functions such as identifying *be* verbs and passive constructions, noting extremely long sentences, identifying clichés and wordy expressions, and so forth. Although these programs can be useful by drawing your attention to some areas where you may be able to tighten or enliven your prose, they have to be used with caution. So-called grammar-checkers can't catch most of the most common errors in usage and grammar that writers make, and they often flag nonexistent problems.

Microtheme Projects on Editing

The following microtheme assignments focus on selected problems of editing and style. Since you never know a concept as well as when you have to teach it to someone else, these assignments place you in a teaching role. They ask you to solve an editing problem and to explain your solution in your own words to a hypothetical audience that has turned to you for instruction.

Your instructor can use these microtheme assignments as individual or group writing projects or as prompts for classroom discussion.

Microtheme 1: Apostrophe Madness Your friend Elmer Fuddnick has decided to switch majors from engineering to creative writing. Poor Elmer has a great imagination, but he forgot to study basic punctuation when he was in high school. He's just sent you the first draft of his latest short story, "The Revenge of the Hedgehogs." Here are his opening sentences:

> The hedgehogs' scrambled from behind the rock's at the deserts edge, emitted what sounded like a series of cats scream's and then rolled themselve's into spiny balls. One of the hedgehogs hunched it's back and crept slowly toward a cactus' shadow.

Although you can't wait to finish Elmer's story, you are a bit annoyed by his misuse of apostrophes. Your job is to explain to Elmer how to use apostrophes correctly.

Begin by correcting Elmer's sentences; then explain to Elmer the principles you used to make your corrections. Your explanation of apostrophes should be clear enough so that Elmer can learn their use from your explanation. In other words, you are the teacher. Use your own language and make up your own examples.

Microtheme 2: Stumped by However You are putting yourself through college by operating an online grammar hot line and charging people for your advice. One day you receive the following e-mail message:

> Dear Grammarperson:
>
> I get really confused on how to punctuate words like "however" and "on the other hand." Sometimes these words have commas on both sides of them, but at other times they have a comma in back and a semicolon in front. What's the deal here? How can I know whether to use a comma or a semicolon in front of a "however"?
>
> Bewildered in Boston

Write a response to Bewildered explaining why words such as *however* are sometimes preceded by a comma and sometimes by a semicolon (or a period, in which case *however* starts with a capital letter). Use your own language and invent your own examples.

Microtheme 3: The Comic Dangler Here is another message received at the grammar hot line (see Microtheme 2):

> Dear Grammarperson:
>
> My history teacher was telling us the other day that editing our papers before we submitted them was really important. And then she mentioned in passing that some editing mistakes often create comic effects. She said that the dangling participle was her favorite because it often produced really funny sentences. Well, maybe so, but I didn't know what she was talking about. What are dangling participles and why are they funny?
>
> Not Laughing in Louisville

Explain to Not Laughing what dangling participles are and why they are often funny. Illustrate with some examples of your own and then show Not Laughing how to correct them.

Microtheme 4: How's That Again? The grammar hot line is doing a great business (see Microtheme 2). Here is another e-mail message:

> Dear Grammarperson:
>
> It has often been said by some instructors that I have had in the various educational institutions that I have attended that a deadening effect is achievable in the prose produced by writers through the transformation of verbs into nouns and through the overuse of words that are considered empty in content or otherwise produce a redundant effect by the restating of the same idea in more words than are necessary for the reader's understanding of the aforementioned ideas. Could these teachers' allegations against the sentence structure of many writers be considered to be at least partially true in the minds of those persons who read these writers' prose?
>
> Verbose in Vermont

Help Verbose out by rewriting this question in a crisper style. Then explain briefly, using your own language and examples, the concepts of wordiness and nominalization.

Microtheme 5: The Intentional Fragment Advertisers frequently use sentence fragments purposely. Find an advertisement that makes extensive use of fragments in its copy. Rewrite the copy to eliminate all sentence fragments. Then write a one-paragraph microtheme in which you speculate why the advertiser used fragments rather than complete sentences. Try to suggest at least two possible reasons.

Microtheme 6: Create Your Own Following the model of the five preceding assignments, create your own microtheme assignment on an editing problem related to any section of this handbook (or to a section assigned by your instructor). Then exchange assignments with a classmate and write a microtheme in response to your classmate's assignment. Be prepared to write a microtheme in response to your own assignment also.

PEARSON mycomplab For support in learning this chapter's content, follow this path in **MyCompLab**: Resources ⇒ Writing ⇒ The Writing Processes ⇒ Finishing and Editing. Review the Instruction and Multimedia resources, then complete the Exercises and click on Gradebook to measure your progress.

2 UNDERSTANDING SENTENCE STRUCTURE

This chapter provides a basic review of English grammar. Throughout, we emphasize that you already have an innate understanding of grammar, based on your ability to speak and understand English. In this chapter we want to give you a more conscious understanding of the structures you subconsciously use all the time. We also introduce some useful terms and labels that will facilitate your learning of the rules for usage and punctuation.

In this chapter, you will learn:

- The concept of the sentence
- Basic sentence patterns
- Parts of speech
- Types of phrases
- Types of clauses
- Types of sentences

The Concept of the Sentence

The *sentence* is perhaps the most crucial grammatical concept for writers to understand. A sentence is a group of related words with a complete subject and a complete predicate. The subject names something, and the predicate makes an assertion about the thing named.

Name Something	Make an Assertion about It
Cheese	tastes good on crackers.
Lizards and snakes	are both kinds of reptiles.
Capital punishment	has been outlawed in many countries.

Every sentence must include at least one subject and one predicate. These components answer two different questions: (1) Who or what is the sentence about? (subject); and (2) What assertion does the sentence make about the subject? (predicate). Consider the following example:

Tree ants in Southeast Asia construct nests by sewing leaves together.

What is this sentence about? *Tree ants in Southeast Asia* (subject). What assertion is made about tree ants? (They) *construct nests by sewing leaves together* (predicate).

Grammarians sometimes distinguish between simple and complete subjects and between simple and complete predicates. A simple subject is the single word or phrase that the sentence is about. In our example, *ants* is the simple subject and *tree ants in Southeast Asia* is the complete subject (the simple subject plus all its modifiers). A simple predicate is the main verb (along with its helping or auxiliary verbs) that makes the assertion about the subject. In our example, *construct* is the simple predicate (the verb) and *construct nests by sewing leaves together* is the complete predicate (the main verb plus modifiers and nouns needed to complete its meaning).

Ordinarily a sentence begins with the subject, followed by the verb. Sometimes, however, word order can be changed. In the following examples, the subjects are underlined once and the verbs are underlined twice.

Normal Word Order	The most terrifying insects wander through the countryside seeking prey.
Question	What are the most terrifying insects?
Imperative	Watch for the driver ants. ("You" is understood as the subject.)
"There" Opening	There are various kinds of terrifying insects.
Inverted Order	Across the jungles of Africa marched the driver ants.

Sentences can also have more than one subject or predicate.

Compound Subject	The army ants of South America and the driver ants of Africa march in long columns.
Compound Predicate	The hunters at the head of a column discover a prey, swarm all over it, and eventually cut it apart.

Basic Sentence Patterns

All sentences must have a complete subject and a complete predicate. However, the predicates of sentences can take several different shapes, depending on whether the verb needs a following noun, pronoun, or adjective to complete its meaning. These words are called *complements*. The four kinds of complements are *direct objects, indirect objects, subject complements,* and *object complements.*

Pattern One: Subject + Verb (+ Optional Adverb Modifiers)

adverb modifiers

The eagle soared gracefully across the summer sky.

In this pattern, the predicate contains only a verb and optional adverbial modifiers. Because the verb in this pattern does not transfer any action from a doer to a receiver, it is called "intransitive."

Pattern Two: Subject + Verb + Direct Object (DO)

DO

Peter was fixing a flat tire over in Bronco County at the very moment of the crime.

Direct objects occur with *transitive verbs,* which transfer action from a doer (the subject) to a receiver (the direct object). Transitive verbs don't seem complete in themselves; they need a noun or pronoun following the verb to answer the question What? or Whom? Peter was fixing *what*? The *flat tire.*

Pattern Three: Subject + Verb + Subject Complement (SC)

SC
My mother is a professor.

SC
The engine in this car seems sluggish.

In this pattern, verbs are *linking verbs,* which are followed by subject complements rather than direct objects. Unlike direct objects, which receive the action of the verb, subject complements either rename the subject (a noun) or describe the subject (an adjective). You can best understand a subject complement if you think of the linking verb as an equals sign (=).

Pattern Four: Subject + Verb + Direct Object + Object Complement (OC)

DO OC
That woman called me an idiot.

Whereas a subject complement describes the subject of the sentence, an object complement describes the direct object, either by modifying it or by renaming it. Compare the patterns.

Pattern Three	I am an idiot. (SC: an idiot)
Pattern Four	The woman called me an idiot. (DO: me; OC: an idiot)

Pattern Five: Subject + Verb + Indirect Object (IDO) + Direct Object

IDO DO
My mother sent the professor an angry letter.

IDO DO
My father baked me a cake on Valentine's Day.

Sometimes transitive verbs take an *indirect object* as well as a direct object. Whereas the direct object answers the question What? or Whom? following the verb, the indirect object answers the question To what or whom? or For what or whom? My mother sent *what? A letter* (direct object). She sent a letter *to whom? The professor* (indirect object). My father baked what? *A cake* (direct object). My father baked a cake *for whom*? For *me* (indirect object).

Parts of Speech

Although linguists argue about the best way to classify the functions of words in a sentence, the traditional eight parts of speech listed here are most often used in dictionaries and basic introductions to grammar.

Parts of Speech

nouns (N)	adverbs (Adv)
pronouns (PN)	prepositions (P)
verbs (V)	conjunctions (C)
adjectives (Adj)	interjections (I)

Each part of speech serves a different function in a sentence and also possesses structural features that distinguish it from the other parts of speech. Because many words can serve as different parts of speech in different circumstances, you can determine what part of speech a word plays only within the context of the sentence you are examining.

Nouns

Nouns are the names we give to persons (*Samuel, mechanic*), places (*Yellowstone, the forest*), things (*a rock, potatoes*), and abstract concepts (*love, happiness*). Nouns can be identified by structure as words that follow the articles *a*, *an*, or *the*; as words that change their form to indicate number; and as words that change their form to indicate possession.

a rock several rock*s* the rock'*s* hardness

But not: a *from*; several *froms*; the *from's* coat.

Pronouns

Pronouns take the place of nouns in sentences. The noun that a pronoun replaces is called the pronoun's *antecedent*. English has the following types of pronouns:

Type of Pronoun	Examples
Personal	I, me, you, he, him, she, her, it, we, us, they, them
Possessive (with Noun)	my, your, his, her, its, our, their
Possessive (no Noun)	mine, yours, his, hers, ours, theirs
Demonstrative	this, that, these, those
Indefinite	any, anybody, someone, everyone, each, nobody
Reflexive/Intensive	myself, yourself, himself, herself, itself, ourselves, yourselves, themselves
Interrogative	who, what, whom, whose, which, whoever, whomever
Relative	who, whom, whose, which, that

Verbs

Verbs are words that express action (*run, laugh*) or state of being (*is, seem*). Structurally, they change form to indicate tense and sometimes to indicate person and number. A word can function as a verb if it can fit the following frames:

I want to ____________. I will ____________.

I want to *throw*. I will *throw*.

But not: I want to *from*; I will *from*.

Verbs are used as complete verbs or as incomplete verbs, often called "verbals." When used as complete verbs, they fill the predicate slot in a sentence. When used as incomplete verbs, they fill a noun's, adjective's, or adverb's slot in a sentence. Verbs often require helping verbs, also called "auxiliary verbs," to fulfill their function.

Person and Number In many instances, verbs change form to agree with the person or number of the subject.

Person	Singular	Plural
First person	I give. I am giving.	We give. We are giving.
Second person	You give. You are giving.	You give. You are giving.
Third person	He (she, it) gives. He (she, it) is giving.	They give. They are giving.

Principal Parts Verbs have five principal parts, which vary depending on whether the verb is *regular* or *irregular*.

Principal Part	Regular Verb Examples	Irregular Verb Examples
Infinitive or Present Stem (infinitives begin with *to*; the word following the *to* is the *present stem*)	to love to borrow	to begin to get
Present Stem + -s (used for third-person singular, present tense)	loves borrows	begins gets
Past Stem (regular verbs add *-ed* to present stem; irregular verbs have different form)	loved borrowed	began got
Past Participle (same as past stem for regular verbs; usually a different form for irregular verbs)	loved borrowed	begun gotten
Present Participle (add *-ing* to present stem)	loving borrowing	beginning getting

The irregular verb *to be* has more forms than do other verbs.

Infinitive	to be
Present Forms	am, is, are
Past Forms	was, were
Past Participle	been
Present Participle	being

Tenses Verbs change their forms to reflect differences in time. A verb's time is called its "tense." There are six main tenses, each with three forms, sometimes called "aspects"—simple, progressive, and emphatic. For two of the tenses—the simple present and simple past—a complete verb is formed by using one word only. For all other tenses, two or more words are needed to form a complete verb. The additional words are called "helping," or "auxiliary," verbs. In some tenses the main verb or one of the helping verbs changes form to agree with its subject in person and number.

Simple Form. Here are regular and irregular examples of the simple form of the six main tenses:

See pp. 668–671 on subject-verb agreement.

Simple Present	She *enjoys* the pizza. They *begin* the race.
Simple Past	She *enjoyed* the pizza. They *began* the race.
Simple Future	She *will enjoy* the pizza. They *will begin* the race.
Present Perfect	She *has enjoyed* the pizza. They *have begun* the race.
Past Perfect	She *had enjoyed* the pizza. They *had begun* the race.
Future Perfect	She *will have enjoyed* the pizza. They *will have begun* the race.

Progressive Form. Each tense also has a progressive form to indicate actions that are ongoing or in-process.

Present Progressive	Sally *is eating* her sandwich.
Past Progressive	Sally *was eating* her sandwich.
Future Progressive	Sally *will be eating* her sandwich.
Present Perfect Progressive	Sally *has been eating* her sandwich.
Past Perfect Progressive	Sally *had been eating* her sandwich.
Future Perfect Progressive	Sally *will have been eating* her sandwich.

Emphatic Form. Several tenses have an emphatic form, which uses the helping verb *to do* combined with the present stem. The emphatic form is used for giving special stress, for asking questions, and for making negations.

I *do go*. I *did go*.

Did the dog *bark*?

Do you *like* peanuts?

The child *does* not *sit* still.

See the section on subjunctive mood below.

Modal Forms. Additionally, a variety of other helping verbs, often called "modals," can be used to form complete verbs with different senses of time and attitude.

will, would	may, might
can, could	must
shall, should	

Mood Verbs have three moods: indicative (by far the most common), subjunctive, and imperative. These three moods indicate the attitude of the writer toward the statement the verb makes.

Indicative Mood. The indicative mood is so common that you might call it the "default mood." It is used for both statements and questions.

The dog *rode* in the back of the pickup. Where *is* Sally?

Subjunctive Mood. The subjunctive mood is used to indicate that a condition is contrary to fact and, in certain cases, to express desire, hope, or demand. The subjunctive is formed in the present tense by using the infinitive stem.

I request that Joe *pay* the bill.

Compare with the indicative: Joe *pays* the bill.

In the past tense, only the verb *to be* has a distinctive subjunctive form, which is always *were*.

If I *were* the teacher, I would give you an A for that project.

Here the subjunctive *were* means "I am *not* the teacher"; it expresses a condition contrary to fact.

The subjunctive frequently causes problems for writers in sentences with *if* clauses. If an *if* clause uses the indicative mood, then the independent clause uses the simple present or the simple future. However, if an *if* clause uses the subjunctive mood, then the independent clause uses a modal auxiliary such as *would, could, might,* or *should*.

Indicative in *If* Clause	If he *takes* chemistry from Dr. Jones, he *will learn* a great deal.
Subjunctive in *If* Clause	If he *were* a serious science student, he *would have taken* chemistry from Dr. Jones.

The subjunctive in the second sentence implies the following meaning: "He is not a serious science student, so he didn't take chemistry from Dr. Jones."

Imperative Mood. Finally, the imperative mood conveys a command or request. For most verbs the imperative form is the same as the second-person present tense. An exception is the verb *to be*, which uses *be*.

Be here by noon. *Pay* the bill immediately.

Voice The voice of a verb indicates whether the subject of the verb acts or is acted on. The concept of voice applies only to *transitive* verbs, which transfer action from a doer to a receiver. In the active voice, the subject is the doer of the action and the direct object is the receiver.

Active Voice The professor graded the paper.

In the passive voice, the subject is the receiver of the action; the actor is either omitted from the sentence or made the object of the preposition *by*. The passive voice is formed with the past participle and some form of the helping verb *to be*.

For advice on when to use active and passive voice, see pp. 687–688.

Passive Voice The paper was graded (by the professor).

Adjectives and Adverbs

Adjectives and adverbs describe or *modify* other words.

Adjectives Adjectives modify nouns by answering such questions as Which ones? (*those* rabbits); what kind? (*gentle* rabbits); how many? (*four* rabbits); what size? (*tiny* rabbits); what color? (*white* rabbits); what condition? (*contented* rabbits); and whose? (*Jim's* rabbits).

Articles (*a, an, the*) form a special class of adjectives. *A* and *an* are indefinite and singular, referring to any representative member of a general class of objects.

I would like *an* apple and *a* sandwich.

The is definite and can be singular or plural. It always specifies that a particular object is meant.

I want *the* apple and *the* sandwich that were sitting on my desk a few minutes ago.

Adverbs Adverbs modify verbs, adjectives, or other adverbs. They answer the questions How? (he petted the rabbit *gently*); how often? (he petted the rabbit *frequently*); where? (he petted the rabbit *there* in the corner of the room); when? (he petted the rabbit *early*); and to what degree? (he petted the rabbit *very* gently).

Conjunctive adverbs, such as *therefore, however*, and *moreover*, modify whole clauses by showing logical relationships between clauses or sentences.

Positive, Comparative, and Superlative Forms A distinctive structural feature of adjectives and adverbs is that they take positive, comparative, and superlative forms.

Positive	This is a *quick* turtle. It moves *quickly*.
Comparative	My turtle is *quicker* than yours. It moves *more quickly* than yours.
Superlative	Of the three turtles, mine is the *quickest*. Of all the turtles in the race, mine moves *most quickly*.

Conjunctions

Conjunctions join elements within a sentence. *Coordinating* conjunctions (*and, or, nor, but, for, yet,* and *so*) join elements of equal importance.

John *and* Mary went to town.

The city rejoiced, *for* the rats had finally been exterminated.

Subordinating conjunctions (such as *when, unless, if, because, after, while, although*) turn an independent sentence into a subordinate clause and then join it to an independent clause.

For more on coordinating and subordinating conjunctions, see p. 665.

After I get off work, I will buy you a soda.

She won't show him how to use the TiVo *unless* he apologizes.

If you are going to the city, please get me a magazine at Caesar's.

Prepositions

Prepositions show the relationship between a noun or pronoun (the object of the preposition) and the rest of the sentence. The preposition and its object together are called a "prepositional phrase." Common prepositions include *about, above, across, among, behind, between, from, in, into, of, on, toward,* and *with.*

The cat walked *under* the table.

The vase was *on* the table.

The table is a mixture *of* cherry and walnut woods.

Interjections

Interjections (*Yippee! Sweet! Ouch!*) are forceful expressions, usually followed by exclamation marks, that express emotion. They can be removed from a sentence without affecting the sentence grammatically.

Hooray, school's out! *Ugh*, that's disgusting!

Types of Phrases

A phrase is a group of related words that does not contain a complete subject and a complete verb. There are four main kinds of phrases:

1. prepositional
2. appositive
3. verbal (participial, gerund, and infinitive)
4. absolute

Prepositional Phrases

A preposition connects a noun, pronoun, or group of words acting as a noun to the rest of the sentence, thereby creating a prepositional phrase that serves as a modifying element within the sentence. Prepositional phrases usually begin with the preposition and end with the noun or noun substitute, called the "object of the preposition."

We watched the baby crawl *under the table.*

The man *in the gray suit* is my father.

Appositive Phrases

Appositive phrases give additional information about a preceding noun or pronoun. They sometimes consist of only one word.

Jill saw her friend *Susan* in the café.

We stopped for a mocha latte at Adolpho's, *the most famous espresso bar in the city.*

Verbal Phrases

Verbals are incomplete forms of verbs that can't function as predicates in a sentence. Similar to verbs, verbals can show tense and can take complements, but they also function as other parts of speech in that they fill noun, adjective, or adverb slots in a sentence. When a verbal is accompanied by modifiers or complements, the word group is called a "verbal phrase." There are three kinds of verbals and verbal phrases:

1. participial
2. gerund
3. infinitive

Participial Phrases Participles have two forms: the present participle and the past participle. The present participle is the *-ing* form (*swimming, laughing*); the past participle is the *-ed* form for regular verbs (*laughed*) and an irregular form for irregular verbs (*swum*). Participles and participial phrases always act as adjectives in a sentence. In the following examples, the noun modified by the participle is indicated by an arrow.

I saw some ducks *swimming in the lake.*

Laughing happily, Molly squeezed Jake's arm.

The 100-meter freestyle, a race *swum by more than twenty competitors last year,* was won by a thirteen-year-old boy.

Gerund Phrases Gerunds are always the *-ing* form of the verb, and they always serve as nouns in a sentence.

Swimming is my favorite sport. *[serves as subject]*

I love *swimming in the lake.* *[serves as direct object]*

I am not happy about *losing my chemistry notebook in the student union.* *[serves as object of preposition]*

Infinitive Phrases An infinitive is the dictionary form of a verb preceded by the word *to* (*to run, to swim, to laugh*). Infinitives or infinitive phrases can serve as nouns, adjectives, or adverbs in a sentence.

To complete college with a major in electrical engineering is my primary goal at the moment.

The person *to help you with that math* is Molly Malone.

Absolute Phrases

An absolute phrase is comprised of a noun or noun substitute, followed by a participle. It is *absolute* because it doesn't act as a noun, adverb, or adjective; rather, it modifies the whole clause or sentence to which it is attached.

Her face flushed with sweat, the runner headed down Grant Street.

The assistant hunched over the keyboard, *his fingers typing madly*.

Types of Clauses

Clauses have complete subjects and complete predicates. Some clauses can stand alone as sentences (*independent*, or *main*, clauses), whereas others (*dependent*, or *subordinate*, clauses) cannot stand alone as sentences because they are introduced by a *subordinating conjunction* or a *relative pronoun*.

Here are two independent sentences that could serve as independent clauses:

Sam broke the window.

Lucia studied the violin for thirteen years.

Now here are the same two sentences converted to subordinate clauses:

because Sam broke the window

who studied the violin for thirteen years

In the first example, the subordinating conjunction *because* reduces the independent clause to a subordinate clause. In the second example, the relative pronoun *who*, which replaces *Lucia*, also reduces the independent clause to a subordinate clause.

Finally, here are these subordinated clauses attached to independent clauses to form complete sentences.

Because Sam broke the window, he had to pay for it out of his allowance.

Lucia, who studied the violin for thirteen years, won a music scholarship to a prestigious college.

Subordinate clauses always act as nouns, adjectives, or adverbs in another clause.

Noun Clauses

A noun clause is a subordinate clause that functions as a noun in a sentence. Noun clauses act as subjects, objects, or complements.

He promised *that he would study harder.* [serves as direct object]

Why he came here is a mystery. [serves as subject]

He lied about *what he did last summer.* [serves as object of preposition]

Adjective Clauses

An adjective clause is a subordinate clause that modifies a noun or a pronoun. Adjective clauses are formed with the relative pronouns *who, whom, whose, which,* and *that.* For this reason they are sometimes called "relative clauses."

Peter, *who is a star athlete,* has trouble with reading.

The future threat *that I most fear* is a stock market collapse.

Adverb Clauses

An adverb clause is a subordinate clause that modifies a verb, an adjective, or another adverb. Adverb clauses begin with subordinating conjunctions, such as *although, because, if,* and *when* (see p. 665 for a list of subordinating conjunctions).

Because he had broken his leg, he danced all night using crutches.

When he got home, he noticed unusual blisters.

Types of Sentences

Sentences are often classified by the number and kinds of clauses they contain. There are four kinds of sentences:

1. simple
2. compound
3. complex
4. compound-complex

Simple Sentences

A sentence is *simple* if it consists of a single independent clause. The clause may contain modifying phrases and have a compound subject and a compound predicate.

John laughed.

John and Mary laughed and sang.

modifying phrase

Laughing happily and holding hands in the moonlight, John and Mary walked

independent clause (with compound subject and predicate)

along the beach, wrote their names in the sand, and threw pebbles into the crashing waves.

Compound Sentences

See the discussion of comma splices and run-ons, pp. 662–664.

A sentence is *compound* if it consists of two independent clauses linked either by a semicolon or by a comma and a coordinating conjunction. Each clause may contain modifying phrases as well as compound subjects and predicates.

independent clause / independent clause

John laughed, and Mary sang.

modifying phrase / independent clause (with compound subject) / independent clause

Laughing happily, John and Mary walked hand in hand toward the kitchen, but they weren't prepared for the surprise on the countertop.

Complex Sentences

A sentence is *complex* if it contains one independent clause and one or more subordinate clauses.

independent clause / subordinate clause

John smiled to himself while Mary sang.

subordinate clause / independent clause / subordinate clause

When John and Mary saw the surprise on the countertop, they screamed uncontrollably until John fainted.

Compound-Complex Sentences

A *compound-complex sentence* has at least one subordinate clause and two or more independent clauses joined by a semicolon or by a comma and a coordinating conjunction.

independent clause / subordinate clause / independent clause

John smiled to himself while Mary sang, for he was happy.

subordinate clause / independent clause / independent clause

When John and Mary saw the surprise on the countertop, they screamed uncontrollably; soon John collapsed on the floor in a dead faint.

PEARSON mycomplab

For support in learning this chapter's content, follow this path in **MyCompLab**: Resources ⇒ Grammar ⇒ Sentence Grammar. Review the Instruction and Multimedia resources, then complete the Exercises and click on Gradebook to measure your progress.

PUNCTUATING BOUNDARIES OF SENTENCES, CLAUSES, AND PHRASES

3

Readers can quickly get lost if writers fail to signal sentence boundaries accurately. Readers also rely on internal punctuation, primarily commas, to help them recognize the boundaries of clauses and phrases within a sentence. Periods, capital letters, commas, and, occasionally, semicolons are to readers what stop signs and yield signs are to drivers: They guide the reader through the twists and turns of prose.

You will have mastered the skills of this chapter if you can create sentences of your own that follow these patterns.

__________ . __________.

__________; __________.

__________; however, __________.

__________; __________, however, __________.

__________, and __________.

__________ and __________.

__________, __________.

Because __________, __________.

__________ because __________.

This chapter focuses on punctuation rules that help readers recognize the boundaries of sentences and of clauses and phrases within sentences.

In this chapter, you will learn:

- Why readers need punctuation
- Four basic punctuation rules for signaling internal sentence elements
- Guidelines for identifying and correcting sentence fragments
- Guidelines for identifying and correcting comma splices and run-on sentences
- A reference chart summarizing the rules for joining clauses within a sentence

Why Readers Need Punctuation

To understand why it is important to punctuate sentence and clause boundaries, try to read the following passage:

> RECENTLY A GROWING NUMBER OF COMMENTATORS HAVE BEEN FOCUSING ON THE MENTALLY ILL HOMELESS IN RESPONSE TO THE VIOLENT MURDER OF AN ELDERLY PERSON BY A HOMELESS MENTALLY ILL MAN NEW YORK CITY RECENTLY INCREASED ITS EFFORTS TO LOCATE AND HOSPITALIZE DANGEROUS HOMELESS MENTALLY ILL INDIVIDUALS THEIR PLAN WILL INCLUDE AGGRESSIVE OUTREACH SUCH AS ACTIVELY GOING OUT INTO THE STREETS AND SHELTERS TO LOCATE MENTALLY ILL INDIVIDUALS AND THEN INVOLUNTARILY HOSPITALIZING THOSE DEEMED DANGEROUS ALTHOUGH MANY CRITICS OBJECT TO THIS APPROACH MANY APPLAUD THE CITY'S ACTION.

In this passage the use of all capital letters and the deletion of punctuation eliminates all visual clues for sentence boundaries. How many complete sentences do you find in this passage? Where do they begin and end?

Rules for Punctuating Clauses and Phrases within a Sentence

If writers used nothing but short, simple sentences, a capital letter and a period would suffice to signal sentence structure. But when writers combine clauses to form compound, complex, or compound-complex sentences, they must use internal punctuation to help readers perceive the boundaries of these elements. This section explains four main punctuation rules for marking the boundaries of clauses and phrases within a sentence. Once you understand these rules, you will find it easier to mark the boundaries of complete sentences and thus to avoid fragments, run-ons, and comma splices.

Rule 1: Join two independent sentences with a semicolon or with a comma and a coordinating conjunction. You can join two complete sentences to form a compound sentence in two ways: (1) with a semicolon, or (2) with a comma and a coordinating conjunction. You should learn the seven coordinating conjunctions:

and but or nor for yet so

When you join two sentences using either of these methods, each sentence becomes an independent clause in the compound sentence; the punctuation signals the joining point.

Two Sentences	Melissa hasn't changed the oil in her car. However, she is still willing to take it to the game.
Joined with Semicolon	Melissa hasn't changed the oil in her car; however, she is still willing to take it to the game.
Joined with Comma and Coordinating Conjunction	Melissa hasn't changed the oil in her car, but she is still willing to take it to the game.

Rule 2: Use a single comma to set off an introductory adverb clause. Another common way to join sentences is to use a subordinating conjunction to convert one sentence to an adverb clause. Subordinating conjunctions are words such as *because, when, if, although*, and *until*. If the resulting adverb clause comes at the start of the sentence, set it off from the independent clause with a comma. If it follows the independent clause, don't set it off.

See p. 665 for a longer list of subordinating conjunctions.

Adverb Clause Preceding Independent Clause	If the sun is shining in the morning, we'll go for the hike.
Adverb Clause Following Independent Clause	We'll go for the hike if the sun is shining in the morning.

Note that no comma is used in the latter example because the adverb clause follows, rather than precedes, the independent clause.

An exception to this rule occurs with the subordinating conjunction *although*. You should use a comma to set off a clause introduced by *although* even if it comes at the end of a sentence.

The police officer still gave me a ticket, although I explained to her that my speedometer was broken.

Rule 3: Inside a sentence core, use pairs of commas to set off interrupting elements. The core of a sentence consists of the subject, verb, and direct object or subject complement. Within the core of a sentence, never use a single comma; either omit commas or use commas *in pairs* to set off interrupting elements.

Sentence Core	My dog chased the cat around the room.
Interrupting Element Inside the Core	My dog, barking loudly and snapping his teeth, chased the cat around the room.

Note that *a pair* of commas—a comma preceding the element and a comma following the element—marks the boundaries of the interrupting element.

Sentence Core	The police officer still gave me a ticket.
Interrupting Element Inside the Core	The police officer, however, still gave me a ticket.

Rule 4: Use a single comma to set off some introductory or concluding phrases. An introductory phrase often precedes the core of a sentence. Set off an introductory phrase if it is long or if your voice pauses noticeably between the phrase (or single word such as *however*) and the start of the sentence core. Similarly, use a single comma to set off long concluding elements if your voice pauses noticeably after the core. In either case, the comma signals the boundary between the sentence core and the introductory or concluding element.

INTRODUCTORY ELEMENT

Barking loudly and snapping his teeth, my dog chased the cat around the room.

According to many authorities, this author's treatment of women is historically inaccurate.

However, I disagree.

CONCLUDING ELEMENT

My dog chased the cat around the room, his jaws snapping angrily.

The scholar's claim bothered Jensen, leaving him bewildered and possibly angry.

Your familiarity with these four rules will help you understand the logic for punctuating sentences that combine two or more clauses or that include introductory, interrupting, or concluding phrases. Knowing these rules, in turn, will help you learn to signal sentence boundaries to readers.

Exercise

Return to the sentence templates on page 657 that show blank lines punctuated with commas, semicolons, and periods and use the words *and, however,* and *because.* On a separate sheet of paper, create sentences of your own to fill in these templates. Share your sentences with class members.

Identifying and Correcting Sentence Fragments

A sentence fragment is a nonsentence (any structure lacking a complete subject or a complete predicate) that is punctuated either as a sentence or as an independent clause.

Types of Fragments

There are two kinds of sentence fragments.

1. *Phrase fragments* may lack either a subject or a complete predicate or both. In the following passage, the phrase fragments are italicized.

   Paul and Sarah love their mountain home. *Going fishing in the morning. Watching the deer graze in the meadows.* Outside their cabin, a pair of majestic eagles nest in the top of a lone pine; *with only the starry sky as a night roof.*

   The first two fragments are participial phrases punctuated as complete sentences. The last fragment is a prepositional phrase punctuated as an independent clause. The semicolon signals to readers that two independent clauses are joined together.

2. *Subordinate clause fragments* have a subject and a complete predicate, but they begin with either a subordinating conjunction or a relative pronoun, which prevents them from standing alone as a sentence. In the following examples, the subordinate clause fragments are italicized.

   Sarah and Paul often go for a hike. *As soon as the sun comes up.* At night they love to watch the eyes of owls. *Which blink at them from the branches of nearby trees.*

   The first fragment is created by the subordinating conjunction *as soon as*; the second is created by the relative pronoun *which.*

Methods for Correcting Sentence Fragments

There are various ways to correct a fragment; each method produces a slightly different variation in meaning and emphasis.

Method 1: Change a phrase fragment to a complete sentence by converting an incomplete verb into a complete verb or by adding a verb. This method emphasizes the material in the fragment by giving it the weight of a full sentence.

Fragment The buffalo began to stampede. Their heads flailing wildly.

Revised The buffalo began to stampede. Their heads flailed wildly.

The fragment has been converted to a complete sentence by changing the participle *flailing* to the complete verb *flailed.*

Method 2: Change a clause fragment to a complete sentence by removing the subordinator. This method also emphasizes the ideas in the original fragment.

Fragment For Native Americans, killing buffalo was very dangerous. Because the stampeding buffalo herd had to be guided toward the cliff by braves shaking wolf skins.

Revised For Native Americans, killing buffalo was very dangerous. The stampeding buffalo herd had to be guided toward the cliff by braves shaking wolf skins.

Removing the subordinating conjunction *because* converts the fragment into a complete sentence.

Method 3: Correct the fragment by joining it to the sentence that precedes or follows it, whichever makes more sense. This method subordinates the material in the fragment and can work for either phrase or clause fragments. With this method, you may need to use a comma to signal the joining point.

Fragment The buffalo crashed to their deaths. Although the braves killed the animals that were still alive. The squaws did most of the work in preparing the hides and meat.

Revised The buffalo crashed to their deaths. Although the braves killed the animals that were still alive, the squaws did most of the work in preparing the hides and meat.

The original passage contains a subordinate clause fragment beginning with *although.* The revised passage attaches the *although* clause to the second sentence.

Exercise

Proofread the following passage adapted from a student paper. Underline all of the sentence fragments. Then, on a separate sheet of paper, revise the fragments using one of the main correction methods—turn the fragment into a

(continued)

complete sentence or connect the fragment to a neighboring sentence. Choose the correction method that seems most appropriate for the context of the passage.

> Another difference between a taxi driver and other occupations being the way that taxi drivers interact with people. Driving a taxi is one of the few jobs where you really get to "know the customer." In other service jobs, you rarely get to know the customer's name. Such as waiter or bartender. In those jobs you can wait on one hundred people in a night or mix drinks for two hundred. Without personally talking to five of them. In a taxi, however, each customer spends at least ten to fifteen minutes in a quiet car. Having little to do but talk with the driver.

Identifying and Correcting Run-Ons and Comma Splices

Writers make run-on errors or comma splices whenever they fail to show where one sentence ends and the next begins.

A *run-on error* occurs when two sentences are fused together without any punctuation.

> I explained to the police officer that my speedometer was broken she still gave me a ticket.
>
> Two sentences come together between *broken* and *she*, but no period and capital letter or semi-colon marks the boundary.

A *comma splice* occurs when a writer marks the end of a sentence with a comma instead of with a period and a capital letter or a semi-colon.

> I explained to the police officer that my speedometer was broken, she still gave me a ticket.
>
> A comma by itself cannot mark the boundary between two sentences.

Methods for Correcting Run-Ons and Comma Splices

Run-ons and comma splices can be corrected in a variety of ways, depending on the meaning you wish to convey. You may choose to separate the ideas by placing them in two separate sentences, or you may wish to join the ideas into a single sentence. To choose the most appropriate method, consider the rhetorical context of the passage you are writing.

Method 1: Separate the sentences with a period and a capital letter. This method gives equal emphasis to both sentences. If you wish to indicate a logical relationship between the two sentences, you can add a conjunctive adverb (such as *therefore* or *nevertheless*) somewhere in the second sentence.

Revised I explained to the police officer that my speedometer was broken. She still gave me a ticket.

Revised I explained to the police officer that my speedometer was broken. However, she still gave me a ticket.

Method 2: Join the sentences with a semicolon. This method creates a compound sentence with two equally strong independent clauses.

Revised I explained to the police officer that my speedometer was broken; however, she still gave me a ticket.

Method 3: Join the sentences with a comma and a coordinating conjunction. This method also creates a compound sentence with two equally strong independent clauses.

Revised I explained to the police officer that my speedometer was broken, but she still gave me a ticket.

Method 4: Join the sentences with a subordinating conjunction or a relative pronoun. This method creates a complex sentence with an independent clause and a subordinate clause. The material in the independent clause receives more emphasis than the subordinated material does.

Revised Although I explained to the police officer that my speedometer was broken, she still gave me a ticket.

Method 5: Convert one of the sentences into a phrase. This method creates a simple sentence with an added or embedded phrase. The phrase has less importance than the rest of the sentence.

Revised Despite my explanation of the broken speedometer, the police officer gave me a ticket.

Choosing the Most Appropriate Method for Correction Although each of these methods of correcting run-ons and comma splices will produce a grammatically correct solution, the method to be used in a given situation depends on the meaning and emphasis you intend. Consider the following example:

Comma Splice The weather is beautiful, my neighbor is washing her car.

To determine the best way to correct this comma splice, you need to consider the passage in which it occurs. Different correction methods create different effects.

Revised It is a great day. The weather is beautiful. My neighbor is washing her car. Kids are playing in the street. The dog is sleeping in the sun.

Here the focus is on the writer's sense of a great day. The beautiful weather and the neighbor washing her car are only two of four separate pieces of evidence the writer uses to support the feeling. By putting them all in separate sentences, the writer emphasizes each one.

But consider how the comma splice might be corrected in a different context:

Revised I was hoping to invite my neighbor over to watch the football game with me this afternoon. But because the weather is beautiful, she is washing her car.

In this version, the main point is the writer's disappointment that the neighbor isn't coming over to watch football. The beautiful weather is the cause of her washing the car, but the subordinating conjunction *because* makes that information secondary. The writer isn't interested in the beautiful weather for its own sake, so a separate sentence such as the one in the first example would be inappropriate.

These differences illustrate that punctuation is a way of controlling and signaling meaning for readers. As you learn ways of correcting comma splices and run-ons, you will also become aware of the wide variety of options available to convey subtleties of thought and feeling.

Exercise

In the following sentences, underline the comma splices or run-ons (some sentences may be correct). Then, on a separate sheet of paper, revise the underlined sentences.

1. I love to hear coffee perking in the pot on lazy Saturday mornings another of my favorite sounds is rain on a tin roof.
2. When the ice cream wagon begins playing its song in our neighborhood, the children run to greet it, clasping their dimes and quarters in grubby little hands.
3. Freud assumed that the unconscious was the basis for human behavior, therefore, he believed that the pleasure audiences receive from art comes from art's embodiment of unconscious material.
4. Because St. Augustine's conception of God was Neoplatonic, Augustine believed that existence in itself is good.
5. Although scientists don't know for sure how much dinosaurs actually ate, they know that the food intake of the great reptiles must have been enormous, a question they ask themselves, therefore, is what the dinosaurs actually ate.
6. The doctor told me that my MRI revealed nothing to be alarmed about, nevertheless, she wants me to come back in six months for another checkup.
7. Juan and Alicia began taking the engine apart they worked diligently for four hours and then discovered that they didn't have the right tools to continue.
8. I should apologize for the snide e-mail I wrote you last week, although I must admit that I am still angry.
9. In a home aquarium fish will sometimes die from overeating the instructions on fish food boxes, therefore, stress that you feed fish a specified amount on a strict schedule.
10. The upgrade on Manuel's antivirus program seems more trouble than it's worth, so he has decided not to install it.

Overview of Methods for Joining Clauses

Figure HB3.1 (on p. 665) summarizes the methods used in standard written English to join two sentences.

FIGURE HB3.1 Methods for Joining Sentences

Methods for Joining Two Sentences

Coordination

;

, and
, but
, for
, or
, nor
, so
, yet

— **Coordinating conjunctions**

In coordinated sentences, logical relationships are frequently expressed with *conjunctive adverbs* or *transitional expressions*.

Examples of conjunctive adverbs

accordingly	instead
also	likewise
anyhow	meanwhile
besides	moreover
consequently	nevertheless
furthermore	otherwise
hence	still
henceforth	then
however	therefore
indeed	thus

Examples of transitional expressions

after all	in addition
after a while	in fact
as a result	in other words
at any rate	in particular
at the same time	in the first place
for example	on the contrary
for instance	on the other hand

Punctuation pointers

- In coordinated sentences, a semicolon or a coordinating conjunction with a comma must be used where the two independent clauses come together.
- Set off conjunctive adverbs or expressions with commas if your voice pauses around them.

Subordination

with relative pronoun

which
who
whom
whose
that

— **Relative pronouns**

Punctuation pointers

- With relative pronouns, set off the relative clause with commas if the information in the clause is not needed to identify the noun the clause modifies.
- Do not set off the relative clause if the information is needed to identify the noun being modified.

with subordinating conjunction

after
although
as
as if
as though
because
before
if
in order that
since
so that
that
though
unless
until
when
whenever
where
wherever
while

— **Subordinating conjunctions**

Punctuation pointers

- Set off adverb clauses with commas if the adverb clause comes before the independent clause.
- Do not set off adverb clauses at the end of a sentence unless they reverse the direction of thought (for example, *although*).

PEARSON mycomplab For support in learning this chapter's content, follow this path in **MyCompLab**: Resources ⇒ Grammar ⇒ Sentence Grammar. Review the Instruction and Multimedia resources, then complete the Exercises and click on Gradebook to measure your progress.

4 EDITING FOR STANDARD ENGLISH USAGE

In this chapter we address common errors in sentence structure, or usage. In this chapter, you will learn to recognize and correct the following kinds of errors:

- Grammatical tangles such as mixed constructions or faulty predication
- Consistency errors (unnecessary shifts in verb tense or pronoun person)
- Agreement errors (lack of subject-verb agreement or pronoun-antecedent agreement)
- Nonparallel constructions
- Dangling or misplaced modifiers
- Pronoun case errors
- Verb form errors
- Adjective/adverb errors

Fixing Grammatical Tangles

Among the most frequent errors in rough drafts are grammatically tangled sentences that result in *mixed constructions* or *faulty predication.*

Mixed Constructions

In the heat of composing a first draft, a writer sometimes starts a sentence with one kind of construction and shifts midway to another construction.

Faulty By buying a year's supply of laundry soap at one time saves lots of money.

This sentence opens with a prepositional phrase that cannot serve as a sentence subject. The writer can correct the error by eliminating the preposition or by supplying a subject.

Revised Buying a year's supply of laundry soap at one time saves lots of money.

or

By buying a year's supply of laundry soap at one time, the average consumer can save lots of money.

Faulty Predication

Another kind of grammatical tangle, called "faulty predication," occurs when the action specified by the verb can't logically be performed by the subject.

Faulty Throughout *The Scarlet Letter,* Hester Prynne's "A" is imbibed with symbolic significance.

Imbibe means "to drink," so its use makes no sense in this sentence.

Revised Throughout *The Scarlet Letter,* Hester Prynne's "A" is invested with symbolic significance.

Maintaining Consistency

Consistency errors occur whenever a writer illogically shifts verb tenses or shifts the person or number of pronouns.

Shifts in Tense

Readers can become confused when writers change tenses without explanation. You should avoid shifting verb tenses in a passage unless you mean to signal a shift in time.

Faulty The display cases of the little bakery were filled with cakes, pies, doughnuts, and special pastries. From the heated ovens against the back wall *drifts* the aroma of buttery croissants.

The verbs in the first sentence are all in the past tense. The verb in the second sentence shifts to the present without an explanation.

Revised The display cases of the little bakery were filled with cakes, pies, doughnuts, and special pastries. From the heated ovens against the back wall *drifted* the aroma of buttery croissants.

Shifts in the Person and Number of Pronouns

Pronouns have three persons: first (*I, we*); second (*you*); and third (*he, she, it, one, they*). Keep your point of view consistent by avoiding confusing shifts from one person to another or from singular to plural.

Confusing As readers, we are not prepared for Hamlet's change in the last act. When one sees Hamlet joking with the grave diggers, you forget momentarily about his earlier despair.

For advice on avoiding sexist language when using third-person pronouns, see pp. 689–690.

The pronouns shift from first to third to second person.

Revised As readers, we are not prepared for Hamlet's change in the last act. When we see Hamlet joking with the grave diggers, we forget momentarily about his earlier despair.

Maintaining Agreement

Writers often have to choose between singular and plural forms of verbs and pronouns to ensure that verbs match their subjects and pronouns match their antecedents. In some cases, special rules determine whether a subject or an antecedent is singular or plural.

Subject-Verb Agreement

In many tenses a verb changes its form to agree in number with its subject.

Singular	This violin *is* beautiful.
Plural	These violins *are* beautiful.

In most cases, it is easy to determine whether the subject is singular or plural, but some cases are tricky. The following rules cover most of these tricky cases.

Plural Words between Subject and Verb It may be difficult to find the subject when it is separated from the verb by intervening words, phrases, or embedded clauses or when an indefinite word such as *one, each,* or *kind* is followed by a prepositional phrase beginning with *of.* In the latter case the object of the preposition is often mistaken for the subject.

Faulty	One of the recent shipments of boxes containing computers, printers, and monitors *were* delayed.
Revised	One of the recent shipments of boxes containing computers, printers, and monitors *was* delayed.

In this sentence, *one* is the subject, not any of the intervening plural words.

Similarly, prepositional phrases beginning with *as well as, in addition to, along with,* and *including* can trick writers into thinking that a singular subject is plural.

Faulty	My mother, along with several of her coworkers, *are* getting a special award for excellence in customer relations.
Revised	My mother, along with several of her coworkers, *is* getting a special award for excellence in customer relations.

In this sentence the subject is *mother*; the intervening prepositional phrase should be ignored.

Compound Subjects Joined by *and* Use a plural verb for singular or plural subjects joined by *and* unless the nouns joined by *and* are thought of as one unit, in which case the verb is singular. Notice the different meanings of the following sentences:

My brother and my best friend *is* with me now.

This sentence means that my brother is with me now and that my brother is my best friend.

My brother and my best friend *are* with me now.

This sentence means that two people are with me—my brother and my best friend.

Compound Subjects Joined by *or, nor, either . . . or, neither . . . nor* The coordinating conjunctions *or, nor, either . . . or,* and *neither . . . nor* take singular verbs if they join singular subjects and plural verbs if they join plural subjects. If they join a singular subject to a plural subject, the verb agrees with the nearer subject.

Either a raccoon or a dog *is* getting into the garbage pails.

Both subjects are singular, so the verb is singular.

Either raccoons or dogs *are* getting into the garbage pails.

Both subjects are plural, so the verb is plural.

Either some raccoons or a dog *is* getting into the garbage pails.

The subject closer to the verb is singular, so the verb is singular.

Indefinite Pronoun as Subject Some indefinite pronouns are always singular; others can be singular or plural depending on context.

Always Singular		Singular or Plural
anybody	none	all
anyone	each	any
anything	everybody	some
either	neither	
nobody		

The indefinite pronouns in the left-hand columns are always singular.

Faulty	Each of the dogs *are* thirsty.
Revised	Each of the dogs *is* thirsty.

The indefinite pronouns in the right-hand column can be singular or plural. These words are generally followed by a prepositional phrase beginning with *of.* The number of the pronoun depends on whether the object of the preposition is singular or plural.

Some of the table *is* sanded.

The object of the preposition (*table*) is singular, so the verb is singular.

Some of the tables *are* sanded.

The object of the preposition (*tables*) is plural, so the verb is plural.

Inversion of Subject and Verb Locating the subject may be tricky in inverted sentences, in which the subject comes after the verb.

Just beyond the fence line on the other side of the road are some pheasants.

The subject is *pheasants*, so the verb is plural.

Be especially careful with inverted sentences that begin with *here, there,* or *where.* Errors occur most frequently when a writer uses these words in contractions or in questions.

Faulty Where's my belt and sweater?

The subject is *belt and sweater,* so the verb should be plural.

Revised Where are my belt and sweater?

Relative Pronoun as Subject Relative pronouns used as subjects (*who, that, which*) are singular or plural depending on their antecedents.

A person who *builds* glass houses shouldn't throw stones.

Who is singular because its antecedent, *person,* is singular; hence the verb should be singular.

People who *build* glass houses shouldn't throw stones.

Who is plural because its antecedent, *people,* is plural; hence the verb should be plural.

Be especially careful when the antecedent is the object of the preposition *of.*

One of the reasons that *are* frequently given is inflation.

The verb of the main clause (*is*) is singular because its subject is the singular pronoun *one.* But the verb of the relative clause (*are*) is plural because its subject (*that*) has a plural antecedent (*reasons*).

Subject Followed by Linking Verb and Subject Complement Linking verbs should agree with the subject of the sentence, not with the subject complement.

Sleeping, eating, and drinking *are* his whole life.

The verb *are* agrees with the plural subject, not with the singular subject complement.

His whole life *is* sleeping, eating, and drinking.

In this case, the verb agrees with the singular subject, not with the plural subjective complement.

Collective Noun as Subject With collective nouns such as *group, committee, crew, crowd, faculty, majority,* and *audience,* use a singular verb if the collective group acts as one unit; use a plural verb if the members of the group act individually.

The faculty at Hogwash College *is* delighted with the new president.

Here the faculty functions as a single unit.

The faculty at Hogwash College *are* arguing at this very moment.

Here *faculty* refers to individuals who act independently.

Some collective nouns present special problems or follow special rules, for instance, *a number* versus *the number. A number* refers to a collection of individual items and takes a plural verb. *The number* refers to a unit and takes a singular verb.

A number of students *are* studying grammar this semester.

The number of students studying grammar *is* declining every year.

Titles or words referred to as words use singular verbs.

Snow White and the Seven Dwarfs is a famous Disney movie.

The italics indicates a title, which takes a singular verb. If you were referring to the characters rather than the title, the verb would be plural: "Snow White and the seven dwarfs are my favorite Disney characters."

Exercise

In the following sentences, underline the true subject or subjects of the verb in parentheses. Then underline the correct verb form twice.

1. Under a pile of old rags in the corner of the basement (is/are) a mother mouse and a squirming family of baby mice.
2. Hard work, together with intelligence, initiative, and a bit of good luck, (explains/explain) the success of many wealthy businesspeople.
3. The first thing she emphasized (was/were) the differences between Pacific and Atlantic breeding patterns of these fish.
4. The myth, legend, prayer, and ritual of primitive religions (contains/contain) many common themes.
5. Unfortunately, neither of the interviewers for the local TV station (has/have) read any of her works.
6. There (is/are) a number of students who (is/are) waiting to see the teacher.
7. (Does/Do) one of the students still have my notebook?
8. One of the students who (is/are) trying out for the play (wants/want) to become a professional actor.
9. He is the only one of all the students in the theater arts class who really (has/have) professional ambitions.
10. The committee (is/are) writing individual letters to the judge.

Pronoun-Antecedent Agreement

Just as a subject must agree in number with its verb, so must a pronoun agree in number with its antecedent (the noun that the pronoun stands for). To apply this rule, you must first determine the antecedent of the pronoun and then decide whether the antecedent is singular or plural, following the rules presented in the previous section. Pronoun-antecedent agreement occasionally presents some difficulties. The following rules cover most cases.

Compound Construction as Antecedent If a compound antecedent is joined by *and*, choose a plural pronoun; if a compound antecedent is joined by *or*, the pronoun should agree in number with the closer antecedent.

Rebecca and Paul invited us to their party.

Either Brian or Luis will bring his volleyball to the party.

Either Brian or his sisters will bring their volleyball.

Collective Noun as Antecedent Use a singular pronoun to refer to a collective noun that acts as one unit; use a plural pronoun if members of the group act individually.

The committee reported its opinion.

The committee began arguing among themselves.

Indefinite Pronoun as Antecedent Generally, if the antecedent is an indefinite pronoun such as *either, neither, everyone, everybody, someone, somebody, anyone,* or *anybody*, you use a singular pronoun.

Everybody coming to the party should bring his or her own drinks.

See p. 704 for suggestions on alternative constructions.

Note: Sentence constructions such as this one can lead to the use of non-inclusive language.

Maintaining Parallel Structure

When joining items in series or lists, make sure that each item has the same grammatical structure: Nouns should be joined to nouns, verbs to verbs, prepositional phrases to prepositional phrases, clauses to clauses, and so forth. Parallelism greatly increases the clarity and force of your sentences.

A nonparallel construction occurs whenever a writer fails to maintain the same grammatical structure for each item in a series.

Faulty Shanelle likes playing soccer and to roller-skate.

Here the writer has joined a gerund phrase (*playing soccer*) to an infinitive (*to roller-skate*). The problem can be solved by making both items gerunds or both infinitives.

Revised Shanelle likes playing soccer and roller-skating.

or

Shanelle likes to play soccer and to roller-skate.

Faulty As a teacher, he was a courteous listener, helpful during office hours, and he lectured in an exciting way.

Revised As a teacher, he was a courteous listener, a good helper during office hours, and an exciting lecturer.

In this revision the writer converts all items in the series to nouns.

Faulty This term paper is illogical, poorly documented, and should have used more primary sources.

Here the first two items are parallel (the adjectives *illogical* and *poorly documented*), but the last item is a verb phrase (*should have used more primary sources*).

Revised This term paper is illogical, poorly documented, and poorly researched.

or

This term paper, which should have used more primary sources, is illogical and poorly documented.

To increase clarity, writers often repeat function words such as articles, prepositions, conjunctions, or the infinitive word *to* at the beginning of each item in a parallel series.

Confusing The drill sergeant told the recruits that there would be no weekend passes and they would be on KP instead.

Revised The drill sergeant told the recruits that there would be no weekend passes and that they would be on KP instead.

The repetition of *that* clarifies the writer's intention: to report two things the drill sergeant told the recruits.

Placement of Correlative Conjunctions

When using correlative conjunctions (such as *either ... or, neither ... nor, both ... and*, and *not only ... but also*), make sure that each unit of the correlative precedes the same grammatical structure.

Faulty I not only like ice cream but also root beer.

Here the writer places *not only* in front of a verb (*like*), but places *but also* in front of a noun (*root beer*).

Revised I like not only ice cream but also root beer.

Use of *and which/that* or *and who/whom*

Be sure that a clause beginning with *and which, and that, and who*, or *and whom* is preceded by a parallel clause beginning with *which, that, who*, or *whom*.

Faulty Of all my friends, Paul is the one with the greatest sense of courage and who most believes in honesty

The writer links a pronoun (*one*) to a relative clause (*who most believes ...*), creating a nonparallel structure.

Revised Of all my friends, Paul is the one who has the greatest sense of courage and who most believes in honesty.

Exercise

In the following sentences, underline the nonparallel constructions. Then, on a separate sheet of paper, revise the sentences to create parallel structures.

1. We improved our old car's acceleration by resetting the spark plug gaps and also we boiled out the carburetor.

(*continued*)

2. Race car driving requires much practical experience, and your reactions must be quick.
3. After reading the events calendar, we decided to go to a festival of Japanese anime and on attending the battle of the bands afterward.
4. I want to read a biography of a flamboyant figure working in volunteer organizations and who has altered history.
5. Sasha not only does volunteer work in the school, but also coaching soccer every fall.
6. Either you must leave early or leave after the major rush hour.
7. The harvest moon shone brightly, pouring its light over the surrounding water, and which made the evening a special moment in their lives.
8. You can avoid a comma splice by joining main clauses with a comma and a coordinating conjunction, with a semicolon, or by changing one of the main clauses to a subordinate clause.
9. Again and again psychologists explore the same questions: Are we shaped by our heredity, by our environment, or do we have free will?
10. To make friends you must first be a friend and then listening carefully.

Avoiding Dangling or Misplaced Modifiers

Dangling Modifiers

When a sentence opens with a modifying phrase, the phrase must be followed immediately by the noun it modifies, which is usually the grammatical subject of the sentence; otherwise, the phrase is said to dangle. You can correct a dangling modifier by (a) recasting the sentence so that the subject is the word modified by the opening modifier; or (b) expanding the modifying phrase into a clause that has its own subject.

modifier — subject

Faulty Walking down the street, a flowerpot fell on my head.

This sentence brings to mind a walking flowerpot.

modifier — subject

Revised Walking down the street, I was struck on the head by a flowerpot.

or

modifying clause with subject

While *I* was walking down the street, a flowerpot fell on my head.

modifier — subject

Faulty With only a dollar in change, the meal was too expensive.

Does the meal have only a dollar in change?

modifier subject

Revised With only a dollar in change, I couldn't afford the meal.

or

modifying clause with subject

Because *I* had only a dollar in change, the meal was too expensive.

Misplaced Modifiers

A modifier is said to be misplaced when a modifying word or phrase is separated from the element it modifies. To correct this type of error, change the location of the modifier so that it is next to the word or phrase it modifies.

Faulty The students gave a present to their teacher in a big box.

This sentence suggests that the teacher is in a big box.

Revised The students gave their teacher a present in a big box.

Note: Be careful to place limiting adverbs, such as *only, just*, and *merely*, next to the words they limit. As the following example shows, changing the location of *only* can often change the meaning of a sentence.

Only I baked the cake. (I am the person solely responsible for baking the cake.)

I only baked the cake. (I baked it, but I didn't put the frosting on it.)

I baked only the cake. (Someone else baked the cookies.)

Place limiting adverbs *directly in front of* the words they modify.

Faulty I should get a higher grade because I only failed one exam.

The writer intends to modify *one exam* rather than *failed* and thus needs to move *only*.

Revised I should get a higher grade because I failed only one exam.

Exercise

In the following sentences, underline the dangling or misplaced modifiers (some sentences may be correct). Then, on a separate sheet of paper, revise the faulty sentences.

1. Feeling cold, tired, and depressed, tears streamed from my friend's eyes.
2. Their heads tilted back in awe, the children on this summer's night began trying to count the stars.
3. Seen through a telescope that magnifies things sixty times, Jupiter appears as big as the moon.
4. By studying the light reflected by Jupiter, its clouds are a poisonous mixture of ammonia floating in hydrogen.
5. Having long expected to return to Harlem after graduation, the young accountant was not prepared for the changes he saw on Lenox Avenue.

(*continued*)

6. While cruising at 10,000 feet 45 miles east of Albuquerque, New Mexico, on July 16, 1945, at approximately 5:30 A.M., a brilliant flash of light, brighter than the sun, blazed across the horizon.
7. We were absolutely startled, unable to explain the sunlike flash or to grasp the meaning of the huge mushroom cloud that soon appeared above the desert floor.
8. Reporting what we had seen by radio to ground authorities, no satisfactory explanation could be found.
9. The following morning, still plagued by the event, the newspapers only reported that an ammunition dump had exploded in the approximate area where we had seen the flash.
10. Listening to the radio on August 6, 1945, a similar flash of light occurred over Hiroshima, Japan; then we realized what we had seen several weeks earlier—the first explosion of an atomic bomb.

Choosing Correct Pronoun Cases

Many pronouns change their form according to the grammatical slot they fill in a sentence.

Case Name	Used for These Slots	Personal Pronouns	Relative Pronouns
subjective	subject, subject complement	I, we, he, she, they	who, whoever
objective	direct object, indirect object, object of preposition, subject of infinitive	me, us, him, her, them	whom, whomever
possessive	adjective showing possession	my, our, his, her, their	whose

The case of a pronoun is determined by its slot in the sentence.

She and *I* are good friends. *[subjects]*

Paul likes *her* and *me*. *[direct objects]*

Give *her* and *me* the present. *[indirect objects]*

Paul did it for *her* and *me*. *[objects of preposition]*

The winners were *she* and *I*. *[subject complements]*

Patricia asked *her* and *me* to write the final report. *[subjects of infinitive]*

Although writers generally handle pronoun cases accurately, the following instances give special trouble.

Cases of Relative Pronouns

In relative or noun clauses, the pronouns *who, whom, whoever,* or *whomever* take their case from their function in their own clause, not from the function of that clause in the rest of the sentence.

Faulty Give the prize to *whomever* says the secret word.

Although *whomever* at first seems to be the object of the preposition *to*, it is actually the subject of the verb *says* and should be in the subjective case. The object of the preposition *to* is actually the whole noun clause.

Revised Give the prize to *whoever* says the secret word.

Faulty I voted against Ralph Winkley, *who* big business especially supports.

In this case the relative pronoun fills a direct object slot in its own clause. Compare: Big business especially supports *him*. The writer should choose *whom*.

Revised I voted against Ralph Winkley, *whom* big business especially supports.

Intervening Parenthetical Clauses

When choosing the case of relative pronouns, don't let such words as *I think* or *he supposes* influence your choice. These are parenthetical expressions that can be discarded from the sentence.

Faulty I voted for Marion Fudge, *whom* I think is the most honest candidate.

Here the relative pronoun is the subject of the verb *is*, not the direct object of *I think*, and hence it should be subjective.

Revised I voted for Marion Fudge, *who* I think is the most honest candidate.

Pronouns as Parts of Compound Constructions

Case errors are especially frequent in compound constructions. Many people who were reprimanded as children for saying "Him and me are going outside" overcorrect by using "he and I" even when "him and me" is warranted. Pronouns that fill object slots (or subjects of infinitives) must be in the objective case. You can usually avoid case errors in compound constructions by choosing the same case that you would select if you were using the pronoun alone.

Faulty Isobel appointed Ralph and *I* to the committee.

The pronoun is a direct object and should be in the objective case. Compare: Isobel appointed *me* to the committee.

Revised Isobel appointed Ralph and *me* to the committee.

Note that subjects of infinitives are in the objective case.

Faulty The dean of students wants *she* and *I* to represent the student council at the convention.

Compare: The dean of students wants *me* to represent the student council. . . .

Revised The dean of students wants *her* and *me* to represent the student council at the convention.

Be especially careful with pronouns appearing in front of infinitives that omit the *to*.

Faulty Let's you and *I* go to the show this evening.

The pronoun is the subject of the infinitive *(to) go* and should be in the objective case. Compare: Let *me* go to the show.

Revised Let's you and *me* go to the show this evening.

Pronouns in Appositive Constructions

In appositive constructions, in which the pronoun is followed by an identifying noun, use the pronoun case that would be correct if the noun were not there:

The principal told *us* boys to go home.

Compare: The principal told us to go home.

We boys hid around the corner until the principal went back to her office.

Compare: We hid around the corner.

Pronouns as Parts of Implied Clauses

When a pronoun occurs after a *than* that is introducing an implied clause, choose the pronoun's case according to the pronoun's use in the implied clause. Both of the following sentences are correct, but their meanings are different.

I like Paul better than he.

This sentence means "I like Paul better than he likes Paul."

I like Paul better than him.

This sentence means "I like Paul better than I like him."

Pronouns Preceding Gerunds or Participles

Use the possessive case before gerunds (*-ing* verbals used as nouns) and the subjective or objective case before present participles (*-ing* verbals used as adjectives).

I saw *him* running away from the police.

In this sentence, *running* is a participle modifying the direct object *him*.

I think *his* running away from the police was his biggest mistake.

Here, *running* is a gerund, the subject of *was*.

Exercise

In the following sentences, underline the correct pronoun from the choices given in parentheses.

1. (We/Us) girls want to bike to the store.
2. Natalie, (who/whom) received the scholarship, will study microbiology.

3. If you and (he/him) can visit Tim and (I/me) next month, we will tour the national park.
4. Jessica and Lin-Ju will bring (her/their) skis.
5. (His/Him) playing loud music annoyed the neighbors.
6. He is the racer (who/whom) I believe fell at the finish line.
7. This vacation was necessary for you and (I/me).
8. A burglar stole our computer, but no one saw (his/him) entering the house.
9. Stephen or Tom will do (his/her/their) practicing before school.
10. Emily and Amy do (his/her/their) practicing faithfully every day.

Choosing Correct Verb Forms

As we explained in Handbook 2 (pp. 644–656), English verbs change structure to make different tenses. *Regular* verbs add *-ed* to the base form to create the past and past participle; *irregular* verbs form the past and past participle through internal spelling changes.

Verb form errors occur when the writer uses a nonstandard form, often with irregular verbs.

Faulty I *seen* Aram in the back room at 8:00.

The past form of *to see* is *saw*.

Revised I *saw* Aram in the back room at 8:00.

Another verb form error arises when the preposition *of* is substituted for the auxiliary verb *have*. In spoken English, *have* often sounds like *of*, especially in contractions: "I should've finished my paper earlier." In written English, be sure not to confuse the two words.

Faulty I should *of* finished my paper earlier.

Revised I should *have* finished my paper earlier.

Choosing Correct Adjective and Adverb Forms

Although adjectives and adverbs are both modifiers, they cannot be used interchangeably because adjectives modify nouns or pronouns whereas adverbs modify verbs, adjectives, other adverbs, and sometimes whole phrases, clauses, or sentences.

For more on adjectives and adverbs, see p. 651.

Problems with adjectives and adverbs can occur in the following cases.

Confusion of Adjective and Adverb Forms

Do not use adjectives when adverbs are warranted.

Faulty I did *real good* on that test.

The adverb form is *well*, not *good*. Similarly, *real* is an adjective, which cannot modify an adverb.

Revised I did *really well* on that test.

Be careful to use the appropriate modifier after verbs that can be either linking verbs or action verbs. Linking verbs (such as *is, are,* and *seem*) take subject complements, which are either nouns or adjectives. Certain linking verbs, especially the sense verbs *feel, look, taste, smell,* and *sound* as well as a few others, can also be action verbs. After such verbs, choose an adjective if the word modifies the subject and an adverb if it modifies the verb.

The captain looked *angry*.

Here, *angry* is an adjective modifying *captain*. Compare: The angry captain ...

The captain looked *angrily* at the crew.

Here, *angrily* is an adverb telling how the captain did the looking.

Problems with Comparative and Superlative Forms

Short adjectives (with one syllable or two syllables ending in *-y* or *-le*) form their comparative and superlative degrees by adding *-er* and *-est* to the simple form. Other adjectives and most adverbs generally use *more* (or *less*) for the comparative and *most* (or *least*) for the superlative. A few modifiers are irregular.

Choosing Comparatives Versus Superlatives Use the comparative degree for two persons or things and the superlative for three or more.

Of the two players, Maria is the *better*.

Of the whole team, Maria is the *best*.

Misuse of Comparatives with Absolute Adjectives Do not use comparative and superlative degrees with absolute adjectives, such as *unique* or *impossible*.

Faulty Her dress was the *most unique* one I had ever seen.

Unique already means "one of a kind" and can't be further modified.

Revised Her dress was *unique*.

or

Her dress was the *most unusual* one I had ever seen.

Double Comparatives Avoid double comparatives or superlatives.

Faulty Raphael is *more smarter* than George.

Revised Raphael is *smarter* than George.

Illogical Comparisons Avoid making illogical comparisons between items that are not actually comparable. Sometimes illogical comparisons result from a missing word such as *other*.

Faulty Our Volvo is better than any car on the road.

This sentence inadvertently implies that this Volvo isn't on the road.

Revised Our Volvo is better than any *other* car on the road.

At other times an illogical comparison arises when the grammar of the sentence mixes apples and oranges.

Faulty Handwritten papers are harder to read than typing.

Papers cannot be compared with typing.

Revised Handwritten papers are harder to read than typed papers.

Ambiguous Adverbs

Problems rarely occur with adverbs except when they are used ambiguously to modify whole sentences. Normally an adverb modifies a single word or a group of words in a sentence. Sometimes, however, writers use an adverb to modify an entire sentence. Occasionally such sentences are ambiguous.

Ambiguous Unluckily, the wide receiver dropped the pass.

Who has the bad luck here? The wide receiver? Or the speaker of the sentence, who hopes her team will win? The ambiguity can be eliminated by clarifying what *unluckily* modifies.

Revised The wide receiver unluckily dropped the pass.

or

Unluckily for us, the wide receiver dropped the pass.

PEARSON mycomplab

For support in learning this chapter's content, follow this path in **MyCompLab**: Resources ⇒ Grammar ⇒ Basic Grammar. Review the Instruction and Multimedia resources, then complete the Exercises and click on Gradebook to measure your progress.

5 EDITING FOR STYLE

In Handbook 4 we focused on sentence-level errors. In this chapter we consider stylistic concerns, with the goal of making your prose more lively, interesting, and clear. The problems we address in this chapter are not errors. Rather, they are more like noise or interference in a radio broadcast; they annoy your reader and can sometimes distort your message.

In this chapter, you will learn to:

- Prune your prose to cut out deadwood
- Enliven your prose by eliminating nominalizations, noun pileups, pretentious diction, and clichés and by varying sentence structure and using specific details
- Avoid broad or unclear pronoun references
- Put old information before new
- Make informed decisions about the use of the active or passive voice
- Use inclusive language

Pruning Your Prose

In most rhetorical contexts, conciseness is a virtue. Readers like efficient prose that makes its point without padding. Avoiding wordiness does not mean eliminating details or cutting into the muscle of an essay; it means eliminating inefficient words and bulky phrases that take up space without adding meaning.

Cutting Out Deadwood

See also Chapter 4, Concept 11.

Good writers typically write first drafts that are much longer than their final versions. Eliminating unneeded words and phrases is an essential part of revision.

Wordy At the present time it can be considered a truism that families with incomes neither too far above nor too far below the median income can send their children to expensive colleges with no more out-of-pocket charges and expenses than it would cost to send these same children to colleges whose tuition and related expenses are much lower.

Revised The truth is that for average-income families, an expensive college costs no more than a cheap one.

When eliminating deadwood, watch out for common wordy phrases such as the following:

at the present time (use *now*)
because of the fact that (use *because*)
are of the opinion that (use *believe*)
have the ability to (use *can*)
in spite of the fact that (use *although*)

You can easily delete these expressions—and dozens more like them—without sacrificing meaning.

Combining Sentences

Another cause of wordiness is the inefficient use of short, choppy sentences. Try to recast a choppy passage by combining sentences, thus saving words while creating more complex and graceful structures.

Wordy Jim Maxwell took two years to build his solar building. Building his solar building included nearly one year of planning. His solar building was intended mainly as a grain drier. But it also provided a warm winter shop. Additionally he had the advantage of a machinery shed. This shed kept his machinery dry. His new solar building would pay dividends for years to come.

Revised It took two years to build, including nearly one year of planning, but when Jim Maxwell finished his solar building, he had a grain drier, a warm winter shop, and a dry machinery shed that would pay dividends for years to come.

Exercise

On a separate sheet of paper, improve the style of the following sentences by cutting out deadwood, recasting the words, or combining elements to eliminate wordiness.

1. It appears to me that he seems to be an unusually quiet person but also that he is the kind of person who really cares a lot about other people.
2. If a person is the kind of person who hurries rapidly when that person tries to do things, then that person is apt to find that he or she has wasted a lot of valuable time and material by trying to do the events too rapidly.
3. Ilana was interested in finding out the answer to a question that she had recently been puzzling about. The question was this: What is the important and essential difference between a disease that most people would call "mental illness" and a disease that is simply a disease of the brain?
4. It is unfortunate that the mayor acted in this manner. The mayor settled the issue. But before he settled the issue he made a mistake. He fostered a public debate that was very bitter. The debate pitted some of his subordinates against each other (and these were key subordinates, too). It also caused many other people to feel inflamed passions and fears as a result of the way the mayor handled the whole affair.

Enlivening Your Prose

You can often revise your prose to make the tone livelier and more interesting.

Avoiding Nominalizations

Lively writers express actions with verbs. Lifeless writers often *nominalize* their sentences by converting actions into nouns (for example, by writing, "arrive at a conclusion" rather than "conclude"). A highly nominalized style characterizes much bureaucratic and administrative prose, making it sound stilted, impersonal, and dead.

Nominalized	For the production of effective writing, the expression of an action through the use of a verb is the method most highly preferred.
Revised	Effective writers express actions with verbs.

A nominalized sentence is not only long and dull, but also confusing. Nominalized sentences often include two additional problems: overuse of the verb *to be* and a pileup of prepositional phrases. To revise a nominalized sentence, ask yourself who is doing what; then make the doer of the action the subject and make the action a verb.

Nominalized	Jim's receiving of this low grade was the result of his reading of the material too quickly.
Revised	Jim received a low grade because he read the material too quickly.

By putting *Jim* in the subject slot, the writer eliminates the weak verb *was* as well as three prepositional phrases.

Exercise

On a separate sheet of paper, revise the following sentences to eliminate nominalizations.

1. The person who received the rewards is the person who was the victor.
2. The killing of a goose from which the laying of golden eggs is frequent is usually seen to be a mistake.
3. The socialization of children in the avoidance of risky behaviors often results in their timidity as adults.
4. Juanita came to the realization that her preference of major was changing from history to mathematics.
5. The teacher's examination of the student's locker was caused by the teacher's suspicion of the possibility of the hiding of drugs by the student.

Avoiding Noun Pileups

Noun pileups result from the tendency, again common in bureaucratic prose, to use nouns as adjectives.

Noun Pileup Consideration of an applicant physical disability access plan by the student services reform committee will occur forthwith.

Revised The committee to reform student services will soon consider a plan for improving access to buildings for physically disabled applicants.

Avoiding Pretentious Language

Unless you are intentionally imitating a long-winded style, strive for language that sounds natural and clear rather than pretentious (or developed through overuse of a thesaurus).

Stilted The tyro in the field of artistic endeavors commenced to ascertain the suitability of different constituencies of pigment.

Revised The student artist began wondering which color paint would be most suitable.

Avoiding Clichés, Jargon, and Slang

Clichés are tired, frequently repeated phrases such as "last but not least," "easier said than done," or "a chill ran up my spine." Replace them with fresh language.

Deciding when to avoid jargon and slang is more problematic because their use may be appropriate depending on your audience, purpose, and genre. Technical jargon is acceptable if you are writing for an audience who understands it within a genre that uses it; slang is also fine if it suits your purpose, audience, and genre. In general, you should avoid jargon that may not be understood by your audience, and you should avoid slang in most formal contexts.

Inappropriate Jargon for a Teacher's Letter to Parents

Your child displays maladaptive socialization behaviors.

Revised Your child is sometimes rude to classmates.

Inappropriate Slang for a College Essay

The gods are all bent out of shape because Oedipus killed his dad.

Revised The gods are angry because Oedipus killed his father.

Creating Sentence Variety

Prose can feel wooden or choppy if each sentence has the same construction and length. Skilled writers combine sentences in various ways for emphasis and grace.

Monotonous Martin watched carefully for loose rocks. He picked his way along the edge of the cliff. Martin didn't hear the rattles at first. Then he suddenly froze with fear when he heard them. A timber rattler was about two feet away. It was coiled like a garden hose. The rattler's neck was arched. Its fangs looked like twin needles of death.

In this passage, each sentence starts with the subject, and all the sentences are approximately the same length.

Revised Watching carefully for loose rocks as he picked his way along the edge of the cliff, Martin suddenly froze with fear. At first he didn't hear the rattles. Then he heard them for sure. About two feet away, coiled like a garden hose, was a timber rattler, its neck arched, its fangs looking like twin needles of death.

Here the longest sentence is twenty-four words and the shortest is six words. The two short sentences emphasize dramatically important moments.

Using Specific Details

See also Chapter 4, Concept 11.

Except in philosophical or theoretical writing, which uses abstract language precisely, abstract prose can be dull. You can enliven abstract prose by replacing abstract terms with concrete words or by adding specific, colorful details for support.

Abstract The poor are often stereotyped as beggars, drunks, or people with uncared-for children. We think of them as being without spirit or hope.

Revised We often stereotype poor people as panhandlers demanding our spare change, as scruffy drunks holding a bottle in a paper bag, or as barefoot children with matted hair, filthy clothes, and tears streaking down their dirty faces as they tug on their mother's arm. We picture the poor as spiritless or hopeless, isolated in their own world, eyes glazed with despair.

Note that in this example, adding concrete language makes the passage *longer*, whereas pruning deadwood makes a passage shorter. What is the difference between deadwood and detail?

Avoiding Broad or Unclear Pronoun Reference

Each time you use a pronoun, make sure that the noun to which it refers, its *antecedent*, is clearly apparent. Unclear use of pronouns can confuse readers.

Avoiding Broad Reference

For more on *this* as a pronoun, see p. 647.

A broad reference occurs whenever a pronoun—usually *this, that,* or *it*—stands for an idea or a whole group of words rather than for a single noun. Although this usage is sometimes acceptable, it is often ambiguous or vague.

Broad Reference Harold Krebs in Hemingway's "Soldier's Home" rebels against his parents. He does *this* by refusing to accept their values, and *this* is why his parents are so upset by *it.*

In this sentence the italicized pronouns refer not to specific nouns but to ideas, which shift with each pronoun, confusing the reader.

Revised Harold Krebs in Hemingway's "Soldier's Home" rebels against his parents by refusing to accept their way of life. His rejection of their values explains why his parents are so upset by his later actions.

Do not make broad references with the pronoun *which*, which must have a single noun for its antecedent.

Faulty	He drinks a lot, which is something I disapprove of.
Revised	I disapprove of his heavy drinking.

In the original sentence, *which* has no noun antecedent.

Avoiding Unclear Antecedents

To avoid confusing your readers, make sure that every pronoun has a clear antecedent. Avoid using pronouns that seem to stand for two different antecedents.

Unclear Antecedent	Chris explained to his son the reasons he couldn't go to the meeting.
Revised	Chris explained the reasons his son couldn't go to the meeting.

In the original sentence, *he* could stand for either *Chris* or *son*, making it unclear whether Chris or his son couldn't go to the meeting.

Putting Old Information before New Information

In closed-form prose, clear writers begin sentences with old information—a key word or concept from the previous sentence, from the paragraph's topic sentence, or from the essay's thesis statement or purpose,—to keep their readers on track. Revise the structure of sentences that violate this rule.

The old/new contract is one of the chief principles of clarity in closed-form prose. See Skills 17.1 and 17.7 for more details.

New Information before Old	When the experts disagree, therefore, what advice can be given? Ferreting out the facts that all sides agree on is a first step that we can take.
Revised	What advice can we give, therefore, when the experts disagree? First, we try to ferret out the facts that all sides agree on.

Deciding between Active and Passive Voice

You must choose active or passive voice whenever you use a transitive verb—an action verb that has a receiver of the action as well as a doer. The active voice makes the doer of the action the subject and the receiver of the action the direct object; the passive voice makes the receiver of the action the subject and either omits the doer or makes the doer the object of the preposition *by*.

Active Voice	Our cat just caught a mouse.
Passive Voice	A mouse was just caught by our cat.

Strength of the Active Voice

Experienced writers usually prefer the active voice because it is stronger and more economical. The passive voice requires *to be* helping verbs and prepositional phrases for the doer of the action.

Weak	The cake and ice cream were eaten, and then games were played.
Revised	The children ate the cake and ice cream and then played games.

However, the passive voice isn't always inappropriate. The choice of voice depends on the context of your sentence.

When to Use the Passive Voice

Writers sometimes choose the passive voice to create appropriate emphasis or to evade responsibility.

Passive Voice When Doer Is Unimportant The passive voice is appropriate whenever the receiver of the action is more important than the doer. It is often used in scientific writing, which tends to emphasize the material acted on rather than the doer of the action.

The distillate is then removed from the liquid.

Passive Voice to Place Old Information before New The passive voice is also appropriate when the old information in a sentence is the receiver of the action rather than the doer.

Graphs are essential tools for economic analysis. They *are* commonly *used by* economists to display both concrete economic data and abstract economic concepts.

In the second sentence, the passive voice allows the writer to begin with old information. The pronoun *they* refers to *Graphs* in the previous sentence.

Passive Voice to Evade Responsibility Sometimes writers use the passive voice intentionally to avoid naming a responsible party. This practice is ethically questionable. Avoid it when you can.

Evasive	The decision has been made to raise the dues.
Forthright	The president and the treasurer have decided to raise the dues.

Exercise

On a separate sheet of paper, convert the transitive passive sentences to transitive active, and convert the transitive active sentences to transitive passive. Leave the intransitive sentences unchanged. In converting some transitive passive sentences to transitive active, you may have to add an actor or agent. For each sentence, explain in which rhetorical situations the active-voice version would be better and in which the passive would be better.

1. The wrong carpets were installed by the carpet layers while the owners were away.
2. Smoke rose in thick billows above the burning house.

3. Beth ladled hot liquid blackberry jelly into sterilized jars.
4. The little girl in the green sunsuit slowly covered her sleeping father with piles of sand.
5. Some of the most important scientific principles have been discovered accidentally.
6. The motor was probably ruined by the turbine bearing's being rusted out.

Using Inclusive Language

For much of the history of the English language, grammarians accepted the use of masculine pronouns ("Everyone should bring *his* own lunch") and the use of *man* ("Peace and goodwill to *men* everywhere") as generic references for both men and women. Many contemporary writers believe that these usages reflect pro-male bias. Many writers are also now aware of other ways in which language subtly reflects attitudes toward gender, culture, and ethnicity. In this section, we offer suggestions that will help you construct sentences free of biased language.

Avoiding Sexist Labels and Stereotypes

Avoid language that labels or stereotypes women. Referring to women as "the weaker sex," "the ladies," "the girls," or "the distaff side" implies that women are not equal to men. Similarly, it is inappropriate to identify women as wives or mothers in a context where their professional or work status is more relevant or to refer to a woman's appearance unless the context demands it. Let the same considerations guide you whether you are describing a man or a woman.

Sexist Janet Peterson, stunning in her new, blue-sequined evening gown, gave the keynote address at the annual mayors' conference.

Would you say, "Robert Peterson, stunning in his new tuxedo, ruffled shirtfront, and cummerbund, gave the keynote address at the annual mayors' conference"?

Revised Janet Peterson, newly elected mayor of the state's third-largest city, gave the keynote address at the annual mayors' conference.

Avoiding Use of Masculine Pronouns to Refer to Both Sexes

Whenever possible, revise sentences to avoid using the masculine pronouns *he, him, his,* and *himself* to refer to people of both sexes. Often you can use plural pronouns (*they, them, their,* and *themselves*), which do not indicate gender.

Problematic If a student wants to bring his text to the exam, he may.

Revised If students want to bring their texts to the exam, they may.

In informal writing, you can also use *you* and *your* to avoid sexist language; in formal prose you can use *one* and *one's*, although this usage sometimes sounds stilted.

Revised	If you want to bring your texts to the exam, you may.
Revised	If one wants to bring one's text to the exam, one may.

Another strategy is to alternate between masculine and feminine forms.

> At the revising stage, the writer should go over *his* draft carefully, making sure that the central idea of each paragraph is clear. At the editing stage a writer's focus shifts. Now *she* should check for sentence-level problems, paying particular attention to spelling, punctuation, and problems of usage.

(Note: This practice, although common in some academic journals, is not yet widely accepted in the popular media.)

Avoid bureaucratic constructions such as *him/her* or *s/he*, which are cumbersome and inelegant. Occasional use of the combined forms *he or she* or *him or her* is acceptable, but overuse of this construction is tiresome.

Avoiding Inappropriate Use of the Suffix *-man*

Use of *-man* as a suffix in such words as *repairman, mailman*, and *policeman* or as a prefix in *mankind* seems to ignore the presence of women in the workforce and in the human race. The suffix *-person* may be an acceptable substitute; *chairperson* and *salesperson* are becoming increasingly common in formal usage. However, *weatherperson* still sounds odd, as does "Joan is a new *freshperson* at state college." Look for alternative expressions.

Avoid	Prefer
chairman	chairperson
coed	student
congressman	representative, member of Congress
forefathers	ancestors
mailman	mail carrier
man (generic)	person, people, humans, human beings
wives, husbands	spouses
manmade	synthetic
policeman	police officer
salesman	sales representative, salesclerk
waiter, waitress	waitperson, server
newsman	reporter, journalist
fireman	firefighter
weatherman	weather announcer, meteorologist
sportsman	sports enthusiast, athlete
stewardess	flight attendant

Avoiding Language Biased Against Ethnic or Other Minorities

Avoid language that reflects stereotypes against ethnic or other minorities. Language referring to minorities evolves rapidly. In the 1980s *black* and *Afro-American* were preferred terms, but in the 1990s these largely gave way to *African-American*. Similarly, the terms *Latino* and *Latina* are replacing *Hispanic*. Homosexual people now prefer the terms *gay man* and *lesbian* and in some contexts are reviving the word *queer*. Today the term *people of color* is in favor, but the term *colored person* is an intense insult.

As a writer, you need to be sensitive to the subtle ways in which language can make people feel included and welcomed or excluded and insulted. Nowhere is the evolving and charged nature of language more evident than in the connotations of words referring to cultural minorities.

PEARSON mycomplab

For support in learning this chapter's content, follow this path in **MyCompLab**: Resources ⇒ Grammar ⇒ Usage and Style. Review the Instruction and Multimedia resources, then complete the Exercises and click on Gradebook to measure your progress.

6 EDITING FOR PUNCTUATION AND MECHANICS

This chapter provides a handy compendium of rules and guidelines for using punctuation marks, italics, and capital letters. It also includes a section on manuscript form.

In this chapter, you will learn how to use:

- Periods, question marks, and exclamation points
- Commas
- Semicolons
- Colons, dashes, and parentheses
- Apostrophes
- Quotation marks
- Italics (underlining)
- Brackets, ellipses, and slashes
- Capital letters
- Numbers
- Abbreviations
- Manuscript form

Periods, Question Marks, and Exclamation Points

For a full discussion of sentence boundaries, including advice for avoiding fragments, comma splices, and run-ons, see Handbook 3.

Periods, question marks, and exclamation points, sometimes called "terminal punctuation" or "endmarks," signal the end of a sentence. These marks generally raise few problems for writers except in the case of sentence fragments (when an endmark follows a nonsentence), comma splices (when a comma is substituted for an endmark), and run-ons (when two sentences are fused together without an endmark).

A few other situations that sometimes pose problems for writers are discussed next.

Courtesy Questions

Courtesy questions—mild commands phrased politely as questions—normally end with a period.

Would you please return the form in the enclosed envelope.

The absence of a question mark makes this a mild command, not a real question.

Indirect Questions

Although direct questions require a question mark, indirect questions end with a period.

Direct Question	He asked me, "Where are you going?"
Indirect Question	He asked me where I was going.

Placement of Question Marks with Quotations

If quotation marks and a question mark appear together, the question mark goes inside the quotation marks when only the quotation is a question and outside when the whole sentence is a question.

QUOTATION IS QUESTION

The professor asked, "Can you solve the fox-and-chicken puzzle?"

ENTIRE SENTENCE IS QUESTION

Did you hear the professor talk about the "fox-and-chicken puzzle"?

Note: When the question mark goes inside the quotation marks, do not follow the question mark with a comma or period.

Faulty	"Can we go with you?," she asked.
Revised	"Can we go with you?" she asked.

Exclamation Points

An exclamation point is used after a sentence or word group to express strong emotion. Exclamation points are used primarily in dialogue to indicate shouting or an especially strong feeling. Avoid using them in most other instances— especially academic prose—because they rarely have the effect on a reader that the writer intends. Expressing emotion through word choice, sentence structure, and tone is more effective. When an exclamation point goes inside a quotation, do not follow the exclamation point with a comma or period.

Commas

The comma is the most frequently used mark of internal punctuation. A comma mistakenly used as an endmark creates a comma splice. The main rules for use of commas to mark the boundaries of phrases, clauses, and sentences are covered in depth in Handbook 3. These rules are reviewed in this section, along with additional guidelines.

Using Commas

Using Commas with Coordinating Conjunctions Use a comma and a coordinating conjunction (*and, or, nor, for, but, yet,* and *so*) to join two independent clauses.

I released the dog's leash, and the dog trotted off across the field.

If the main clauses are very short, it is acceptable to omit the comma before the coordinating conjunction, but it is never acceptable to omit the coordinating conjunction; doing so will create a comma splice.

Comma Splice	We crossed the meadow, then we headed toward the mountain.
Revised	We crossed the meadow, and then we headed toward the mountain.

Comma after Introductory Adverb Clauses and Long Introductory Phrases Use a comma to set off introductory adverb clauses and long introductory phrases from the rest of the sentence.

Introductory Adverb Clause	When I get home from work, I always fix myself a big sardine sandwich.
Introductory Phrase	Having lost my balance, I began waving my arms frantically.

Note: Initial gerund phrases or infinitive phrases used as sentence subjects should not be set off because they are part of the sentence core.

Faulty To know him, is to love him. Playing her guitar every evening, is Sally's way of relaxing.

These introductory phrases serve as the subjects of their sentences and should not be set off.

Revised To know him is to love him. Playing her guitar every evening is Sally's way of relaxing.

See Figure HB3.1 on p. 665 for a list of transitional expressions.

Comma after Introductory Transitional Words and Expressions Set off most introductory transitional words and phrases such as *on the other hand, in sum, however, moreover,* and *for example* with a comma.

On the other hand, bicycle racing involves an astonishing amount of strategy.

Writers often do not use a comma to set off *thus* and *therefore* and some other transitional expressions that do not noticeably interrupt the flow of the sentence. In such cases let your voice be your guide. If you pause noticeably after the transitional expression, set it off with a comma.

Commas to Set Off Absolute Phrases An absolute phrase comprises a noun followed by a participle or participial phrase. These phrases are *absolute* because they are complete in themselves; they modify the entire sentence rather than an individual word within the sentence. Absolute phrases are always set off with commas.

See p. 653 for an explanation of verbal phrases.

His hand wrapped in a blanket, Harvey hobbled toward the ambulance.

The bear reared on its hind legs, *its teeth looking razor sharp in the glaring sun.*

Comma before Concluding Participial Phrases Use commas to set off participial phrases at the ends of sentences if they modify the subjects.

The doctor rushed quickly toward the accident victim, fumbling to open his black bag.

In this example, it is the doctor who fumbles to open his bag. The comma indicates that *fumbling* modifies *doctor* (the sentence subject) and not *victim* (the noun immediately preceding the participle).

Do not use a comma to set off a participial phrase at the end of a sentence if the phrase modifies the immediately preceding noun.

The doctor rushed quickly toward the accident victim lying face forward on the soft shoulder of the road.

Here the participial phrase modifies the preceding noun, *victim*, instead of the sentence subject. It is not set off with commas.

Commas to Avoid Confusion Use commas to separate sentence elements if failure to separate them would create confusion.

Confusing	Every time John ate his dog wanted to be fed too.
Revised	Every time John ate, his dog wanted to be fed too.

Commas to Set Off Nonrestrictive Clauses and Phrases Adjective modifiers following a noun are either *restrictive* or *nonrestrictive*, depending on whether they are needed to identify the noun they modify. Use commas to set off nonrestrictive clauses and phrases.

Restrictive and Nonrestrictive Clauses. An adjective clause is *nonrestrictive* if it is not needed to identify the noun it modifies. In such cases, set off the clause or phrase with commas.

Nonrestrictive Clause	My father dislikes Bill Jones, who rides a noisy motorcycle.

In this case, you know whom the father dislikes: Bill Jones. The fact that Bill rides a noisy motorcycle is additional information about him.

If the modifying clause is needed to identify the noun it is modifying, then it is *restrictive* and is not set off with commas.

Restrictive Clause	My father dislikes people who ride noisy motorcycles.

Here the meaning is "My father doesn't dislike all people, just those people who ride noisy motorcycles." The adjective clause restricts the meaning of *people*; that is, it narrows down the class "people" to the subclass of "people who ride noisy motorcycles." Because the phrase is needed to identify which people the father dislikes, it is a restrictive clause used *without* commas.

To help you remember this rule, think of this saying: Extra information, extra commas; needed information, no commas.

Nonrestrictive Clause My grandmother, who graduated from college when she was eighty-two years old, deserves a special award.

You know who deserves a special award: my grandmother. The adjective clause provides extra information, so the sentence needs extra commas.

Restrictive Clause Anyone who graduates from college at age eighty-two deserves a special award.

Here, *who graduates from college* is needed information. Otherwise the sentence would mean that "anyone" deserves a special award, rather than only those people who graduate from college at age eighty-two. This sentence follows the rule "needed information, no commas."

Restrictive and Nonrestrictive Phrases. The same extra information/needed information rule holds for adjective phrases.

Restrictive Phrase The man wearing the double-breasted suit is an accountant.

Here the phrase *wearing the double-breasted suit* identifies which man is an accountant. The sentence implies that there are two or more men. (Which man is the accountant? The one wearing the double-breasted suit.) Because the phrase is needed to identify which man is meant, it is not set off with commas.

Nonrestrictive Phrase Elvis Dweezle, wearing a double-breasted suit, looked at himself briefly in the mirror before knocking on his boss's door.

Here the phrase *wearing a double-breasted suit* merely adds extra information about the already-identified Elvis Dweezle.

Commas to Set Off Nonrestrictive Appositives An *appositive* is a noun or noun phrase that immediately follows another noun, renaming it or otherwise referring to it. Appositives also follow the extra information/needed information rule. An appositive is restrictive (needed information) if it serves to identify the preceding noun; it is nonrestrictive (extra information) if it simply contributes additional information to an already-identified noun. As with nonrestrictive adjective clauses and phrases, set off nonrestrictive appositives with commas.

Nonrestrictive Appositive Angela, a good friend of mine, has just been promoted to chief accountant.

In this example you know who has just been promoted: Angela. The appositive *a good friend of mine* adds extra information about Angela.

Restrictive Appositive	My friend Angela offered to do my income taxes for me.

Here the appositive *Angela* is needed to identify which friend offered to do the taxes. No commas are used.

Commas to Separate Items in a Series Use commas to separate items in a series of three or more words, phrases, or clauses. The first comma leads readers to anticipate a list, with the last two elements joined by *and* or *or*. Place commas after each item in the series except the last.

He especially likes golf, jogging, and swimming.

We went to the movies, had dinner downtown, and then went bowling.

(Note: Although British writers and some American writers omit the comma before the coordinating conjunction in a series, sentences are generally clearer if the comma is included.)

Confusing	I like three kinds of pizza: pepperoni, Canadian bacon and pineapple and Italian sausage.
Clearer	I like three kinds of pizza: pepperoni, Canadian bacon and pineapple, and Italian sausage.

In the first version, the reader initially thinks that the first *and* marks the end of the series when, in fact, it simply joins one of the elements (*Canadian bacon and pineapple*). Placing a comma before the final *and* in the series clarifies the sentence.

Commas to Separate Coordinate Adjectives Preceding a Noun Coordinate adjectives in a series are separated by commas. Adjectives are coordinate if they can be separated by *and* or if they can be placed in a different order.

Coordinate Adjectives	A nearsighted, tall, thin, grumpy-looking man walked slowly down the street.

In this case you could say a "thin and grumpy-looking and nearsighted and tall man," thus separating the elements with *and* and placing them in a different order. These are coordinate adjectives separated by commas.

Noncoordinate Adjectives	Three copper-plated frying pans sat on the shelf.

These adjectives are not coordinate because you cannot say "frying and copper-plated and three pans." Hence these adjectives are not separated by commas.

Note: Do not place a comma after the last coordinate adjective in a series.

Faulty	A lightweight, sleekly designed, racing, bicycle was my summer's dream.
Revised	A lightweight, sleekly designed, racing bicycle was my summer's dream.

Commas to Set Off Parenthetical or Interrupting Elements Use commas to set off parenthetical words, phrases, or clauses and other similar elements that interrupt the flow of the sentence. By reading your sentences aloud in a natural voice, you can generally identify parenthetical material that interrupts the flow of a sentence. Such material should be set off by pairs of commas. The following are common examples of interrupting material:

CONTRASTING ELEMENTS INTRODUCED BY BUT, NOT, OR ALTHOUGH

The man at the front desk, not the mechanic, was the one who quoted me the price.

WORDS OF DIRECT ADDRESS, *YES* AND *NO*, AND MILD INTERJECTIONS

I tell you, Jennifer, your plan won't work.

TRANSITION WORDS AND EXPRESSIONS

She will, however, demand more money.

TAG PHRASES CITING SOURCES

This new car, according to the latest government reports, gets below-average mileage.

ATTRIBUTIVE TAGS IDENTIFYING SPEAKERS

"To be a successful student," my adviser told me, "you have to enjoy learning."

Commas to Set Off Elements of Places, Addresses, and Dates Use commas to set off each separate element in a date, place, or address.

He drove to Savannah, Georgia, on July 5, 1971, in an old blue Ford.

Do not place a comma in front of zip codes in addresses.

I live on 23 Elm Street, Seattle, WA 98115.

Omitting Commas

Many beginning writers tend to use too many commas rather than too few. Do not use a comma unless a specific rule calls for one. "When in doubt, leave commas out" is a good rule of thumb. Learn to recognize the following situations that do *not* require commas. These are frequently sources of error in student papers.

Do Not Use a Comma to Separate a Subject from Its Verb or a Verb from Its Complements

Faulty The man in the apartment next to mine, swallowed a goldfish.

Here a comma mistakenly separates the subject from the verb.

Revised The man in the apartment next to mine swallowed a goldfish.

Do Not Use a Single Comma within a Sentence Core

Faulty My brother, who recently won a pole-sitting contest swallowed a goldfish.

Here a comma occurs on one side of a nonrestrictive clause but not on the other side.

Revised My brother, who recently won a pole-sitting contest, swallowed a goldfish.

Do Not Use a Comma before *and* If It Joins Only Two Words or Phrases

Faulty She pedaled uphill for twenty minutes, and won the race by several lengths.

The *and* joins two verbs rather than two main clauses.

Revised She pedaled uphill for twenty minutes and won the race by several lengths.

Do Not Use a Comma after *such as*

Faulty They forgot some key supplies such as, candles, matches, and trail mix.
Revised They forgot some key supplies such as candles, matches, and trail mix.

Exercise

Insert commas where needed in the following sentences.

1. Whenever I go home to Bismarck North Dakota for Christmas vacation the dinner conversation turns to cross-country skiing.
2. On my last visit during dessert my dad who is an expert skier asked me if I wanted to try dogsled racing.
3. "I've wanted to try dogsledding for years" Dad said "but we've never had the equipment or the dogs. Now however my friend Jake Jackson the new agent for Smith Insurance has just bought a team and wants his friend to give it a try."
4. Rock shrimp unlike some other species have hard shells that make them difficult to peel.
5. Hiking or biking through southern Germany you will discover a rich mosaic of towns regional foods colors sounds and smells of the rural countryside and historic Black Forest region.
6. Instead of riding on busy boulevards you can pedal on a network of narrow paved roads built for farm vehicles or on graveled paths through lush green forests.
7. According to historian Daniel T. Rodgers a central question that divided workers and employers in the nineteenth and early twentieth centuries was how many hours a day the average worker should work.
8. Believing strongly in tradition the early factory owners thought their workers should follow the old sunrise to sunset work schedule of agricultural laborers.

(*continued*)

9. This schedule which meant fourteen-hour workdays during the summer could also be maintained during the winter thanks to the invention of artificial light which owners rapidly installed in their factories.
10. Spurred on by their desire to create a shorter working day laborers began to organize into forerunners of today's labor unions and used their collective powers to strive for change.

Semicolons

A semicolon is stronger than a comma. It can be used to join two independent clauses to form a single sentence or to separate the main items in a list that already contains commas.

Semicolon to Join Main Clauses

When a semicolon is used to join main clauses, it signals a close relationship between the meanings of the two main clauses and creates a sentence with two balanced, equal parts.

I asked the professor for an extension on my essay; she told me I was out of luck.

Semicolons are frequently used to connect main clauses when the second clause contains a conjunctive adverb or transitional phrase such as *however, therefore, nevertheless,* and *on the other hand.*

Comma Splice	He spent all morning baking the pie, however, nobody seemed to appreciate his efforts.
Revised	He spent all morning baking the pie; however, nobody seemed to appreciate his efforts.

The new airport won't be finished until June; therefore we'll have to land at Fitzsimmons Field.

For more on comma splices, see pp. 662–665.

Note: Joining two main clauses with only a comma creates a comma splice.

Semicolon in a Series Containing Commas

Use a semicolon to separate elements in a series when some of those elements already contain commas.

On vacation we went to Laramie, Wyoming; Denver, Colorado; Salt Lake City, Utah; and Boise, Idaho.

Since commas are used to separate the cities from the states, the semicolons are needed to separate the elements of the series.

Exercise

In the following sentences, insert semicolons and commas as needed. Some sentences may need no additional punctuation. Make sure that your marks of punctuation can be easily read.

1. The two men defended themselves before the justice of the peace in Bilford across the river a similar case was being tried with attorneys and a full jury.
2. She claimed that most teenage shoplifters are never caught moreover those who are caught are seldom punished.
3. I admit that I went to the party I did not however enjoy it.
4. I admit that I went to the party but I did not enjoy it.
5. Although I went to the party I did not enjoy it.
6. When the party ended our apartment was in chaos from one end of the living room to the other end of the bedroom a fine layer of confetti blanketed everything like snow.
7. Within twenty minutes of leaving the trail we saw an antelope two elk one of which had begun to shed the velvet on its antlers an assortment of squirrels gophers and chipmunks and most startling of all a large black bear with two cubs.
8. An effective education does not consist of passive rote learning rather it consists of active problem solving.
9. Failure to introduce and to use calculators and computers in elementary school creates needless barriers for teachers and learners furthermore computer literacy is a basic skill in the new millennium.
10. We watched the slide show of their vacation for what seemed like an eternity—Toledo Ohio Columbus Missouri Topeka Kansas Omaha Nebraska and on and on across the continent.

Colons, Dashes, and Parentheses

Colons

The most frequent uses of a colon are to introduce a list; to announce a word, clause, or phrase predicted in a preceding main clause; or to introduce a block quotation. Colons are generally preceded by main clauses and are not used as internal punctuation within a clause.

Colon to Introduce a List Use a colon to introduce a list when the list follows a grammatically complete independent clause.

> We can win in two ways: changing our defense or adding Jones to the offensive lineup.

Do not use a colon in the middle of a clause or after the words *such as, for example,* or *including.*

Faulty The things you should bring to the party are: chips, salsa, and your own drinks.

Revised The things you should bring to the party are chips, salsa, and your own drinks.

or

Please bring to the party the following: chips, salsa, and your own drinks.

In the first example the offending colon is removed. In the second, the structure preceding the colon has been expanded to a main clause by adding *the following,* which serves as the direct object of *bring.*

Faulty We have many opportunities to improve our score, such as: retaking the exam, doing an extra credit project, or doing a longer paper.

Revised We have many opportunities to improve our score, such as retaking the exam, doing an extra credit project, or doing a longer paper.

Colon to Introduce a Predicted Element Following an Independent Clause Following an independent clause, use a colon to introduce a predicted element, which can be a word, a phrase, or a clause.

The professor agreed to something remarkable: grading contracts for all students.

The professor agreed to something remarkable: He allowed Jack to submit a late paper.

Note on capitalization: If what follows the colon is a main clause, you have the option of beginning the clause with a capital letter; if what follows the colon is not a complete sentence, use a lowercase letter.

For an explanation of block quotations, see pp. 568–569.

Colon to Introduce Block Quotations or Quotations Receiving Special Emphasis A colon is used to introduce a block quotation if what precedes the colon is a main clause. You can also use a colon to introduce a short quotation that you want to emphasize.

His father replied slowly, carefully, thoughtfully: "Buying the SUV now, when we are already too deeply in debt, is not a good idea."

A comma could also be used to introduce this quotation; a colon is more formal and emphatic.

Colon in Salutations, Time Notations, Titles, and Biblical Citations Colons are sometimes used in letter salutations and within titles. They are also used in time expressions and biblical notations.

Salutation	Dear Sarah:
Time Notation	4:30 A.M.
Titles	*Teaching Critical Thinking Skills: Theory and Practice*
Biblical Citations	Proverbs 3:16

Dashes

Think of the dash as a strong comma that gives special emphasis to the material being set off. (To make a dash, type two hyphens; leave no space before, after, or between the hyphens.)

> Sir Walter Raleigh brought the potato—as well as tobacco—to Queen Elizabeth I on his return from Virginia.
>
> In this example a pair of commas could replace the pair of dashes. The dashes emphasize the material between them by calling for a greater pause when reading.

Sometimes a dash is used to set off nouns placed for special emphasis at the beginning of a sentence. The nouns are then summarized by a pronoun following the dash.

> Joy, happiness, prosperity—all this is promised to investors in the new Veggi-burger fast-food chain.

Parentheses

Parentheses are used to enclose nonessential, supplemental information and to enclose citations or list numbers.

Supplemental Information The most common use of parentheses is to enclose supplemental information.

> He took one look at my computer (an old Kaypro from the early 1980s) and started to laugh.

Citations and Numbered Items in a List Parentheses are also used to enclose citations in many documentation systems and to enclose numbers or letters identifying parts of a list.

For an explanation of the MLA and APA documentation systems, see Chapter 22.

> To graduate, a student must fill out three forms: (1) the transcript summary, (2) the request form, and (3) the adviser's sign-off sheet (*Junebug State Bulletin* 32).
>
> Parentheses enclose the list numbers and the citation to the *Junebug State Bulletin*, page 32, where this information is found.

Punctuating Sentences That Include Parentheses When you place a complete sentence within parentheses, the concluding endmark goes inside the parentheses. When you end a sentence with parenthetical elements, the endmark goes outside the parentheses.

> When visiting England, we watched a lot of cricket. (Cricket is a British game something like American baseball.)
>
> When visiting England, we watched a lot of cricket (a British game somewhat similar to American baseball).

Apostrophes

The apostrophe is used mainly for showing possession, but it is also used to indicate missing letters in contractions and to form special plurals.

Apostrophe to Show Possession

Use the apostrophe to indicate possession of nouns and indefinite pronouns. Possessive constructions show both a possessor and a thing possessed: The thing possessed occurs last in the construction; the person or thing that possesses (the possessor) comes first and contains an apostrophe.

Possessor	Thing Possessed	Alternative Construction
Sally's	car	car belonging to Sally
men's	coats	coats for men
cats'	fur	fur of cats
three minutes'	work	work lasting three minutes

Because plurals and possessives both add an *s* sound to words, they are identical to the ear. To the eye, however, they are easily distinguished by the use of the apostrophe in the possessive. Be sure that you don't confuse your reader by mixing possessives and plurals.

Faulty Our neighbor's have two horse's and ten cat's on their grandfathers old farm.

Revised Our neighbors have two horses and ten cats on their grandfather's old farm.

Neighbors, horses, and *cats* are plurals, not possessives; *grandfather's* is a possessive, not a plural.

Forming the Possessive

To make a noun possessive, you must first determine whether it is singular or plural. Add an apostrophe and an *s* (*'s*) to singular nouns and to plural nouns that do not end in *s;* add an apostrophe only (') to plural nouns that end in *s*.

The man's car *[the car belonging to the man]*

The men's cars *[the cars belonging to the men]*

The cats' food dish *[the food dish belonging to the cats]*

The cat's food dish *[the food dish belonging to the cat]*

To form the possessive of hyphenated words, compound words, and word groups, add an apostrophe and an *s* (*'s*) to the last word only.

her mother-in-law's lawn mower

the ladies-in-waiting's formal gowns

Do Not Use Apostrophes for Possessives of Personal Pronouns Do not use apostrophes with the possessive forms of personal and relative pronouns (*yours, his, hers, ours, theirs, its, whose*). When an apostrophe is used with personal or relative pronouns, it indicates a contraction. Be especially careful to distinguish between *it's* ("it is") and *its* (possessive).

Possessive	Contraction
The dog chases its tail.	It's (it is) a funny dog.
Your tie is crooked.	You're (you are) a sloppy dresser.
Whose dog is that?	Who's (who is) at the door?

Apostrophes with Contractions

Use an apostrophe (') to indicate omitted letters in contractions.

you're (you are)	isn't (is not)
it's (it is)	spring of '34 (spring of 1934)

Note: Be sure to insert the apostrophe exactly where the missing letters would be.

Faulty is'nt
Revised isn't

Apostrophes to Form Plurals

Use an apostrophe and an *s* (*'s*) to form the plural of letters and words used as words. Underline (italicize) the letter or word but not the plural ending.

See pp. 708–709 on italics and underlining.

> On your test I can't distinguish between your t's and your E's. You also use too many *very*'s and *extremely*'s.

Quotation Marks

Use quotation marks to enclose words, phrases, and sentences that are someone's spoken words or that you have copied from a source. Also use quotation marks to set off titles of short works and to indicate words used in a special sense. Quotation marks always occur in pairs, one marking the beginning and the other the ending of the quoted material.

See Chapter 21, for details on how to quote sources and avoid plagiarism.

Punctuating the Start of a Quotation

When a quotation is introduced with an attributive tag (such as "my instructor says" or "Sharon Smith acknowledges"), the tag can be followed by a comma, a colon, or *that*. If you use a comma or a colon, begin the quotation with a capital letter. If you introduce a quotation with *that*, do not capitalize the first letter of the quotation even if it is capitalized in the original. In this case, you do not precede the quotation with a comma.

Columnist E. J. Dionne says, "Terror is designed to paralyze."

For use of brackets, see p. 709.

Columnist E. J. Dionne says that "[t]error is designed to paralyze."

If you work a short quotation into the structure of your own sentence, use no punctuation other than quotation marks around the quoted passage.

According to E. J. Dionne, all acts of terror are "designed to paralyze."

Placement of Attributive Tags

Attributive tags can be placed before, inside, or after the quotation. When an attributive tag is placed between the two halves of a quotation, the second half is not capitalized unless it begins a new sentence.

Michael Karnok says, "To be a father is to know the meaning of failure."

"To be a father," says Michael Karnok, "is to know the meaning of failure."

"To be a father is to know the meaning of failure," says Michael Karnok.

Punctuating the End of a Quotation

Put commas and periods inside quotation marks.

He told me to "buzz off," and then he went about his business.

He told me to "buzz off." Then he went about his business.

Note that both the comma (first sentence) and the period (second sentence) go inside the quotation mark.

In documented papers that place citations inside parentheses at the end of the quotation, put the comma or period after the parenthetical citation.

According to Immunex Chief Executive Edward Fritzky, "Genetic Institute is doing very, very well" (Lim C5).

Note the order: quotation mark, parenthetical citation, final period.

Place colons and semicolons outside the ending quotation mark.

He told me to "buzz off"; then he went about his business.

My sexist husband wants his "privileges": Monday night football and no household chores.

Note that the semicolon (first sentence) and the colon (second sentence) go outside the quotation mark.

See p. 693 for an example.

Place question marks and exclamation points inside quotation marks if they belong to the quotation; place them outside the ending quotation mark if they belong to the whole sentence.

Indirect Quotations

Use quotation marks for *direct* quotations—the actual words spoken by someone—but not for *indirect* quotations, which report what someone said without using the exact words.

Direct Quotation	"Do you want to go to the library?" Sally asked Harry.
Indirect Quotation	Sally asked Harry whether he wanted to go to the library.

Indented Block Method for Long Quotations

When quoting more than four typed lines (MLA style) or forty words (APA style), use the indented block method rather than quotation marks to indicate direct quotations. Double-space the quotation for both styles. For the MLA style, indent each line ten spaces from the left margin. Indent five spaces for the APA style. Do *not* put quotation marks around the blocked passage.

See pp. 568–569 for an example.

Single Quotation Marks

In American practice, use a single quotation mark, made with an apostrophe on most keyboards, to enclose a quotation within a quotation.

> Molly angrily told her discussion group, "Every time I ask my husband to help me with the ironing, he says that 'men don't iron clothes' and stalks out of the room in a huff."
>
> Inside Molly's directly quoted words is a direct quotation from Molly's husband: *men don't iron clothes*. The husband's words in this case are enclosed in single quotation marks.

With the block indentation method, use regular quotation marks to enclose a quotation within a quotation.

Quotation Marks for Titles of Short Works

Use quotation marks for titles of essays, short stories, short poems, songs, book chapters, and other sections that occur within books or periodicals.

> I liked Spenser's sonnet "Most Glorious Lord of Lyfe" better than *The Faerie Queene*.
>
> In this sentence, both the sonnet and *The Faerie Queene* are poems, but the former is in quotation marks because it is short, and the latter is italicized (underlined) because it is long.

Quotation Marks for Words Used in a Special Sense

Use quotation marks to call attention to a word or phrase used in a special sense. Often your intention is to show that you disagree with how someone else uses the word or phrase.

> My husband refuses to do what he considers "woman's work."
>
> In this example, the quotation marks indicate that the writer would not use the phrase *woman's work* and that she and her husband have different ideas about what the phrase means.

Although you may set off words used in a special sense with quotation marks, avoid using quotation marks for slang and clichés as an attempt to apologize for them. Rephrase your sentence to eliminate the triteness.

Weak	I've been "busy as a bee" all week, so I'm exhausted.
Revised	I've been so busy this week that I'm exhausted.

Exercise

In the following sentences, insert apostrophes and single or double quotation marks as needed.

1. My mother told me that she didn't want me to buy a car until I had a permanent part-time job.
2. Jake has his little quirks, as Molly calls them, but he is still lovable.
3. My adviser recently remarked: The nervous student who encounters a professor who states, Twenty percent of this class usually fails, must learn to say, Not I, instead of giving up.
4. Did your friends teacher really say Attendance is necessary in this class?
5. We are guilty of gross misuse of language, continued the speaker, whenever we use disinterested to mean uninterested.
6. I spent two hours worth of good homework time, complained Thomas friend Karen, trying to invent a tongue twister that would make people stand up and shout, That's a masterpiece.

Italics (Underlining)

In handwritten papers, indicate italics with underlining. In papers prepared using a computer, italicizing is usually acceptable. Check with your instructor.

Italics for Titles of Long Complete Works

Use italics for titles of books, magazines, journals, newspapers, Web sites, plays, films, works of art, long poems, pamphlets, and musical works. Capitalize and italicize *a, an*, and *the* only if they are part of the title.

Moby-Dick	Michaelangelo's *David*	*YouTube*
Newsweek	the *Encyclopaedia Britannica*	*MySpace*
Star Wars	*The Sound and the Fury*	*The Jupiter Symphony*

Note: The Bible and its books, as well as the Qur'an (Koran), are not underlined or italicized.

the Bible	Exodus	Revelations	the Qur'an

Italics for Foreign Words and Phrases

Use or italics for foreign words and phrases.

You should avoid the *post hoc ergo propter hoc* fallacy.

Italics for Letters, Numbers, and Words Used as Words

Use italics for letters, for numbers, and for words when they are referred to as words and phrases and not as what they represent.

> To spell the word *separate* correctly, remember there is *a rat* in *separate.*

Brackets, Ellipses, and Slashes

Brackets and ellipses (three spaced dots) indicate changes within quotations and occasionally have other uses. Slashes are used primarily to indicate line breaks in quoted poetry or, in informal or bureaucratic prose, to indicate an option of alternative words or phrases.

Brackets

Brackets [ ] are made with straight lines and should not be confused with parentheses ( ), which use curved lines.

Brackets to Set Off Explanatory Material Inserted into Quotations Use brackets to set off explanatory material inserted into a quotation.

> According to Joseph Menosky, "Courses offered to teach these skills [computer literacy] have popped up everywhere."

The original source of this quotation did not contain the words *computer literacy,* since the context of the original source explained what *these skills* meant. In this example, *computer literacy* is inserted in brackets to make up for the missing context. The brackets indicate that the material they enclose did not occur in the original version.

Brackets to Indicate the Writer's Alteration of the Grammar of a Quotation Use brackets when you need to change the grammar of a quotation to make it fit the grammar of your own sentence.

Original Source	I see electric cars as our best hope for reducing air pollution. —Jean Haricot
Correct Use of Brackets	Jean Haricot says that "electric cars [are] our best hope for reducing air pollution."

In this example the writer has to change the original *as* to *are* to make the quotation fit the grammar of his or her own sentence. This change is placed in brackets.

Brackets to Enclose *Sic* to Indicate a Mistake in a Quotation If you quote a source that contains an obvious mistake, you can insert *sic* in brackets to indicate that the mistake is in the original source and is not your own.

> According to Vernon Tweeble, not your greatest sportswriter, the home-run king is still "Baby [*sic*] Ruth."
>
> Here the *sic* indicates that Tweeble said "Baby Ruth," not "Babe Ruth." The mistake belongs to Tweeble, not to the writer.

Ellipses

For more on the use of ellipses in quotations, see pp. 567–568.

An ellipsis, made with three spaced periods, is used to indicate an omission within a quotation. When an ellipsis occurs at the end of a sentence, a period is used before the ellipsis to mark the sentence boundary.

Original Before the dam, a float trip down the river through Glen Canyon would cost you a minimum of seven days' time, well within anyone's vacation allotment, and a capital outlay of about forty dollars—the prevailing price of a two-man rubber boat with oars, available at any army-navy surplus store. A life jacket might be useful but not required, for there were no dangerous rapids in the 150 miles of Glen Canyon.

—Edward Abbey, "The Damnation of a Canyon"

Correct Use of Ellipses According to Edward Abbey, before the dam was built "a float trip down the river through Glen Canyon would cost you a minimum of seven days' time . . . and a capital outlay of about forty dollars. . . . A life jacket might be useful but not required . . ." (351).

Here the first ellipsis indicates words omitted in the middle of a sentence. The second ellipsis shows words omitted at the end of a sentence and hence includes a period to mark the sentence boundary. In the last example, the period marking the sentence boundary goes after the parenthetical citation, which indicates the page number of the source.

When quoting poetry, use a line of dots to indicate that one or more full lines of the poem have been omitted, as in this example using Ben Jonson's "Come, My Celia":

Come, my Celia, let us prove,
While we can, the sports of love;
. . . .
Why should we defer our joys?
Fame and rumor are but toys.

Slashes

The main use of the slash is to divide lines of poetry written as a quotation within a sentence.

Ben Jonson evokes the *carpe diem* tradition when he says: "Come, my Celia, let us prove, / While we can, the sports of love."

If you quote more than four lines of poetry, use the indented block method rather than quotation marks with slashes.

Slashes are sometimes used to indicate options, but this use is too informal for most essays.

Informal He told me to take algebra and/or trigonometry.

Formal He told me to take either algebra or trigonometry or both.

Capital Letters

Most writers agree on the conventions for using capital letters, but on occasion usage varies. When in doubt about whether to capitalize a particular word, consult a good dictionary.

Capitals for First Letters of Sentences and Intentional Fragments

Capitalize the first letter of the first word in every sentence and also in sentence fragments used intentionally for effect. In fragmentary questions in a series, initial capital letters are optional.

> That man is a liar and a scoundrel. What do you want me to do? Like him? Invite him to dinner? Offer him my money?
>
> **or**
>
> What do you want me to do? like him? invite him to dinner? offer him my money?

Capitals for Proper Nouns

Use capitals for all proper nouns. The following rules cover most cases you will encounter.

Capitalize the names of people.	Pete Rose; Muhammed Ali; Ho Chi Minh
Capitalize titles of people when the title precedes the name or when the title follows the name without an article.	Doctor Sarah Smith; John Jones, Professor of Mathematics
Do not capitalize titles of people that include an article (*a* or *an*).	Sarah Smith, a medical doctor; John Jones, a mathematics professor
Capitalize family relationship names (Mother, Uncle) when used with a name. When used in place of a name, capitalization is optional.	Please, Aunt Eloise, tell Grandfather (or grandfather) that dinner is ready.
Do not capitalize relationship words when not used with a name or as a name.	I hear that my uncle and your father are going to visit Tony's grandfather.
Capitalize the names of specific geographic locations, areas, and regions, including compass directions if they are part of a name.	Mount Everest; the Pacific Northwest; Main Street; the Hudson River; the South; Illinois
Do not capitalize geographic locations indicated by compass directions but not considered actual names.	the northeast part of the United States; a mountain south of here
Capitalize historical events, names, movements, and writings.	the Korean War; the Oregon Territory; Articles of Confederation; the Renaissance; the Impressionist Period
Capitalize the names of ships and buildings and capitalize brand names.	USS *Missouri*; the Empire State Building; Pepsi

Capitalize specific academic courses but not academic subject areas, except "English" and foreign languages.	This term I am taking Chemistry 101, Integral Calculus, and French. But: This term I am taking chemistry, calculus, and French. (In the first sentence, the writer names specific courses; in the second sentence, the writer names subject areas only.)
Capitalize specific times, days, months, and holidays, but not names of seasons.	Monday; the Fourth of July; Halloween; last year; autumn; winter
Capitalize abbreviations derived from proper names.	NFL; U.S.A.; RCA; NAFTA; U. of W.

Capitals for Important Words in Titles

In titles of books, articles, plays, musical works, and so forth, capitalize the first and last words, any word following a colon or a semicolon, and all other words except articles, prepositions, and conjunctions of fewer than five letters.

"Ain't No Such Thing as a Montana Cowboy"

Famous Myths and Legends of the World: Stories of Gods and Heroes

Capitals in Quotations and Spoken Dialogue

Capitalize the first word of spoken dialogue, but do not capitalize the first word in the second half of a broken quotation that follows an attributive tag.

She said, "Because it is raining, we won't go."

"Because it is raining," she said, "we won't go."

Do not capitalize indirect quotations.

She said that we wouldn't go because it is raining.

Consistency in Use of Capitals

Use capitals consistently and avoid unnecessary capitals. Contemporary writers generally use capitals sparingly. Once you make a decision in optional or ambiguous cases, stick with it throughout your essay.

Numbers

Writers often have to decide whether to write numbers as words (ten) or as numerals (10). Follow the conventions of the genre in which you are writing.

Numbers in Scientific and Technical Writing

Scientific and technical writers generally use numerals for all numbers. Check with your instructor about how to handle numbers in lab reports and other formal papers in science, mathematics, and engineering.

Numbers in Formal Writing for Nontechnical Fields

In the humanities and other nontechnical fields and in most business and professional writing, writers usually adhere to the following conventions:

Use Words Instead of Numerals

For single-word number	eight dogs; a hundred doughnuts
For common fractions	one-third of a cup; half a pie
In the humanities, for two-word numbers	twenty-three students (however, business and professional writers prefer numerals for two-word numbers—23 students)
For numbers greater than a million, use a combination of words and numerals.	72 billion dollars

Use Numerals Instead of Words

For addresses	1420 Heron Street
For times and dates	I'll be there at 10:00 A.M. on November 5th.
For percentages and statistics	At least 30 percent of the students scored above 15 on the standardized test.
With decimals	The average score was 29.63
For amounts of money that include cents	That notebook cost around $3.95.
With symbols	20° C, 5′4″
For scores	The Yankees beat the Indians 5 to 3.
To refer to chapters, pages, and lines	You'll find that statistic in Chapter 12 on page 100 at line 8.

Numbers at the Beginning of a Sentence

Spell out in words any number that begins a sentence. If the result is awkward, rewrite the sentence.

Faulty 375 students showed up for the exam.

Revised Three hundred seventy-five students showed up for the exam.

or

We counted 375 students at the exam.

Plurals of Numbers

Do not use an apostrophe for the plural form of numbers.

Faulty Most of my quiz scores are in the low 90's.

Revised Most of my quiz scores are in the low 90s.

Numbers in a Series for Comparison

Use numerals instead of words to express numbers in a series when easy comparison is important.

There were 700 persons at the professor's first public lecture, 270 at the second, and 40 at the third.

Abbreviations

Whenever it is necessary to save space, such as in tables, indexes, and footnotes, you may use abbreviations. In the main text of formal writing, however, you should generally spell out rather than abbreviate words. Abbreviations are acceptable in the following cases.

Abbreviations for Academic Degrees and Titles

Use abbreviations for academic degrees and for the following common titles when used with a person's name: *Mr., Ms., Mrs., Dr., Jr., Sr., St.* (*Saint*). Other titles, such as *governor, colonel, professor,* and *reverend,* are spelled out.

> The doctor asked Colonel Jones, Ms. Hemmings, and Professor Pruitt to present the portrait of St. Thomas to Judge Hogkins on the occasion of her receiving a Ph.D. in religious studies.

Abbreviations for Agencies, Institutions, and Other Entities

Use abbreviations for agencies, groups, people, places, or objects that are commonly known by capitalized initials.

FBI	UCLA
IOOF	DNA molecules
Washington, D.C.	CD-ROM

If you wish to use a specialized abbreviation that may be unclear to your audience, write out the term in full the first time it appears and place in parentheses the abbreviation that you will use subsequently.

> The Modern Language Association (MLA) recently issued new guidelines for citing electronic sources.
>
> This example indicates that the writer will henceforth use the abbreviation *MLA*.

Abbreviations for Terms Used with Numbers

Use abbreviations for terms commonly used with numbers, especially times, dates,* amounts, and other units of measure.

1200 C.E.	$15.05
500 B.C.E.	no. 12 in a series
2:45 P.M.	

*If used, A.D. always precedes the date while B.C. follows it. The abbreviations B.C. ("before Christ") and A.D. (anno domini, "in the year of the Lord") are now often replaced with B.C.E. ("before the common era") and C.E. ("common era"). In both cases the abbreviation appears after the date. Thus A.D. 500 would be rewritten 500 C.E.

Note that you should use abbreviations for units of measure only when they appear with numbers; never use abbreviations by themselves.

Faulty	I will meet you sometime in the P.M.
Revised	I will meet you sometime in the afternoon.

There is no clear rule about when to use a period with abbreviations (*U.S.A.* or *USA; kg.* or *kg*). Most publishing houses establish their own guidelines, which they follow consistently.

Abbreviations for Common Latin Terms

Use abbreviations for common Latin terms used in footnotes, bibliographies, or parenthetical comments. In the main text, spell out the English equivalents.

e.g.	for example
i.e.	that is
c.f.	compare

This rule also applies to *etc.* (*et cetera,* meaning "and so forth"). Avoid using *etc.* in formal writing. Instead, use the English *and so forth* or *and so on,* or rewrite your sentence to make it more inclusive, thus eliminating the need for *and so forth.* Never write *and etc.,* because *et* is Latin for "and."

Weak	During my year in London I went to ballets, the opera, Shakespeare plays, etc.
Revised	During my year in London I saw many cultural events, including two ballets, one opera, and four Shakespeare plays.

Plurals of Abbreviations

Do not use an apostrophe when forming the plural of an abbreviation.

Faulty	I've misplaced two of my CD's.
Revised	I've misplaced two of my CDs.

Manuscript Form

An attractive manuscript contributes to your *ethos* as a writer. A sloppily prepared, visually unattractive manuscript, or one that violates standard conventions or your instructor's special instructions, creates a negative first impression and weakens the rhetorical effectiveness of your writing.

For more on *ethos,* see Chapter 3, Concept 9.

Unless told otherwise by your instructor, use the following format for all your college papers:

1. Use white, twenty-pound, $8^1/_2$-by-11-inch paper.
2. Print the paper in black using an inkjet or laser printer. The type should be dark and readable. Do not use colored inks.

3. Avoid fancy typefaces and icons. Make the text look like a typed manuscript rather than a published document unless the assignment calls for such an appearance.
4. Double-space the text throughout, including quotations and notes.
5. Use one-inch margins at the top and bottom, and left and right sides.
6. Indent five spaces for paragraphs. Leave one or two spaces after periods and other terminal punctuation; leave one space after commas and other marks of punctuation.
7. Distinguish between brackets [ ] and parentheses ( ) and make ellipses with spaced periods.
8. Proofread carefully. Type in your corrections, and print a clean copy of the paper. If you can't use a computer to make the corrections, write them neatly in ink by crossing out typographical errors and writing corrections above the crossouts.
9. Do *not* make a separate title page unless you are using the APA style or have been given special directions by your instructor. Rather, follow the MLA style, which places "cover page" information on the first page of the paper itself.
10. Staple your pages in the upper left-hand corner. Do *not* place your essay in a binder unless your instructor requests that you do so.

For rules on the use of brackets, parentheses, and ellipses, see pp. 703 and 709–710.

For a paper formatted in MLA style, see pp. 590–598. For an APA-style paper, see pp. 231–240.

PEARSON mycomplab

For support in learning this chapter's content, follow this path in **MyCompLab**: Resources ⇒ Grammar ⇒ Punctuation and Mechanics. Review the Instruction and Multimedia resources, then complete the Exercises and click on Gradebook to measure your progress.

ACKNOWLEDGMENTS

Page 6. David Rockwood, "Letter to the Editor" from *The Oregonian*, January 1, 1993. Copyright © 1993 David Rockwood. Used with permission.

Page 7. From *Raids on the Unspeakable* by Thomas Merton. Copyright © 1966 by The Abbey of Gethsemani, Inc. Reprinted by permission of New Directions Publishing Corp.

Page 35. E.E. Cummings, "next to of course god america i" from *Complete Poems: 1904–1962* by E.E. Cummings, edited by George J. Firmage. Copyright 1926, 1954, © 1991 by the Trustees for the E.E. Cummings Trust. Copyright © 1985 by George James Firmage. Used by permission of Liveright Publishing Corporation.

Page 36. Figure 2.2: Copyright © Health Sentinel

Page 56. Jimmy Carter, "Make this national treasure a national monument." The New York Times, December 28, 2000, p. A23. Copyright © 2000, The New York Times. Reprinted by permission of the New York Times Company.

Page 65. Carl Pope, "Nuclear Power is not the way forward." Copyright © 2009 Carl Pope. Reprinted by permission.

Page 78. "Simulations of Global hurricane climatology, interannual variability, and response to global warming using a 50-km resolution GCM" by Zhao et al., from *Journal of Climate*, Vol. 22, pp. 6653–6678, December 15, 2009. Copyright © 2009 American Meteorological Society. Used with permission.

Page 78. Copyright © 2010 Foundation for National Progress. Reprinted by permission from July/August issue of Mother Jones.

Page 79. Copyright © 2010 *Providence Journal*. Reprinted with permission.

Page 79: Copyright © American Museum of Natural History. Used with permission.

Page 88. Reprinted by permission of International Creative Management, Inc. Copyright © 2008 by Michael Pollan for *The New York Times*.

Page 90. Graphics by Charles M. Blow, *New York Times Magazine,* April 1, 2008. Copyright © 2008 The New York Times Company, Inc.

Page 96. From "Dangers of Disarming" by Robert B. Cullen, *Newsweek*, October 27, 1986. Copyright © 1986. All rights reserved. Reprinted by permission.

Page 111. Kyle Madsen, "Can a green thumb save the planet?" Copyright © Kyle Madsen. Used with permission.

Page 124. From "Dangers of Disarming" by Robert B. Cullen, *Newsweek*, October 27, 1986. Copyright © 1986. All rights reserved. Reprinted by permission.

Page 125. Stephanie Malinowski, "Questioning Thomas L. Friedman's Optimism in '30 Little Turtles'." Copyright © 2007 Stephanie Malinowski. Reprinted with the permission of the author.

Page 130. Froma Harrop, "New Threat to Skilled U.S. Workers." *Seattle Times,* April 17, 2007. Copyright © 2007 Froma Harrop. Reprinted with permission.

Page 135. Excerpt from *Black Boy* by Richard Wright. Copyright 1937, 1942, 1944, 1945 by Richard Wright; renewed © 1973 by Ellen Wright. Reprinted by permission of HarperCollins Publishers.

Page 143. Copyright © 2007, Megan Lacy. Used with permission.

Page 143. Copyright © 2007, Jeffrey Cain. Used with permission.

Page 146. Kris Saknussemm, "Phantom Limb Pain." Reprinted by permission of Kris Saknussemm.

Page 148. Patrick José, "No Cats in America?" student essay. Reprinted with the permission of the author.

Page 150. Stephanie Whipple, "One Great Book." Copyright © Stephanie Whipple. Used with permission.

Page 169. James Gardiner, How Do Online Social Networks Affect Communication?" Copyright © James Gardner. Used with permission.

Page 174. James Gardiner, "The Effect of Online Social Networks on Communications Skills—Annotated Bibliography." Copyright © James Gardner. Used with permission.

Page 178. Copyright © EnchantedLearning.com. Used by permission. From enchantedlearning.com/subjects/arachnids/spider/tarantualprintout.shtml

Page 179. "Myths about "Dangerous" Spiders" from www.washington.edu/burkemuseum/spidermyth/index.html. Copyright © Burke Museum. Reprinted by permission of Burke Museum, Seattle, WA.

Page 192. "Muslim Americans: Middle Class and Mostly Mainstream," May 22, 2007. Copyright © 2007 Pew Research Center. Used with permission.

Page 195. Kerri Ann Matsumoto, "How much does it cost to go organic?" Copyright © 2008 Kerri Ann Matsumoto. Used with permission.

Page 196. Shannon King, "How Clean and Green are Hydrogen Fuel-Cell Cars?" Copyright © 2008 Shannon King. Used with permission.

Page 199. Eugene Robinson, "You have the right to remain a target of racial profiling," *Washington Post,* May 1, 2007. Original title, "Pulling Over for Prejudice." © 2007, The Washington Post Writers Group. Reprinted with permission.

Page 225. "Women and Smoking in Hollywood Movies: A Content Analysis" by Gina Escamilla et al., *American Journal of Public Health*, March, 2000. Copyright © 2000 APHA. Used with permission.

Page 231. Lauren Campbell, Charlie Bourain, and Tyler Nishida, "A Comparison of Gender Stereotypes in Spongebob Square Pants and a 1930s Mickey Mouse Cartoon," Reprinted by permission of the authors.

Page 240. Lauren Campbell, Charlie Bourain, and Tyler Nishida, "Spongebob Squarepants has Fewer Gender Stereotypes." Reprinted by permission of the authors.

Page 281. Evelyn Dahl Reed, "Medicine Man" from *Coyote Tales from the Indian Pueblos* by Evelyn Dahl Reed. Copyright © 1988 by Evelyn Dahl Reed. Reprinted with the permission of Sunstone Press, P.O. Box 2321, Santa Fe, NM 87504-2321.

Page 292. "Everyday Use" from *In Love and Trouble: Stories of Black Women* by Alice Walker. Copyright © 1973 by Alice Walker. Reprinted by permission of Houghton Mifflin Harcourt Publishing Co.

Page 298. Elizabeth M. Weiler, "Who Do You Want to Be?" student essay. Reprinted with the permission of the author.

Page 302. Nikki Swartz, "Mobile Phone Tracking Scrutinized," *Information Management Journal,* March/April 2006. Copyright © 2006. Used with permission.

Page 303. Terry J. Allen, "Reach Out and Track Someone" *In These Times*, May 2006. Copyright © 2006 Terry J. Allen. Used with permission.

Page 324. http://immigrationmexicanamerican .blogspot.com used with permission.

Page 325. Byron Williams, "Immigration Frenzy Points Out Need for Policy Debate." Copyright © 2006 Byron Williams. Used with permission.

Page 326. Victor Davis Hanson, "The Global Immigration Problem" Tribune Media Services, June 6, 2007. Copyright © 2007.

Page 328. Blog.thehill.com

Page 328. Jake McIntrye, "Progressive Case Against the Immigration Bill" by Trapper John, posted on www.dailykos.com. Copyright © 2007. Used with permission.

Page 359. Ross Taylor, "Paintball: Promoter of Violence or Healthy Fun?" student essay. Reprinted with the permission of the author.

Page 362. William Sweet, " Better Planet: Dirty Coal Plants are Killers ..." Copyright © 2007 William Sweet. Used with permission.

Page 367. "No to Nukes," *Los Angeles Times*, July 23, 2007. Copyright © 2007. Used with permission.

Page 370. Leonard A. Pitts, Jr., "Spare the Rod, Spoil the Parenting," *The Seattle Times*, September 6, 2001. Copyright © 2001 by the Miami Herald. Reprinted by permission.

Page 372. A. J. Chavez, "The Case for (Gay) Marriage, student essay. Reprinted with the permission of the author.

Page 394. Jackie Wyngaard, "EMP: Music History or Music Trivia?" student essay. Reprinted with the permission of the author.

Page 396. Diane Helman and Phyllis Bookspan, "Sesame Street: Brought to You by the Letters M-A-L-E," *The Seattle Times,* July 28, 1992. Reprinted with permission.

Page 398. Teresa Filice, "Parents: The Anti-Drug; A Useful Site." Copyright © Teresa Filice. Reprinted with the permission of the author.

Page 420. Sam Rothchild, "Reward Work, Not Wealth." Copyright © Sam Rothchild. Used with permission.

Page 423. Lucy Morsen, "A Proposal to Improve the Campus Learning Environment." Copyright © Lucy Morsen. Used with permission.

Page 427. Jennifer Allen, "The Athlete on the Sidelines," *New York Times,* 2/20/04. Copyright © 2004 The New York Times. Reprinted by permission.

Page 429. Dylan Fujitani, "'The Hardest of the Hardcore': Let's Outlaw Hired Guns in Contemporary American Warfare." Copyright © Dylan Fujitani. Used with permission.

Page 498. "Being Prey" by Val Plumwood. First published in the *Utne Reader,* July, August 2000. Copyright © 2000 Val Plumwood. Used by permission of the author.

Page 499. Excerpt from "Leaves" by Richard Brautigan from *The Tokyo-Montana Express*. Copyright Richard Brautigan. Used with permission.

Page 500. Excerpt from *Into Thin Air* by Jon Krakauer. Copyright © 1997 Jon Krakauer. Publishing by Anchor Books.

Page 501. "A Strange Old Man" by Hitomaro, translated by Kenneth Rexroth from *One Hundred Poems from the Japanese*. Copyright © New Directions Publishing Corp. Used with permission.

Page 515. © 2007 Woman Against Gun Control. www.wagc.org

Page 531. Copyright © EBSCO, Inc.

Page 533. Copyright © Google, Inc.

Page 548. © 2007 Million Mom March Chapters of the Brady Campaign to Prevent Gun Violence. Used with permission. www.millionmommarch.org

Page 553. From *Gunfighters, Highwaymen, and Vigilantes: Violence on the Frontier* by Roger D. McGrath. Copyright © 1984 The Regents of the University of California. Used with permission.

Page 584. Copyright © 2007 EBSCO

Page 584. Matsuba et al., "Searching for Self and Relationships Online," *CyberPsychology & Behavior*, June 1, 2006. Copyright © 2006 Mary Ann Liebert, Inc. Used with permission.

Page 585. Copyright © 2009 The Bryan College Station Eagle. Used with permission.

Page 604. Scharrer, E., et al, "Working hard or hardly working? Gender, humor and the performance of domestic chores in television commercials," *Mass Communication & Society* 9(2), pp. 215-238. Copyright © 2006 Routledge. Used with permission.

Page 633. Jaime Finger, "Single Reflection." Copyright © Jaime Finger. Used with permission.

Page 634. Bruce Urbanik, "Comprehensive Reflection." Copyright © Bruce Urbanik. Used with permission.

Illustrations

Page 3. Bob Jacobson/Corbis

Page 15. Ennio Leanza/epa/Corbis

Page 53. Jon Carr

Page 61. Clockwise from top left: Tom Walker/Getty; Accent Alaska/Alamy; James Balog/Getty; Simon Bruty/Sports Illustrated/Getty

Page 63. Clockwise from top left: Jose Luis Pelaez Inc./Blend Images/Corbis; Corbis Premium RF/Alamy; Ken Seet Photography/Corbis; Richard G. Bingham II/ Alamy

Page 93. Thomas Hannich/Bransch/NY Times

Page 128. David Horsey/2003/Seattle Post Intelligencer

Page 129. Mike Lane

Page 137. Clockwise from top left: Ken Bube; Debra McClinton/Taxi/Getty; Ken Bube; Photos Alyson/Getty

Page 180. From left: Courtesy Manuel J. Cabrero; Courtesy Ron Taylor

Page 240. From top: Walt Disney Co./Everett Collection; Paramount/Everett Collection

Page 242. Clockwise from top left: Karen Kasmauski/Corbis; Guillermo Arias/AP; Carlos Barria/ Corbis; J. Emilio Flores/Corbis

Page 244. Clockwise from top left: Steven James Silva/Reuters/Landov; Det. Greg Semendinger/NYPD/ AP; David Turnley/Corbis

Page 250. Peter Turnley/Corbis

Page 251. Jean-Christophe Bott/Keystone/AP

Page 254. Scala/Art Resource, NY

Page 255. Albright-Knox Art Gallery/Art Resource, NY

Page 256. June Johnson (2 images)

Page 259. Lars Halbauer/DPA/Landov

Page 264. Coors Brewing Company

Page 266. Advertising Archives

Page 267. Advertising Archives (2 images)

Page 276. Stephen Crowley/The New York Times/Redux

Page 277. Dorothea Lange

Page 366. Stan Eales/Cartoon Stock

Page 380. The Authority of the People

Page 381. Courtesy of the University of Massachusetts (bottom)

Page 387. Courtesy of Experience Music Project

Page 420. Top left: Bill Jacobus; top right: Spencer Platt/Getty; center left: Don Jon Red/Alamy

Page 548. MillionMomMarch.org

Page 607. Courtesy of American Indian College Fund. All rights reserved.

Page 637. Poster available at AwarenessIDEAS.com, 800-875-1725

INDEX

Abbreviations, 714–715
Absolute phrases
  commas to set off, 694–695
  explanation of, 654
Abstraction, ladder of, 71–75, 501–502, 504
Abstracts, 99, 220. *See also* Summaries
Academic degrees, 714
Academic disciplines
  as field of inquiry and argument, 27–28
  scholarly questions for assorted, 28–29
Academic writing. *See also* Research source documentation; Scholarly publications
  closed-form prose for, 22
  document design for, 75–77
  examples of, 21
  graphics in, 491
  stating point for, 26
  synthesis as component of, 301
  titles for, 465–466
Accidental criteria, 385
Active voice
  explanation of, 651
  use of, 687–688
Ad hominem, 352
Adjective clauses, 655
Adjectives
  choosing correct form of, 679–680
  coordinate, 697
  explanation of, 651
  forms of, 651, 680–681
Adverb clauses
  commas with, 659, 694
  explanation of, 655, 659
Adverbs
  ambiguous, 681
  choosing correct form of, 679–680
  comparative form of, 680–681
  conjunctive, 651, 662, 665
  explanation of, 651
  forms of, 651
Advertisements
  advocacy, 401, 406–408
  analysis of, 261–268
  examples of, 256, 259, 264, 266, 267
  goals of, 258
  media for, 257, 258
  MLA style for citing, 588
  overview of, 256–257
  strategies for effective, 258–260
  target audience for, 257, 258
Advocacy, degree of, 544
Advocacy advertisements
  document design features of, 412–413
  exploring and generating ideas for, 412–413
  function of, 401, 406–408
  peer review for, 414
  revision of, 414
  shaping and drafting, 413
Agreement
  pronoun-antecedent, 671–672
  subject-verb, 668–671
all about writing, 457–458
Allen, Jennifer, 427–428
Allen, Paul, 387
Allen, Terry J., 303–305
Alley, Michael, 416
although, 39, 40, 659
American Express ad, 267
American Psychological Association (APA). *See* APA style
Amis, Martin, 67
Analogy
  argument from, 405
  false, 351
Analysis. *See also* Idea analysis and synthesis; Image analysis; Literary analysis
  of angle of vision, 55–57
  of essay exam questions, 614, 621
  explanation of, 241, 301
and then chronology, 456–457, 496. *See also* Chronological order
Anecdotal conclusions, 493
Angle of vision
  analysis of, 55–56
  examples of, 56–57
  explanation of, 52, 538
  of images, 58–64, 245
  persuasion through, 52–57
  recognition of, 52–54
  of research sources, 542–544
  strategies to construct, 56–57
  thought exercise on, 52
Annotated bibliographies
  examples of annotations for, 165–166
  explanation of, 153, 164
  features of, 165
  functions of, 164–165
  peer reviews for, 167–168
  shaping, drafting, and revising, 167
  writing critical preface for, 166–167
Antecedents
  agreement between pronouns and, 671–672
  avoiding unclear, 686–687
  collective nouns as, 672
  compound construction as, 671–672
  explanation of, 647, 671
  indefinite pronouns as, 672
Anthologies
  APA style for citing, 603
  MLA style for citing, 582–583
Anxiety, test, 618–619
APA style, 26*n*
  for articles in magazines and newspapers, 601–602, 604
  for articles in scholarly journals, 600–601, 604
  for books, 602–603
  for citing online databases, 603
  for edited anthologies, 603
  for films, 605
  for government publications, 605
  in-text citations in, 599–600
  for manuscripts and papers, 77
  for podcasts, 605
  References list in, 600
  for sound recordings, 605
  for television programs, 605
  for Web and Internet sources, 603–605
Apostrophes, 704–705
Appeals
  bandwagon, 352
  to *ethos,* 21, 58, 59, 104, 106, 348, 349

to false authority, 352
to *logos,* 58, 59, 104, 105, 349
to *pathos,* 58–60, 104, 106, 348–350
Appositive constructions, 678
Appositives, 653, 696–697
Arctic National Wildlife Refuse (ANWR) example, 56–57, 61, 104, 107, 108
Argument. *See also* Classical argument; Evaluation argument; Proposal writing
addressing objections and counterarguments in, 343–345
appeals to *ethos* and *pathos* in, 348–350
articulating reasons in, 336–337
articulating underlying assumptions in, 337–338
audience-based reasons for, 347–348
components of, 331–332
from consequence, 405
evaluating evidence for, 342–343
exploration of, 332–333
fallacies in, 351–352
finding issue for, 335
framework for classical, 353
generating and exploring ideas for, 354–355
misleading views of, 332
peer review for, 357–358
from precedent or analogy, 405
from principle, 404
process of nutshelling, 460–461
readings in, 359–376
responding to objects, counterarguments, and alternative views in, 346–347
revision of, 357
shaping and drafting, 355–357
stages of development of, 333–335
stating claim for, 336
structure of, 338*n*
truth seeking in, 331, 334, 377, 378, 382
types of evidence for, 339–342
use of sources based on, 555–557
visual, 406–408
Aristotle, 16, 58
Articles
APA style for citing, 600–604
MLA style for citing print, 580–581
Articles (parts of speech), 651
Assumptions, articulating underlying, 337–338
"The Athlete on the Sidelines" (Allen), 427–428
Attributive tags
to avoid ambiguities, 563–564
explanation of, 561–562
to frame source material rhetorically, 564–565
methods to use, 562–563, 566, 577
placement of, 706
to shape reader response, 564–565
in summaries, 100, 101
Audience
for advertisements, 257, 258
analysis of, 20, 439–440
for arguments, 347–348
attempts to change views of, 19, 38–39
desire for clarity, 38, 452–453, 504–505
point of view of, 19, 38–39
shared problems uniting writers and, 12
voice to match, 74–75
writer's view of, 19–21
writing for, 16
Audience-based reasons
explanation of, 347–348
process to identify, 356
Autobiographical narratives
characters in, 135–136, 140
elements of, 133–134
explanation of, 132
generating and exploring ideas for, 139
opposition of contraries in, 134
peer reviews for, 140–141
plot in, 133–135, 139, 140
revision of, 140
setting in, 136–137
shaping and drafting, 139–140
theme in, 137–138
Auxiliary verbs, 649, 650

Background knowledge, 96–97
Bain, Ken, 26
Bandwagon appeals, 352
Banking method of education, 26
Bar graphs, 489
because clauses, 337, 380
Believing and doubting game, 33–34, 49–50
Berlin Wall, 249–251
Biblical citations, 702
Bibliographic citations, 165, 539
Bibliographies, 164. *See also* Annotated bibliographies
Billboard advertisements, 256, 259
"The Bird and the Machine" (Eisley), 505
Black Boy (Wright), 135–136
Blended response
example of, 111–113
explanation of, 110, 114
Block quotations, 568–569, 702, 707
Blogs
APA style for citing, 605
explanation of, 32
MLA style for citing, 586
Boldface, 76
Bonnin, Gertrude. *See* Zitkala-Sa (Gertrude Bonnin)
Books
APA style for citing, 602–603
MLA style for citing, 580–583
Bookspan, Phyllis, 396–397
Boolean search commands, 530
Bott, Jean-Christophe, 251
Bourain, Charlie, 231–240
Brackets, 567, 709
Branding, 258
Brautigan, Richard, 499–500
Burke, Kenneth, 16, 51, 55, 451, 504
Bus advertisements, 256
Bush, George W., 59

Cain, Jeffrey, 143
Campbell, Lauren, 231–240
"Can a Green Thumb Save the Planet? (Madsen), 111–113
Capital letters, 711–712
Carter, Jimmy, 56, 61
Cartoons, 53
MLA style for citing, 588
political, 128, 129, 380
"The Case for (Gay) Marriage" (Chavez), 372–376
Category questions, 211
Causality, 215–216
Celeste, Manoucheka, 273–275
Chanda, Nayan, 51
Chaney, Michael A., 69
Characters
asking questions about, 283
in autobiographical narratives, 135–136, 140

Chat rooms, 32
Chavez, A. J., 372–376
Chronological order
  closed-form prose and, 456–457
  open-form prose and, 496–497
Chronological structure, 456–457
Chunks, 459–460
Citations. *See* Research source citations
Claims
  evaluation, 392
  explanation of, 25*n*, 336
  qualifying, 347
  reasons for, 338, 386
Clarity, reader's desire for, 38, 452–453, 504–505
Classical argument. *See also* Argument; Evaluation argument
  addressing objections and counterarguments in, 343–345
  articulating reasons in, 336–337
  articulating underlying assumptions in, 337–338
  evaluating evidence for, 342–343
  explanation of, 353
  fallacies in, 351–352
  generating and exploring ideas for, 354–355
  peer reviews for, 357–358
  readings in, 359–376
  responding to objects, counterarguments, and alternative views in, 346–347
  revision of, 357
  shaping and drafting, 355–357
  stages of development in, 333–335
  structure of, 338*n*
  types of evidence for, 339–342
Clauses
  adjective, 655
  adverb, 655, 659, 694
  because, 337, 380
  explanation of, 654
  if, 650
  independent, 654, 656, 659
  methods for joining, 654, 664–665
  noun, 654–655
  parenthetical, 677, 698
  subordinate, 654, 656
Closed-form introductions, 466–468
Closed-form prose
  for academic writing, 22, 25
  binding sentences together in, 477–481
  choice of, 10
  conclusions in, 492–494
  example of, 6–7
  explanation of, 8–9
  forecasting and fulfillment in, 454–455
  graphics in, 486–492
  humor in, 510
  introductions in, 42–46
  level of specificity in, 72–73
  old-before-new principle in, 453–454, 506
  open vs., 10–11
  organizing and developing ideas in, 116, 481–486
  planning and visualizing structure in, 459–464
  points in, 47–48
  purpose statements in, 19
  reader expectations for, 452, 464
  rhetorical critiques as, 105
  thesis in, 37–38, 46–49
  thesis/support structures in, 455–458
  titles and introductions for, 464–470
  topic sentences for paragraphs in, 470–473
  transitions and signposts in, 474–477
  unity and coherence in, 452–453
  using open-form elements to create voice in, 510–512
Clothing, rhetoric of, 62–64
Coherence
  in closed-form prose, 452, 453
  explanation of, 440
Coleridge, Samuel Taylor, 282
Collective nouns, 670–672
Colons, 701–702
Color
  effects of, 80
  in images, 249, 254
Commas
  with absolute phrases, 694–695
  with adverb clauses, 659, 694
  to avoid confusion, 695
  with coordinate adjectives preceding nouns, 697
  with coordinating conjunctions, 694
  to correct run-ons and comma splices, 663
  to correct sentence fragments, 661
  explanation of, 693
  with interrupting elements, 659, 698
  with introductory or concluding phrases, 659–660, 694
  with introductory transitional words and expressions, 694
  with items in series, 697
  to joint independent sentences, 658
  with nonrestrictive appositives, 696–697
  with nonrestrictive clauses and phrases, 695–696
  with participial phrases, 695
  with places, addresses, and dates, 698
  when to omit, 698–699
Comma splices
  explanation of, 662
  methods for correcting, 662–664
Companion pieces, 628
Comparatives, 651, 680–681
Comparison/contrast move, 485–486
"A Comparison of Gender Stereotypes in *Spongebob Squarepants* and a 1930s Mickey Mouse Cartoon" (Campbell, Bourain, and Nishide), 231–240
Complements, 645, 670
Complete subjects, 645
Complex sentences, 656
Compound-complex sentences, 656
Compound predicates, 655
Compound sentences, 656
Compound subjects, 655, 668–669
"A Comprehensive Reflective Letter" (Urbanik), 634–635
"Comprehensive Immigration Reform: PROs and ANTIs" (Dee), 324
Comprehensive reflection, 623, 629–632, 634–635
Conclusions
  in autobiographical narratives, 140
  delayed-thesis, 493
  to essay examination responses, 621
  hook and return, 493
  larger significance, 492
  proposal, 493
  scenic or anecdotal, 493
  simple summary, 492
  strategies for writing, 492–493
Concrete language
  effects of, 502–503
  use of, 71

Conference presentations, 588
Conjunctions
  coordinating, 652, 663, 665, 669, 694
  correlative, 673
  explanation of, 652
  subordinating, 652, 654, 659, 663, 665
Conjunctive adverbs, 651, 662, 665
Connectedness, 499–500
Connolly, Kelly Ann, 549
Consequence, argument from, 405
Consumer items, rhetoric of, 62–64
Content, reading for, 114–117
Content knowledge, 630–631
Coordinate adjectives, 697
Coordinating conjunctions
  commas with, 658, 694
  to correct run-ons and comma splices, 663
  explanation of, 652, 665
  to joint independent sentences, 658
  list of, 665
  use of, 669
Coors Light ad, 263–265
Correlative conjunctions, 673
Council of Writing Program Administrators, 4
Counterarguments
  methods of addressing, 343–345
  responses to, 346–347
Courtesy questions, 692
Cradock, Angie L., 225–230
Crapo, Mike, 328
Crawford, Rod, 179–180, 183
Creative imitation, 508, 509
Credibility, of research sources, 541
Criteria
  accidental, 385
  establishment of, 382–383
  necessary but not sufficient, 385
  in order of importance, 389
  problems related to establishment of, 384–385
  purpose and context in determining, 384, 388
  sufficient, 38
Criteria-match process, 382–383
Critical knowledge, 631
Critical thinking
  connection between writing and, 5, 11
  explanation of, 26
  skills for, 27
Critiques, rhetorical, 104–106
Cullen, Robert B., 96
cummings, e. e., 35
Cyberspace. *See* Internet; Web sites; World Wide Web

Dangling modifiers, 674–675
Dashes, 703
Data
  factual, 339
  presentation of numerical, 486–492
Databases
  APA style for citing material from, 603
  licensed, 529–530, 532, 534
  methods to search, 529–533
  MLA style for citing material from online, 583
Data collection
  interviews for, 208–210
  methods for, 202
  observation for, 207–208
  questionnaires for, 210–213
Delayed-thesis conclusions, 493
Dependent clauses. *See* Subordinate clauses
Descriptions, opposing, 82
Design. *See* Document design
Details
  sensory, 83
  use of specific, 71–73, 686
Dialectic, 156
Dialectic discussion
  explanation of, 31–32
  for exploratory essays, 156
Dialectic talk, 31–33
Dillard, Annie, 506
Dinesen, Isak, 507
"Disturbing Media Images of Haiti Earthquake Aftermath Tell Only Part of the Story" (Celeste), 273–275
Division-into-parallel-parts move, 484–485
Doctorow, E. L., 495
Documentary photographs. *See also* Photographs
  analysis of, 245–251, 268
  angle of vision and credibility of, 245
  effects of, 246
  examples of, 244, 250, 251
  function of, 243, 245
  persuasive effects of, 247–249, 251
  rhetorical contexts of, 246
Documentation. *See* Research source documentation
Document design
  for advocacy advertisements, 412, 413
  color and, 80
  explanation of, 75
  for manuscripts and papers, 75–77
  for published works, 76, 78–81
  space and layout and, 80
  type and, 76
Domain-specific skills, 27–28
Double-entry research notes, 159–160
Doubting game, 33. *See also* Believing and doubting game
Drafts. *See also* Revision
  for advocacy advertisements, 413
  for annotated bibliographies, 167
  for autobiographical narratives, 139–140
  for classical argument, 355–357
  for evaluation argument, 392–393
  for exploratory essays, 161–163
  first, 443
  function of multiple, 438–440
  for image analysis, 269
  for informative writing, 186, 189–190
  for literacy narratives, 144–145
  for literary analysis, 290
  methods used to produce, 116–117, 443
  peer review of, 444–448
  for proposal writing, 410
  read aloud, 640
  read backward, 640–641
  for research reports, 219
  of response essays, 122–123
  for synthesis writing, 318, 319

Eales, Stan, 265, 366
E-books, 583, 605
EBSCOhost, 529, 531, 533
Edited anthologies
  APA style for citing, 603
  MLA style for citing, 583
Editing
  by adding specific details, 686
  for clichés, jargon, and slang, 685
  combining sentences when, 683
  for correct adjective and adverb forms, 679–680
  for correct verb forms, 679
  for dangling modifiers, 674–675
  for deadwood, 682–683
  for faulty prediction, 667
  importance of, 639
  for inclusive language, 689–691

Editing (*continued*)
methods for improving skills in, 640–641
microtheme projects on, 641–643
for misplaced modifiers, 675
for mixed constructions, 666
for nominalizations, 684
for noun pileups, 684–685
for old before new information, 687
for parallel structure, 672–673
for pretentious language, 685
for pronoun-antecedent agreement, 671–672
for pronoun cases, 676–678
for sentence variety, 685–686
for sexist pronoun use, 689–690
for subject-verb agreement, 668–671
for unclear pronoun reference, 686–687
for voice, 687–688
for wordiness, 70
Eisley, Loren, 505
Either/or reasoning, 352
Elbow, Peter, 33, 37
Electronic databases. *See* Databases
Electronic discussion boards, 32
Ellipses, 567, 710
E-mail, MLA style for citing, 586
"EMP: Music History or Music Trivia?" (Wyngaard), 43, 394–395
Empathic listening, 98
Emphatic form, of tenses, 649
EnchantedLearning.com, 178–179, 183
Encyclopedia Britannica, 527
Encyclopedias, 527
Encyclopedic structure, 457–458
Engfish writing, 458
Escamilla, Gina, 225–230
Essay examinations
analysis of questions on, 612–613, 617–618
function of, 609, 610
handling test situation during, 618–620
key terms on, 614–617
organizational cues for, 613
preparation for, 610–612
successful responses on, 620–621
use of outside quotations on, 613
Essays. *See also specific forms of writing*
five-paragraph, 9
incorporating graphics into, 490–492
old-before-new principle in, 454
Ethical guidelines
to avoid plagiarism, 570
for research, 217–218, 570–571
Ethos
appeals to, 21, 58, 59, 104, 106, 349
explanation of, 348
research and, 217
Evaluation argument
criteria-match process for, 382–383
distinguishing necessary, sufficient and accidental criteria for, 385
establishing criteria for, 384–385
generating and exploring ideas for, 391–392
method to conducting, 387–390
overview of, 378–380
peer reviews for, 393
readings in, 394–400
revision of, 393
shaping and drafting, 392–393
using planning schema to develop, 386–387
Evaluative annotations, 164, 165
"Everyday Use (For Your Grandmother)" (Walker), 292–297
Evidence
in essay examination responses, 621
explanation of, 339
STAR criteria for evaluation of, 342–343, 351
types of, 339–342
Examinations. *See* Essay examinations
Examples, as evidence, 339–340
"Excerpt from 'Immigration Policy Must Help Economy While Preserving Ideals'" (Crapo), 328
"Excerpt from 'The Progressive Case Against the Immigration Bill'" (Trapper John), 328–330
Exclamation points, 693
Exigency, 18
Experience Music Project (EMP), 387–388
Exploratory writing
analysis of, 154–155
double-entry research notes for, 159–160
elements of, 155–156
examples of, 154–155
explanation of, 153
function of, 29, 443
generating and exploring ideas for, 35–37, 157–159
peer reviews for, 163–164
revision of, 163
shaping and drafting, 161–163
Exploratory writing strategies
believing and doubting game as, 33–34
dialectic talk as, 31–33
focused freewriting as, 31
freewriting as, 29–31
idea mapping as, 31

Facebook.com, 30
"Face to Face with Tragedy" (Hoyt), 271–273
Factual data, 339
Fallacies, 351–352
The Fall of the Berlin Wall (Turnley), 249–251
False analogy, 351
Faulty prediction, 667
Feminism and the Mastery of Nature (Plumwood), 498
"A Festival of Rain" (Metron), 7
Field research. *See also* Research papers
analyzing results from, 214–217
ethical standards for, 217–218
explanation of, 201
posing research questions and, 204–206
reporting results from, 213–214
scientific posters and, 222–224
Field research data. *See also* Research papers
analysis of, 201–202
empirical research report structure and, 202–204
interviews to gather, 208–210
observation to gather, 207–208
questionnaires to gather, 210–213
Field research reports
designing and drafting introduction and method sections of, 219
examples of, 225–240
generating ideas for, 218–219
graphics in, 213, 214
method to read, 204
peer reviews for, 220, 224
posing research question of, 204–206
research and writing guidelines for, 219–220
revision of, 220
structure of, 202–204
team writing for, 221–222

Figurative language, 506–507
Filice, Teresa, 392, 398–400
Films, MLA style for citing, 588
Finger, Jaime, 633
First drafts, 443
FirstSearch Databases, 530
Five-paragraph essays, 9
Fixed-choice questions, 211
Flowcharts, 463, 464
"Flying Elsewhere" (Markham), 509
Focused freewriting, 31. *See also* Freewriting
Fonts, 76
Forecasting
  in closed-form prose, 454–455
  in open-form prose, 505
  strategies for, 469–470
  with thesis statement purpose statement, or blueprint statement, 468–470
Foreign words, 708, 715
Forester, E. M., 499
for example move, 482
The Foundling (Piccinini), 14, 15
Fragments. *See* Sentence fragments
Framing, 248
Freewriting
  example of, 30
  explanation of, 29–31
  focused, 31
  functions of, 35, 37
Freire, Paulo, 26
Friedman, Thomas L., 122, 124–125
Frye, Northrop, 138
Fujitani, Dylan, 158–159, 429–433
Fulkerson, Richard, 342
"Funnel" introductions, 464–465

Gardiner, James, 30, 44, 153, 158, 159, 165, 169–176, 461, 462, 468, 531, 589–598
Gehry, Frank, 387
Geico Gecko billboard ad, 259–260
Generic Peer Review Guide, 447–448
Genre
  in college-level reading, 96
  document design and, 76
  examples of, 21
  explanation of, 16, 21
  how writers think about, 21–22
  voice to match, 74–75
Gerund phrases, 653
Gerunds, 678
"The Global Immigration Problem" (Hanson), 326–327
Global revision, 440–442
Google, 533
Government publications
  APA style for citing, 605
  MLA style for citing, 588–589
Grace, Kevin Michael, 69
Grammar checkers, 641
Graphics. *See also* Images; Photographs; Visual aids
  guidelines for using, 80–81, 486
  incorporated into essays, 490–492
  in research reports, 213, 214
  used to tell stories, 487–490
Graphs, 381
Graves, Michael, 511
"Greenpeace Climate Change Protest" (Bott), 251
Groups, idea generation in, 188–189
Guns web sites, 547–550

Hanson, Victor Davis, 326–327
"'The Hardest of the Hardcore': Lets Outlaw Hired Guns in Contemporary American Warfare" (Fujitani), 429–433
Harrop, Froma, 130–131
Hasty generalization, 351
Headings, to signal transitions, 477
Hegel, George Wilhelm Friedrich, 156
Helman, Diane, 396–397
Helping verbs. *See* Auxiliary verbs
Hendrix, Jimi, 387
Hitomaro, 501
Home pages
  library, 528–529
  MLA style for citing, 586
Hook and return conclusions, 493
Horsey, David, 128
Howard, Rebecca Moore, 560*n*
"How Clean and Green Are Hydrogen Fuel-Cell Cars? (King), 187, 196–198
"How Do Online Social Networks Affect Communication?" (Gardiner), 169–173
"How Much Does It Cost to Go Organic" (Matsumoto), 181, 195
Hoyt, Clark, 271–273
Humor, 510
Hypothesis, 201

Idea analysis and synthesis. *See also* Synthesis writing
  exploring main themes and similarities and differences for, 314–315
  formulating your synthesis views and, 317–318
  generating and exploring your own ideas for, 316–317
  learning logs and, 311–312
  organization for, 320, 321
  overview of, 302
  peer review for, 321–322
  readings in, 302–305, 308–310, 312–313
  revision of, 320
  rhetorical strategies and, 313–314
  shaping and drafting, 318, 319
  summary/strong response writing and, 306–307
  synthesis questions and, 305–306
  writing thesis for, 320
Idea generation
  for advocacy advertisements, 412–413
  for autobiographical narratives, 139
  for classical argument, 354–355
  for empirical research reports, 218–219
  for evaluation argument, 391–392
  for exploratory essays, 35–37, 157–159
  for image analysis, 268–269
  for informative writing, 185–186, 188–189
  for literacy narratives, 144
  for literary analysis, 288–290
  for proposal writing, 409–410
  reading for structure and content for, 114–117
  for synthesis writing, 316–317
Idea mapping
  example of, 32
  explanation of, 31
  functions of, 36–37
Ideas critique
  explanation of, 106–107
  question-answering strategies for writing, 107–108
Ideology, 332–333
if clause, 650
"The Iguana" (Dinesen), 507
Ill-structured problems, 26*n*
Image analysis
  for advertisements, 256–267 (*See also* Advertisements)
  exploration of, 241–243
  generating and exploring ideas about, 268–269
  overview of, 241
  peer reviews of, 270
  readings about, 271–279
  revision of, 269
  shaping and drafting, 269

Images. *See also* Photographs; Visual aids
in advertisements, 256–268
angle of vision of, 58–64, 245
concrete language to evoke, 502–503
documentary and news photographs, 243–252
paintings as, 252–256
persuasion through, 247–249, 263
rhetorical effect of, 59–62
use of, 81
Imitation, creative, 508, 509
"Immigration Frenzy Points Out Need for Policy Debate" (Williams), 325–326
Immigration reform, 241–243, 323–330
Imperative mood, 650
Indefinite pronouns, 669, 672
Independent clauses
colons with, 701, 702
explanation of, 654
semicolons with, 658
in sentences, 655, 656
Independent redundancy, 491
Indicative mood, 650
Indirect questions, 693
Indirect quotations, 706–707
Infinitive phrases, 654
Infinitives, 648, 649
Inflated voice, 74
Informal voice, 74
Information
converted to meaning, 46–47
data collection methods to gather, 207–213
presentation of old to new, 477–479
Informative writing
categories of, 177
examples of, 178–180, 192–200
exploration of, 178–179
function of, 180–181
generating and exploring ideas for, 185–186, 188–189
peer reviews for, 187–188, 191
reports as, 181–182
revision of, 186, 190
shaping and drafting of, 186, 189–190
surprising-reversal strategy in, 177, 182–185
Informed consent, 217
Interjections, 652
Internet. *See also* Web sites; World Wide Web
APA style for citing sources from, 603–605
evaluating sources on, 545–550
MLA style for citing sources from, 583–587
print sources vs. sources from, 524, 526–527
rhetorical environment of, 544–545
search engines for, 533–534
strategies for searching, 533–535
Interpretive questions, 285
Interrupting elements, 659
Interviews
methods to conduct, 208–210
MLA style for citing, 588
In-text citations
APA style for, 599–600
explanation of, 575
MLA style for, 576–580
"Into Thin Air" (Krakauer), 500
Introductions
closed-form, 466–468
in closed-form prose, 42–46
example of, 43
in exploratory writing, 158–159
features of good, 43–44
in research reports, 219
Irregular verbs, 648, 649, 679
Issue questions, 335
Issues
explanation of, 335
stock, 409–410
strategies to find arguable, 354
Italics, 76, 708–709

Jensen, William, 623
José, Patrick, 138, 148–150, 505
Journals. *See also* Scholarly publications
MLA style for citing articles in, 579–580, 583
JSTOR, 530
Justification, in proposals, 402, 404–405
Juxtapositions, 505–506

Kawachi, Ichiro, 225–230
Key terms, on essay exams, 614–616
Keyword searches
library catalog, 528–529
methods for, 530
Kilcup, Rodney, 5
King, Shannon, 187, 189, 196–198
Knowledge
applied on essay exams, 611
background, 96–97
content, 630–631
critical, 631
rhetorical, 544–550
self-, 630
Krakauer, Jon, 500

"Labor Day Blues" (Lane), 129
Lacy, Megan, 143
Ladder of abstraction, 71–75, 501–502, 504
La Loge (Renoir), 253–255
Lane, Mike, 129
Language
aesthetic use of, 496
bias in, 689–691
concrete, 71, 502–503
figurative, 506–507
inclusive, 689–691
pretentious, 685
revelatory, 503–504
specific, 71–73
technical, 95
Larger significance conclusions, 492
Latin terms, 715
Layout, 80
Learning logs, 311–312
"Leaves" (Brautigan), 499
Lectures, MLA style for citing, 588
"A Letter to the Editor" (Rockwood), 6–7
Letters
comprehensive reflective, 631–632, 634–635
of recommendation, 54–55
Lexis-Nexis Academic Universe, 530
Libraries
home page for, 528–529
searching licensed databases in, 529–534
Library of Congress Subject Headings, 528
Licensed databases. *See also* Databases
explanation of, 529
searches using, 529–530, 532–534
Line graphs, 487, 489
Linking verbs, 670
Lists, 703
Literacy, visual, 241
Literacy narratives
examples of, 143
explanation of, 132, 141–142
features of, 142

generating and exploring ideas for, 144
revision of, 145
shaping and drafting, 144–145
Literary analysis
generating and exploring ideas for, 288–290
guidelines for understanding, 282–285
guidelines for writing, 285–286
overview of, 280
peer reviews for, 291
reading logs and, 286–288
readings for, 292–299
shaping, drafting and revising, 290
Literary nonfiction, 10, 495. *See also* Open-form prose
"Living Like Weasels" (Dillard), 506
Local revision, 440–442
Logos
appeals to, 58, 59, 104, 105
explanation of, 348, 349
Los Angeles Times, 367–369

MacAulay, Kate, 308–310, 312
Macrorie, Ken, 458*n*
Madsen, Kyle, 111–113, 122
Magazines
APA style for citing, 601–602
document design for, 76, 78
MLA style for citing, 580–581
writing style in, 511–512
Main clauses. *See* Independent clauses
Malinowski, Stephanie, 122, 123, 125–127
Manuscripts
document design for, 75–76
format for, 77, 715–716
Markham, Beryl, 509
MasterCharge advertisements, 266, 267
Matsumoto, Kerri Ann, 181, 186, 195
McCarthy, Lucille, 25, 378
McGrath, Roger D., 553–557, 561–563, 573
McIntyre, Jake. *See* Trapper John
McPhee, John, 502–503
Meaning, points converting information to, 46–47
Media, advertising, 257, 258
"The Medicine Man" (Reed), 281, 282
Memory, working, 438
Memory-soaked words, 503–504
Mencken, H. L., 135
Merton, Thomas, 7, 8, 11
Messages
effects of, 51
nonverbal, 58–63
persuasive power through angle of vision, 52–57
persuasive power through appeals, 58
Metacognition, 627
Metaphors, 507
Microsoft PowerPoint, 408, 416
Million Mom March, 547, 548
Mirror effect, 258
Mirrors and windows principle, 258–259
Misplaced modifiers, 675
"Mission Accomplished" photograph, 59–60
Mixed constructions, 666
MLA style, 26*n*
for anthologies, 582–583
for articles in scholarly journals accessed in print, 579–580
for books, 580–583
citation system in, 576
for citing online databases, 583
example using, 590–598
formatting in, 576
for interviews, 588
in-text citations in, 576–580
for magazine and newspaper articles accessed in print, 580–581
for manuscripts and papers, 75–77
for podcasts, 586
for Web and Internet sources, 583–587
for "Works Cited" list, 579
"Mobile Phone Tracking Scrutinized" (Swartz), 302–303
Modal form, 650
Modals, 650
Modern Language Association (MLA) style. *See* MLA style
Modifiers
dangling, 674–675
explanation of, 651
misplaced, 675
Mood
imperative, 650
indicative, 650
observing scenes in different, 82
subjunctive, 650
Morsen, Lucy, 423–426
Motivation, for writing, 18, 19
"Muslim Americans: Middle Class and Mostly Mainstream" (Pew Research Center for the People and the Press), 182, 192–193
MySpace.com, 30
"Myths about 'Dangerous' Spiders" (Crawford), 179–180, 183
"The Myth of Violence in the Old World" (McGrath), 553–555
"My Turn: Hunks and Handmaidens" (Register-Freeman), 508

Narrative
autobiographical, 132–152 (*See also* Autobiographical narratives)
examples of, 146–152
explanation of, 456
literacy, 132, 141–145 (*See also* Literacy narratives)
open-form prose as, 456, 496–498
as story, 496–497
Narrators, 284
Natural speaking voice, 74
Necessary but not sufficient criteria, 385
Newsmagazines, 526
Newspapers
APA style for citing, 601–602, 604
document design for, 76, 79
MLA style for citing, 580, 581, 586
as research source, 526
News photographs. *See* Documentary photographs
"New Threat To Skilled U. S. Workers" (Harrop), 130–131
"next to of course god america i" (cummings), 35
Nishida, Tyler, 231–240
"No Cats in America?" (José), 136, 138, 148–150, 505
Nominalizations, 684
Nonrestrictive appositives, 696–697
Nonrestrictive clauses, 695–696
Non sequitur, 352
Nonverbal messages
clothing and consumer items as, 62–64
explanation of, 55
visual, 59–62
Notes
avoiding plagiarism and, 571
double-entry, 159–160

Notes (*continued*)
for focused descriptions, 82–83
research, 159–160
taking purposeful, 539–541
"No to Nukes" (Los Angeles Times), 367–369
Noun clauses, 654–655
Nouns
collective, 670–672
explanation of, 647
pileups of, 684–685
proper, 711–712
Nuclear power passages, 65–66
Number, 670–671
Numbers
abbreviations for terms used with, 714–715
writing out, 712–713

Object complements, 645
Objections
anticipation of, 344–345
methods for addressing, 343–344
responses to, 346–347
Observation, to gather information, 207–208
Old-before-new principle, 453–454, 687
Old/new contract
links to old in, 479–480
open-form prose and, 506
in sentences, 454, 477–478
"One Great Book" (Whipple), 150–152
"One Hundred Poems from the Japanese" (Hitomaro), 501
Open-ended problems
explanation of, 27
for research, 204–205
Open-ended questions, 9, 26, 211
Open-form prose
closed vs., 10–11
concrete language in, 502–503
connectedness in, 499–500
depicting events through time in, 498–499
disrupting predictions and making odd juxtapositions in, 505–506
disrupting reader's desire for direction and clarity in, 504–505
example of, 7
explanation of, 9–10, 495, 496
figurative language in, 506–507
leaving gaps in, 506
as narrative, 456, 496–498
reflection writing as, 109
resolution, recognition, or retrospective interpretation in, 500–501
revelatory and memory-soaked language in, 503–504
tension and conflict in, 500
used to create "voice" in closed-form prose, 510–513
use of styles in, 508–509
Oral presentations, 401
Organization
of essay examination responses, 620
for synthesis writing, 320, 321
Organizational cues, 613
Outlines
for closed-form prose, 461–462
for proposal speeches, 415–416, 418–419
scratch, 459–460
Overly informal voice, 74

"Paintball: Promoter of Violence or Healthy Fun?" (Taylor), 359–361
Paintings
analysis of, 252–255, 268
compositional features of, 255
Paragraphs
topic sentences for, 470–471
unity in, 472–473
Parallel structure, 672–673
Paraphrases
guidelines for, 572
of research source information, 558–561
Parentheses, 703
Parenthetical citations, 562–564, 572
Parenthetical clauses, 677, 698
"Parents: The Anti-Drug: A Useful Site" (Filice), 398–400
Participial phrases, 653, 695
Participles
past, 648, 649
present, 648, 649
pronouns preceding, 678
Particulars, to support points, 46–47, 473
Passive voice
explanation of, 651
use of, 687–688
Past participle, 648
Past participles, 648, 649
Patchwriting, 560–561, 572
Pathos
appeals to, 58–60, 104, 106, 349–350
explanation of, 348–349
Peer reviews
for advocacy advertisements, 414
for annotated bibliography, 167–168
for autobiographical narrative, 140–141
for classical argument, 357–358
of drafts, 444–448
for evaluation argument, 393
for exploratory essays, 163–164
function of, 445–448
for image analysis, 270
for informative essays, 187, 191
for literacy narratives, 145
for literary analysis, 291
for proposal writing, 411
for research reports, 220, 224
responding to, 450
for scholarly manuscripts, 527
for scientific posters, 224
for seeing rhetorically, 104
for synthesis writing, 321–322
Peer review workshops, 449–450
Periodicals. *See also specific types of periodicals*
databases of, 529–530
as research sources, 524
rhetorical overview of, 525–526
Periods
to correct run-ons and comma splices, 662
placement of, 692
Persona, 68
Personal pronouns, 705
Personal writing, examples of, 21
Persuasion. *See also* Argument; Classical argument; Evaluation argument
explanation of, 331
images and, 247–249, 251, 263
through appeals, 58, 59
Pew Research Center for the People and the Press, 182, 192–193
"Phantom Limb Pain" (Saknussemm), 146–147
Photographs. *See also* Documentary photographs; Graphics; Image analysis; Visual aids
analysis of, 245–251
angle of vision and credibility of, 245
function of, 243, 245
rhetorical effect of, 59–62
Phrase fragments, 660
Phrases
absolute, 654, 694–695
appositive, 653

gerund, 653
infinitive, 654
introductory or concluding, 659–660
nonrestrictive, 695–696
participial, 653, 695
prepositional, 652–653, 668
restrictive, 695–696
verbal, 653
Piccinini, Patricia, 14, 15
Pie charts, 489–490
Pirsig, Robert, 639
Pitts, Leonard, Jr., 370–372
Plagiarism
ethical use of sources and, 570
explanation of, 569
guidelines to avoid, 571–572
identification of possible, 573
note-taking strategies to avoid, 571
paraphrasing and, 572
unwitting, 569
Planning schema
to anticipate argument objections, 344–345
to develop evaluation arguments, 386–387
Plot
asking questions about, 282–283
in autobiographical narratives, 133–135, 139, 140
explanation of, 134
Plumwood, Val, 498–499, 502
Plurals, 713, 715
Podcasts, 586, 605
Point of view
asking questions about, 283–284
changing reader's, 19, 38–39
in exploratory writing, 155–156
Points
adding particulars to support, 46–47, 473
used in revision, 48–49
Policy proposals, 401. *See also* Proposal writing
Political cartoons, 128, 129, 380
Political stance, 542–544
Pollan, Michael, 87–94
Popular magazines
as research sources, 526
techniques used in, 511–512
Portable document format (.pdf) files, 526–527
Portfolios
collecting work for, 624
electronic, 624
function of, 624
overview of, 623
reflective writing to introduce work in, 625–626
selecting work for, 625
Positive form, 651
Possessives, 704–705
Posters, 222–223, 381. *See also* Scientific posters
Post hoc, ergo propter hoc argument, 351
PowerPoint (Microsoft), 408, 416
Practical proposals, 401. *See also* Proposal writing
Precedent, argument from, 405
Predicates, 644, 645, 655, 656
Predictions
disruption of, 505–506
faulty, 667
Prefaces, for annotated bibliography, 166–167
Premise, 336
Prepositional phrases, 652–653, 668
Prepositions, 652
Presentations. *See* Oral presentations
Presentation software, 408
Present participle, 648, 649
Pretentious language, 685
Primary sources, 523–524
Principle, argument from, 404
Print sources. *See also specific sources*
cyberspace sources vs., 524, 526–527
in libraries, 529–530
reliability of, 524
rhetorical overview of, 525–526
Problematic questions, 290
Problematizers, 26
Problems
description of, 402
ill-structured, 26*n*
open-ended, 27
posing initial, 157–158
for proposal writing, 12–14, 402–404
strategies to introduce, 45
Problem statements, mistakes in, 410
Process, 332
Process logs, 628
Product, 332
Progressive tenses, 649
Pronoun-antecedent agreement, 671–672
Pronouns
in appositive constructions, 678
avoiding broad or unclear reference to, 686–687
cases of, 676–677
consistency in use of, 667
explanation of, 647, 667
indefinite, 669, 672
as parts of compound constructions, 677–678
personal, 705
possessive, 704–705
preceding gerunds or participles, 678
relative, 654, 670, 676–677
sexist use of, 689–690
types of, 647
Proofreading, methods to improve, 641
Proper nouns, 711–712
Proposal conclusions, 493
Proposal speeches
components of, 414
delivery of, 421
explanation of, 415
peer review for, 422
revision of, 422
strategies to creating, 415–416
visual aids for, 416–420
"A Proposal to Improve the Campus Learning Environment by Banning Laptops and Cell Phones from Class" (Morsen), 423–426
Proposal writing
as advocacy advertisements, 412–414
developing justification section in, 404–405
elements of, 402–403
exploration of, 401–402
generating and exploring ideas for, 409–410, 412–413
peer reviews for, 411, 414
readings in, 423–433
revision of, 411, 414
shaping and drafting, 410
strategies to solve problems of, 403–404
types of, 401
visual aids to enhance, 406–408, 414
ProQuest, 529
Prose. *See also* Closed-form prose; Open-form prose
closed-form vs. open-form, 6–11, 495
methods to streamline, 70
writer-based vs. reader-based, 440
Protagonists, 283
Prototype, 43

Public affairs magazines, 525
Punctuation. *See also specific types of punctuation*
apostrophes, 704–705
brackets, 567, 709
colons, 701–702
commas, 658–661, 663, 694–699
to correct run-ons and comma splices, 662–664
to correct sentence fragments, 661
dashes, 703
ellipses, 567, 710
exclamation points, 693
function of, 658
parentheses, 703
periods, 692
question marks, 693
quotation marks, 705–706
of quotations, 565–568, 705–708
semicolons, 658, 700
slashes, 710
Purpose
as desire to change reader's view, 19
in determining criteria, 384
as response to motivating occasion, 18–19
as rhetorical aim, 17–18
taking notes according to, 539–541
voice to match, 74–75

"Questioning Thomas L. Friedman's Optimism in '30 Little Turtles'" (Malinowski), 125–127
Question marks, 693
Questionnaires
construction of, 210
ethical guidelines for, 218
example of, 212
random sampling and, 213
types of questions used in, 211
Questions
about characters, 283
about plot, 282–283
about point of view, 283–284
about setting, 283
about theme, 284–285
category, 211
courtesy, 692
on essay exams, 612–613
fixed-choice, 211
freewriting and discussion to generate, 35
idea mapping and discussion to generate, 36–37
indirect, 693
interpretive, 285
interview, 209
in introductions, 43–44
issue, 335
open-ended, 6, 26, 204–205, 211
problematic, 290
punctuation of, 692–693
questionnaire, 211
research, 204–206, 223
scaled-answer, 211
significant, 44
synthesis, 305–306, 310–311
thesis, 11
thesis statements developed from, 41–42
turning-point starter, 288–289
for writing ideas critique, 107–108
for writing rhetorical critique, 105–106
Quotation marks, 100, 101, 566–568, 705–707
Quotations
block, 568–569, 702, 707
brackets in, 709
capitalization in, 712
of complete sentences, 566
ellipses in, 710
in examination questions, 613
explanatory material in, 709
indirect, 706–707
inserted, 566
modification of, 567
omissions from, 567–568
punctuation of, 565–566, 705–709
question marks with, 693
within quotations, 568
of research source information, 561
with and without attributive tag, 562, 563

Radio programs, 587
Random samples, 13
Raynor, Bruce, 102–104
"Reach Out and Track Someone" (Allen), 303–305
Reader-based prose, 440
Readers. *See* Audience
Reading
expert strategies for, 97–99
with and against the grain, 87, 98–99, 106
research sources, 536–539
rhetorical, 87–99 (*See also* Rhetorical reading)
for structure and content, 114–117
Reading logs, 285–288
Reasons
audience-based, 347–348, 356
explanation of, 336
Recognition, 500–501
Red herring fallacy, 352
Reed, Evelyn Dahl, 281
"Reefer Madness" (Schlosser), 183
Reference books, 525, 527
References List, 600
References list, 575
Reflection, 109
Reflective writing
comprehensive, 623, 629–632
explanation of, 108–109, 625
readings in, 633–635
single, 623, 627–629
strong responses as, 109–110
Register-Freeman, Victoria, 508, 509
Regular verbs, 648, 679
Relative pronouns
cases of, 676–677
explanation of, 654
punctuation of, 665
as subjects, 670
Reliability, of research sources, 541
Renoir, Pierre-Auguste, 253–255
Repetition, in images, 249
Reports, 181–182
Research. *See also* Field research; Field research data
analyzing results from, 214–217
ethical standards for, 217–218, 570–571
as evidence, 340
reporting results from, 213–214
scientific posters and, 222–224
Research data
analysis of, 201–202
empirical research report structure and, 202–204
interviews to gather, 208–210
observation to gather, 207–208
posing research questions and, 204–206
questionnaires to gather, 210–213
reading research reports and, 204
Research notes, double-entry, 159–160
Research papers. *See also* Field research; Field research data; Field research reports
arguing your own thesis in, 518–522
characteristics of good, 517–518
designing and drafting introduction and method sections of, 219

documentation in, 518
examples of, 225–240
generating ideas for, 218–219
graphics in, 213, 214
method for reading, 204
peer reviews for, 220, 224
research and writing guidelines for, 219–220
revision of, 220
structure of, 202–204
team writing for, 221–222
Research questions, 204–206, 223
Research source citations
APA style for, 599–605
in-text vs. end-of-paper list of cited works, 575–576
MLA style for, 576–598
overview of, 574–575
parenthetical system of, 572
Research source documentation
APA style for, 26*n* (*See also* APA style)
MLA style for, 26*n* (*See also* MLA style)
parenthetical method for, 577
role of, 518
Research sources. *See also* Libraries; Web sites; *specific types of research sources*
angle of vision and political stance of, 542–544
avoiding plagiarism when using, 569–573
credibility of, 541
database searches for, 529–533
evaluation of Web, 544–550
incorporated into your own prose, 558–559
letting your own argument determine your use of, 555–557
library, 528–529
method to read, 536–539
note taking from, 539–541
primary and secondary, 523–527
reliability of, 541
rhetorical overview of, 525–526
taking notes from, 539–541
use of attribution tags to distinguish your ideas from, 561–565
Web searches for, 533–535
when and how to summarize, paraphrase, and quote from, 558–561, 565–569
Resolution, 500–501
Response writing. *See also* Essay examinations
blended, 110–114
examples of, 111–113, 121–122
exploring ideas for, 118–119, 121
function of, 104
ideas critique as, 106–108
reflection as, 108–110
revision of, 123
rhetorical critique as, 104–106
shaping and drafting for, 122–123
thesis for strong, 121–122
Restrictive clauses, 695–696
Retrospective interpretation, 500–501
Revelatory words, 503
Revision. *See also* Drafts
of advocacy advertisements, 414
of autobiographical narratives, 140
of classical argument, 357
of evaluation argument, 393
of exploratory essays, 163
function of, 116–117, 438–440
global and local, 440–442
of image analysis, 269
of informative writing, 186, 189–190
of literacy narratives, 145
of literary analysis, 290
of material for popular audiences, 512
of proposal writing, 411
of research reports, 220
of response writing, 123
strategies for, 443–444
of synthesis writing, 320
use of points and particulars in, 48–49
Rhetoric
angle of vision and, 52–53
explanation of, 16
logos, ethos, and *pathos* and, 58–60, 104, 106
purpose as aim of, 17–19
visual, 59–62
Rhetoric: Discovery and Change (Young et al.), 38*n*
Rhetorical analysis
of research sources, 523–527
of Web sites, 546–550
Rhetorical context
in college-level reading, 95–96
exploration of, 313–314
of photographs, 246
Rhetorical critique
explanation of, 104–105
strategies for writing, 105–106
Rhetorical effects, of images, 242–243
Rhetorical knowledge
to evaluate Web sources, 544–550
explanation of, 631
Rhetorical reading
exploration of, 87–88
reasons for difficulties in, 95–96
of research sources, 537–539
strategies for, 97–99
Rhetorical thinking
about audience, 16, 19–21
about genre, 16, 21–22
about purpose, 16–19
Rhetorical triangle, 59
Robinson, Eugene, 199–200
Rockwood, David, 6–8, 11, 18, 38, 60, 347–348
Rogers, Carl, 98
Run-ons
explanation of, 662
methods for correcting, 662–664

Saknussemm, Kris, 146–147
Salutations, 702
Sans serif fonts, 76
Satisfice, 444
Scaled-answer questions, 211
Scenarios, 340
Scenic conclusions, 493
Schema, planning, 344–345
Scholarly publications. *See also* Academic writing
APA style for citing, 600–601, 604
document design in, 76–81
MLA style for citing, 579–580, 586
as research sources, 525, 527
style in, 68–69
Scientific posters
content of, 222–223
design and revision of, 223
example of, 240
explanation of, 222
features of, 223
peer reviews for, 224
Search engines, 533–534
Secondary sources
analysis of, 524–527
explanation of, 523
Self-knowledge, 630
Self-reflection. *See* Reflective writing
Semicolons
in compound-complex sentences, 656
to correct run-ons and comma splices, 663
to join main clauses, 658
to joint independent sentences, 658
in series containing commas, 700
Sensory details, awareness of, 83

Sentence fragments
correction of, 661
explanation of, 660
types of, 660
Sentences
absolute phrases in, 654
adjective clauses in, 655
adjectives in, 651
adverb clauses in, 655
adverbs in, 651
appositive phrases in, 653
complex, 656
compound, 656
compound-complex, 656
conjunctions in, 652
dangling modifiers in, 674–675
editing to combine, 683
explanation of, 644–645
faulty prediction in, 667
inserting quoted words and phrases into, 566
interjections in, 652
misplaced modifiers in, 675
mixed constructions in, 666
nominalized, 684
noun clauses in, 654
nouns in, 647
old-before-new principle in, 454, 477–478
in outlines, 461
parallel structure in, 672–673
parentheses in, 703
patterns of, 645–646
prepositional phrases in, 652–653
prepositions in, 652
pronoun-antecedent agreement in, 671–672
pronoun case in, 676–677
pronouns in, 647
punctuating clauses and phrases within, 658–660
quoting complete, 566
simple, 655
topic, 470–473
types of clauses in, 654–655
variety in, 685–686
verbal phrases in, 653–654
verbs in, 648–651
Sentence structure
to control emphasis, 70–71
style and, 68
Series
commas with items in, 697
numbers in, 713
semicolons with items in, 700
Serif fonts, 76
"Sesame Street: Brought to You by the Letters M-A-L-E" (Helman & Bookspan), 396–397
Setting
asking questions about, 283
in autobiographical narratives, 136–137, 140
Sexist language, 689–690
Shading, 76
Sherman, A. Kimbrough, 25, 27
Short stories. *See* Literary analysis
Short-term memory, 438
sic, 709
Signaling phrases. *See* Attributive tags
Simon, Herbert, 444
Simple sentences, 655
Simple subjects, 645
Simple summary conclusions, 492
"A Single Reflection on an Exploratory Essay" (Finger), 633
Single reflection, 623, 627–629
Slashes, 710
Slater, Wayne, 511
Slides, 416–420
Slippery slope fallacy, 352
Small groups, idea generation in, 188–189
Software
grammar-check, 641
presentation, 408, 416
spell-check, 641
word processing, 461
Sound recordings, 588
Source documentation. *See* Research source documentation
Sources. *See* Research sources
Space, in document design, 80
"Spare the Rod, Spoil the Parenting" (Pitts), 370–372
Specialty fonts, 76
Speeches
MLA style for citing, 588
outlines for, 415–416, 418–419
peer reviews of, 422
proposal arguments as, 415–422
revision of, 422
strategies for delivery of, 421
visual aids for, 416–420
Spell-checkers, 641
STAR criteria for evaluating evidence, 342–343, 351
Statistics, 340–341
Stereotypes, 689
Stock issues, 409–410
"The Stolen Watch," 496–497, 499
Story. *See also* Narrative
criteria for, 497–498
narrative as, 496–497
Stress position, 478
Strong response writing. *See* Response writing
Structure
chronological, 456–457
for closed-form prose, 455–458
drafts to improve, 440
encyclopedic, 457–458
engfish, 458
planning and visualizing, 459–463
reading for, 114–117
thesis/support, 455–458
Study plans, 612
Style
expanding your repertoire of, 508–509
explanation of, 68
factors affecting, 68
strategies to improve, 69–75
Subarguments, 341–342
Subject complements, 645, 670
Subject matter
changing reader's view of, 19, 38–39
for essay exams, 610–612
of images, 52, 247–248
Subject-matter questions, 37–38
Subject searches, 528
Subjects (sentence)
agreement between verbs and, 648
complex, 645
compound, 655, 668–669
explanation of, 644
inversion of verbs and, 669–670
simple, 645
Subject-verb agreement
explanation of, 648, 668
rules for, 668–671
Subjunctive mood, 650
Subordinate clause fragments, 660
Subordinate clauses
explanation of, 654
in sentences, 656
Subordinating conjunctions
to correct run-ons and comma splices, 663
examples of, 665
explanation of, 652, 654, 659, 665
Sufficient criteria, 385
Summaries
challenges of writing, 100–102
criteria for incorporating, 102

examples of, 100–104
explanation of, 99
exploring texts through, 312–313
function of, 100
removing particulars to create, 47–48
of research, 340
of research sources, 558, 559
thematic, 138
usefulness of, 99–100
Summary/however move, 483
Summary-only annotations, 164
Superlatives, 651, 680
Surprise
structure without, 458
in thesis, 37–38
Surprising-reversal strategy
examples of, 40–41, 183–185
explanation of, 39–40, 183
informative writing using, 177, 182–185
Swartz, Nikki, 302–303
Sweet, William, 362–365
Swift, Jonathan, 437
Symbols, rhetorical power of, 16
Synthesis, 301. *See also* Idea analysis and synthesis
Synthesis questions, 305–306, 310–311
Synthesis writing. *See also* Idea analysis and synthesis
developing your views for, 317–318
as extension of summary/strong response writing, 306–307
generating ideas for, 316–317
organization of, 320
overview of, 301
revision of, 320–321
student examples of, 307–310, 312–313
thesis for, 320

Tables, 487, 488, 491
Talk-back assignments, 628
Talk-to assignments, 628
"Tarantulas" (EnchantedLearning.com), 178–179
Taylor, Ross, 339–340, 359–361
Team writing, for research reports, 221–222
"Technology's Peril and Potential" (MacAulay), 308–310
Television programs
APA style for citing, 605
MLA style for citing, 587
Tenses. *See* Verb tenses
Tension
in autobiographical writing, 134
in thesis, 39–41
Terrorist attacks of September 2001, 243–245
Test anxiety, 618–619
Testimony, 341
Tests. *See* Essay examinations
Themes
asking questions about, 284–285
in autobiographical narratives, 137–138
process for clarifying, 314–315
Theroux, Paul, 33–34
Thesis
in closed-form prose, 37–38, 46–49
creating tension in, 39–41
elements of strong, 37–38
for response essays, 121–122
for synthesis writing, 320
Thesis questions, 11
Thesis statements
in closed-form prose, 46–49, 468–470
creating working, 461
explanation of, 11, 25*n*
function of strong, 37–38
questions to develop, 41–42
in research reports, 214–215
for response essays, 620
Thesis/support structures
chronological, 456–457
encyclopedic, 457–458
engfish and, 458
explanation of, 455
"30 Little Turtles" (Friedman), 124–125
this, 481
"This Is the End of the World" (Tuchman), 509
Tiehen, Katie, 390
Time
depicting events through, 498–499
point of view and, 284
Time/Life writers, 511–513
Time management, during essay exams, 619–620
Time notation, 702
Titles
capitalization of, 712
for closed-form prose, 464–466
punctuation of, 702, 707
underlining or italics for, 708
Titles (personal), 714
to be, 650
"Today's Economic Indicator" (Horsey), 128
Tomalin, Nicholas, 506–507
Tone, style and, 68
Topic position, 478
Topic sentences
for paragraphs, 470–472
revision to match paragraphs, 472–473
Toulmin, Stephen, 338*n*
Trade books, 525, 527
Trade magazines, 526
Transitions
headings to indicate, 477
between parts, 476
signaling relationships with, 474–476
Transition words/phrases
in closed-form prose, 474–477
commas with, 694
examples of, 665
Trapper John, 328–330
Tree diagrams
example of, 463
explanation of, 462–463
Truth seeking. *See also* Argument
in argument, 331, 334, 377, 378, 382
increasing attention to, 380
Tuchman, Barbara, 509
Tufte, Edward, 67
Turning points, 288–289
Turnley, Peter, 249–251
"Two Photographs Capture Women's Economic Misery" (Wheeler), 275–279
Type, 76

Underlining, 76, 708–709
Underlying assumptions, 337–338
Unity
in closed-form prose, 452, 453
in paragraphs, 472–473
U.R. Riddle activity, 54–57, 70
Urbanik, Bruce, 634–635
URLs (universal resource locators), 534–535

Verbal phrases, 653–654
Verbals, 648, 678
Verbs
agreement between subjects and, 648, 668–671
auxiliary, 649, 650
choosing correct forms of, 679
explanation of, 648
in inverted sentences, 669–670

Verbs (*continued*)
  irregular, 648–649, 679
  linking, 670
  mood of, 650
  position of, 645
  principal parts of, 648–649
  regular, 648, 679
  voice of, 651
Verb tenses
  consistency in use of, 667
  explanation of, 648, 649
  literary analysis and, 284
  types of, 649–650
Video recordings, MLA style for citing, 588
Vision. *See* Angle of vision
Visual aids. *See also* Graphics; Graphs; Images
  for proposal arguments, 406–408
  for proposal speeches, 416–420
Visual literacy, 241
Visual rhetoric, 59–62. *See also* Graphics; Image analysis
Vocabulary, in college-level readings, 95
Voice
  active, 651, 687–688
  differences in, 74
  open-form elements to create, 510–512
  passive, 651, 687–688
  for purpose, audience and genre, 74–75
  style and, 68

Walker, Alice, 292–297
Walvoord, Barbara, 25, 378
Watterson, Kara, 312–314, 316–317
Web sites. *See also* World Wide Web
  analyzing purpose for using, 546–550
  APA style for citing, 603–605
  domain identifiers for, 546
  evaluation of, 545–546
  library, 528–529
  MLA style for citing, 583–587
  as research sources, 524, 526–527
  strategies for searching, 533–535
Web videos, 586, 605
Weiler, Betsy, 298–299
"Welcome to Sellafield" (Eales), 366
"What Is the Effect of Online Social Networks on Communication Skills?" (Gardiner), 174–176
Wheeler, Lydia, 275–279
which/that, 673
Whipple, Stephanie, 150–152
White, E. B., 498
"Who Do You Want to Be?" (Weiler), 298–299
who/whom, 673
"Why Bother" (Pollan), 88–94
"Why Facebook Might Not Be Good For You: Some Dangers of Online Social Networks" (Gardiner), 590–598
"Why Uranium Is the New Green" (Sweet), 362–365
Wikipedia, 527
Wikis, 527
Williams, Byron, 325–326
Window effect, 258
Windows in 21 Days, 510
Wolfe, Tom, 503
"Women and Smoking in Hollywood Movies: A Content Analysis" (Escamilla, Cradock, & Kawachi), 225–230
"Women Are the Real Victims of Handgun Control" (Connolly), 549
Word choice, style and, 68
Wordiness, 70, 682–683
Words
  concrete, 502–503
  foreign, 708
  memory-soaked, 503–504
  revelatory, 503
  transition, 474–477, 665, 694
Working memory, 438
"Works Cited," 575, 579, 597–598
World Wide Web. *See also* Internet; Web sites
  APA style for citing sources from, 603–605
  methods to search, 529–533
  MLA style for citing sources from, 583–587
  print sources vs. sources from, 524, 526–527
  rhetorical environment of, 544–545
  search engines for, 533–534
Wright, Richard, 135–136
Writer-based prose, 440
Writers
  as questioners, 5
  rhetoric for college, 4
  shared problems uniting readers and, 12
  view of audience, 19–21
  view of genre, 21–22
Writer's memo, 628
Writing. *See also specific types of writing*
  closed vs. open, 8–10
  connection between critical thinking and, 5, 11
  expert habits to improve, 442–444
  motivation for, 18, 19
  purpose for, 17–19
  reasons to study, 5
  recursive, 440
  as recursive process, 440
  reflective, 108–109, 625–635
  response, 104–114
  strategies to improve, 442–444
  summary, 99–104
  team, 221–222
  thinking rhetorically about good, 5
Wyngaard, Jackie, 43, 392, 394–395

Yancey, Kathleen Blake, 623
"You Have the Right to Remain a Target of Racial Profiling" (Robinson), 199–200
Zitkala-Sa (Gertrude Bonnin), 142